FROM
SCRIPT
TO
STAGE

RINEHART PRESS
San Francisco

FROM SCRIPT TO STAGE

eight modern plays

Randolph Goodman

Brooklyn College
City University of New York

iv

For BERTHA KAHN GOODMAN

"Upon such sacrifices, . . .
The gods themselves throw incense."

Preface

For those who are interested in the drama chiefly as literature, there are available for study numerous texts for every historical period from the Greeks to the present. But for the student of drama as performed under complex theatrical conditions, the records are sparse and tantalizing.

A play on a printed page is "like a patient etherized upon a table," fit only for dissection and analysis, but on the stage it breathes, it amuses, it soothes, it excites. Like all living organisms, however, the produced play is extremely ephemeral—a thrilling production very quickly becomes merely a matter of hearsay, and a great performance is often forgotten during the performer's own lifetime. When the actor is gone, when the costumes and scenery have disappeared, when the playhouse is dark or has been demolished, it is difficult for the reader to envision the play in the rich context of the actual production. The reader's imagination can be stimulated, however, by an account of the theatrical conditions under which the play was produced, and by a more intimate acquaintance with the personalities and practices of the playwright's corps of collaborators—the actors, directors, scene and costume designers, lighting and sound technicians, and musicians— whose combined talents make possible the play's successful translation from script to stage.

We must be grateful, therefore, to those literate playgoers, critics, and members of the theatrical profession who have left us their "remembrance of things past," enlivened in many instances by drawings, engravings, and photographs, which help us to recapture the pleasure and excitement of drama on stage. That, in essence, is the purpose of the interviews with contemporary artists and technicians that introduce each of the plays in this volume. Such statements can help the reader to restage these plays more effectively in the theatre of his mind. Studied in the light of the explicit procedures of the professional craftsmen who have actually brought it to life, a script tends to lose the smell of the lamp and begins to emit the seductive aroma of grease paint.

The plays chosen for this volume represent the dramatic styles that have been dominant in the theatre during the twentieth century. Included are examples of psychological and poetic realism, naturalism, expressionism, and theatricalism—from the well-made play through the unstructured one-acter to the nonverbal Happening—and, in addition, an example from the musical theatre. The student of modern drama will discover that a strong relationship exists between the work of such seemingly disparate writers as Ibsen and Albee, Strindberg and Ionesco, O'Neill and Aspenström, and that so-called avant-garde plays and the extreme theatrical techniques employed in their presentation are neither as new nor as traditionless as they appear to be.

A book of this sort could not have been written without the cooperation and active assistance, the advice and suggestions, of many people. I owe a great debt of gratitude to the professional theatre artists, mentioned by name in the text, who generously consented to talk with me about their work; but I must also express my thanks to the following individuals and institutions:

In New York: To the late George Freedley, former curator, and to Paul Myers, present curator, and the entire staff of the Theatre Collection, Library and Museum of the Performing Arts at Lincoln Center; to the staffs of the Art, Dance, Music, Periodical, and Photographic Divisions, New York Public Library; to Louis Rachow and Carl Willers of the Walter Hampden Memorial Library, The Players; to Elizabeth B. Burdick, Archivist of the International Theatre Institute; to Beatrice Buda of the Theatre Collection, Museum of the City of New York; to Rose Sellers, Alexander Preminger, and the staff of the Brooklyn College Library; to the staff of the Columbia University Library; to Marna Feldt and Karin Friberg of the Swedish Information Service; to J. P. Lustenberger, Vice-Consul for Switzerland; to Torstein Sando, United States representative for Norwegian Broadcasting; to the Cultural Division of the French Embassy; to the French Institute; to Leo Wilder, Public Relations Department, Warner Brothers-Seven Arts; to Sallie Jones, Photography Department, CBS-TV; to Professor Bernard Beckerman, Theatre Arts Department, Columbia University; to Kurt and Elsa Pinthus; to Jacqueline d'Arcole; to Donald Madison; to Cameron Brown, Lawrence Gundersen, Edvin B. Lian, Osa Lindberg, and Dr. Louise R. Schub, for assistance with translations from Swedish, Norwegian, and French; and to the British, French, German, Norwegian, Soviet, and Swiss information offices.

In London: To George Nash, G. M. Johnson, and the staff of the Gabrielle Enthoven Collection, Victoria and Albert Museum; to the British Museum; to the National Film Archive; and to Frank Marcus.

In Paris: To Violette Novy of the Centre Français du Théâtre; to André Veinstein, Jacques M. Guignard, Robert Bellé, and Michèle Thomas of the Bibliothèque de l'Arsenal; to the Bibliothèque Nationale; to Gilles Daziano of the American Cultural Center; to Erica Bosché of the International Theatre Institute; to Michèle and Ernest Ostrowsky; to Lotte Eisner; to Francesca Bray, Catherine Girardeau, Pierre Combescot, and Christopher Mankowski for assistance with translations from the French; to the publishers Editions de Minuit, Bernard Grasset, and Gallimard; to Solange de la Baume, editor-in-chief of *La Revue de Paris*; and to Gisèle Teyssoneau of Bordeaux.

In Stockholm: To Maud Frohm of Swedish Broadcasting; to Gerard Bonnier and Sven Lindner of Bonniers Förlag; to Ulla Aberg of the Royal Dramatic Theatre; to Lenn Hjortzberg; to Lennart Ahlbom of the Park Theatre; to the Library of the University of Stockholm; and to Palle Granditsky and Anita Blom of the Upsala-Gävle Stadsteater.

In Oslo: To Rigmor Ottho and Hilda Lundgren Olsen of Norwegian Broadcasting; to the administrative staff of the National Theatre; and to Tormod Skagestad, Director of the Norwegian Theatre.

In East Berlin: To H. Wolff, of the Press Department, Deutsche Staatsoper, Berlin.

And, finally, I must express my thanks to the personal friends who have given me limitless help and encouragement: in New York— Valborg Anderson, Margarete Bieber, Rolf Fjelde, Leonard Fleischer, David M. Glixon, Mildred C. Kuner, Inger and Leif Sjöberg, and Jerome and Jean Trichter; in London—David Magarshack, Leslie Reade, and the Alexander family. I owe a special debt of gratitude to Caleb Smith, whose spirit is everywhere in this book, and to Ruth Chapman and Betsy Hirsch of Holt, Rinehart and Winston; also to Blanche Applebaum and Anita Stein, who assisted me in the preparation of the manuscript. To those whose names I may inadvertently have omitted, I offer both thanks and apologies.

R. G.

New York
August 1970

Contents

THE SEVEN DEADLY SINS
of the LOWER MIDDLE CLASS

THE OLD TUNE

THE APES SHALL INHERIT THE EARTH

FROM
SCRIPT
TO
STAGE

Theatre Since the Restoration

The physical theatre, in the architectural structure most familiar to us today, made its appearance under the aegis of Charles II with the restoration of the English monarchy in 1660; and the plays that filled that theatre reflected the pleasure-loving attitude of London society. In subject matter, point of view, and form, Restoration drama foreshadowed many of the elements that have assumed significance in the plays of our time. John Dryden, the foremost poet, critic, and dramatist of the Restoration, asserting that "the drama's laws the drama's patrons give," recognized the central importance of audience and playwright in the development of the drama.

Audience and Playwright

The playwright, like any member of his audience, is molded by the social and cultural conditions of his time, and faces the same pressures and problems, but his special gifts enable him to express a personal view of the world, its customs, mores, and institutions. He may defend or defy them. Earlier playwrights, including Shakespeare, worked mainly within the traditions of their age; modern dramatists, on the other hand, have distinguished themselves as iconoclasts, critics, and rebels, whose defiance of authority has been esthetic as well as social or political, manifesting itself not only in the subject matter but also in the very structure of their plays.

Traditional drama—whether an ancient Greek tragedy or a romantic play of the nineteenth century—mirrored a highly structured society in a well-defined artistic form. Modern drama, on the contrary, reflects a chaotic world—ambiguous in its moral precepts and in its rules both of conduct and of art—displaying as a result eclecticism and formlessness in its structure. When a playwright of the past dealt with such subjects as alienation, violence, war, sex, and pollution, he was able to explore their ethical and political implications within a clearly ordered system of values. The modern playwright has no such fixed standards; he treats these subjects according to his own predilections, and usually on a purely physical level. More often than not, his primary aim is to titillate or shock a bored and cynical audience. The changeover from traditional to modern drama did not occur in a single leap; step by step, over a period of two and a half centuries, it has reflected the shift in man's view of himself, of his fellow men, and of the world in which he lived.

In the latter part of the seventeenth century, the religious feeling that had given the drama its initial impetus in the medieval period and had sustained it through its flowering in the Renaissance, was clearly waning. Men no longer submitted unquestioningly to the authority of Church or State, but took a more personal and secular view of existing realities and began to believe that the universe could be understood in logical, mathematical, and

1

mechanical terms. Reason, it seemed, would eventually solve all human problems.

The return of the drama to the English stage in 1660, similar to the early days of the Enlightenment, created an atmosphere of optimism and high spirits. The Restoration audience was a privileged group: aristocratic, wealthy, sophisticated, and pleasure-seeking. Its favorite plays were of two types: the cynical, witty, sexual comedies, in which such writers as Etherege, Congreve, Wycherley, and Dryden projected the audience's hedonistic views and lampooned its manners; and the bombastic heroic tragedies, such as Nathaniel Lee's *The Rival Queens* and Thomas Otway's *Venice Preserved*. Though the ostensible purpose of the heroic tragedy was to instruct and elevate, its theatrical appeal lay in great, declamatory parts for the performers and spine-tingling moments for the audience. In both comedy and tragedy, the Restoration playwright lost no opportunity to point an irreverent finger at cracks in the structure of the Establishment for his new audience had a strong taste for social, political, and ecclesiastical satire.

The eighteenth century saw a growing interest in science and a rationalistic approach to social, economic, and educational problems. But the approach was largely theoretical for, despite an increasing awareness of the existence of the poor and the exploited, the members of this class played no important part in society or as characters in the serious plays of the period. Prosperous merchants now filled the theatres, and their middle-class morality dictated the taste and types in plays, which ran to sentimental comedies and domestic tragedies. Examples of the first genre may be found in Richard Steele's *The Conscious Lovers* and Hugh Kelly's *False Delicacy;* and of the second, in George Lillo's *The London Merchant* and Edward Moore's *The Gamester*. Heroic tragedy had become by now only a subject for burlesque, as in Henry Fielding's *Tragedy of Tragedies; or, The Life and Death of Tom Thumb the Great*. The very concepts of "heroism" and "tragedy" seemed ridiculous, until revived in the romantic plays of the next century, when men dreamed of unfettered individualism and longed to escape from the drudgery of the humdrum world.

What had been theory in the seventeenth and eighteenth centuries became technology in the nineteenth. The growth of industry and its mechanization caused radical alterations in the life of the common man. He awoke from the dreams of the Enlightenment to find himself a mere cog in a great machine, and grew more and more alienated from his work and from other men. Industrialization brought with it an intensification of capitalism, which subjected workers to such intangible external influences as the fluctuations in foreign markets and on the stock exchange. Before the middle of the century, Balzac had written a play in which a financial wheeler-dealer, Mercadet, put off his creditors with the alibi that his partner had absconded with their funds but was sure to return and that he was simply "waiting for Godeau!"

The American and French Revolutions and several minor ones had already taken place, but the liberation of man had not; pessimism had set in. Still, social revolt seemed the only way to restore the individual's power to act, and this became the theme and substance of many of the romantic plays of the period. Beginning with Goethe and Schiller, romanticism spread over Europe and proved the ideal mode of expression for such dramatists as Victor Hugo, Georg Büchner, Heinrich von Kleist, and Adam Oehlenschläger, the last-named having a profound influence on the young Ibsen. The usual romantic protagonist was a larger-than-life hero, who was torn between love and duty to an ideal (social or political), and who doggedly pursued the good, the true, and the beautiful; he lived and died (and therein lay the tragedy) for an "impossible dream." The romantic play was, of course, at the farthest remove from reality; it was written in verse, and dealt always with historical persons and places, never contemporary ones, which made it possible to preserve the fiction that man was a creature of free will with the attributes of a tragic hero. By this time, the average playgoer was a wage slave, a prisoner in a shop or factory.

Melodrama (drama plus music), like romantic drama, presented a theatrical avenue of escape. It pictured ordinary people in sentimental situations or exciting adventures, with morality always triumphant. Good examples of the style may be found in the work of Tom Taylor and Dion Boucicault. Boucicault, an Irish actor-playwright, who settled in America, filled his plays with Gaelic patriots, Negro slaves, and virtuous maidens.

The "well-made play"—a mechanical construction as serviceable as the other machine-made products of the time—was perfected by Eugene Scribe, who wrote over four hundred pieces of various sorts for the theatre and turned playwriting into big business. He sacrificed thought and characterization to clever intrigue, which proved tremendously popular with the ever growing audiences that flocked to the theatre as a result of the spread of education and the growth of affluence and democracy. Following in Scribe's footsteps, Victorien Sardou produced mechanical art full of sensationalism and moral platitudes. Between them, Scribe and Sardou provided the transition from the airy, romantic fantasy to the minutiae of the commonplace.

Side by side with melodrama and the play of intrigue, there developed the musical extravaganza, a pastiche of songs, dances, and comedy in a sentimental plot—the forerunner of the modern musical—which helped to inject some color and gaiety into the workaday world.

But life was becoming more drab and trivial and the dramas that mirrored the everyday world—those of Dumas *fils* and Augier, for example—were almost as dull as social documents. Yet men were building great hypotheses. The systems of Darwin and Marx (and later of Freud and Einstein) led to the popular belief that everything in life could be dissected and controlled, all the mysteries of life explained. But two contemporary philosophers, Kierkegaard and Nietzsche, were not impressed; their writings expressed the wasteland psychology to which all men were about to succumb. These precursors of modern existentialism had no faith in any system or in the idea of progress; they held the intellect suspect as it tended to reduce reality to immobility. Existence, they felt, was in continual and dynamic flux and challenged each man from moment to moment to solve his problems by intuition and improvisation. According to Kierkegaard, a man was isolated from everyone but God—not the God of organized religion but the individual deity each person had to become worthy of facing. Meanwhile, in his loneliness and isolation, man lived in fear and trembling. Nietzsche, going beyond Kierkegaard, felt that an individual might possibly become a "superior man" by the supreme exercise of his will but would first have to discard all mental and emotional crutches, particularly religion. Nietzsche saw the world as a raging chaos, considered every system a lie, challenged the Establishment at every point, and called for the transvaluation of all existing values. It was he who announced, "God is dead!"

In two closely related dramatic styles—realism and naturalism—that have been dominant in the theatre from the 1870s to the present, we find the synthesis that marks the beginning of modern drama: in form the "well-made play"; in subject matter the people and problems of everyday life; in point of view and tone cynical, ironic, iconoclastic.

Here Ibsen was the pace-setter. He very early discarded the form of romantic drama for the trim, stark structure of the "well-made play," abandoning poetry for prose, as more suitable to the spare images and staccato speech of real life. In one sense Ibsen's work was a clear reflection of the rigidity and rationalism of late nineteenth-century society; in another it was the beginning of streamlined drama. Here, too, the intellectual seeds of Kierkegaard and Nietzsche took hold, blossoming into a whole gallery of modern characters—isolated, bored, frustrated—prototypes of the anti-heroes to come. Before the end of the century, Alfred Jarry wrote *Ubu Roi,* which is generally accounted the first Absurdist drama; it satirized the illogical nature of the world, but it had no immediate successors.

It was August Strindberg who made the first effective break with realism and naturalism. Although he had written two masterpieces in those genres (*The Father* and *Miss Julie*), he found their tight, logical structure too inflexible to contain his mercurial and flamboyant thoughts and feelings. His material came from explosive, personal experiences and neurotic fantasies, and his creative genius provided dramatic styles in which he could portray the subjective, savage, and irrational side of man's nature. With these styles, Strindberg anticipated Freud's work with dreams and laid the foundation of expressionistic drama. Ibsen and Strindberg must thus be considered the most influential figures in modern drama, since it was they who established the two basic styles—realism and theatricalism—which have held the stage from their day to ours. All modern dramatists have written in one or both of these styles. Theatricalism, it should be explained, is not representational but presentational.

During the opening years of the twentieth century, a feeling of hollowness and dissatisfaction continued to gnaw at many people, who considered it a personal and local affliction until World War I disclosed its universal proportions. That conflict shattered many fixed ideas, shocked a number of sensitive souls into the belief that not only was God dead, but reason also. Artists in general became anti-intellectual, abstract, eclectic, and symbolic. In several major plays Luigi Pirandello, a former professor of philosophy, questioned the existence of objective truth and showed that it was impossible to differentiate clearly between illusion and reality. The Dadaists and Surrealists went even further and depicted in various genres an insane world in the process of disintegration. Antonin Artaud withdrew from the camp of the Surrealists and became a seminal figure in avant-garde drama when he founded the Theatre of Cruelty. The theatre, as Artaud conceived it, was not an escape from life, but a reattachment to it—fearful as life was. He wrote: ". . . If there is still one hellish, truly accursed thing in our time, it is our artistic dallying with forms, instead of being like victims burnt at the stake, signaling through the flames." These words, written during World War II, were an urgent plea that the theatre reflect the facts of current life— the slaughter, devastation, and suffering that had become the commonplaces of the world.

After Auschwitz and Hiroshima the absurd, the grotesque, and the totally irrational were in the ascendant. Men seemed to have grown cold, callous, and withdrawn, sensible only of feelings of nausea and anxiety. Since the mid-twentieth century, the reactions, predictably, have been violence, escape, or simply apathy, with many now viewing murder as a spectator sport, using sex and drugs as a way out, or hiding behind dark glasses.

In today's theatre, realism is no longer considered adequate for an in-depth portrayal of the absurdity and meaninglessness of our lives, computerization having reduced the individual to a hole in an IBM card. Various avant-garde styles—grouped under the heading of theatricalism and exemplified by the plays of Ionesco, Beckett, Genet, and of many younger more experimental writers—seem better able to reflect the volatile and fragmented nature of our culture.

As we enter the Space Age, the horrors of nuclear threats, of organized crime, of racial and religious strife, of worsening relations among the peoples of the world, seem unspeakable; while astounding technological advances promising transplantation of the organs of the body and transportation to distant planets leave us speechless. This state of affairs helps to account, perhaps, for the recent development of nonverbal drama. In such a play as Werner Aspenström's *The Apes Shall Inherit the Earth,* which entirely eliminates the interchange of speech, there is a heavy reliance on music, sound, gesture, and movement (mime, dance, and acrobatics). Performances of this sort have been variously called Happenings, Events, Pieces, and so on.

The "writer" of a Happening is reduced to supplying a synopsis of the action (and occasionally some words, sounds, or speeches to be utttered at random)—the action being of a surrealistic nature and of greater importance than the words. Ken Dewey, who started as a playwright but has turned to improvisational, psychedelic, and action theatre, and calls his own presentations Crossings, has said: ". . . I was trying to get out. I mean that literally: out of the text, out of the building, and, most earnestly, out of theatre's way of doing things. . . . The further out one moves, the simpler becomes one's understanding of what theatre is. I now would accept only that theatre is a situation in which people gather to articulate something of mutual concern."

The playwright thus becomes superfluous, as does the theatre, since streets, parks, subways, or any other environment will serve for the performance. And if no one happens to be around to see what is going on, the players themselves constitute the audience.

Just as the audience and the playwright have undergone a noticeable transformation from the seventeenth century to the present, so have the playhouses and the productional arts. The following is a brief overview.

The Physical Theatre

With the restoration of the English monarchy in 1660, the king issued licenses to Thomas Killigrew and William D'Avenant for the formation of new acting companies, and a sumptuous theatre was built for each of these men. The new theatres did not resemble the old, Elizabethan, open-air playhouses, which had been shut down eighteen years before. They were modeled instead on the opera houses of the Italian Renaissance, which were being imitated all over Europe and, later, in America. The basic structure of the building is the one with which we are still most familiar.

The theatre, constructed of brick and faced with stone or plaster, is two or more stories high. The house is entered from the street, and the entryway, under an overhanging marquee, is often decorated with sculptured figures, tall columns, or other architectural ornaments. The lobbies and foyers may be gilded, mirrored and carpeted to appeal to the desire of the public for luxury. The entrance to the stage is at the back of the house, usually at the end of a dim passageway, leading into a maze of iron steps, unadorned walls, and a welter of stage scenery and machinery. The contrast between the gilt and brocades in the foyer and the pipes and ropes backstage dramatizes the difference between illusion and reality.

The interior of the theatre is shaped roughly like a horseshoe and is divided into two main parts, the auditorium and the stage. In the seventeenth and eighteenth centuries, balconies rose in tiers—sometimes as many as six in height—around the walls of the auditorium. These balconies were divided into private boxes, little cubicles reserved for the use of the royal family, the members of the nobility, and the upper classes. They were the most expensive seats in the house. The seats in the orchestra were less expensive and were occupied by members of the middle class. The working class, including servants, sat on benches in the cheapest location, above the boxes and just under the roof, in an undivided area called the gallery. Theatres built during the nineteenth century reflected the increasing patronage of the middle classes. There were usually only two or three balconies and a limited number of private boxes. The aristocratic, individual box began to disappear and the undivided tier or balcony allowed all social classes to mingle. Theatres built today for the costly presentation of operas or musicals usually have several balconies for economic reasons; if the building is intended to house dramatic works, there is a single balcony and a thrust stage, which helps to bring actor and audience closer. Private boxes have been almost entirely eliminated from the modern theatre, although the new Metropolitan Opera House at Lincoln Center has retained them all around the Grand Tier and at the sides of the Dress Circle and Balcony.

The stage of the traditional theatre is separated from the auditorium by a proscenium arch, in which the front curtain hangs. The stage setting fills the entire proscenium opening. In the older theatres, it took up almost all the backstage area. In the eighteenth century, for instance, it was practically impossible to walk around behind the set as the wings and drops were close to the walls of the house. In more recent theatre buildings, the set may occupy as little as half of the stage space, thus allowing more room for the movement of actors and scenery. Offices, workshops, or storerooms may even be situated in the backstage area. Revolving and rolling platforms, as well as mechanical and lighting equipment, are on the stage. The stage floor usually has trap doors in it supported by elevators for special effects, and beneath the stage there may be a rehearsal room, the wardrobe, or a place for the musicians (if the house does not have an orchestra pit). Above the stage, and behind the proscenium arch, is an overhead storage space in which scenery and large properties can be hung from the gridiron (a metal structure high above the stage), and raised and lowered by means of a counterweight system. The machinery was formerly worked by hand, now by electric power. The actors' dressing rooms are ranged along corridors on various levels backstage.

The basic structure described above is typical for most commercial theatres in operation today. Since the 1920s, however, architects, designers, and producers have attempted to vary the shape of the theatre both outside and in. The most notable change has been made in the relative position of auditorium to stage. Many theatres are now specially designed for open staging, of which there are two main types: the arena stage, where the actors are completely surrounded by the audience; and the thrust stage, where the actors are surrounded on three sides. These theatres have eliminated front curtains in order to reduce the elements separating actor from audience and to increase communication between them.

The avant-garde producer looks upon the traditional playhouse as an antiquated building, where classical and contemporary texts can only be recited in a routine and stultifying manner. For his productions he wants no stage, no sharp line of demarcation between the actor and the audience. The actor must be able to move freely around the spectator, speak to him directly, touch him, and startle him by frequent surprise effects. The primary intention is to create a physical and emotional response in the audience. The place of performance is almost never a conventional theatre but a location chosen for its availability or suitability; it may be a large room, a converted garage, an art gallery, or it may be out of doors—a street, a park, a rooftop. These locations, in which the spectators are completely surrounded by the actors, are called "environments."

Acting

The appearance of women on the Restoration stage had a significant effect on the actors' art, particularly in those scenes in which both sexes were involved. When boys had played the female parts—a convention that existed until the closing of the theatres in 1642—the love scenes had been more or less formal and stylized. With women on the stage, these scenes become more physical, sensual, and realistic. Realism, as we understand it, however, was unknown, and acting continued to be exaggerated and artificial for the next two centuries. When a performer completed an especially showy speech or scene, he was applauded, as are our opera singers today.

In the eighteenth century there was no dearth of theories concerning the relative merits of nature and art in acting. The great controversy then arose, and still goes on, as to whether actors should feel the emotions they portray or simply feign them. In a pamphlet titled "The Paradox of Acting," Denis Diderot, the French philosopher and critic, spoke out strongly for external acting and the *imitation* of emotion. The opposite view was expressed by Charles Macklin, the English actor, who first performed Shylock as a serious character rather than as a low comedian. An exponent of naturalism long before the term came into use, Macklin believed that the actor should completely identify with the character and deeply feel his emotions.

Such theoretical discussions had little effect on actual practice, however, for actors throughout the Romantic period continued to use flamboyant gestures and to declaim to the point of ranting. The celebrated Rachel, in the formal plays of Racine, and Edmund Kean, in Shakespearean roles, were both noted for acting that went beyond passion to violence. "To see Kean," said Coleridge, "was to read Shakespeare by flashes of lightning."

The widespread interest in sociology and psychology led late nineteenth-century writers and actors to study human emotions, motivations, and relationships, as well as the effect of the environment on character and personality. This resulted in realistic acting as we know it.

The great exponent of internal acting in modern drama was Constantin Stanislavsky. By the Stanislavsky method, the performer draws upon his own psyche to achieve emotional identification with the character he is portraying. To stimulate affective and sense memories and to achieve relaxation and concentration, the actor is required to do special exercises and improvisations. He attempts to awaken within himself emotions he has felt in the past in specific situations related or adaptable to the character or scene he is to play. Since each actor must draw on his own psychological and emotional equipment and must depend on a free flow of psychic energy from his unconscious, method acting is plastic and variable. At present there are many variations of the Stanislavsky method; no modern actor or teacher of acting ignores it completely, though some question its value. Acting is an evolving art; and as the present realistic phase, which is as much of a convention as were the masks and robes of Greece, seems to be waning, if not passing, new techniques for external acting in theatricalist drama have been developed.

Just as Stanislavsky, in a sense, implemented the theories of Macklin, so Jerzy Grotowski, a Polish director, has been able to work out in the last ten years a system of non-naturalistic acting based, consciously or unconsciously, on the ideas of Vsevolod Meyerhold. The actors who are members of Grotowski's "laboratory" meet every morning at ten and go through three hours of basic exercises: gymnastics, acrobatics, breathing, rhythmic dance, plastic action, concentration, mask composition, and pantomime. After that they rehearse the play that is currently in preparation, working straight through until the time of the evening performance. The actors depend on the elements of primitive ritual: fascination, suggestion, magic words and signs, and acrobatics that compel the body to go beyond its natural, biological limitations. The actors use no make-up, but control their facial muscles to give the impression that they are wearing masks. The actors' gestures and movements are grotesque; their speech is a series of whispers, shouts, chants, grunts, sighs, and groans. The texts they use, including the classics, are cut or altered to suit their point of view and style of acting. Each actor plays many parts, regardless of age or sex, and the parts are interchangeable—Romeo becomes Juliet; and Juliet, Romeo. But in no case does the actor identify with the character. The actors perform in a room without a stage and completely surround the spectators, who very often are treated as characters in the play; in Marlowe's *Doctor Faustus,* for instance, the audience represented guests at a banquet and were seated on both sides of long, bare tables, on the tops of which the actors performed the play. Strange as it may seem, Grotowski's experiments have certain aims and elements in common with Greek tragedy: the actors wear "masks" (their own faces fixed in masklike expressions), the audience is part chorus (though silent), and the hoped-for effect of the performance is catharsis.

The Living Theatre, the Open Theatre, and other modern companies have for a long time been using techniques like Grotowski's to a similar end; as a process of self-discovery for both actor and audience. This is not surprising in view of the depersonalization of man in our society, which is reflected in the dehumanization of the theatricalist actor and in many of the characters which the realistic actor is now called on to portray. Depersonalization is largely responsible, too, for the prevalence of nudity and obscenity —shock treatments for audience and actor alike.

Directing

The theatrical director, as we know him today, first made his appearance less than a hundred years ago. Before that time the task of coordinating the various elements of a production was left to the playwright, the star, or a stage manager. There was no actual need for a director—the very title was unknown—in the Greek, medieval, Elizabethan, or neoclassical theatre, in each of which dramatic presentations had more or less fixed forms, established by traditions that the actors observed and the audiences recognized.

By the seventeenth century, social values had shifted, conventions had lost ground, and the playwright no longer held a central position in the theatre. The indoor playhouse had brought with it the picture-frame stage, on which the leading actor took over the pictorial arrangements, placing himself in the foreground center. The only unity in the production was supplied by the imposing personality and style of such stars as Thomas Betterton, Colley Cibber, and James Quin, who drew attention entirely to themselves.

Some attempts were made in the eighteenth century to achieve more realistic effects in acting, costuming, and scenery and to integrate these arts in a unified production. The most notable steps in this direction—though they did not proceed very far—were taken by David Garrick and Charles Macklin in England, Mlle. Claire Hippolyte Clairon and Henri-Louis LeKain in France, and Konrad Ekhof and Friedrich Schroeder in Germany. These influential actors, most of whom were also managers, insisted upon the careful casting of minor parts, adequate readings and rehearsals, less posturing and declamation in the acting, and more carefully planned sets and costumes.

The passion for truth, for reform, and for historical authenticity spurred nineteenth-century actor-managers to ever greater efforts toward integration and accuracy in productions. John Philip Kemble, William Charles Macready, Samuel Phelps, and several others attempted, by careful preparation, to bring order and harmony into the movement of their actors, and to their sets, costumes, and lighting. Charles Kean went beyond his contemporaries, insisting upon the historical accuracy of all the visual elements in his productions and upon the careful "blocking" (arrangement) of stage crowds as well as of featured players. Kean was assisted by a staff of stage managers and technical experts, including scholars and historians.

The first modern stage director, the man who surpassed all his predecessors in achieving a totally integrated production, was George II, Duke of Saxe-Meiningen (1826–1914), the ruler of a small state in central Germany. The Duke was a painter and draughtsman who had a passion for the theatre and who designed and directed every detail that went into his meticulous productions. His wife, who had been an actress, and his stage manager, Ludwig Chronegk, worked under his orders. The Duke realized that every aspect of a production must be related both to the script and to the actor; with iron discipline he forged all the theatrical elements required for the play into a unified work of art. From the very first rehearsal the actors used the sets, costumes, and properties designed for the play, so that they would be thoroughly familiar with them during the performance. The Duke himself conceived every gesture, movement, and position for the actor. He treated each extra in a crowd scene as an individual and rehearsed him separately. This took weeks and even months of intensive work, but the Duke set no limits on either time or money. The work of this inspired amateur revealed, according to Lee Simonson: "the necessity for a commanding director who could visualize an entire performance and give it unity as an interpretation by complete control of every moment of it; the interpretive value of the smallest details of lighting, costuming, makeup, stage setting; the immense discipline and the degree of organization needed before the performance was capable of expressing the 'soul of the play.' "

Between 1874 and 1890 the Duke's company traveled throughout Europe and gave some 2600 performances in such cities as Berlin, London, Brussels, Stockholm, Basel, and Moscow. Where they were seen, these productions created a sensation and set in motion a chain reaction of imitation and innovation. They had enormous influence on the work of André Antoine, Otto Brahm, and Constantin Stanislavsky, the great exponents of realism and naturalism among modern directors. Stanislavsky, taking his cue from Ludwig Chronegk, behaved at first like a drillmaster toward his actors, prescribing their every gesture, movement, and inflection, which he had worked out in advance and set down in his production book. By his own admission, it took him about twenty-five years to realize that this technique would produce only an external realism. By throwing away his production notes, planning nothing in advance, working creatively with his actors step by step through a play, he was finally able to achieve an inner, or psychological, realism of greater validity.

The generation of directors that came after Stanislavsky felt liberated by the Russian Revolution and mounted plays in a variety of non-naturalistic styles. Vsevolod Meyerhold, who had played Konstantin in Stanislavsky's production of *The Seagull,* was the most creative of the experimentalists; he attempted to mirror the mechanistic world in his sets and in the movement of his actors. In a constructivist setting, a complex arrangement of bare pipes and platforms, his actors performed in a highly stylized and mechanistic way. Meyerhold's directorial ideas were based on the art of improvisation. A script was merely a springboard for his conceptions, and the actors were his puppets. At his school each day's work began with the practice of "biomechanics" —exercises intended to train the actor's body, tone up his nervous system, sharpen his reflexes, and develop his energy and control. Meyerhold felt that the most important subjects for the actor to master were athletics, acrobatics, and music. Ideas similar to Meyerhold's were later expressed by Antonin Artaud, Jerzy Grotowski and other contemporary theatricalist directors. One of Meyerhold's students, Nikolai Okhlopkov, founded the Realistic Theatre in Moscow and abolished the fixed stage; this was an early attempt to force actors and audience to mingle in what is currently called an "environment."

The social upheaval created by World War I had an unsettling effect on the director trying to achieve unity in his productions. If the play is a microcosm of the world, and the world is shattered, looking at the stage would be like looking into a broken mirror. This accounts for the theatricalist techniques that the more innovative directors began to adopt in the 1920s. Antonin Artaud attempted to create "total theatre," which would combine all visual and aural elements; Erwin Piscator developed his Epic Theatre, which made social and political statements by means of multimedia: narration, acting, films, projections, maps, music, and so on; and Bertolt Brecht, Piscator's disciple in directing, mounted his own plays in multimedia and according to his theory concerning the alienation of the actor.

Talented and original directors, such as Tyrone Guthrie, Jean-Louis Barrault, Elia Kazan, José Quintero, Peter Brook, Roger Blin, Judith Malina, Jerzy Grotowski, and many others have had to impose their personal visions on both realistic and theatricalist plays in this fragmented age; and the contemporary director will be forced to continue to work in an individualistic manner until plays are once again able to mirror the "form and pressure" of a cohesive culture, an eventuality not likely to occur in the foreseeable future.

Scenery

The painters of the Renaissance discovered the laws of perspective, and stage designers soon put them to use to create the illusion of space, size, and distance in the limited area at their disposal. The Restoration stage was two or three times the size of the auditorium (these proportions were reversed in the eighteenth century) and, framed by a proscenium arch, lent itself admirably to pictorial treatment. When the curtain went up, the audience was delighted by an eye-filling scene depicting a castle in the midst of a forest, a fleet of ships at sea, a town square, or whatever locale was called for by the text. These pictures were created by the use of "wing-and-drop" scenery.

The stage floor sloped up from the footlights to the rear wall and was covered with a green baize cloth. On either side of the stage and parallel to each other were six rows of side wings (canvas stretched over wooden frames); these diminished in size and converged toward each other as they neared the backdrop (a painted cloth that completed the stage picture) the wings and drop forming a visual unit. Two additional wings downstage, called shutters, could be brought together in the center to hide the changes of scene, though the scenery was often changed in full view of the audience to the accompaniment of music. This could be done very quickly as the wings ran on tracks and one set could be pulled in while another was being pushed out; or the wings formed three sides of a pyramid, which revolved on a central axis, and merely had to be turned; the drops meanwhile were raised and lowered from the flies. These sudden transformations gave the audience great pleasure.

During the eighteenth century the stage became smaller and the auditorium larger. Painted scenery was still in vogue and the members of the Bibiena family, and other designers, were creating scenes of such complexity and grandeur as to fill us to this day with admiration and wonder. But tentative efforts were being made to provide more authentic visual settings. To begin with, the privileged spectators who had for over a century been allowed to sit on the stage during the performance were driven off by David Garrick in England and by Voltaire in France, in order to increase the illusion of reality within the picture frame. Garrick's stage designer, Philippe Jacques de Loutherbourg, provided several scenic innovations: one was the introduction of "ground rows," which represented low walls, rocks, or distant mountains and could be placed anywhere on stage; another, the beginning of local color, was the reproduction of actual locales, which were familiar to the audience.

In the early part of the nineteenth century, the wing-and-drop system was still in use. Actual stage furnishings were rather meager, but backdrops were painted in minute detail. The great hall of a castle, for instance, showed paneled walls, mullioned windows, stags' antlers, coats of arms, a banquet table fully set, and rich rugs; while the interior of humbler homes had rough plaster walls, rickety tables and chairs, pots and pans around the hearth, and even trash on the floor. As stages became shallower, the actor was forced to stand closer to the painted drop, which showed up the false perspective and completely destroyed the illusion of reality.

The cult of realism brought with it a revolution in stage settings. The box set, a room with the "fourth wall" removed, became the standard interior.

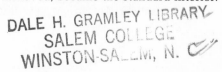

At first the walls of the room were entirely constructed of painted canvas, with openings for practical doors and windows; gradually such architectural elements as cornices, columns, and panels, and even some of the walls, came to be built of sturdier materials. From the beginning the rooms were elaborately furnished; for the set of his first production, André Antoine moved the furniture from his own home to the stage of the Théâtre Libre. Hedda Gabler's home was fitted out with real curtains, pictures, rugs, plants, and bric-a-brac. Conventional, realistic plays still use this type of set.

Two leaders in the revolt against naturalistic settings were Gordon Craig and Adolphe Appia. These influential theoreticians objected to papier-mâché buildings, painted canvas, and cluttered stages; they advocated instead the use of simple platforms, screens, and draperies to which light—the unifying element—would give mass, line, and color. It was a form of theatrical impressionism which, when accompanied by music, would appeal primarily to the emotions. These ideas strongly influenced such American designers as Robert Edmond Jones, Norman Bel Geddes, Lee Simonson, and Jo Mielziner. In 1952 Sheldon Cheney wrote, "Today the setting is flat, perspectiveless, simplified almost to bareness; surface reality no longer is pictured, but only faintly suggested, the 'atmosphere' is caught in color and light. Progress today seems all in the direction of space stages and honestly architectural stages. Painting on the stage seems to have gone into almost complete eclipse."

The newer styles in scene design, which include expressionism, constructivism, and theatricalism, range from the sculptural and the architectural to the symbolic, antirealistic, and fantastic. Happenings and Events, whether presented indoors or out, use more props than scenery, not arranged formally but as if by chance.

Lighting

Lighting the stage of an indoor theatre presented a problem in the seventeenth century because candles were the only source of illumination, though for special optical effects they burned various substances, such as moss, and set off fireworks. Candles, even in large quantities, did not shed much light, nor could the light be altered to suit a particular scene. Large chandeliers, containing hundreds of wax tapers, were suspended over the stage and auditorium and burned throughout the performance. Candles in tin sconces served as footlights, and sconces were also attached to the backs of the side wings to light the painted drop at the rear of the stage. Actors performed downstage, close to the footlights, so that their faces could be clearly seen. Lanterns directed from offstage, like primitive spotlights, cast a bit of extra light on certain characters and acting areas. Undoubtedly, there was more smoke, smell, and heat than light in the theatre. The Restoration comedies, whose texts are so brilliant and glittering, were performed in a rather dim and flickering atmosphere.

By the eighteenth century, stage lighting was somewhat improved by the use of oil lamps, which could be controlled to a certain extent. They could be made brighter or dimmer, and the color of the light they cast could be altered if bottles of tinted liquid or pieces of colored glass were placed between them and the stage. This enabled the designer to show changes in the time of day and of the weather, and to create such special effects as fire and storm.

In the first quarter of the nineteenth century, oil lamps were replaced by gaslight. The bright new illumination showed up the tawdriness of painted drops and hastened the introduction of more realistic scenery. By 1850 a dimmer-switchboard, which regulated the flow of gas to all parts of the stage, made it possible to control the intensity of the light with some accuracy.

In 1846 an electric arc lamp was first used at the Paris Opera House to create the illusion of sunlight; about fifteen years later the Paris Opera introduced the floodlight and follow spot. By the end of the century, electricity was in use in all the important theatres in Europe, and not long afterward in the United States as well. This made it possible for stage lighting to develop into a full-fledged art.

The principles of stage lighting were worked out by Adolphe Appia in the last years of the nineteenth century. He drew a distinction between two types of lighting: diffused or general illumination, floodlighting, which casts an even radiance over the stage; and focused, mobile light, spotlighting, which gives three-dimensionality to the actor. One effect of his theories was to change the concept of space onstage: an actor stepping out of a "hot" spot into the semidarkness just a few feet away appears to have moved farther than one who goes clear across the stage in bright and even light. Before Appia's principles could be fully worked out in practice, however, a great deal of sophisticated electrical equipment, such as lamps, lenses, projectors, and switchboards, had to be developed. The creative lighting designer today is able, by a sensitive control of the intensity, color, distribution, and movement of light, to achieve enormous plasticity, the most subtle psychological effects, and the exact mood called for by each moment of the play. Modern stage lighting has become so flexible and expressive that changes in the level of the illumination may go unnoticed by the spectator and yet intensify his emotional reactions to the performance. One advanced instrument that makes such precise control possible is the electronic switchboard, which permits the presetting of hundreds of light cues in the most complicated combinations.

Lighting, like acting and scenery, may be naturalistic, symbolic, stylized, or theatricalist. In such a work as Strindberg's *Dream Play,* all four styles may be used in a single production. For their "Epic" plays, Piscator and Brecht preferred to use only general illumination, as if the stage were a lecture platform; this did not rule out films and slide projections. Glen Tetley's production of the Brecht-Weill *Seven Deadly Sins* relied entirely upon lights and projections in place of built or painted scenery. Happenings, Events, and other forms of avant-garde theatre, either because of their artistic principles or their limited budgets, have not made use of sophisticated lighting equipment but seem to favor general illumination or simple spotlighting; for their outdoor performances they only require, as did the ancient Greeks, the natural light of day.

Costumes

From 1660 to about 1850, theatrical costumes were neither accurate nor consistent, so far as the period of the play or the individuality of the character was concerned. Each production showed a welter of styles in dress, which depended on the wardrobe of the performer or on a theatrical tradition. The actor usually wore the fashionable clothes of his own day: in the Restoration, for instance, Thomas Betterton played Hamlet in frilled lace, full-bottomed wig, and petticoat breeches, while in the eighteenth century David Garrick acted the role in the smallclothes of his day. Female performers, like their male counterparts, were generally attired in the height of current fashion;

for almost two centuries women's dresses showed a number of variations of low-cut necklines, full sleeves, and narrow waists, though the silhouette of the skirt went from broad panniers to straight shift to huge hoops. In addition to contemporary fashions, there were some conventional costumes, inherited from the Elizabethan theatre, for warriors, for Orientals, and for other types. The actor impersonating a soldier, of whatever time or place, wore a fanciful costume that resembled a Roman military uniform, consisting of a tunic, breastplate, plumed helmet, high cross-gartered boots, and a shield or spear to complete the outfit. The costume for Orientals was distinguished by full pantaloons secured at the ankles and worn by both men and women, with a long robe, a plumed turban, and a scimitar or dagger for the actor, and an overskirt, an elaborate commode headdress, and flying streamers, for the actress.

During the first half of the nineteenth century, only sporadic efforts were made to achieve some degree of individuality and historical accuracy in theatrical costumes. But in 1850 Charles Kean began to dress the actors in his Shakespearean productions with meticulous care, and the growing interest in realism extended that care from the plays of Shakespeare to those of contemporary writers.

The costume designer today seeks to embody in the clothes he creates some indication of the time and place, mood and style of the play, as well as the psychology and taste of the character who wears the garment. Modern stage costumes are of four main types: historical, contemporary, symbolic, and theatricalist.

Designers of historical costumes now strive for authenticity of silhouette, texture, and color. Before going to work on a play that takes place in the past, the designer will study the records and pictures of the period in which he is interested in order to reproduce the clothing with a high degree of believability. That does not mean that the stage costume will be identical to the actual one; it will *appear* to be so if the style of the production is realistic, but merely suggest the original if it is treated non-naturalistically. It is often necessary to make minor modifications in the structure of historical clothing to enable the actor to move with greater ease or to speed the change from one costume to another; certain materials, such as satin brocades, may be too expensive or too difficult to handle, but the clever designer is able to treat a cheaper and lighter fabric in such a way as to simulate a rich and luxurious texture. Properties and make-up are also specially designed to evoke a particular time in the past.

Contemporary stage clothing creates a realistic effect, but stage costumes usually differ from clothing worn offstage. A designer may buy a dress off the rack and then treat it in such a way as to make a special point—the bad taste of a frumpish woman, for instance—which must be visible to the entire audience. To achieve the effect he wants, he may alter the lines of the garment or elaborate the ornamentation. Colors are modified or made to cover larger areas; fabrics are specially selected for ease of treatment by the designer and of handling by the actor. A common practice is the employment of a famous couturier to supply the dresses for the star, as he does for a society woman; the creations of such designers as Mainbocher, Schiaparelli, Valentina, Castillo, and Dior have been seen on professional stages here and abroad.

Symbolic costumes and properties indicate the character's profession (policeman, nurse, astronaut); his social or economic status (top hat and tails, soiled work clothes); his interests or beliefs (football uniform, ecclesiastical garments). Symbolic clothing has a dramatic value because it supplies information in "visual shorthand" and at the same time arouses certain expectations in the audience.

Theatricalist costumes are the stylized or fantastic creations used generally in non-naturalistic plays. Fright wigs, abstract make-up, and a mélange of colors and styles alter the actor's appearance and help him to present a new conceptual image. A leotard often serves as the basis of a costume, and significant bits of clothing are added to it. In such a play as Aspenström's *The Apes Shall Inherit the Earth*, the furry monkey skin, which totally masks and dehumanizes the actor, is, like the facial masks used in earlier times, a theatricalist device. Nudity on the stage, a current trend, is the farthest extremity of theatricalism as it destroys all the subtleties of posture, gait, and movement, of social, economic, and professional differentiation, of characterization, and of historicity, and, as a result, has a limiting rather than a liberating effect on the drama; it eliminates, in addition, the creative contributions of an important theatrical artist—the costume designer.

Music and Dance

Music and dance, which are basic elements in ballet, opera, and musical comedy, are also valuable components of the serious drama in modern times. These independent arts are now integrated into the dramatic structure of the play. This was not always the case; from the seventeenth to the last quarter of the nineteenth century, incidental music and dance interludes were thrust into plays for no dramatic or logical reason except that they gave pleasure to the audience. William D'Avenant, the famous Restoration playwright and theatre manager, staged *Macbeth* "with alterations, amendments, additions, and new songs and divertissements [short ballets or dance numbers]," which grew more elaborate from year to year until Shakespeare's play resembled a patchwork opera.

The custom of interpolating music and dance numbers into plays, with total disregard for their relevance, continued in the eighteenth century. In 1747, Charles Macklin, who was celebrated for portraying Shylock as a serious, almost tragic, figure, did not hesitate, however, to offer a spectacular dance interlude performed by the ballet stars of the day, in the midst of his production of *The Merchant of Venice*. The sentimental comedies and domestic tragedies then in vogue gave pleasure to their audiences by reducing them to tears, and counted heavily on incidental music of a melancholy kind to achieve the desired effect. The dance, at this time, began to move out of the drama and into the burlesques and pantomimes, which were the forerunners of musical comedy.

The characteristic features of the romantic and sentimental plays of the eighteenth century reached their full development in the melodramas of the nineteenth; the close connection between music and melodrama is clear from the very name of the genre, the music being of the kind that was referred to as "hearts and flowers" because of its maudlin sentimentality. The big Romantic plays of the period were equally dependent upon musical accompaniment for the creation of mood, and the same might be said about the Shakespearean productions of Charles Kean. When Kean appeared in *Hamlet*, a contemporary critic wrote: "The house was filled in every part long before the rising of the curtain—all present being anxious to catch a glimpse of the 'greatest actor of the day.' The discussion as to his merits or demerits, during the performance of the overture, was such as to drown all the beauty of the music, which was performed on this occasion for the sole amusement of the gentlemen of the orchestra." The practice of playing an overture, and music between the acts, persisted well into the twentieth century and is still occasionally heard.

The arrival of realism, however, brought with it the distinction between incidental music and integrated (or dramatic) music and dance. Incidental music accompanies a play but is not an integral part of it; it serves to create a mood, to heighten the emotion, or to bridge scenes. It was used frequently in the theatre until the arrival of motion pictures, which adopted the practice of "sneaking in" mood music behind the action in the manner of the nineteenth-century melodrama. At present, incidental music serves to indicate moments of unreality in realistic plays, or as accompaniment to non-naturalistic drama.

Integrated music, or dance, is built into the structure of the play and is carefully motivated and developed. It has a specific dramatic function: to advance the action, to characterize, to heighten the mood, to reinforce the theme, or to do several of these things. When Hedda Gabler bangs out a wild dance tune on the piano in the last moments of Ibsen's play, she is not only indicating her frame of mind but is setting the scene for the fatal shot to follow; when, in Desire Under the Elms, old Ephraim dances joyously to the music of a fiddle to celebrate the birth of a son, the drama is infused with pathos and bitter irony; and when, in The Seven Deadly Sins, Brecht and Weill wrote what they called a ballet-cantata, they managed to create a highly didactic play on a social theme entirely in music, song, and dance.

Adolphe Appia and Gordon Craig, pioneers in the use of music and light as a unifying element in the drama, turned their backs on realism and envisioned a symbolic and poetic theatre. Appia wrote: "Music and music alone can coordinate all the elements of scenic presentation into a completely harmonious whole in a way which is utterly beyond the capacity of our unaided imagination. Without music the possibility of such harmony does not exist and therefore cannot be discovered. . . ." Craig, whose first job as a stage director was the mounting of Purcell's opera Dido and Aeneas, was equally aware of the importance of wedding movement to music in the creation of drama; he was composing dances for the opera and, in a letter to his sister, spoke of one dance for the last scene at Dido's death: "One dance I'll make a dance of arms—white white arms—The rest of the scene dark—and out of it, the voices—with arm accompaniment—exciting if done well."

Theatricalist plays lean more heavily upon music and dance than do those plays that attempt to create the illusion of reality. Expressionistic and Epic theatre have made brilliant use of choreographed movement, of song, and of specially composed scores to heighten emotional power and dramatic impact. Avant-garde drama has introduced atonal and electronic music, sound effects, and noise to accompany abstract movement and acrobatics, and has achieved stirring and startling effects.

The art of the theatre, as Gordon Craig pointed out, is comprised of three elements—sound, light, and movement—which encompass speech and music, scenery, costumes, and illumination, gesture and dance. These separate arts have, with the passage of time, been adapted to a variety of styles and conventions, the most recent of which may be seen in modern drama on stage.

HEDDA GABLER

Henrik Ibsen

Signe Hasso as Hedda takes vicious delight in burning Lövborg's manuscript. National Repertory Theatre production, 1964–1965. Photograph: Van Williams. ANTA Collection, The Players.

Henrik Ibsen

Henrik Ibsen, who is generally considered the Father of Modern Drama, was born on March 20, 1828, in Skien, a small trading center on the southeastern coast of Norway. He was the eldest of five surviving children born to Mariechen and Knud Ibsen. At the time of Henrik's birth, Knud Ibsen was a prosperous merchant and a prominent member of local society, living extravagantly in a large house in the center of town. But in 1836 his business failed, and he was driven into bankruptcy, which in those days meant social disgrace. When friends began to shun the family, the Ibsens moved to a decrepit farm, their last remaining property, in the isolated countryside. Knud Ibsen never recovered in spirit or finances from this failure. Bitter and sharp-tongued, he browbeat his hard-working wife and the children.

Henrik's reaction to the cheerlessness of his home was to withdraw into himself. He refused to play outdoors with his brothers and sister, but sat in a little room off the kitchen, drawing, painting, reading, and playing with a toy theatre he had built. Although silent and withdrawn, he was extremely observant and imaginative, and much that he read, thought, and experienced at this time later found its way into his plays. To the lonely and poverty-stricken boy the future seemed bleak, but it was his responsibility, he felt, to restore the family name and fortune, though the only means at his disposal were painting and poetry. His success was to depend largely on the strength of his will.

When Henrik was fifteen and a half, the family decided to move back to Skien, but he, not wanting to be a burden to them any longer and thinking that he might like to be a doctor, took off for the little town of Grimstad, where he apprenticed himself to an apothecary. From that day to the end of his life, he was self-supporting and independent, though he suffered through many lean years.

By choice, Ibsen cut himself off entirely from his birthplace, never setting foot in it after 1850 and severed all personal contact with his family. Except for a few notes to his sister Hedvig and a letter to his uncle at the time of Knud Ibsen's death in 1877, he never again communicated with his parents or relatives. Yet he achieved his purpose: the family name, at his death, was known far beyond Skien and Norway; his fame was world-wide.

That Ibsen was deeply marked by his struggle to realize his goal is evident from the subject matter of his dramas. In play after play Ibsen explored the suffering caused by the exercise of the will, the ruthlessness involved in the single-minded pursuit of a mission in life, and the questionable value of success if its price included terrible personal sacrifices. In his loneliness at Grimstad, Ibsen read voluminously; and he began to write poetry in earnest.

When he was eighteen, Ibsen fathered a child with a servant in the house, a woman ten years his senior, and for the next fifteen years had to contribute to the child's support. Before he was nineteen, Ibsen held strongly unorthodox views about marriage, morals, and religion.

The democratic revolutions of 1848 were spreading through Europe like a brush fire, and the young poet adopted a radical point of view toward social and political events. By temperament, he took the side of freedom for the individual in all things, and at this time he wrote poems and essays in praise of the rebels, particularly the Hungarians. He was reading widely in folklore, philosophy, and history, and felt impelled to speak out against the old social order. The career of Catiline, the Roman politician who was accounted a rebel and crushed by Cicero, especially attracted him. In 1849 at the age of twenty-one, Ibsen completed *Catiline*, his first full-length play in verse. The play was not produced, but a friend managed to have a small edition printed. *Catiline* contained many of the themes and situations Ibsen was to deal with in his later work, among them, as the playwright himself pointed out, "Two opposing women who struggle for the man and thus reveal the duality within him." Interestingly enough, this is one of the central situations in *Hedda Gabler*, which was written forty years after *Catiline*.

In 1850 Ibsen went to Christiania, the capital of Norway, intending to enter the university. After cramming for the stiff entrance examinations, he passed eight out of the eleven tests, but was not permitted to matriculate. He had already written an essay called "The Importance of Self-Knowledge" and so he turned independently to intensive reading and writing. He was interested at this time in Scandinavian folk tales and legends, and he wrote a short play, *The Warrior's Grave*, which was based on native material; it inaugurated a period of historical and romantic verse dramas. The play was submitted to the Christiania Theatre, was accepted, and was given three performances. Ibsen, watching his work being performed, shrank back in his seat when he realized how little he knew about playwriting.

In 1851 the celebrated violinist Ole Bull, who had recently founded a theatre in Bergen, on the west coast of Norway, came to Christiania to recruit talent for his playhouse. He met Ibsen and hired him as playwright-in-residence and assistant stage manager at a salary of about $22 a month. When it was discovered that Ibsen knew very little about the theatre, he was sent off to Denmark and Germany to study theatrical production, with the understanding that upon his return, he would remain at Bergen for five years. At the theatres he visited, he gained a wealth of knowledge about stagecraft and was particularly impressed by a little pamphlet from Germany called "The Modern Drama." Its author, Hermann Hettner, who was a scholar and critic, made a strong plea for psychological truth in dramatic characters, even those in historical plays. Hettner's pamphlet called Ibsen's attention to the work of the German playwright Friedrich Hebbel, who had made the transition from romantic, historical drama in verse to modern social drama in prose. Hebbel had written in his diary, "Ideas are to drama what counterpoint is to music; they are in themselves nothing, but they underlie everything the drama represents." In this statement we have an expression of the later aims of Ibsen as well as the aims of almost all the playwrights who have come after him.

A very much wiser Ibsen returned to Bergen to assume the duties of stage manager, which included taking charge of costumes and properties; he was learning his business, both as technician and playwright, from the ground up. During his five years at Bergen, Ibsen had a chance to study closely all the plays produced there, including those of the French playwright Eugene Scribe, outstanding exponent of the "well-made play." Ibsen observed, "These works have mostly a perfected technique, and therefore they please the public; they have nothing to do with poetry, and therefore perhaps they please the public still more."

Despite his apparent scorn for the French playwright, Ibsen was indebted to Scribe for a foundation upon which he could build. It was Ibsen's addition of psychologically observed characters and controversial social problems to the Scribean technique that later produced the celebrated Ibsenic drama.

Until 1864 the young playwright continued to turn out poetic, romantic, historical plays, most of which failed. These plays include *St. John's Night* (1853); *Lady Inger of Ostraat* (1855); *The Feast at Solhaug* (1856), Ibsen's first success; *Olaf Liljekrans* (1857); *The Vikings in Helgeland* (1857); *On the Uplands* (1859); *Love's Comedy* (1862); and *The Pretenders* (1864), his second success. Though each play showed an advance in style and power, his career as a writer had thus far brought him few financial returns. In 1857 he had left Bergen to become the director of the Norwegian Theatre in Christiania; in 1858 he married Suzannah Thoresen, and in 1859 their son, Sigurd, was born. When the Norwegian Theatre failed in 1862, Ibsen began to borrow money. In 1864, with the slim profits from the production of *The Pretenders*, he left Norway, and for the next twenty-seven years lived in voluntary exile with his wife and child, mainly in Italy and Germany. The furniture he had left behind in Norway was sold to discharge his debts.

Although Ibsen spent more than half of his adult life outside his native land, Norway provided the locale for all but one of his plays. His physical distance from home enabled him to view his past life with greater objectivity, as well as to evaluate current events in Scandinavia with a sharper eye. Isolated, like an island, in a foreign environment, he carefully explored his own background and personality and poured his findings into his work. In a creative life that spanned half a century, Ibsen's unremitting dedication to his art is impressive: Seven days a week, Ibsen rose at six-thirty, had his tea at seven, wrote at his desk until one, lunched, walked and meditated from two until five, dined, then read late into the night.

During his first thirteen years abroad, Ibsen wrote four important plays, three of which were monumental verse dramas; the fourth, in prose, was a tentative step in the direction that was later to lead him to world renown.

Brand (1866) was a character study of a young pastor with an indomitable will, whose motto "All or nothing" resembled Kierkegaard's "Either-Or" and who, in fulfilling his idealistic mission, did not hesitate to sacrifice his mother, wife, son, neighbors, and, finally, himself, in the frenzy of his religious zeal. Ibsen noted, however, that Brand might very well have been a scientist or an artist as well as a pastor; it was the character, not the calling, that was important.

In his next play, *Peer Gynt* (1867), Ibsen drew a lying, irresponsible rascal, completely devoid of idealism or integrity, always ready to agree to half-measures and compromises, the very antithesis of Brand. Both characters—egoistic extremists with whom it is difficult to identify or sympathize—are prototypes of the antihero. The adventures of Peer are presented episodically and combine fantasy with frivolity; in its theatricalism, it is Ibsen's dream play.

Both *Brand* and *Peer Gynt* appeared in book form long before they were produced on the stage, yet even as literature, they caused an outburst of excitement in Scandinavian countries, where politicians and other public figures, particularly those of a religious bent, imagined that they personally were being ridiculed by the playwright. In commenting on the hostile review of a Danish critic who had belittled his powers as a poet, Ibsen wrote to his friend Björnson: "I feel my powers grow with my anger. If it is to be war, let it come! I shall try my luck as a photographer. My contemporaries up there, I shall deal with one by one . . . I shall not spare the child in its mother's womb . . ."

This statement was more than a threat; it was a prophecy. For Ibsen's next play, *The League of Youth* (1869), was his first excursion into photographic realism in prose. Its protagonist, Stensgaard, is a lawyer-politician, who proves to be a demogogue and opportunist. The "war" was on in earnest, for Björnson, the leader of the Liberals in Norway, saw himself in the character of Stensgaard and was sure that Ibsen had gone over to the Conservatives. The play was produced successfully in Christiania in 1869, and was often mounted in the other Scandinavian countries during the next thirty years. Although it prefigures his later, and greater, plays, *The League of Youth* is as machine-made as anything by Scribe. Ibsen did, however, take pride in the fact that he had managed in this play to do without soliloquies and asides.

The success of this prose work did not immediately encourage Ibsen to cut short his career as a dramatic poet. His next play, *Emperor and Galilean* (1873), dealt with Roman history and religion in ten acts; it was his greatest failure and the last play he was to write in verse. With Julian the Apostate as its protagonist, the drama presented the conflict between the freedom of paganism and the repressiveness of Christianity, ending with the triumph of the latter, but expressing the hope that the future would bring a synthesis of the two ways of life. This work is almost never performed on the stage and is seldom read, yet it was Ibsen's favorite.

At the age of forty-nine, Ibsen was ready to turn away for good from historical and legendary material, episodic structure, and dialogue in verse and to develop the style of drama that was to take his name and bring him to the attention of the world.

In subject matter Ibsenic drama dealt iconoclastically with contemporary social, moral, and political problems. In structure, it was a miracle of compression and economy, surpassing even that of the French practitioners, for the main events of the story have taken place long ago, while the drama concerns itself primarily with revelations and the consequences of their former deeds to the characters. In style Ibsen the poet renounced verse dialogue for the poetry of mood, of symbolism, and of dramatic metaphor.

In the thirteen years from 1877 to 1890, which constitute his realistic period, Ibsen wrote eight masterful plays, so arranged as to present opposing points of view.

Earlier, in *The League of Youth,* he had been blamed for attacking the Left. In *Pillars of Society* (1877), the first of his truly modern plays and an unalloyed triumph in Scandinavia, he openly assailed the Right. *A Doll's House* (1879) explores an unhappy marital relationship, which ends with the woman leaving her husband. This play brought Ibsen international notoriety and fame. *Ghosts* (1881) deals with an unhappy marital relationship, in which a woman comes to grief because she does not leave her husband. *An Enemy of the People* (1882) portrays an idealist who is stoned and reviled when he attempts sincerely to help his fellow man. *The Wild Duck* (1884) depicts an idealist who causes only suffering when he puts his idealism into practice. *Rosmersholm* (1886) is the portrait of an alienated and guilt-ridden man, who has lost his old faith but cannot find a new one and sees death as the only proof of love. With this play, Ibsen began to explore his characters in depth, exercising an intuitive kind of ego psychology. *The Lady from the Sea* (1888) concerns a neurotic woman whose husband helps her to find her identity. *Hedda Gabler* (1890) has for its protagonist a neurotic woman who is unable to find her identity and destroys herself.

"What Ibsen insists on," says George Bernard Shaw in *The Quintessence of Ibsenism,* "is that there is no golden rule; that conduct must justify itself by its effect upon life and not by its conformity to any rule or ideal."

All of these plays, it should be noted, show a mixture of styles, including irony, satire, and bitter humor, as well as deep seriousness; they are tragicomedies that verge on the grotesque and thus foreshadow many of the plays of the contemporary theatre.

Upon the completion of *Hedda Gabler,* Ibsen returned to Norway, chiefly for the benefit of his son, Sigurd, who was in the Norwegian diplomatic service and who had fallen in love with, and was soon to marry, Bergliot Björnson, daughter of Ibsen's old friend and rival. Ibsen, now well-to-do and universally known, settled down in Oslo, where he composed his last four plays. The works of the final period are moody, symbolic, mystical, and often enigmatic; they are personal and nostalgic enough to be considered the playwright's spiritual autobiography.

The Master Builder (1892) is a retrospective and somber play about old age, its fascination for and destruction by youth. Solness, the protagonist, has already been stricken with an existential despair. *Little Eyolf* (1894) portrays a rejected child, very much like Hedvig in *The Wild Duck,* who is destroyed by indifferent parents. *John Gabriel Borkman* (1896) depicts the last days of a bankrupt, who is loveless and half mad. *When We Dead Awaken* (1899), Ibsen's last play, has much in common with *Brand,* one of his first, but here it is a sculptor rather than a preacher who, in his coldness in human relations and unswerving pursuit of his ideal, dies in an avalanche on an icy mountaintop.

Ibsen had called this play *When We Dead Awaken: A Dramatic Epilogue.* When asked by a newspaper editor to explain what he meant by the last word in the title, the playwright replied, ". . . The play forms an epilogue to the series of plays which began with *A Doll's House* and which now ends with *When We Dead Awaken.* . . . It completes the cycle, and makes an entity of it, and now I am finished with it. If I write anything more, it will be in another context; perhaps, too, in another form."

It is interesting to note that Brian Johnston, in a recent article ("The Corpse and the Cargo," in *The Drama Revue,* Winter, 1968) shows the close connection between what he calls Ibsen's "naturalistic cycle"—the twelve plays from *The Pillars of Society* to *When We Dead Awaken*—and Hegel's ideas concerning the evolution of spirituality in history, as set forth in the German philosopher's *The Phenomenology of Mind.* In each of the plays in the cycle, Johnston points out, Ibsen, closely following Hegel, dramatized a "spiritual confrontation and collision" in a different period of history. *Hedda Gabler,* for example, depicts the conflict between paganism and Christianity, reduced to the scale "of nineteenth-century bourgeois and suburban life." "The 'Christian' forces of the play," says Johnston, "are represented by the pious little phrases of Aunt Julie and Thea's foolish but brave self-sacrificial character (with her halo of golden hair that so infuriates Hedda). The pagans—Hedda, her alter-ego Diana, and the dionysiac Lövborg —are similarly 'reduced,' yet through these unpromising characters, their setting and their dialogue, Spirit manages to fight much the same campaign, and witness much the same defeat, as that of the emperor Julian [in *Emperor and Galilean*]."

Ibsen clearly realized that he had taken realism and naturalism as far as they could go and that now some completely new departure was called for in the drama. Symbolism, expressionism, and other forms of theatricalism had already made their appearance; Ibsen's work was finished. In 1900 he suffered the first of a series of paralytic strokes, which brought his life to an end on May 23, 1906.

Because he dealt with ideas then rarely discussed in public and because he questioned the validity of generally accepted moral and ethical beliefs, Ibsen was reviled as a vicious scandalmonger, sensationalist, and muckraker. In vain he protested that he was not a reformer but a poet. Yet as each new play appeared in country after country, hidebound critics, nurtured on senti-mental, conventional, and romantic drama, let out howls of protest and torrents of vituperation. Even such a literary light as Henry James viewed the playwright, at first, with contempt, though later he was to undergo a partial conversion. Strindberg despised Ibsen but called him "Master"; Chekhov thought *Ghosts* was a "rotten play" but admitted, "Ibsen is my favorite author." Shaw, from the very first, praised Ibsen enthusiastically and, during the older playwright's lifetime, coined the terms Ibsenism and Ibsenite. Pirandello said, "After Shakespeare, without hesitation, I put Ibsen first. . . ."

To readers and audiences throughout the world, there came at length a recognition of Ibsen's clarity of thought, objectivity, psychological insight, poetic vision, and human and emotional impact—the end products of this master builder's consummate craftsmanship. As a result Ibsen's plays im-mediately recommended themselves to the European stage directors who were just then introducing realistic techniques of theatrical production. The Duke of Saxe-Meiningen, André Antoine, Otto Brahm, J. T. Grein, and Stanislavsky, among others, used Ibsen's plays as vehicles for the develop-ment of psychological acting, the handling of stage crowds, the creation of mood and atmosphere in stage settings, and the imaginativeness and aptness of stage business. The old playwright saw and applauded some of the modern productions his artistry had made possible.

Regrettably Ibsen's success, and the honors bestowed upon him in old age, did not bring him happiness; but his technical and artistic innovations won him scores of disciples among critics, playwrights, and directors and have had a lasting effect upon modern drama.

Hedda Gabler

Hedda Gabler is Ibsen at the height of his creative powers. It is a drama that depicts a type of neurotic personality that has become more universally recognized in our day than it was at the turn of the century. Long before the advent of Freud, Ibsen understood intuitively that there are internal pressures that drive people to commit inexplicable and wanton acts. In his full-length portrait of Hedda, the dramatist has given us an authentic study of a pathological type, which Dr. Karen Horney has dealt with in detail in her book, *The Neurotic Personality of Our Time*. According to Dr. Horney, the individual who grows up under rigid discipline and without affection will feel anxious, hostile, and alienated from the world, and will attempt to mask his feelings of helplessness and insignificance by a show of strength. By seeking power and prestige, the neurotic imagines he will be in a position to control others without being controlled. Too cowardly to give vent to his deepest feelings, whether of love or hate, or to take an active part in life, the neurotic shuns responsibilities and commitments, yet envies those who are able to pursue their aims in competition with others, begrudges them their success, and attempts to belittle and destroy them.

Hedda, in effect, represents Ibsen's conception of the New Woman in an individualistic and competitive society. In contrast to her, there are the old-fashioned types, Aunt Julie and Thea, whose greatest joy comes from serving those they love, even, as in Thea's case, when it means defying conventions to do so.

Eilert Lövborg and George Tesman are contrasted intellectual types—the undisciplined talent and the unimaginative hack. Ibsen seems to pity the one and to scorn the other and ends the play on a heavy note of irony. It would take more than Thea's inspiration to spark George Tesman; between them they can hardly hope to recreate Eilert's vision, for all their eagerness to do so.

Judge Brack is, to a certain degree, the male counterpart of Hedda; he is a secret lecher who seeks freedom from the responsibilities of marriage in affairs with prostitutes and the seduction of married women.

Inspiration for the writing of *Hedda Gabler* is generally thought to have come from the playwright's brief romance with Emilie Bardach, a Viennese girl whom he met at a resort in the Alps late in 1889 and with whom he corresponded until February, 1890, shortly after he began this play. The dramatist was sixty-one, the girl eighteen; the encounter, apparently, was platonic. If the incident stirred the spirit of creativity in the aging playwright, it provided little identifiable or significant dramatic material for the play. *Hedda Gabler* does contain, however, unmistakable allusions to the life and heavily autobiographical works of August Strindberg, the Swedish playwright, who was twenty-one years Ibsen's junior and in Ibsen's view an impetuous "youth knocking at the door."

Strindberg had begun to attack Ibsen after the appearance of *A Doll's House* (1879), a play in which an "emancipated" woman leaves her husband. Strindberg, who feared that his own wife would leave him (as all three of his wives eventually did), was rabid on the subject of male-female relations, and he firmly believed that woman's place was in the home. He promptly accused the Norwegian playwright of starting the "Nora cult" that was infecting Scandinavian life and called him, among other things, a defender of masculine women and effeminate men—degenerates who would bring ruin to European civilization. In Strindberg's collection of short stories entitled *Married,* one of the tales, "A Doll's House," actually refers to Ibsen and his play by name, and states plainly that the writer of such a work is a mischief-maker, a "devil," a disrupter of happy homes. Strindberg continued to snipe at Ibsen in public and in private (in plays, books, stories, letters, and conversations), with ever mounting venom, throughout the 1880s. Ibsen, though living on the Continent, was an avid reader of Scandinavian newspapers, periodicals, and books and was well aware not only of Strindberg's scurrilous remarks but also of the younger man's scandalous escapades.

Strindberg had fallen in love with Siri von Essen, a society girl who was unhappily married to a military man much older than herself. Wishing to be "emancipated" and "to live dangerously," Siri got a much publicized divorce, married Strindberg, and went on the stage under her own name. These events caused a great deal of gossip and were fully reported in the press. By 1882 Strindberg had won a reputation for being a wild genius much given to drink, was working at the Royal Library, and had written several books about cultural history. At the time, he was about thirty-three, the age of George and Eilert in *Hedda Gabler.*

In 1884 Strindberg published *Utopias of Reality,* which contained his vision of the bright civilization of the future. It was a safe book, in that it stirred up no controversy, and was well received. This was true also of Eilert's first book, which its author considered inconsequential; Strindberg's subject matter, however, was the same as that of Eilert's second book. Strindberg's next work, *Married* (1884–86), expressed his deepest feelings about the unsoundness of the institution of marriage and of all the institutions of church and state. *Married* was immediately banned, and the author was threatened with a sentence of two years at hard labor, which brought him to the verge of insanity and suicide. This episode put Strindberg's name in the headlines of the major European newspapers and could not have escaped Ibsen's notice. In *Hedda Gabler* it is the loss to Eilert of his outspoken second book, into which he had put his "true self," that unsettles him emotionally and causes his death.

In his preface to *Married,* Strindberg remarked that women ought to keep their maiden names when they take a husband—a point Ibsen makes in the very title of *Hedda Gabler.* Helena, the heroine, of Strindberg's "Corinna," a story in this volume, is the daughter of a general and is brought up to excel in horseback riding, gymnastics, and other masculine sports. She despises women, holds men in contempt, is revolted by sex, and, like Hedda, is afraid of the responsibilities of motherhood. Out of financial necessity she marries a college teacher, a weakling she looks down upon but helps him to acquire a professorial chair. Though she treats him disgracefully, he is madly in love with her. All of these elements, of course, are fundamental to the plot of *Hedda Gabler.*

"Love and Bread," another Strindberg story in the same volume, also has for its heroine the daughter of a military man and for its "hero" a weakling who has been raised by a doting elderly maiden aunt. This man courts the girl in her living room under the surveillance of her father. After they have married, the young couple establish a home, which is described, in part, as follows: "The bride had her own little alcove, which was screened off by a Japanese screen. The drawing-room, which was also dining-room, study and morning-room, contained her piano . . . [and] his writing-table. . . ." Here are further correspondences with *Hedda Gabler:* George's overzealous aunt Julie, Eilert's meeting with Hedda under the eye of General Gabler, Hedda's alcove and piano, George's writing-table.

In his play *Comrades* (1886), Strindberg attempted to demonstrate that comradeship can never exist between a man and a woman because of the inveterate battle of the sexes. Eilert wished to be a "comrade"—his favorite word—to Hedda and to Thea, and failed. In *Miss Julie* (1888), a play that achieved international fame, Strindberg portrayed a neurotic society girl who destroyed herself with a weapon provided by a "lover" and under the influence of the power of suggestion—not unlike the way in which Eilert receives from Hedda both the weapon and the idea of using it. Miss Julie, a sexually disturbed woman, is described as "a relic of the old warrior nobility," and Strindberg spoke of "keeping the unhappy spirit of the father above and behind the action." The spirit of General Gabler, an "old warrior," remains "above and behind the action" in *Hedda Gabler,* and the prostitute, in whose room Eilert dies, Ibsen calls Mademoiselle Diana. Miss Julie is the owner of a wayward bitch who happens to be called Diana; the use of the name of the goddess of chastity and of the hunt having ironic implications in both plays.

After reading *Hedda Gabler,* Strindberg maintained, in his book *A Madman's Defence,* that he had "fathered" the play, just as earlier he was sure that he and Siri had been ridiculed by Ibsen in *The Wild Duck* (1884). Strindberg pointed out the close resemblance of Hedda to several of his own female characters; Eilert Lövborg he considered a weak and unreliable person, apparently unaware that he himself might have served as the model. So sure was he of his influence on the Norwegian playwright that after the appearance of *The Master Builder* (1892), Strindberg said in a letter to Birger Mörner, a young Swedish writer, "My seed has fallen in Ibsen's brain-pan—and germinated."

If, in *Hedda Gabler,* Ibsen used material from Strindberg's life and work as a subtle retaliation for ten years of insults, his impeccable craftsmanship transformed the subject matter into a masterpiece of universal significance. Although the two men never met, there is no doubt that Ibsen was psychologically involved with his Swedish rival. In 1895, Ibsen bought a portrait of Strindberg—with his "devilish eyes"—which he hung over his desk, saying, "I am not now able to write a word without having that madman staring down at me."

In *Hedda Gabler,* Ibsen presents, a concatenation of themes with which he had dealt separately in earlier plays: In *Catiline,* we find a man torn between two women, his Good and Evil Angels, as in the Thea-Eilert-Hedda relationship; in *A Doll's House,* a woman commits a reprehensible act for the benefit of her husband and falls into the power of an unscrupulous man; in *The Wild Duck,* a meddler, who is determined to improve the lives of others, succeeds only in destroying them; and in *The Lady from the Sea,* a woman marries for security but is bound in her fantasies to a former lover. It is remarkable that from such diverse materials Ibsen was able to construct a unified work that is a masterpiece of economy, force, and originality.

It has been fashionable for critics, with few exceptions, to call Ibsen's plays dated, since modern drama has veered sharply from quiet, subtle irony and has moved headlong into violence and vituperation. Edward Albee's *Who's Afraid of Virginia Woolf?* is perhaps one of the most notable recent examples of the drama's excursion into overt hostility. When the play opened on Broadway in October, 1962, Howard Taubman, of *The New York Times,* said, "It is a modern variant on the theme of the war between the sexes. Like Strindberg, Mr. Albee treats his women remorselessly, but he is not much gentler with his men." Other critics, too, have seen the ghost of Strindberg haunting Albee's play. What is curious in this—and has been generally overlooked—is that the Strindbergian spirit seems to have been transmitted through the medium of Ibsen. Indeed, the resemblances in both situations and characters between *Virginia Woolf* and *Hedda Gabler* are astonishingly numerous.

Both plays are concerned with people in academic life.

Ibsen deals with the interrelations of four characters: Hedda, George, Eilert, Thea; Albee does the same with Martha, George, Nick, Honey. Brack, a fifth figure of importance in Ibsen's play, is a man of strong sexual inclination, a characteristic Albee gives to Nick.

Both Hedda and Martha are the daughters of imposing fathers, whose almost physical presence stands behind the action. Hedda's father is literally a part of the stage setting: "Above the sofa hangs the portrait of a handsome elderly man in a General's uniform." Martha says of hers: "Daddy built this college. . . . He *is* the college."

Hedda's husband, George, is a professor of history, unaggressive and undistinguished; Martha's husband, George, has the same profession, same status, same personality.

Both Hedda and Martha hold their husbands in contempt.

Hedda has married George Tesman with certain expectations (". . . it may very well be that he will get some place, in time") but is disappointed in him as a man ("Scholars are not exactly entertaining. . . . To hear someone talk cultural history early and late—"). Martha has similar expectations, similar disappointments: "So, here I am, stuck with this flop . . . this BOG in the History Department . . . some bookworm, somebody who's so damn . . . contemplative, he can't make anything out of himself. . . ."

Both Hedda and Martha lead bored and aimless lives. Ibsen suggests that Hedda is a pagan (she envisions Eilert "with vine leaves in his hair") and a romantic (she wishes him to die "beautifully"). Albee has George characterize Martha directly: "Martha is the only true pagan on the eastern seaboard." "Martha's a Romantic at heart."

Eilert is presented as a rival to George at the university, mainly because he has published a book on cultural history. His second book, in manuscript, "deals with the forces that will determine the civilization of the future." Martha makes much of Nick as a rival to George, and the two men express opposite views of the civilization of the future, George regarding Nick and the growing influence of science as a cultural threat.

All the women in both plays are childless. Hedda does not want children. When Brack says ". . . suppose that there comes—what people—in rather elegant language—call a serious, demanding responsibility on you?" Hedda responds: "Be quiet. You will never live to see anything like that. . . . I have no leaning towards such things, Mr. Brack. Not for responsibilities."

Honey's pregnancies are false and fruitless; she is afraid of having children: "I DON'T WANT THEM . . . I . . . don't . . . want . . . any . . . children. I'm afraid. I don't want to be hurt. . . ."

Hedda destroys Eilert's and Thea's "child" (the manuscript); George destroys his and Martha's imaginary child. Both "mothers" are deeply upset by the destruction of their fictional offspring.

Hedda fires her pistol at Brack "in fun." "Hedda: Now I shall shoot you, Mr. Brack! Brack: Have you gone mad—! Hedda: Goodness—did I hit you, possibly? . . . Brack (gently takes the pistol out of her hand): With your permission, madam! . . . Because we won't play that game any more today." George "shoots" Martha with a trick shotgun out of which pops a Chinese parasol. Their hostility is verbalized. "George: Did you think I was going to kill you, Martha? Martha: (Dripping contempt) You? . . . Kill me? . . . That's a laugh. George: Well, now, I might . . . some day. Martha: Fat chance."

In structure *Virginia Woolf* consists of a series of "games," for each of which Albee provides a title; the identical games, untitled, are played in *Hedda Gabler:*

Humiliate the Host—In Ibsen's version, Hedda clearly expresses her contempt for George's aunts and for his work and his manhood.

Get the Guests—Ibsen begins the game when Hedda sits between Eilert and Thea; she taunts Eilert, starting him on the path to self-destruction, and torments both by revealing information Thea has told her in confidence.

Bringing up Baby—Eilert and Thea discuss the manuscript of his second book as if it were their child, now mistreated, lost, abandoned, destroyed.

Hump the Hostess—Brack's persistent advance upon Hedda is foiled by her suicide; Nick's encounter with Martha is frustrated by his excessive drinking.

Hedda freely admits that she is a coward and dies a coward's death; when for the last time, Albee's George asks Martha, "Who's afraid of Virginia Woolf?" Martha, a coward too, says, "I am . . . George . . . I am . . ."

One of the crucial events in *Hedda Gabler,* though it occurs offstage, is an all-night liquor and sex orgy that ends at dawn; this is a concise description of *Who's Afraid of Virginia Woolf?* in its entirety.

George Bernard Shaw found the ending of *Hedda Gabler* faulty; he called the heroine's suicide "operatic." Shaw said that the "tragedy" of a person of Hedda's type is that she would *not* destroy herself but would go on living, a nuisance to herself and to everyone around her. This is, it appears, precisely what Martha will do after the end of *Virginia Woolf.* It is impossible to believe that she will find any real reconciliation with George, as the closing lines of the play suggest, since we see no change in George nor any remission in Martha's neuroticism. It has often been said that Hedda would have found ample outlets for her energy and hostility had she but had the social and professional opportunities of the woman of today; Martha, with all these modern opportunities, is more openly hostile and neurotic than Hedda.

Written seventy years after *Hedda Gabler,* Albee's play depends for its appeal mainly on the naked violence of its action and the shock value of its outspoken dialogue; Ibsen's play offers a subtler exploration of character, deeper psychological insights, muted ironies, and the tantalizing ambiguities of human drives and desires. Each play deals with barrenness and creativity —physical, psychological, and literary—in the idiom of its own time. It is difficult, perhaps, to realize that Ibsen was once considered an avant-garde playwright and that *Hedda Gabler* was greeted with cries of "too outspoken," "obscene," "sewage."

Production Record

Hedda Gabler was published in Copenhagen in December, 1890, and had its first performance on January 31, 1891, at the Residenz Theater in Munich, where the playwright was living at the time. Ibsen attended the première. He found fault with the star, Frau Conrad-Ramlo, who, instead of speaking in a straightforward and natural manner, "declaimed" her lines in a way that indicated to the author that she did not understand the part. The audience whistled and jeered. In Stockholm, Göteborg, Copenhagen, and Christiania, its audiences greeted the play with hisses, boos, and laughter. Ibsen saw the play for the second time at the Lessing Theater in Berlin and again found the leading lady's performance inadequate. The actors of the day were not accustomed to naturalistic playing; the public and the critics found the subject matter "unpleasant," if not downright "disgusting."

Ibsen was of the opinion that powerful realistic performances would make the difference between failure and success. Through Kristina Steen, an actress at the Christiania Theater, he had learned that Mrs. Wolf, a notable member of the company, was not willing to play the part of Berta. The playwright wrote to Miss Steen:

Mrs. Wolf wishes to be released from playing the said, Berta, in my new play, since she believes that this rôle can easily be filled by any other actress in the company.

She is mistaken. There is no one else at the theater who can play Berta as I wish her to be played. Only Mrs. Wolf can do it. She has obviously not taken the trouble to read the play carefully, or she would certainly have realized this.

George Tesman, his old aunts, and their housekeeper, Berta, together create a picture that is unified and complete. They have common thoughts, common memories, and a common attitude towards life. To Hedda they represent a foreign and hostile force which is a threat to her individuality. The harmony that exists between them must be made clear by the actors. And this can be done if Mrs. Wolf plays the part. But only if she does.

I have too much respect for Mrs. Wolf's common sense to believe seriously that she considers it beneath her dignity as an artist to play the part of a maid. I surely did not regard it as beneath my artistic dignity to create this competent, honest, middle-aged woman.

Here in Munich this simple creature is to be played by one of the

Hoftheater's leading actresses, and she has undertaken the task with interest and love. For she is not merely an actress, she is also an artist. By that I mean that she is not satisfied simply to "play a part" but strives to bring to life the character she impersonates.

Mrs. Wolf persisted, however, in her refusal to play Berta.

Translated into one language after another, *Hedda Gabler* has served as a vehicle for some of the foremost actresses in the Western world, among them Mrs. Fiske, Eleonora Duse, Mrs. Patrick Campbell, Alla Nazimova, Peggy Ashcroft, and Eva Le Gallienne.

The first performance of the play in English, in William Archer's translation, was put on at the Vaudeville Theatre, London, in 1891, by an American actress, Elizabeth Robins. Although the play was a resounding success with the public, the critics showered it with ridicule and abuse. The play was first seen in America when Miss Robins brought her production to New York in 1898 for a single performance.

In October, 1903, Mrs. Minnie Maddern Fiske, the most glamorous star in the American theater at that time, appeared as Hedda for a week's engagement at the Manhattan Theatre, with George Arliss playing Judge Brack. The production was such an enormous success that Mrs. Fiske revived it for a month in 1904, and later included it in her traveling repertory. A reporter from the New York *Herald* interviewed the star in her dressing-room and asked her why she "chose to glorify gloom and impersonate such an unsympathetic and detestable character as Hedda." Mrs. Fiske replied:

Ibsen has come to be a force in the theater . . . and the player must be catholic in his selection of plays. Why should Ibsen . . . be played in all the dramatic centers of Europe and be neglected here? Moreover, there is that in Ibsen that well repays representing him. The great number of modern plays are neither good literature nor good stage-craft. Even many among those that are the more pretentiously represented will not repay a reading. . . . They are produced with every art of the scene painter and the stage mechanic, and are adorned with all possible detail that pleases the eye, but they have no substance as drama and are bad literature." The reporter then inquired whether it paid financially to produce Ibsen. Mrs. Fiske's response was, "Yes, it does. It is a mistake to think, as many do, that Ibsen does not attract the public. . . . I don't think an Ibsen play would run for a season, as so many other plays do, but I do think . . . that *Hedda Gabler* would run for two months, and it would draw intelligent people. . . ." On the value of Ibsen to the performer, Mrs. Fiske remarked: "Ibsen is splendid practice for the actor. He makes the intellect alert, and one must study carefully to reach any of his depths. . . . He brings out of actors of even the minor parts things that they themselves never dreamed they possessed. The character of Hedda requires long study, years of study. . . . It would be impossible for me to give my idea of Hedda Gabler without long thought . . . there are so many things about the character that impress the student.

Soon other American stars essayed the role. In 1904 Nance O'Neill appeared as Hedda at the Columbia Theatre, Boston, and in the same year

Robert Edmond Jones' setting (unlighted) for *Hedda Gabler,* 1918. Nazimova stands in the curtained doorway. The portrait of General Gabler is down-stage of her (left), not in the inner room. Courtesy Museum of the City of New York Theatre Collection.

Blanche Bates was seen in the part in Philadelphia. The *Record* spoke of Miss Bates as a "hysterico-neurotic heroine," and the *Ledger* said,

> The performançe was well managed. Acted with the realistic, natural method, the dramatist's power carried the mind of the spectator toward Hedda's inevitable punishment with an irresistible impetus. Here and there a jarring note appeared in theatricalisms, which seemed utterly out of place in a drama of this sort. The tendency to increase the tempo at the ends of the acts and the casting of a green light on the face of the dead Hedda were noticeable blemishes.

The Russian actress, Alla Nazimova, who became a great star of the American stage and screen, first appeared in the role of Hedda at the Princess Theater in New York on November 13, 1906. She played the role many times after that, over a period of thirty years. It was also the first part in which Nazimova spoke English, having learned the language in seven months. After seeing her performance, William Archer, Ibsen's English translator, said: "In her manipulation of the [Lövborg] manuscript, throughout this scene she departed from Ibsen's intentions, but in such a splendidly imaginative way that I am sure he would have forgiven her." Nazimova later explained: "Mr. William Archer opened my eyes to the value of a little thing in *Hedda Gabler* that was purely a matter of accident. I had always hidden Lövborg's manuscript under a sofa pillow, but at this performance [the one Archer attended], Mr. Blair [who played Lövborg] came in sooner than I expected, and I could not reach the pillow in time. So I thrust the manuscript under my wrapper and held it against my breast. But when Mrs. Elvsted said to Lövborg, 'I shall think of it to my dying day, as though you had killed a little child,' the thought of clasping a dead child filled me with such horror that my hands shrank from the touch of the manuscript, and it fell to the floor. Luckily I was able to cover it with my wrapper, and the scene was saved. I thought no more of it, till Mr. Archer spoke of it as the greatest moment in the play."

On this occasion, Nazimova wore a costume that was intended to have symbolic significance. A critic described her appearance as follows:

Robed in a strangely mottled fabric of green, a glorified kimono, falling straight from chin to toe and neck to heel, her dark head rising upon a slim, long neck above the shining folds, Madame Alla Nazimova looked not unlike the most beautiful, most glittering and powerful of serpents . . . an ominous shining thing that might have trailed its length unnoticed in the grass.

Nazimova played the part again in 1907 at the Bijou Theatre, in 1908 at the Majestic Theatre, and ten years later at the Plymouth Theatre. The production at the Plymouth opened on April 8, 1918; it was produced and directed by Arthur Hopkins, with sets by Robert Edmond Jones. The star had long since abandoned the theatrical, reptilian costume, but her performance was more remarkable than ever. Heywood Broun concluded his flattering review with the words: "Nazimova has never appeared to better visual advantage than in the first act of the present production of *Hedda*." The actress continued to apear intermittently in the role until 1936 when, after her run at the Longacre Theatre, she took the play on a final national tour that included Boston, Chicago, Syracuse, and Detroit.

On November 14, 1907, Mrs. Patrick Campbell, a reigning British star, was seen as Hedda at the Lyric Theatre in New York. Mrs. Campbell had played the part many times in London and considered it one of her triumphs. Max Beerbohm, the celebrated English critic, preferred Mrs. Campbell's interpretation of Hedda to Duse's. It should be noted, however, that Beerbohm understood no Italian, the language in which the great Duse played; of her performance, he wrote: "She was spiritual, statuesque, somnambulistic, what you will, always in direct opposition to eager, snappy, fascinating, nasty little Hedda Gabler. . . . Resignation, as always, was the keynote of her performance. And here, as often elsewhere, it rang false." Beerbohm thought that Duse showed no real feeling for the part, whereas Mrs. Campbell enacted it perfectly. He said: "Mrs. Campbell's only fault is one over which she has no control: she is physically too beautiful; Hedda should be *mesquine* [mean-looking]." Mrs. Campbell, according to Beerbohm, was successful as Hedda because she could brood disdainfully, had a sense of humor which she communicated to her audience, especially in her wicked mockery, and suggested that Hedda was a "good sport" in a sexual sense.

Emily Stevens, who had studied the role of Hedda with her cousin Mrs. Fiske and had played the part of Berta in Mrs. Fiske's production of 1904, starred in the Actors' Theatre version of the play at the Comedy Theatre, January 26, 1926. Although she met with general approval, one reviewer pointed out that Miss Stevens was "mannered and occasionally over-emphatic," conceding that her interpretation of Hedda was "continuously arresting and often brilliant in its quick shifts of mood, its concentration, and its impulsiveness."

The American actress most frequently seen as Hedda in recent times is Eva Le Gallienne, who played the part at almost regular intervals from 1928 to 1948, first at her Civic Repertory Theatre in New York, then on Broadway, and finally in summer stock and in tours around the country. In her first appearance as Hedda, Miss Le Gallienne wore modern dress, which, the critics agreed, seemed to date the play rather than give it a contemporary look; in subsequent productions, the actress reverted to period costumes.

Scene from Actors' Theatre production, New York 1926. Emily Stevens (Hedda) and Frank Conroy (Judge Brack). Courtesy Museum of the City of New York.

Eva Le Gallienne (at head of table) reads from her own translation of *Hedda Gabler* at the first rehearsal of the National Repertory Theatre production which she directed, New York 1964. At her right, Dolores Sutton (Thea) and Farley Granger (Lövborg); at her left, cigarette in hand, Signe Hasso (Hedda). Photograph: Van Williams. ANTA Collection, The Players.

The most scintillating and impressive production of *Hedda Gabler* done in our day was mounted in 1954 by Peter Ashmore at the Lyric, Hammersmith, in London, with Peggy Ashcroft as the star of this "mordant comedy." W. Macqueen Pope, a British critic, wrote: "Nobody who sees this *Hedda* will ever forget it. . . . Here is the supreme egotist whose world revolves around herself. Miss Ashcroft makes not the slightest gesture for sympathy—she is content to be horrible, as Ibsen meant her to be. . . . She is determined to repel and she does, yet she fascinates at the same time. She does more damage to her victims with a smile, a look, a movement of her hands and even her feet, than by the bitterest line Ibsen put in her mouth. This is great acting." After a run of several months at the Lyric Theatre, the production was moved to the Westminster Theatre in the West End, after which it toured the Scandinavian countries for three weeks. The actors faced their severest test in Oslo, Ibsen's own city, but audiences were wildly enthusiastic and the critic for the leading newspaper, *Aftenposten*, wrote as of a revelation: "It is curious to have to register the fact that an English

Anne Meacham (Hedda) seated, Lester Rawlins (Tesman), and Lois Holmes (Aunt Julie) in the David Ross production, New York 1960. Courtesy ANTA Collection, The Players.

actress has shown the Norwegian public how Hedda should be played." The King of Norway set his seal on the general acclamation by giving Miss Ashcroft the King's Medal in gold.

Hedda Gabler achieved the longest run in its history when the play was put on by David Ross at the Fourth Street Theater, New York, in November 1960. In Michael Meyer's translation this production chalked up 340 consecutive performances. In his review in the New York *Herald Tribune,* Walter Kerr spoke of "the peacock cries of the superb Anne Meacham in the title role" and mentioned "the dry-ice brilliance of [her] work." For her acting in this part, Miss Meacham won an Obie [Off-Broadway] Award.

The most recent production of note was the one directed by Ingmar Bergman at the Royal Dramatic Theatre, Stockholm, and described by Richard Roud in the *Guardian* [London], under date of January 7, 1965. Mr. Roud wrote:

> Most productions of *Hedda* try to capture the claustrophobic and stultifying nature of Hedda's world by covering the stage with tons of more-or-less Norwegian bric-a-brac and filling every corner with over-stuffed furniture.
>
> Bergman's solution to the problem is quite simple. When the curtain rises we see that the back and side walls of the stage have been painted a dull bilious red. By way of flats, there is a more or less semi-circular series of screens around the stage, also painted dull red. Props are reduced to a minimum: there is an old-fashioned oblong piano, an armchair, and a couch, covered in dull red felt, and outlined with matt black wood. Stage left, a black wood mirror frame is stuck onto one flat; stage right there is a *trompe-l'oeil* book-case with the book spines covered in dull red felt.
>
> Nowhere is there a window, nowhere a real door, nowhere any realistic light source. This solution seems to me quite brilliant because it certainly renders the stuffy, airless atmosphere of Hedda's life without forcing the eye to look at hideous furniture and knick-knacks for two hours. Another contribution specifically by Bergman is a two-minute mime scene for Hedda as the play begins. Dressed in a white négligé she wanders distractedly around the library, picking out a few notes on the piano, lighting a cigarette, playing with her pistols.
>
> Purists might object to such additions to the play, but there is no denying that the scene is extremely effective. A later interpolation is less happy: when Brack discovers Hedda has killed herself he vomits into his handkerchief. . . .
>
> As far as the cast goes, however, I do not think it was any better than that of the recent Volanakis production [of *Hedda Gabler*] in London with Joan Greenwood. Gertrud Fridh—who has acted in many Bergman films—has been made to play it very straight, and very restrained. So much so that if one had not read the play or seen other productions, one might wonder why this seemingly self-contained lady was behaving quite so peculiarly.

In 1962 Raymond Rouleau directed a production of *Hedda Gabler* at the Théâtre Montparnasse in Paris, with Ingrid Bergman acting the title role in

French. Five years later Rouleau cast Delphine Seyrig as Hedda for his television version of the play, which ran for one hour and forty-five minutes. The director made some minor cuts of repetitious lines in the opening scenes, but then interpolated a scene of his own invention in which Hedda dreams of George and Eilert at the stag party at which her father, the General, appears and criticizes her severely. The dream sequence, according to Rouleau, was intended to represent Hedda's hopes and fears and to turn the play into a drama of guilt. Other television adaptors have mutilated the play by cutting it to fit a sixty- or ninety-minute time slot; these television productions have featured such performers as Jessica Tandy, Tallulah Bankhead, and Pamela Brown; or Ingrid Bergman, this time speaking English, heading an all-star cast that included Ralph Richardson, Michael Redgrave, Trevor Howard, and Ursula Jeans, on CBS-TV in 1963.

In addition to receiving innumerable productions in countries on every continent, *Hedda Gabler* has been presented literally hundreds of times in colleges and universities throughout the United States, and often with unusual distinction. The mystery of Hedda's personality, and the dire consequences of it, will, it is safe to say, continue to offer a challenge to future actresses, directors, and producers and to hold a fascination for future readers and playgoers.

Ibsen's Writing Process

Before I write down one word, I have to have the character in mind through and through. I must penetrate into the last wrinkle of his soul. I always proceed from the individual; the stage setting, the dramatic ensemble, all of that comes naturally and does not cause me any worry, as soon as I am certain of the individual in every aspect of his humanity. But I have to have his exterior in mind also, down to the last button, how he stands and walks, how he conducts himself, what his voice sounds like. Then I do not let him go until his fate is fulfilled.

As a rule, I make three drafts of my dramas which differ very much from each other in characterization, not in action. When I proceed to the first sketch of the material I feel as though I had the degree of acquaintance with my characters that one acquires on a railway journey; one has met and chatted about this or that. With the next draft I see everything more clearly, I know the characters just about as one would know them after a few weeks' stay in a spa; I have learned the fundamental traits in their characters as well as their little peculiarities; yet it is not impossible that I might make an error in some essential matter. In the last draft, finally, I stand at the limit of knowledge; I know my people from close and long association— they are my intimate friends, who will not disappoint me in any way; in the manner in which I see them now, I shall always see them.

A. E. Zucker, *Ibsen: The Master Builder* (New York: Henry Holt, 1929), pp. 194, 208. Copyright 1929, Henry Holt and Company. Reprinted by permission of Holt, Rinehart and Winston, Inc.

Michael Redgrave (Tesman) standing, Trevor Howard (Lövborg), Ingrid Bergman (Hedda), and in the background, Ralph Richardson (Brack) in the CBS television production, 1963. Courtesy Columbia Broadcasting System.

Ibsen made fuller preliminary notes for *Hedda Gabler* than for any of his other plays. This is the first page of his small notebook on which he discusses his dramatic theories. From Else Höst, *Hedda Gabler:* A Monograph.

From Ibsen's Notes

Henrik Ibsen made preliminary notes for his plays on scraps of paper, on the backs of telegram forms, and, later in his career, in small notebooks. He jotted down ideas for characters, situations, and bits of dialogue. His notes for *Hedda Gabler* are the playwright's most voluminous, running to twenty-one pages in the Centennial Edition of his Collected Works (Vol. XI, pp. 496–516), edited by Francis Bull, Halvdan Koht, and Didrik Arup Seip; Gyldendal, Oslo, 1928–58. Written in the winter and spring of 1889–90 and probably in chronological order, the following excerpts are representative of Ibsen's preparatory work on this play:

> The aunt asks all sorts of indirect questions about those things that tease her imagination the most.

> Notes: One evening as Hedda and Tesman, together with some other people, were on their way home from a party, Hedda remarked, as they were passing a handsome villa, that she would like to live there. She meant it, but said it mainly to keep the conversation with Tesman going. "Because he just can't carry on a conversation."
> The villa happened to be up for rent or sale. Tesman had been spoken of as a man with a bright future. Later when he asked her to marry him, and mentioned that he too had dreamed of living there, she accepted him.
> The house had also appealed to him very much.
> So they get married. And rent the villa.
> Both of them, each in his own way, see a bond of sympathy in their mutual love for this house. As if they were seeking and were drawn to a common home. Then he rents the villa. They get married and go abroad. The house is bought, and furnished by his aunt at his expense. Now it is their home. It is theirs, yet it is not theirs, since it has not been paid for. Everything depends on his getting the professorship. The villa had belonged to the old widow of a cabinet minister who is now dead.
> But when Hedda returns as a young wife, with a vague idea of her responsibilities, it all seems repugnant to her. She begins to feel an intense dislike for the house just because it has become her home. She reveals this to Brack. To Tesman she says absolutely nothing about it.

> The play will concern itself with "the unattainable," that is, the aiming at and striving for something which is against social conventions, against approved and accepted beliefs—including Hedda's.

> Lövborg leans towards a "bohemian" way of life. Hedda is drawn in the same direction, but does not dare to take the leap.

> Hedda realizes that she, much more than Thea, has deserted her husband.

> Hedda is typical of women in her position and of her character.

One marries a Tesman, but fills one's fantasies with an Eilert Lövborg. She leans back in her chair, closes her eyes, and imagines his adventures. Here is the great difference: Mrs. Elvsted "works for his moral betterment." But for Hedda he is the object of cowardly, seductive daydreams. In reality she does not have the courage to be involved in such affairs. Then she realizes her condition. Trapped! Can't understand it. Ridiculous! Ridiculous!

The commonly held foolish notion that for one man there is one woman. Hedda is steeped in the conventional. She marries Tesman but in her imagination she has Eilert Lövborg—She despises his flight from life. He thinks that it has increased her regard for him.—Thea Elvsted is the conventional, sentimental, hysterical woman with pretentions to culture.

Eilert Lövborg has a double nature. It is a fiction that one loves only one person. He loves two—or more—(to speak frivolously) alternately. But how can he explain his personal situation? Mrs. Elvsted, who forces him to behave with restraint, runs away from her husband. Hedda, who goads him beyond all limits, retreats at the thought of a scandal.

This is something that neither he nor Mrs. [Ibsen crossed out the words "Elvsted understands" and wrote] Hedda understands.

In the manuscript that was left behind, Tesman reads about "the two ideals." Mrs. Elvsted cannot explain to him what E. L. meant. Then comes the burlesque conclusion: Both T. and Mrs. E. will devote the rest of their lives to solving the puzzle.

The great misfortune in this world is that so many have nothing else to do but to hunt for happiness without being able to find it.

Hedda: To dream of a scandal,—yes, I understand that very well. But to commit one—no, no, no.

Tesman is nearsighted. He wears glasses. Oh, what a beautiful rose! So he stuck his nose in the cactus. Since that time—!

The demonic desire in Hedda is this: She wants to have an influence on another person. When she succeeds, she despises him—The manuscript?

Life for Hedda becomes a huge joke which is not "worth playing out to the end."

Brack cannot stand to be in a house where there are small children. . . .

H. agrees that children have always been abhorrent to her too.

Main Points:
1. They are not all made to be mothers.
2. They are full of lust but they are terrified of scandal.
3. They see that the times offer many causes worth devoting one's life to, but they cannot find out what they are.

Hedda is completely occupied with the child that is to come, but after it is born she is afraid of what will follow—

NB!! Eilert Lövborg believes that a comradeship must be established between a man and a woman out of which the truly exceptional person can emerge. Whatever else these two may do is irrelevant. That is what the people around him do not understand. To them he is a licentious person. Inwardly he is not.

If a man may have many male friends, why may he not also have many women friends?

It is for that very sensuality—aroused in him in the company of his female "friends" or "comrades"—that he seeks an outlet in his excesses.

Conclusion: Life is not tragic.—Life is absurd—And that is what I cannot bear.

On page 44 of the small notebook, Ibsen jotted down two possible speeches for Hedda: "That's what I want: to know—to know—to know—" and "If only I could have lived like him!" These express Hedda's hunger for experience and her envy of Lövborg. From Else Höst, *Hedda Gabler,* A Monograph.

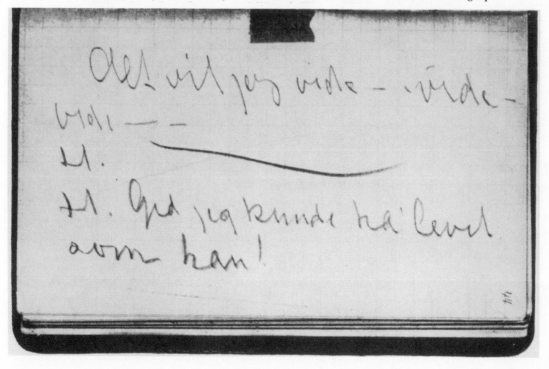

Brack understands very well that it is repression and hysteria which entirely motivate Hedda's behavior.

Hedda, on her part, surmises that Brack sees through her, though he does not believe that she is aware of it.

When Hedda talks to B. in the Fifth Act[1] about those two sitting there putting together the manuscript without having the talent for it, she bursts into laughter.—Then she plays the piano—then—d—

NB!! It is really a *man's* life that she wants to live completely. But then come apprehensions. Her heritage and what has been implanted in her.

This deals with "underground forces and powers." Women as miners. Nihilism. Father and mother belong to different eras. The female underground revolution in thought. The slave's fear of the world outside.

NB!! Why should I conform to society's morals which I know won't last more than half a generation? When I am on the loose, as they call it, it's just an escape from the present. Not that I find any pleasure in my excesses. I'm completely stuck in the existing order of things—
Thea, that little fool, doesn't understand anything about it. But she is lovely anyway. There is an uncertain future in store for her.

Hedda. Slim figure and medium height. Nobly formed, distinguished face with a fine, wax-colored skin. The eyes have a veiled expression. The hair medium brown. Not especially thick hair. Dressed in loose-fitting morning-robe, white with blue trimming. Quiet in her manners. The eyes steel-gray but without luster.
Mrs. Elvsted of delicate build. Her eyes round, slightly protruding, almost a watery blue. Weak face with soft lines. Nervous gestures, frightened expression—

See above. E. L.'s belief in the comradeship between man and woman—A life-saving thought!

If society will not let us live morally with them (women), then we'll have to live with them immorally—

Hedda's basic demand is: I want to know everything, but keep myself clean.

. . . She [Hedda] thinks that Tesman really feels only a vain pride in having won her. His concern for her is like that a man shows for a

---

[1] The play as we have it is in four acts.

thoroughbred horse or an expensive hunting-dog.—This, however, does not upset her. She just accepts is as a fact.

Hedda tells Brack that she does not think Tesman can be called ridiculous. But in reality she feels that he is. Later on she considers him pitiable as well. . . .

In the Third Act we are informed of one thing after another concerning Lövborg's escapades during the night. Finally he himself arrives in quiet despair. "Where is the manuscript?" "Didn't I leave it behind me here?" He does not know whether he did or not. But of what use can the manuscript be to him now! He is writing about "the morality of the future"! When he himself has just been turned loose by the police!

Ibsen as a Stage Craftsman

Article by P. F. D. Tennant

It is a matter of considerable importance to remember that Ibsen's development as a dramatist was intimately connected with his practical association with the stage. His years of apprenticeship were spent first as salaried dramatist and instructor at the Bergen National Theatre (1851–7) and then as "artistic director" of the Christiania Norwegian Theatre (1857–62), while for a short period he was literary adviser to the Christiania Theatre (1863). After leaving Norway in 1864 his connexion with the stage was severed and, apart from schemes for the establishment of a new theatre in Christiania, he no longer evinced any interest in the stage, though he was considerably influenced by the performances of the Meininger company, which he saw first in 1876 when Duke Georg invited him as his guest to attend a performance of his own play, *The Pretenders,* and decorated him with the Ernestine Order. Ibsen's most characteristic works, his social dramas, cannot fully be explained without reference to his particular exeprience of the stage in his early days, and it was this experience which stereotyped the dramatic form which he later adopted. Unlike his contemporary, Strindberg, he was uninterested in the practical innovations of the theatre which occurred toward the end of the century, and his last plays were written with reference to the formal picture stage of his own experience with all its conventional resources of lighting and mechanism. The only instance of an experimental stage effect in Ibsen's later dramas is in his *John Gabriel Borkman,* in the last act of which Borkman takes a walk through the forest while the scenery moves past him. The following examination of his experience as a stage craftsman endeavours to assess the influence of the practical theatre on his work as a dramatist.

Reprinted from *The Modern Language Review* for October 1939, vol. 34, pp. 557–68, by permission of the Modern Humanities Research Association and of the Editors.

Ibsen wrote *Catiline,* practically speaking, without any knowledge of the stage. His next play, *The Warrior's Barrow,* was also written without much acquaintance with the practical side of the theatre, but it procured him a free ticket to the performance of the Christiania Theatre which he was otherwise too poor to frequent. He there became familiar with the current repertoire, and in his criticisms we find him paying considerable attention to the style of acting and the setting of the plays. But it is also obvious from these articles that Ibsen had not as yet "got behind the scenes." His chance came when Ole Bull summoned him to the Bergen National Theatre in 1851. On 6 November he signed a contract to "assist the theatre as dramatic author." This post as salaried dramatist was rather an anomaly in a theatre of such small means, and in order to initiate Ibsen into the intricacies of the stage the management decided in February 1852 to give him a traveling grant for the purpose of studying European stages. On 15 April Ibsen left Bergen for Copenhagen in the company of the actors Johannes and Luise Brun, who were to study dancing and acting with Danish instructors. Ibsen was to produce a report of his studies and had been promised the position of stage-manager and producer in the theatre on his return.

Ibsen installed himself in a room in Reverentsgaden 205. He had a personal introduction from Judge Hansson in Bergen to the manager of the Royal Theatre, the philosopher-critic-poet J. L. Heiberg, and was received very kindly. He was handed on to the care of the stage-manager of the theatre, Thomas Overskou, who was most helpful. The season was then approaching its close, no new plays were being rehearsed, and Ibsen was advised to spend the first part of his time in the auditorium watching the finished products. He was given a free pass to all performances and this "little hardbitten Norwegian with his watchful eyes," as Overskou called him, had excellent opportunities to witnesss a very extensive repertoire. He saw Phister play in Holberg, N. P. Nielsen in Oehlenschläger; he saw for the first time Michael Wiehe, whose performances he recalled many years afterwards, and, most important of all, he saw Höedt play his realistic version of Hamlet in direct opposition to the idealistic manner which was favoured by J. L. Heiberg and the Germans. He saw Shakespeare's *Lear, Romeo and Juliet,* and *As You Like It,* saw plays by Scribe and admired their stage structure, and also plays by Hertz, Hostrup, and Heiberg. Besides the Royal Theatre there were two others in Copenhagen at the time, the Casino and the Royal Court Theatre, both of which he visited. The latter Ibsen attended for a gala performance at which Hostrup's play, *Master and Apprentice,* was produced for the first time. This work probably influenced Ibsen's future production in its attack on the morals of journalism, while Hostrup's use of supernatural creatures may have played its part in the forming of the fantastic play Ibsen was writing at the time, *Midsummer Eve.*

When the season was over Overskou at last took Ibsen behind the scenes at the Royal Theatre. Of Ibsen's impressions we can only judge from a letter he wrote a few days before (30 May 1852). "The theatre's season ended last Friday," he writes. "Mr. Overskou has promised to make me acquainted with the theatre machinery etc., which was impossible during the season; however, the machinery at the Copenhagen theatre is not of the best, and I hope in this respect that the German theatres will make a much more profitable study." Ibsen remained in Copenhagen another week studying the stage and procuring copies of plays, a costume book and musical scores for the Bergen theatre. His choice of repertoire in Bergen was profoundly influenced by his stay in Copenhagen, in his productions of Scribe and of Scribe's Danish imitators, a repertoire well suited to the public with which he had to reckon at home.

Ibsen left Copenhagen on 6 June and arrived in Dresden on the 9th, where he stayed with a veterinary surgeon, Tröitzk, at Töpfergasse 13. He had letters of introduction to the Norwegian painter and art professor, J. C. Dahl, but on account of the latter's absence on holiday had to wait till the 16th before he met him. On 24 June he wrote: "He (Dahl) has now managed to procure me access behind the scenes at the theatre, which I am certain will be of great value to me, since everything is in excellent condition." He had to pay for his admission to the performances, but in spite of straitened circumstances managed to see some sterling productions. He saw the Pole Bogumil Dawison play Hamlet, and he also saw Emil Devrient. Of other Shakespearean plays here he saw *A Midsummer Night's Dream* and *Richard III*. Hettner's book, *Das moderne Drama*,[1] had just come out and here he was once more able to find support for his admiration of Scribe and Shakespeare. Hettner's book he had probably already read in Copenhagen, as the paper *Faedrelandet* advertised the opening of a new newspaper reading room in Silkegade where Hettner's *Das moderne Drama* and *Die romantische Schule* were displayed for the benefit of the readers.

In September Ibsen returned to Bergen. Here he took up his new post as stage-manager and producer. He was not independent, as he had hoped, but under the control of Hermann Laading, who was also given the same title, a situation which annoyed Ibsen and even resulted in making him challenge his superior to a duel. Whatever his official position may have been, Ibsen nevertheless both wrote and produced plays on his own. He was now able to put into practice the results of his studies abroad. His producer's notebook for the years 1852 to 1854 is preserved in the Bergen Museum, and this not only gives a very good idea of how he set to work but is also instructive in throwing light on his own dramatic technique.

For the period 1852–3 his method of preparation was as follows. In a broad column on the left side of the page he drew a painstaking diagram of the stage setting. In every case we find him using flats set behind one another, whether for indoor or outdoor scenery. These were of course painted in perspective to give an illusion of reality. The theatre museum of Bergen has some amusing relics from this period which show with what skill the scene-painters could use their two dimensions. The diagrams were then filled in with the positions of the characters, whose movements were indicated by dotted lines. To the right of this diagram was a smaller column for cues and to the right of this again a broad column with notes indicating the movements and gestures of the characters. Pages without diagrams contained four columns, two for cues and two for notes on the movements of the actors. In 1853 the arrangement of his notes takes another form, more detailed and more practical for reference. Each page has four different columns, one for stage directions, one for positions, one for properties and a fourth for notes. The column of stage directions is

---

[1] In this short critical work, the scholar Hermann Hettner praised Friedrich Hebbel for introducing psychological analysis into his historical plays, and urged other playwrights to do the same. Ibsen took Hettner's advice and put it into practice.

filled in either with written descriptions of the setting or diagrams, the latter often in two planes, vertical and horizontal, and frequently executed in colour. The stage directions are divided into scenes according to exits and entrances in the French tradition, a convention which Ibsen used with his own plays at the time and only gave up when he wrote *Love's Comedy* in 1862. The directions are written and the diagrams are drawn with "right" and "left" as seen from the stage, in direct contradiction to his later custom and in conformity with the French models which he so closely followed in his own earlier plays. In a letter to August Lindberg (22 November 1884) he wrote: "In reply to your question I hasten to inform you that *The Wild Duck,* like all my plays, is set from the auditorium and not from the stage. I set everything as I see it before me when writing." When Ibsen made this change it is impossible to say with any certainty, but it would seem to date from *The League of Youth,* which was written with the conscious intent to create a realistic illusion, or from *Ghosts,* where Ibsen declared his intention to be "to give the reader the impression that he was experiencing a piece of reality while reading." It is at any rate connected with the intention to write for the reader and not for the producer, an intention which is not obvious with Ibsen until he has left Norway and has severed his connexion with the stage.

This producer's note-book, together with the plays Ibsen wrote on his return to Norway, show clearly what he learnt from his study tour. He had grasped the importance of the visual stage effect. Not only can we follow this in the diagrams and notes of his producer's book but also in the wealth of stage directions which now fill his plays. The contrast between *Catiline* and *Midsummer Eve,* the play he wrote during his tour, is very striking in this respect. The first act of *Catiline* is headed: "On the Flaminian highway outside Rome. A wooded slope. In the background rise the heights and walls of the town. It is evening." The setting of the first act of *Midsummer Eve* is described as follows: "Mrs. Berg's garden, which is cut off from the highroad in the background by a fence with a gate. On the right the main building, erected in an attractive modern style; on the left farther up stage an old-fashioned timbered house." The stage directions in *Catiline* give only a hint of locality, they give no indication of the distribution of the various sets about the stage. There could, however, be no doubt about the stage plan in *Midsummer Eve.* The setting here is bounded by foreground, background and the right and left wings, which is not the case in *Catiline.* Ibsen has begun to set his plays in relation to a definite stage. The stage directions in *Catiline* and *The Warrior's Barrow,* with their sign-board curtness, are an inheritance from Shakespeare's editors, handed down via Schiller and Oehlenschläger. The extensive stage directions which we meet for the first time with Ibsen in *Midsummer Eve* are taken direct from the contemporary French drama of intrigue, which in this respect as in many others was a direct offshoot of the realistic English bourgeois drama of the eighteenth century.

The lavish settings and numerous changes of scene in Ibsen's Bergen plays would lead one to believe that the Beregn stage possessed extensive technical resources. This was by no means the case. The theatre was built in 1800 in neo-classic style with a stage which was singularly ill equipped. In 1825 a Danish portrait painter was engaged to furnish the stage with modern machinery. This consisted of a variation of the apparatus which was employed in the eighteenth century court theatres, and as far as scene-shifting was concerned it was very efficient. The flats in the wings were mounted in grooves and connected to a central winch below the stage. Each flat had a group of two, three or four grooves in which the successive sets could be mounted simultaneously. The winch could then in a very short time pull into position or withdraw any one of the sets. The sets worked in combination with a backcloth which was quickly changed by folding or rolling. This expeditious method of scene-shifting, together with the scene-painter's proficiency in perspective painting, made practically speaking any scene possible. Ibsen's later demands for realism discarded two-dimensional perspective scenery and introduced three-dimensional scenery with walls and solid properties. The wagon or lift stage had by then not been invented, no one yet thought of using curtains, and it took much more time to change scenes of this kind. This latter consideration no doubt contributed to Ibsen's artistic economy in the unity of place which dominates in his early realistic plays.

Lighting was always of supreme importance to Ibsen in creating the atmosphere of a setting. In a letter to Schroder with reference to the setting of *The Wild Duck* he wrote: "The lighting also has its significance; it is different for each act and is intended to correspond to the mood which gives each of the acts its special character." This symbolical use of light is characteristic of Ibsen even in his earliest works. In his preface to the second edition of his first work, *Catiline*, he dwells on the fact that the play was written at night and adds: "I believe that this is the unconscious reason for nearly all the action taking place at night." The play was undoubtedly written with a sense of the importance of the lighting in order to give it atmosphere, but certainly without regard for the technical possibilities. Not until Ibsen came to Dresden did he realize the possibilities of the lighting effects embodied in gas illumination. Oil lamps were used in Bergen until 1856, when gas was introduced in the theatre. His appreciation of the importance of being able to control the strength of the lighting with gas illumination can be seen in *Midsummer Eve,* the play which he wrote abroad under the influence of his impressions there. The first act begins in the evening and a stage direction tells us that it "begins to get dark." In the second act "it is night; the moon is in the sky." The scene is then suddenly lit up by the opening of the fairy mound, a purely operatic stage effect, and the third act shows us the whole stage in bright daylight again. The play was a failure, and this no doubt was largely due to the fact that the theatre machinery and lighting were not equal to Ibsen's demands. Anyhow, it is noticeable how Ibsen's next play, *Lady Inger,* follows the model of *Catiline* and passes in a crescendo of gloom, completely abandoning the effects of light contrasts which he developed to such an art later, and only indulging in such effects as would conform to the demands of realism on a lamp-lit stage. Ibsen, in his dual position of dramatist and stage-manager, would naturally advocate such a reform as the introduction of gas into the theatre, and it appears not unlikely that he was responsible for its installation. Gas illumination was used in Bergen for the first time in 1856 and the theatre was one of the first institutions to take advantage of it. *The Feast of Solhaug,* which was produced in January 1856, shows as yet no signs of the effect of the new illumination, but the next play, *Olaf Liljekrans,* is full of lighting effects, dusk, dawn and a midnight fire. The next play, *The Warriors of Helgeland,* with its full-blooded realism of setting, spares no opportunity for stage effect, and it is significant that Ibsen first sent his play to the Christiania Theatre before producing it at his own, because he knew among other things that it possessed a very much better technical equipment. From now on Ibsen's stage directions never omit indications of lighting. Here, in the first act, the curtain rises on "thick snowy weather and storm." This is followed later by the stage direction: "The storm has ceased during the previous scene; the midday sun appears like a red disk on the horizon." The second act is by contrast illuminated by a log fire, the third is daylight, and the fourth act is lit by torches and the rising moon, which spreads an atmosphere of peace after the passing storm. Light is from now onwards used by Ibsen, not only to indicate the passage of time, but also as a symbolical accompaniment to the action. His early appreciation of the importance and possibility of light effects on the stage he owed to his visit to Dresden in 1852.

Final scene from the production at the Little Theatre, October 4, 1920, directed by Mme. Borgny Hammer. Hedda (Mme. Hammer) on sofa, Tesman (Charles Laite) and Berta (Ellen Prom) bend over her. Thea (Mercedes Desmore) and Judge Brack (Rolf Fjell) react to her suicide.

During his tour in Denmark and Germany, Ibsen became acquainted with contemporary stage machinery and lighting, together with the routine of producing. We have seen the fruit of his experience in the detailed settings and stage directions of the plays he wrote at the time, which form a parallel to the painstaking plans in his producer's note-book. So far we have watched him exploiting the technical resources with which he became acquainted. If we now turn to the individualization of Ibsen's technique of setting and stage directions, we find here as everywhere a growing tendency towards a realistic illusion combined with an equally strong inclination to romantic symbolism. It is the latter which dominates in the later plays.

In *Catiline* and *The Warrior's Barrow* there is no conscious attempt at realistic setting. *The Ptarmigan of Justedal* and *Midsummer Eve* offer only vague indications of conventional sets and properties. The disposition of the various scenes is indicated, but not the nature of the individual objects. In the former we meet with a "wild but beautiful part of Justedalen," which only evokes a very vague picture. In the latter we know that the main building is "erected in an attractive modern style" while the building on the left is an "old-fashioned timbered house." This tells us nothing of the peculiarities of the two buildings, but is rather an indication for the property-man as to what sets are to be used. In *Lady Inger* and *The Feast at Solhaug* we find a slight increase in detail, but we are dealing with standard props all the time, "a magnificent room," "an old-fashioned carved high seat," and so forth. The same is the case with *Olaf Liljekrans*. *The Warriors of Helgeland* is the first play with a specifically realistic setting, and it is significant that it was written in the year that Ibsen left Bergen and no longer had to reckon with the theatre stock of properties and sets. The setting of the first scene is as follows: "A high shore which slopes steeply down to the sea in the background. On the left a boat-house, on the right mountains and pine woods. The masts of two warships can be seen down in the bay; far away on the right rocks and high islands; the sea is very rough, it is winter with thick snowy weather and storm." The striking feature about this setting is not so much the absence of standard props and scenery but the way in which Ibsen sets an outdoor scene and overcomes false perspective. He uses a high foreground which masks receding perspective, behind which the backcloth can represent the middle and far distance without risk of showing up the actors out of proportion. The foreground is the only area of the stage on which the actors appear and their size is then always in proper relation to the scenery. This method of giving an illusion of reality to outdoor settings was in future always employed by Ibsen with only two variations. The first was the high foreground which we meet again in *The Lady from the Sea*, *John Gabriel Borkman* and *When We Dead Awaken*, the second the fenced-in garden where the fence has the function of masking the perspective, a setting which we remember as far back as *Midsummer Eve*, and which recurs in *The Lady from the Sea*, *Little Eyolf* and *When We Dead Awaken*.

One frequently hears of the stuffy atmosphere of Ibsen's plays, the atmosphere which pervades the indoor settings of his modern tragedies. From 1877, when *The Pillars of Society* was published, until 1886, the date of the publication of *Rosmersholm*, all his plays were set indoors, while the first three of these six take place in one and the same room. After this date there is only one totally indoor play, *Hedda Gabler*, two are set entirely out of doors (*The Lady from the Sea, When We Dead Awaken*), and the remaining three have both outdoor and indoor settings. The indoor setting is the direct result of Ibsen's conscious effort to create a realistic illusion, while its abandonment coincides with his reversion to romantic symbolism. Even more than in the case of the outdoor setting, the interior had to overcome the difficulties of perspective. As we can see from Ibsen's diagrams for interior settings, the Bergen theatre used the type of scenery which was common at the time; that is to say, that the side walls of a room were represented by transverse flies set parallel behind one another as in the outdoor scenes, while the back wall was represented by a flapping backcloth perforated with doors and windows. The whole proscenium opening was used for rooms of all dimensions and the illusion of varying size was brought about by the false perspective of the scene-painter. In the setting of Ibsen's *Lady Inger,* for instance, the room in the first act would occupy as much stage space as the knight's hall in the third, though the latter might of course use a little deeper stage. In the impoverished theatre at Bergen economy was everything as regards properties and scenery, and the painter was in consequence called upon to include in his settings flat pasteboard cupboards, chairs and ornaments which the theatre could not afford to procure in the solid. The effect of these settings as a peep-show panorama was often very illusory, but the impression was immediately destroyed by the movements of the actors. A reaction against this type of indoor setting began to make itself felt in Europe about this time. The study of the Elizabethan stage which had begun with Tieck led to various attempts at reconstruction, especially in the use of the little inner stage and the curtain background. Laube, in his historical productions, had already begun to simplify his scenery and had set his actors against a plain background, but the tendency of the day was for historical realism and against stylization, and here it was that the Meininger company seemed to have impressed Ibsen with their solid realistic scenery. Solid interior walls and ceilings for modern settings had already been introduced previously in France and England, and it may well be that Ibsen, during his residence in Germany, had seen imitations of this in modern plays. The settings of *Emperor and Galilean* are mostly outdoor ones and the few interiors show as yet no signs of modern realism. But when we come to *The Pillars of Society* it is a different matter. The earliest notes for this play date from 1870 and it was not finished until 1877, the year after Ibsen saw the first Meininger performances. As far as we can judge from the notes and sketches before 1876, the scene was removed in each act. The first act took place in Consul Bernick's morning-room, the second in the garden, the third on a road by the shore and the fourth in a wood. After 1876 the setting immediately took shape and was restricted to Consul Bernick's morning-room for all the acts, while the directions give the most detailed description of the stage that Ibsen had hitherto indulged in. In this setting he has tranferred the historical realism of the Meininger into modern surroundings, and has combined the interior with the fenced-in garden exterior to give a complete illusion of the "fourth wall." We have only to compare this scene with a corresponding scene in *The League of Youth,* its predecessor as a modern play, to see how Ibsen had individualized his technique. The second act of the latter play has the following setting: "The chamberlain's morning-room. Elegant furniture, a piano, flowers and rare plants. Entrance door in the background. On the left a door into the dining-room; on the right several glass doors opening into the garden." In this case we are still dealing with props and standard sets. In *The Pillars of Society* we find the following setting: "A spacious morning-room in Consul Bernick's house. In the foreground on the left there is a door leading into the Consul's room; farther back on the same wall is a similar door. The wall in the background is almost entirely composed of mirrors, with an open door leading out on to broad garden steps, over which is stretched an awning. At the bottom of the steps one can see part of the garden, which is enclosed by a fence with a little gate. On the other side of the fence, and parallel to it, runs a street which is flanked on the opposite side by small brightly painted wooden houses. It is summer and the sun is shining warmly. People pass by in the street from time to time; they stop and converse; they go and make purchases in a shop on the corner etc. . . ." Here there is no question of standard props or sets, the whole scene is an individual solid structure. We find Ibsen for the first time giving directions for a realistic setting and following the example of contemporary producers. The producers had hitherto looked to the past for their dramatists, and now Ibsen appeared and immediately carried them off their feet.

With *Pillars of Society* Ibsen inaugurates his series of modern indoor plays, and he becomes a master in electrifying these settings with dramatic potentiality. The dramatic importance of the ground plan and elevation of the houses in which his plays are set, together very often with the locality in which the houses stand, is very great in Ibsen's work. He transforms and adapts to his own use the secret stairs and trapdoors and sliding panels of romantic melodrama so that his doors and curtains and windows are equally pregnant with secrets in spite of their prosaic surroundings. Ibsen once spoke of himself as a builder, and there is no doubt that he had a supreme sense of the dramatic in architecture. We remember houses and parts of houses from Ibsen's plays as well as we know our own. His insistence on architecture begins with *A Doll's House*. The room in this case has four doors, each of them having its function, while two of them, the door to Helmer's study and the one into the hall, become the focus of dramatic tension, especially when Krogstad's letter is lying in the hall letter-box. In the course of the action we learn that the flat is on the first floor, we know where the kitchen and the nursery and Nora's bedroom are, and we hear the music from the fancy-dress party in the flat above. The effect of this technique is to give one a sense of tremendous dramatic activity focused on the one room visible on the stage, and also to give this one room an extension far beyond its real dimensions. This latter effect is increased by noises off and talking off the stage. In *John Gabriel Borkman* a similar illusion of architectural solidity is brought about by the continuity of the four acts in which the action progresses without any time interval. At the end of the first act in Mrs. Borkman's room on the ground floor we hear music from Borkman's room above. The second act opens in Borkman's room where Frida Foldal is playing the piano, in the third Borkman comes downstairs and at the end rushes out of the hall door into the snow. The fourth act shows the outside of the house and Borkman walking out. The door to Borkman's room is also charged with dramatic tension. He is always waiting for the knock which will announce the arrival of the delegation which is to clear his reputation. A similar dramatic door we have in *The Master Builder,* when Solness says, "One of these days youth will come here knocking at the door," in response to which Hilde Wangel seals his fate by her prompt knocking. In *Rosmersholm* we find a genuine survival of romantic melodrama in the curtain behind which Rebekka overhears Rosmer's conversation with Mortensgard.

Ibsen's appreciation of the dramatic value of a realistic setting is well illustrated in the case of *The Wild Duck*. In this case a study of the drafts of the play shows exactly with what care he worked out the details. The last four acts of the play pass in Hjalmar Ekdal's studio, and in the back wall we see the door which leads into the weird garret where the duck and the rabbits and pigeons are kept. In the second draft the stage directions describe the door as follows: "A large double door in the middle of the back wall constructed so that it can be pushed aside." When Ekdal insists on showing Gregers the attic, the directions state: "Ekdal and Hjalmar have gone to the back wall and each pushes aside the upper part of his half of the door." In the third act the same process is repeated: "Hjalmar and Ekdal open the upper part of the half-doors to the garret." Ekdal squeezes himself into the garret by opening the lower half of the doors slightly. Then Hjalmar "pulls a string; a piece of stretched fishing-net slides down in front of the door opening." In the play the door into the garret is constructed differently. Instead of being divided into four parts, which enables the upper half to be open while the lower remains shut, it is made of only two partitions, one on each side, which open and disclose the whole floor of the garret. It is a "broad double sliding door." In the second act Hjalmar and Ekdal disclose the whole attic in the moonlight, the animals being hidden in the shadow, whereas formerly the floor was not visible. In the third act Hjalmar and Ekdal again open each of the sliding doors and disclose the whole attic in the sunshine, together with its inhabitants. After this full glimpse, Hjalmar "pulls a string; from inside a curtain is lowered, the bottom part of which consists of a strip of old sailcloth, the upper of a piece of stretched fishing net. Thus the floor of the garret is no longer visible." In the earlier version the contents of the garret were seen by the actors alone and the duck still remained a formless figure for the audience. In the play the garret is fully revealed to the spectators with its bizarre display of animals and rubbish. The momentary glimpse of what is behind gives the sailcloth and the closed door a weird suggestive power which was absent when the duck remained unseen and unreal. This is only one instance of Ibsen's capacity for increasing the dramatic effect by a pure arrangement of scenery.

This constructive sense in Ibsen's indoor settings is equally strong in all his later plays and it is combined with great economy of material. His stages were set with regard to the function of the various units, the doors, windows and pieces of furniture, and he cleared the stage of all the superfluous junk that was popular in the dazzling settings of French social dramas. His settings were inspired with a sympathy for the effect of milieu on the characters and often possess a *dramatic quality* independent of the characters themselves. Concentration and elimination were his principles in developing dialogue and character, and it was the same principles he applied to realistic settings; his dramatic sense was greatly aided by his painter's eye in their conception, and they form one of the characteristic features of Ibsen's drama.

Mrs. Minnie Maddern Fiske (Hedda) and George Arliss (Brack) in the second American production of the play, Manhattan Theatre, New York, 1903. Photograph: Byron. Courtesy Museum of the City of New York.

Mrs. Fiske as Hedda Gabler

Review by William Winter

William Winter, who was probably America's most influential drama critic at the turn of the century, wrote regularly for the New York *Tribune*. He was puritanical in his view of the stage and vigorously opposed the realistic movement in plays and in acting. His predilection for the romantic and sentimental dramatic fare of his youth, to which he remained loyal to the end of his days, won him the nickname "Weeping Willie." Following is Winter's review of Mrs. Fiske in *Hedda Gabler*:

All persons are, in one sense, diseased and hastening toward the grave. In some cases the disease is known and named, and the time of the inevitable obsequies can be predicted with approximate precision. In other cases the disease is incipient, and hope fluctuates as to the probable arrival of the final catastrophe. But there is no doubt as to either the present condition or the ultimate result. All flesh is grass; all grass will be cut down, dried up, and,

necessarily, withered; and, sooner or later, the universal hay crop will be gathered in.

> "You are bones, and what of that?
> Every face, however full,
> Padded round with flesh and fat,
> Is but modelled on a skull."

Those remarkably sapient views were, in general, the views of the late Mr. Ibsen, of Norway, and those views,—with others, about hereditary disease, original sin, miscellaneous humbug, and taxes,—he was at great pains to divulge, in a series of plays, some of which are nasty and all of which are ponderous and dull. Mrs. Fiske, at the Manhattan Theatre, New York, on October 5, 1905, produced one of those dreary compositions (a tolerably clean one), called "Hedda Gabler," and acted the principal character in it. The character, *Mrs. Tesman,* is sick. Functional derangement has disordered her brain and destroyed her moral sense. She is vain, selfish, malicious; a thief, a liar, a traitor; she exults in cruelty and depravity; and,—figuring through a series of inexpressibly tiresome colloquies,—she closes a life of hypocrisy and guilt by the crime of suicide. A nastier little female reptile has not been depicted, even by Ibsen,—"whose spirits toil in frame of villainies," and whose whole fabric of dramatic writing is a pollution to the Stage, a wearisome burden upon contemporary thought, a darkness to the eyes of hope, and a blight to everything that it can touch of nobility, beauty, and joy. Perhaps such persons as *Hedda Gabler* exist: the Lunatic Asylum is the place for them; not the Theatre. Mrs. Fiske presented that ailing and eccentric female in a manner to awaken solicitude, and with an elocution irresistibly suggestive of an additional "b" in the middle of her surname. Early in the depressing services it became obvious that *Hedda* had made a mistake in marrying *Professor Tesman* and that the society of that respectable scientific ass had become almost intolerable to her. Later it was observed that she became experimental and analytic, and that she wanted, in particular, to diversify existence by making mischief. To this end she insulted her husband's aunt; flirted with the tax man [Brack]; badgered a fugacious female who had sought her help and protection; tempted a former sweetheart of her own to get drunk and go to ruin; stole that lover's precious manuscript and put it in the fire; goaded him to desperation by her ironical taunts, and armed him with a pistol with which to shoot himself; and, finally, when no more deviltry seemed to be feasible, played a piano and shot herself. All this from mere wanton jealousy that anybody else should be happy!

The play of "Hedda Gabler" is a long-winded, colloquial exposition of disease, and its heroine is an insane cat. No other phrase can as well describe such a monstrous union of vanity and depravity. Some excellent acting was done in the presentment of this vicious and depressing picture of dulness and morbid, madhouse wickedness. Mrs. Fiske, indeed, considerably exaggerated her icy, piercing, stridulous, staccato speech, but she has the talent of sarcasm, and can say heartless words in a way to bite the sense of hearing and almost to sting the heart. Her performance was remarkably effective,—being mordant with sarcasm, keen with irony, dreadful with suggestion of watchful wickedness, and bright with vicious eccentricity. Not long before her first production of "Hedda Gabler" Mrs. Fiske, in writing about Henrik Ibsen, condemned that author, in terms no less trenchant than true,—declaring, in a New York magazine, that Ibsen "by his example as well as by his work, has almost *banished beauty, nobility, picturesqueness, and poetry from the Stage."* and that "some of us must believe that *his influence on the whole of the contemporary drama has been baneful."* That being the fact, and that fact being recognized by the actress, it seemed a little singular that Mrs. Fiske should contribute to a possible extension of a "baneful" influence by producing and acting in Ibsen's plays. But it is lovely woman's inalienable right to be inconsistent. Her exploit, however, in producing Ibsen's plays has amply substantiated her condemnation of them. There is, surely, enough good in human nature, enough romance in human experience, enough beauty in the natural world, whereon to base a drama of loveliness and light: and, surely, it is neither unreasonable nor unkind to hold that a woman of genius, like Mrs. Fiske, has no need to stoop to the baneful drama of feculence, prolixity, depression, and disease,—the drama that banishes poetry, beauty, and nobility from the Stage, the drama of crack-brained pessimists or charlatans, made of "all that is at enmity with joy."

Hedda at the Norwegian National Theatre

Interviews with Knut Hergel, Christian Stenersen, and Lita Prahl

In 1861 Henrik Ibsen and Björnsterne Björnson, then the two most important theatrical figures in Christiania (Oslo), were demanding the establishment of a national theatre, in which the work of Norwegian playwrights would be presented by Norwegian actors, directors, and designers, all under government subsidy. Such a theatre was not founded until 1899, too late to make use of the personal services of its two early proponents; but in front of the imposing old theatre building, which still stands in the center of town, there are larger-than-life-size statues of Ibsen and Björnson.

A state-supported theatre has many advantages: it fosters native talent, raises the cultural level of the community, and can operate without slavish regard to the profit motive. But it also has its disadvantages: it usually works under severe budgetary limitations, is open to political interference from without and to domination by cliques within; it is apt to become traditional and stale, avoiding or attempting only timidly new or experimental ideas and techniques.

The version of *Hedda Gabler* presented at the Norwegian National Theatre in 1951 was produced under the conditions just described. Knut Hergel, then General Director of the Theatre, was approached by Gerd Nissen Grieg and asked if he would direct the Ibsen play, giving her the title role. Mrs. Grieg, who was related by marriage to the composer Edvard Grieg, was a great dramatic star in her own right. In 1932 she had appeared in a production of *Hedda Gabler,* which had won great praise and continued to serve as a measure of excellence. *Hedda* was one of Hergel's favorite plays, and he was very eager to direct it. He knew that Mrs. Grieg had been hailed for her

Scene from the National Theatre production, Oslo, 1951. Gerd Grieg (Hedda) in the old-fashioned dress she insisted upon wearing, and Thea (seated) in the more modern dress designed by Lita Prahl. The scenery, made up of architectural units and draperies, was designed by Christian Stenersen. Courtesy of the National Theatre, Norway.

interpretation, but he had his own conception of the part, and he foresaw difficulties. Finally he agreed to do the play, sure that with the collaboration of his scenery and costume designers, he could establish a style for the production so strong that the actress would have to play within it. Lita Prahl was selected to design the costumes; Christian Stenersen, the sets; Hergel and Stenersen had worked together on many successful plays, and their ideas were mutually complementary.

The scenery for the play was to be both modern and semisymbolic, created mainly with draperies and a few architectural pieces; the period was to be suggested rather than definitely established. The lighting would be very cold, as suitable to the atmosphere of Hedda's inner life; when Lövborg entered, the air would appear to grow warmer and sunnier. The lighting was to be arbitrary and used plastically, as music often is, to heighten the mood. Naturalism was to be avoided at all costs; all the little decorative details of the period were to be omitted, furniture and props were chosen for a definite purpose and significance. The costumes would merely suggest the period of Ibsen; the actual colors and lines would be altered to make the clothes appear more modern.

At the end of the play, Hergel introduced a brief "visual climax," in which the lighting was used to make a symbolic point. After Hedda shoots herself in the inner room, Tesman draws the curtain aside. Hedda is seen lying on a divan beneath a large painting of her father. A spotlight picks out the General's face and "throws light" on the daughter's suicide. Though this was done very casually, it did not fail to make the desired impression.

Hergel saw Hedda as a timid and frightened girl, brought up in a conservative household and dominated by a stern military father. Her behavior seemed to Hergel more masculine than feminine. He saw Hedda's weak esthetic feelings blocked and stifled by her own conventionalism. When she wanted to break out of the prison of her life, she was afraid to act. She had hoped to escape through the efforts of Tesman but felt more thwarted than ever by the discovery that she was pregnant. In Hergel's view, Hedda was a frigid and frustrated woman. But this was not Gerd Grieg's conception: she saw Hedda as a warm, almost passionate woman, whose love had been perverted, but who nonetheless continually strove to express it. As finally presented, the character of Hedda showed a merging of the two conceptions in, what might be called most kindly, an "uneasy compromise."

Scenery by Christian Stenersen

When Knut Hergel decided that he would not use the conventional, built scenery for the play, which had been standard practice since Ibsen's own day, he set to work with the designer to devise a new plan. He and Stenersen created a set that seemed to them to be original and interesting and at the same time to preserve a feeling for the period. Their solution was a design that combined architectural units with free-hanging draperies.

Three panels—representing a rear wall and two side walls—arranged like a triptych, with spaces between them, were erected on the stage. The ceiling was hung from the flies but did not rest upon the walls. Black velvet draperies enclosed the entire set, while dark-green velvet draperies hung behind the set pieces. In the center panel there was an alcove with tall, thin columns at each side of it; three steps led up from the stage floor to this inner room, which could be closed off by a green velvet curtain. In the right panel was a doorway; in the left were French windows with lace curtains and green velvet draperies.

The side panels were not as tall as the center panel, but all three were topped by pearl-gray architectural borders, and decorated with acanthus leaves. All the woodwork, doors included, was finely constructed; and the furniture, in rich materials, was expensive and in excellent taste. In the alcove there was a sofa, table and chairs, and a crystal chandelier; above the sofa hung a portrait of General Gabler. In the larger room downstage were several units of tables and chairs, and up left was a highboy of exquisite marquetry.

Since the scenery was not realistic, the furniture and costumes had to supply the sense of period. The draperies especially helped to establish the era of the play. "The draperies had many other advantages," said Stenersen. "A room enclosed by draperies seems more suitable than one with solid walls for a woman of Hedda's character and personality, which are unusual, not to say abnormal. Draperies have a suffocating, secretive effect when closed and can hide one from the world. Dark green seemed the most suitable color for them, as the hue and the somberness suggest both deep sea and dense forest, something mysterious and interior. As a final practical consideration, draperies are better to light than walls; lights falling on draperies create a depth, mood, and interesting shadows, which are unobtainable with painted or built scenery."

Concerning the technical facilities at the Norwegian National Theatre, which is still in use, Stenersen said that the house is very old and rather cramped; both building and storage space are inadequate, which makes it difficult to create large or complex sets. Scene-changing in this theatre is in itself a major problem. The scene designer must work within the limitations of the physical plant, and these limitations affected the designs for *Hedda Gabler.* The director and designer cannot always do what they want to do but must often contrive workable substitutes. "So, although the old and inadequate equipment of the theatre limits creativity in one way," said Stenersen, "it provides an opportunity for the designer to exercise his ingenuity in another way."

Costumes by Lita Prahl

"This production of *Hedda Gabler* was very difficult to design," said Lita Prahl, "because I did not have a free hand." Gerd Grieg had held on to the costume she wore in 1932 and insisted upon wearing it again because she was 'comfortable in it.' In my original sketches, the dresses suggested the year 1890 but also satisfied modern tastes because I had simplified the lines, fabrics, and colors. Mrs. Grieg's costume, on the other hand, was definitely a museum-piece. When she refused to abandon the old dress, I had to discard my original designs, modify the concept, and pray that the styles would not clash."

Miss Prahl described the working procedures for the costume designer at the Norwegian National Theatre. The first step, she said, is to have a series of discussions with the director and the scene designer to work out the style of the production and the basic shapes and colors in the scenery, which will serve as the background against which the costumes will be seen.

The next step is to make sketches of the clothes each character will wear, taking into consideration the character's age, social status, personality, habits, and such special items as Aunt Julia's bonnet. For *Hedda Gabler,* the high fashion of the 1890s served as the model both for the men's and the women's clothes. No specially formulated color scheme was used, beyond making sure that the colors were appealing and did not clash. If Miss Prahl cannot produce in her sketch the exact color she wants in the fabric (she does not render well in paint), she finds swatches of material in the shades and textures she desires and pastes the cloth to the page. Sometimes the swatch indicates both color and texture, sometimes just one or the other. The cloth is often dyed, or treated in other ways, to get the desired shade. If the play has a large cast, Miss Prahl designs only three or four key costumes, gets the approval of the director and scene designer, and then proceeds with the designs for the entire company.

In addition to the scenery itself, the lighting of each scene must be taken into consideration. The costume and lighting designers should work in close cooperation in order to bring out the exact textures, tints, and shades of the fabric. As Miss Prahl reads a script, she makes a special note of the time, place, and weather conditions of each scene, as these elements have an important effect upon clothing.

A danger involved in creating period costumes is the tendency to mix the silhouettes or accessories of one period with those of another. Before the nineteenth century nobody worried about such anachronisms; but with the growing interest in history and archeology, even theatrical productions have to be "scientifically" accurate. Audiences today are so knowledgeable and observant that even minor errors must be avoided. That is why, Miss Prahl said, she was so disturbed when Mrs. Grieg insisted upon wearing her "ancient" gown; it left her with the unhappy choice of bringing all the costumes into conformity with it, or of selecting a costume style for the production, which would not cause blatant confusion when seen beside the star's costume. She chose the latter course. "The designer must be equally careful when creating modern dresses," said Miss Prahl. "Modern clothes may be bought in shops and may be in the latest style, but they are not costumes. Costumes must be designed to characterize—to tell the audience something about the character's environment, taste, and personality."

A final important consideration in the designing of costumes should be the actor's comfort (Mrs. Grieg's argument). Stage clothing must be wearable"—the actor must feel free, at home, and able to move easily in everything he wears, whether it is modern or period; he should also be able to get into and out of the costume without difficulty. "But," said Miss Prahl, "if an actor tells a designer, 'I don't like green or brown,' it is not necessary for the designer to take the actor's personal preference into consideration, as the actor is not playing himself but portraying a character who might like those colors." In that connection, Miss Prahl recalled an incident that occurred during her first year at the Theatre. She was assigned the task of designing the gowns for Johanna Dybwad, a very great and celebrated actress who was to play the part of Queen Elizabeth. Miss Dybwad, it was well known, had a peculiar penchant for red. No one ever remembered her appearing on stage in any other color. Miss Prahl had a conference with the actress, during which she explained how effective it would be if each of the five gowns the queen was to wear were of a different color—green, brown, purple, black, and, of course, a magnificent red. The actress gave her complete approval, and the young designer felt that she had achieved a great triumph. Then, each day thereafter, the actress had misgivings and, when the gowns were finally completed, they were all in various shades of red, except for one in green. It was a small victory, but still a memorable one!

Miss Prahl remarked that she had started her career at the Norwegian National Theatre and has never been connected with any other producing organization. The great advantages of government-subsidized employment are the continuity of work and the opportunity to do great plays and to work with the finest talents in the country; the one significant disadvantage that the young designer feels is the weight of tradition, which curbs originality and independence. "It seems to me," said Miss Prahl, "that a young designer starting out with a young company would have more opportunities to be creative and experimental, and might even evolve new ideas and new styles. But maybe I'm only rationalizing or dreaming."

The Critics on Gerd Nissen Grieg

Writing about the production directed by Ingolf Schanches in 1932, Kristian Elster said:

She avoided the trap that most actresses fall into; she shunned tragedy and declamation and played naturalistically. Her personally marvelous and sensitive performance was slowed down occasionally by the un-hurried tempo of the production, especially in the first act which in itself is slow getting started. The direction was excellent but full of superfluous and delaying details. In the second act the tempo accelerated but not sufficiently to allow Gerd Nissen's characterization to take shape. Her interpretation, nevertheless, is highly believable and brought Hedda to life; her acting was close to reality, muted and yet strong, with the shivering undertone of hysteria which suddenly broke through on several occasions. She was captivating as Hedda can very often be, but the cold-ness of her barrenness and of her spite come through even when she is most tempting and alluring; she stimulates our fantasies without stirring our imaginations. She is a social sphinx whose riddle is a terrible and frightening emptiness. There is something admirable in the way Gerd Nissen reveals and conceals at the same time. In scene after scene, par-ticularly in the masterful scene with Judge Brack, we see her driven by the lascivious curiosity that she never dared to put into action and that existed only in her fantasy, not in her active life. Gerd Nissen surrounds Hedda with all the mystery and glamor of womankind which makes her a wonderful bait to men's minds. The actress, furthermore, is capable of remarkable variety; it is not the same woman who burns Lövborg's manu-script, who gives Lövborg the pistol; and she is different again in the final scenes when she suddenly reveals herself; still she is always strong, natural, and interesting without making Hedda seem more valuable as a human being than she really is. Gerd Nissen's acting is never melo-dramatic and yet she was able to show that occasionally there are melodramatic trends in Hedda's mind. More successfully than any other actress I have ever seen, Gerd Nissen made Hedda's suicide under-standable in the way she built up her determination and then immediately collapsed into a feeling of deep revulsion.

Writing about the production directed by Knut Hergel in 1951, Paul Gjesdahl said:

Gerd Grieg plays Hedda with the same revealing intelligence and with the same half-reluctant sympathy that characterized her performance a number of years ago. She shows great security in revealing the many details in Hedda's makeup. She does not attempt to mystify the audience, but her Hedda has grown and changed during these years. She has added new and interesting moments. She shows us how lonely Hedda is, how useless she is to everyone except to the professional seducer Judge Brack. Occasionally the actress emphasizes too many unimportant details in the character; at such moments one has the feeling that the actress is not playing the part but is standing beside the character and commenting on her. [This is what Bertolt Brecht called the "alienation-effect," which he wished all actors to achieve; Gjesdahl considers it a fault.—R.G.] From the Third Act on, however, the performance is clean and free; the actress's portrayal and the author's meaning and aim merge. In directing the play, Knut Hergel seems to have recreated the conception of Ingolf Schanches.

An English Hedda

Interview with Peggy Ashcroft

One of the most important actresses in England, Peggy Ashcroft has served as leading lady with John Gielgud, Laurence Olivier, and Paul Robeson. She has appeared in some of the greatest plays in the dramatic repertory from the Greeks to the present, but, until 1954, had never performed in a drama by Ibsen.

George Devine (Tesman) and Peggy Ashcroft (Hedda) at the Lyric Theatre, Hammersmith, London 1954. For her performance in this production Miss Ashcroft received a gold medal from the King of Norway. Angus McBean. Photograph: Theatre Collection New York Public Library.

"For some reason," said Miss Ashcroft, "I was never drawn to playing Ibsen, but for a long time I was interested in Hedda. Some critics have called her an ordinary woman, the sort 'one might take in to dinner any evening,' while others have spoken of her as an extraordinary person, a *femme fatale*. The contradiction fascinated me, and when I was offered the opportunity to play the part I was delighted."

It was a first-rate company the producer assembled—George Devine as Tesman, Alan Badel as Eilert, Michael MacLiammoir as Brack, and Rachel Kempson as Thea. The play was directed by Peter Ashmore, with scenery and costumes designed by Motley.

When she began to study her part, Miss Ashcroft was amazed to discover how taut and economical Ibsen's writing was, how every word revealed his intentions. The playwright, it seemed, was making a satiric comment on the provincialism, the narrowness of outlook and morality, of the upper-middle and professional classes in Norway. Into this milieu he injected the powerful, restless personality of Hedda, a woman who was as cold as ice yet burned with a terrible fire, a coward with an inverted kind of courage. The more Miss Ashcroft thought about the character, the more the personality traits emerged. Hedda is clever, full of energy, personally fascinating, but she lacks a conscience, depth of feeling, and good judgment. She wrecks another woman's happiness, drives a man to disgrace and death, and finally shoots herself, for no more important reason than to import some color and excitement into her humdrum life. Through all this, Hedda lacks tragic intensity but is rather grimly amusing. She is a vixen, a nasty minx, and ridiculously pretentious. We are aware at every moment that all Hedda's claims to esthetic taste, aristocracy of spirit, and nobleness of despair are preposterous. And that was the clue to the presentation of the role: the entire performance—and the production as well—was pervaded by a comic spirit, which cast an ironic light upon Hedda's actions, but was never allowed to fall into burlesque.

Miss Ashcroft smiled or laughed cruelly without mirth; it was the unpleasant sort of sound that Katherine Mansfield described as "a spoon tinkling against a medicine-glass." Hedda laughed as she threatened to burn Thea's hair, and the controlled hysteria of her repeated laughter reached its height in the final scene with Lövborg. Her most polite remarks dripped with acid; her white, tense face was twisted with spite. One felt that she was frigid, a cold-blooded harlot.

"Although the play begins like Victorian melodrama," said Miss Ashcroft, "since the strains of a piano take the curtain up and a servant sets out Hedda's defects of character before the lady appears, it ends like the most potent and modern existentialism. In sending Lövborg to the party, in burning his manuscript, and in Hedda's suicide, there is the existentialist insistence on choice decided without respect to any kind of morality except that evolved by the individual's own actions."

Because Hedda's character is not only complex but "unnatural," Miss Ashcroft found the role of Ibsen's heroine a particularly difficult one to master. Thea, the modern woman of her time, a sort of suffragette, weak where Hedda is strong and vice versa, has, at least, normal feminine traits. Hedda, the daughter of a general, is atypical: she has masculine tendencies but is antifeminist, is oversexed yet severely repressed. "All of that is of the utmost importance," said Miss Ashcroft. "The actress has to present the character, strange as she may be, so that within the first few moments after she comes on stage the audience will believe in her. That's why the bonnet scene is so brilliant—it immediately illuminates one of Hedda's basic traits. In the manuscript-burning scene, however, Ibsen seems to suggest that as Hedda puts Eilert's book into the fire with the words, 'I am burning your child,' she does so with great deliberation. But I could not do it that way. Ibsen invests this moment with enormous sexuality; the fire is a sexual symbol and Hedda, an inverted nymphomaniac, is aroused. Hedda is deriving a perverse pleasure from what she is doing, and so I thought she would burn the manuscript hysterically, with frenzy, trembling and laughing. A bit earlier, when Thea speaks of the manuscript as 'our child,' Hedda reacts to the idea of George's child with loathing; and, after Thea leaves, Hedda has an attack of nausea because of her pregnancy. Some members of the audience got it, some didn't."

In Miss Ashcroft's production, Hedda was not played as the star. "It was a remarkable company," said the actress. "Every member of the cast was excellent, and we played as an ensemble. It was amazing how George Devine managed to make Tesman pathetic and ridiculous at the same time; Alan Badel had the demonic quality that Eilert needs; and Michael MacLiammoir was a sparkling, debonair, and lecherous Brack."

The play opened originally at the Olympia Theatre, Dublin, on July 5, 1954. It went into the Lyric Hammersmith, London, on September 8 and ran until November 27. It was so well attended that it recovered its production costs within the first five weeks of its run at the Lyric. On November 29, it was moved to the Westminster Theatre in London's West End for a limited engagement, with Michael Warre in the role of Eilert and Noel Willman as Brack. The company then went abroad on a six-week tour but continued to work on the script and the performances, sharpening dialogue, characterization, and meaning.

In Holland audiences showed no sympathy for Hedda; apparently, such a character was totally inconceivable to the Dutch. In Copenhagen and Oslo, however, the play was greeted with great warmth, not because the audiences felt compassion for Hedda, Miss Ashcroft noted, but because they understood that such women exist. The reception in Oslo was particularly gratifying; playgoers and critics raved over the play. Tancred Ibsen, grandson of the playwright, told Miss Ashcroft, "Henrik Ibsen never went to the theatre because actors always played him with the cothurnus, instead of portraying realistic, down-to-earth people." As the King of Norway presented Miss Ashcroft with a gold medal for her performance, he said, "You are very brave to come into the lion's den." This production actually influenced later Norwegian productions of Ibsen. Although the play was performed in period costume and decor so authentic that Miss Ashcroft even wore a pair of genuine Victorian corsets stiffened with whalebone, the impression it created was of enlarged realism, modern in both its bitterness and its humor.

Having portrayed many great roles created by such dramatists as Sophocles, Shakespeare, Sheridan, and Webster, Miss Ashcroft was in a position to say, "There is a mystery about classic parts which has to be discovered imaginatively, but a serious actress should be prepared to present the dilemmas of ordinary women, of the women in the audience, in addition to the more exotic predicaments of classical heroines. If she specializes in one or the other, she will tend to work to a method or formula, and staleness will inevbitably set in. I welcome a new type of part because it brings fresh problems and new difficulties with it, demanding new solutions and giving new satisfactions."

After appearing in *Hedda Gabler,* Miss Ashcroft was praised for her interpretation of Rebecca West in *Rosmersholm* in 1959 and of Mrs. Alving in *Ghosts* in 1967.

Costumes and Scenery for an
Ingmar Bergman Production

Interview with Mago

In July, 1964, Ingmar Bergman and his designer, Mago, held discussions about a new stage production of *Hedda Gabler,* which was to be mounted at the Royal Dramatic Theatre in Stockholm that fall. Mago had created most of the costumes for Bergman's films since 1953, and now he was to undertake the scenery as well as the costumes for the stage. In their preliminary talks, the men began with a conventional concept: the set was to be a beautiful reproduction of an interior of the period—Oslo, 1890. There were to be leather-covered walls with gold tooling, ample bookshelves, a fireplace with a portrait of General Gabler above it. All the other pictures in the room were to be painted in sepia, as was the backdrop, which was to represent a garden. With that much decided, Mago went off to Portugal for a brief holiday.

When he returned from Lisbon a few weeks later, he had a portfolio bulging with completed sketches based on the ideas upon which he and Bergman had agreed. At the end of July, he went to the theatre to meet with the director. Rehearsals were to start at the beginning of August. Bergman began to ponder over Mago's sketches. Three or four days later he said that he felt the set was "too beautiful" and would have to be changed. Both men agreed, however, that what they liked about the original design was the way the bookshelves at the rear seemed to contain the set and hem in the lives of the occupants. After all, Eilert and George, as well as Hedda and Thea, were completely involved with books, almost to the exclusion of life.

The rehearsal space was cleared and seven screens were put up to delimit the acting areas. One screen, stage right, was set at a right angle to the others and marked the separation of Hedda's alcove from the living room; this screen was movable—pushed upstage, Hedda's door was open, pushed downstage, Hedda's room was shut off. Two screens at the rear could be opened like double doors.

Bergman wanted the lower edge of the dark-red theatre curtain to be seen during the play, and he thought that the screens ought to be done in natural color. Mago felt that a natural color would be too flat, suggesting instead red screens and a red floor, an idea which Bergman accepted. All the books, and many other stationary objects, were covered in the same shade of red, while the wooden furniture in the room—piano, mirror, desk—were of dark walnut, almost black.

The ceiling of the room was set very low, not more than ten or twelve feet from the stage floor, to provide a boxlike and oppressive atmosphere. The permanent decoration on the theatre's proscenium arch was highly ornamented and gilded and was made to serve as the rich exterior of the house. This arrangement was meant to contrast the community's illusion concerning the expansive life of the occupants with the reality of their constrained existence. When the audience entered the theatre, the curtain was up and the set could be seen. As the play was about to begin, spotlights lit up the entire proscenium as if it were part of the house. With the entrance of the actors, the lights on the proscenium dimmed down slowly and went out while the stage lights became hotter.

It was immediately apparent to the director and the designer that with the stylized set they had devised, they could not use completely realistic costumes. They decided, therefore, to give the characters a uniform appearance, which might suggest the strict conventions of the time, the place, and the social class. They agreed upon a single silhouette for the women and another one for the men; the silhouettes chosen were of about the year 1910. Although all the women were to wear the identical dress and all the men the same suits, the individualization of the characters was provided for in the colors.

On her first entrance Aunt Julia's dress was a medium gray (which appeared lighter against the red background); she had a short cape, and a small light-gray hat over her dark-brown hair. In her second appearance, after her sister's death, her dress, cape, and hat were black. Berta, the housekeeper, wore the identical dress in navy blue and over it an apron, just a few shades lighter in blue-gray. Berta was played by an elderly actress who dressed her own gray hair.

Hedda's first costume was a dressing gown made of dull silk in champagne color; its severe lines were relieved by a touch of lace at the wrists. Another dress was of peacock green—a dark blue-green—that picked up the lights slightly. Gertrud Fridh, who played Hedda, has natural golden-red hair which, worn very simply, provided a remarkable contrast to the red background.

Thea wore the silhouette in dark brown, with accessories to match—small hat, coat, bag, and gloves—and a wig of neutral-brown hair.

The men's suits as has already been mentioned, were, for the most part, of identical style. On his first entrance, George had a normal-length jacket of heavy wool in medium gray; for his evening out, however, he changed into a Prince Albert coat of the same color. Eilert's suit was a shade of gray slightly darker than George's; and Judge Brack's was a still darker shade of gray.

"We had no intention of making the costumes symbolic," said Mago. "We wanted them to be simple, uniform, and suggestive of another time, only vaguely dated, vaguely period. At first I had misgivings about not doing it in exact period style, with Hedda in a riding-habit and all the trimmings, but as the concept evolved I realized that what we were doing worked well for the play and for Hedda. She is the forerunner of one 'type' of modern woman."

Bergman himself did the lighting for the production; the morning scenes were brilliant and hot, the evening scenes dim and cool. The scheme was entirely arbitrary, since there were no windows in the set or any other obvious sources of light.

An interesting bit of direction and design was displayed in the placing of the stove in which Hedda burned Eilert's book. A feature of almost all European theatres is the prompter's box (a small cavelike structure located at the footlights, downstage center, where the prompter sits, script in hand, ready to come to the aid of the forgetful actor; a hood conceals this functionary from the audience). Bergman used this hooded opening to represent the stove. The idea was planted during the play as characters approached the hood and stood warming themselves in its fiery glow. Thus, during the burning of the book, Hedda was able to come down to the very edge of the stage and face the audience full front as she tore up the manuscript and cast the pages into the prompter's box.

This production aroused a great deal of comment, even controversy but achieved enormous success in Sweden and on the Continent.

In 1950 Alec Clunes asked Irene Worth to play Hedda Gabler but, despite the actress's tremendous admiration for Ibsen, she said no, emphatically no, because she wasn't ready for it.

"What worried me very much, indeed embarrassed me, was Hedda's line, 'Do it beautifully!' " says Miss Worth. "It is not until one has a deeper understanding of human nature that one begins to appreciate what lies behind that enormous cry of Hedda's. Now I can see that it is perhaps over-elaborate, over-intense, almost violent, because by nature she is basically a very refined woman."

Now Miss Worth feels she is as ready for the part as she will ever be ("I now know how to cope with that line").

From an interview with Ian Woodward in the
Christan Science Monitor, April 29, 1970.

In the summer of 1970, Miss Worth appeared in *Hedda Gabler* at the Shakespeare Festival, Stratford, Ontario. In his review of her performance, Walter Kerr said:

"The actress is brilliant at every turn, and she is never not turning. She can straighten her spine in swift, silent alarm, telling us in the hushed movement that she has known all along there is to be no professorship for her husband, no crowded future for herself; from the beginning she has intuited that life would walk away from her without warning. She can glide past Judge Brack, smiling but nonetheless going as though to say that she understands and enjoys him but is permanently not his. She can give a terrible shrug, when asked why she has always had impulses to torment other people to no purpose, and simply say "I don't know" in a candor that is shattering.

"... She even wakes up properly, lying still long after you know she is listening, turning and opening her eyes when she decides to be awake. I have never seen an actress do that before. It is astonishingly true."

Kerr concludes that "Miss Worth is just possibly the best actress in the world."

From "In 'Hedda Gabler,' Irene Proves Her Worth,"
by Walter Kerr, *Sunday Times,* June 21, 1970.

Hedda
Gabler   *A Play in Four Acts*

HENRIK IBSEN
English Version by Randolph Goodman

Characters

George Tesman, a research fellow in cultural history
Hedda, his wife
Miss Juliana Tesman, his aunt
Mrs. Elvsted
Judge Brack
Eilert Lövborg
Berta, The Tesmans' housekeeper

Scene: The Tesmans' home in Christiania (Oslo)
Time: About 1890

Act One

A large, handsome, and tastefully furnished drawing-room, decorated in dark colors. At the rear, a wide doorway with portieres drawn back, leading into a smaller room decorated in the same style as the drawing-room. In the front room, at the right, a folding door leads out to the hall. In the opposite wall, at the left, a glass door, also with curtains drawn back; through the panes may be seen part of the veranda and trees covered with autumn foliage. Standing well forward in the drawing-room is an oval table, with a cover on it, and chairs around it. By the wall, down right, a large stove of dark porcelain, a highbacked armchair, an upholstered footstool, and two small side-tables. A sofa, with a small round table in front of it, is in the upper right-hand corner. Standing slightly away from the wall, down left, is another sofa. Above the glass door, a piano. On either side of the wide doorway, rear, a bric-a-brac stand with terra-cotta and majolica ornaments. Against the rear wall of the inner room a sofa, with a table and one or two chairs. Over the sofa hangs the portrait of a handsome, elderly man in the uniform of a general. Over the table a hanging lamp, with an opalescent glass shade. Many bouquets of flowers are arranged about the drawing-room in vases and glasses, others lie upon the various tables. The floors in both rooms are covered with thick carpets. It is early morning; the sun shines in through the glass door.

Miss Juliana Tesman, *wearing a hat and carrying a parasol, comes in from the hall, followed by* **Berta,** *who carries a bouquet wrapped in paper.* **Miss Tesman** *is a handsome and pleasant-looking woman of about sixty-five. She is well-dressed in a simple, grey, tailored outfit.* **Berta,** *a middle-aged woman, is plain and rather countrified in appearance.*

Miss Tesman: [*Stops just inside the door, listens, then says softly.*] Dear me, I don't think they're awake yet!
Berta: [*Also softly.*] That's what I told you, Miss Juliana. You know how late the steamer got in last night. And after they came home, good heavens, the young mistress just had to un-

pack everything before she would go
to bed.

Miss Tesman: Well, let them sleep as
long as they like. But when they get
up, they ought to have a breath of
fresh air.

[*She goes to the glass door and
opens it wide.*]

Berta: [*Beside the table, not knowing
what to do with the bouquet in her
hand.*] There's not a bit of room left
anywhere. I'll just put them down
here, Miss Juliana.

[*She puts the bouquet on the
piano.*]

Miss Tesman: So you've got a new mistress now, Berta dear. Heaven knows
it was hard for me to let you go.

Berta: [*Almost weeping.*] Don't you think
it was hard for me too, Miss Juliana?
After all those blessed years I spent
with you and Miss Rina.

Miss Tesman: We've got to make the
best of it, Berta. What else can we
do? You know George can't get along
without you—he just can't. You've
looked after him ever since he was a
little boy.

Berta: Yes, Miss Juliana. But I'm worried
about poor Miss Rina lying there
helpless. And that new girl—she'll
never learn to take proper care of an
invalid.

Miss Tesman: Oh, I'll be able to train
her. Of course, I'll have to do most
of the work myself at first. Now don't
you worry about my poor sister,
Berta dear.

Berta: But there's something else, Miss
Juliana. I'm so afraid I'll never be
able to please the young mistress.

Miss Tesman: Oh, heavens, there may
be one or two things at first—

Berta: But I'm sure she'll be very particular.

Miss Tesman: Well, it's no wonder—
General Gabler's daughter! You can
imagine how she was pampered
when her father was alive! We used
to watch them as they went by—the
two of them—galloping down the
road. She wore a long, black riding-
habit—and feathers in her hat! Don't
you remember?

Berta: Oh, I remember, all right. But
good Lord, I never would have
dreamed that she and our Georgie
would team up some day!

Miss Tesman: Nor would I! But, Berta
dear—before I forget—from now on
you mustn't call him Georgie. You
must call him Doctor Tesman.

Berta: Yes, that's what the young mistress told me last night—the minute
they set foot in the house. Is it really
true, Miss Juliana?

Miss Tesman: It certainly is. Just think,
Berta, some foreign university made
him a doctor—while he was abroad.
I didn't know a thing about it, but he
told me so himself last night on the
pier.

Berta: Well, he's clever enough to do
anything. But I never thought he'd
go in for doctoring people.

Miss Tesman: No, no, he's not that kind
of doctor. [*Nods significantly.*] But
let me tell you, it won't be long
before we have to call him something
much grander!

Berta: You don't say so! And what's
that, Miss Juliana?

Miss Tesman: [*Smiles.*] Wouldn't you
like to know! [*With emotion.*] Oh,
dear, if only my poor brother were
alive now to see what an important
man his little boy has become!
[*Glances around.*] But what have you
done, Berta? Taken all the covers off
the furniture?

Berta: Mistress told me to. She said she
can't stand slipcovers.

Miss Tesman: Do they intend to use this
as their living room now?

Berta: That's what I understood her to
say, but he—I mean the Doctor—
didn't say anything.

[**George Tesman** *enters the inner
room from the right, humming to
himself, and carrying an empty,*

unstrapped suitcase. He is a youthful-looking man of thirty-three, medium height, rather stout, with a round, open cheerful face, fair hair and beard. He wears glasses and is rather carelessly dressed in a comfortable old suit.]

Miss Tesman: Good morning, good morning, George.

Tesman: *[In the doorway between the rooms.]* Auntie Julie! Dear Auntie Julie!

[Goes to her and shakes her hand warmly.]

Way out here—so early in the morning, eh?

Miss Tesman: I had to come and see how you were getting along.

Tesman: Even though you were up half the night?

Miss Tesman: Oh, that doesn't bother me at all.

Tesman: You got home all right from the pier, eh?

Miss Tesman: Yes, of course, I did. Judge Brack was kind enough to see me right to my door.

Tesman: We were sorry we couldn't give you a lift. But you saw what a pile of luggage Hedda had.

Miss Tesman: Yes, she certainly had a lot!

Berta: *[To* **Tesman.***]* Shall I go in and see if there's anything I can do for Mrs. Tesman?

Tesman: No, thanks, Berta—you don't have to. She said she'd ring if she wanted anything.

Berta: *[Starts to leave, right.]* All right.

Tesman: Wait a minute, though—you can take this suitcase with you.

Berta: *[Takes it.]* I'll put it up in the attic. *[She goes out by the hall door.]*

Tesman: You wouldn't believe it, Auntie, but that bag was packed full of notes from all the old documents I went through—in libraries and archives— wonderful material that no one else knew existed.

Miss Tesman: You don't seem to have wasted your time on your honeymoon, George.

Tesman: Oh, I certainly didn't. But why don't you take your hat off, Auntie? Let me help you, eh?

Miss Tesman: *[While he does so.]* My, my, this is just like old times when you were still at home with us.

Tesman: *[Turns the hat in his hand and looks at it with admiration.]* Oh, what an elegant hat you've got yourself!

Miss Tesman: I bought it for Hedda's sake.

Tesman: For Hedda's sake, eh?

Miss Tesman: Yes, so that Hedda wouldn't be ashamed of me if we happened to go out together.

Tesman: *[Pats her cheek.]* You always think of everything, Aunt Julie. *[Puts the hat on a chair beside the table.]*

Now, look here—let's sit down on the sofa and be comfortable. We can have a little talk till Hedda comes. *[They sit down. She stands her parasol against the corner of the sofa.]*

Miss Tesman: *[Takes both his hands and looks at him.]* How wonderful it is to have you home again, Georgie, where I can feast my eyes on you! My George—my dear brother's own boy!

Tesman: And it's wonderful to see you again, Auntie Julie. You've been both a father and mother to me.

Miss Tesman: I know you'll always keep a place in your heart for your old aunts.

Tesman: Oh, how is Auntie Rina? No better, eh?

Miss Tesman: No, I'm afraid she'll never be any better. She's as helpless as ever, poor thing. But I pray to God I won't lose her. I don't know what I'll do with myself if she goes. Especially now, George, that I don't have you to look after any more.

Tesman: *[Pats her back.]* There, there, there . . .

Miss Tesman: *[Suddenly changes her tone.]* It's hard for me to believe that you're a married man now, George, and married to Hedda Gabler—the beautiful Hedda Gabler! And that you won out over all her admirers!

Tesman: *[Hums a little tune and smiles with self-satisfaction.]* Yes, I suppose some of my friends would like to be in my shoes right now, eh?

Miss Tesman: And then your lovely long wedding trip! More than five months —nearly six . . .

Tesman: But the trip was important for my research work, too, Auntie. All those libraries I had to go through— and the books I had to read!

Miss Tesman: Yes, of course. *[Lowers her voice, confidentially.]* But George dear, isn't there something—something special you want to tell me?

Tesman: About our trip?

Miss Tesman: Yes.

Tesman: I can't think of a thing I didn't mention in my letters. I had a doctor's degree conferred on me—but I told you that last night.

Miss Tesman: Yes, you did. But what I mean is—haven't you any—any expectations—?

Tesman: Expectations?

Miss Tesman: For heaven's sake, George. You can tell your old auntie!

Tesman: Why, of course, I have expectations.

Miss Tesman: Yes!

Tesman: I have every expectation of becoming a professor one of these days.

Miss Tesman: Oh, yes, a professor, but—

Tesman: In fact, I'm sure of it. But Auntie dear, you know all about that already!

Miss Tesman: *[Laughingly.]* Yes, of course, I do. You're quite right, dear. *[Changes the subject.]* But we were talking about your trip. It must have cost a good deal of money, George.

Tesman: Well, that fellowship I had was pretty generous. It went a long way.

Miss Tesman: But I can't understand how you made it do for two.

Tesman: No, I suppose that's not so easy to understand, eh?

Miss Tesman: Especially traveling with a lady—they tell me that makes it much more expensive.

Tesman: Yes, of course it's a little more expensive. But Hedda had to have this trip, Auntie! She really had to. It's the way things are done.

Miss Tesman: Yes, I suppose so. It seems a honeymoon abroad is absolutely essential nowadays. But tell me— have you had a chance to look through the house?

Tesman: I certainly have. I've been wandering from room to room ever since it grew light.

Miss Tesman: And what do you think of the place?

Tesman: I'm delighted! Just delighted! But I can't imagine what we'll do with the two empty rooms between the back parlor, there, and Hedda's bedroom.

Miss Tesman: *[Laughs.]* Oh, George dear, I'm sure you'll find some use for them—a little later on.

Tesman: Of course, you're right, Aunt Julie! You mean as my library grows, eh?

Miss Tesman: That's it, my dear boy. It's your library I was thinking of.

Tesman: But I'm very happy for Hedda's sake. She always had her eye on this place. Even before we were engaged she often used to say she would never want to live anywhere but in Secretary Falk's house.

Miss Tesman: What a coincidence—that this very house should be put up for sale just after you left!

Tesman: That certainly was lucky, Aunt Julie, wasn't it, eh?

Miss Tesman: But think of the expense, George dear! You'll find it very expensive—keeping all this up.

Tesman: *[Looks at her unhappily.]* Yes, I suppose so, Auntie.

Miss Tesman: It will take an awful lot of money.

Tesman: How much do you think? Approximately, eh?

Miss Tesman: I can't even guess. We'll have to wait until all the bills come in.

Tesman: Well, anyway, Judge Brack was able to arrange the most favorable terms for me. That's what he said in a letter to Hedda.

Miss Tesman: Don't you worry about it, my dear boy. At least I was able to put up security for the furniture and carpets.

Tesman: Security? You? But Aunt Julie —what sort of security could *you* give?

Miss Tesman: I took a loan against our annuity.

Tesman: *[Jumps up.]* What! Your annuity!

Miss Tesman: I didn't know what else to do.

Tesman: Have you gone out of your mind, Auntie! The annuity is all that you and Aunt Rina have to live on.

Miss Tesman: Now, don't get excited. Judge Brack said it was just a formality. He was kind enough to arrange the whole thing for me. A mere formality, that's what he said.

Tesman: That's all very well, but still—

Miss Tesman: You'll have your own salary to live on now. And suppose we do have to help out a bit in the beginning—we'd be only too happy to do it!

Tesman: Oh, Auntie, won't you ever get tired of making sacrifices for me!

Miss Tesman: *[Rises and puts her hands on his shoulders.]* The only happiness I have in this world is to make things easier for you, my dear boy. You had no mother or father to help you. Sometimes, of course, it was pretty hard to make ends meet, but now we're successful and we have nothing to fear.

Tesman: Yes, it's really remarkable how everything has turned out for the best.

Miss Tesman: Now you can look down on those who stood in your way. They've fallen behind you, George. Your most dangerous rival fell the lowest of all. He's made his bed and he must lie in it, poor foolish creature.

Tesman: Have you had any news of Eilert? Since I went away, I mean.

Miss Tesman: Only that he's supposed to have published a new book.

Tesman: A new book? Eilert Lövborg! Recently, eh?

Miss Tesman: That's what they say. But how can a book of his be worth anything! When your book appears, it'll be a different story! What's it about, George?

Tesman: It will deal with the domestic industries of Brabant during the Middle Ages.

Miss Tesman: Fancy being able to write about things like that!

Tesman: But it may be quite some time before the book is ready. You see, first I have to arrange all the notes I've collected.

Miss Tesman: Yes, collecting and arranging—no one can beat you at that. That's where you take after your poor dear father.

Tesman: I just can't wait to get started, especially now that I have my own wonderful home to work in.

Miss Tesman: And more than that, dear, now that you have the wife your heart was set on.

Tesman: *[Embraces her.]* Oh, yes, yes, Aunt Julie. Hedda is the most wonderful part of it all! *[Glances toward the inner room.]* I think she's coming in now, eh?

> *[***Hedda** enters from the left through the inner room. She is a woman of twenty-nine whose face and figure show refinement and distinction. Her complexion is pale and opaque. Her steel-*

grey eyes express a cold, un-
ruffled calm. Her hair is medium
brown but not particularly abun-
dant. She is dressed in an
attractive, somewhat loose-fitting
housecoat.]

Miss Tesman: *[Going to meet* **Hedda.***]*
Good morning, Hedda dear! Good
morning and welcome home!

Hedda: *[Extends her hand.]* Good morning, Miss Tesman! Such an early call!
That was kind of you.

Miss Tesman: *[Slightly embarrassed.]*
Well—has the bride slept well in her
new home?

Hedda: Yes, thank you. Fairly well.

Tesman: *[Laughs.]* Fairly well! That's a
good one, Hedda! You were sleeping
like a rock when I got up.

Hedda: Fortunately. But, of course, Miss
Tesman, one has to get used to new
surroundings little by little. *[Glancing
toward the left.]* Oh, that maid's left
the door open and let in a whole
flood of sunshine.

Miss Tesman: Well, then, we'll shut it.

Hedda: No, no, not that! Tesman, will
you please draw the curtains. It will
give a softer light.

Tesman: *[At the door.]* Of course. There
now, Hedda, you have both shade
and fresh air.

Hedda: We certainly must have fresh
air, with all these stacks of flowers—
But won't you sit down, Miss
Tesman?

Miss Tesman: No, thank you. Now that
I've seen that everything here is all
right, I must be getting home to my
poor sister.

Tesman: Be sure to give her my love,
Auntie, and tell her I'll drop in to
see her later in the day.

Miss Tesman: Yes, George, I'll be sure to
tell her. Oh, I almost forgot—*[Feels
in her pocket.]* I have something here
for you.

Tesman: What is it, Auntie? Eh?

Miss Tesman: *[Produces a flat parcel
wrapped in newspaper and hands it
to him.]* Here, dear, look!

Tesman: *[Opens the parcel.]* Well, good
heavens! You kept them for me, Aunt
Julie! Hedda, isn't this touching, eh?

Hedda: *[Beside the bric-a-brac stand on
the right.]* What is it?

Tesman: My slippers! My old bedroom-
slippers!

Hedda: Oh, yes, I remember. You often
talked about them on the trip.

Tesman: Because I missed them so
much.

[Going up to her.]

Now you can have a look at them,
Hedda.

Hedda: *[Moving toward the stove.]*
Thanks, but I really don't care to.

Tesman: *[Follows her.]* Just think, Aunt
Rina embroidered them for me—sick
as she was. You can't imagine how
many memories they bring back!

Hedda: *[At the table.]* Not for me.

Miss Tesman: Of course not for Hedda,
George.

Tesman: But now that she's a member
of the family, I thought—

Hedda: *[Interrupting.]* I don't think we'll
get along with this maid, Tesman.

Miss Tesman: Not get along with Berta?

Tesman: Why, dear, what makes you
think that, eh?

Hedda: *[Pointing.]* Look—she left her old
hat on the chair over there.

Tesman: *[Appalled, drops the slippers.]*
Why, Hedda—!

Hedda: Just imagine if someone should
come in and see it!

Tesman: But Hedda—that's Aunt Julie's
hat.

Hedda: Is it!

Miss Tesman: Yes, indeed, it is. And
what's more, it's not old, Mrs.
Tesman.

Hedda: I really didn't look at it very
closely, Miss Tesman.

Miss Tesman: *[Putting on the hat.]* This
is the first time I've worn it. The very
first.

Tesman: And it's a very nice hat—very
elegant.

Miss Tesman: Oh, it's not worth all that
praise, George. *[Looks around.]* My

parasol—? Here it is! [Takes it.] And this is mine, too—[Under her breath.] not Berta's.

Tesman: A new hat and a new parasol! Just think, Hedda!

Hedda: Very nice—lovely.

Tesman: Yes, aren't they, eh? But Auntie, take a good look at Hedda before you go! Isn't she lovely?

Miss Tesman: My dear boy, that's nothing new. Hedda's always been lovely.

[She nods and goes toward the right.]

Tesman: [Following her.] Yes, but haven't you noticed how plump she is? She's filled out a bit on the trip, eh?

Hedda: [Crosses the room.] Oh, be quiet—!

Miss Tesman: [Who has stopped and turned.] Filled out?

Tesman: Of course, you don't notice it so much because of the dress she's wearing. But I'm able to see—

Hedda: [At the glass door, impatiently.] Oh, you can't see anything.

Tesman: It must have been the mountain air in the Tyrol—

Hedda: [Curtly, interrupting.] I'm exactly the same as I was when we left.

Tesman: Yes, so you say. But you certainly aren't. Don't you agree with me, Auntie?

Miss Tesman: [Who has been gazing at her with folded hands.] Hedda is lovely—lovely—lovely.

[Draws **Hedda's** head downwards with both hands and kisses her hair.]

God bless you and keep you Hedda Tesman, for George's sake.

Hedda: [Frees herself gently.] Oh—! Let me go, please.

Miss Tesman: [With quiet emotion.] I won't let a day pass without coming to see you.

Tesman: You will do that, won't you, Auntie, eh?

Miss Tesman: Good-bye! Good-bye!

[She goes out by the hall door.

Tesman accompanies her. The door remains half open. **Tesman** can be heard repeating his message to **Aunt Rina** and his thanks for the slippers.

In the meantime, **Hedda** walks about the room, raising her arms and clenching her hands as if in desperation. Then she flings back the curtains from the glass door and stands there looking out.

Presently **Tesman** returns and closes the door behind him.]

Tesman: [Picks up the slippers from the floor.] What are you looking at, Hedda?

Hedda: [Now calm and controlled.] I'm just looking at the leaves. They're so yellow—so withered.

Tesman: [Wraps up the slippers and puts them on the table.] After all, we're well into September.

Hedda: [Restless again.] Yes, yes— already in September—

Tesman: Didn't Aunt Julie behave strangely today, dear? She was so formal. What do you think was the matter with her, eh?

Hedda: Why, I scarcely know her. Doesn't she usually act that way?

Tesman: No, not as she did today.

Hedda: [Moving away from the door.] Do you think she was offended about the hat?

Tesman: Oh, no. Maybe a little, just for a moment—

Hedda: But what a way to behave, to toss her hat just anywhere in the drawing room! People don't do such things.

Tesman: Well, I'm sure Aunt Julie won't do it again.

Hedda: Anyway, I'll manage to make it up to her.

Tesman: Yes, Hedda dear, I'm sure you will.

Hedda: When you go to see them this afternoon, you might ask her to come over for the evening.

Tesman: Oh yes, I will. And there's one

more thing you could do that would make her very happy.

Hedda: Yes? What's that?

Tesman: If you could only show her a little more affection and call her Auntie. For my sake, Hedda, eh?

Hedda: No, no, Tesman—you can't expect me to do that. I've told you before, I'll try to call her Aunt Juliana—that's all I can do.

Tesman: All right. Only I think now that you're a member of the family, you—

Hedda: H'm—I really don't see why— [She moves toward the doorway to the inner room.]

Tesman: [After a pause.] Is there anything the matter with you, Hedda, eh?

Hedda: I'm just looking at my old piano. It doesn't go well with the rest of the furniture.

Tesman: As soon as I draw my first salary, we can go and trade it in for a new one.

Hedda: Trade it in! Never! I don't want to part with it. We could put it there in the back room and get a new one in here. Later on, I mean, when we can afford it.

Tesman: [Slightly taken aback.] Yes—of course we could do that.

Hedda: [Picks up the bouquet from the piano.] These flowers weren't here when we came in last night.

Tesman: Aunt Julie must've brought them for you.

Hedda: [Examines the bouquet.] Here's a card. [Takes it out and reads it.] "Will be back later." You'll never guess who it's from!

Tesman: Who is it, eh?

Hedda: It says "Mrs. Elvsted."

Tesman: Really? Thea Elvsted. Her maiden name was Thea Rysing.

Hedda: Exactly. The girl with that irritating head of hair she was always showing off. I heard she was an old flame of yours.

Tesman: [Laughs.] Oh, that didn't last long. Anyway, it was before I knew you, Hedda. But imagine her being in town!

Hedda: Funny that she'd call on us. I've hardly seen her since we were in school.

Tesman: I haven't seen her either for— Lord knows how long. I wonder how she can stand living in such a God-forsaken place, eh?

Hedda: [Suddenly, after a moment's thought.] Tell me, Tesman—isn't it somewhere up there that he—that— Eilert Lövborg went to live?

Tesman: Yes, he's somewhere around there.

Berta: [Enters by the hall door.] That lady, ma'am, that left some flowers a little while ago is back again. [Pointing.] The flowers you have in your hand, ma'am.

Hedda: Oh, is she? Well, ask her to come in.

[Berta opens the door for Mrs. Elvsted and goes out herself. Mrs. Elvsted is a delicate-looking woman, with pretty, soft features. Her eyes are light blue, large, round, and somewhat prominent, with a startled, inquiring expression. Her hair is almost flaxen, and unusually thick and wavy. She is a couple of years younger than Hedda. She wears a dark dress, in good taste, but not quite in the latest fashion.]

Hedda: [Greeting her warmly.] How do you do, my dear Mrs. Elvsted? How nice to see you again after all these years.

Mrs. Elvsted: [Nervously, trying to control herself.] Yes—it's a long time since we met.

Tesman: [Shaking hands.] And it's been quite a while since we've met too, eh?

Hedda: Thank you for your lovely flowers.

Mrs. Elvsted: Oh, don't mention it—I would have come to see you yesterday but I heard you were away.

Tesman: Have you just come to town, eh?

Mrs. Elvsted: I got in yesterday at noon.

I was terribly upset not to find you at home.

Hedda: Upset? Why?

Tesman: Yes, why, my dear Mrs. Rysing —I mean Mrs. Elvsted—eh?

Hedda: You're not in any trouble, are you?

Mrs. Elvsted: Yes, I am. And I don't know another living soul I can turn to.

Hedda: [Puts the bouquet on the table.] Come—let's sit down here on the sofa—

Mrs. Elvsted: Oh, I'm much too nervous to sit down.

Hedda: Oh no, you're not. Now come here—
[She draws **Mrs. Elvsted** down on the sofa and sits beside her.]

Tesman: Well, Mrs. Elvsted, what is it, eh?

Hedda: Has anything gone wrong at home?

Mrs. Elvsted: Well, yes—and no. Oh, I hope you won't misunderstand me—

Hedda: Then the best thing to do is to tell us the whole story, Mrs. Elvsted.

Tesman: I suppose that's why you've come here, eh?

Mrs. Elvsted: Yes, yes, of course. But first let me tell you—if you haven't already heard—Eilert Lövborg is in town, too.

Hedda: Lövborg!

Tesman: What! Has Eilert Lövborg come back? Think of that, Hedda!

Hedda: Good heavens, I heard what she said.

Mrs. Elvsted: He's been here for a week —a whole week! Alone—in this awful town—it would be so easy for him to get into trouble.

Hedda: But, my dear Mrs. Elvsted, why should you be so worried about him?

Mrs. Elvsted: [With a startled expression, says rapidly.] He was the children's tutor.

Hedda: Your children's?

Mrs. Elvsted: No, my husband's. I have no children.

Hedda: Your stepchildren, then.

Mrs. Elvsted: Yes.

Tesman: [Hesitantly.] But was he—I don't know how to put it—was he— regular enough in his habits to hold such a position, eh?

Mrs. Elvsted: For the last two years his conduct has been irreproachable.

Tesman: Has it, really? Think of that, Hedda!

Hedda: Yes, yes, I heard it.

Mrs. Elvsted: Absolutely irreproachable, I assure you! But now that he's alone here in town, with quite a lot of money in his pocket—I'm worried to death about him.

Tesman: Why didn't he stay where he was? With you and your husband, eh?

Mrs. Elvsted: After his book was published he became too restless to stay on with us.

Tesman: Oh, yes, Aunt Julie told me he had published a new book.

Mrs. Elvsted: Yes, an enormous book—a sort of outline of civilization. It came out a couple of weeks ago. It's had a tremendous sale and made a great sensation—

Tesman: Has it, really? It must be something he wrote in his better days.

Mrs. Elvsted: You mean, years ago?

Tesman: Yes.

Mrs. Elvsted: Oh, no. He wrote every word of it while he was with us— recently—in the last year.

Tesman: Think of that, Hedda! Isn't that good news?

Mrs. Elvsted: Oh, yes, if only he'd keep it up!

Hedda: Have you seen him here in town?

Mrs. Elvsted: No, not yet. I had to go to a lot of trouble to find out where he was staying, but this morning I finally managed to get his address.

Hedda: [With a searching look.] You know, it seems rather odd that your husband—

Mrs. Elvsted: [With a nervous start.] That my husband—what?

Hedda: That he'd send you here on such an errand—that he didn't come down himself to look after his friend.

Mrs. Elvsted: Oh, no—my husband is terribly busy. And besides, I had some shopping to do.

Hedda: [With a faint smile.] Oh, yes, of course!

Mrs. Elvsted: [Uneasy, rises quickly.] I beg you, Mr. Tesman, be kind to Eilert Lövborg if he should come to see you. And I'm sure he will. You were such good friends in the old days—and you're interested in the same subject. As far as I can understand, you both work in the same field.

Tesman: We used to, at any rate.

Mrs. Elvsted: That's why I knew I could ask you to keep an eye on him, too. You will do that, Mr. Tesman—promise me you will?

Tesman: I'd be very glad to, Mrs. Rysing—

Hedda: Elvsted!

Tesman: I assure you I'll do everything in my power for Eilert. You can depend on that.

Mrs. Elvsted: Oh, how very, very kind of you! [Seizes his hand.] Thank you, thank you! [Suddenly frightened.] You see, my husband is so fond of him.

Hedda: [Rises.] I think you ought to write to him, Tesman. He might not come here on his own.

Tesman: Perhaps that would be the best thing to do, Hedda, eh?

Hedda: And the sooner the better. Why not right now?

Mrs. Elvsted: [Imploringly.] Oh, yes, would you?

Tesman: This very moment. Have you got his address, Mrs.—Mrs. Elvsted?

Mrs. Elvsted: Yes. [Takes a slip of paper from her pocket and hands it to him.] Here it is.

Tesman: Fine, fine. I'll go inside— Oh, wait— [Looks around.] Where are my slippers? Here they are! [Takes the parcel and starts out.]

Hedda: Be sure you write him a nice friendly letter—and a good long one, too.

Tesman: I certainly will.

Mrs. Elvsted: But please don't say I suggested it!

Tesman: Of course not. What makes you think I would, eh? [He goes out, right, through the inner room.]

Hedda: [Goes up to **Mrs. Elvsted,** smiles and says in a low voice.] There! Now we've killed two birds with one stone.

Mrs. Elvsted: What do you mean?

Hedda: Couldn't you see I wanted him to leave us?

Mrs. Elvsted: Yes, to write the letter.

Hedda: And so I could talk to you alone.

Mrs. Elvsted: About the same thing?

Hedda: Precisely.

Mrs. Elvsted: [Alarmed.] But there's nothing more to tell, Mrs. Tesman! Absolutely nothing!

Hedda: Oh, yes, there is. I can see that. There's lots more to tell. Now let's sit here and have a nice, quiet little talk.

[She forces **Mrs. Elvsted** to sit in the easy-chair beside the stove and seats herself on the footstool.]

Mrs. Elvsted: [Anxiously glances at her watch.] But, really, Mrs. Tesman, I'm afraid I must be going.

Hedda: Oh, you can't be in such a hurry. Come now, tell me something about your life at home.

Mrs. Elvsted: I'd rather not speak about that.

Hedda: But to me, dear! Why, we went to school together!

Mrs. Elvsted: Yes, but you were in the class ahead of me, and I was terribly afraid of you then.

Hedda: Afraid of me?

Mrs. Elvsted: Yes, dreadfully. When we met on the stairs you always used to pull my hair.

Hedda: Did I, really?

Mrs. Elvsted: Yes—and once you said you were going to burn it all off.

Hedda: Oh, I was just teasing you!

Mrs. Elvsted: I was so silly in those days — And then we drifted apart and moved in such different circles.

Hedda: Well, now we must try to drift together again. At school we called each other by our first names—

Mrs. Elvsted: Oh, I think you're mistaken.

Hedda: No, no. I remember it distinctly. *[Draws the footstool closer to* **Mrs. Elvsted.***]* And now we're going to be close friends again. *[Kisses her on the cheek.]* So you must call me Hedda.

Mrs. Elvsted: *[Presses and pats* **Hedda's** *hands.]* Oh, how kind you are! I'm not used to such kindness!

Hedda: There, there! I'll call you my dear little Thora.

Mrs. Elvsted: My name is Thea.

Hedda: Oh, of course! I meant Thea. *[Looks at her with compassion.]* So my dear little Thea is not used to kindness—even in her own home?

Mrs. Elvsted: Oh, if I only had a home! But I haven't. I never had one.

Hedda: *[With a long look.]* I thought it was something like that.

Mrs. Elvsted: *[Stares helplessly before her.]* Yes—yes—yes.

Hedda: Thea, I don't quite remember— didn't you go to the Elvsteds at first as their housekeeper.

Mrs. Elvsted: I really was hired as a governess, but Mrs. Elvsted—his first wife—was an invalid, and rarely left her room, so I had to look after the house as well.

Hedda: And finally you became mistress of the house, yourself.

Mrs. Elvsted: *[Sadly.]* Yes, I did.

Hedda: How long ago was that?

Mrs. Elvsted: That I married him?

Hedda: Yes.

Mrs. Elvsted: Five years ago.

Hedda: Yes, it must be all of that.

Mrs. Elvsted: Oh, those five years—! Anyway, the last two or three of them! Oh, Mrs. Tesman, you just can't imagine—

Hedda: *[Gives her hand a little slap.]* Mrs. Tesman! Shame on you, Thea!

Mrs. Elvsted: Yes, I'll try— Hedda, if you only knew—

Hedda: *[Lightly.]* Eilert Lövborg's been living somewhere out your way for about three years now, hasn't he?

Mrs. Elvsted: *[Looks at her uncertainly.]* Eilert Lövborg? Oh, yes—he has.

Hedda: Did you know him before that— here in town?

Mrs. Elvsted: No, hardly. I knew him by name, of course.

Hedda: But you must have seen a good deal of him in the country?

Mrs. Elvsted: Yes, he came to our house every day. He gave the children lessons. After all, I had so many other things to take care of, I couldn't do that as well.

Hedda: Certainly not. Especially with your husband away from home so much. He is, isn't he?

Mrs. Elvsted: Oh, yes. As sheriff, he has to keep traveling around in his district.

Hedda: *[Leans against the arm of* **Mrs. Elvsted's** *chair.]* Thea, my dear little Thea, you must tell me everything— exactly as it is.

Mrs. Elvsted: I don't know where to begin. What can I tell you?

Hedda: What sort of man is your husband, Thea? To live with, I mean. Is he good to you?

Mrs. Elvsted: *[Evasively.]* I'm sure he always means well.

Hedda: But isn't he much too old for you? There must be a difference of at least twenty years between you.

Mrs. Elvsted: *[Irritably.]* Yes, that's true. I just can't stand him! We haven't a single thought in common. Nothing— nothing, at all.

Hedda: But he must be fond of you, just the same, in his own way!

Mrs. Elvsted: Oh, I don't know. He thinks I'm something useful to have around. And it doesn't cost much to keep me. I'm not expensive.

Hedda: That's stupid of you.

Mrs. Elvsted: [Shakes her head.] But that's the way it is—with him. I don't think he really cares for anyone but himself—and maybe a little for the children.

Hedda: And for Eilert Lövborg, Thea.

Mrs. Elvsted: [Looks at her.] For Eilert Lövborg? What makes you say that?

Hedda: Well, it seems quite clear, when he sends you all the way to town to look after him— [With a slight smile.] You said so yourself, to Tesman.

Mrs. Elvsted: [Nervously.] Did I? Yes, I suppose I did! [Intensely, but not loudly.] Well, I might as well tell the truth. It's all bound to come out, anyway.

Hedda: What—?

Mrs. Elsted: Well then—my husband didn't know I was coming here.

Hedda: He didn't know it!

Mrs. Elvsted: No, of course not. He was away from home himself when I left. I couldn't stand it any longer, Hedda. I really couldn't—being alone like that—up there—

Hedda: Yes, and then—?

Mrs. Elvsted: I just packed some of my things—those I needed most—as quickly and quietly as possible—and I left the house.

Hedda: Without saying a word to anyone?

Mrs. Elvsted: Yes—and I took the very next train to town.

Hedda: But, Thea, my dear! How did you dare to do it!

Mrs. Elvsted: [Rises and moves about the room.] What else could I possibly do?

Hedda: But what do you think your husband will say when you go back home?

Mrs. Elvsted: [At the table, looks at her.] Back to him?

Hedda: Yes, of course.

Mrs. Elvsted: I'll never go back to him again.

Hedda: [Rises and goes toward her.] You mean, you've really left home for good?

Mrs. Elvsted: Yes. There was nothing else I could do.

Hedda: But to walk out like that—so openly.

Mrs. Elvsted: You can't very well keep such a thing a secret.

Hedda: But what will people say about you, Thea?

Mrs. Elvsted: Let them say what they like, for all I care.
[Sits wearily and sadly on the sofa.]
I only did what I had to do.

Hedda: [After a short silence.] What are your plans now? How will you live?

Mrs. Elvsted: I don't know. I only know I have to live here, where Eilert Lövborg is, if I'm to live at all.

Hedda: [Takes a chair from the table, sits beside **Mrs. Elvsted,** and strokes her hands.] Thea, dear, tell me. How did this friendship, between you and Eilert Lövborg, come about?

Mrs. Elvsted: Oh, it just grew gradually. I had some sort of influence over him, it seems.

Hedda: Really?

Mrs. Elvsted: He gave up his old habits, even without my asking him to. I wouldn't have dared to do that. But he knew how much they upset me, so he dropped them.

Hedda: [Conceals a scornful smile.] So my dear little Thea has reformed him!

Mrs. Elvsted: Yes, he says so himself. And, in exchange, he's made a real human being of me. He's taught me to think and to understand so many things.

Hedda: Then he gave you lessons, too?

Mrs. Elvsted: Well, not lessons, exactly, but he talked to me seriously about so many things. And then came the wonderful, happy time when he let me share his work—let me help him.

Hedda: Oh, he did?

Mrs. Elvsted: Yes! He never wrote anything without my help.

Hedda: Like two good comrades!

Mrs. Elvsted: [Excitedly.] Comrades! Yes, Hedda, that's exactly the word he used! Oh, I ought to be very happy, but I'm not. I'm so afraid it's not going to last.

Hedda: Then you're not very sure of him, are you?

Mrs. Elvsted: [Gloomily.] There seems to be a shadow between Eilert Lövborg and me—the shadow of a woman.

Hedda: [With a look of deep interest.] Who can that be?

Mrs. Elvsted: I don't know. Someone he knew long ago—someone he's never completely forgotten.

Hedda: Has he told you anything about her?

Mrs. Elvsted: He mentioned her only once—quite vaguely.

Hedda: What did he say?

Mrs. Elvsted: He said that when they parted she threatened to shoot him.

Hedda: [With cold composure.] That's nonsense! The people here don't do such things.

Mrs. Elvsted: No. That's why I think it must have been that red-haired singer he used to—

Hedda: Yes, I suppose so.

Mrs. Elvsted: I remember they said she carried loaded pistols.

Hedda: Well—naturally, she must be the one!

Mrs. Elvsted: [Wrings her hands.] But just think, Hedda—now I hear this woman is in town again! Oh, I'm desperately afraid—

Hedda: [Glances toward the inner room.] Ssh! Here comes Tesman.

[Rises and whispers.]

Thea—all this was just between you and me.

Mrs. Elvsted: [Rises quickly.] Oh, yes, yes—for God's sake—!

[**George Tesman,** with a letter in his hand, comes from the right through the inner room.]

Tesman: There now—I've written the letter.

Hedda: Good. And Mrs. Elvsted was just going. Wait a minute—I'll go with you to the garden gate.

Tesman: Would you ask Berta to mail the letter, Hedda dear?

Hedda: [Takes it.] I'll tell her to.

[**Berta** enters from the hall.]

Berta: Judge Brack wants to know if you'll see him.

Hedda: Yes, show the Judge in. And here—drop this letter in the mailbox.

Berta: [Takes the letter.] Yes, ma'am.

[She opens the door for **Judge Brack** and goes out herself. **Brack** is a man of forty-five, heavy-set but well-built and energetic in his movements. He has a roundish face and an aristocratic profile. His hair is short, still almost black, and carefully groomed. His eyes are lively and sparkling; his eyebrows thick. His moustache is also thick, but neatly trimmed. He wears a well-tailored suit, a little too youthful for his age. He uses an eye-glass, which he lets drop now and then.]

Brack: [With his hat in his hand, bows.] I hope I'm not calling too early in the day.

Hedda: Of course not.

Tesman: [Shakes his hand.] You're always welcome, you know that. [Introduces him.] Judge Brack—Miss Rysing—

Hedda: Oh—!

Brack: [Bows.] Delighted.

Hedda: [Looks at him and laughs.] It's nice to see you by daylight, Judge!

Brack: Do you find me—so different?

Hedda: A little younger, I think.

Brack: Oh, thank you so much.

Tesman: But what do you think of Hedda, eh? Isn't she blooming? She's actually—

Hedda: Oh, leave me out of it. You haven't thanked Judge Brack for all the trouble he went to—

Brack: Nonsense! It was a pleasure, believe me.

Hedda: Yes, you're a very good friend.

But here stands Mrs. Elvsted impatient to go—so forgive me, Judge. I'll be back in a moment.

[An exchange of goodbyes. **Mrs. Elvsted** *and* **Hedda** *go out by the hall door.]*

Brack: Well—is your wife more or less satisfied with everything?

Tesman: Oh, we can't thank you enough. Of course, she talks of making a few changes here and there, and of wanting to buy one or two more little things.

Brack: Really!

Tesman: But you needn't bother about them. Hedda says she'll take care of all that herself. Why don't we sit down, eh?

Brack: Thanks—just for a moment.

[Sits beside the table.]

There's something I want to talk to you about, Tesman.

Tesman: Oh, yes, I understand!

[He sits down.]

Now comes the serious business of paying the piper, eh?

Brack: No, we don't have to discuss money matters right now—but I must say, I wish we had been a bit more economical.

Tesman: No, no, not at all. You know Hedda—and the things she was accustomed to—I couldn't ask her to live like an ordinary housewife—

Brack: No, that's just the trouble.

Tesman: Fortunately, it won't be long before I get my appointment.

Brack: But, you know, sometimes those things are held up.

Tesman: Have you heard anything definite, eh?

Brack: Not exactly definite— *[Interrupts himself.]* Oh, but I can give you one bit of news.

Tesman: What's that?

Brack: Your old friend Eilert Lövborg is back in town.

Tesman: So I've heard.

Brack: Is that so? Who told you?

Tesman: That lady who went out with Hedda.

Brack: Really? What's her name? I didn't quite catch it.

Tesman: Mrs. Elvsted.

Brack: Oh, the sheriff's wife— Of course —and Lövborg was staying up in their neck of the woods.

Tesman: I'm so glad to hear he's living a regular life again!

Brack: So they say.

Tesman: And he's even published a new book, eh?

Brack: Yes, he has.

Tesman: And I hear it's made quite a sensation!

Brack: An extraordinary sensation.

Tesman: Just imagine—isn't it delightful! He has such amazing talents—I felt so sorry to think he'd completely ruined himself.

Brack: That's what everybody thought.

Tesman: But I can't imagine what he'll do now! How in the world will he make a living, eh?

[During the last words, **Hedda** *enters by the hall door.]*

Hedda: *[To* **Brack,** *with a slightly scornful laugh.]* Tesman is forever worrying about how people will make a living.

Tesman: We were talking about Eilert Lövborg, dear.

Hedda: *[Glances quickly at him.]* Oh, really?

[Sits in the armchair by the stove and asks casually.]

What's the matter with *him*?

Tesman: Well—he's probably squandered everything he owned, and he can't write a new book every year, eh? So I really don't see how he's going to get along.

Brack: Perhaps I can tell you something about that.

Tesman: You can?

Brack: You must remember he has some very influential relatives.

Tesman: His relatives? They've completely washed their hands of him.

Brack: They used to call him the hope of the family.

Tesman: Yes, at one time. But he's managed to convince them otherwise.

Hedda: Who knows? *[With a slight smile.]* I hear they've reformed him up at the Elvsteds'—

Brack: And then this book he's published—

Tesman: Well, I hope they're able to find something for him to do. I just wrote him a letter—and I asked him to come and see us this evening, Hedda dear.

Brack: But you're coming to my stag party this evening. You promised you would last night on the pier.

Hedda: Did you forget that, Tesman?

Tesman: Yes, completely.

Brack: Well, don't worry about it. You can rest assured that he won't show up.

Tesman: What makes you think so, eh?

Brack: *[Hesitates, then rises and rests his hands on the back of his chair.]* Now, Tesman—and you, too, Mrs. Tesman—I think I ought to tell you something that—that—

Tesman: That concerns Eilert, eh?

Brack: Yes, and you as well.

Tesman: Both of us? What is it?

Brack: I'm afraid that your appointment is going to be held up for a while.

Tesman: *[Jumps up nervously.]* Why—what's the hitch, eh?

Brack: The final decision may depend on a competition—

Tesman: Competition! Imagine that, Hedda!

Hedda: *[Leans farther back in the chair.]* Aha!

Tesman: But who's my competitor? Certainly not—

Brack: Precisely—Eilert Lövborg.

Tesman: *[Clasps his hands.]* Oh, no—it's impossible! Absolutely inconceivable, eh?

Brack: But that's the way it is, all the same.

Tesman: But, Judge Brack, they're not being fair to me. *[Waves his arms.]* Just think, I'm a married man. Hedda and I got married on the strength of these prospects. We're deep in debt —we even owe money to Aunt Julie. Why, they practically promised me the appointment, eh?

Brack: Oh, there's no doubt you'll get it —they just want you to compete for it.

Hedda: *[Without moving.]* Just think, Tesman, it'll be a sort of sports event.

Tesman: But, Hedda dear, how can you be so cool about it?

Hedda: *[As before.]* Cool? Not at all! I can hardly wait to see who wins.

Brack: In any case, Mrs. Tesman, it's best that you know how things stand. I mean—before you go out and get those little extras I hear you're thinking of buying.

Hedda: I'm sure this won't make any difference.

Brack: Really! Then I've no more to say. Goodbye! *[To **Tesman**.]* On the way back from my afternoon walk, I'll drop in and pick you up.

Tesman: Yes, yes—but I'm terribly upset—

Hedda: *[Reclining, holds out her hand.]* Good-bye, Judge. I hope to see you later.

Brack: Thank you. Good-bye.

Tesman: *[Accompanies him to the door.]* Judge Brack, you must really excuse me— Good-bye—

   *[**Judge Brack** goes out by the hall door.]*

Tesman: *[Crosses back.]* Oh, Hedda—one should never rush into adventures, eh?

Hedda: *[Looks at him and smiles.]* Do you do that?

Tesman: Wasn't it adventurous to get married and set up house on nothing but expectations, eh?

Hedda: You may be right about that.

Tesman: Well, at least we have our delightful home, Hedda! The house we both dreamed of—and I might almost say—fell in love with, eh?

Hedda: *[Rises slowly and wearily.]* You know, it was part of our agreement

that we'd do a lot of entertaining—
and keep open house.

Tesman: Good Lord, I can't tell you how
much I was looking forward to it—
seeing you as a great hostess—in a
very select circle! Well, for the time
being, we'll just have to get along
with each other's company. Of
course, we can invite Auntie Julie in
now and then. But I really did want
you to lead an utterly different sort
of life, Hedda dear.

Hedda: Then I don't suppose I can have
my butler just yet.

Tesman: Oh, no—a butler is out of the
question.

Hedda: And what about the saddle-horse
you promised me—?

Tesman: *[Aghast.]* The saddle-horse!

Hedda: I mustn't even think of that now,
I suppose!

Tesman: Not now, Hedda.

Hedda: Well, at least I have one thing I
can amuse myself with.

Tesman: *[Beaming.]* Thank heaven for
that! What is it, Hedda, eh?

Hedda: *[In the doorway to the inner
room, looks at him with barely concealed scorn.]* My pistols, George.

Tesman: *[In alarm.]* Your pistols!

Hedda: *[With cold eyes.]* General Gabler's pistols.
     *[She goes out through the inner
     room, to the left.]*

Tesman: *[Rushes up to the middle doorway and calls after her.]* No, Hedda,
darling, please don't touch those
dangerous things. For my sake,
Hedda, eh?

CURTAIN

Act Two

The rooms at the **Tesmans'** *as in the first
act, except that the piano has been removed and in its place stands a beautiful
desk with bookshelves attached. A small
table has been placed near the sofa on
the left. Most of the bouquets have been*
taken away. **Mrs. Elvsted's** *bouquet is on
the large table, front. It is afternoon.*

     *[***Hedda,*** *in afternoon dress, is
     alone in the room. She stands at
     the open glass door, loading a
     pistol. The mate to it lies in an
     open pistol case on the desk.]*

Hedda: *[Looking down into the garden,
calls.]* So you've come back again,
Judge!

Brack: *[Off, at a distance.]* Yes, I have!

Hedda: *[Raises the pistol and takes aim.]*
I'm going to shoot you, Judge Brack!

Brack: *[Off, voice closer.]* No, no! Don't
aim that at me!

Hedda: This is what you get for trying
to come in through the back door!
[She fires.]

Brack: *[Nearer, cries out.]* Are you out
of your mind—!

Hedda: My goodness, I didn't happen
to hit you, did I?

Brack: *[Still outside.]* I wish you'd stop
playing these games!

Hedda: Oh, come in, Judge!
     *[***Judge Brack,*** *dressed for his stag
     party, enters by the glass door.
     He carries a light overcoat over
     his arm.]*

Brack: What the devil—aren't you sick
of that sport yet? What are you
shooting at?

Hedda: Oh, I was only shooting at the
sky.

Brack: *[Gently takes the pistol out of
her hand.]* With your permission, madam! *[Examines it.]* Oh—I recognize
this pistol! *[Looks around.]* Where's
the case? Ah, here it is. *[Puts the
pistol in it and shuts it.]* Now we
won't play that game any more
today.

Hedda: Then what do you suggest I do
with myself?

Brack: Haven't you had any visitors?

Hedda: *[Closes the glass door.]* Not one.
I suppose everybody we know is
still away.

Brack: Isn't Tesman here either?

Hedda: *[Puts the pistol-case in a desk*

drawer, which she shuts.] No. He rushed off to see his aunts right after lunch. He didn't expect you so early.

Brack: H'm—I didn't think of that! It was stupid of me.

Hedda: *[Turns to look at him.]* Why stupid?

Brack: Because then I would have come here even earlier.

Hedda: Then you wouldn't have seen anyone at all. I've been in my room, dressing, ever since lunch.

Brack: But isn't there a little crack in the door through which we could have—negotiated?

Hedda: You forgot to provide one.

Brack: That was stupid of me, too.

Hedda: So we'll just have to sit down here and wait for Tesman. He may not be back for some time.

Brack: That's all right. I won't be impatient.

[**Hedda**, *seats herself in the corner of the sofa.* **Brack** *lays his overcoat over the back of the nearest chair and sits down, but keeps his hat in his hand. A short pause, while they look at each other.]*

Hedda: Well?

Brack: *[In the same tone.]* Well?

Hedda: I spoke first.

Brack: *[Bends forwards slightly.]* All right, let's have a nice little talk.

Hedda: *[Leans further back in the sofa.]* It seems ages since our last one. Of course I don't count the few words we exchanged last night and this morning.

Brack: You mean, since the two of us last talked—confidentially?

Hedda: Well, yes—if you want to put it that way.

Brack: Not a day passed but I wished you were home again.

Hedda: And I wished the same thing.

Brack: Really, Hedda? And I thought you were enjoying your trip so much!

Hedda: Ha!

Brack: But Tesman's letters always said you were.

Hedda: Oh, Tesman! Don't you know his greatest delight is to go rooting around in libraries—and to sit and make copies of old parchments—or whatever you call them!

Brack: *[With a touch of malice.]* Well, that's his life's work, you know—or part of it, anyway.

Hedda: Yes, I know—it's one thing when it's your life's work—But I— Oh, my dear Judge, I've been so desperately bored.

Brack: *[Sympathetically.]* Do you mean that? Seriously?

Hedda: Yes, I do. Imagine going for six whole months without meeting a soul you knew or could talk to. How would you like that?

Brack: I'm afraid I wouldn't!

Hedda: But the thing I found most unbearable of all—

Brack: What?

Hedda: —was being forever alone with one and the same person.

Brack: *[Nods in agreement.]* Morning, noon, and night—every hour of the day—

Hedda: I said—forever.

Brack: Yes, but Tesman's such a good person, I should have thought that—

Hedda: Tesman is a specialist, my dear Judge.

Brack: No question about it.

Hedda: And specialists are not very amusing to travel with—not for long, anyway.

Brack: Not even—the specialist you happen to love?

Hedda: Ugh! Don't use that nauseating word!

Brack: *[Taken aback.]* Hedda, what are you saying?

Hedda: *[Half laughing, half annoyed.]* Well, you just try it—listening to nothing but the history of civilization, morning, noon, and night—

Brack: Forever.

Hedda: Yes, yes! And all that business about the domestic industries in the

Middle Ages! That's the most sick-ening part of it!

Brack: [*Looks searchingly at her.*] But if that's true—I just don't understand why you—H'm—

Hedda: Why I married George Tesman, is that what you mean?

Brack: Well, let's put it that way.

Hedda: Is there anything so astonishing in that?

Brack: Well, yes and no—Hedda.

Hedda: I really had danced myself tired, my dear Judge—and I wasn't getting any younger. [*With a slight shudder.*] Oh no, I won't say that—I won't even think it!

Brack: You certainly have no reason to.

Hedda: Oh, reasons—[*Observes him closely.*] And George Tesman, you must admit, is a very proper person.

Brack: Oh, yes. He's proper and de-pendable—there's no question about that.

Hedda: And I don't see anything es-pecially ridiculous about him.—Do you?

Brack: Ridiculous? No. I—I wouldn't exactly say that—

Hedda: Well, anyway, when it comes to research he's untiring. I see no rea-son why he shouldn't go pretty far some day.

Brack: [*With hesitation.*] I thought that you, like everyone else, expected him to become a very famous man.

Hedda: Yes, I did. And when he abso-lutely insisted upon being allowed to support me, I really didn't see why I shouldn't accept his offer.

Brack: No, of course not—when you put it that way—

Hedda: It was more than any of my other admirers were willing to do for me, my dear Judge.

Brack: [*Laughs.*] Well, I can't speak for the others, but so far as I'm con-cerned, you know very well that I've always had the greatest respect for the institution of marriage. I mean, in principle, Hedda.

Hedda: [*Jokingly.*] Oh, I never had any hopes as far as *you* were concerned.

Brack: All I need is a nice, intimate fam-ily circle where I can offer help and advice and feel free to come and go as a trusted friend—

Hedda: Of the man of the house, you mean?

Brack: [*With a slight bow.*] Well, frankly, of the lady, first—but then of the man, too, of course. I think such triangular friendships, so to speak, are very convenient for everyone concerned.

Hedda: Yes, I often longed for someone to talk to on the trip—a third per-son—Oh, those interminable train-rides—*tête-a-tête*—!

Brack: You ought to be happy—now your honeymoon is over!

Hedda: [*Shakes her head.*] There's a long, long way to go. I've just come to a station on the line.

Brack: Then the passengers jump out and wander off a bit, Hedda.

Hedda: I never jump out.

Brack: Why not?

Hedda: Because there is always some-one standing there waiting to—

Brack: [*Laughs.*] To look at your legs, you mean?

Hedda: Precisely.

Brack: But, Good Lord—!

Hedda: [*With a gesture of repulsion.*] I detest that sort of thing. I'd rather stay where I am on the train—and go on with the *tête-a-tête*.

Brack: But what if a third person were to jump in and join the couple.

Hedda: Oh—that's an entirely different thing!

Brack: A trusted, understanding friend—

Hedda: —lively and entertaining in all sorts of ways—

Brack: —but in no way—a specialist!

Hedda: [*Sighs audibly.*] Oh, what a great relief that would be!

Brack: [*Hears the front door open and glances in that direction.*] The tri-angle is completed.

Hedda: [*Half aloud.*] And the train goes on.

[**George Tesman,** *in a gray tweed suit, with a soft felt hat, enters from the hall. He has a number of paperbound books under his arm and in his pockets.*]

Tesman: [*Goes up to the table beside the corner sofa.*] Whew—! What a load to carry in this heat—all these books! [*Lays them on the table.*] I'm actually sweating, Hedda. Well, what's this? Are you here already, my dear Judge, eh? Berta didn't tell me.

Brack: [*Rises.*] I came in through the garden.

Hedda: What are all those books you've got there?

Tesman: [*Stands looking through them.*] Some new books in my special field—I had to have them.

Hedda: Your special field?

Brack: [*Exchanges a confidential smile with* **Hedda.**] Yes, in his special field, Mrs. Tesman.

Hedda: Do you still need more books in your special field?

Tesman: You can never have too many of them. Hedda dear. One must keep up with all the new publications.

Hedda: Yes, I suppose one must.

Tesman: [*Searches among his books.*] And look here, I got hold of Eilert Lövborg's new book, too. [*Offers it to her.*] Would you like to glance through it, Hedda, eh?

Hedda: No, thank you. Well, perhaps—later on.

Tesman: I leafed through it a bit on my way home.

Brack: Well, what do you think of it? As a specialist, I mean.

Tesman: I think it shows very sound judgment. It's remarkable! He never wrote like that before.
[*Gathers the books together.*]
I'll take these into my study. I just can't wait to cut the leaves—! And then I must change my clothes. [*To* **Brack.**] We needn't go just yet, eh?

Brack: Oh no, there's no hurry.

Tesman: Then I'll take my time.

[*Starts to go with his books, then stops in the doorway and turns.*]
Oh, by the way, Hedda, Aunt Julie isn't coming over this evening.

Hedda: Why not? Is she still offended about the hat?

Tesman: Oh, far from it! How could you think such a thing of Aunt Julie? Just imagine! It's Auntie Rina—she's very ill.

Hedda: Isn't she always?

Tesman: Yes, but today she's much worse than usual, poor thing.

Hedda: Then, naturally, her sister would want to stay there with her. And I'll just have to bear my disappointment.

Tesman: You have no idea, Hedda, how delighted Auntie Julie is that you've come back home—and filled out so nicely!

Hedda: [*Half aloud, rises.*] Oh, those everlasting aunts!

Tesman: What's that, dear?

Hedda: [*Goes to the glass door.*] Nothing —nothing at all!

Tesman: Oh! Then excuse me, eh?
[*He goes through the inner room, out to the right.*]

Brack: What's that you were saying about a hat?

Hedda: Oh, something that happened this morning. Miss Tesman left her hat on that chair—[*Looks at him and smiles.*] and I pretended to think it was the maid's.

Brack: [*Shakes his head.*] Why, Hedda, how could you do such a thing to that nice old lady!

Hedda: [*Nervously crosses the room.*] I don't know! These impulses suddenly come over me and I can't control them.
[*Throws herself down in the armchair by the stove.*]
Oh, I just can't explain it.

Brack: [*Behind the armchair.*] The trouble is—you're not really happy.

Hedda: [*Looks straight before her.*] And why should I be—happy? Can you tell me that?

Brack: Well, for one thing, you're living in the house you've always had your heart set on.

Hedda: [*Looks up at him and laughs.*] Do you believe that story, too?

Brack: You mean, there's nothing to it?

Hedda: Oh; yes, there's *something* to it.

Brack: Well?

Hedda: Last summer I made use of Tesman to escort me home from some evening parties—

Brack: Unfortunately, *I* had to go in a different direction.

Hedda: Oh, yes. I know you were going in quite a different direction last summer.

Brack: [*Laughs.*] Shame on you, Hedda. Well, then—you and Tesman—?

Hedda: We happened to pass here one evening. Tesman was struggling desperately to make conversation, so I took pity on the great scholar—

Brack: [*Smiles wryly.*] Took pity on him—?

Hedda. Yes, I really did. Just to help him out of his agony—I said, without even thinking, I'd always wanted to live in this house.

Brack: Is that all?

Hedda. That was all—that evening.

Brack: But later?

Hedda: My thoughtlessness had its consequences, my dear Judge.

Brack: Unfortunately, thoughtlessness usually does.

Hedda: Thanks! So you see it was my burning desire for Secretary Falk's house that brought George Tesman and me together. And in its wake came our engagement, our wedding, our honeymoon, and all the rest of it. Oh, yes, Judge—I was about to say—as you make your bed you must lie in it.

Brack: This is priceless! The fact is—the house really didn't mean a thing to you!

Hedda: Certainly not.

Brack: And not even now—that we've made it so comfortable for you?

Hedda: Ugh! The whole place smells of lavender and dried rose leaves. But maybe Aunt Julia brought that odor in with her.

Brack: [*Laughs.*] No, I think you've inherited it from the late Mrs. Falk.

Hedda: Yes, there's the smell of death about it. It reminds me of flowers—the day after the dance. [*Clasps her hands behind her head, leans back in her chair and looks at him.*] Oh, my dear Judge, you can't imagine how horribly bored I'm going to be out here.

Brack: Hedda, why don't you take a special interest in something—as others do?

Hedda: An interest—that would really excite me?

Brack: If possible, yes.

Hedda: God knows what sort of interest that could be! I've often wondered if—[*Breaks off.*] But that wouldn't work—

Brack: What are you thinking of?

Hedda: If I could get Tesman to go into politics.

Brack: [*Laughs.*] Tesman? In politics? No, he wasn't cut out for anything like that—!

Hedda: Perhaps not. But suppose I could get him into it just the same?

Brack: What satisfaction would that give you? If he's not fit for it, why drive him into it?

Hedda: Because I'm bored, I tell you!
   [*After a pause.*]
So you think it's impossible for Tesman ever to become a member of the cabinet?

Brack: H'm—well—you see, Hedda, to do that he'd have to be a fairly rich man.

Hedda: [*Rises impatiently.*] Yes, that's it! This cramped little corner I've got myself into—!
   [*Crosses the room.*]
That's what makes life so unbearable! So utterly ridiculous—because that's what it is!

Brack: But *I'd* say the fault lies else-where.

Hedda: Yes? Where?

Brack: You've never experienced anything that has really moved you.

Hedda: Anything serious, you mean?

Brack: Yes, you can call it that. But it's bound to happen soon.

Hedda: [*Tosses her head.*] Oh, you're thinking of the fuss over that ridiculous professorship! But that's Tesman's affair. Believe me, I won't waste a moment's thought on it!

Brack: No, I'm sure you won't. But, Hedda, suppose you were to have what people delicately call [*Smiles.*] a new responsibility—?

Hedda. [*Angrily.*] Be quiet! You'll never live to see it!

Brack: [*Warily.*] We'll talk about it again next year—at the very latest.

Hedda: [*Curtly.*] I have no talent for anything like that, Judge Brack. No new responsibilities for me!

Brack: Are you so different from most other women that you have no talent for something that—

Hedda: [*At the glass door.*] Oh, be quiet, I tell you! There's only one thing in this world I have any talent for—!

Brack: [*Draws close to her.*] And what's that, may I ask?

Hedda: [*Stands looking out.*] Boring myself to death—now you know it!— [*Turns, looks toward the inner room, and laughs.*] Yes, as I thought! Here comes the professor!

Brack: [*Softly, in a warning tone.*] Now, now, Hedda!

[**George Tesman,** *dressed for the party, with his gloves and hat in his hand, enters from the right through the inner room.*]

Tesman: Hedda, have you had any message from Eilert, eh?

Hedda: No.

Tesman: Then he'll be here soon, you'll see.

Brack: Do you really think he'll come?

Tesman: Yes, I'm almost sure of it. That must have been one of those rumors that gets around—what you told us this morning.

Brack: You think so?

Tesman: Anyway, Auntie Julie said she didn't believe for a moment he'd ever stand in my way again. Imagine that!

Brack: Well, then, that's fine.

Tesman: [*Puts his hat, with his gloves in it, on a chair, at the right.*] I'd like to wait for him as long as possible, though.

Brack: We still have plenty of time. I don't expect anyone to show up at my place before seven—seven-thirty.

Tesman: We can keep Hedda company meanwhile—and see what happens, eh?

Hedda: [*Moving* **Brack's** *hat and overcoat to the corner settee.*] And if worse comes to worst, Mr. Lövborg can stay here with me.

Brack: [*Offering to take his things.*] Oh, allow me, Mrs. Tesman!—What do you mean by the "worst"?

Hedda: If he won't go with you and Tesman.

Tesman: [*Looks at her dubiously.*] But, Hedda dear—do you think it's proper for him to stay here with you, eh? Remember, Aunt Julie isn't coming.

Hedda: No, but Mrs. Elvsted is. And the three of us can have a cup of tea together.

Tesman: Well, then, that'll be all right.

Brack: [*Smiles.*] And perhaps that would be safest for him, too.

Hedda: Why so?

Brack: Well, you know, Mrs. Tesman, you always disapproved of my little stag parties. You said they were only fit for men of the strictest principles.

Hedda: Oh, I'm sure that Mr. Lövborg's principles are strict enough now. A reformed sinner—

[**Berta** *appears at the hall door.*]

Berta: There's a gentleman asking if you're at home, ma'am.

Hedda: Well, show him in.

Tesman: [*Softly.*] I'm sure its Eilert! Imagine that!

[*Eilert Lövborg enters from the hall. He is slim and gaunt; about* **Tesman's** *age, he looks older and somewhat dissipated. His hair and beard are dark brown, his face long and pale, but with patches of color on the cheekbones. He is well dressed in a new black suit, and has dark gloves and a top hat. He stops near the door and makes a rapid bow; he is somewhat embarrassed.]*

Tesman: [*Goes up to him and shakes hands warmly.*] Welcome, my dear Eilert—so at last we meet again!

Lövborg: [*In a subdued voice.*] Thanks for your letter, George.
[*Approaches Hedda.*]
May I shake hands with you, too, Mrs. Tesman?

Hedda: [*Takes his hand.*] I'm very glad to see you, Mr. Lövborg. [*With a gesture.*] I don't know if you two gentlemen—

Lövborg: [*Bows slightly.*] Judge Brack, I believe.

Brack: [*Returns the bow.*] Oh, yes—we met some years ago—

Tesman: [*To* **Lövborg,** *both hands on his shoulders.*] Now you must make yourself right at home here, Eilert! Mustn't he, Hedda?—I hear you are going to stay in town again, eh?

Lövborg: Yes, I am.

Tesman: Well, that makes sense. Listen, I just got hold of your new book—but I haven't had time to read it yet.

Lövborg: You can save yourself the trouble.

Tesman: Why? What do you mean?

Lövborg: There's very little in it.

Tesman: Imagine that! How can you say that?

Brack: But it's won very high praise, I hear.

Lövborg: That's exactly what I wanted! So I wrote a book everyone would agree with.

Brack: Very clever.

Tesman: Yes, but my dear Eilert—!

Lövborg: I intend to make a fresh start —and win a proper position for myself.

Tesman: [*Slightly embarrassed.*] Oh, is that what you want to do, eh?

Lövborg: [*Smiles, puts his hat down, and takes a packet, wrapped in paper, from his coat pocket.*] But when this one comes out, George Tesman, you'll have to read it! This is the *real* book—the one in which I actually speak my mind!

Tesman: Really? What is it?

Lövborg: It's the sequel.

Tesman: The sequel? To what?

Lövborg: To my book.

Tesman: To the one that just came out?

Lövborg: Yes.

Tesman: But my dear Eilert—that brings us right down to our own time!

Lövborg: Yes, it does—and this one deals with the future.

Tesman: The future! But, good heavens, we don't know anything about the future!

Lövborg: No—but there are one or two things that can be said about it just the same. [*Opens the packet.*] Look here—

Tesman: But that's not your handwriting!

Lövborg: I dictated it. [*Leafs through the manuscript.*] It's in two sections. The first part deals with the forces that are shaping the civilization of the future—[*Leafs through the pages towards the end.*]—and the second part predicts the course that civilization will probably take.

Tesman: That's amazing! I'd never have thought of writing about anything like that.

Hedda: [*At the glass door, drums on the pane.*] No—of course not.

Lövborg: [*Replaces the manuscript in its wrapper and lays the packet on the table.*] I brought it with me because I thought I might read a little of it to you this evening.

Tesman: That was very good of you, Eilert. But this evening—? [*Looks* *at* **Brack.***]* I don't think we can manage it—

Lövborg: Well, then, some other time. There's no hurry.

Brack: You see, Mr. Lövborg, I'm giving a little party at my house this evening to welcome Tesman back—

Lövborg: *[Looks for his hat.]* Oh—then I won't detain you—

Brack: No, but listen—I'd like to have you join us.

Lövborg: *[Curtly and decisively.]* I'm sorry—I can't—thank you very much.

Brack: Of course you can! Come on! There'll be just a few close friends. And I promise you we'll have a "lively time"—as Hed—as Mrs. Tesman puts it.

Lövborg: I don't doubt that. But all the same—

Brack: You can bring your manuscript with you and read it to Tesman at my place. I'll even give you a room to yourselves.

Tesman: Yes, think of that, Eilert! Why not come, eh?

Hedda: *[Breaks in.]* But, dear, if Mr. Lövborg doesn't really want to! I'm sure he'd much rather stay here and have supper with me.

Lövborg: *[Looks at her.]* With you, Mrs. Tesman?

Hedda: And with Mrs. Elvsted.

Lövborg: Oh—*[Casually.]* I saw her for a moment this morning.

Hedda: Did you? Well, she'll be here later on. So you simply *must* stay, Mr. Lövborg, or she'll have no one to see her home.

Lövborg: That's true. Thank you, Mrs. Tesman—I'll stay.

Hedda: Good! Then I'll just give the maid one or two orders—
[She goes to the hall door and rings. **Berta** *enters.* **Hedda** *talks to her in a whisper and points towards the inner room.* **Berta** *nods and goes out.]*

Tesman: *[While* **Hedda** *and* **Berta** *are talking, to* **Lövborg.***]* Tell me, Eilert —is that the subject—the future—you'll be lecturing on, eh?

Lövborg: Yes.

Tesman: Because I heard at the bookstore you'll be giving a series of lectures here this fall.

Lövborg: I intend to. I hope you have no objections, Tesman.

Tesman: No, none at all, but—

Lövborg: I can readily understand that it might bother you.

Tesman: *[Dejectedly.]* Well, I can hardly expect that just for my sake you'd—

Lövborg: But I'll wait until you get your appointment.

Tesman: You'll wait? But—but aren't you competing for it, eh?

Lövborg: No, I only want to win out over you—in public opinion.

Tesman: But, good Lord—Aunt Julie was right after all! Yes, I knew it. Hedda! Just imagine—Eilert Lövborg won't stand in our way!

Hedda: *[Curtly.]* Our way? Please leave me out of it!
[She goes up toward the inner room, where **Berta** *is placing a tray with decanters and glasses on the table.* **Hedda** *nods in approval and comes forward again.* **Berta** *goes out.]*

Tesman: *[While* **Hedda** *is busy with* **Berta.***]* And what do *you* say about all this, Judge Brack, eh?

Brack: Well, I say a moral victory—h'm —may be all very fine but—

Tesman: Yes, of course. But still—

Hedda: *[To* **Tesman** *with a cold smile.]* You look as if you'd been struck by lightning—

Tesman: Yes—close to it—I almost feel—

Brack: That's because a thunderstorm just passed over us, Mrs. Tesman.

Hedda: *[Points toward the inner room.]* Now won't you gentlemen go in and have a glass of cold punch?

Brack: *[Looks at his watch.]* You mean, one for the road? That's not such a bad idea!

Tesman: An excellent idea, Hedda. Excellent! I feel like it, now that I've heard—

Hedda: Won't you join them, Mr. Lövborg?

Lövborg: No, thank you. Nothing for me.

Brack: But, good Lord— cold punch isn't poison, you know.

Lövborg: Perhaps not for everyone.

Hedda: Then I'll kep Mr. Lövborg company meanwhile.

Tesman: Yes, Hedda dear—you do that. *[He and* **Brack** *go into the inner room, sit down, drink punch, smoke cigarettes, and engage in a lively conversation, during the following scene.* **Eilert Lövborg** *remains standing beside the stove.* **Hedda** *goes to the desk.]*

Hedda: *[Raises her voice a little.]* Would you like to look at some photographs, Mr. Lövborg? You know, Tesman and I took a trip through the Tyrol on our way home.
[She takes an album from the desk and places it on the table beside the sofa, in the far corner of which she seats herself. **Eilert Lövborg** *approaches, stops and looks at her; then he takes a chair and sits down to her left, with his back toward the inner room.]*

Hedda: *[Opens the album.]* Do you see this range of mountains, Mr. Lövborg? That's the Ortler group. Look, Tesman has written the name underneath: "The Ortler group near Meran."

Lövborg: *[Who has never taken his eyes off her, says softly and slowly.]* Hedda—Gabler!

Hedda: *[Looks hastily at him.]* Sssh!

Lövborg: *[Repeats softly.]* Hedda Gabler!

Hedda: *[Her eyes on the album.]* That was my name in the old days—when you and I knew each other.

Lövborg: And from now on—and for the rest of my life—I must keep myself from saying Hedda Gabler?

Hedda: *[Still turning the pages.]* Yes,

you must—and you ought to practice it—the sooner the better, I'd say.

Lövborg: *[With indignation.]* Hedda Gabler married? And married to— George Tesman!

Hedda: Yes—so it turned out!

Lövborg: Oh, Hedda, Hedda—how could you throw yourself away like that!

Hedda: *[Looks sharply at him.]* Now that's enough of that!

Lövborg: What do you mean?
*[***Tesman** *comes into the room and goes toward the sofa.]*

Hedda: *[Hears him coming and says in a casual tone.]* And this is a view from the Ampezzo Valley, Mr. Lövborg. Just look at those peaks! *[Glances affectionately up at* **Tesman.** *]* Now what's the name of these curious peaks, dear?

Tesman: Let me see. Oh, those are the Dolomites.

Hedda: Yes, that's it! Those are the Dolomites, Mr. Lövborg.

Tesman: Hedda dear—I just wanted to ask—would you like me to bring you some punch? Just for you, I mean, eh?

Hedda: Yes, I'd like some, thank you—and perhaps a few cookies.

Tesman: No cigarettes?

Hedda: No.

Tesman: Good.
[He goes into the inner room and out to the right. **Brack,** *who remains seated in the inner room, turns a watchful eye from time to time on* **Hedda** *and* **Lövborg.**]*

Lövborg: *[Softly, as before.]* Answer me, Hedda—how could you bring yourself to do this?

Hedda: *[Apparently absorbed in the album.]* If you intend to get so personal, I won't talk to you.

Lövborg: Not even when we're alone?

Hedda: No. You can think what you like, but you mustn't say it.

Lövborg: Oh, I understand. It's an offence against your love for George Tesman.

Hedda: [Glances at him and smiles.] Love? Don't be silly!

Lövborg: You don't love him, then?

Hedda: That doesn't mean I intend to be unfaithful. Absolutely not!

Lövborg: Hedda—tell me just one thing—

Hedda: Sssh!

[**Tesman** enters with a small tray from the inner room.]

Tesman: Look! Here come the goodies! [He puts the tray on the table.]

Hedda: Why are you serving it yourself?

Tesman: [Fills two glasses.] Because I think it's such fun to wait on you, Hedda.

Hedda: But now you've poured out two glasses. And Mr. Lövborg said he doesn't want any—

Tesman: No, but Mrs. Elvsted will be here soon, won't she?

Hedda: Yes, of course—Mrs. Elvsted—

Tesman: Did you forget about her, eh?

Hedda: We were so absorbed in these pictures. [Shows him one.] Do you remember this little village?

Tesman: Oh, that's the one just below the Brenner Pass. We spent the night there—

Hedda: —and met all those lively tourists.

Tesman: Yes, that's the place. Just imagine—if only you could have been with us, Eilert, eh?

[He returns to the inner room and sits beside **Brack**.]

Lövborg: Just answer one question for me, Hedda—

Hedda: What?

Lövborg: Didn't you ever feel any love for me, either? Not a spark—not the faintest glimmer of it?

Hedda: I wonder if I did! It seems to me we were just two good comrades—two very good friends. [Smiles.] No one could have been more outspoken than you.

Lövborg: You wanted me to be that way.

Hedda: Now, as I look back on it all, I think there was something beautiful—fascinating—and even daring, about our comradeship—our secret intimacy—that not a soul in the world suspected.

Lövborg: Yes, Hedda, you're right! Whenever I came to visit you in the afternoon—the General would always sit by the window reading his paper—with his back turned—

Hedda: While you and I were on the corner sofa—

Lövborg: Holding that same magazine up in front of us—

Hedda: Because we didn't have an album then.

Lövborg: Yes, Hedda, that's when I confessed to you—and only you—about the insane things I did—the drunken orgies that went on night and day. What made me tell you those things? Hedda, what power did you have?

Hedda: You think it was some power I had?

Lövborg: Yes, how else can I explain it? All those devious questions you used to ask—

Hedda: Which you understood perfectly well—

Lövborg: But how could you bring yourself to ask such intimate questions?

Hedda: In a devious way, please remember.

Lövborg: But intimate, all the same. Questions about such things!

Hedda: And how could you bring yourself to answer them, Mr. Lövborg?

Lövborg: That's just what I can't understand—as I look back on it. Tell me, Hedda, wasn't there love at the bottom of our friendship? When you made me confess, wasn't it because you wanted to cleanse me of my sins? Was that it?

Hedda: No, not quite.

Lövborg: What made you do it, then?

Hedda: Can't you understand that a young girl—if she could possibly do it in secret—

Lövborg: Yes?

Hedda: Would be eager to find out—

Lövborg: What?

Hedda: What goes on in a world that—

Lövborg: That?

Hedda: That she's forbidden to know anything about?

Lövborg: So that's what it was!

Hedda: Yes—partly.

Lövborg: You had a thirst for life—like me. We were comrades in that! But why did it have to end?

Hedda: It was your fault.

Lövborg: But you broke it off.

Hedda: Yes, when our friendship took a serious turn. Shame on you, Eilert Lövborg! How could you think of making advances to your trusting comrade?

Lövborg: [Clenches his hands.] Oh, why didn't you shoot me down—when you threatened to?

Hedda: Because I'm much too afraid of a scandal.

Lövborg: Yes, Hedda, you're a coward at heart.

Hedda: A terrible coward. [Changes her tone.] But it was lucky for you. You've found so much consolation at the Elvsteds'.

Lövborg: I know what Thea has been telling you.

Hedda: And perhaps you've been telling her—about us!

Lövborg: Not a word. She's too stupid to understand such things.

Hedda: Stupid?

Lövborg: About such things—she's stupid.

Hedda: And I'm a coward. [Leans toward him and says softly, without looking directly at him.] Now I'll tell you something.

Lövborg: [Tensely.] What?

Hedda: My not daring to shoot you—

Lövborg: Yes—?

Hedda: —that was not the worst of my cowardice that night!

Lövborg: [Looks at her a moment, understands, and whispers passionately.] Oh, Hedda! Hedda Gabler! Now I begin to see what really drew us together—you and I! Yes, it was your thirst for life—

Hedda: [Softly, with a sharp glance.] Be careful! Don't you believe it!

[It has begun to get dark. **Berta** opens the hall door.]

Hedda: [Closes the album with a bang and calls out smilingly.] At last! Thea darling! Come in!

[**Mrs. Elvsted** enters from the hall. She is in evening dress. The door is closed behind her.]

Hedda: [Still seated, stretches out her arms toward her.] Thea, my sweet— I thought you were never coming!

[**Mrs. Elvsted,** in passing, exchanges slight greetings with the gentlemen in the inner room, then goes up to the table and gives **Hedda** her hand. **Eilert Lövborg** has risen. He and **Mrs. Elvsted** greet each other with a silent nod.]

Mrs. Elvsted: Don't you think I ought to go in and say hello to your husband?

Hedda: No, leave those two alone. They'll be going out soon.

Mrs. Elvsted: Are they going out?

Hedda: Yes, on a drinking party.

Mrs. Elvsted: [Quickly, to Lövborg.] Not you, though?

Lövborg: No.

Hedda: Mr. Lövborg is staying here with us.

Mrs. Elvsted: [Takes a chair and is about to seat herself at **Lövborg's** side.] Oh, how nice it is to be here!

Hedda; No, no, Thea dear! Not there! You must come over here next to me. I'll sit between you.

Mrs. Elvsted: Any place you say!

[She goes around the table and seats herself on the sofa on **Hedda's** right. **Lövborg** sits down again on his chair.]

Lövborg: [After a short pause, to **Hedda.**] Isn't she lovely to look at?

Hedda: [Lightly stroking **Mrs. Elvsted's** hair.] Only to look at?

Lövborg: Yes—she and I are two real comrades. We trust each other completely, so we can be absolutely frank with each other—

Hedda: Not devious, Mr. Lövborg?

Lövborg: Well—

Mrs. Elvsted: *[Clings softly to* **Hedda.***]* Oh, how happy I am, Hedda! You know, he says I've actually inspired him, too.

Hedda: *[Looks at her with a smile.]* Really! Does he say that, dear?

Lövborg: And she has such courage, Mrs. Tesman—when she's called on to act!

Mrs. Elvsted: Good heavens—me, courage?

Lövborg: Enormous courage—where I'm concerned.

Hedda: Oh, yes—if one only had courage!

Lövborg: Then what?

Hedda: Then life might be bearable! *[With a sudden change of tone.]* But now, Thea dear, you must have a nice glass of cold punch.

Mrs. Elvsted: No, thank you—I never drink anything like that.

Hedda: Then how about you, Mr. Lövborg?

Lövborg: None for me, thanks.

Mrs. Elvsted: No, none for him either!

Hedda: *[Looks fixedly at him.]* But if I insist?

Lövborg: It makes no difference.

Hedda: *[Laughs.]* Poor me! I have no power over you at all, have I?

Lövborg: Not in that way.

Hedda: But seriously, I really think you ought to drink it—for your own sake.

Mrs. Elvsted: Why, Hedda—!

Lövborg: What do you mean?

Hedda: Or rather for other people's sake.

Lövborg: Why?

Hedda: Because people may think that you don't really feel secure—that you have no confidence in yourself.

Mrs. Elvsted: *[Softly.]* Oh, Hedda, don't—!

Lövborg: People can think what they like, for all I care.

Mrs. Elvsted: *[Joyfully.]* Yes, let them!

Hedda: Well, if you'd seen Judge Brack's face a minute ago—

Lövborg: What did you see?

Hedda: The contempt in his smile because you were afraid to join them in there for a drink.

Lövborg: Afraid? I just wanted to stay here and talk to you.

Mrs. Elvsted: Oh, that's so obvious, Hedda!

Hedda: Not to the Judge. I saw him smile and look at Tesman when you were afraid to accept the invitation to his horrible little party.

Lövborg: Afraid? You say I'm afraid?

Hedda: No, I don't say so! But that's how Judge Brack sees it!

Lövborg: Well, let him.

Hedda: Then you're not going with them?

Lövborg: No, I'm staying right here with you and Thea.

Mrs. Elvsted: Yes, Hedda—of course, he is.

Hedda: *[Smiles and nods approvingly to* **Lövborg.***]* You're firm as a rock! Faithful to your principles, now and for ever That's how a man should be! *[Turns to* **Mrs. Elvsted** *and caresses her.]* There, Thea, what did I tell you this morning, when you came here in such terrible despair—?

Lövborg: *[Surprised.]* Despair!

Mrs. Elvsted: *[Terrified.]* Hedda—oh Hedda—!

Hedda: Don't you see—there was absolutely no reason for you to be so worried to death about—*[Interrupts herself.]* Well, now we can all relax and enjoy ourselves!

Lövborg: *[Startled.]* What's this all about, Mrs. Tesman?

Mrs. Elvsted: Oh, my God, Hedda! What are you saying? What are you doing?

Hedda: Don't get so excited! That disgusting Judge Brack is watching you.

Lövborg: You were worried to death about me?

Mrs. Elvsted: *[Softly, unhappily.]* Oh, Hedda—you're making me so miserable!

Lövborg: [*Looks intently at her for a moment; his face is distorted.*] So that's how completely you trusted me!

Mrs. Elvsted: [*Imploringly.*] Oh, my dearest, you must listen to me—

Lövborg: [*Takes one of the glasses of punch, raises it to his lips and says in a low, husky voice.*] Your health, Thea! [*He empties the glass, puts it down and takes the second.*]

Mrs. Elvsted: [*Softly.*] Oh, Hedda, Hedda —how could you do this?

Hedda: *I* do it? *I?* Are you crazy?

Lövborg: Here's to your health, too, Mrs. Tesman. Thanks for the truth. To the truth! [*He empties the glass and is about to fill it again.*]

Hedda: [*Puts her hand on his arm.*] All right—that's enough for now. Remember you're going to a party.

Mrs. Elvsted: No, no, no!

Hedda: Ssh! They're watching you.

Lövborg: [*Puts down the glass.*] Now, Thea—tell me the truth—

Mrs. Elvsted: Yes.

Lövborg: Does your husband know that you followed me?

Mrs. Elvsted: [*Wrings her hands.*] Oh, Hedda—just listen to him—

Lövborg: Did the two of you agree you were to come here to look after me? I suppose he forced you to do it! No doubt he wants my help in his office. Or needs an extra hand for his card game!

Mrs. Elvsted: [*Softly, grief-stricken.*] Oh, Eilert, Eilert—!

Lövborg: [*Seizes a glass and is about to fill it.*] Let's drink one to the old Sheriff, too!

Hedda: [*Stops him.*] No more now. Remember you've got to read your manuscript to Tesman.

Lövborg: [*Calmly, puts down the glass.*] It was stupid of me, Thea—to act this way, I mean. Please don't be angry with me, my dear, dear friend. You'll see—and so will the others— even though I was down—I'm on my feet again! Thanks to you, Thea.

Mrs. Elvsted: [*Radiant with joy.*] Oh, thank God—!

[**Brack,** *in the meantime, has looked at his watch. He and* **Tesman** *rise and enter the drawing room.*]

Brack: [*Takes his hat and overcoat.*] Well, Mrs. Tesman, our time is up.

Hedda: I suppose it is.

Lövborg: [*Rises.*] Mine too, Judge Brack.

Mrs. Elvsted: [*Softly, imploringly.*] Oh, Eilert, don't!

Hedda: [*Pinches her arm.*] They can hear you!

Mrs. Elvsted: [*Faintly.*] Oh!

Lövborg: [*To* **Brack.**] You were kind enough to invite me to join you.

Brack: So you're coming after all?

Lövborg: Yes, if you don't mind—

Brack: I'm delighted.

Lövborg: [*Puts the manuscript in his pocket; to* **Tesman.**] I'd like to show you one or two things before I send this to the publishers.

Tesman: Just imagine—how delightful! But, Hedda dear, how will Mrs. Elvsted get home, eh?

Hedda: Oh, we'll manage somehow.

Lövborg: [*Looks toward the ladies.*] Mrs. Elvsted? I'll come back and get her, of course. [*Comes nearer*] About ten o'clock, Mrs. Tesman? Will that be all right?

Hedda: Yes, that will be fine.

Tesman: Well, then, that's settled. But you mustn't expect *me* so early, Hedda.

Hedda: Oh dear, you can stay—just as long as you like.

Mrs. Elvsted: [*Tries to conceal her anxiety.*] Well, then, Mr. Lövborg—I'll wait here until you come.

Lövborg: [*With his hat in his hand.*] I understand, Mrs. Elvsted.

Brack: All right, gentlemen, the excursion train is about to leave! I'm sure we'll have a lively time, as a certain fair lady puts it.

Hedda: Oh, if only that fair lady could be there—but invisible—!

Brack: Why invisible?

Hedda: To listen to a little of your un-censored liveliness, Judge Brack.

Brack: [Laughs.] I wouldn't advise the fair lady to try it.

Tesman: [Also laughing.] Oh, you're a nice one, Hedda! Imagine that!

Brack: Well, good-night—good-night, ladies.

Lövborg: [Bows.] About ten o'clock, then. [**Brack, Lövborg,** and **Tesman** go out by the hall door. At the same time, **Berta** enters from the inner room with a lighted lamp, which she places on the table, front center; she goes out again through the inner room.]

Mrs. Elvsted: [Who has risen and is wandering restlessly about.] Hedda—Hedda—what's going to come of all this?

Hedda: At ten o'clock—he'll be here. I can see him now—with vine-leaves in his hair—flushed and confident—

Mrs. Elvsted: Oh, if only that were true!

Hedda: And then, you'll see,—he'll be in full control of himself—and he'll be a free man for the rest of his life.

Mrs. Elvsted: Oh, God—if he'd just come back as you see him!

Hedda: He will! Exactly as I see him—and no other way! [Rises and approaches **Thea.**] Go on and doubt him as much as you like. I believe in him. Now we'll see—

Mrs. Elvsted: You have some hidden reason for what you're doing, Hedda!

Hedda: Yes, I have. For once in my life, I want to have power over a human being.

Mrs. Elvsted: But don't you have that?

Hedda: No, I haven't—and I've never had it.

Mrs. Elvsted: But what about your husband?

Hedda: Do you think he's worth the trouble? Oh, if you only knew how poor I am—While you're allowed to be so rich! [Clasps her passionately in her arms.]

I think I'll have to burn your hair off, after all!

Mrs. Elvsted: Let me go! Let me go! I'm afraid of you, Hedda!

Berta: [In the doorway to the inner room.] Supper's on the table in the dining-room, ma'am.

Hedda: All right, we're coming.

Mrs. Elvsted: No, no, no! I'd rather go home alone! Right now!

Hedda: Nonsense! First you'll have something to eat, you silly thing—then at ten o'clock—Eilert Lövborg will be here—with vine-leaves in his hair. [She drags **Mrs. Elvsted** almost by force toward the doorway to the inner room.]

CURTAIN

Act Three

The same rooms at the **Tesmans'.** *The portieres are drawn across the doorway to the inner room, and the curtains across the glass door. The lamp on the table sheds a faint light. The door of the stove is open; the fire is nearly burnt out.*

[**Mrs. Elvsted,** *wrapped in a large shawl, her feet on a footstool, lies back in the armchair which is close to the stove.* **Hedda,** *fully dressed, is asleep on the sofa, with an afghan over her.*]

Mrs. Elvsted: [After a pause, suddenly sits up in her chair and listens intently. Then she sinks back again wearily, moaning to herself.] Not yet! —Oh God!—Oh God!—Not yet!—

[**Berta** enters cautiously by the hall door. She has a letter in her hand.]

Mrs. Elvsted: [Turns and whispers eagerly.] Did someone come in?

Berta: [Softly.] A girl just brought this letter.

Mrs. Elvsted: [Quickly, holds out her hand.] A letter! Give it to me!

Berta: It's for Doctor Tesman, ma'am.

Mrs. Elvsted: Oh!

Berta: It was Miss Tesman's maid that

brought it. I'll leave it here on the table.

Mrs. Elvsted: Yes, do.

Berta: [Puts the letter down.] I think I'd better put out the lamp. It's smoking.

Mrs. Elvsted: Yes, put it out. It'll be daylight soon.

Berta: [Puts out the lamp.] It's daylight already, ma'am.

Mrs. Elvsted: Broad daylight! And no one's come back yet—!

Berta: So help me, ma'am—I knew this would happen.

Mrs. Elvsted: You knew?

Berta: Yes, when a certain gentleman— who's back in town—went along with them—I knew it. We heard plenty about him before.

Mrs. Elvsted: Don't talk so loud! You'll wake Mrs. Tesman.

Berta: [Looks toward the sofa and sighs.] Oh, my—let her sleep, poor thing. Shall I put some wood on the fire?

Mrs. Elvsted: Not for me, thanks.

Berta: All right. [She goes out quietly by the hall door.]

Hedda: [Awakened by the shutting of the door, looks up.] What's that?

Mrs. Elvsted: It was only the maid—

Hedda: [Looks around.] Oh, we're here! I remember now.

> [Sits up on the sofa, stretches herself, and rubs her eyes.]

What time is it, Thea?

Mrs. Elvsted: [Looks at her watch.] It's after seven.

Hedda: When did Tesman get home?

Mrs. Elvsted: He hasn't come back.

Hedda: Not home yet?

Mrs. Elvsted: [Stands up.] No one's come in!

Hedda: And we sat up and waited, like fools, till four in the morning—

Mrs. Elvsted: [Wrings her hands.] Oh, this waiting for him is terrible!

Hedda: [Yawns and speaks with her hand over her mouth.] Well—we might have spared ourselves the trouble.

Mrs. Elvsted: Did you get a little sleep?

Hedda: Oh, yes—I think I slept pretty well. Didn't you?

Mrs. Elvsted: No, Hedda, not a wink! I just couldn't—!

Hedda: There, there! There's nothing to be so worried about. I know exactly what happened.

Mrs. Elvsted: Then tell me! Where are they?

Hedda: Well, I'm sure the Judge's party broke up very late—

Mrs. Elvsted: Yes, of course, but then—

Hedda: Tesman didn't want to wake us up in the middle of the night— [She laughs.] Maybe he didn't want us to see him, either—after a party like that.

Mrs. Elvsted: But where could he have gone?

Hedda: To his aunts', of course, to sleep it off. They always keep his old room ready for him.

Mrs. Elvsted: No, he can't be there. He just got a note from Miss Tesman. It's on the table.

Hedda: Really? [Looks at the envelope.] Yes, this is Aunt Julia's handwriting. Well, then, he stayed at Judge Brack's. And Eilert Lövborg—he's sitting there with vine-leaves in his hair, reading away.

Mrs. Elvsted: Oh, Hedda, you don't believe a word of that yourself!

Hedda: You really are a little idiot, Thea.

Mrs. Elvsted: Yes, I suppose I am.

Hedda: And you look dead tired.

Mrs. Elvsted: I am dead tired.

Hedda: Why don't you do as I say—go into my room and lie down for a little while.

Mrs. Elvsted: No, no—I wouldn't be able to sleep, anyway.

Hedda: Of course, you would.

Mrs. Elvsted: But your husband should be coming home any minute now, and I want to know right away—

Hedda: I'll call you as soon as he gets here.

Mrs. Elvsted: Promise me you will, Hedda!

Hedda: Yes, you can trust me. You just go in and take a nap in the meantime.

Mrs. Elvsted: Thanks—I'll try to. *[She goes out through the inner room.]*

*[**Hedda** goes up to the glass door and draws back the curtains. Daylight fills the room. Then she takes a little mirror from the desk, looks at herself and arranges her hair. Then she goes to the hall door and presses the call-button. After a short pause **Berta** appears at the hall door.]*

Berta: Did you want something, ma'am?

Hedda: Yes, you can put some more wood in the stove. I'm absolutely frozen.

Berta: My goodness—I'll have a nice fire going in a minute. *[She rakes the embers, then puts a piece of wood on them; suddenly she stops and listens.]* That was the front doorbell, ma'am.

Hedda: Go see who it is. I'll take care of the fire.

Berta: It'll start to burn soon. *[She goes out by the hall door.]*

*[**Hedda** kneels on the footstool and puts several pieces of wood in the stove. After a shout pause, **George Tesman** enters from the hall. He looks tired and rather serious. He tiptoes toward the doorway to the inner room and is about to slip through the portieres.]*

Hedda: *[At the stove, without looking up.]* Good morning.

Tesman: *[Turns.]* Hedda! *[Approaches her.]* Good heavens—are you up so early, eh?

Hedda: Yes, I got up very early this morning.

Tesman: And I thought you'd still be sound asleep. Imagine that, Hedda!

Hedda: Don't talk so loud. Mrs. Elvsted is trying to rest.

Tesman: Did Mrs. Elvsted stay here all night?

Hedda: Of course—since no one came to take her home.

Tesman: No, I guess not.

Hedda: *[Closes the door of the stove and rises.]* Well, did you enjoy yourselves at Judge Brack's?

Tesman: Were you worried about me, eh?

Hedda: No, that never occurred to me. I just asked you if you had a good time.

Tesman: Yes, I really did for once. But the beginning was the best part of it —when Eilert read to me. Just imagine —we got there more than an hour early! And the Judge had all sorts of things to attend to—so Eilert read me a good part of his book.

Hedda: *[Sits at the right of the table.]* Yes, but tell me about—

Tesman: *[Sits on a footstool near the stove.]* Oh, Hedda, you can't imagine what a book that's going to be! I believe it's one of the most remarkable things ever written. Think of that!

Hedda: Yes, yes. But I don't care about that—

Tesman: I have a confession to make, Hedda. I must tell you—when he finished reading—the most terrible feeling came over me.

Hedda: Terrible feeling?

Tesman: I was jealous of Eilert—for being able to write such a book. Think of that, Hedda!

Hedda: Yes, I am thinking!

Tesman: And just think—that with all his gifts—he's absolutely incorrigible.

Hedda: You mean he has more courage than the rest of you!

Tesman: Oh, no—I mean he just can't take his pleasures in moderation.

Hedda: Why, what happened?

Tesman: Well, to tell you the truth, Hedda, the only thing I can honestly call it is an orgy.

Hedda: Did he have vine-leaves in his hair?

Tesman: Vine-leaves? No, not that I noticed. But he made a long, rambling speech in honor of the woman who had "inspired him in his work"— that's the phrase he used.

Hedda: Did he mention her name?

Tesman: No, he didn't. But it seems to

me it can't be anyone but Mrs. Elvsted. See if I'm not right!

Hedda: Well—where did you leave him?

Tesman: On the way back. When the party broke up—the last of us left Brack's place all together—and Brack came with us for a little fresh air. Then we all decided to take Eilert home, because he was pretty much under the weather—

Hedda: I don't doubt it.

Tesman: But now comes the strangest part of it, Hedda—or maybe I should say the saddest part. I'm almost ashamed to tell you—for Eilert's sake—

Hedda: Go on, will you!

Tesman: Well, as we were going along the street, you see, I happened to walk a little behind the others for a while—think of that!

Hedda: Yes, yes—?

Tesman: And then as I hurried to catch up with them—what do you think I found in the gutter, eh?

Hedda: Oh, how should I know!

Tesman: You mustn't tell a soul, Hedda—do you hear! Promise me, for Eilert's sake. [Pulls a parcel, wrapped in paper from his coat pocket.] Just imagine, dear—I found this.

Hedda: Isn't that the thing he had with him yesterday?

Tesman: Yes—his precious, irreplaceable manuscript! All of it, right here. He lost it—and didn't even know it was missing. Think of that, Hedda! It's really sad—

Hedda: Why didn't you give it right back to him?

Tesman: The state he was in— I didn't dare to!

Hedda: Didn't you tell any of the others you'd found it?

Tesman: No, no—don't you see, for Eilert's sake, I couldn't do that.

Hedda: Then no one knows you have Eilert Lövborg's manuscript?

Tesman: No—and no one must know it.

Hedda: But what did you say to him afterwards?

Tesman: I didn't have a chance to say anything to him, because he and a couple of the others suddenly took off and disappeared. Imagine that!

Hedda: Then I suppose they saw that he got home.

Tesman: Yes, I guess so. And Brack left us, too.

Hedda: And where have you been since then?

Tesman: Well, some of the others and I went home with one of the fellows for an early breakfast—or maybe I ought to call it a late supper, eh? But just as soon as I've rested a bit—and I give poor Eilert enough time to sleep it off—I'll take this back to him.

Hedda: [Holds out her hand for the parcel.] No—don't give it back! Not right away, I mean. Let me read it first.

Tesman: No, Hedda dear, I can't, I really can't.

Hedda: Why can't you?

Tesman: Don't you realize how desperate he'll be when he wakes up and misses the manuscript? He hasn't even got a copy of it—he told me so himself.

Hedda: [Looks closely at him.] Well, can't he write it all over again?

Tesman: No, I don't think that's possible. You see, the inspiration is—

Hedda: Yes, I suppose that's necessary. [Casually.] By the way, there's a note for you.

Tesman: Imagine—!

Hedda: [Hands it to him.] It came early this morning.

Tesman: It's from Aunt Julie! What can it be?
[He puts the parcel on a footstool, takes the note out of the envelope, reads it hastily, and jumps up.]
Oh, Hedda—she says poor Auntie Rina is dying!

Hedda: Well—we were expecting it.

Tesman: And if I want to see her again I'd better hurry. I'll run over there right away.

Hedda: [Suppresses a smile.] You'll run?

Tesman: Oh, Hedda dear—can't you

bring yourself to come with me? Just think!

Hedda: [Rises and says wearily, shuddering at the idea.] No, no, don't ask me to. I can't bear to look at sickness and death. I loathe anything ugly.

Tesman: Well, then—! [Dashes around.] My hat—? My overcoat—? Oh—in the hall—I hope I don't get there too late, Hedda, eh?

Hedda: Not if you run—
    [Berta appears at the hall door.]

Berta: Judge Brack is here and is asking to see you.

Tesman: Now! No, I can't possibly see him now.

Hedda: But I can. [To **Berta**.] Ask the Judge to come in.
    [Berta goes out.]

Hedda: [Whispers quickly.] Tesman, the manuscript! [She snatches it up from the stool.]

Tesman: Yes, give it to me!

Hedda: No, no. I'll keep it till you come back.
    [She goes to the desk and puts it in the bookcase. **Tesman**, in his hurry, cannot get his gloves on. **Judge Brack** enters from the hall.]

Hedda: [Nods to him.] Well, aren't you an early bird!

Brack: Yes, don't you think so? [To **Tesman**.] And are you on your way, too?

Tesman: Yes, I must rush off to my aunts! Imagine—Auntie Rina is dying, poor thing.

Brack: She is? Then don't let me keep you. At a time like this, every minute counts—

Tesman: Yes, I really must run—Goodbye! Goodbye!
    [He hurries out by the hall door.]

Hedda: [Approaches **Brack**.] It seems you had a pretty lively party at your place last night, Judge Brack.

Brack: I haven't even changed my clothes, Hedda.

Hedda: Not you, either?

Brack: No—don't I look it? But what's Tesman been telling you about last night's adventures?

Hedda: Oh, some boring story about having breakfast someplace with someone or other—

Brack: I've heard about the breakfast-party already. Eilert Lövborg wasn't with them, I understand?

Hedda: No, they took him home before that.

Brack: Tesman, too?

Hedda: No, some of the others, he said.

Brack: [Smiles.] George Tesman is really an innocent creature, Hedda.

Hedda: Yes, God knows he is. But tell me, is there something more to all this?

Brack: Yes, there is.

Hedda: Well, then, my dear Judge, why not sit down and be comfortable while you tell me the story?
    [They seat themselves at the table; **Hedda** at the left, and **Brack** near her.]

Hedda: Now then?

Brack: I had special reasons for keeping an eye on my guests—or rather on certain guests—last night.

Hedda: And Eilert Lövborg was one of them perhaps?

Brack: Frankly—yes.

Hedda: Now I'm really interested—

Brack: Do you know where he and a couple of the others wound up after my party, Hedda?

Hedda: No, tell me—if it's not absolutely unmentionable!

Brack: It's not unmentionable at all. They went to another party that made mine look sober.

Hedda: To an orgy?

Brack: Yes, an orgy—to put it mildly.

Hedda: Go on, Judge, tell me more—

Brack: Lövborg and the others were invited to this affair a long time ago. I knew all about it. But Lövborg turned down the invitation after he was "reformed"—

Hedda: Up at the Elvsteds', you mean. But he did go, anyway?

Brack: Well, you see, Hedda—unfortunately, at my place last night, the spirit moved him—

Hedda: Yes, I hear he was inspired.

Brack: Pretty violently inspired. And I suppose that brought on a relapse. We men, I must admit, are not always as true to our principles as we ought to be.

Hedda: I'm sure you're an exception, Judge Brack. But you were speaking of Lövborg—?

Brack: Well, to make a long story short —he wound up at Mademoiselle Diana's establishment.

Hedda: Mademoiselle Diana?

Brack: Yes, she was giving a party for a few of her very special admirers— male and female.

Hedda: Is she a red-haired woman?

Brack: Yes.

Hedda: A singer—of sorts?

Brack: Oh, yes—that, too. And a mighty huntress—of men! You must've heard of her, Hedda. Eilert Lövborg was one of her warmest friends—in his palmy days.

Hedda: And how did it all end?

Brack: Not in a very friendly way, it seems. Mademoiselle Diana greeted him with open arms, but it wasn't long before she was in a fist-fight—

Hedda: With Lövborg?

Brack: Yes. He accused her and her friends of robbing him. He said his wallet was gone—and other things, too. It seems he started a near riot.

Hedda: And what happened?

Brack: It turned into a free-for-all, with the ladies and gentlemen trading blows. Luckily, the police finally showed up.

Hedda: The police?

Brack: Yes, it's going to be a pretty expensive little caper for Eilert Löv-borg, that crazy fool.

Hedda: How so?

Brack: It seems he put up a violent resistance—punched one of the officers in the ear and ripped his coat to shreds. So they dragged him off to the station house with the others.

Hedda: Where did you hear all this?

Brack: From the police themselves.

Hedda: [Gazes straight before her.] So that's the way it was—no vine-leaves in his hair!

Brack: Vine-leaves, Hedda?

Hedda: [Changes her tone.] But tell me, Judge—what's your real reason for going around like that spying on Eilert Lövborg?

Brack: Well, in the first place, it would certainly concern me if it's brought out in the investigation that he came straight from my house.

Hedda: Will there be an investigation?

Brack: Of course. But things will work themselves out! I thought that, as a friend of the family, it was my duty to give you and Tesman a full account of his adventures last night.

Hedda: Why is that?

Brack: Because I have a strong suspicion that he intends to use you as a sort of front.

Hedda: Oh, how can you think such a thing!

Brack: Good Lord, Hedda—we have eyes in our heads, haven't we? Just wait and see! This Mrs. Elvsted won't be in such a hurry to go home.

Hedda: Well, even if there *is* something going on between them, I'm sure there there are plenty of other places where they can meet.

Brack: Not in anyone's home. From now on, every respectable house will be closed to Eilert Lövborg again.

Hedda: And mine ought to be, too, you mean?

Brack: Yes. I must say I'd be very unhappy if you allowed him to come here. If you let such a worthless person force his way into—

Hedda: —into the triangle?

Brack: Precisely It would simply mean that I'd find myself homeless.

Hedda: [Looks at him with a smile.] So you want to be cock-of-the-walk, Judge. Is that your aim?

Brack: [Nods slowly and lowers his voice.] Yes, that is my aim. And that's what I'll fight for—with every weapon I can command.

Hedda: [Her smile vanishes.] I see you're a dangerous person—when it comes right down to it.

Brack: Do you think so?

Hedda: I'm beginning to think so. And I'm certainly glad you have no hold of any kind over me.

Brack: [With an ambiguous laugh] Well, Hedda, you may be right about that. If I had, who knows what I might not do!

Hedda: Now listen here, Judge Brack! That sounds very much like a threat!

Brack: [Rises.] No, not at all! The triangle, you know, ought to be formed, if possible, on a voluntary basis.

Hedda: I agree with you there.

Brack: Well, now I've said all I have to say, and I'd better be getting back to town. Goodbye, Hedda. [He goes toward the glass door.]

Hedda: [Rises.] Are you going through the garden?

Brack: Yes, it's a short cut for me.

Hedda: And it's the back way, too!

Brack: Well, I have no objection to back ways. They can be quite exciting at times.

Hedda: When there's shooting going on, you mean?

Brack: [In the doorway, laughs.] Oh, no one ever shoots a tame rooster!

Hedda: [Laughs.] Especially if he's cock-of-the-walk—

[They laugh and nod to each other as he goes. She closes the door behind him. **Hedda,** now serious, stands looking out for a moment. She then goes over and glances through the portieres to the inner room. She moves down to the desk, takes **Lövborg's** parcel out of the bookcase and is about to look through it. **Berta** is heard speaking loudly in the hall. **Hedda** turns and listens. Then she quickly locks up the parcel in a draw and puts the key on the inkstand.

Eilert Lövborg, in his overcoat and with his hat in his hand, tears open the hall door. He enters, excited and somewhat confused.]

Lövborg: [Looks back toward the hall.] I must see them—and I will go in I tell you—So there!

[He closes the door, turns, sees **Hedda,** immediately regains his self-control, and bows.]

Hedda: [At the desk.] Well, Mr. Lövborg, isn't this rather late to be calling for Thea?

Lövborg: You mean rather early to be calling on you. Please forgive me.

Hedda: How do you know Thea's still here?

Lövborg: They told me at her lodgings she'd been out all night.

Hedda: [Goes to the oval table.] Did they give you a strange look when they said that?

Lövborg: A strange look?

Hedda: I mean, didn't they seem to think it odd?

Lövborg: [Suddenly understands.] Oh, I see what you mean! I'm dragging her down with me! But I didn't notice their looks—I suppose Tesman isn't up yet?

Hedda: No— I don't think so—

Lövborg: When did he get home?

Hedda: Very late.

Lövborg: Did he tell you anything?

Hedda: Yes, it seems you all had a wonderful time at Judge Brack's.

Lövborg: Anything else?

Hedda: No, I don't think so. But then I was so terribly sleepy—

[**Mrs. Elvsted** enters through the portieres which close off the inner room.]

Mrs. Elvsted: [Goes toward him.] Oh, Eilert! At last—!

Lövborg: Yes, at last. And too late!

Mrs. Elvsted: [Looks anxiously at him.] What's too late?

Lövborg: Everything's too late now. I'm finished.

Mrs. Elvsted: Oh, no—don't say that!

Lövborg: You'll say the same thing when you hear—

Mrs. Elvsted: I won't hear anything!

Hedda: If you'd like to talk to her alone —I'll leave.

Lövborg: No; stay—you, too. Please stay

Mrs. Elvsted: But I tell you, I don't want to hear anything.

Lövborg: It has nothing to do with last night.

Mrs. Elvsted: Then what is it?

Lövborg: It's that—our ways must part now.

Mrs. Elvsted: Part!

Hedda: [Involuntarily.] I knew it!

Lövborg: I have no further use for you, Thea.

Mrs. Elvsted: You can stand there and say that! No more use for me! Can't I help you now, as I did before? Can't we go on working together?

Lövborg: I'm through with work—from now on.

Mrs. Elvsted: [In despair.] Then what have I to live for?

Lövborg: You must try to live as though you'd never known me.

Mrs. Elvsted: But you know I can't do that!

Lövborg: You must try, Thea. You must go home again—

Mrs. Elvsted: [Adamantly.] No, never! Wherever you are, that's where I'll be! You can't drive me away. I intend to stay here! I'm going to be with you when the book appears.

Hedda: [In a tense whisper.] Oh, yes— the book!

Lövborg: [Looks at her.] My book and Thea's—that's what it is!

Mrs. Elvsted: Yes, that's true—it is. That's why I have a right to be with you when it appears! I want to see all the respect and honor that will come to you—and the joy! I want to share that with you, too.

Lövborg: Thea—our book will never appear.

Hedda: Oh!

Mrs. Elvsted: Never appear!

Lövborg: Can never appear.

Mrs. Elvsted: [In an agony of foreboding.] Lövborg—what have you done with the manuscript?

Hedda: [Looks anxiously at him.] Yes, the manuscript—?

Mrs. Elvsted: Where is it?

Lövborg: Thea, don't ask me about it!

Mrs. Elvsted: Yes, I must know! I have a right to know!

Lövborg: Well, then—if you must know —I've torn it into a thousand pieces!

Mrs. Elvsted: [Shrieks.] Oh, no—no!

Hedda: [Involuntarily.] But that's not—

Lövborg: [Looks at her.] Not true, you think?

Hedda: [Collects herself.] Of course, if you say so. But it sounded so incredible—!

Lövborg: It's true, all the same.

Mrs. Elvsted: [Wrings her hands.] Oh, God—Oh, God! Hedda, he's torn his own work to pieces!

Lövborg: I've torn my whole life to pieces—why shouldn't I tear up my work as well—?

Mrs. Elvsted: And you did that last night?

Lövborg: Yes, you heard me! In a thousand pieces! And scattered them on the fjord—far out—where, at least, there's clean, salt water. Let them drift there—with the wind and current—till they sink—deeper and deeper. Like me, Thea.

Mrs. Elvsted: Do you know, Eilert—what you've done to the book—will haunt me for the rest of my life—as though you'd killed a little child.

Lövborg: Yes, you're right. It was like murdering a child.

Mrs. Elvsted: Then how could you do it—! The child belonged to me, too!

Hedda: [Almost inaudibly.] Oh, the child—

Mrs. Elvsted: [Breathes heavily.] Then it's all over. Yes—yes—I'll go now, Hedda.

Hedda: But you're not leaving town?

Mrs. Elvsted: I don't know what I'll do. There's nothing but darkness ahead of me.

[She goes out by the hall door.]

Hedda: [*Waits for a moment.*] Aren't you going to see her home, Mr. Lövborg?

Lövborg: I? Through the streets? And let people see her with *me*?

Hedda: Of course, I don't know what else may have happened last night. But is it so utterly irreparable?

Lövborg: It won't end with last night— I know that very well. And I don't even care for that kind of life any more. Maybe I haven't got the nerve to begin it again—because she broke my spirit—and destroyed my courage.

Hedda: [*Looks straight before her.*] So that pretty little fool had power over a man's life! [*Looks at him.*] But all the same, how could you treat her so heartlessly?

Lövborg: Don't say it was heartless!

Hedda: You destroyed something that filled her whole life for months and years. And you don't call that heartless?

Lövborg: Hedda, I can tell *you* the truth.

Hedda: The truth?

Lövborg: But first promise me—give me your word—you'll never let Thea know what I tell you now.

Hedda: You have my word.

Lövborg: Good. Then I want you to know—there wasn't a word of truth in the story I told her—

Hedda: About the manuscript, you mean?

Lövborg: Yes. I didn't tear it to pieces— or throw it into the fjord.

Hedda: Oh, no—? But then—where is it?

Lövborg: I've destroyed it just the same. Utterly destroyed it, Hedda!

Hedda: I don't understand.

Lövborg: Thea said that what I did was like murdering our child.

Heda: Yes—so she said.

Lövborg: But to kill his child—is not the worst thing a father can do to it.

Hedda: Not the worst?

Lövborg: No. I wanted to spare Thea from hearing the worst.

Hedda: And what *is* the worst?

Lövborg: Look, Hedda—suppose a man comes home in the early hours of the morning—after a wild, drunken night —and says to his child's mother, "Listen, I've been here and there—in this place and that—and I had our child with me. But now it's lost— gone! And God knows whose hands it's fallen into—whose fingers are all over it!

Hedda: Yes, but after all, it was only a book—

Lövborg: Thea's pure soul was in that book.

Hedda: Yes, so I understand.

Lövborg: Then you surely also understand that she and I can have no future together.

Hedda: And what will you do now?

Lövborg: Nothing. Put an end to it all. The sooner the better.

Hedda: [*Takes a step nearer to him.*] Eilert Lövborg—listen to me. Won't you try to—to do it beautifully?

Lövborg: Beautifully? [*He smiles.*] With vine-leaves in my hair—that old dream of yours—?

Hedda: Oh, no. I don't believe in vine-leaves any more. But beautifully, all the same! Just this once!—Goodbye! You must go now—and you mustn't come here again.

Lövborg: Goodbye, Mrs. Tesman. And give George Tesman my best wishes. [*He is about to go.*]

Hedda: No, wait! I want to give you something to take with you—as a gift—

[*She goes to the desk and opens the drawer and the pistol-case, then returns to* **Lövborg** *with one of the pistols.*]

Lövborg: [*Looks at her.*] That? Is that the gift?

Hedda: [*Nods slowly.*] Do you recognize it? It was aimed at you once.

Lövborg: You should have used it then.

Hedda: Here. Use it now.

Lövborg: [*Puts the pistol in his breastpocket.*] Thanks!

Hedda: And beautifully, Eilert Lövborg. Promise me that!

Lövborg: Goodbye, Hedda Gabler.

[He goes out by the hall door. **Hedda** *listens for a moment at the door. Then she goes to the desk, takes out the packet with the manuscript, looks under the cover, pulls out a few sheets part way and glances at them. She goes to the armchair beside the stove and sits down, with the packet in her lap. After a moment, she opens the stove door and unwraps the manuscript.]*

Hedda: *[Throws handfuls of sheets into the fire and whispers.]* Now I'm burning your child, Thea!—You and your curly hair! *[Throws more handfuls into the stove.]* Your child and Eilert Lövborg's! *[Throws the rest in.]* I'm burning—I'm burning your child.

CURTAIN

Act Four

The same rooms at the **Tesmans'**. *It is evening. The drawing-room is dark. The inner room is lit by the hanging lamp over the table. The curtains are drawn across the glass door.* **Hedda,** *dressed in black, walks back and forth in the dark room. Then she goes into the inner room and disappears for a moment to the left. She is heard to strike a few chords on the piano. She appears again and returns to the drawing-room.* **Berta** *enters from the right, through the inner room, with a lighted lamp, which she places on the table in front of the corner settee in the drawing-room. Her eyes are red from crying, and she has black ribbons on her cap. She goes quietly out to the right.* **Hedda** *goes up to the glass door, lifts the curtain aside slightly, and looks out into the darkness. After a few moments,* **Miss Tesman,** *in mourning, wearing a hat with a veil, comes in from the hall.* **Hedda** *goes toward her and holds out her hand.*

Miss Tesman: Yes, Hedda, here I am in mourning—and my poor sister's suffering is finally over.

Hedda: I've already heard—as you see. Tesman sent me a note.

Miss Tesman: Yes, he promised he would. But, all the same, Hedda, I thought I ought to come to this house, where life is beginning, to bring news of the death myself.

Hedda: That was very kind of you.

Miss Tesman: But Rina shouldn't have left us just now. This is no time for mourning in Hedda's house.

Hedda: *[Changes the subject.]* Did she die peacefully, Miss Tesman?

Miss Tesman: Yes, her end was so beautiful, so calm—and she was so happy to see George again—to say goodbye. —Hasn't he come home yet?

Hedda: No. He wrote that I was not to expect him too early. But won't you sit down?

Miss Tesman: No, thank you, my dear, blessed Hedda. I really would like to, but I have so little time. Now I must go home and prepare her as best I can. I want her to look beautiful when they carry her to her grave.

Hedda: Isn't there anything I can do to help?

Miss Tesman: Oh, you mustn't think of it! This is nothing for Hedda Tesman to have her hand in—or to let her thoughts dwell on, either. Not at this time, no!

Hedda: Oh, thoughts—We're not always mistress of our thoughts—

Miss Tesman: *[Continues.]* Well, that's life for you. At my house we'll be sewing a shroud—and here there will soon be sewing, too, I suppose—but of a different kind, thank God!

*[***George Tesman*** enters by the hall door.]*

Hedda: Well, that's good—you've finally come back.

Tesman: You here, Auntie Julie? With Hedda? Imagine that!

Miss Tesman: I was just going, my dear boy. Well, did you do all the things you promised me you'd do?

Tesman: No, I'm really afraid I forgot half of them. I'll have to come to see you again tomorrow. Today my brain's in a whirl. I can't keep my thoughts together.

Miss Tesman: But, George dear, you mustn't take it that way.

Tesman: I mustn't? What do you mean?

Miss Tesman: Don't grieve. We should be glad, for her sake—she's found peace at last.

Tesman: Oh, yes, yes. You're thinking of Auntie Rina.

Hedda: It will be very lonely for you now, Miss Tesman.

Miss Tesman: For a while, yes. But not for very long, I hope. My blessed Rina's little room won't stay empty, I'm sure.

Tesman: No? Who do you think would move into it, eh?

Miss Tesman: Unfortunately, there's always some poor invalid who needs care and attention.

Hedda: Would you really take such a burden on yourself again?

Miss Tesman: A burden? God forgive you, child—it was anything but a burden to me.

Hedda: But it's different with a total stranger—

Miss Tesman: Oh, it's easy to make friends with sick people. And I must have someone to live for—for my own good. And, God willing, there'll be something here in this house, too, to keep an old aunt busy.

Hedda: Oh, don't worry about us.

Tesman: Yes, just imagine what a nice time we three could have together if—

Hedda: If what?

Tesman: [Uneasily.] Oh, nothing. Everything'll be all right. Let's hope so, eh?

Miss Tesman: Well, I suppose you two have things to say to each other. [Smiles.] And Hedda may also have something to tell you, George. Goodbye. Now I must go home to Rina. [Turns at the door.] Heavens, it's strange, when you come to think of it!—Now Rina is with me and with our blessed brother, at the same time.

Tesman: Yes, just imagine, Auntie Julie, eh?

[**Miss Tesman** goes out by the hall door.]

Hedda: [Gives **Tesman** a cold, searching look.] I almost believe this death affects you more than it does her.

Tesman: Oh, it's not only the death. It's Eilert I'm all upset about.

Hedda: [Quickly.] Is there any news of him?

Tesman: I went around to see him this afternoon—to tell him his manuscript was in good hands.

Hedda: Well, did you find him?

Tesman: No, he wasn't at home. But later I met Mrs. Elvsted and she said he was here early this morning.

Hedda: Yes, right after you left.

Tesman: And he claimed he tore his manuscript to pieces, eh?

Hedda: Yes, that's what he said.

Tesman: Good heavens, he must have gone completely insane! So I suppose you didn't dare give it back to him, Hedda?

Hedda: No, I didn't give it to him.

Tesman: But of course you told him we had it?

Hedda: No. [Quickly.] Did you tell Mrs. Elvsted?

Tesman: No, I thought it best not to. But you should have said something to him. Just imagine, if he should go off in desperation and harm himself! Give me the manuscript, Hedda. I'll take it back to him right away. Where did you put it?

Hedda: [Cold and motionless, leans against the armchair.] I don't have it anymore.

Tesman: You don't have it! What on earth do you mean by that?

Hedda: I've burned it—the whole thing.

Tesman: [Starts up in terror]. Burned it! Burned Eilert's manuscript!

Hedda: Stop shouting. The servant can hear you.

Tesman: Burned it! But good God Almighty—No, no, no—that's utterly impossible!

Hedda: Yes, but it's true, all the same.

Tesman: Do you realize what you've

done, Hedda! It's the illegal appropriation of lost property! Imagine that! You just ask Judge Brack—he'll tell you what that means!

Hedda: It would be wiser not to mention it—to Judge Brack or to anyone else.

Tesman: But what made you do such an incredible thing? What put it into your head? What possessed you? Tell me that, eh?

Hedda: [Suppresses a faint smile.] I did it for your sake, George.

Tesman: For my sake!

Hedda: When you came home this morning and told me he had read to you—

Tesman: Yes, yes—what about it?

Hedda: You admitted you were jealous of that book.

Tesman: Oh, my God, I didn't mean it so literally.

Hedda: All the same, I couldn't bear the thought of anyone putting you in the shade.

Tesman: [In an outburst of doubt mixed with joy.] Hedda! Is it true—what you're saying? But—but I never knew you would show your love for me like that. Just imagine!

Hedda: Well, you might as well know—that right now—[Breaks off impatiently.] No, no—you can ask your Aunt Julia. She'll tell you all about it.

Tesman: Oh, I almost think I understand you, Hedda! [Clasps his hands together.] Good heavens, no! Can it really be that, eh?

Hedda: Stop shouting. The servant can hear you.

Tesman: [Laughs with uncontrollable glee.] The servant! Oh, Hedda, you're really priceless! The servant—that's Berta! I want to run out and tell Berta myself.

Hedda: Oh, I'll die—I'll die of all this!

Tesman: Of what, Hedda, eh?

Hedda: Of all this—nonsense—George.

Tesman: Nonsense! Because I'm so overjoyed at the news? But after all, perhaps I'd better not say anything to Berta.

Hedda: Oh, yes—why not?

Tesman: No, no, not just now. But Auntie Julie certainly must hear about it—and that you've started to call me George, too. Just imagine! Oh, Auntie Julie will be so happy—so happy!

Hedda: When she hears I burned Eilert Lövborg's manuscript—for your sake?

Tesman: Oh, no—no one must know about the manuscript—the burning—but for love of me, Hedda—Auntie Julie will be as happy as I am when she hears that! I wonder if that sort of thing is usual in young wives, eh?

Hedda: I think you'd better ask Auntie Julie about that, too.

Tesman: Yes, I certainly will, when I get a chance. [Looks uneasy and downcast again.] But the manuscript—! Good God, it's terrible when you think of poor Eilert, just the same.

[**Mrs. Elvsted,** dressed as on her first visit, wearing a hat and coat, enters by the hall door.]

Mrs. Elvsted: [Greets them hurriedly and in evident agitation.] Oh, Hedda dear, please forgive me for coming here again.

Hedda: What's the matter, Thea?

Tesman: Is it about Eilert Lövborg again, eh?

Mrs. Elvsted: Yes, I'm terribly afraid he's met with some kind of accident.

Hedda: [Seizes her arm.] Oh—you think so?

Tesman: Good Lord, Mrs. Elvsted, where did you get that idea?

Mrs. Elvsted: The people at the place I'm staying at were talking about him—just as I came in. I've heard the most incredible rumors about him today—

Tesman: Yes, just imagine, so have I! But I can swear he went straight home to bed last night. Imagine that!

Hedda: Well, what were those people saying about him?

Mrs. Elvsted: I couldn't make it out. It all seemed very vague—and they stopped talking when they saw me. Oh, I didn't dare to ask.

Tesman: [Moves about uneasily.] Let's

hope—let's hope you misunderstood them, Mrs. Elvsted.

Mrs. Elvsted: No, I'm sure they were talking about him. They said something about the hospital or—

Tesman: The hospital?

Hedda: No, no—that's impossible!

Mrs. Elvsted: Oh, I was so terrified—I went to his lodgings and asked for him there.

Hedda: You could bring yourself to do that, Thea!

Mrs. Elvsted: What else could I do? I just couldn't bear the suspense any longer.

Tesman: But you didn't find him there, neither, eh?

Mrs. Elvsted: No, they didn't know anything about him. They said he hadn't been home since yesterday afternoon.

Tesman: Yesterday! Imagine, how could they say that?

Mrs. Elvsted: There's only one answer— something terrible must have happened to him.

Tesman: Hedda dear—suppose I go around to a few places and try to find out—?

Hedda: No, no—don't you get mixed up in this.

[**Judge Brack,** with his hat in his hand, enters by the hall door, which **Berta** opens and closes behind him. He looks serious and bows in silence.]

Tesman: Oh, is that you, Judge, eh?

Brack: Yes, it's important that I see you right now.

Tesman: Oh, you've heard the news about Aunt Rina?

Brack: Among other things, yes.

Tesman: Isn't it sad, eh?

Brack: Well, my dear Tesman, that depends on how you look at it.

Tesman: [Looks at him doubtfully.] Has something else happened?

Brack: Yes.

Hedda: [Tensely.] Something dreadful, Judge?

Brack: That, too, depends on how you look at it, Mrs. Tesman.

Mrs. Elvsted: [Unable to restrain herself.] Oh, it's something about Eilert Lövborg!

Brack: [With a glance at her.] What makes you think that, Mrs. Elvsted? Perhaps you've already heard something—?

Mrs. Elvsted: [Confused.] No, no, nothing at all, but—

Tesman: Oh, for heaven's sake, tell us!

Brack: [With a shrug.] Well—I'm sorry to say—Eilert Lövborg's been taken to the hospital. He's dying.

Mrs. Elvsted: [Cries out.] Oh God, oh God—!

Tesman: To the hospital! And he's dying!

Hedda: [Involuntarily.] So soon—!

Mrs. Elvsted: [Moans.] And we parted in anger, Hedda!

Hedda: [Whispers.] Thea—Thea—be careful!

Mrs. Elvsted: [Pays no attention to her.] I want to go to him! I want to see him alive!

Brack: It's useless, Mrs. Elvsted. No one is allowed to see him.

Mrs. Elvsted: But at least tell me what happened to him? What is it?

Tesman: You don't mean to say that he himself—eh?

Hedda Yes, he did, I'm sure of it.

Tesman: Hedda, how can you—?

Brack: [Watches her closely.] Unfortunately, you've guessed absolutely right, Mrs. Tesman.

Mrs. Elvsted: Oh, how horrible!

Tesman: Did it himself! Imagine that!

Hedda: Shot himself!

Brack: You've guessed right, again, Mrs. Tesman.

Mrs. Elvsted: [Tries to control herself.] When did it happen, Mr. Brack?

Brack: This afternoon—between three and four.

Tesman: But, good Lord, where did he do it then, eh?

Brack: [Hesitates.] Where? Well—where he was staying, I suppose.

Mrs. Elvsted: No, that can't be right, because I was there myself between six and seven.

Brack: Well, somewhere else, then. I

don't know exactly. I only know that he was found—he'd shot himself—in the chest.

Mrs. Elvsted: Oh, it's terrible to think of it! That he should die like that!

Hedda: *[To Brack.]* Was it in the chest?

Brack: Yes—I told you so.

Hedda: Not in the temple?

Brack: In the chest, Mrs. Tesman.

Hedda: Well—the chest is just as good.

Brack: What do you mean, Mrs. Tesman?

Hedda: *[Evasively.]* Oh, nothing—nothing.

Tesman. And you say the wound is serious, eh?

Brack: Absolutely fatal. He's probably dead already.

Mrs. Elvsted: Yes, I know it. It's over—It's all over! Oh, Hedda—!

Tesman: But tell me—how did you get to know all this?

Brack: [Curtly.] From a police officer—I had some business with.

Hedda: *[In a loud voice.]* At last, someone did something worth doing!

Tesman: *[Terrified.]* God help me—what are you saying, Hedda?

Hedda: I say that there's beauty in this.

Brack: H'm, Mrs. Tesman—

Tesman: Beauty! Imagine that!

Mrs. Elvsted: Oh, Hedda, how can you see any beauty in such an act?

Hedda: Eilert Lövborg has settled accounts with himself. He had the courage to do—what had to be done.

Mrs. Elvsted: No, you mustn't believe that! What he did—he did in delirium!

Tesman: In despair!

Hedda: No, never. I'm sure of that.

Mrs. Elvsted: Of course, he was delirious —as he was when he tore our book to pieces.

Brack: *[With a start.]* The book? The manuscript, you mean? He tore that up?

Mrs. Elvsted: Yes—last night.

Tesman: *[In a whisper.]* Oh, Hedda, we'll never get out of this.

Brack: H'm that's very strange.

Tesman: *[Moves about the room.]* To think of Eilert dying this way! And not even leaving behind the book that would have made him famous—

Mrs. Elvsted: Oh, if only it could be put together again!

Tesman: Yes, just imagine, if only it could! What I wouldn't give—

Mrs. Elvsted: Perhaps it can, Mr. Tesman.

Tesman: What do you mean?

Mrs. Elvsted: *[Searches in the pocket of her dress.]* Look. I've kept all the notes he used, to dictate from.

Hedda: *[Takes a step toward her.]* Oh!

Tesman: You've kept them, Mrs. Elvsted, eh?

Mrs. Elvsted: Yes, I have them. I took them with me when I left home—and here they are still in my pocket—

Tesman: Oh, just let me have a look!

Mrs. Elvsted: *[Hands him a bundle of small sheets of paper.]* But they're not in the right order—they're all mixed up.

Tesman: Just imagine, if we could sort them out! Perhaps if we worked together—

Mrs. Elvsted: Oh, yes—at least we can try—

Tesman: It *will* work! It *must*. I'll devote my life to it!

Hedda: You, George? Your life?

Tesman: Yes, or at least all the time I can spare. My own work will just have to wait. You understand me, Hedda, eh? I owe this to Eilert's memory.

Hedda: Perhaps you're right.

Tesman: And now, my dear Mrs. Elvsted, we must pull ourselves together. Good Lord, there's no use brooding over what's happened, eh? We've got to have peace of mind in order to—

Mrs. Elvsted: Yes, yes, Mr. Tesman, I'll try very hard.

Tesman: Well, come on, then. We'll start looking through the notes right away. Where shall we sit? Here? No, in there, in the back room. Excuse us, Judge. Come with me, Mrs. Elvsted.

Mrs. Elvsted: Oh, God—if only we could do this!

*[**Tesman** and **Mrs. Elvsted** go into*

the inner room. She takes off her hat and coat. They sit at the table under the hanging lamp and begin to examine the papers with deep concentration. **Hedda** *crosses to the stove and sits in the armchair. After a moment,* **Brack** *draws near her.]*

Hedda: *[In a low voice.]* Oh, what a sense of freedom there is in this act of Eilert Lövborg's.

Brack: Freedom, Hedda? Oh, yes, it certainly freed him—

Hedda: I mean, for me. It gives me a sense of freedom to know it's still possible to act with a free will and with courage in this world—to do something that's shining and beautiful because it's spontaneous.

Brack: *[Smiles.]* H'm—my dear Hedda—

Hedda: Oh, I know what you're going to say—because you're a kind of specialist, too, like—well, you know!

Brack: *[Looks hard at her.]* Eilert Lövborg meant more to you than you're willing to admit—even to yourself. Or am I wrong about that?

Hedda: I won't answer such a question. I only know that Eilert Lövborg had the courage to live his life in his own way. And that his final act—was beautiful! He had the strength and will to turn away from the banquet of life—so early.

Brack: I'm sorry, Hedda—but I'm afraid I must deprive you of your beautiful illusion.

Hedda: Illusion?

Brack: Which would have been destroyed very soon, anyway.

Hedda: What do you mean?

Brack: He didn't shoot himself—of his own free will.

Hedda: He didn't—?

Brack: No. Eilert Lövborg's death didn't happen exactly as I said it did.

Hedda: *[Tensely.]* You've concealed something? What is it?

Brack: For poor Mrs. Elvsted's sake, I made a few small alterations in the story.

Hedda: What were they?

Brack: First, that he's actually already dead.

Hedda: At the hospital?

Brack: Yes—without regaining consciousness.

Hedda: What else have you concealed?

Brack: The incident didn't take place in his room.

Hedda: Well, that doesn't make much difference.

Brack: No, not very much. But I think I ought to tell you—Eilert Lövborg was found shot in—in Mademoiselle Diana's bedroom.

Hedda: *[Starts to rise, then sinks back.]* That's impossible, Judge Brack! He couldn't have gone there again today!

Brack: He was there this afternoon. He went there, he said, to get something they'd taken from him. He kept raving about a lost child—

Hedda: Oh, that's why—

Brack: I thought possibly he meant his manuscript—but now I hear he destroyed that himself. So it must have been his wallet.

Hedda: Yes, I suppose so. And that—that's where they found him?

Brack: Yes. With a discharged pistol in his breast pocket. The bullet had wounded him fatally.

Hedda: In the chest. Yes.

Brack: No—in the bowels.

Hedda: *[Looks up at him with an expression of disgust.]* That, too! Oh, what a curse—everything I touch turns ridiculous and ugly!

Brack: There's something else, Hedda. Something equally ugly!

Hedda: And what's that?

Brack: The pistol he was carrying—

Hedda: *[Breathlessly.]* Well, what about it?

Brack: He must have stolen it.

Hedda: *[Leaps up.]* Stolen it! That's not true! He didn't steal it!

Brack: No other explanation is possible. He must have stolen it—Sssh!

*[***Tesman*** *and* **Mrs. Elvsted** *have risen from the table in the inner*

room and come into the drawing room.]

Tesman: [His hands full of papers.] Hedda dear—it's almost impossible to see under that lamp in there. Just think!

Hedda: Yes, I am thinking.

Tesman: Will it be all right if we use your desk for a little while, eh?

Hedda: Yes, if you like. [Quickly.] No, wait! Let me clear it off first.

Tesman: Oh, you don't need to, Hedda. There's plenty of room.

Hedda: No, no, let me do it, I say. I'll put all these things in on the piano for the time being. There, now!

[From under the bookshelves, she has taken an object covered with sheet music and piles several other sheets of music on it, all of which she carries into the inner room, to the left. **Tesman** lays the scraps of paper on the desk, then moves the lamp there from the corner table. He and **Mrs. Elvsted** sit down and proceed with their work. **Hedda** returns.]

Hedda: [Stands behind her chair and gently ruffles **Mrs. Elvsted's** hair.] Well, my sweet Thea—how are you getting on with Eilert Lövborg's memorial?

Mrs. Elvsted: [Looks dispiritedly up at Hedda.] Good heavens—it's going to be terribly hard to straighten all this out.

Tesman: But we'll do it! There's no question about it! After all, arranging other men's papers is just the sort of thing I do best.

[**Hedda** goes over to the stove and seats herself on the footstool. **Brack** stands over her, leaning on the armchair.]

Hedda: [Whispers.] What were you saying about the pistol?

Brack: [Softly.] That he must have stolen it.

Hedda: Why stolen it?

Brack: Because every other explanation seems impossible, Hedda.

Hedda: Really?

Brack: [Glances at her.] Of course, Eilert Lövborg was here this morning. Wasn't he?

Hedda: Yes.

Brack: Were you alone with him?

Hedda: Yes, for a while.

Brack: Didn't you leave the room while he was here?

Hedda: No.

Brack: Try to remember. Weren't you out of the room—even for a moment?

Hedda: Well, perhaps for just a moment —out in the hall.

Brack: And where was your pistol case?

Hedda: I had it down in—

Brack: Yes, Hedda?

Hedda: The case was there on the desk.

Brack: Have you looked since to see if both pistols are there?

Hedda: No.

Brack: Well, you needn't. I saw the pistol Lövborg had with him, and I recognized it immediately. I had not only seen it yesterday—but before that, too.

Hedda: Do you happen to have it with you?

Brack: No, the police have it.

Hedda: What will they do with it?

Brack: Try to find the owner.

Hedda: Do you think they'll succeed?

Brack: [Bends over her and whispers.] No, Hedda Gabler—not so long as I keep quiet.

Hedda: [With a frightened look.] And if you don't keep quiet—then what?

Brack: [Shrugs.] It's possible to swear that the pistol was stolen.

Hedda: [Firmly.] I'd rather die!

Brack: [Smiles.] People say such things— but they don't do them.

Hedda: [Ignores the remark.] And suppose the pistol was not stolen—and they find the owner. What happens then?

Brack: Then, Hedda—there'd be a scandal.

Hedda: A scandal!

Brack: A scandal, yes—which frightens you to death. Naturally, you'll have to appear in court—both you and Mademoiselle Diana. She'll have to explain how the thing happened. Whether it was an accident or murder. Was he trying to take the pistol out of his pocket to threaten her—and did it go off accidentally? Or did she grab it out of his hand, shoot him, and stick it back in his pocket again? She could very well have done that—she's a pretty powerful woman, this Mademoiselle Diana.

Hedda: But all those revolting things have nothing to do with *me*.

Brack: No. But you'll have to answer the question: Why did you give Eilert Lövborg the pistol? And what conclusion will people draw from the fact that you did give it to him?

Hedda: [*Lowers her head.*] That's true. I didn't think of that.

Brack: Well, fortunately, there is no danger as long as I keep quiet.

Hedda: [*Looks up at him.*] So you have me in your power, Judge. You have a hold over me from now on.

Brack: [*Whispers softly.*] Hedda dear, believe me, I won't abuse my advantage.

Hedda: But I'm in your power, just the same. A slave to your will and your demands. Not free! Not free! [*Rises impetuously.*] No—I can't bear the thought of it! Never.

Brack: [*Looks at her half-mockingly.*] People somehow adjust to the inevitable.

Hedda: [*Returns his look.*] Yes, perhaps so.

[*She crosses to the desk. Suppressing an involuntary smile, she imitates **Tesman's** way of speaking.*]

Well? Making any headway, George, eh?

Tesman: Heaven knows, dear. It will take months of work, in any case.

Hedda: [*As before.*] No! Imagine that!

[*Passes her hands softly through **Mrs. Elvsted's** hair.*]

Doesn't it seem strange to you, Thea? Sitting here now with Tesman—just as you used to sit with Eilert Lövborg?

Mrs. Elvsted: If I could only inspire your husband in the same way!

Hedda: Oh, I'm sure you will—in time.

Tesman: Yes—you know, Hedda—I'm really beginning to feel something of the sort! But why don't you go and talk to Judge Brack again?

Hedda: Isn't there anything I can do to help you two?

Tesman: No, not a thing in the world. [*Turns his head.*] From now on, Judge, I'm depending on you to keep Hedda company.

Brack: [*With a glance at **Hedda**.*] It will give me the greatest of pleasure!

Hedda: Thanks. But I'm rather tired this evening. I think I'll go in and lie down on the sofa for a while.

Tesman: Yes, do that dear, eh?

[**Hedda** *goes into the inner room and closes the portieres behind her. A short pause. Suddenly she is heard playing a wild dance tune on the piano.*]

Mrs. Elvsted: [*Starts up from her chair.*] Oh—what's that?

Tesman: [*Runs up to the doorway.*] But, Hedda dear—don't play dance music tonight! Just think of Auntie Rina! And of Eilert!

Hedda: [*Puts her head out between the portieres.*] And of Auntie Julie! And everybody else!—From now on, I'll be quiet.

[*Closes the portieres again.*]

Tesman: [*At the desk.*] It's not good for her to see us at this distressing work. I'll tell you what, Mrs. Elvsted—you can take the empty room at Auntie Julie's, and I'll come over in the evenings, and we'll sit and work there, eh?

Mrs. Elvsted: Yes, perhaps that would be better—

Hedda: [*From the inner room.*] I hear very well what you're saying, Tesman.

But how will I get through the evenings out here—alone?

Tesman: [As he looks through the papers.] Oh, I'm sure Judge Brack will be good enough to come out to see you now and then.

Brack: [In the armchair, calls out gaily.] Every single night, Mrs. Tesman! We'll have a rollicking time here together, you and I!

Hedda: [In a loud, clear voice.] Yes, that's what you'd like, Judge, wouldn't you? To be cock-of-the-walk—!

[A shot is heard within. **Tesman, Mrs. Elvsted,** and **Brack** leap to their feet.]

Tesman: Oh, now she's playing with those pistols again.

[He throws back the portieres and runs into the inner room, followed by **Mrs. Elvsted. Hedda** lies stretched on the sofa, lifeless. Confusion and cries. **Berta** enters in alarm from the right.]

Tesman: [Shrieks to **Brack**.] Shot herself! Shot herself in the temple! Imagine that!

Brack: [On the point of collapse, in the armchair.] Good God!—but—people don't do such things!

CURTAIN

A
DREAM
PLAY

August Strindberg

John Elfström (The Glazier) and Ingrid Thulin (Indra's Daughter) in the open-ing scene of Ingmar Bergman's television production of *A Dream Play*, Stock-holm, 1963. The window, lower right, lighting slowly created the illusion of the castle growing, as though it had "put out a wing." Photograph: Roland Andersson. Courtesy Swedish Broadcasting System.

August Strindberg

August Strindberg, the intense, fiery, and tortured genius, Sweden's greatest playwright, was, after Ibsen, the most influential figure in the development of modern drama. Strindberg was born in Stockholm, on January 22, 1849, to a merchant who claimed aristocratic ancestors and a woman who had been a servant. His mother bore his father three sons before she married him, just prior to August's birth, and several children afterward—eight in all survived. Soon after August was born, his father went into bankruptcy, and the lonely, sensitive boy grew up in an atmosphere of poverty and discord. He had a limitless need for affection, but his father was cold and severe, and his mother slighted him for her oldest and favorite son. August was tormented by the thought that he was the son of a servant and considered himself the victim of injustice, a grievance that persisted and grew throughout his life until it became a mania. Although his tubercular mother could not give August all the attention he craved, she did try to instill in him her deep interest in religion. During his youth he scorned religion and denied the existence of God; but when a mental crisis overtook him in middle age, he turned to religion in an effort to retain his sanity.

When August was thirteen, his mother died, and his father married the housekeeper. The boy was disturbed by sexual conflicts; in his fantasies he saw his mother and stepmother, on the one hand, as pure and virginal and, on the other, as promiscuous and destructive. It was the beginning of the alternation of attraction and repulsion that he felt for the feminine sex throughout his life. This ambivalence, which recurs as a theme in much of his writing, was to ruin his marriages, in which he sought mothers and comrades rather than wives.

August did not get along with his stepmother or with his teachers. Although his unusual abilities were recognized at school, he refused to submit to discipline and did poorly in his studies. He read widely, however, laying the foundation of the enormous knowledge of poetry, drama, philosophy, and the natural sciences that later revealed itself in his literary, scientific, and pseudoscientific pursuits. At the age of eighteen, he entered the University of Uppsala, which he attended intermittently for about five years without earning a degree, suffering all the while from poverty, minor neuroses, and the effects of a dissolute life. He tried teaching but gave that up and went to live in the home of Dr. Axel Lamm, where he hoped to learn something about medicine and to earn some money by tutoring the doctor's young sons. In the Lamm home, Strindberg experimented with chemicals in the doctor's laboratory, read omnivorously in the excellent library, and met the professional writers and artists who were guests of the Lamms.

When he failed in chemistry at the entrance examinations for the study of medicine, Strindberg decided to become an actor. At the Dramatic Theatre, he was given a small part but was advised to enroll at the Dramatic Academy for some acting courses. Full of rage and frustration at the suggestion that he return to school, Strindberg went back to the attic in which he lived, took an opium pill, expecting to die; instead, he fell into a deep sleep. When he awoke, his mind was seething with memories of his childhood and adolescence, which were as vivid as a play in the theatre. He arranged his thoughts feverishly and set them down in dramatic form. In four days of furious writing, he completed a two-act comedy, and he felt an enormous sense of release. It was then that he knew he would be a writer.

Almost all of Strindberg's literary and dramatic work shows a close relationship to his first play. Nearly everything he wrote was autobiographical, was written feverishly, had the quality of hallucination, provided him with therapeutic relief, or was motivated by rage, revenge, or the need to bolster his ego. Often during his life, Strindberg was close to suicide and insanity; yet even when it appeared to others that he had gone beyond the bounds of reason, he managed to retain his hold on reality, with the aid of his remarkable powers of self-analysis and his compulsion to write.

Although at twenty he was in a state of mental turmoil, Strindberg began to write poetry and plays, which won him a measure of recognition but no money. He tried to support himself by journalism but failed at that. Then he applied for a civil service job and, in spite of not having a college degree, was the winning candidate for the position of assistant librarian at the Royal Library of Stockholm. During eight years there (1874–1882), he read and wrote with great intensity and began to publish stories and essays about Sweden and to gather the material he made use of later in his historical plays. He had come under the influence of Darwin's theory of evolution, Schopenhauer's pessimism, Buckle's relativistic theory of history, Kierkegaard's existentialism, and von Hartmann's *Philosophy of the Unconscious*. In 1879 he wrote his first autobiographical novel, *The Red Room*. This bitterly incisive and realistic attack upon his country's institutions won him the name of the Swedish Zola, although at the time he knew nothing of that writer's work. The novel created a scandal and was a great success.

Four years earlier, in 1875, when Strindberg was twenty-six, he had met Siri von Essen and had fallen in love with her. She was the wife of Baron Wrangel, a man much older than herself, and the mother of a young daughter. As a frequent visitor at the Wrangels' house, Strindberg began to regard Siri and the Baron as his mother and father. The young writer was looking for a home and for a woman to mother him; Siri found home life dull and had a desire to go on the stage. At Strindberg's insistence, Siri left the Baron; their widely publicized divorce caused a great scandal. As long as she had been the wife of the Baron, Siri had appeared to Strindberg to be pure, ethereal, and desirable, but as soon as she married him he began to find fault with her, accusing her of trying to compete with him, of flirting, drinking, bearing him another man's child, trying to drive him mad, and particularly of being a poor housekeeper. (One of Strindberg's compulsions was an excessive neatness and cleanliness.) The couple left Sweden and moved from place to place on the Continent; several times they quarreled, separated, and came together again.

The schoolroom scene in the Royal Dramatic Theatre production, Stockholm, 1955, with Rune Carlsten as The Teacher and Jarl Kulle as The Officer. Photograph: Sven Järlas. Courtesy Royal Dramatic Theatre.

The marriage lasted sixteen years and ended in divorce; Siri, was granted custody of their three children. Throughout his life, Strindberg was haunted by Siri, who figured in almost everything he wrote. In the early and "happier" years of their union, Strindberg wrote mainly nondramatic works, but as his marital relations worsened and his rage increased, he had a burst of dramatic creativity. This pattern was repeated in his later marriages.

In 1893 he met and married Frida Uhl, an Austrian journalist, who was twenty-three years his junior. Frida's sister, Maria, who met the playwright several times before the marriage, wrote a penetrating description of him, which reads, in part:

> He manages to remain absorbed in his thoughts for a quarter of an hour at a time, not saying a word and not hearing what is said to him. I can never shake off the fear of seeing him suddenly go insane. At the same time he more and more impresses me as a great genius. . . . He gave himself up to scientific experiments . . . he also paints; there, too, he is a law unto himself, naturalistic symbolism he calls it. . . . He is so full of talent that he doesn't seem to know what to do with it. But his is not a joyful way of creating. It is more like the savage impulse driving a murderer to his crime. To me he is uncanny. I cannot understand Frida, nor how she dares entrust her future to the hands of such a man.

In less than three months Frida had left him, but she returned and left him again several times after that. They had one child.

Living in Paris alone and in a state of frenzy, Strindberg began to suffer from mental aberrations and hallucinations. Severe "electric shocks" were passing through his body, and he was sure that hostile "Powers" were persecuting him. He became haggard and unkempt, and moved from place to place to avoid his "enemies." In the meantime, he was furiously engaged

119

in chemical experiments designed to produce gold. In the process he burned his hands with sulfur and was hospitalized for several months. He wrote a number of scientific treatises, as well as the two autobiographical volumes *Inferno* and *Legends,* which described in detail the hellish period he had just lived through.

At this time he had begun to study occultism and the mysticism of the eighteenth-century philosopher and theologian Swedenborg. It was the ideas of Swedenborg that turned Strindberg's mind toward religion by suggesting to him that his suffering was a punishment for his sins—loving his mother to excess, taking Siri away from the Baron, deserting his children, and trying to make gold. Hereafter, he vowed, he would do penance; and this resolution helped to restore his mental balance.

In 1899 he returned to Sweden and in the following year saw Harriet Bosse, a beautiful, young Norwegian actress in the role of Puck in *A Midsummer Night's Dream.* To her he offered the leading part in his play *To Damascus* and, although she was twenty-nine years his junior, he married her in 1901. Violent dissensions set in at once, and both of them felt trapped; it was a repetition of his former experiences. Harriet left him and returned to him several times, moving out finally in 1903 and taking with her their child. She agreed, however, to appear in a production of *A Dream Play* in 1907, in the role of Indra's Daughter, which Strindberg had written with her in mind. The playwright hoped for a reconciliation, but in 1908 Harriet married the actor Gunnar Wingard. Thereafter Strindberg lived alone and, though his health was failing, wrote a number of books and articles. After a life of torment and suffering, mainly self-induced, Strindberg died at the age of sixty-three on May 14, 1912.

Strindberg's versatility and productivity were astounding. In addition to his dramatic works, he wrote novels, short stories, essays, fairy tales, and poems. He engaged in scientific experiments, wrote music, and painted; he studied Chinese and wrote in both German and French. He produced books on philology, religion, botany, geology, and economics.

The list of his dramatic works alone is impressive. He was the author of about seventy-five plays, composed at three distinct periods of time.

His apprentice work was done between 1869 and 1876. The plays of this period were imitative and unsuccessful, but attracted the attention of the directors of the Dramatic Theatre and of the public. Written in 1869, *A Name-Day Gift,* his first play, was a domestic comedy; in the same year he wrote *Hermione,* in the manner of Greek tragedy. Both plays were rejected by the Royal Theatre. *In Rome* (1870), a one-act play in verse about the painter Thorwaldsen, was accepted for production but passed almost unnoticed. *The Free-Thinker* (1870), a full-length prose play, concerns a schoolteacher who is punished for having advanced ideas. This play was published but was criticized for its echoes of Kierkegaard and Ibsen. *The Outlaw* (1871) deals with the conflict between paganism and Christianity in old Sweden. The play was produced unsuccessfully, the critics again suggesting that the young playwright had borrowed from Ibsen. It should be noted, however, that both Ibsen and Strindberg had been influenced by the Danish dramatist Ohlenschläger and that both had drawn on material from the Icelandic sagas. *Master Olof,* which Strindberg worked on for five years (1872–76), was an historical play about a religious rebel, set in medieval Sweden in the reign of Gustavus Vasa. The playwright had given up his belief in Kierkegaard's idea of Either/Or and depicted Olof, not with the resolute character of Ibsen's Brand, but as a vacillating human being. The play was originally written in prose, was rejected, and was rewritten in verse; but still no theatre would put it on. Strindberg revised it again and again. It was published in its verse form in 1877 and, after nine years of effort, was finally produced in 1881 in its original prose.

In the early years of his marriage to Siri von Essen, Strindberg wrote *The Secret of the Guild* (1880) to provide a vehicle for his wife's debut on the stage. The subject matter was unusual for him, in that the play deals with the building of a medieval church in Uppsala and demonstrates the power of faith to hold two people together. Put into immediate production, the play proved a success for both dramatist and star. When Siri appeared in her husband's next play, *Herr Bengt's Wife* (1882), she won even greater acclaim. This play, too, had a medieval setting and was a paean in praise of love, marriage, and parenthood. Written in two weeks, *Lucky Peter's Journey* (1882), a romantic fairy play, contained the same message as Strindberg's two previous efforts and drew large and approving audiences. Siri's services as an actress were now in great demand, and she went off to play *Jane Eyre* in Finland, leaving Strindberg to look after the children and the housekeeping.

Siri's success soon worked a change in Strindberg's mood. While she was away from home, he was resentful and suspicious; when she returned, he started bitter quarrels and made wild accusations. He no longer considered her a comrade but a competitor. As their relationship deteriorated during the next four years, Strindberg seemed to store up a charge of resentment, which he finally hurled forth in a bolt of dramatic works. In the period from 1886 to 1892, he explored every stratagem in the battle of the sexes and, with a pen dipped in vitriol, wrote four important full-length plays, a number of one-acters, and an autobiographical novel containing a vicious attack on Siri before his fury was spent.

The four long plays created from 1886 to 1888 represent Strindberg's attempt to write with "scientific truth" in the manner of Emile Zola, the founder of naturalism. But the playwright's bias against women and his passion for revenge are incompatible with the coldly rational objectivity of the naturalist; in their violence and exaggeration they are closer to the manner of the impressionist. In *Comrades* (1886) Bertha and Axel, husband and wife, are both artists, living apparently in great comradeship until Axel discovers that his wife is really a petty, jealous, and deceitful competitor and drives her away. *The Father* (1887), a brilliant study in abnormal psychology, displays Strindberg's uncanny ability to probe the human mind. It also shows clearly his interest in hypnosis and the power of suggestion, as Laura raises doubts in her husband's mind as to the paternity of their child. The heartlessness of this vampire finally drives the man mad. *Miss Julie* (1888) puts the battle of the sexes on a class basis: Jean is a servant; Julie, an aristocrat. This situation reflects Strindberg's feelings about his own social status as against Siri's. In the duel between them, the chief weapon is sex. According to the dramatist, *Miss Julie* was a study of one aspect of evil though it offered no solution; it is Strindberg's most naturalistic play. *Creditors* (1888) introduces another vampire in Tekla, who has written a scurrilous novel about her first husband and is now undermining her second husband by her domination of him. The first husband returns to open the eyes of his successor and, in so doing, destroys him. *The Father* and *Miss Julie* are the authentic masterpieces of Strindberg's so-called naturalistic period.

In the one-act plays that followed, the central theme continues to be the love-hate conflict between men and women. But now we see the influence of Friedrich Nietzsche and Edgar Allan Poe, a greater emphasis on hypnotic suggestion, cynicism, and the horror and futility of life. There is also a heightened use of symbolic and expressionistic techniques. The outstanding plays in this group include *Pariah, The Stronger, Simoom,* and *Playing with Fire.*

The year before *Creditors* appeared, Strindberg had published *A Madman's Defence* (1887), an autobiographical novel written in French, in which he had portrayed Siri as a man-devouring monster. Like Tekla's novel (in *Creditors*), it was a vicious book, which Strindberg himself found disgusting, for he wrote that he was using "his own wife as a rabbit for his vivisections." He was to forbid his second and third wives ever to read this book. *A Madman's Defence* was one of seven autobiographies, written between 1886 and 1898, which reflected Strindberg's internal tensions and traced his bitter marital experiences. For the time being, Strindberg had written himself out.

During the next six years, after marrying Frida Uhl and breaking with her, Strindberg went through the Inferno crisis that took him perilously close to the brink of insanity. His return to Sweden and his third marriage brought forth another flood of dramas; between 1898 and 1909 he wrote thirty plays. Many of these were "dream" plays, heavy with mood and symbolism in the manner of the Belgian playwright Maurice Maeterlinck, and employed such experimental techniques as kaleidoscopic scenes, unnamed characters, lyrical dialogue, and non-naturalistic lighting and scenery. These plays were replete with Strindberg's own "creedless religion," with mystical and ritualistic visions, and with vague expressions of hope, although the dramatist still pictured the world as filled with hypocrisy and filth, meanness and suffering.

The strongly "spiritual" plays of this period include *To Damascus* (Parts I and II, 1898; Part III, 1904), *Advent* (1898), and *Easter* (1900).

Then came a series of plays dealing with medieval Swedish history. In *The Saga of the Folkungs, Gustavus Vasa,* and *Erik XIV,* all written in 1899, Strindberg completed the cycle he had begun years before with *Master Olof.*

In *The Dance of Death* (1901) he returned briefly to naturalism and to the old subject of the horrors of the marital relationship. Yet in that very year he married Harriet Bosse and wrote two of his happiest pieces, the fairy plays *The Bridal Crown* and *Swanwhite,* his only love story. In that year, too, he created one of his undisputed masterpieces, *A Dream Play.*

More historical plays followed. Then, early in 1907, the young actor-director August Falck conceived the idea of founding a Strindberg Theatre, which would be devoted entirely to the production of the dramatist's plays. It was to be an intimate playhouse, and Strindberg was immediately inspired to write a series of "chamber plays" intended as dramatic equivalents of chamber music. The plays were to be short, the casts small, the staging simple. When the Intimate Theatre, which seated 161 people, opened its doors in November, 1907, Strindberg, who had been working at furious speed, had ready for it *The Storm, The Burned Lot, The Ghost Sonata,* and *The Pelican.* Dealing with marital discord, sin, shame, guilt, and retribution, these plays resembled earlier works in themes and situations. In mood and tone they are harsh and somber; in form and style they impress us with the terseness and force of their dialogue and with the compression, distortion, and nightmarish atmosphere later to be identified with expressionism and avant-garde drama. *The Ghost Sonata,* the most inventive work in the group, is the actual forerunner of surrealism in the theatre.

Strindberg's last play, *The Great Highway* (1909), was a pilgrimage into his past, a backward glance at the emotional highlights of his life. Because it did not meet with the approval of either the public or the critics, the play, produced at the Intimate Theatre, had only a single performance. The theatre itself, which had long been in financial difficulties, closed in 1910. In the two years of life remaining to him, Strindberg wrote no more plays.

Though Strindberg lived the greater part of his life in the nineteenth century, his work identifies him as a modern, experimental playwright. Ibsen, who was his older contemporary, had taken realism as far as it could go and knew that the drama was ready for new forms and techniques. These Strindberg developed, crossing the old frontiers of both the romantic-poetic and the well-made play and advancing into the unknown territories of "naturalistic symbolism," expressionism, and surrealism. By the exploration of his dreams and the deep analysis of his hallucinatory states, and by his ability to transfer these experiences in aesthetic form to the stage, Strindberg initiated the Theatre of Cruelty, and theatre as a weapon, as well as absurdist and avant-garde drama. The use of nonlogical structure, the shattering of human identity, ambiguity in motivation and dialogue, supersubjectivity in theme and subject matter, and grotesqueness in scenery, costumes, and lighting are the formal elements that Strindberg has bequeathed to the playwrights of our time. His influence is clearly discernible in the work of Luigi Pirandello, Eugene O'Neill, and Sean O'Casey, to name but a few of the masters. In more recent times such cynical social commentators as Brecht, Ionesco, Beckett, Pinter, and Genet have raised a superstructure of raucous laughter, of cabaret and farce, on the somber foundations laid down by August Strindberg.

A Dream Play

In 1899 Strindberg returned to Stockholm after an absence of about seven years. During that time he had left his second wife, Frida Uhl, had passed through a mental crisis (the Inferno period), and had regained some stability through oriental religions and the mystical ideas of Emanuel Swedenborg.

No doubt, the writing of his first "dream play" hastened his recovery. Parts I and II of *To Damascus* were completed during this period. Fluid in form, unhampered by the dramatic unities, and set in an unreal landscape, *To Damascus* represented a complete departure from naturalism and allowed Strindberg great freedom to work out his emotions about his life with Frida, as well as his memories of his first wife, Siri. The two women were merged in a character called The Lady, while The Stranger (Strindberg himself), a haunted man, went on a perilous journey through life. Unlike an actual dream the play is structured around a single narrative thread.

To Damascus was being considered for production in the fall of 1900, but the part of The Lady had not as yet been cast. It was suggested to Strindberg that he go to see a new, young Norwegian actress, Harriet Bosse, who was appearing as Puck in *A Midsummer Night's Dream*. Strindberg disliked Shakespeare's "dream play" because of its too careful construction, but he enjoyed the antics of the working-class characters, and fell in love with Harriet Bosse. After she had accepted the part of The Lady, Strindberg asked her to marry him. He was bitterly aware of his unstable nature and of the hazards of a union with a girl almost thirty years his junior. Despite his fears and premonitions, they were married in May, 1901, and set up housekeeping at 40 Karlavägen. By June dissensions had arisen, and Harriet went off to visit friends in Denmark. Strindberg was in despair; the pattern of his life was repeating itself; he was sure Harriet would never return.

He brooded over his situation, and in loneliness and terror began a new play, which at first he called *Prisoners*, because it seemed to him that men were locked in themselves as in prisons or lunatic asylums. He followed Harriet to Denmark, brought her home, and was delighted to learn that she was pregnant. But by late summer their life together had again become intolerable, and Harriet left him for the second time. Strindberg went on with his play, a review of his life, which was more a nightmare than a dream. He now referred to the play as the *Corridor Drama*, alluding to the theatre alley where years before he had waited for Siri, and more recently for Harriet, and where he had pondered over a door that had an air hole shaped like a four-leaf clover. At one point he called the play *Setting Up House*, possibly with ironic intent, as Harriet left him and returned several times while he was writing it.

A later version was called *The Growing Castle*. As he wrote in his study in Karlavägen, Strindberg could look out the window and see in the distance, rising above the treetops, the golden dome of the newly built cavalry barracks. Passing the barracks during his walks, he noted the piles of manure that had been swept out of the stables, and it seemed to him that everything struggled and grew up out of filth. As Strindberg worked on the play during the fall and winter, the trees lost their leaves, and more of the barracks building became visible to him, which may have heightened the impression that the "castle" was growing.

His marriage continued to deteriorate, and Strindberg put into the play his feelings of sorrow and loss. He was keenly aware of the disparity between heavenly aspirations and earthly imperfections; he criticized Harriet's housekeeping, her independence, her ambitions—the identical complaints he had leveled at Siri and Frida—yet he envisioned Harriet as a daughter of the gods sent to earth to find out if men's complaints were justified. He wove these visions into what he now called *A Dream Play*.

The Prologue, which introduces Indra's Daughter, is technically not part of the play's structure; it was conceived late in 1901, as we learn from the dramatist's *Occult Diary*:

November 18th. Am reading about Indian religions. The whole world is but an illusion . . . a dream picture. (Consequently my *Dream Play* is a picture of life). . . . The sum total of it all is a ceaseless wavering between sensual orgies and the anguish of repentance. This would seem to be the key to the riddle of the world. . . . Indian religion, therefore, showed me the meaning of my *Dream Play*, the significance of Indra's Daughter, and the secret behind the door—nothing.

Strindberg completed a draft of the play in January, 1902. Two months later his daughter Anne-Marie was born; by the fall of 1903, Harriet and the child had left Karlavägen for good, and the following year she obtained a divorce. Strindberg and Harriet remained on friendly terms, however, and when *A Dream Play* had its première on April 17, 1907, Harriet created the role of Indra's Daughter, which she had inspired.

Tormented not only by the failure of his third marriage but by the whole course of his life, which he reviewed incessantly (it is summarized three times in the play), Strindberg continued to revise the work until it took on the complexity and beauty of a musical composition, in which the themes of human suffering, pity for mankind, and the futility of life were interwoven and restated in brilliant variations, harmonious, discordant, and contrapuntal.

A Dream Play has seemed to many to be entirely lacking in form; actually, the plot follows, in chronological order, the playwright's memories of his three marriages. The outlines are blurred, however, because Indra's Daughter encompasses the characteristics of all three wives. The various facets of the playwright's character are divided among The Officer, The Lawyer, and The Poet. In his preface to the play, Strindberg states that as in a dream, "the characters split, double, multiply, disappear, solidify, blur, and re-emerge. But one consciousness governs them all—that of the dreamer. . . ."

In the opening section of the play, Strindberg identified himself with The Officer, an identification in effect with Siri's first husband, the Baron Wrangel, who had been a Captain of the Guards. For years after Siri's divorce, Strindberg feared that the Baron would seek revenge. By a strange coincidence, on the eve of his wedding to Frida, Strindberg came face to face with the Baron on a street in Berlin and took this as an evil omen. By an even stranger coincidence, the Baron was his neighbor at 40 Karlavägen, where the playwright worked on the *Dream Play* during the breakup of his third marriage. It seemed to him he could not escape from his past or his destiny.

In the next section of the play, Strindberg saw himself as The Lawyer, clearly identifying with Frida's father and maternal grandfather, successful well-known lawyers, who may also have served as models. Strindberg, Frida, and their child lived in the grandfather's home until the playwright was threatened with arrest because of his novel *A Madman's Defence*, which the authorities considered obscene. Frida wished to go on in her profession of journalism, and Strindberg saw this as an attempt on her part to belittle him. He left her and their child and went to live in Paris. In a furnished room in the Latin Quarter, where he lived in grinding poverty and probably sickened on the smell of cabbage, Strindberg sought to produce gold through chemical experiments. He built a smelting furnace in his fireplace and worked until his hands were black and bleeding and he had to be hospitalized. The Lawyer in *A Dream Play* refers to his cracked and bleeding hands, and The Quarantine Master (another image of the playwright) has a furnace that purges and purifies.

In the final section of the play, Strindberg saw himself in the guise of The Poet. Harriet had first come to his attention when she appeared in Shakespeare's poetic dream play at a time when Strindberg himself had begun to write in a more lyrical vein. She was the most childlike and ethereal of his wives, with the slightly oriental features and coloring that caused the playwright to think of her as an exotic messenger from heaven. After an evening with Harriet, he wrote, "the candles burned quietly in prayer and the flowers were lost in thought." She inspired him to write a great deal of verse, much of which found its way into his plays. Her suffering in childbirth is echoed in The Poet's lines, which Indra's Daughter recites:

> Why must you be born in anguish,
> child of man, and cause your mother
> so much pain . . .

The sun gleaming on the golden dome of the cavalry barracks, at the very top of which was a budlike ornament, always attracted Strindberg's attention and, as he noted in his diary, induced in him a feeling of joy. It is possible, therefore, that the fire that consumed the Growing Castle and caused the bud to blossom into a giant chrysanthemum was intended to symbolize an affirmative answer to The Poet's prayer, a hopeful if not happy ending to the dream.

A Dream Play was completed in 1901, less than a year after the appearance of Sigmund Freud's The Interpretation of Dreams, but it is safe to say that Strindberg had never heard of the book. He was familiar, however, with the work of several of Freud's predecessors: Eduard von Hartmann's The Philosophy of the Unconscious and the experiments with hypnotism carried on in the 1880s by Charcot at the Salpetrière in Paris and by Bernheim at Nancy. His keen intuitive faculty and merciless self-analysis enabled Strindberg, like Sophocles and Shakespeare, to achieve an understanding of human motivation and behavior and to dramatize the processes operative in "dream work," such as wish fulfillment, condensation, multiple representation, and symbolism. The dreamer's (Strindberg's) wish that the deity or an intercessor look into the human situation and grant relief to suffering man is fulfilled by the appearance of Indra's Daughter. A "screen memory" enables The Officer to recall the petty injustice he suffered as a child but conceals the greater injustice he committed against his brother, of which his mother reminds him. When, in their discussions, Harriet would defend the rights of women, Strindberg would rush out of the room and she would hear him washing and washing his hands. An object growing out of filth, the Castle, for instance, has been taken as an indication of a cleanliness compulsion, from which Strindberg is known to have suffered, and the bursting chrysanthemum has been seen as a symbol for orgasm.

A Dream Play, however, is not a dream but a play and must be examined as such. Strindberg had once informed his brother that his plays were compounded of fact and fiction but that he could not tell them apart. As early as 1884, he wrote: "My best writing comes when I am suffering from hallucinations . . ."; and in 1887 he remarked in a letter to a young Swedish writer, "It seems to me as though I walk in my sleep—as though reality and imagination are one . . . Through much writing my life has become a shadow-play." After his Inferno crisis, he said, "Human beings live a double life—our fancies, fantasies and dreams possess a kind of reality."

But because it was not the "kind of reality" that could be expressed in a naturalistic style, Strindberg was forced to devise a new form for the dream plays of his last period. He was aware of what he had done, for in a letter written in 1902 to his German translator, Emil Schering, he declared, "The

Dream Play is a new form, which is my invention." This form was later to become the chief influence in the literary movement called expressionism, which flourished in Germany in the twenties; its most notable practitioners were Georg Kaiser, Ernst Toller, and Franz Werfel.

Expressionism, as has been said, represents a strong reaction against the naturalist's goal of scientific objectivity and, consequently, avoids the formal regularity of the well-made play. The characteristic features of expressionistic drama, all of which are exemplified in *A Dream Play*, include:

1. Subjective and autobiographical material, projecting the inner feelings and attitudes of the playwright.

    There is hardly a detail in *A Dream Play* that does not stem from Strindberg's own experiences and moods, from his mother's illness and pietism and his father's pettiness to his domestic quarrels with his three wives. The Schoolroom Scene reflects the hatred he always felt for formal education, and The Four Deans are the figures through whom he attacks the central institutions of the Establishment.

2. Episodic form.

    As a representation of a series of dream images, Strindberg's play tends toward formlessness and phantasmagoria. Unity is provided, however, by several tenuous narrative threads: The Daughter of Indra's pilgrimage, the vain longing of The Officer for The Opera Singer, the unhappy marital relationship of The Lawyer and The Daughter, and the attempt to discover the secret behind the door.

3. Characters are types, not individuals, and bear labels rather than names.

    Since the characters in Strindberg's play represent various facets of the dreamer, their egos are only parts of a single personality; thus no strong, fully developed individual character emerges. No character in the play has the force of a Hedda Gabler or even a Henry Higgins. The nameless figures that make up the *dramatis personae* enable the playwright to achieve a degree of universality; The Officer, The Lawyer, The Poet stand for their professions in general, The Daughter of Indra is a surrogate for all compassionate women, The Coalheavers represent the laboring class, and so on.

4. Dialogue is, on the one hand, telegraphic and abrupt, and on the other, poetic in tone or in form.

    Strindberg's telegraphic style, now much in use by avant-garde playwrights, may be seen in the following rhythmical colloquy:

    Poet: Perhaps I dreamt it.
    Daughter: Or made a poem of it.
    Poet: Or made a poem of it.
    Daughter: Then you know what poetry is.
    Poet: I know what dreaming is.

    In prose-poetry, Strindberg creates such lines as:

    Lawyer: Where are we, sister?
    Daughter: What do you hear?
    Lawyer: I hear drops falling—
    Daughter: Those are the tears of mankind weeping . . .

    There are, in addition, long passages in measured verse, as well as the aphoristic refrain that runs through the play: "Men are to be pitied!"

The cathedral scene, with impressionistic pipe organ, in the Stadttheater production, Bern, Switzerland, 1960. Designed by Hannes Meyer, directed by Christoph Groszer. Courtesy *World Theatre.*

5. A copious use of music and symbolism.

   Throughout the text Strindberg calls for specific musical selections to be played both onstage and off. There is background music from Wagner and Verdi, a Waldteufel waltz, Bach's Toccata and Fugue, No. 10, and a Kyrie. A "battle" actually takes place between the waltz and the toccata, with the latter triumphant. Symbols, which serve as a kind of visual music, are numerous and may admit of one or of many interpretations: a doorknob is made to stand for a heart, a shawl absorbs man's misery, and the clover-leaf door conceals the answer to the mystery of life. The Growing Castle has been variously interpreted and may, perhaps, represent man's body, which is finally destroyed to release his soul. In a sense, the entire play is a symbolic fable, depicting "the ironic experience of immortal spirit immersed in the heavy atmosphere of mortality."

6. Expressionistic drama frequently contains elements of religious feeling and ritual, though no special creed; it is a search for God in an age which believes God is dead. Myths, legends, and the supernatural are much in evidence.

   According to Strindberg, The Daughter of Indra (Indra had no daughter in Indian mythology) comes to earth in a missionary spirit and will presumably report back to the Brahmin heaven with a recommendation for the alleviation of man's sufferings. In the church scene, however, The Daughter places a crown of thorns upon The Lawyer's head, then plays a Kyrie on the organ; the atmosphere is suffused with Christian theology.

7. Expressionistic drama emphasizes human values and the spiritual brotherhood of man.

Positive values are offered in A Dream Play, but the playwright gives them a pessimistic turn. The Officer searches for ideal love yet meets only with disappointment and unhappiness; The Lawyer, who labors to aid his fellow men, is castigated, soiled, and worn out; and The Poet, who yearns for a pure vision, must take mud baths to harden his skin. But The Poet comes closest to The Daughter of Indra in spirituality, for as she departs from earth, she says:

Farewell, you child of man, you dreamer,
you poet, who best knows how to live . . .

8. Expressionistic drama, finally, attempts to reach the intellect through the emotions.

Although it contains powerful scenes of social satire and devastating thrusts at the Establishment, A Dream Play does not plead for a special cause; it is not a thesis play. Like music, painting, and poetry, it aims to evoke a succession of changing images and to arouse strong emotional responses in the audience.

Strindberg's work has exerted a powerful influence, particularly among experimental and avant-garde dramatists, who seem to have taken direct hints from A Dream Play. There appear to be echoes, for instance, of The Coalheavers in O'Neill's The Hairy Ape; of The Quarantine Master's remark, ". . . I often wish I could forget—especially myself. That's why I go in for masquerades, fancy dress, and amateur theatricals" in Pirandello's Henry IV; of The Deans of the Four Faculties and The Poet in O'Casey's Within the Gates; of the schoolroom scene in Ingmar Bergman's Wild Strawberries and Ionesco's The Lesson; and of The Officer who "waits" near a tree with its sparse leaves in Beckett's Waiting for Godot. This does not exhaust the list.

In the opinion of Professor Walter Johnson, "Strindberg succeeded in depicting the workings of the inner life (the irrational, the disordered, the undisciplined, the senseless) and in revealing what the realistic method cannot reveal, and thereby provided the blueprint for the most advanced drama of the twentieth century."

Production Record

A Dream Play had its first performance at the Swedish Theatre in Stockholm on April 17, 1907, with Harriet Bosse as Indra's Daughter, Ivar Kage as The Officer, Tore Svennberg as The Lawyer, and Ivan Hedqvist as The Poet. The play was produced by Albert Ranft and directed by Victor Castegren. The stage was specially painted and renovated for the production, and a stereop-

Agnes and The Glazier in an experimental production of *A Dream Play* adapted and directed by Alexandro Jodorowsky, presented March 1966 at the Teatro de la Casa de la Paz, Mexico City. All the male parts were played by Carlos Ancira, all the female parts by Maria Teresa Rivas. Courtesy International Theatre Institute Library, New York.

ticon projector was borrowed from a threatre in Dresden, where it had been used for a production of *Faust*. Because the equipment was primitive and Swedish technicians were unskilled in the use of projected scenery, the projector did not work satisfactorily. The audience, however, was excited by the play, and the reviewers commented on its great imaginativeness. One critic, who praised the play for its beauty, was not entirely satisfied with the performances: "The acting was sensitive but perhaps too formal for a dream. ... The characters in a dream consider everything that happens to them natural. As Indra's Daughter, Harriet Bosse ... was marvelous, a perfect apparition, but she sometimes succumbed to the temptation to preach. Mr. Svennberg was the best of all."

In November, 1907, Strindberg's own Intimate Theatre opened its doors, but *A Dream Play* was never performed there because its director, August Falck, considered his tiny stage with its limited equipment inadequate for the proper presentation of so complex a play.

On March 17, 1916, the play had its first production outside of Sweden. It was performed in German in Berlin, as *Ein Traumspiel*, with an excellent cast under the direction of Rudolph Bernauer. The play was well received, with special praise going to the Danish-born scene designer, Svend Gade, who, with the aid of improved technical equipment, created a brilliant, expressionistic production that came close to recreating Strindberg's vision. On October 28 of the same year, the celebrated director Mauritz Stiller produced the play in Göteborg, Sweden, with an original musical score by Wilhelm Stenhammar.

In October, 1921, the internationally famous Max Reinhardt went as a guest-director to the Royal Dramatic Theatre in Stockholm, where he mounted an elaborate production of *A Dream Play*, with scenery by the Austrian designer Alfred Roller and a musical score by the Bulgarian composer Pantscho Wladigeroff. Most of Reinhardt's clever and creative directorial touches met with the approval of the public and the critics, but some fault was found with his more extreme innovations, such as the wall of real human faces—white, distorted, and staring—he used as a background for the scene in The Lawyer's office; furthermore, it was noted that the tempo of the play, which was performed in Swedish, was "painfully slow"—a weakness due possibly to Reinhardt's directing in a language that was unfamiliar to him.

Later in 1921 the play was translated into German, recast, redesigned, and put on by Reinhardt at the Deutsches Theater in Berlin, with the blond and dignified Helene Thimig (Reinhardt's wife) as Indra's Daughter, Eugen Klöpfer as The Lawyer, and the great character actor Werner Krauss in five different minor roles. This production was an unqualified success. Four years later *Ein Traumspiel*, Julius Weissmann's opera based on Strindberg's play, had its première in Duisburg, Germany.

Under the title of *Le Songe, ou Jeu des Rêves*, the play was presented in France for the first time at the Théâtre de l'Avenue, Paris, on two Saturday afternoons, June 2 and 9, 1928. This production was directed and designed by Antonin Artaud and presented by his company, which was called the Théâtre Alfred Jarry. In the cast were Tania Balachova as Indra's Daughter, Raymond Rouleau as The Officer, Maxime Fabert as The Lawyer, Auguste Boverio as The Poet, and Antonin Artaud as The Dean of Theology. Strindberg's own French version of the play was used, but the Prologue and Scenes 6, 12, and 14 were omitted. Artaud, the originator of the concept of the

Harriet Bosse, for whom Strindberg created the part of Indra's Daughter, in the simple costume she wore in the first production of the play, Stockholm, 1907. The headdress, earrings, and hair style were meant to suggest the character's exotic origin. Theatre Collection, New York Public Library.

Theatre of Cruelty, adapted the play to conform to his ideas and directed it in what has come to be known as avant-garde style. Artaud added many unusual and startling details to the action, such as having The Lawyer bring a ladder on stage and climb to the top of it in order to get his overcoat from a hanger attached to the ceiling. The play did not succeed, but the performances were long remembered because the audiences insisted upon taking part in the proceedings, replying to the lines spoken by the actors and indulging in crude jokes and jeers, which finally led to fist fights.

The most frequent and most important interpreter of Strindberg's plays was the Swedish director Olof Molander, who produced at least six different stage versions and two radio versions of *A Dream Play* in a period spanning thirty years. Molander was forty-three years old when he attempted the play for the first time. This epoch-making production was put on at the Royal Dramatic Theatre in Stockholm on October 25, 1935. The scenery, designed by Isaac Grünewald, was minimal but highly suggestive, combining fantasy and realism; many scenes were projected on a cyclorama, while some were played in spotlights against a background of impenetrable darkness. Often the designer achieved a misty, dreamlike landscape and scenes that flowed into each other with a shadowy naturalness. The acting, too, was natural. Tore

Scene in The Lawyer's combination home and office in Max Reinhardt's production at the Royal Dramatic Theatre, Stockholm, 1921. Agnes (Jessie Wessel) stands beside the cradle while The Lawyer (Gustaf Molander, brother of the famous Olof) reads his briefs. Against the dark curtains in the background and in the open doorway may be seen the pale faces of suffering clients. Theatre Collection, New York Public Library.

Teje played Indra's Daughter with "a calm, melancholy air." Lars Hanson, as The Officer, acted with a boyishness that "made it seem natural for him suddenly to find himself back in school." Gabriel Alw gave an excellent performance as The Lawyer "with the furrowed and anguished face of Christ and the bent back that seemed to be carrying the worries of the world." Alw's acting in the graduation scene was the high point of the play. Ivar Kage, as The Poet, wore a portrait mask of Strindberg and played with an "intense and overflowing warmth." Each of Molander's later versions of the play was new and interesting, and each showed omissions, additions, and rearrangements of Strindberg's material.

Molander presented his next version in Copenhagen in 1940. Here the elements of fantasy were de-emphasized so that they would not appear to be extraordinary or "profound." The director attempted to make the dream completely believable. When the third version of the play was put on at the Malmö Civic Theatre in the spring of 1947, the critics noted that an excessive amount of Catholic ritual had been introduced into the action and remarked that Molander, with the enthusiasm of the newly converted, had infused the drama with a Catholicism that had no place in Strindberg's work. In this production Inga Tidblad played Indra's Daughter like "a little social worker in a black dress"; Carl Ström, as The Lawyer, was a commonplace man harried by too many petty cases. In the final scene, in place of the offerings to a fire, Molander substituted offerings to an altar, over which there was a cross inscribed with the words, "Ave Crux Spes Unica" (Hail, Cross, our only hope), the epitaph Strindberg wanted placed on his grave.

For his next version, presented at the Göteborg Civic Theatre in the fall of 1947, Molander took an entirely different approach. Here he was far less lyrical and more bitter, and the action of the play was made to refer to events in World War II. In the final scene, for instance, a large plain wooden

The graduation scene in the Royal Dramatic Theatre production, Stockholm, 1955. Photograph: Sven Järlas. Courtesy Royal Dramatic Theatre.

The Gatekeeper (Tilla Durieux) in the Oscar Fritz Schuh production, Hamburg, Germany, 1963. Miss Durieux, a star of the German stage for over sixty years, had played Eliza Doolittle in Shaw's *Pygmalion,* Berlin, 1913. (See p. 305.) Photograph: Rosemarie Clausen. Courtesy *Theater Heute.*

cross was seen against a background of black ruins, which the audience associated with the destruction of Hamburg. Because of these topical references, many of the scenes were frighteningly ugly yet incredibly moving.

In February, 1955, Molander presented still another production of the play at the Royal Dramatic Theatre in Stockholm. This time there was a heavy emphasis on unusual visual and sound effects. During long periods of silence, the Growing Castle and The Officer's home appeared as if by magic; then other visions took their place; suddenly sharp sounds—piercing sirens, whistles, and words—were heard; then silence again. The designer, Marik Vos, provided dazzling colors—a blue-green castle, a bright-blue top hat. The production had a mixed reception. Those critics in a position to compare Molander's various versions of the play tended to praise most highly the 1935 production.

In 1959 the brilliant actor-director Bengt Ekerot, who has been closely associated with Ingmar Bergman, produced the play at the Malmö Civic Theatre, with Annika Tretow as Indra's Daughter, Sture Lagerwall as The Officer, and Max van Sydow as The Lawyer. The critics were most enthusiastic about designer Per Falk's pale-pastel light projections, which "created distance, simplicity, a rhythmical monotone, and a quiet beauty."

During the 1940s and 1950s *A Dream Play* was produced in various countries in Europe, including Austria, Germany, Finland, and Switzerland; it was done in radio and television versions, as well as on the stage. In Denmark a radio production of the play was presented in 1949 to celebrate the one hundredth anniversary of Strindberg's birth.

The play was presented in Great Britain on radio in 1948 and again in 1957 but never done in English on the stage. It was performed at Sadler's Wells in German by the Kurfürstendamm Theater Company of Berlin in 1957; the production was directed by Oscar Fritz Schuh, had costumes and scenery by Caspar Neher, and incidental music by Heimo Erbse. The critic for the London *Stage* said that the play was produced "with tremendous care and achieved some exciting moments, but generally the pace seemed too slow, the rhythms rather monotonous. After each scene a gauze curtain was lowered and the sets were changed in a half-light while screens carried changing projections. This seemed overelaborate and not always meaningful. Much more effective was an instantaneous change from a church interior to a crypt, achieved by simply lowering the Gothic roof trusses."

A Dream Play has to date not had an adequate professional production in the United States. It was first done here in 1925 at the tiny Provincetown

The Lawyer (Will Quadflieg) and Agnes (Joana Maria Gorvin) in their squalid home. Oscar Fritz Schuh's production, Hamburg, 1963. Schuh had directed the play in Berlin in 1955 with scenery by Caspar Neher. Neher's designs were reconstructed from photographs and used again in 1963. Photograph: Rosemarie Clausen. Courtesy *Theater Heute*.

Playhouse in New York under the direction of James Light. The critics found no merit in the play but praised the scenery. Richard Watts, Jr., of the *Tribune* said, "The most interesting feature of the production at the Playhouse is . . . the sets of Cleon Throckmorton. All of them are of interest and some of them, particularly the Cave of Fingal, with its jagged opening against the purples and greens of the clouds, achieved a striking beauty." A still less successful production of the play was attempted in New York in 1960 at Theatre East, about which the critic for *The New Yorker* commented, "The Theatre East is one of those miniscule, subterranean theatres-in-the-round through which a runaway next-door subway might crash, and the notion of trying to realize the bulging and diffuse eccentricities of *A Dream Play* in it is dismaying, to say the least."

The best nonprofessional productions of the play in America have been done on college and university campuses, notably at Minnesota, Columbia, and Illinois.

Two recent Swedish productions of *A Dream Play* have confirmed its vitality and value. On May 2, 1963, Ingmar Bergman's television version was broadcast from Stockholm. Although Bergman made several cuts in the script, both artistically and technically, it was the most elaborate and expensive TV drama ever aired in Sweden. The enormous cast was headed by Ingrid Thulin as Indra's Daughter, Uno Henning as The Officer, Allan Edwall as The Lawyer, and Olof Widgren as The Poet; the scenery and costumes were designed by Cloffe, the music composed by Sven-Erik Bäck, and the masks created by Börje Lundh. Broadcast to all Scandinavian countries, the play attracted a record audience and elicited an enthusiastic response.

On January 22, 1965, Olof Molander's final production of *A Dream Play* opened at the Norwegian Theatre in Oslo with Rut Tellefsen as Indra's Daughter and Per Theodor Haugen as The Officer. Arne Walentin created the scenery and costumes. After a successful run in Norway, Molander took the play to Sweden where it played to great acclaim. In a Swedish radio interview a few months before his death in May, 1966, Olof Molander asserted that in none of his productions of *A Dream Play* had he been completely successful but that the Oslo version had been his best, for in it he had achieved about seventy-five percent of his intention.

Indra's Daughter (Mary Fowler), surrounded by flames, as she leaves for heaven in the last scene of the play at the Provincetown Playhouse, New York, 1925. Theatre Collection, New York Public Library.

On August 13, 1968, Malcolm Williamson's *The Growing Castle*, an opera in English based on Strindberg's play, was performed in the music room in Dynevor Castle, Wales, before an audience of fewer than a hundred persons. The leading roles were sung by Jennifer Vyvyan, Nancy Evans, Benjamin Luxon, and Geoffrey Chard. The music was played by the composer—piano, harpsichord, and percussion—a one-man band. Although the reviews were mixed, the music critics from the leading British newspapers found much to praise in the work.

Strangely enough, *A Dream Play* has never been produced as a motion picture, a form for which it seems ideally suited, though images from it may be seen in the work of Ingmar Bergman, as well as in the films of other masters of the cinema.

Falck, Strindberg, and *A Dream Play*

Notes by August Falck

In his book *Five Years With Strindberg*, August Falck recalled his association with the Swedish playwright in the founding of the Intimate Theatre and the playwright's efforts to have *A Dream Play* produced there. Falck's material is a collection of more or less random notes.

As a young actor-director profoundly impressed by Strindberg's plays, Falck conceived the idea of establishing a theatre in which only that dramatist's work would be presented. The young man submitted to the playwright his idea for a Strindberg Theatre, and along with it a production plan for *A Dream Play*. Both suggestions met with the approval of Strindberg, who, in his enthusiasm, hastily composed for the new house his so-called chamber plays. Early in 1907 Strindberg and Falck rented a large ground-floor room near the Central Station in Stockholm and converted it into a playhouse. The theatre contained only 161 seats and had very limited stage space. They called it the Intimate Theatre and opened its doors to the public on November 26, 1907. In April of that year, *A Dream Play* had had its première at the Swedish Theatre, but had closed after twelve performances. Strindberg was looking forward to a new production of the play; however, when Falck had submitted his original plan he had not envisioned working in so small a house. Now Falck felt that Strindberg's chamber plays and one-acters, which required a limited number of sets and small casts, would work much better than a play that presented overwhelming production problems.

Strindberg was well aware of the problems and, in a letter to Falck dated June 11, 1909, offered one of his innumerable suggestions for solving them:

> You see, if we had triangular side-wings △ with side a) showing columns, side b) showing a city, and side c) showing a forest, and they

From, August Falck, *Five Years with Strindberg*, Stockholm, Wahlström and Widstrand, 1935; pp. 271–76. Published by permission of the copyright owners.

rotated on an axis, it would serve very well. But we'll work out something, of course.

Falck recalls: "So he continued to make new plans for a production of *A Dream Play*, although he had already drawn up a detailed outline in the spring. Repeatedly, he urged me to present the play on every possible occasion. 'Do the *Dream Play* after *Crimes and Crimes* (or some other play we were considering),' he would mention casually in his notes to me. But *A Dream Play* is hardly the sort of work you just 'do' in any way whatsoever. I knew that we did not have anything like adequate resources at the Intimate Theatre for the proper production of that wonderful play, which requires to begin with a large stage in order to give the impression of space and perspective in an external sense. The production plan that I had submitted long before, and that we had discussed at the very beginning of our acquaintanceship, called for a unit set backed up by draperies and the use of set-pieces and a few other simple devices. This plan had met with his approval at first, but later he used it as a springboard for his own ideas which developed partially in a different direction. From the production of the play which had been done in Christiania [Oslo], he got the idea of painting symbols on flats."

According to Strindberg's plan, there were apparently to be six flats on the stage, each one bearing one or two different symbols. Falck provides the following list in which only five items are enumerated:

A Dream Play
Flat-Symbols

1. A poppy, red, with seedpods—Sleep and Dreams.
2. A blue monkshood flower—Deceptive Hope. A green sink-net—Fulfilled wishes which do not satisfy.
3. For the Lawyer: Bulletin boards with notices and bills.
4. In the Church scene, the bulletin boards show the numbers of the hymns; for the Graduation scene, the laurel wreaths are hung there.
5. Statues: One white for Fairhaven; one black for Foulstrand.

The ending—When the Daughter of Indra goes into the castle while it is burning, you can open the backdrop and show a burning castle; (?) or perhaps let her go through a sheet of fire.

A little later on, Falck continues, he [Strindberg] felt that he had to be rather cautious in the use of symbols, so "that one does not become either too realistic or too baroque." And if the play were to be performed in draperies "which would raise the piece to an abstract level," then he wanted to free everything else from the appearance of reality.

"Fantastic costumes might be introduced (after the manner of those of [Edward Gordon] Craig or the style of *L'Art Nouveau*). Agnes can certainly wear a white tunic; the Poet, a Roman toga, with such props as a lyre or a scimitar; the Lawyer, in an 18th century wig, which English barristers wear to this day . . .

Strindberg also suggested that Anna Flygare and Fanny Falkner, the leading actresses at the Intimate Theatre, be given three ballets to dance at the following points in the play:

1. The corridor in the opera house; the singer who was rehired and the singer who was not rehired.
2. In the Graduation scene, where the two girls put the laurel wreath aside and engage in a mimed fight over the crowning of The Lawyer.
3. At Fairhaven, where Flygare, representing Bach's Fugue, outdances Falkner, who is Waldteufel's Waltz.

" 'But let the ladies work this out for themselves in the grand style of [Isadora] Duncan.

" 'And consider the costumes again! A masquerade-ball or anything else is allowable in dreams only if it is beautiful.

" 'And you will have to have five string-instruments (Halldén will be helpful!). An organ for Bach would outdo the piano.

" 'Ask the ladies about this! One should listen to advice, but needn't take it!'

"Strindberg's suggestions were meant to serve our special needs. [Earlier he had sent me a book containing reproductions of Turner's paintings with a note saying, 'The scenery for the *Dream Play* at the Intimate Theatre should be painted in this misty way.'] For a production of the play on a larger stage he suggested the use of projected scenery by means of a stereopticon, a bold innovation in the Swedish theatre. The process had been developed in Germany, but an attempt to use it in Sweden had not turned out well; first, because the light source had been visible through the screen, and then because, in order for the projected scenery to be sharp and clear, the stage in front of it had to be in almost total darkness [obscuring the actors]. But Strindberg thought these problems could be solved. 'I believe, on the basis of my own experiments [he said], that if one were to employ various light sources it would be possible to use projected scenery. You must, for instance, use a carbon arc-lamp (violet) behind the screen, while on the figures in front of the screen you must throw the red light from a bulb or white light from an Auer-lamp; in that way the actors could be lighted while the scenery is visible.'

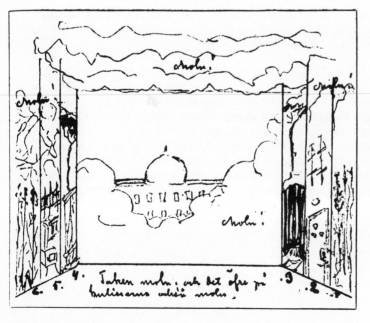

Scene design sketched by Strindberg for *A Dream Play*. The borders were to represent clouds, and the castle in the background was to be half hidden by clouds. Three painted panels on each side of the stage would revolve and suggest the locales of the various scenes. From Falck, *Five Years with Strindberg*.

"But the play was so huge and complex that it seemed impossible for us to squeeze it onto our stage, so Strindberg's plans for a production of *A Dream Play* at the Intimate Theatre never materialized."

Falck includes in his book a scene design made by Strindberg for *A Dream Play*. The sketch shows three painted and numbered wings on each side of the stage, a backdrop depicting the dome of a castle rising above the clouds, the borders also representing clouds. The playwright has written on the sketch, "The ceiling clouds, and the upper part of the wings also clouds." Underneath the sketch are the following descriptions of the paintings that are to appear on each wing:

The Dream Play

One permanent set

The backdrop: Cloudcaps. The castle is only visible when lit from behind.

Wing 1: Hollyhocks.

Wing 2: Below, the clover-leaf door. Above, the masts of a training ship and of other ships.

Wing 3: Below, Fingal's Cave, or the organ. Above, a pine tree—Italy.

Wing 4: A piece of furniture from the Lawyer's office. Above, cypress. Pine.

Wing 5: An iron stove—Foulstrand (Quarantine), or the Lawyer's home. Above, an iron fence. Mastheads.

Wing 6: Hollyhocks.

A spotlight apparently was to illuminate that part of the wing related to the scene being played.

Then follows a list headed "Music for *The Dream Play*," and a note giving the edition of the text to which the page numbers refer. [NB: Several of the words and abbreviations in Strindberg's scrawl are undecipherable.]

P. 206 Choir . . . Kyrie from Beethoven's *Fidelio*, Act II, No. 12 . . . First thirteen bars. Continue with Swedish text etc.

P. 207 Sound ensemble of wave and winds from Mendelssohn's "The Hebrides" Fingal's Cave Overture in B Minor. Only the first few bars of the main theme which is repeated.

P. 222, 223 Piano offstage. "Music and dance up there on the hill" A Boston waltz.

P. 228 Behind the orchestra "a dissonant chord."

P. 229 Piano offstage. Bach's Toccata in D Minor and a Boston wind orchestra.

P. 248 Ditto in orchestra. "The Song of the Waves" from Beethoven's "Adelaide" bars 39–70 but only the accompaniment.

P. 249 "The Wailing of the Winds" Beethoven's Lied No. 32, "An die Hoffnung": only the accompaniment from the first movement.

P. 252 "Why are you born in pain" (in orchestra) Beethoven's Lied No. 3 "Vom Tode" only the accompaniment.

P. 274 "Our parting is near" from Beethoven's *Fidelio*, Act II, somber, as long as is required.

P. 199 Offstage, themes from "Meistersinger" and "Aida"

X Beethoven . . . with Swedish text according to the original.

P. 195 Music in dance-time?

Translated by Leif Sjöberg

Scene from an unproduced play conceived by Antonin Artaud in the twenties to exemplify his theory of the Theatre of Cruelty. One woman and three men suggest Agnes, The Officer, The Lawyer, and The Poet in *A Dream Play*, which Artaud produced in the season 1927–1928. Photograph: Mme. Colomb-Gérard. Courtesy Bibliotheque de l'Arsenal.

A Dream Play and the Theatre of Cruelty

Comments by Antonin Artaud and Robert Aron

> [The following is one of the manifestoes issued by Antonin Artaud and Robert Aron, directors of the Théâtre Alfred Jarry at the time of its founding in 1926.]

Theatrical conventions have had their day. We, such as we are now, are unable to accept a theatre that would continue to trick us. We must be able to believe what we see. A production that repeats itself every evening according to rites that are always the same, always identical to themselves, can no longer win our approval. We want the show we are attending to be unique, to give the impression of being as spontaneous and as incapable of repeating itself as any action in life, as any event whatsoever cast up by circumstances.

With this theatre, in a word, we re-attach ourselves to life instead of separating ourselves from it. The playgoer, and we ourselves, will only be able to take ourselves seriously, if we very clearly give the impression that a profound part of our life is engaged in the action that is framed by the stage. Comic or tragic, our play will be one of those at which at a given moment you laugh bitterly. That's what we are commiting ourselves to.

It is in that *human* anguish that the playgoer will have to respond to us. He will be shaken and offended by the internal force of the production that unfolds before his eyes. And this force will be in direct relation to the suffering and anxieties of his entire life.

Such is the fatality that we evoke, and the production will be that very fatality. The illusion we seek to create will not depend on the degree of verisimilitude of the action, but on the communicative force and reality of that action. Each production will become by that very fact a sort of happening. The spectator must feel that a scene from his own life, and a truly important scene, is being acted out before him.

In a word, we demand of our public an intimate, profound adhesion. Discretion is not our aim. In every production we mount, we take a serious risk. If we are not ready to pursue the consequences of our principles to the very end, we consider that the risk is not really worth taking. The spectator who comes to us will be aware that he is coming to expose himself to a genuine performance in which not only his spirit but his senses and flesh come into play. If we were not certain that we could achieve this in the most serious way possible, we would consider that we were falling short of our basic goal. The spectator must be fully convinced that we are capable of making him scream.

This need which we have for being as honest and vital as possible shows very clearly the contempt we feel for theatrical methods as such, for everything included in what has conveniently been labeled the *mise en scène,* such as lighting décor, costumes, and so on. In all of that there is an artificial picturesqueness, which we are not expending our efforts to convey. It wouldn't take much for us to go back to candles. For us the theatre resides in something imponderable, which in no way accommodates itself to progress.

What will give value in reality and revelation to the productions put on by us will generally be an unconscious discovery, but one capable of creating the maximum illusion in the mind of the spectator. That is to say that when it comes to *mise en scene* and principles we shall trust bravely to chance. In the theatre we wish to create, Chance will be our god. We are not afraid of failure, of catastrophe. If we did not have faith in a possible miracle, we would not commit ourselves to such a hazardous course. But only a miracle could repay us for our efforts and our patience. And we are counting on that miracle.

The director who obeys no rules but follows his own inspiration will or will not make the happy find that is necessary for us. According to the play that he will have to produce, he will or will not make a discovery, will or will not hit upon an ingenious device, will or will not find *the disturbing element proper for throwing the spectator into the sought-for uncertainty.* Our entire success depends on that alternative.

It is quite evident, however, that we will be working from specific texts; the plays we will be doing, no matter what is said about them, belong to literature. How are we going to reconcile our desire for freedom and independence with the necessity of conforming to a certain number of directions imposed by the texts?

For that definition we are trying to give the theatre, one thing alone seems unassailable to us, one thing alone seems to us to be valid: the text. But the text, insofar as it is a distinct reality, existing by itself, sufficient unto itself, not with regard to its spirit, which we are as little disposed as possible to respect, but simply with regard to the displacement of air which the speaking of the words produces. Period, that's all.

For what seems to us essentially disturbing in the theatre, and above all essentially destructible, is what distinguishes theatrical art from pictorial and literary art; it is that entire despicable and cumbersome paraphernalia that makes a production out of a written play instead of allowing it to remain within the limits of speech, images, and abstractions.

It is that—that paraphernalia, that visual display—that we want to reduce to its impossible minimum and to cover with the look of seriousness and the disturbing character of the action.

Le Théâtre Alfred Jarry

[During its second season, 1927–28, the Théâtre Alfred Jarry presented Antonin Artaud's production of A Dream Play, about which
Artaud made the following comments.]

Strindberg's *Dream Play* is part of the repertory of an ideal theatre and constitutes one of those plays of the kind whose realization is the crowning point of a director's career. The gamut of emotions that is to be found, translated, and brought together in it, is infinite. One discovers in it at the same time the interior and exterior of a complex and thrilling conception. And in it are represented and evoked the deepest problems in a form that is at the same time both concrete and cryptic. It is really the universality of spirit and of life whose magnetic vibration is sent out to us and stirs our most precise and fruitful awareness of humanity. The success of such a production necessarily sanctifies a designer, a director. The Théâtre Alfred Jarry owed it to itself to put on such a play. The *raison d'être* and the princi-ple of this new company are well-known. The Théâtre Jarry would like to reintroduce into the theatre the meaning, not of life, but of a certain truth situated in the depths of the mind. Between real life and dream life there exists a certain set of mental combinations, of interrelated gestures, of events translatable into acts and constituting very exactly that theatrical reality which the Théâtre Jarry has taken upon itself to resuscitate. The meaning of genuine reality in the theatre has been lost. The idea of theatre has been erased from the human mind. It exists, however, at a halfway point between reality and dream. But to the extent that it is not found again in its most absolute and fruitful integrity, the theatre will not stop disintegrating. The theatre of today portrays life and seeks by means of more or less realistic décor and lighting to give back to us the commonplace truths of life, or else it cultivates *illusion*—and then it is worst of all. There is nothing less capable of giving us an illusion than the illusion of false "props," of painted boards and cloths that the modern stage offers us. One must resign himself to the inevitable and not seek to vie with life. In the simple presentation of real objects, in their combinations, in their order, in the relationship between the human voice and light, there is an entire reality that is sufficient unto itself and has no need of the other in order to live.

The *mise en scène* for *A Dream Play*, therefore, obeys that necessity of not presenting anything to the eyes of the public which could not be used immediately and exactly as it is by the actors: characters in three dimensions who may be seen moving among the "props," among objects, in the midst of an entire reality equally three-dimensional. The false in the midst of the true—that is the ideal definition of this *mise en scène*. A meaning, a utilization of a new spiritual order given to the ordinary objects and business of life.

[Shortly before founding the Théâtre Alfred Jarry, Artaud had severed his connection with the surrealists. André Breton, the leader of that movement, retaliated by instigating riots at the two performances of A Dream Play. *After the second disturbance, Robert Aron, Artaud's colleague, sent the following letter to the press.]*

The Théâtre Alfred Jarry and the Surrealists

On Thursday, June 7, 1928, the surrealists, invoking reasons, some of which were defensible, others not, but all of which, compared to the spiritual importance of the Théâtre Alfred Jarry, had only an anecdotal value, forbade the Théâtre Alfred Jarry to present the second performance of Strindberg's *Dream Play*, which was to take place on the matinée of Saturday, June 9, at the Théâtre de l'Avenue. Whatever the reasons they gave, the surrealists had no right to formulate such a prohibition. The Théâtre Alfred Jarry, created alongside them and in spite of them, did not have to take any orders from them, notwithstanding the spiritual affinities that might have existed between them and it.

Antonin Artaud and I decided, therefore, to ignore this prohibition. Having explored in turn the various means of resistance that are available to two isolated individuals against thirty troublemakers, and having concluded that none of them was of any use, we sent a special delivery letter to André Breton on the evening of June 8 to warn him that we would not yield to his threats and that, in order to prevent him from entering the theatre we would employ, whatever it might cost us, all means, "even those that were most repugnant to us."

This circumlocution reappeared in a leaflet we distributed on Saturday, June 9, at the entrance to the theatre, and which was worded thus:

After the incidents that took place last Saturday during the performance of *A Dream Play*, and forced by new threats to defend its freedom of action at all costs, the Théâtre Alfred Jarry, accepting no restraints, declares itself determined to employ all means, even those most repugnant to it, to safeguard its liberty.
The possible troublemakers have been warned.

Antonin Artaud–Robert Aron, June 9, 1928.

The issue was thus clearly and frankly stated: we felt as cruelly as anyone, what a contradiction lies in even the limited help of the police for a theatre of which we wanted to make an enterprise in a revolutionary spirit. But the destructive will of our opponents forced us into this dilemma: either to yield to the surrealists' orders and renounce our freedom of action, or, despite our repugnance, to resist by the only effective means, the police.[1]

In order to point out what is inadmissible in the attitude of the surrealists, it is necessary to recall that in the first year of its existence, the Théâtre Alfred Jarry provided, on its own initiative, the only courageous and dangerous displays of surrealist spirit to have taken place in at least two years. The performance of *Le Partage du Midi* [a play by Paul Claudel] on January 14, 1928, without the author's permission, followed by Antonin Artaud's statement denouncing Paul Claudel's treason, as well as the public declaration of revolt made on June 2, 1928 by Antonin Artaud in the course of the first performance of *A Dream Play,* meant the serious risk of legal punishment that no surrealist demonstration had faced for a long time.

With that they ceased being surrealist demonstrations, to tell the truth, and became almost revolutionary demonstrations—the two words having long ago become unreconcilable.

That there had formerly been among the surrealists a certain revolutionary spirit, or sentimentality, cannot be denied. And certain passages in their proclamation of January 27, 1925,[2] promised action, in comparison to which a few disorders without consequences and without risks in theatres or at literary banquets appear to be ridiculous.

Not willing to run any real danger and incapable of being effective, thus lacking the two properly revolutionary qualities, the surrealists remaining, willy-nilly, on the literary or artistic battlefield, incur no other risk than that—wished for as the consecration of their puerile activity—of a brief sojourn at the police station.

To put an end to this dictatorship of nothingness, whose ridiculous activity compromises the very ideas it pretends to defend, all means have seemed to me provisionally good, even those which are the most repugnant to me. That is why, having no other practical way of resisting an empty authority, without concealing from myself the baseness of the requested help, and having decided not to forgive André Breton for reducing me to the most compromising equivocation, I had the courage—greater than that of thirty people invading a theatre—to call the police, whatever it might cost me, whatever misunderstanding it might expose me to, whatever disgust with myself I might have to live with.

Written in my own name and involving no one but myself.

Robert Aron
June 10, 1928.

[1] It should be noted that the only help requested by us of the police was that they forbid the demonstrators to enter the theatre. All the police activity in the theatre and in the street had been called for by others without our knowledge and *before our request.*

[2] "We hurl at Society this solemn warning. Let it pay attention to its mistakes, to every error of its spirit, we will not miss it. At every turn of its thought, Society will find us there. We are the specialists of rebellion. There is no type of action we would not be capable of using if necessary."

An Actor for Artaud

Interview with Raymond Rouleau

Raymond Rouleau, a French director of international repute, worked as a young man with Antonin Artaud and appeared as The Officer in Artaud's production of *A Dream Play.*

"Antonin Artaud was my friend and counsellor," said Rouleau. He was one of the founders of the Théâtre Alfred Jarry and originated the Theatre of Cruelty but he had no theatre of his own. We just traveled around and performed where we could. Most of us were then studying with Charles Dullin, a brilliant teacher, who rehearsed us unmercifully but seldom gave us a chance to perform. Artaud chose his actors from among these students and held his rehearsals very late at night since many of us also had jobs in various Paris theatres. It was a courageous enterprise— thirty nights of rehearsal in order to give one or two performances.

For his production of *A Dream Play,* Artaud used Strindberg's text, with the omission of several scenes and with great freedom of interpretation. Rouleau recalled Artaud's method: "He did not prepare his productions in any precise way; he did not have that mania for planning that makes our theatre so anemic today. His direction was a kind of introspection; he seemed to listen attentively to the promptings of his subconscious. At the first rehearsal, Artaud rolled around on the stage, assumed a falsetto voice, contorted himself, howled, and fought against logic, order, and the "well-made" approach. He forbade anyone to pay too close attention to the "story" at the expense of its spiritual significance. He sought desperately to translate the "truth" of the text, and not the words. It was only after he felt that he had found the truth, which his interior voyage had disclosed to him, that he fixed it meticulously, often with amazing profundity."

As a confirmed antinaturalist, Artaud tried to arouse and develop the individual emotions of the actor. He managed to do this perfectly with mimed demonstrations. He wanted the actor to alter his personality and to break the identity of the character, in short, to find a new approach to each role. He made suggestions to his actors but never imposed movements or line readings upon them. "I remember to this day," said Rouleau, "how in my role as The Officer my emotional states—my anguish, my tenderness, my ardor—grew out of Artaud's hints and impelled me toward the dénouement."

Although Artaud worked for movement and speech that was anarchistic and unusual, he used period costumes and furniture, and normal lighting in his productions. Because of his limited funds, the scenery was extremely simple, the stage practically bare. "But the productions must have seemed very strange to the audiences;" said Rouleau, "here's an example of the sort of performance Artaud called for: The actor might begin a speech while standing up, but as he continued to speak he would fall to his knees, then lie down on the stage, and finally finish the speech on his knees. The audience thought the actors were ridiculing them."

Concerning his performance in *A Dream Play,* Rouleau recalled that it had been very taxing mainly because of the many quick changes of make-up required; he played The Officer both in youth and in old age and went

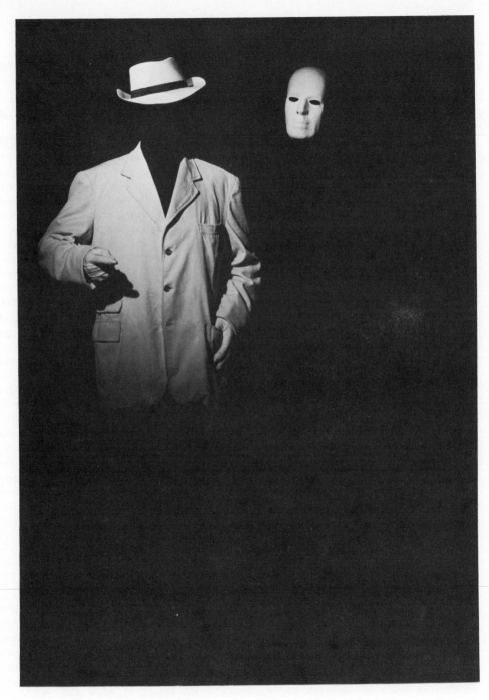

Les Baladins, French dancers and mimes, in 1967 performed a playlet concerning the transportation of a packet of LSD from Paris to New York, in which, by the use of "black light," they were able to carry out Artaud's visual conception. Courtesy Les Baladins.

back and forth between the two. The work proceeded along improvisational lines, with Artaud providing little specific help but enormous inspiration for the actors. He managed somehow to draw the actor out of himself, which gave a sense of greater breadth and depth to the performance. The company worked in utter exhaustion but complete exhilaration, and when Artaud did occasionally offer a direct suggestion to an actor, it was accepted almost with ecstasy. Rouleau explained that there had been a sort of "mystical brotherhood" among the members of the company. The actors were aware of Artaud's intellectual gifts but knew that some of his most startling effects were the result of emotional excitement induced by the use of drugs. Drugs were also at the root of Artaud's grotesque visions, of which he had drawings and photographs made to illustrate the violent spirit of the plays of his Theatre of Cruelty. These scenes—reproduced in his collected works—suggest the Grand Guignol; they were not presented on the stage but are meant to indicate what Artaud was trying for. Despite the hard work, the poor pay, and the scant publicity, the young actors in the company were completely convinced of the rightness of what Artaud was doing. The only explanation that Rouleau can offer today for that whole-hearted dedication was that Artaud "had a magnetic personality that com-pelled the actors to accept his concept of theatre." Rouleau added, however, that after working with Dullin for twelve hours a day, the actors desperately needed the complete release Artaud gave them.

Artaud's total lack of restraint was partially responsible for the riots that broke out in the theatre at both performances of *A Dream Play*. Artaud had managed to get the Swedish ambassador in Paris to make a modest contribution to the production of Strindberg's play. At the first performance Robert Desnos stood up and shouted at Artaud, "You have sold yourself to the Swedish people. You are a traitor." Artaud, replying from the stage in a characteristic and surrealistic way, shouted back, *"J'emmerde la Suéde et les Suédois."* Whereupon the Swedish ambassador and the other Swedish members of the audience rose and left the theatre. When Artaud made the same remark about France and the French, Desnos urged his countrymen to leave, but only one or two people responded, and the play continued. It was believed that the trouble had been started by the surrealists, who considered Artaud a traitor for having withdrawn from that group. At the next performance the following week, the surrealists initiated a full-fledged riot.

Concerning the manner in which Artaud attempted to "energize" his actors, Rouleau said, "I have seen nothing since then to equal or approach his method, except perhaps the one that Tania Balachova, who was one of his disciples, uses in her dramatic art courses. I myself have been conscious of the influence of Artaud on my work as an actor, director, and teacher."

Rouleau recalled that at the Community Theatre in the Rue Mouffetard, which he established in 1965, and in which he has experimented with some of Artaud's principles, two students recently produced separate versions of *A Dream Play;* the first, in conventional style, Rouleau considered unsatis-factory and canceled; the second production of the play was done by a highly inventive and talented Israeli student, Ram Goffer, in a strong balletic style. About ten percent of the dialogue was cut, and a great deal of music was added. What impressed Rouleau most about Goffer's production was the use the young director had made of gestures, movements, and vocal expressions that were unmistakably reminiscent of Artaud. In place of music, however, Artaud always called for sound effects and noises that were "unbearably piercing."

Raymond Rouleau believes that Artaud's influence may be seen not only in the work of today's performing artists and directors but also in the ideas and practices of our critics and playwrights.

An Actress for Artaud

Interview with Tania Balachova

In Antonin Artaud's production of *A Dream Play,* Tania Balachova, French actress and drama coach, played the role of Indra's Daughter. Mme. Balachova recalled that the production was a hectic experience from the very beginning. All the members of the company were engaged in other activities, so that the rehearsals were catch-as-catch-can. But the actors were devoted to Artaud, who had the amazing ability of stimulating their imaginations and fantasies for their utilization in the service of the play. Artaud denied the actor all customary, automatic, and technical devices. Every character, every line had to be approached in a fresh way. A new *tone* was demanded—not conventional poetry, not everyday naturalistic speech—no *alienation* and no systems, but an extraordinarily free fantasizing, like a dream. Strangely enough, despite the fact that Artaud had quarreled with the surrealists and had separated himself from them, he was using a surrealistic approach, based on magic, dreams, and cultism. "We did not know it then," said Mme. Balachova, "but Artaud was actually the precursor of our avant-garde theatre."

Among Artaud's many apparent eccentricities were a number of genuine innovations. For instance, in 1928 all professional French actors used a great deal of ocher in their make-up, but for his productions Artaud insisted upon the use of the ivory tints that were to come into use at a later date. At that time, too, it was rare for actors to wear period costumes except for historical plays, but Artaud wanted all costumes to be exactly right for the specific moment indicated in the script.

Mme. Balachova said: "The costumes for *A Dream Play* were beautiful; they had been lent to us by a woman in high society and had come from her own wardrobe. It was very much like the practice of Molière and of the Elizabethans. The men's clothes were provided by a theatrical costumer, but each suit had something unusual or strange about it. The décor was starkly simplified; it was practically a bare stage. Yet it was all very real without being naturalistic. Objects were placed in very strange places; it was pop-art in embryo. But this 'pop-art' did not give the impression of a music-hall act; Artaud made it poetic. The lighting was not extreme, and there were no histrionics or declamation.

"The actors who worked with Artaud believed implicitly in what he was doing; some felt that his was not the only way to proceed; but all of us looked upon it as an 'adventure.' Appearing in the Artaud productions helped the actors, many of them for the first time, to call on their subconscious. Of course, the actor always calls on his subconscious without knowing it, but with Artaud it became a conscious process. He had been under the care of a psychiatrist, Dr. Allendy, and knew about Freud's theories, but he did not use a formal psychological approach. In fact, he scorned such an approach. He considered the theatre ritualistic, poetic, moral, and metaphysical. Artaud was also acquainted with Stanislavsky's method, but his own "system" differed radically from Stanislavsky's.

At this point Mme. Balachova commented, *"Stanislavsky fait appel à la vérité du jour; Artaud fait appel à la vérité de la nuit"* (Stanislavsky called upon the truth of daytime; Artaud called upon the truth of night). Artaud then is clearly closer to Freud than to Stanislavsky. One of his strongest influences was Alfred Jarry, the early absurdist playwright, for whom he named his "theatre."

The actress spoke of the fracas that marked Artaud's first performance of *A Dream Play*. Before the play began, Artaud stepped before the curtain to address the audience. Someone stood up and accused Artaud of being a traitor to France for accepting money from the Swedish ambassador. Artaud made an obscene remark, and the Swedes left; he added in his impulsive way that he felt the same way about the French. Then the man in the audience shouted, "Let all good Frenchmen follow me." Apparently very few did, but interruptions and disturbances continued throughout the play, and these were blamed on the surrealists.

"Because of the intensity with which I worked under Artaud's direction," Mme. Balachova said laughingly, "I missed half of the fun of the riot that took place in the theatre the following week. I was facing upstage, deeply engrossed in the speech I was delivering and completely lost in my part, when I became aware that much more of a commotion was going on about me than usual. I heard shouts and screams and people running. When I turned around I saw that all the technicians—the stage hands and the three electricians—and all the members of the company were down at the footlights looking out into the house. I joined them and peered out into the dark auditorium. Halfway back on the left side, two people were cowering down behind the row of seats as if afraid for their lives, while on the right side of the house most of the members of the audience were involved in a violent fist fight. André Breton, who had probably instigated the riot, was in the midst of the fray. At the moment the riot had broken out, apparently, a photographer who was in the theatre took a picture of the stage from the back of the house; for the photograph shows the people in the first rows standing up and looking back into the theatre, the front of the stage crowded with the technicians and actors, all except me. There I am with my back to the audience, still acting."

At the time they were working with Artaud, no one, including Mme. Balachova, thought that he would become such a significant figure in the modern theatre. "Of course," she said, "we were all aware of his great creativity and its enormous value in helping us to perform, but we thought that his influence would be limited to our generation of actors. Now I realize that Artaud, who had the sensitivity of a poet, became aware long before most other people that there is a deep strain of malice and violence in our society. And I suppose that's the reason why there has been such universal acceptance of Artaud's Theatre of Cruelty."

Notes from Director to Designer

Correspondence of Olof Molander

[Excerpts from the letters of director Olof Molander in Stockholm to designer Arne Walentin in Oslo regarding the scenery for *A Dream Play*.]

October 29, 1964

Dear Arne Walentin!

Thanks for the ground plans. . . . They are excellent, though I can't understand how you will manage the scene-changes in full view of the audience. It seems to me, for example, that the small stage-opening of the [Norwegian] theatre would make it necessary to place the walls in Scenes 2 and 3 of Act I as I marked them in red on Plate I, in order not to obstruct the projected image, which is very important. After the Daughter and the Glazier finish their dialogue, and while they are walking upstage, the walls for Scenes 2 and 3 may be pushed into their correct positions. But the wall with the clover-leaf door has to be moved in far enough so that the entire door will be visible to everyone in the theatre.

[*Molander makes specific comments of the above sort for each scene in the play, and then remarks:*]

Well, this has been the traditional solution [of the problem of scenery for *A Dream Play*] up to now, and though I am by no means criticizing such a solution, what I am asking you is—Couldn't we make one composition out of all the sets, with a platform serving as mid-axis, around which chairs, tables, doors, wardrobe, etc. are placed? We would only have to give the revolving-stage a slight turn in order to get a new view. But all the furnishings would remain on the stage all the time! The objection might be made that in such a case the backs [of walls and furniture] would show. So what?

The projected images constitute a sustained backdrop, "the description of the atmosphere in the atmosphere," so to speak. But what we place on the stage can be more ephemeral. Couldn't we, for instance, remove the wall in Scene 2 and use only a *grating*? And also take away the wall around the clover-leaf door and fasten the frame to the side of the door? And eliminate the entire wall in the theatre-corridor behind the Doorkeeper's chair? Also skip the bookcase in the Lawyer's home and just have the window with curtain-rods and curtains and lattice-work only suggested, but no wall for the window? Is it necessary to have the balustrade in the Church? The furnace and the gymnastic equipment cannot be left out, of course, as the actors use them in the same way that they use the furniture. But the dance-pavilion could be simplified by merely suggesting it, while the piano, which is the important thing, remains, etc. etc.

It would be a good thing if you could, within reason, clear away everything that is superfluous. (When the Officer goes out to telephone, he has to change clothes, of course, but at the same time he could be visible at the telephone beyond the Doorkeeper's table and chair—if we use a stand-in in similar costume!!!) You would make theatre history if you could arrive at a solution along these lines: I mean, keeping the basic set-up of furniture, windows, doors, etc., but doing away with unnecessary walls.

Indra's Daughter (Tora Teje) and The Poet (Ivar Kage) wearing a Strindberg portrait-mask in Olof Molander's celebrated production at the Royal Dramatic Theatre, Stockholm, 1935. Theatre Collection, New York Public Library.

Perhaps we have to create a neutral zone in the center, for one purpose or another, framed by black screens. But I don't think even that would be necessary.

As an experiment, make a large production blueprint and send it to me as soon as possible. If you can, send back at the same time the copies of the small production blueprints that I am returning now with notes.

November 2, 1964

Thanks for the letter and production blueprints. I think you have succeeded excellently . . .

Now only a few comments, some of which may be due to my inability to penetrate your intentions completely.

Scene 1. In this set (the Castle), which is, figuratively speaking, outside this world, this life, we must try to have the stage as uncluttered as possible; that is, there must not be the slightest glimpse of the Officer's table, chair or wall, nor of the clover-leaf door and the billboard, nor of the table and chair at the right for the Mother. It makes no difference if in the following scenes all sorts of worldly objects are visible, for inside the castle we are, of course, in life on earth, but in the first scene [we should see] only gigantic hollyhock bushes, the castle with its golden dome, and the piles of hay covering the horse-droppings, the manure. Perhaps we should have at the front of the stage a scrim that one can see through, with hollyhocks painted on it. If we place the two performers a good way upstage, would we be able to light them somehow without having to use front lighting? Perhaps we could make the hollyhock-scrim so dense towards the sides that we could conceal the furniture for Scenes 2 and 3 behind it, at the left and right, and only have to push in the wall on the left and the clover-leaf door on the right. We probably could try this on a model stage to see if it would work. What do you think? The platform, covered in black, can of course be there in Scene 1 in the same position as in the following scenes!!! . . .

The final scene. This too should be relieved of "things temporal," that is, be just as uncluttered as Scene 1, but naturally one can envision flowers —not arranged in orderly fashion, though—to hide the gymnastic equipment and the furnace! My dear Walentin, please try to get rid of them sooner. I realize that the gymnastic equipment takes up space, but the third dimension of the furnace can probably be tampered with a good deal. Perhaps we could show the patients using the equipment in a projection or in a photograph enlarged beyond normal scale, and in that way make all the physical culture equipment easily moveable and *dreamlike in its frightfulness!* The whole thing would simply amount to a screen.

Concerning the dance-pavilion in Fairhaven, why not make a façade in Swiss-villa style adorned with leaves and with paper garlands and Chinese lanterns, a gingerbread-architecture; you know the type that was so much in style during the 90s. The whole archipelago, outside Stockholm, was full of houses in this awful style. The piano is created only in low relief, a prop that can be brought in easily on wheels. The stool could be a so-called folding-chair that Edith herself would bring in. It is wild but fine!!!! . . .

The clover-leaf door should appear in as many scenes as possible, even in the two Fingal's Cave scenes. It should always remain in the same spot. But once it has been opened, in the last theatre-corridor scene, we could, during the uprising against the Daughter, get it out to the right if we wish. We merely change the light on it and on the contents of the frame. In the Church, we *could,* if we wanted to, gild the frame and perhaps add a sculptured cornice, but that is not necessary. . . .

The school desks: It is important, as perhaps I have written earlier, that the Officer just barely be able to sit at the school desk, which, of course, was really meant for a small boy. The desk should look *outgrown,* so to speak. On top of that, I am wondering if it wouldn't be well to have his desk placed somewhat away from those of the other boys', so that the Schoolmaster would be able to walk around the Officer's desk, and he would seem more *isolated.*

I don't think I can say anything more now before I have seen a model. . . .

In every way, this is a very great improvement in simplification. Congratulations and thanks!

November 4, 1964

Since mailing my last letter to you, in which I particularly pointed out that Scene 1 (The Growing Castle) has a set that differs completely from the others because it represents the world beyond human vision and the comprehension of the senses, I have been thinking a lot about it.

For my other productions of the play, the scenic artists—probably influenced by Strindberg's own sketch, which appears in the book about Strindberg by Falck—have always imagined the hollyhock bushes planted in neat rows in front of the Castle, as if it were situated in a botanical garden. But that doesn't communicate the essence of the play, even if Strindberg himself pictured the gigantic hollyhocks that way.

The castle, which continues to grow, symbolizes existence, and blooms in the middle of a jungle paradise, with emphasis on the *jungle*. It should give the impression of an orgy of colors and a network of undergrowth that indicates a moist and fertile soil. It is in that sort of atmosphere that a castle can turn into a flower or a flower look like a castle, with a wing [sprouting] on the sunny side, and so on. Wouldn't you say that there is sound reasoning in this?

On the other hand, Scenes 2 to 13, which take place *on the earth,* are as naturalistic or realistic as possible; all the details that you consider suitable to include have three dimensions and are in colors corresponding to those of reality. But the forest and castle should have four dimensions (or at least three!!!), and tints and shades that simply don't exist in the color range used in Scenes 2 to 13, so that it will be quite clear that one is getting a glimpse of something that is not on this earth.

It would be easy enough to paint the forest on a projection slide and a theatrical gauze curtain so that it is not completely representational, but modernistic, in style. (But above all it is the *color* that is most important in the first set.) The Glazier is not able to see the castle until the Daughter points it out, as when an old person stands in front of a modern painting and asks comically, "What is it supposed to be?" It is not supposed to be anything, but it stimulates the imagination of the viewer and helps to create something that has meaning for him, isn't that right? Have you seen any of Strindberg's own pictures? He himself painted that way.

I know that you are not yet ready to work on the sketches for the projections, but I bring this up now because one forgets earlier ideas when one gets into the rehearsal routine.

What would you think of using projections of actual photographs as backgrounds for Scenes 2 to 13, but not for [the growing castle and] the fire in the castle? That, perhaps, is something to consider, in order to separate those two scenes from the others.

P. S. Do you think it would be a good idea if I arrived a day before the rehearsals start so that we can go over the running order of the play on a model? I won't have time to write up my production-book before then, but of course I can "improvise" à la Mowinckel[1] if I am only slightly briefed on the new ideas and requirements. . . .

November 9, 1964

How are you doing with our (and Strindberg's) *Dream Play?* Since I haven't heard from you, I assume that everything is going well and you don't need me. But it would be a good thing for me to familiarize myself with your solutions to the scenic problems before rehearsals start, so that I will know where to place the actors. I suppose the scheme will be very much as we have worked it out, but the completely open stage will require an entirely different arrangement of entrances and exists. And then there is the question of where the Officer will make his very quick changes of costumes and wigs. He will have to do this as close as possible to his place of entrance, don't you think? Perhaps we ought to provide a small dressing-room for him—about 6 × 9, backstage center—where a dresser and makeup man can help him.

[1] Agnes Mowinckel, temperamental Norwegian actress and director, died 1963.

I believe we will have to devote Monday the 23rd to going over the technicalities. . . . According to the Agreement, the rehearsals should begin on November 23, but I don't suppose there is anything to prevent such an arrangement. Will you please check this with Skagestad [Tormod Skagestad, Director of the Norwegian Theatre]? . . .

November 17, 1964

Thanks for the letter! Everything sounds excellent and it will be interesting to work it out on the model on Monday. . . .

See you in Oslo!

Yours sincerely,
Olof Molander

[After two months of rehearsal, *A Dream Play* opened at the Norwegian Theatre, Oslo, on January 22, 1965.]

Designing *A Dream Play*

Interview with Arne Walentin

Arne Walentin, the Norwegian designer, provided the costumes and scenery for Olof Molander's final production of *A Dream Play,* which had its première at the Norwegian Theatre (*Det Norske Teatret*) in Oslo, in January, 1965. Preparations for the production started in October, 1964, when Walentin went to Stockholm to confer with the director. Because there was so little time for preparation, Molander decided that he would do the play in one of the many ways he had done it before. The two men agreed, however, that the basic silhouettes for both costume and scenery would suggest the period in which the play was written—about 1900.

Walentin went back to Oslo and began to think about some of the details Molander had mentioned concerning the writing of the play. Strindberg had been living on Karlavägen and, while working at his desk, could see from his window the recently built army barracks and stables. Walentin studied pictures of these buildings, which suggested certain architectural shapes. Molander had also said that Strindberg was reading in Indian philosophy and religion at the time and that Oriental ideas had permeated the play—in the concept of Indra's Daughter, for instance. Molander had thought that it would be good if an Eastern atmosphere could be recreated in the design. Walentin looked at pictures of ancient Indian temples; they had a sort of vegetable form and seemed to be growing out of the ground. By merging the shapes of army barracks and Indian temples, Walentin was able to create a castle suitable for a dream. He sent his drawings and plans to Molander, who was delighted with them and was inspired to approach the play in a new way, with "the reality of the dream-world."

Walentin knew that most of Molander's former productions of the play had been done on very large stages, which were highly mechanized. Although it had a revolve and cyclorama, the stage at the Norwegian

Scenery by Arne Walentin for Olof Molander's last production of *A Dream Play,* 1965. Some elements were permanent and remained throughout the play (the bulletin board and the door with the clover-leaf pattern); various elements appeared in some scenes and not in others (the street lamp, the gate, the table and chair); still other elements took various forms (the tree became a clothes-tree and then a candelabrum.) The foliage was projected. The shifts were as rapid as in a dream. Photograph: Sturlason. Courtesy Arne Walentin.

Theatre was not large. Its limited space would, in fact, pose many problems, as the plan was to do the play without interruption, one scene fading into another as in a dream, and the changes taking place without the audience's being aware of them. To accomplish this, Walentin put two platforms on the stage at right angles to each other, one platform two steps above the other. Beside the platform, stage left, was a wardrobe and the door with the clover-leaf design. These were set pieces that remained throughout the play but could be altered easily; on the door, for example, was hung a picture, then a billboard, then a blackboard, and so on. On one of the platforms was a fence of iron railings, which served various purposes; and the changing backgrounds were projected onto the cyclorama.

For this production Molander eliminated the Prologue spoken by Indra's Daughter, because, he explained, it was written a number of years after the play in order to give Harriet Bosse, then Strindberg's wife, a big entrance and at the same time to clarify the situation for the audience. But since Freud, Molander felt that the audience required no special preparation for the use of the dream technique.

Walentin's scene-plot follows:

1. A projection on the cyclorama of the Growing Castle, surrounded by flowers as described in the text.

157

2. The Castle fades out, the stage revolves, and the scene with the Officer is ready stage right: a table and a few chairs.

3. Lights out. Scene with mother on stage left: candle on the table, etc.

4. Lights up on the cyclorama which shows the corridor of the Opera House. The Stage-hands who carry in the scenery for *Aida*, take off the table and chairs used in Scene 3. The street lamp and the tree, both in green, are swung around. The window for Victoria is dropped in from the flies; it has red curtains and a light behind them. The walls representing the backs of the buildings are dark, but the center panel is a bright green. During the scene the background changes imperceptibly from Spring to Autumn and from day to night. Then the blue monkshood flowers appear in a special projection; they fade and die, the bush turns brown, and collapses.

5. The Lawyer's Office. Behind the crowd of people, clients clamoring for legal services, the props are changed, and the projection on the cyclorama dissolves into a row of slum tenements. The tree becomes a clothes-rack.

6. The Church. Projection of a rose-window and organ pipes. The clothes-rack becomes a standard candelabra. The iron railing is rolled off and an organ console rolled on.

7. The Grotto. The Lawyer and the Daughter move down to the forestage and a dull black curtain is dropped in behind them. They play their short scene in front of the curtain.

8. During the preceding scene, the Lawyer's Home is set up behind the curtain. A wall is dropped in containing a window, a door, and a picture; on the cyclorama is seen another backyard slum. The props consist of a table, chairs, crib, iron stove with cabbage cooking on it, limp candles on the table, in short, everything Strindberg called for in the script.

An Intermission occurs at this point.

9. The scene is Foulstrand; there is a huge furnace with red and orange pipes. On a dock there is a sign that reads SKAMSUND (Foulstrand); a post with a life-preserver on it; and a little white boat with a light-blue sail and floral decorations. To the right of the furnace is an open-air pavilion containing gymnastic equipment; the men using it are fat and deformed. The colors are sickly pinks and greens. On the cyclorama is shown Fairhaven, on the other side of a body of water; in the distance it looks very beautiful and enticing. Houses, boats, and trees, Swedish banners and flags are all done in pale shades of green, blue, and white. As the scene comes to an end, the Daughter and the Officer move down to the forestage, the black curtain descends, and the scene changes behind the curtain.

10. Foulstrand and Fairhaven were set back to back, so that by a simple revolve Fairhaven was brought into view. Now Foulstrand is projected; it is seen in the distance and, done in greys, blues, blacks, and browns, looks cold and icy. The architecture at Fairhaven is that of the 1880s, the buildings are yellow with white trim and covered with snow. Banners and flags are dropped in from the flies; later, when the cannon is fired, a large signal flag is projected. At stage right is the schoolroom, the students who come in running and screaming bring

Though the permanent and semipermanent elements remain, the entire projected background now shows decaying tenement houses. Photograph: Sturlason. Courtesy Arne Walentin.

For the cathedral scene only the bulletin board on which the hymn numbers are written and the clover-leaf door remain intact. The table and chair had been removed and have been brought back; the tree is a candlestand. The organ console is a prop, while the pipes and rose-window are projections. Photograph: Sturlason. Courtesy Arne Walentin.

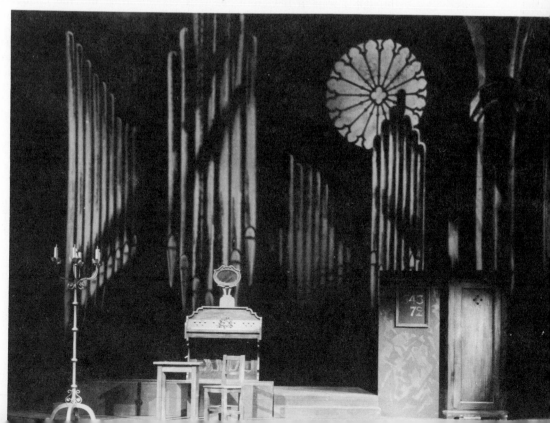

in their own benches. At stage left is the dance pavilion and in front of it the piano on which Edith plays. The end of the scene is acted on the forestage in front of the black curtain.

[The Mediterranean resort scene was omitted from this production by Dr. Molander. "He cut it," said Walentin, "because he felt that it was redundant, that it contained no new thoughts, and no really new dramatic situation. It would, furthermore, have violated the style of the production; our intention was to make the play completely 'Swedish' with innumerable details peculiar to Stockholm and its environs; the only exceptions were the Growing Castle and Fingal's Cave. But the Castle opened and closed the play and served as a frame for the dream, and the name Fingal sounds Swedish. The intention also was to simplify and unify the production. If the Mediteranean scene had been included, it would have created many technical difficulties and added new problems to an already complex design."]

11. Fingal's Cave. Stage right, a flight of steps and a platform. Stage left, a pile of jetsam—the baby's crib from Scene 8 now broken down, life preservers, a ship's figurehead, nameplates from old vessels, and various other things. A projection of the grotto, the interior of the cave in blue-green and black with ear-shaped reflections on the wall and ceiling; outside a light sky and a wild, running sea.

12. The corridor of the Opera House as in Scene 4. It is here that the clover-leaf door is opened—to disclose nothing.

13. A bare stage except for a platform on which is a blue door-frame that appears to be the entrance to the Growing Castle. The Castle is projected on the cyclorama and stands in the midst of the blue monkshood, the aconite, and other flowers which grow all around. The fire Strindberg called for was eliminated. Instead, the actors enter in procession, say their final lines, go through the door-frame, and exit through a trap in the platform, as if disappearing into the Castle. As this goes on, the Castle slowly turns a fiery red as though being consumed by flames, then the Castle disappears completely. The cyclorama is flame-colored but slowly fades down to a midnight blue and on it appears the sorrowful face of a woman; her image is repeated over and over, and covers the entire cyclorama. This is intended to represent suffering humanity the world over.

[At first, an effort was made to show the faces of people of all races and colors, but Molander and Walentin discarded the idea because it seemed to them that suffering was the same for all people and that one face could communicate it.]

The faces fade out to black and the play is over.

Molander arranged the musical score which was made up of selections from Bach, Chopin, and other composers, as called for by Strindberg. In The Officer's scene, for instance, the music used was Brahm's "Songs My Mother Taught Me."

After its presentation in Oslo, this production was done in Stockholm. Walentin felt highly gratified when one of the critics remarked that the scenery was "more Swedish than was ever done in Sweden."

Molander worked out new business and movement for this production, as well as new characterizations in depth. With the individual actor he developed the life story of each character, and every speech had to tell, or grow out of, that story. The aging of The Officer alone took hours of work during the six or seven weeks of rehearsal. Molander and the actor, Per Theodor Haugen, who played The Officer, went over and over each period of the character's life—how would he speak, gesture, sit, stand, move—as a young man, in middle age, when old? When Rut Tellefsen, who played The Daughter, was told that the Prologue was to be cut, she was very unhappy; later she realized that it would be better for the play, and a greater challenge to her as an actress to have to suggest the divinity of the earth-bound goddess.

Molander's imagination supplied the basis for the acting style, which emerged as a kind of "heightened realism." The actors took up the challenge and made a special effort to carry out his ideas. Molander's most brilliant conception for this production was his idea that people and situations in dreams seem larger than life and more intense, and so he devoted enormous attention to every detail of each scene in order to achieve a dreamlike vividness.

Indra's Daughter

Interview with Rut Tellefsen

Rut Tellefsen was a regular member of the company at the Norwegian Theatre in 1964 when Tormod Skagestad, its general director, who was casting for Molander, selected her for the role of Indra's Daughter. Miss Tellefsen did not meet Molander until the first reading of the play, when the entire cast gathered at the theatre to start work. The company read through the play slowly, discussing the characters and the situations as they proceeded.

This was to be Molander's final production of a play he had been working on for almost thirty years. He had thought deeply about the significance of every word that Strindberg had set down and was able to make enlightening remarks and suggestions about every aspect of the play. It took several days to read through the script; then the actors started work on the stage. There were seven or eight weeks of rehearsal.

Miss Tellefsen described in detail Molander's method with the actors. The stage floor was marked out according to Walentin's floor plan. The actors read the script before or after each scene, and Molander made comments about what was to be done or what had been done in the scene. Molander had great respect for the actors, and from his inexhaustible knowledge about the play, he "spoon-fed" them details bit by bit; the actors were eager to learn more and more of Molander's "secrets." With Molander's inspiration the actor was given every opportunity to use his talents to his fullest capacity: he was given several chances to work out an interpretation

The Officer (Per Theodor Haugen) holds a bunch of roses for Victoria and sings out her name. Indra's Daughter (Rut Tellefsen) is seated and The Gatekeeper stands behind her. Molander production Norway and Sweden, 1965. Photograph: Sturlason. Courtesy Arne Walentin.

for himself; if he failed, Molander turned "dictator" and gave specific directions.

But it was part of Molander's genius that he was seldom arbitrary; none of his insights or directions was hard and fast. He would set a scene one way and later change it completely if he got a better idea. Or he would very consciously make changes just to keep the actors on their toes; he did not want them to feel that there was a definite and final blueprint they had to follow. The scene between The Lawyer and The Daughter is a case in point. The character of Agnes was never referred to as anything but The Daughter (meaning Indra's Daughter), because she remained a goddess in all her guises.

Miss Tellefsen recalled that her scene with The Lawyer proved especially difficult: "We could not find the 'melody.' Molander suggested that we play it as if The Lawyer were merely pretending to be hateful in order to demonstrate to The Daughter how evil the world is. When we tried the scene that way it proved completely false and Molander objected. We had to alter it so that there was a balance between 'acting' and acting 'reality.' It was such subtle nuances as these that gave the production its distinction."

While molding the play, Molander kept working on the players, stirring up their imaginations and enthusiasm. He did this by "association." "He had all kinds of stories—funny stories and horrifying stories—that he kept telling us all the time, before, during, and after rehearsals, in order to put us in the proper mood. The stories were exactly right for the mood of the scene being played. Molander was very precise about every detail of the production. Among the sound effects, for example, a foghorn was called for. The stage manager brought in a real foghorn and used it at the appropriate moment; Molander objected, 'It may be real, but it is not Strindberg's foghorn.' The stage manager kept bringing in horns but none proved satisfactory; finally Molander produced the sound he wanted with his voice—it was unreal but dramatic. It could only be reproduced, it turned out, with a bell that was rung wildly like a danger signal on a ship."

In Molander's production Indra's Daughter made her first entrance with her "father," The Glass Cutter. She noticed that the Castle had grown (being divine she was the first to be aware of it); The Glass Cutter, a mortal, was puzzled but agreed. These figures were presented in a dreamlike way. The Daughter asks her father, "Why do flowers grow up out of dirt?" He replies, "They don't like the dirt, so they push up into the light as fast as they can—to bloom and die." Here Molander commented, "But they need the dirt for their growth," and pointed out that these were key lines for the meaning of the play. After The Daughter and The Glass Cutter entered the Castle, they were considered to be in life-on-earth and their speech and movements ceased to be dreamlike and became realistic.

This was the first time that Molander had done the play without the Prologue. He found it more interesting and challenging to suggest The Daughter's divinity scene by scene than to state it clearly in advance; he felt that her scenes would be more mysterious and provocative and that greater ingenuity and experimentation would be required to make them so. At those moments when Molander did not like what was being done on the stage, he would call out, "Now the public is falling asleep!"

As the play progressed, The Daughter became more and more depressed by the conditions of life on earth until, at the end, she was delighted to return to her home in heaven. Rut Tellefsen had seen an earlier Molander production of *A Dream Play,* at the Royal Dramatic Theatre in Stockholm, and remembered that The Daughter had become more human and trivial as her involvement in earthly affairs deepened until she finally had lost all of her divinity. But for the present production Molander and Miss Tellefsen wanted The Daughter to retain some of her divinity to the very end; starting with a bright heavenly aura, which would fade gradually as her contacts with reality increased, there would still be a faint glimmer of it at her departure.

In the scene in which The Lawyer complains of The Daughter's poor housekeeping, they quarrel, and she says, "I'm beginning to hate you after all this." Miss Tellefsen uttered the line as a mortal would, with deep hostility, but Molander explained that she must say it with wonder at the fact that even a goddess could be reduced to hatred on this planet. The Daughter is prepared to leave The Lawyer, but he reminds her of their child; suddenly remembering that she is a mother, she clutches at the crib and cries out, "That's true—for the child's sake! Yes, yes, we must go on!" But it is as if she were saying, "I'm trapped!" There is a note of horror in her voice at the realization of her human predicament. At that point Miss Tellefsen raised an objection. She reminded Molander that The Daughter is not really trapped, since she does leave her husband and child. When she next meets The Lawyer, two scenes farther on, he asks her to come home, but she refuses. Molander's comment was, "But it's a dream!" Miss Tellefsen realized then that it could not be approached as if it were a conventional play; here each scene made its own psychological point and had its own "build."

The Officer (Per Theodor Haugen) stands beside Indra's Daughter (Rut Tellefsen). The Lawyer kneels and begs her to return home while The Quarantine Master, with arms folded, is amused. It is the Foulstrand scene with furnace and pipes visible in the background. Photograph: Sturlason. Courtesy Arne Walentin.

When The Daughter and The Poet met each other, they immediately felt a close affinity; each recognized at once the other's divinity, and The Daughter seemed to know much more about The Poet than he knew about himself. The relationship grew stronger and more meaningful as the play went on.

"Ingmar Bergman told the actors in Oslo the following story," said Miss Tellefsen. "When Molander was a young man, he saw Max Reinhardt's production of *A Dream Play*. Reinhardt had The Officer sing out the name 'Vic-to-ri-a' to a particular melody, which Molander remembered and has used in every production of this play he has done. From version to version, Molander has changed everything else but that melody!"

In the scene in which Edith plays Bach on the piano, Molander arranged the action so that he could build to a tableau that was an exact reproduction of a famous painting by Edvard Munch: As Edith played, dancing couples appeared to come "crawling" out through the doorway of the pavilion, then the dancers "froze" with their mouths open, and the picture formed, to the audience's amazement. One of Molander's great contributions to this play was his ability to make it surge with life and excitement.

After the play opened, Molander remarked to Miss Tellefsen that this production "hung together about seventy-five percent of the time," and the actress admitted that that was the way she felt about her characterization of The Daughter. But in a radio interview granted shortly before his death in 1966, Molander said that he considered this production better than any other he had done of the play.

The Lawyer (Allan Edwall) tormenting Indra's Daughter (Malin Ek) says, "I'll smile so hard my back teeth will show." Ingmar Bergman's 1970 production of *A Dream Play*. Photograph: Beata Bergström. Courtesy Ingmar Bergman.

An earlier scene from Bergman's 1970 production with Indra's Daughter and The Lawyer (in the shawl of misery). Photograph: Beata Bergström. Courtesy Ingmar Bergman.

A Dream Play

AUGUST STRINDBERG
English Version by Randolph Goodman

Copyright © 1969 by Randolph Goodman

Characters[1]

The God Indra (A Voice)
Indra's Daughter
The Glazier
The Officer
The Father
The Mother
Lina
The Gatekeeper
The Billposter
The Ballet Girl
The Chorus Girl
The Prompter
The Policeman
The Lawyer
The Chancellor
The Dean of Theology
The Dean of Philosophy
The Dean of Medicine
The Dean of Law
Kristin
The Quarantine Master
The Dandy (Don Juan)
The Coquette
The Friend
The Poet
He
She
The Pensioner
Ugly Edith
Edith's Mother
The Naval Officer
The Schoolmaster
Nils
The Husband
The Wife
The Blind Man

The First Coalheaver
The Second Coalheaver
The Gentleman
The Lady
Victoria
Members of the Opera Company, Clerks, Graduates, Maids, Schoolboys, Children, Ship's Crew, The Right-Minded, Voices.

A Reminder

In this dream play, as in his earlier dream play *To Damascus,* the author has attempted to recreate the disconnected but seemingly logical form of the dream. Anything can happen; everything is possible and probable. Time and space do not exist. On a slight foundation of reality, the imagination spins and weaves new patterns: a blending of memories, experiences, free fancies, absurdities, and improvisations.

The characters split, double, multiply, disappear, solidify, blur, and re-emerge. But one consciousness governs them all— that of the dreamer; for him there are no secrets, no incongruities, no scruples, no laws. He neither criticizes nor approves, he merely narrates. And since a dream is usually painful rather than pleasant, a note of sadness and of pity for all human beings runs through the wavering tale. Sleep, the liberator, is often terrifying, but when the pain is at its worst, the dreamer awakes and is reconciled with reality, which, however depressing it may be, nevertheless seems a joy in comparison to the tormenting dream.

A. S.

[1] Strindberg did not include a list of characters

Prologue

In the background there are banks of clouds, which resemble crumbling stone cliffs, with here and there the ruins of castles and fortresses.

The constellations Leo, Virgo, and Libra are visible in the sky, and in their midst the planet Jupiter shines brightly.

[**The Daughter of Indra**[1] *stands on the topmost cloud.]*

Indra's Voice: *[From above]*

    Where are you, Daughter, where?

Daughter:

    Here, Father, here.

The Voice:

    You've lost your way, my child—
      watch out, you're sinking . . .
    How did you get there?

Daughter:

    I followed a bolt of lightning from
      the ethereal heights
    and took a cloud for a carriage . . .
    But the cloud sank, and is still
      sinking . . .
    Tell me, great Father Indra, what
      region
    am I coming to? Why is the air so
      dense,
    so hard to breathe?

The Voice:

    You've passed beyond the second
      world and now you're in the third,
    you've left Cukra, the morning star,
    far behind you and are about to enter
    the foggy circle of the earth. There
      you'll see
    the sun in its seventh stage, called
      Libra;
    there the day-star is weighed in au-
      tumn's scales
    and day and night stand in even bal-
      ance.

Daughter:

    You spoke of the earth . . . Is that the
      dark

[1] Indra was the Hindu god of the heavens. Brahma was the god of creation. According to myth, Indra had no daughter.

    and heavy world the moon lights up?

The Voice:

    It is the heaviest and densest
    of all the spheres that wander in
      space.

Daughter:

    Tell me, don't the sun's rays ever
      reach it?

The Voice:

    Yes, the sun shines there—now and
      then . . .

Daughter:

    Now there's a rift in the clouds, and
      I can see below . . .

The Voice:

    What do you see, my child?

Daughter:

    I see . . . that it's beautiful . . . with
      green forests,
    blue water, white mountain peaks,
    and yellow fields . . .

The Voice:

    Yes, as beautiful as everything Brah-
      ma made . . .
    but it was even more beautiful
    in the dawn of time; then a strange
      thing happened—
    a shifting of the orbit, or something
      else—
    rebellion was followed by crime, that
      had to be put down . . .

Daughter:

    Now I hear sounds rising from be-
      low . . .
    What sort of beings live down there?

The Voice:

    Go down and see . . . I won't speak
      ill of the Creator's children,
    but what you hear is the language
      they speak.

Daughter:

    It sounds as if . . . it's not a happy
      sound.

The Voice:

    I agree with you! Their mother-
      tongue
    is called Complaint. Yes, those who
      live on earth
    are a discontented, thankless lot . . .

Daughter:

    Oh, don't say that. I hear cries of joy,

and the roll of thunder. I see flashes
of lightning.
Now bells are ringing, and fires blaze,
and thousands upon thousands of
voices
are singing praise and thanks to
heaven.
[Pause.]
Oh, Father, you judge them too
harshly!

The Voice:
Go down and see and hear . . . then
come back
and tell me if they have good reason
for their lamentations and complaints
. . .

Daughter:
Well, then, I'll go—but, Father, come
with me!

The Voice:
No. I can't breathe down there . . .

Daughter:
Now the cloud is sinking . . . how
sultry it's getting . . .
I'm choking! I'm not breathing air,
but smoke and steam . . .
It's so heavy it drags me down and
down,
and now I feel it rolling;
the third world surely is not one of
the best . . .

The Voice:
It's neither the best nor the worst;
it's called Dust, and it rolls like all
the rest,
so that sometimes the people there
grow dizzy,
and seem to be half foolish and half
mad.
Have courage, my child . . . this is
only a test.

Daughter:
[Kneels as the cloud descends.]
I'm sinking!

[The curtain rises on the Growing
Castle.]

The background represents a forest of
giant hollyhocks in bloom. They are white,
pink, crimson, sulphur-yellow, violet. Rising above them may be seen the gilded
dome of a castle, the apex of which is
shaped like a bud resembling a crown.
At the foot of the castle walls lie heaps
of straw and the sweepings from the
stable. The "wings," which remain un-
changed throughout the play, show stylized representations of interior décor,
architecture, and landscape.

[**The Glazier** and **The Daughter**
enter.]

Daughter: The castle keeps growing up
out of the earth . . . Do you see how
much it's grown since last year?

Glazier: [To himself.] I've never seen
this castle before . . . I've never
heard of a castle growing, but . . .
[To **The Daughter,** with conviction.]
Yes, it's grown six feet, but that's
because they've manured it . . . if
you look closely, you'll see it's put
out a wing on the sunny side.

Daughter: Shouldn't it be blooming soon,
now it's past the middle of the summer?

Glazier: Don't you see the flower up
there?

Daughter: Yes, I see it! [Claps her hands
joyfully.] Tell me, father, why do
flowers grow out of dirt?

Glazier: [Simply.] Because they're not
happy in the dirt, so they hurry up
into the light to bloom and die.

Daughter: Do you know who lives in
that castle?

Glazier: I used to know, but I can't remember.

Daughter: I think a prisoner is kept in
there . . . and he's surely waiting
for me to set him free.

Glazier: But at what price?

Daughter: You don't bargain when it's
your duty. Let's go into the castle!

Glazier: Yes, let's go.
[As they move upstage, the scene
changes.]

They are now in a plain, bare room,
which contains only a table and a few
chairs. **The Officer,** dressed in a very
unusual but modern uniform, sits in one
of the chairs; he tilts back and keeps
beating on the table with his sword.

Daughter: [Goes up to **The Officer** and gently takes the sword out of his hand.] Stop that! Stop it!

Officer: Oh, Agnes dear, let me keep the sword!

Daughter: No, you're ruining the table. [To **The Glazier.**] Now you go down to the harness room and put in the windowpane. We'll meet later.

[**The Glazier** goes out.]

Daughter: You're a prisoner in your own room. I've come to set you free.

Officer: I've certainly been waiting for that, but I didn't know if you'd want to.

Daughter: The castle is strong. It has seven walls, but—it can be done! Do you want to be set free, or don't you?

Officer: Frankly speaking, I don't know. Whatever I choose will mean suffering. Every joy in life has to be paid for with a double measure of sorrow. Living here is bad enough, but if I buy the joys of freedom I'll suffer threefold for it. Agnes, I'm willing to endure life as it is, if only I can see you!

Daughter: What do you see in me?

Officer: Beauty, which is the harmony of the universe. The lines of your body are nowhere to be found but in the orbits of the solar system, in strings that sing softly, in vibrations of light. You're a child of heaven . . .

Daughter: So are you!

Officer: Then why must I tend the horses, clean out the stables, and have the straw carted away?

Daughter: So that you'll long to get away from here.

Officer: Oh, how I long to, but it's so hard to pull yourself out.

Daughter: But it's your duty to seek freedom in the light.

Officer: Duty? Life has never done its duty by me!

Daughter: You feel you've been wronged by life?

Officer: Yes, it's been unjust . . .
[Now voices are heard from behind a partition, which a moment later is pulled aside. **The Officer** and **The Daughter** look in that direction and stop as if paralyzed in the midst of a gesture.]

At a table sits **The Mother,** looking very ill. In front of her burns a tallow candle, which she trims from time to time with a pair of snuffers. The table is piled with the shirts she has just made and which she is marking with a quill and ink. To the left stands a wardrobe, dark brown in color. **The Father** offers a silk shawl to **The Mother.**]

Father: [Gently.] Don't you want it?

Mother: A silk shawl for me, my dear? What's the use of that when I'm going to die soon.

Father: Do you believe what the doctor says?

Mother: Yes, I believe what he says, but even more what the voice in here says.

Father: [Sadly.] It's true then? And you think of your children first and last.

Mother: They've been my life . . . my reason for living . . . my joy and my sorrow . . .

Father: Kristina, forgive me . . . for everything!

Mother: What have I to forgive? Dearest, you forgive me! We've been tormenting each other. Why? We don't know! We couldn't do anything else. Anyway, here's the children's new linen. See that they change twice a week, Wednesdays and Sundays, and see that Louisa bathes them—their whole bodies . . . Are you going out?

Father: I have to be at a staff meeting at eleven o'clock.

Mother: Ask Alfred to come in before you go.

Father: [Pointing to **The Officer.**] But, dearest, he's standing right here.

Mother: Think of that, my eyes are failing, too . . . Yes, it's getting dark . . . [Trims the candle.] Come here, Alfred.

[**The Father** disappears through the wall, nodding goodbye as he

leaves. **The Officer** *goes over to*
The Mother.*]*

Mother: Who's that girl over there?

Officer: *[Whispers.]* That's Agnes.

Mother: *[Whispers.]* Oh, is that Agnes?
Do you know what they say? That
she's a daughter of the god Indra, and
she begged her father to let her come
down to earth to see how men really
live . . . But don't say anything!

Officer: She *is* a child of the gods!

Mother: *[Aloud.]* Alfred, my son, I'll
soon be leaving you and your
brothers and sisters . . . Let me tell
you one thing . . . and remember it
for life.

Officer: *[Sadly.]* Tell me, Mother.

Mother: Just this: Never quarrel with
God.

Officer: What do you mean, Mother?

Mother: Don't go around feeling that life
has wronged you.

Officer: But when I'm treated unjustly—

Mother: You're thinking of the time you
were punished unjustly for having
taken a penny that turned up later.

Officer: Yes! And that one injustice
changed the course of my whole
life . . .

Mother: That may be. But now go to
that wardrobe there—

Officer: *[Embarrassed.]* So you know
about that! That was—

Mother: The book—*Swiss Family Robin-
son*—that—

Officer: Don't say any more!

Mother: That your brother was punished
for—and that *you* tore up and hid!

Officer: Just think, that old wardrobe is
still standing there after twenty years
—We've moved so many times, and
my mother died ten years ago.

Mother: Yes, what of it? You're always
questioning everything, and spoil the
best years of your life that way!
Look, there's Lina!

Lina: *[Enters.]* Thanks very much, dear
lady, but I can't go to the christening.

Mother: Why not, my child?

Lina: I have nothing to wear.

Mother: You can borrow this shawl of
mine.

Lina: Oh, dear, no . . . that wouldn't be
right!

Mother: I don't understand you! I won't
ever be going to any more parties . . .

Officer: What will father say? After all,
it was a present from him . . .

Mother: What small minds!

Father: *[Puts his head in through the
wall.]* Are you going to lend my present to the servant girl?

Mother: Don't talk like that! Remember
I was a servant girl once myself! Why
should you hurt an innocent girl?

Father: Why should you hurt me, your
husband?

Mother: Oh, this life! If you do something nice, someone is sure to think
it nasty; if you're kind to one person,
another is hurt! Oh, this life!

    *[She snuffs out the candle and her
area of the stage goes dark. The
partition is pushed back to its
former position.]*

Daughter: Men are to be pitied.

Officer: You find that's so?

Daughter: Yes, life is hard, but love conquers all! Come and see.

    *[**The Daughter** moves upstage;
The Officer goes out.]*

The background changes and becomes an
old, dilapidated wall, in the center of
which is a gate closing a passageway.
This opens upon a green, sunlit plot of
ground where an enormous blue monkshood (aconite) is growing. To the left of
the gate sits **The Gatekeeper.** Her head
and shoulders are covered by a shawl,
and she is crocheting a bedspread with a
starlike pattern. To the right of the gate
is a billboard, which **The Billposter** is
cleaning. Beside him stand a fish-net with
a green handle [and a green fish-box].
Further to the right is a door that has an
air-hole shaped like a four-leaf clover. To
the left of the gate stands a small linden
tree with a coal-black trunk and a few

pale-green *leaves. Near it is a small air-hole leading into a cellar.*[2]

Daughter: *[Goes up to* **The Gatekeeper.***]* Isn't that star spread finished yet?

Gatekeeper: No, my little friend. Twenty-six years isn't long for such a piece of work.

Daughter: And your lover never came back?

Gatekeeper: No, but it wasn't his fault. He *had* to go away, poor thing! That was thirty years ago.

Daughter: *[To* **The Billposter.***]* She was with the ballet, wasn't she? Right here in the opera house?

Billposter: She was the leading dancer . . . but when *he* went away, it seems as if he took her dancing with him . . . so she didn't get any more parts.

Daughter: Nothing but complaints . . . in people's eyes and voices . . .

Billposter: I don't complain very much . . . not since I have my net and my green fish-box!

Daughter: And that makes you happy?

Billposter: Yes, very happy, very . . . I dreamed of them as a boy, and now it's come true. I'm more than fifty years old, of course . . .

Daughter: Fifty years for a fish-net and a fish-box . . .

Billposter: A green fish-box, a green one . . .

Daughter: *[To* **The Gatekeeper.***]* Let me have the shawl now, and I'll sit here and watch the children of mankind! But you must stand behind me and tell me about them.

[She takes the shawl and sits down in **The Gatekeeper's** *place.]*

Gatekeeper: This is the last day of the season, the opera house is closing. They'll find out today if they've been rehired for next year.

[2] Later stage directions indicate a door and a window behind the place occupied by **The Gatekeeper;** both lead into her room or lodge where there is a telephone.

Daughter: What about those they let go?

Gatekeeper: Oh, dear God, I can't bear to see it . . . I pull the shawl over my head, I . . .

Daughter: Poor human beings!

Gatekeeper: Look, here comes one of them! She wasn't chosen. You see how she's crying . . .

*[***The Singer*** *enters from the right; rushes through the gate with her handkerchief to her eyes; stops for a moment in the passageway beyond the gate, and leans her head against the wall; then runs out quickly.]*

Daughter: Men are to be pitied!

Gatekeeper: But look at this one. That's the way a happy human being looks!

*[***The Officer*** *enters through the passageway wearing a frock coat and high hat, and carrying a bunch of roses; he is radiantly happy.]*

Gatekeeper: He's going to marry Miss Victoria!

Officer: *[Far downstage; looks up and sings.]* Victoria!

Gatekeeper: The young lady will be down in a minute.

Officer: Good! The carriage is waiting, the table is set, the champagne is on ice . . . Let me hug you, ladies.

[He embraces **The Daughter** *and* **The Gatekeeper.** *He sings.]*

Victoria!

A Woman's Voice: *[From above, sings.]* I am here!

Officer: *[Paces up and down.]* Well, I'm waiting!

Daughter: Do you know me?

Officer: No, I know only one woman . . . Victoria! For seven years I've come here to wait for her . . . at noon, when the sun touches the chimneys, and in the evening, when darkness begins to fall. Look at the pavement here, and you'll see it's worn down by the steps of a faithful lover. Hooray, she's mine!

[Sings.]

Victoria!
[There is no reply.]
Well, she's dressing now, I suppose.
[To The Billposter.] There's the fish-net, I see. Everybody in the opera is crazy about fish-nets—or rather about fish—because the fishes are dumb and can't sing. What does a thing like that cost?
Billposter: It's very expensive.
Officer: *[Sings.]* Victoria!
[Shakes the linden tree.]
Look, now it's turning green again. For the eighth time.
[Sings.]
Victoria! Now she's combing her hair. *[To The Daughter.]* Listen now, Madam, let me go up and get my bride!
Gatekeeper: No one's allowed to go backstage.
Officer: For seven years I've been coming here. Seven times three hundred and sixty-five makes two thousand five hundred and fifty-five!
[Stops and pokes at the door with the clover-shaped hole.]
I've looked at that door two thousand five hundred and fifty-five times and still don't know where it leads to. And that clover-leaf that lets in the light! Lets in the light for whom? Is anyone in there? Does anyone live there?
Gatekeeper: I don't know. I've never seen it opened.
Officer: It looks like a pantry door I saw once when I was only four years old and went visiting with our maid one Sunday afternoon. We went from house to house, calling on other maids, but I never got beyond the kitchen in any of them, and I had to sit between the water barrel and the salt box. I've seen so many kitchens in my day . . . and the pantries were always out in the hall and their doors had round holes and a clover-leaf bored in them! But there can't be a pantry in the opera house because they don't have a kitchen!

[Sings.]
Victoria! Listen, Madam, she can't come out any other way but here, can she?
Gatekeeper: No, there's no other way.
Officer: Well, then, I'm sure to meet her.
*[**Members of the Opera Company** rush out and are closely watched by **The Officer** as they pass.]*
Officer: Now she's sure to come out soon . . . Madam, that blue monkshood outside . . . I've seen it since I was a child. Is it the same one? I remember it from a country parsonage where I stayed when I was seven years old . . . There were two doves, under the hood . . . but then a bee came and flew into the hood. I thought: now I have you! And I grabbed hold of the flower. But the sting of the bee went through it, and I started to cry. The minister's wife came out and put mud on it . . . and then we had wild strawberries and milk for supper . . . I think it's getting dark already! *[To The Billposter.]* Where are you going?
Billposter: I'm going home to eat supper.
[He goes out with the fish-net and fish-box.]
Officer: *[Draws his hand across his eyes.]* Supper? At this time of day?— Listen, may I go in for a moment and telephone the Growing Castle?
Daughter: What must you do there?
Officer: I must tell the glazier to put in double windows, because it's almost winter and I'm freezing to death!
[He goes into The Gatekeeper's lodge.]
Daughter: Who is Miss Victoria?
Gatekeeper: She's the woman he loves.
Daughter: That's a good answer! What she is to us or to others doesn't matter to him! It's only what she is to *him*, that she really *is*!
[It suddenly grows dark.]
Gatekeeper: *[Lights a lantern.]* It's getting dark early today.
Daughter: For the gods a year is no more than a minute!

Gatekeeper: And for human beings a minute can be as long as a year!

Officer: *[Enters again, looking dusty; the roses are withered.]* Hasn't she come down yet?

Gatekeeper: No.

Officer: She *will* come! She *will* come! *[Paces back and forth.]* To tell the truth, maybe I ought to call off the luncheon . . . after all, it's time for supper. Yes, I think I'll do that.
    [He goes back into the lodge to telephone.]

Gatekeeper: *[To **The Daughter**.]* May I have my shawl now?

Daughter: No, my friend, you rest for a while. I'll take care of your duties . . . because I want to get to know men and life, and see if things are really as bad as they say.

Gatekeeper: But you can't sleep here on the job . . . never sleep . . . night or day . . .

Daughter: No sleep at night?

Gatekeeper: Oh, yes, if you can, but only with the bell string tied to your wrist . . . because there are night watchmen in the theatre and they have to be relieved every three hours . . .

Daughter: That's pure torture!

Gatekeeper: So you think! But the rest of us are glad to get a job like this, and if you only knew how people envy me!

Daughter: Envy you? They envy those who are being tortured?

Gatekeeper: Yes! But I'll tell you what's worse than this drudgery and staying awake nights, and much harder to bear than the drafts, the cold, and the dampness—that's listening to the tales of woe of all those unhappy people up there. They all come to me. Why? They must read the lines engraved in my face by suffering as an invitation to confide in me. That shawl, my friend, has absorbed thirty years of agony—my own and others.

Daughter: That's why it's so heavy . . . and it stings like nettles.

Gatekeeper: Go on wearing it, if you want to. If it gets too heavy, call me, and I'll come and relieve you!

Daughter: Goodbye. What you can do, I ought to be able to do!

Gatekeeper: We'll see! But be kind to my little friends, and don't lose patience with their complaints.

    *[**The Gatekeeper** disappears through the passageway.]*

The stage is blacked out. When the lights come up again, we see that the linden tree has lost its leaves, the blue monkshood has withered, and the grass at the end of the passageway has turned brown.

    *[**The Officer** enters. His hair and beard are gray. His clothes are shabby, his collar is soiled and wrinkled. He still carries the bouquet of roses but the petals have disappeared.]*

Officer: *[Paces up and down.]* Judging by the look of things, summer is gone and fall is here. I see that in the linden tree and the monkshood. *[He paces.]* But the autumn is my spring, because that's when the opera opens again! And then she's sure to come! Dear lady, may I sit on this chair for a while?

Daughter: Yes, my friend, sit down. I can stand.

Officer: *[Sits down.]* If only I could get a little sleep, I'd feel better . . .
    [He dozes off for a few moments, then jumps up and starts pacing. He finally stops in front of the door with the clover-leaf pattern and pokes at it.]
This door won't give me any peace. What's behind it? There must be something!
    [Faint ballet music is heard from above.]
So . . . now the rehearsals have begun!
    [The lights go on and off rhythmically, like the beam of a lighthouse.]
What's that? *[He speaks in time with

the flashing of the light.] Light and dark . . . light and dark?

Daughter: [Imitates him.] Day and night . . . day and night! A merciful providence wants to shorten your waiting. So the days fly along on the heels of the night.

[The light is constant now. **The Billposter** enters with his fish-net and his implements.]

Officer: There's the billposter with the fish-net. Was the fishing good?

Billposter: I should say so! The summer was hot and a little long. The net was pretty good, but not exactly what I thought it would be.

Officer: [Emphasizes each word.] "Not exactly what I thought it would be!" That's a good one! Nothing was ever what I thought it would be—because the thought is more than the action, more than the thing.

[He walks up and down, striking the wall with the stems of the roses until the last leaves fall off.]

Billposter: Hasn't she come down yet?

Officer: No, not yet, but she'll come soon! Billposter, do you know what's behind that door?

Billposter: No, I've never seen that door open.

Officer: I'm going to telephone for a locksmith to come and open it. [Goes in to telephone.]

[**The Billposter** puts up a poster and moves off to the right.]

Daughter: What was wrong with the fish-net?

Billposter: Wrong? Well, there wasn't anything wrong exactly . . . but it didn't turn out as I thought it would . . . I didn't enjoy it as much.

Daughter: What did you expect the net to be like?

Billposter: What? That's hard to say . . .

Daughter: Let me tell you! You imagined it to be something it wasn't! It was to be green, but not that shade of green!

Billposter: You understand, Madam, you do! You understand everything. And

that's why everyone comes to you with his troubles. If you'll listen to me, too, sometime . . .

Daughter: But I will, gladly. Come in here and pour out your heart . . .

[**The Daughter** goes into the lodge. **The Billposter** remains outside and speaks to her through the window.]

The stage is blacked out. Then the lights come up slowly and reveal that the tree is covered with leaves, the monkshood is blooming, and the sun is shining on the green grass beyond the passageway.

[**The Officer** enters. Now he is old and white-haired, his clothes in rags, his shoes worn out. He carries the remnants of the rose stems. He walks up and down with the gait of a very old man, then stops to read the poster.]

[**A Ballet Girl** comes out of the opera house.]

Officer: Has Miss Victoria gone?

Ballet Girl: No, she hasn't left yet.

Officer: She'll be coming down soon, won't she?

Ballet Girl: [Seriously.] I'm sure she will.

Officer: Don't go away now, if you want to see what's behind that door. I've just sent for a locksmith.

Ballet Girl: Oh, it'll be awfully interesting to see that door opened. That door and the Growing Castle—you've heard of the Growing Castle?

Officer: Have I? Wasn't I held a prisoner there?

Ballet Girl: No, was that you? But why do they keep so many horses there?

Officer: It was a stable castle, you see.

Ballet Girl: [Distressed.] How stupid of me—not to have known that!

[**A Member of the Chorus** (Male) enters from the right.]

Officer: Has Miss Victoria gone?

Member of the Chorus: [Seriously.] No, she hasn't gone. She never leaves.

Officer: That's because she loves me! Look, don't go away now before the locksmith comes. He's going to open this door.

Member of the Chorus: Oh, is the door going to be opened? Well, that'll be fun! I just want to ask the gate-keeper something.

[**The Prompter** enters from the right.]

Officer: Has Miss Victoria gone?

Prompter: No, not so far as I know.

Officer: There, you see! Didn't I say she was waiting for me! Don't go away— the door's going to be opened.

Prompter: Which door?

Officer: Is there more than one door?

Prompter: Now I know—the one with the clover-leaf! Then I'll certainly have to stay! I'm just going to have a word with the gatekeeper.

[He joins **The Member of the Chorus, The Ballet Girl** and **The Billposter** at the window, where they talk by turns to **The Daughter**.]

[**The Glazier** enters through the gate.]

Officer: Are you the locksmith?

Glazier: No, the locksmith had visitors . . . but I'm sure a glazier will do just as well.

Officer: Yes, of course, of course . . . but did you bring your diamond with you?

Glazier: Naturally! A glazier without a diamond—what could he do?

Officer: Nothing. Well, let's get to work.

[**The Officer** claps his hands. Everyone gathers around the door. **Male Members of the Chorus** in costumes of Die Meistersinger, and **Ballet Girls** in costumes from Aida, enter from the right and join the rest.]

Officer: Locksmith—or glazier—do your duty!

[**The Glazier** goes up to the door with the diamond in his hand.]

Officer: A moment like this doesn't happen often in a man's life, and so, my friends, I beg you to . . . pay close attention . . .

Policeman: [Who has entered while **The Officer** was speaking, now steps forward.] In the name of the law, I forbid you to open that door!

Officer: Oh, God! What a fuss they make when you want to do something new and great! But we'll fight this in court! Let's go to the lawyer—and we'll see if this law can be enforced! To the lawyer!

The curtain is not lowered, but the scene changes to **The Lawyer's** office. The gate becomes a railing in the office and runs clear across the stage; the lodge, into which we are now able to see, becomes **The Lawyer's** private room. The leafless linden tree becomes a clothes-tree. The billboard is covered with legal notices and court decisions. The door with the clover-leaf forms part of a cupboard.

[**The Lawyer,** in evening dress and white tie, sits at the left, inside the railing; in front of him is a desk covered with papers. He appears to be suffering terribly. His face is chalk-white and full of wrinkles, and its shadows have a purplish hue. He is ugly, and his features seem to reflect all the crimes and vices with which he has been involved in his profession. Of his two **Clerks,** one has lost an arm, the other an eye.

The people gathered to witness "the opening of the door" remain as before, but they now appear to be clients waiting to see **The Lawyer.** Their attitudes suggest that they have been standing there forever.

The Daughter, still wearing the shawl, and **The Officer** are far downstage.]

Lawyer: [Goes over to **The Daughter.**] Tell me, sister, may I have that shawl? I'll hang it up here till I light a fire in the stove, then I'll burn it with all its sorrows and miseries . . .

Daughter: Not yet, brother, first I want it to be absolutely full . . . and, more than anything, I want it to absorb all the agonies you suffered when your clients spoke to you in confidence about crime, vice, robbery, slander, libel . . .

Lawyer: My little friend, your shawl's not big enough for that! Look at these walls. Doesn't it look as if all those sins stained the wallpaper? Look at these papers in which I write up the records of evil. Look at me! Nobody who comes in here ever smiles. Nothing but angry looks, snarling lips, clenched fists . . . And everyone pours his anger, his envy, his suspicions on me. Look, my hands are black and can never be washed clean. You see how cracked they are, they're bleeding . . . I can never wear my clothes more than a few days, because they stink of other people's crimes. Sometimes I have the place fumigated with sulphur, but it doesn't help. I sleep in the next room and dream of nothing but crimes. Right now I have a murder case in court, which is bad enough, but do you know what's worst of all? Separating husbands and wives. Then it's as if heaven and earth were crying out—crying treason against the primal force, the source of all good—against love! And do you know, after reams of paper have been filled with mutual accusations, if some sympathetic person takes one of them aside, pinches his ear, smiles, and asks the simple question: what have you really got against your husband, or your wife?—then he or she stands there speechless and can't think of a thing. Well, once, it was about a salad, another time about a word, usually about nothing at all. But the suffering, the agony! That's what I have to bear! Do you see what

I look like! Do you think I can win a woman's love with crime written all over my face? Or that anyone would want to be the friend of a man who collects all the debts and liabilities in the city? Oh, it's miserable to be a man!

Daughter: Men are to be pitied!

Lawyer: Yes, they are. And what people live on is a mystery to me. They marry on an income of two thousand, when they need four thousand. They borrow, of course—everyone borrows. They just manage to get along by the skin of their teeth till the day they die . . . and leave nothing but debts. And who pays for it in the end? Tell me that!

Daughter: He who feeds the birds!

Lawyer: Well, if He who feeds the birds would only come down to this earth of His and see what the poor children of men have to go through, He'd be full of compassion . . .

Daughter: Men are to be pitied!

Lawyer: Yes, that's the truth! [To **The Officer.**] What do you want?

Officer: I only want to ask if Miss Victoria has gone.

Lawyer: No, she hasn't. You can rest assured of that—Why do you keep poking at my cupboard over there?

Officer: I thought the door looked exactly like—

Lawyer: Oh, no, no, no!
    [Church bells begin to ring.]

Officer: Is there a funeral in town?

Lawyer: No, it's graduation day for doctoral candidates. And I'm just going up to be made a Doctor of Law. Wouldn't you like to graduate and get a laurel wreath?

Officer: Yes, why not? That would be a little diversion, at least . . .

Lawyer: Perhaps we ought to proceed to the solemn ceremonies right away . . . Just go and change your clothes!
    [**The Officer** goes out.]

The stage goes dark and the scene changes. The railing remains but it now

encloses the chancel of a church. The billboard displays hymn numbers. The linden hat-tree becomes a candelabrum. **The Lawyer's** *desk becomes* **The Chancellor's** *lectern, and the door with the clover-leaf leads to the vestry.*

[**The Male Members of the Chorus** *become ushers with staffs, and* **The Ballet Girls** *carry laurel wreaths. The rest of the people act as spectators.*

In the background there is a huge church organ, with pipes above and keyboard below; over the keyboard, the organist's mirror. Music swells up from the organ.

At the sides stand the four deans of the faculties: Philosophy, Theology, Medicine, and Law.

For a moment the stage is empty, then **The Ushers** *enter from the right;* **The Ballet Girls** *follow with laurel wreaths which they hold in their outstretched hands. One after another,* **Three Graduates** *enter from the left, receive their wreaths from* **The Ballet Girls,** *and go out to the right.* **The Lawyer** *steps forward to get his wreath.* **The Ballet Girls** *turn away from him and refuse to place the wreath on his head. Then they leave the stage.* **The Lawyer,** *shocked, leans against a pillar. All the others go out slowly;* **The Lawyer** *is left alone.*

The Daughter *enters, her head and shoulders covered by a white veil.]*

Daughter: Look, now I've washed the shawl! But why are you standing here? Didn't you get the wreath?

Lawyer: No, I wasn't worthy of it.

Daughter: Why? Because you took the side of the poor, put in a good word for the criminal, lightened the burden of the guilty, and won a reprieve for the condemned? Woe to mankind!

They're no angels, but they must be pitied.

Lawyer: Don't speak ill of men, after all it's my job to defend them.

Daughter: [*Leans on the organ.*] Why do they slap their friends in the face?

Lawyer: They don't know any better.

Daughter: Let's enlighten them. Do you want to? You and I together!

Lawyer: They don't care to be enlightened! Oh, if only our cries could reach the gods in heaven!

Daughter: They'll reach the throne! [*Turns toward the organ.*] Do you know what I see in this mirror? The world turned right side up! Yes—of course, it's upside down as it is!

Lawyer: How did it come to be upside down?

Daughter: When the copy was made—

Lawyer: See, now you've said it! The copy—I've always had the feeling it was a spoiled copy. And when I began to recall the original, I became dissatisfied with everything. People called it fault-finding; they said it was bits of glass the devil put in my eye, and other things like that.

Daughter: It's a crazy world! Look at the four faculties here! The government, which is supposed to preserve society, supports all four of them. Theology, the science of God, is constantly being attacked and ridiculed by Philosophy, which claims to have the sum of all wisdom. And Medicine is always challenging Philosophy, and refusing entirely to consider Theology a science, even insisting on calling it a mere superstition. And they all sit together on the Faculty Council whose function it is to teach young people respect—for the university. It's certainly a madhouse! And woe to him who first comes to his senses!

Lawyer: The first ones to realize it are the theologians. As a preparatory course they take philosophy, which teaches them that theology is nonsense, and then they learn from theology that philosophy is nonsense. Madness isn't it?

Daughter: And then there's the law, which serves everyone but its servants!

Lawyer: And Justice—that wants to be just and puts men to death! Right that so often goes wrong!

Daughter: What a mess you children of men have made of it! Children, indeed! Come here, and I'll give you a wreath—one that really suits you.
[*Puts a crown of thorns on his head.*]
Now I'll play for you.
[*She sits down at the keyboard and plays a Kyrie, but instead of organ music human voices are heard singing.*]

Children's Voices: Eternal One! Eternal One!
[*The last note is sustained.*]

Women's Voices: Be merciful!
[*The last note is sustained.*]

Men's Voices: [*Tenors.*] Save us for Your mercy's sake!
[*The last note is sustained.*]

Men's Voices: [*Basses.*] Spare Your children, O Lord, and be not wrathful against us!

All: Have mercy on us! Hear us! Have pity on mortal men! O Lord eternal, why are You so far from us? Out of the depths we call to You: Let not the burden be too heavy for Your children! Hear us! Hear us!

The stage grows dark as **The Daughter** *rises and draws close to* **The Lawyer.** *The scene changes. The organ disappears and we see the interior of Fingal's Cave. The ground-swell of the ocean can be seen rising and falling between columns of basalt, and the music of winds and waves blend in harmony.*

Lawyer: Where are we, sister?

Daughter: What do you hear?

Lawyer: I hear drops falling—

Daughter: Those are the tears of mankind weeping . . . What else do you hear?

Lawyer: There's sighing . . . and whining . . . and wailing . . .

Daughter: The lamentations of mortals reach this far . . . and no further. But why these never-ending complaints? Isn't there anything in life to rejoice at?

Lawyer: Yes, the sweetest which is the bitterest—love! Wife and home! The highest and the lowest!

Daughter: May I try it?

Lawyer: With me?

Daughter: With you! You know the rocks and the shoals. Let's steer clear of them!

Lawyer: I'm very poor.

Daughter: What difference does that make, as long as we love each other. And a little beauty doesn't cost anything!

Lawyer: There are things I dislike that you may like.

Daughter: We'll have to adjust to them.

Lawyer: Suppose we get tired of it?

Daughter: Then we'll have children who always bring new interests.

Lawyer: You—you will take me, poor and ugly, scorned and rejected?

Daughter: Yes. Let's join our destinies!

Lawyer: So be it then!

The scene changes to **The Lawyer's** *living quarters—a very simple room adjoining his office. On the right, a large double bed with a canopy over it and curtains around it. Near it, a window with double panes. On the left, an iron stove with cooking utensils on it.*

[**Kristin,** *the servant, is pasting strips of paper along the cracks of the window. In the background, through an open door leading to* **The Lawyer's** *office, may be seen a number of poor clients who are waiting to be admitted.*

The Daughter, *now pale and emaciated, sits beside the stove.*]

Kristin: I'm pasting . . . I'm pasting!

Daughter: You're shutting out the air. I'm choking.

Kristin: Now there's only one little crack left.

Daughter: Air! Air! I can't breathe!

Kristin: I'm pasting . . . I'm pasting!

Lawyer: That's right, Kristin! Heat is expensive.

Daughter: Oh, it's as if you were pasting my lips together.

Lawyer: *[Stands in the doorway, with a paper in his hand.]* Is the baby sleeping?

Daughter: Yes, at last!

Lawyer: *[Gently.]* The screaming scares away my clients.

Daughter: *[Gently.]* What can we do about it?

Lawyer: Nothing.

Daughter: We'll have to get a bigger place.

Lawyer: We can't afford it.

Daughter: May I open the window? This bad air is choking me.

Lawyer: That'll let the heat out, and we'll freeze.

Daughter: This is terrible! *[Points to the open door.]* Can't we scrub up out there?

Lawyer: You're not strong enough to do any scrubbing, neither am I . . . and Kristin has to go on pasting. She must paste up the whole house, every crack in the ceiling, in the floor, in the walls.

Daughter: I was prepared for poverty, not dirt.

Lawyer: Poverty is always rather dirty.

Daughter: This is worse than I dreamt!

Lawyer: We're not the worst off! There's still food in the pot.

Daughter: But what kind of food?

Lawyer: Cabbage is cheap, nourishing, and good.

Daughter: For those who like cabbage. To me it's revolting!

Lawyer: Why didn't you say so?

Daughter: Because I loved you, I was willing to sacrifice my own taste.

Lawyer: So I must sacrifice my taste for cabbage for your sake! Sacrifice must be mutual!

Daughter: Then what shall we eat? Fish? But you hate fish.

Lawyer: And it's expensive.

Daughter: This is harder than I imagined!

Lawyer: *[Gently.]* You see how hard it is! And the child who was to be our bond and our blessing . . . is our undoing!

Daughter: Dearest . . . I'm dying in this air . . . in this room . . . looking out on a backyard . . . The baby crying for hours on end, so I can't sleep . . . and those people out there with their whining and bickering and accusations . . . I'm dying in here!

Lawyer: Poor little flower . . . without light . . . without air . . .

Daughter: And you say there are people who are worse off!

Lawyer: I'm one of the envied ones in the neighborhood.

Daughter: Everything would be all right, if only I could have some beauty in my home.

Lawyer: I know, you mean a plant, a heliotrope especially, but that costs as much as six quarts of milk or half a bushel of potatoes.

Daughter: I'd gladly go without food, if only I had my flowers.

Lawyer: There's one kind of beauty that costs nothing . . . and not to find it in his home is the worst torture for a man with a feeling for beauty.

Daughter: What's that?

Lawyer: If I tell you, you'll be angry!

Daughter: We agreed never to get angry.

Lawyer: We agreed to—Everything will be all right now, Agnes, if only we can avoid sharp tones. You've heard them? Not yet!

Daughter: We'll never hear them!

Lawyer: Never as far as I'm concerned!

Daughter: Now tell me!

Lawyer: Well—when I come into a home, the first thing I look at are the curtains . . . to see if they're draped properly.

[He goes to the window and adjusts the curtains in their sashes.]
If they hang like a rope or a rag, I leave in a hurry. Then I glance at the

chairs . . . if they're in their places, I stay.

[*He puts a chair back against the wall.*]

Finally I look at the candlesticks. If the candles lean this way and that, the whole house is crooked.

[*He straightens a candle on the bureau.*]

You see, my little friend, that's the kind of beauty that doesn't cost anything.

Daughter: [*Hangs her head.*] Not those sharp tones, Axel!

Lawyer: They weren't sharp!

Daughter: Yes, they were.

Lawyer: To hell with it!

Daughter: What kind of language is that?

Lawyer: Forgive me, Agnes! But I've suffered as much from your untidiness as you do from the dirt. And I didn't dare lend a hand to straighten things up myself. When I do, you get angry . . . as if I were criticizing you . . . ugh! Shall we stop this now?

Daughter: It's terribly hard to be married—harder than anything else. You have to be an angel, I think.

Lawyer: Yes, I think so, too.

Daughter: I feel I'm beginning to hate you after all this.

Lawyer: Then it's woe to us! But let's try to avoid hatred! I promise never to mention untidiness again—even if it's torture for me.

Daughter: And I'll eat cabbage—even if it's agony for me.

Lawyer: So we'll live together and suffer! One's pleasure, the other's pain!

Daughter: Men are to be pitied.

Lawyer: You realize that?

Daughter: Yes, but in God's name let's avoid the rocks, now that we know them so well.

Lawyer: Let's do that. We're decent, intelligent people . . . we ought to be able to make allowances and forgive . . .

Daughter: We ought to be able to smile over trifles.

Lawyer: We, only we, can do that! You know, I read in the paper this morning—By the way, where is the paper?

Daughter: [*Embarrassed.*] Which paper?

Lawyer: [*Sharply.*] Do I buy more than one paper?

Daughter: Now smile . . . and don't speak so harshly . . . I used your paper to start the fire—

Lawyer: [*Violently.*] Well, I'll be damned!

Daughter: You must smile! I burned it because it ridiculed something that's holy to me.

Lawyer: Which is unholy to me! Ahh! [*Beside himself, he punches one hand with the other.*] I'll smile . . . I'll smile till my back teeth show! I'll be considerate and hide my opinions, say yes to everything, cringe, and lie! So you've burnt up my newspaper, have you?

[*He pulls at the bed curtains.*]

Look here! Now I'm going to straighten things up again until it makes you angry! Agnes, this is utterly impossible!

Daughter: Of course it is!

Lawyer: All the same, we've got to go on . . . not because of our promises . . . but for the child's sake.

Daughter: You're right! For the child's sake! Oh, oh . . . we've got to go on.

Lawyer: And now I must go out to my clients. Listen! They're growling with impatience to tear one another to pieces, to have each other fined or jailed—Lost souls!

Daughter: Poor, poor mankind!

[**Kristin** *enters with pasting materials.*]

And this pasting! [*She lowers her head in despair.*]

Kristin: I'm pasting . . . I'm pasting!

[**The Lawyer** *stands at the door, twisting the doorknob nervously.*]

Daughter: Oh, how that knob squeaks! It's as if you were twisting my heartstrings . . .

Lawyer: I'm twisting . . . I'm twisting . . .

Daughter: Don't do it!

Lawyer: I'm twisting!

Daughter: No!
Lawyer: I—
  [**The Officer,** in the office, on the other side of the door, takes hold of the knob. (He is now middle-aged.)]
Officer: May I?
Lawyer: [Lets go of the knob.] Certainly . . . since you have your degree!
Officer: Now all of life is mine. All roads are open to me. I've climbed Parnassus, won the laurel wreath . . . Immortality, fame, all are mine!
Lawyer: And what are you going to live on?
Officer: Live on?
Lawyer: You must have a home . . . clothes . . . food, mustn't you?
Officer: You can always find those, if only you have someone to love you.
Lawyer: Think of that now! Think of that! Paste, Kristin, paste . . . until they can't breathe!
  [He goes out backwards, nodding.]
Kristin: I'm pasting . . . I'm pasting . . . until they can't breathe!
Officer: Will you come with me now?
Daughter: This very moment! But where to?
Officer: To Fairhaven. It's summer there and the sun is shining. There are young people there, children and flowers, singing and dancing, feasting and frolicking.
  [Kristin goes out.]
Daughter: I'd like to go there!
Officer: Come!
  [**The Lawyer** enters again.]
Lawyer: Now I'm going back to my first hell—this was the second and worst. The sweetest hell is the worst! Look here, now she's dropped hairpins on the floor again. [He picks them up.]
Officer: Just think, he's discovered the hairpins, too.
Lawyer: Too? Look at this one. There are two prongs, but it's only one pin. There are two, but they're one! Straighten it out and it's a single piece, bend it back and it's two—but it's one just the same. In other words:

these two are one! But if I break it—like this—
  [He breaks the pin.]
then the two are two.
  [He throws the pieces away.]
Officer: He's seen all that! But before it'll break, the parts must separate; if they run together, it'll hold!
Lawyer: And if they're parallel—so they never meet—it neither breaks nor holds.
Officer: The hairpin is the most perfect of all created things. A straight line that equals two parallel ones.
Lawyer: A lock that shuts when it's open.
Officer: It locks in a braid of hair that opens when the lock shuts.
Lawyer: It's like this door. When I shut it, I open the way out for you, Agnes!
  [He goes out and closes the door behind him.]
Daughter: Now what?

The scene changes. The bed with its curtains becomes a tent; the stove remains as it was. The new background shows a beautiful wooded shore. Flags are flying on its piers, where sailboats are moored, some with sails set. Little Italian villas, pavilions, arbors, and marble statues may be glimpsed among the trees along the shore.

In the middle-distance there is a narrow channel of water.

In the foreground, which offers a sharp contrast to the background, are hills stripped of their trees by fire, with red heather growing between the blackened tree stumps. There are red-painted pigsties and outhouses. Beyond these, on the right, is an open-air gymnasium, where sick people are being treated on machines that resemble instruments of torture. On the left, is a section of the quarantine station, consisting of open sheds, with furnaces, boilers, and pipes.

  [**The Quarantine Master,** dressed like a Moor, with his face blackened, is walking along the shore.]
Officer: [Meets him and they shake

hands.] Well, if it isn't old Windbag![3] Is this where you landed?

Q. Master: Yes, here I am.

Officer: Is this place Fairhaven?

Q. Master: No, that's over there. This is Foulstrand.

Officer: Then we've lost our way.

Q. Master: We? Won't you introduce me?

Officer: No, it wouldn't be appropriate. *[In a whisper.]* You see, she's Indra's own daughter.

Q. Master: Indra's? I thought it was Varuna[4] himself. Say, aren't you surprised at my black face?

Officer: Look, my boy, I'm past fifty, and nothing surprises me any more. I immediately took it for granted you were going to a masquerade ball this afternoon.

Q. Master: You're absolutely right! And I hope both of you will come with me.

Officer: Certainly. But right here . . . the place doesn't look very attractive. What kind of people live here?

Q. Master: The sick live here, and the healthy over there.

Officer: Only poor people on this side, I suppose?

Q. Master: No, my boy, these people are rich. *[Points to the gymnasium.]* Look at that one on the rack. He stuffed himself with so much goose liver and truffles and drank so much burgundy his feet are tied up in knots.

Officer: In knots?

Q. Master: Yes, he has a case of knotted feet! And that one lying under the guillotine—he swilled so much brandy they had to put his backbone through a wringer!

Officer: That's not so good either!

Q. Master: What's more, everybody living on this side has some kind of misery to hide. Look at this one coming along, for instance.

[3] In the original, Ordström meaning "stream of words."

[4] In Hindu mythology, an all-powerful god of the sky .

[An old **Dandy** *(Don Juan) is pushed on in a wheelchair. He is accompanied by a gaunt and ugly* **Coquette** *in her sixties, who is dressed in the latest fashion and is being courted by her* **Friend,** *a man of about forty.]*

Officer: It's the Major! He went to school with us!

Q. Master: Don Juan! Look, he's still in love with that old spook at his side. He doesn't even see that she's grown old . . . that she's ugly, faithless, cruel!

Officer: That's true love, that is! I never would've thought such a fickle fellow could fall in love so deeply and so seriously.

Q. Master: That's a very nice way of looking at it!

Officer: I've been in love myself—with Victoria. In fact, I still walk up and down in the alley waiting for her.

Q. Master: Oh, are you the fellow who's waiting in the alley?

Officer: I'm the man.

Q. Master: Well, have you got that door open yet?

Officer: No, the case is still in court . . . The Billposter is out with his fish-net, you see, so there's been a delay in getting the evidence. In the meantime, the Glazier's been fixing the windowpanes in the castle, which has grown half a story higher. This has been an exceptionally good year —warm and wet . . .

Q. Master: *[Points to the furnace.]* But you certainly had no heat to compare with what I have here!

Officer: How hot do you make your ovens?

Q. Master: When we fumigate cholera suspects, we run it up to one hundred and forty degrees.

Officer: Is cholera going around again now?

Q. Master: Don't you know that?

Officer: Of course, I know that, but I so often forget what I know.

Q. Master: And I often wish I *could* forget—especially myself. That's why I go in for masquerades, fancy dress, and amateur theatricals.

Officer: What have you been up to, then?

Q. Master: If I tell anyone, they say I'm bragging; if I don't tell, they call me a hypocrite.

Officer: Is that why you blackened your face?

Q. Master: Yes . . . a little blacker than I really am!

Officer: Who's this coming?

Q. Master: Oh, that's a poet! He's going to take his mudbath.

> [**The Poet** enters; he is looking at the sky and carrying a pail of mud.]

Officer: Good grief, he ought to be taking light baths and air baths!

Q. Master: No, he lives up there in the clouds so much he gets homesick for the mud. When he wallows in it, his skin gets as tough as a pig's and then he can't feel the stings of the gad-flies.

Officer: This is a queer world, full of contradictions!

Poet: [Ecstatically.] Out of clay the god Ptah made man on a potter's wheel, a lathe—

> [Mockingly.]

or some other damned thing!

> [Ecstatically.]

Out of clay the sculptor makes his more or less immortal masterpieces—

> [Mockingly.]

which is mostly a lot of junk.

> [Ecstatically.]

Out of clay they make those objects so essential in the home, which go by the name of pitchers and bowls—

> [Mockingly.]

but I couldn't care less what they're called!

> [Ecstatically.]

That's clay! When clay is fluid, it's called mud. C'est mon affaire!

> [He calls out.] Lina!
> [**Lina** enters with a pail.]

Poet: Lina, let Miss Agnes take a look at you. She used to know you ten years ago, when you were a young, happy, and, you might say, pretty girl. [To **The Daughter.**] Look at her now! Five children, drudgery, screaming, hunger, abuse! You see how her beauty faded and her joy vanished when she did her duty, which should have brought her contentment, a happy face, and a quiet glow in her eyes.

Q. Master: [Puts his hand over **The Poet's** mouth.] Shut up! Shut up!

Poet: That's what they all say! And if you keep quiet, they say, "Talk!" Men are so mixed up!

Daughter: [Goes to **Lina.**] Tell me your troubles.

Lina: No, I don't dare. It would be worse for me if I did.

Daughter: Who would be so cruel?

Lina: I can't tell you. If I do, I'll be beaten.

> [Dance music is heard in the distance.]

Poet: That may be so, but I'll talk about it even if the blackamoor knocks my teeth out. I'll talk about what's unjust now. Agnes, Daughter of the Gods, do you hear music and dancing up there on the hill? Well, that's for Lina's sister, who's come home from the city, where she went astray, you understand . . . Now they're killing the fatted calf! But Lina, who stayed at home, has to take out the garbage pail and feed the pigs.

Daughter: There's joy in that home up there, because the wanderer's given up her evil ways, not just because she's come back. Remember that!

Poet: Then they ought to give a dinner and dance every night for the devoted servant who never strayed down the primrose path. They ought to . . . but they don't! Instead, when Lina has a minute to herself, they make her go to prayer-meetings where she's reprimanded for not being perfect. Is that justice!

Daughter: Your questions are very hard

to answer because—There are so many unknown factors!

Poet: Even the Caliph, Haroun the Just, realized that! Sitting up there quietly on his throne he could never make out what was happening below. Complaints eventually reached his exalted ear, and one fine day he disguised himself and went down among the crowds, unnoticed, to see what kind of justice they were getting.

Daughter: You surely don't think I'm Haroun the Just!

Officer: Let's talk about something else. Here come some visitors.

[*A white boat, shaped like a viking ship, with a dragon for a figurehead, a pale blue silken sail on a gilded yard, and a rose-red pennant flying from the top of a gilded mast, glides through the strait from the left.* **He** *and* **She** *are seated in the stern with their arms around each other.*]

Officer: There you see perfect bliss, absolute happiness, and the ecstasy of young love!

[*The stage grows brighter.*]

He: [*Stands up in the boat and sings.*]
Hail to you, fairest haven,
Where the days of my youth were spent,
Where my first sweet dreams were dreamt—
I've come back to you again,
But not alone as then!
Woods and water,
Sky and sea,
Greet her!
My love, my bride,
My light, my life!

[*The flags on the piers at Fairhaven are dipped in salute; white handkerchiefs are waved from villas and boats; and the air is filled with soft music from harps and violins.*]

Poet: Look at the light that surrounds them! Listen to the music that floats over the water! Eros!

Officer: It's Victoria!

Q. Master: Well, what of it?

Officer: That's *his* Victoria . . . I have my own. But nobody can see mine! Now you hoist the quarantine flag, and I'll pull in the net.

[*The* **Quarantine Master** *waves a yellow flag.* **The Officer** *pulls on a rope that turns the boat toward Foulstrand.*]

Officer: Hold on there!

[*He and* **She** *become aware of the hideous landscape and express their horror.*]

Q. Master: Yes, yes, it's tough! But everyone must stop here . . . everyone who comes from plague-stricken places!

Poet: Imagine talking and acting like that when you see two people so in love! Don't bother them! Don't disturb their love! It's high treason! Woe to us! Everything beautiful must be dragged down nowadays—dragged into the mud!

[**He** *and* **She** *step ashore, looking sad and ashamed.*]

He: Woe to us! What have we done?

Q. Master: You needn't have done anything to suffer life's little pains.

She: Joy and happiness are so brief!

He: How long must we stay here?

Q. Master: Forty days and forty nights.

She: Then we'd rather drown ourselves!

He: Live here . . . among scorched hills and pigsties?

Poet: Love conquers all—even sulphur fumes and carbolic acid![5]

[**The Quarantine Master** *starts a fire in the furnace; blue, sulphurous flames break forth.*]

Q. Master: Now I'm burning the sulphur. Will you kindly step inside!

She: Oh, my blue dress will fade.

Q. Master: And turn white. Your red roses will turn white too.

He: And so will your cheeks—in forty days!

[5] Since the Poet is not mentioned again until the end of the Fairhaven scene, perhaps he goes out here.

She: [*To* **The Officer.**] That will please you.

Officer: No, it won't. Your happiness certainly was the cause of my suffering —but that doesn't matter. I've graduated now and—[*Points across to Fairhaven.*] I have a job over there . . . alas and alack! In the fall I'll be teaching school—teaching boys the same lessons I learned myself all through my childhood and youth— the same lessons I learned all through my manhood and, finally, in my old age—the same lessons! How much is two times two? How many times does two go into four with nothing left over? Until I get a pension and can't do anything at all, but wait around for meals and newspapers— until I'm finally carried off to the crematorium and burnt up . . . Don't you have any pensioners here? That's probably the worst thing, next to two times two is four—going to school again after you've graduated, asking the same questions until you die . . .[6]

[*An* **Elderly Man** *goes by, with his hands clasped behind his back.*]

Officer: Look, there goes a pensioner who's just waiting to die. He's probably a captain who never got to be a major, or a court clerk who missed being a judge. Many are called but few are chosen. He's just walking around, waiting for breakfast—

Pensioner: No, for the paper—the morning newspaper!

Officer: And he's only fifty-four years old. He may go on for another twenty-five years waiting for meals and for newspapers. Isn't that awful!

Pensioner: Is there anything that isn't awful? Tell me that, tell me that!

[6] Elizabeth Sprigge suggests that He, She, and the Quarantine Master go into the shed during this speech. The Quarantine Master returns in time to be asked, "Don't you have any pensioners here?" He and She return five speeches later (as the Officer is clutching his head in despair) and both have been bleached white— clothing, roses, and faces.

Officer: Yes, let him answer that who can! Now I'll have to teach boys that two times two is four, and how many times two goes into four with nothing left over. [*He clutches his head in despair.*] Oh, I loved Victoria and wished her all the happiness in the world . . . and now she is happy, as happy as she can possibly be, and that's why I suffer, suffer, suffer!

She: Do you think I can be happy when I see you suffering? How can you think so? Perhaps it'll relieve your pain to know I'll be a prisoner here for forty days and forty nights. Tell me, does that ease your pains?

Officer: Yes and no. I can't be happy when you're suffering. Oh!

She: And do you think I can build my happiness on your misery?

Officer: We're to be pitied—all of us!

All: [*Raise their arms toward the sky and utter a cry that sounds like a dissonant chord.*] Oh!

Daughter: Eternal One, hear them! Life is evil! Men are to be pitied!

All: [*As before.*] Oh!

The stage goes black for a moment; some of the characters withdraw; those who remain take up new positions. When the lights come up again, Foulstrand is seen in the background lying in deep shadow, but it is clearly a winter landscape, with snow on the ground and on the leafless trees.

The channel of water is still in the middle distance; anchored in the channel is a white warship, brig-rigged, with gunports. On the near side of the channel, in the center, is a pier with white sailboats tied up at it, and flag poles with hoisted flags.

The foreground represents Fairhaven; it and the channel are bathed in summer sunshine.

At the right, a corner of the casino, where dancing couples are visible through the open windows. Three **Maids** are standing outside on top of an empty box with their arms around each other's waists, watching the dancers. On the terrace of the *casino,* **Ugly Edith** *sits on a bench in front of an open piano. She is bare-headed, has long, tousled hair and looks depressed.*

At the left, a yellow wooden house in front of which **Two Children,** *in light summer dresses, are playing ball.*

[**The Daughter** *and* **The Officer** *enter.*]

Daughter: Here there's peace and happiness. It's vacation time! Work put aside . . . parties every day . . . everyone dressed in his best. Music and dancing even in the morning. [*To* **The Maids.**] Children, why don't you go in and dance?

Maids: Us?

Officer: But they're servants!

Daughter: That's true! But why is Edith sitting there instead of dancing?

[**Edith** *buries her face in her hands.*]

Officer: Don't ask her! She's been sitting there for three hours without being asked to dance.

[*He goes into the yellow house on the left.*]

Daughter: What cruel amusement!

[**The Mother,** *in a low-cut dress, comes out of the casino and goes up to* **Edith.**]

Mother: Why don't you go inside as I told you to?

Edith: Because . . . I can't dance by myself. I know I'm ugly, and nobody wants to dance with me, but I don't have to be reminded of it!

[*She begins to play on the piano Bach's Toccata and Fugue, Number 10.*

The waltz music from the casino is heard faintly at first. Then it grows louder as if to compete with the Toccata. **Edith** *triumphs over it and reduces it to silence. The dancers appear in the doorway and stand still, listening reverently, as she plays.*

A Naval Officer *takes* **Alice,** *one*

of the dancers, around the waist and leads her toward the pier.]

Naval Officer: Come . . . hurry!

[*As they move away,* **Edith** *stops playing abruptly, rises, and stares after them with a look of despair; she stands as if turned to stone.*]

The front wall of the yellow house now disappears and reveals three benches on which **Schoolboys** *sit. Among them is* **The Officer,** *who looks worried and depressed. In front of the boys stands* **The Teacher;** *he wears eye-glasses, has a piece of chalk in one hand, and a rattan cane in the other.*

Teacher: [*To* **The Officer.**] Well, my boy, can you tell me how much two times two is?

[**The Officer** *remains seated, trying desperately to think of the answer.*]

Teacher: You must stand up when you're called on.

Officer: [*In agony, rises.*] Two . . . times two . . . Let me see . . . That's two twos!

Teacher: So, you! You haven't done your homework!

Officer: [*Ashamed.*] Yes, I have, but . . . I know what it is, but I can't say it—

Teacher: You're trying to worm your way out of it! You know it, but you can't say it! Maybe I can help you! [*He pulls* **The Officer's** *hair.*]

Officer: Oh, it's awful . . . it's awful . . .

Teacher: Yes, it's awful that such a big boy should have no ambition.

Officer: [*Tortured.*] A big boy—yes, I certainly am big . . . much bigger than the other boys here . . . I'm full-grown . . . I'm through with school . . . [*As if waking up.*] I've even graduated . . . then why am I sitting here? Haven't I got my degree?

Teacher: Yes, of course! But you must sit here and mature, you see! You have to mature . . . Isn't that so?

Officer: [*Puts his hand to his forehead.*] Yes, that's right, a person must mature . . . Two times two . . . is two . . . and I can demonstrate it by analogy, the highest form of proof. Now, listen! One times one is one, therefore two times two must be two. Because what applies in one case must apply in another.

Teacher: The proof is based on the laws of logic, but the answer is wrong!

Officer: Anything based on the laws of logic can't be wrong! Let's test it! One goes into one once, so two must go into two twice!

Teacher: Absolutely right according to analogy! But how much is one times three?

Officer: Three, of course!

Teacher: Then two times three must also be three.

Officer: [Ponders.] No, that can't be right . . . That can't be . . . unless . . .

[Sits down dejectedly.]

No, I'm not mature yet.

Teacher: No, you're not mature by a long shot!

Officer: But how long do I have to sit here, then?

Teacher: How long? Here? You believe that time and space exist? Suppose time does exist, you ought to be able to tell me what it is. What is time?

Officer: Time . . . [Thinks.] I can't say, but I know what it is: ergo, I may also know how much two times two is without being able to say it. Teacher, can you tell me what time is?

Teacher: Of course I can.

All The Boys: Then tell us!

Teacher: Time? Let me see . . . [He stands there motionless with his finger at the side of his nose.] While we speak, time flies. Consequently time is something that flies while I speak.

A Boy: [Rises.] Now the teacher is talking, and while he's talking, I'm flying. That means I'm time.

[He flaps his arms and "flies" out.]

Teacher: That's absolutely right according to the laws of logic.

Officer: Then the laws of logic are absurd. Nils flew out of here, but he can't be time.

Teacher: That's also absolutely right according to the laws of logic—although it's absurd.

Officer: Then logic is absurd!

Teacher: It really looks like it. But if logic is absurd, then the whole world is absurd . . . and I'll be damned if I stay here and teach you absurdities! If anyone offers to buy me a drink, we'll go out and have a swim.

Officer: That's a posterus prius, or the world turned backwards. Usually you go swimming first and then have a drink. You old fogy!

Teacher: Don't be so arrogant, Doctor!

Officer: Captain, if you please. I'm an officer, and I don't understand why I'm sitting here among schoolboys being scolded.

Teacher: [Wags his finger.] We must mature!

Q. Master: [Enters.] The quarantine is beginning.

Officer: So there you are! Just think of it, this fellow is making me sit here in school even though I've graduated.

Q. Master: Well, why don't you go away?

Officer: You say . . . go away? That's easier said than done.

Teacher: So I should think. Just try it.

Officer: [To **The Quarantine Master.**] Save me! Save me from his eyes!

Q. Master: Come along . . . Come and join the dance. We must dance before the plague breaks out. We must!

Officer: Will the ship sail then?

Q. Master: The ship will sail first. A lot of tears will be shed, of course.

Officer: Always tears—when she comes in and when she sails. Let's go.

[They go out. **The Teacher** continues the lesson in pantomime.

The Maids, who were staring through the window of the casino, walk sadly down to the pier.

Edith, *who has been standing like a statue at the piano, follows them.]*

Daughter: *[To* **The Officer.]** Isn't there one happy person anywhere in this paradise?

Officer: Yes, here come two newlyweds. Listen to them.

*[***The Newly Wed Couple*** enter.]*

Husband: *[To his* **Wife.]** My happiness is so complete, I want to die.

Wife: Why die?

Husband: Because at the core of happiness grows a seed of unhappiness. Happiness consumes itself like a flame. It can't burn forever . . . it has to go out! And the presentiment of its end destroys it at its very peak.

Wife: Let's die together then . . . right now.

Husband: Die? All right! Because I'm afraid of happiness—that fraud!

[They go out toward the sea.]

Daughter: Life is evil! Men are to be pitied!

Officer: Look who's coming now. He's the most envied mortal in the place.

*[***The Blind Man*** is led in.]*

He owns all these Italian villas, hundreds of them. He owns all these bays and channels, beaches and forests, along with the fish in the water, the birds in the trees, the game in the woods. All these people are his tenants, thousands of them. The sun rises over his sea and sets over his land.

Daughter: Well—is he complaining too?

Officer: Yes, and with good reason—because he can't see.

Q. Master: He's blind!

Daughter: The most envied of all!

Officer: Now he's come to see the ship sail with his son on board.

Blind Man: I don't see, but I hear! I hear the anchor ripping up the clay bottom like a hook torn out of a fish that drags the heart up with it through the gullet. My son, my only child, is going to strange lands across the wide sea; and I can only follow him with my thoughts. Now I hear the chain clanking . . . and something that flaps and lashes like wash on a clothesline—wet handkerchiefs, perhaps. And I hear sobbing and sighing, like people weeping . . . or maybe the splashing of little waves among the fishing-nets—or maybe girls along the shore, deserted and despairing . . . Once I asked a little boy why the sea was so salty—his father had gone on a long trip across the ocean—and he answered immediately, "It's salty because the sailors cry so much." "And why do the sailors cry so much?" "Well," he said, "because they're always going away . . . and so they always dry their handkerchiefs up on the masts." "And why do people cry when they're sad?" I asked. "Oh," said he, "because the windowpanes in the eyes have to be washed sometimes, so we can see better."

[The ship sets sail and is gliding away. **The Girls** *along the shore alternately wave their handkerchiefs and wipe away their tears with them. Then a signal is sent up the foremast—a red ball in a white field, meaning "Yes." In reply to it,* **Alice** *waves her handkerchief triumphantly.]*

Daughter: *[To* **The Officer.]** What does that flag mean?

Officer: It means "yes." It's the lieutenant's "vow" in red, like the red blood of the heart against the blue cloth of the sky.

Daughter: Then what does "no" look like?

Officer: It's blue, like the tainted blood in blue veins. But look how happy Alice is!

Daughter: And how Edith is crying!

Blind Man: We meet and we part. We part and we meet. That's life. I met his mother. Then she went away. My son was left. Now he's gone.

Daughter: But he'll come back again.

Blind Man: Who's that talking to me?

I've heard that voice before . . . in my dreams . . . in my youth . . . when summer vacations began . . . in the early years of my marriage . . . when my child was born. Whenever life smiled, I heard that voice whispering like the south wind, like the strings of heavenly harps, like the greetings of angels as I imagined them on Christmas Night.

[**The Lawyer** *enters and goes up to whisper something into* **The Blind Man's** *ear.*]

Blind Man: Is that so?

Lawyer: Yes, that's a fact!

[*Goes to* **The Daughter.**]

Now you've seen most of life, but you haven't experienced the worst part of it.

Daughter: What can that be?

Lawyer: Repetitions . . . recurrences . . . Going back . . . Doing your lessons over again . . . Come!

Daughter: Where?

Lawyer: To your duties.

Daughter: What are they?

Lawyer: Everything you dread. Everything you hate to do, but must. It means to abstain, to give up, to do without, to lack—it means everything that's unpleasant, repulsive, painful.

Daughter: Aren't there any pleasant duties?

Lawyer: They become pleasant when they're done.

Daughter: When they no longer exist. So duty is everything unpleasant! Then what's pleasant?

Lawyer: Anything pleasant is a sin.

Daughter: A sin?

Lawyer: Which must be punished, yes! If I spend a pleasant day or evening, my conscience bothers me the next day, and I go through the tortures of hell.

Daughter: How strange!

Lawyer: I wake up in the morning with a headache, and then the repetitions begin, and everything gets twisted. What was beautiful, agreeable, witty, the night before, seems ugly, revolting, and stupid the next morning. Pleasure turns rancid, and joy falls apart. What people call success always leads to their next failure. The successes in my life have been the cause of my downfall . . . because men have an instinctive hatred for other people's good fortune. They think it unfair that fate should favor one man, so they try to even things up by putting stones in his path. And if you have talent, you're in danger of your life—you may very well starve to death! Anyway, you must go back to your duties, or I'll sue you, and drag you through all three courts —Lower, Appeals, Supreme!

Daughter: Go back? To the iron stove, the cabbage pot, and the baby's diapers . . .

Lawyer: Exactly! We have a big wash today, because we must do all the handkerchiefs—

Daughter: Oh, must I do that again?

Lawyer: Life is nothing but doing things over again. Look at the teacher in there . . . Yesterday he got his doctor's degree, won his laurel wreath as the cannons went off, climbed Parnassus, and was embraced by the king . . . and today he starts school all over again, asks how much is two times two, and will go on doing it till he dies . . . Anyway, come back . . . come back to your home.

Daughter: I'd rather die!

Lawyer: Die? You can't do that. In the first place, it's such a disgrace to commit suicide, even your dead body is dishonored. And after that, you're damned . . . it's a mortal sin!

Daughter: It's not easy to be human!

All: Right!

[**The Poet** *might possibly enter here.*]

Daughter: I won't go back with you to the humiliation and dirt. I'm longing to be up there where I came from. But first the door must be opened so I can learn the secret. I want the door to be opened!

Lawyer: Then you'll have to retrace your steps, go back the way you came, and suffer through all the horrors of a lawsuit—the repetitions, revisions, reiterations . . .

Daughter: So be it! But first I must seek solitude . . . go into the wilderness in order to come to myself. We'll meet again! *[To* **The Poet.***]* Follow me!

[Cries of anguish are heard in the distance.]

Voices: Oh! Oh! Oh!

Daughter: What was that?

Lawyer: The lost souls in Foulstrand.

Daughter: Why are their complaints louder than usual today?

Lawyer: Because the sun is shining here . . . because we have music, dancing, and youth here. It makes them feel their own suffering much more deeply.

Daughter: We must set them free!

Lawyer: Try it! Once a liberator came, but he was hanged on a cross.

Daughter: By whom?

Lawyer: By all the right-minded.

Daughter: Who are they?

Lawyer: Haven't you heard about all the right-minded? Then you must get to know them.

Daughter: Were they the ones who refused to give you your degree?

Lawyer: Yes.

Daughter: Then I know them!

The scene changes to the shores of the Mediterranean. In the background, villas, and a casino with a terrace; in the right corner, a view of the blue sea.

In the foreground, on the left, a white wall, and above it branches of an orange tree with ripe fruit on them. On the right, a huge pile of coal and two wheelbarrows.

[Two **Coalheavers,** *naked to the waist, their faces, hands, and bodies blackened by coal dust, are seated on the wheelbarrows. Their expressions show intense despair.*

The Daughter *and* **The Lawyer** *are on the terrace.]*

Daughter: This is paradise!

First Coalheaver: This is hell!

Second Coalheaver: One hundred and twenty degrees in the shade!

First C.: Let's go for a swim.

Second C.: You want the cops to come? No bathing allowed here.

First C.: You allowed to pick the fruit off that tree?

Second C.: No, that'll bring the cops down on you.

First C.: But I can't work in this heat . . . I'll just chuck up the job.

Second C.: Then the cops'll come and pick you up . . .

[Pause.]

and you wouldn't have anything to eat anyway.

First C.: Nothing to eat? We do all the work and get the least food, and the rich don't do a thing and get the most. Would it be a little too free with the truth to call it injustice? What does the Daughter of the Gods up there say about it?

Daughter: I'm speechless! But, tell me, what did you do to get so black and have such a hard life?

First C.: What did we do? We were born poor and had pretty bad parents . . . were in jail maybe a couple of times . . .

Daughter: In jail?

First C.: Yes. The ones that don't get caught hang out up there in the casino and eat eight-course dinners with wine.

Daughter: *[To* **The Lawyer.***]* Can that be true?

Lawyer: More or less, yes.

Daughter: Do you mean that everyone at some time or other deserves to go to prison?

Lawyer: Yes.

Daughter: Even you?

Lawyer: Yes.

Daughter: Is it true those poor men aren't allowed to bathe here in the sea?

Lawyer: Yes. Not even with their clothes on. Only those who try to drown themselves get out of paying a fine —but I hear they get beaten up in the stationhouse.

Daughter: Can't they go out of the city and bathe—out in the country?

Lawyer: There is no country. It's all fenced in!

Daughter: Where it's open and free, I mean.

Lawyer: Nothing is free—everything belongs to somebody!

Daughter: Even the sea, the great, big—?

Lawyer: Everything! You can't sail on the sea and put in to port without registering and paying for it. It's just great!

Daughter: This isn't paradise.

Lawyer: No, I should say not!

Daughter: Why don't people do something to improve their condition?

Lawyer: Oh, they do, of course—but all the reformers end in prison or the madhouse.

Daughter: Who puts them in prison?

Lawyer: All the right-minded, all the upstanding people.

Daughter: Who sends them to the madhouse?

Lawyer: Their own despair—when they see the struggle is hopeless.

Daughter: Hasn't the idea occurred to anyone that for secret reasons things must remain as they are?

Lawyer: Oh, yes, those who are well-off always think so!

Daughter: That everything is all right as it is?

First C.: And yet we're the foundation of society. If we didn't deliver the coal, you'd have no fire for the kitchen, the parlor stove, or the machines in the factory . . . The lights would go out in the streets, the shops, and the homes . . . darkness and cold would plague you. That's why we have to sweat like men in hell to give you that black coal! And what do you give us in return?

Lawyer: [To **The Daughter.**] Help them . . .
[*Pause.*]
Things can't be exactly the same for everyone, I know that . . . but why should they be so different?
[*A **Gentleman** and a **Lady** cross the stage.*]

Lady: Come on, do you want to play a game?

Gentleman: No, I must take a little walk so I'll be able to eat my dinner.

First C.: So he'll be *able* to eat his dinner?

Second C.: So he'll be *able* . . . ?
[**Children** *enter and cry out in horror at the sight of the grimy* **Coalheavers** *(then they run off).*]

First C.: They scream when they see us! They scream . . .

Second C.: Damn it all! I guess we'll have to drag out the chopping-blocks soon, and operate on this rotten system.

Second C.: Yes, damn it, that's what I say! [*He spits.*]

Lawyer: [*To* **The Daughter.**] Things are all wrong! Men aren't so bad but—

Daughter: But . . . ?

Lawyer: But the government . . .

Daughter: [*Goes out, hiding her face in her hands.*] This is not paradise!

Coalheavers: No, it's hell, that's what it is!

The scene changes. Again the interior of Fingal's Cave. In the foreground, a red bell buoy rocks on the waves, no sound comes from it except when indicated. Music of the winds. Music of the waves.

[**The Daughter** *is alone with* **The Poet.**]

Poet: Where have you brought me?

Daughter: Far from the children of men and their murmurs and lamentations —to the outermost edge of the great ocean, to this cave that we call Indra's Ear, for here, it is said, the King of Heaven listens to the complaints of mortals.

Poet: But why here?

Daughter: Don't you see that this cave is built like a shell? Surely, you can see that! And don't you know that your ear is built like a shell? Of course, you know it . . . but you haven't thought about it.

> [She picks up a shell from the beach.]

When you were a child, didn't you hold a shell to your ear and listen—listen to the murmuring of your heart's blood, the whispering of the thoughts in your brain, the snapping of a thousand little worn-out threads in the tissues of your body? If you can hear all that in this little shell, imagine what can be heard in this big one!

Poet: [Listens.] I hear nothing but the whispering of the wind . . .

Daughter: Then I'll interpret for you! Listen! The winds are complaining—

> [She recites to soft music.]

We were born under the clouds in heaven,
but were driven by Indra's fires
down to the dirt-covered earth.
Chaff from the harvests soiled our feet,
dusty highways,
smoky cities,
reeking breaths,
odors of food and drink—
We had to endure all that.
Then we fled to the open sea
to fill our lungs with air,
to shake out our wings,
to bathe our feet.
Indra, Lord of the Heavens,
hear us!
Hear us when we sigh!
Earth is not clean,
life is not kind;
men are not evil,
neither are they good.
They live as they can,
one day at a time.
The sons of dust walk in the dust,
are born of dust,
return to dust.
They were given feet to trudge with—
no wings—

so they're smudged with dust.
Is the fault theirs
or yours?

Poet: I once heard that—

Daughter: Shhh! The winds are still singing.

> [She recites to soft music.]

We, the winds, the children of air,
carry abroad the complaints of men.
Have you heard us
on autumn nights
in the chimneys and stoves,
at keyholes and doors,
when the rain wept on the roof?
Or on wintry nights
in the snowclad, piney woods?
Have you heard us
on the high-heaving sea,
crooning and moaning
in the ropes and sails?
It was we, the winds,
the children of air,
who picked up the tones of torment
as we passed through human breasts
in sickrooms,
on battlefields,
but most of all in nurseries,
where newborn infants
whimper and wail
at the pain of living.
It is we, we the winds,
who are whining and whistling:
Woe! Woe! Woe!

Poet: It seems to me I've already—

Daughter: Be quiet! The waves are singing.

> [She recites to soft music.]

It is we, the waves,
who rock the winds
to rest—
green cradles, we waves!
We are wet and salty
and leap like flames of fire—
wet flames are we—
burning, quenching,
bathing, cleansing,
bearing, creating.
We, we the waves,
who rock the winds
to rest!
False and faithless waves! Everything on earth that's not burned, is

drowned—in the waves. Look here.
[*She points to a pile of debris.*]
Look what the sea has taken and
destroyed. Nothing is left of the
sunken ships but the figureheads . . .
and the names: *Justice, Friendship,
Golden Peace, Hope.* That's all that's
left of *Hope*—false *Hope*—spars,
oarlocks, and buckets! And look—
the lifebuoy; it saved itself but let
the men who needed it drown.

Poet: [*Searching among the wreckage.*]
Here's the nameplate of the ship
Justice. That's the one that left Fairhaven with the Blind Man's son on
board. So she sank! That was the
end of Alice's sweetheart . . . Edith's
hopeless love . . .

Daughter: The Blind Man? Fairhaven? I
must have dreamt that! And Alice's
sweetheart, Ugly Edith, Foulstrand
and the quarantine, sulphur and carbolic acid, the graduation in the
church, the Lawyer's office, the
alleyway and Victoria, the Growing
Castle and the Officer . . . That's
what I dreamt!

Poet: That's what I once wrote poems
about . . .

Daughter: Then you know what poetry
is!

Poet: Then I know what dreams are.
What's poetry?

Daughter: Not reality, but more than
reality. Not dreams, but daydreams . . .

Poet: But the children of men think
poets only waste time . . . invent
things and make believe!

Daughter: It's just as well, my friend, or
otherwise the world would go to
seed for lack of attention. Everybody would be lying on his back,
staring up at the sky. Nobody would
touch a plough or a shovel, a plane
or an axe.

Poet: And you, Indra's Daughter, say
that? You, who half belong up above!

Daughter: You're right to rebuke me. I've
stayed down here too long taking
mudbaths like you . . . My thoughts
can't fly any more. There's clay on

my wings . . . soil on my feet . . .
and I myself . . . [*She raises her
arms.*] I'm sinking, sinking . . . Help
me, Father, God of Heaven!
[*Silence.*]
I can't hear his answer any more. The
ether doesn't carry the sound from
his lips to the shell of my ear. The
silver thread is broken. Alas, I'm
bound to the earth!

Poet: Do you plan to rise . . . soon?

Daughter: As soon as I've burnt off the
dust, because all the waters in the
ocean can't make me clean. Why do
you ask?

Poet: Because I—I have a prayer . . . a
petition . . .

Daughter: What kind of petition?

Poet: A petition from mankind to the
ruler of the universe, drawn up by a
dreamer.

Daughter: Who's going to deliver it?

Poet: Indra's Daughter.

Daughter: Can you recite your poem?

Poet: I can.

Daughter: Then recite it.

Poet: I'd rather you did.

Daughter: Where can I read it?

Poet: In my thoughts—or here.
[*He hands her a scroll.*]

Daughter: [*Takes the scroll.*]
Well, I'll say it then! [*She speaks
without looking at the scroll.*]
"Why must you be born in anguish,
child of man, and cause your mother
so much pain, at the moment
of her motherhood,
the joy above all other joys?
Why do you awake to life,
why do you salute the light,
with cries of fury and of pain?
Why not meet life smiling, child of
man?
For the gift of life should be a joy!
Why must we be born like beasts,
though we come from God and man?
The soul should have a better garment
than this one made of blood and dirt.
Should God's own image lose his
teeth?—"
[*The **Daughter** breaks off, annoyed.*]

Be still! The statue can't find fault
　with the sculptor!
No one yet has solved the riddle of
　life!
　　[She goes on reciting the poem.]
"And thus begins the human journey,
over thistles, thorns, and stones;
if you take a beaten track,
people tell you it's forbidden;
then if you should pick a flower,
you're told at once that it's
　another's;
if a pasture lies before you,
and you dare to tramp across it,
and destroy your neighbor's harvest,
others then will tread yours down,
that you may lose in equal measure.
Every moment you enjoy
brings some grief to someone else,
but your grief makes no one happy,
for from grief comes only grief.
So you journey till you're dead,
and your death gives others bread!"
　　[She turns on **The Poet.**]
Is this the way, O Son of Dust,
that you approach the One Most
　High?

Poet:
　How can a son of dust find words
　so bright, so pure, so airy light
　that they can rise up from the earth?
　Child of the Gods, will you translate
　our cries of pain into the speech
　the Immortals understand?
Daughter: I will.
Poet: [Points to the buoy.] What's that
　floating there? A buoy?
Daughter: Yes.
Poet: It looks like a lung with a larynx.
Daughter: It's the watchman of the sea.
　When there's danger brewing, it
　sings out.
Poet: It seems to me the sea is rising and
　the waves are beginning to swell.
Daughter: That's not unlikely.
Poet: Oh, what am I seeing! A ship . . .
　bearing down on a reef.
Daughter: What ship can that be?
Poet: I think it's the ghost ship.
Daughter: What's that?
Poet: The *Flying Dutchman.*

Daughter: Oh, that one? Why is he being
　punished so severely, and why
　doesn't he go ashore?
Poet: Because he had seven unfaithful
　wives.
Daughter: Should he be punished for
　that?
Poet: Yes. All the right-minded con-
　demned him . . .
Daughter: What a strange world! But
　how can he be freed from this curse?
Poet: Freed? Oh, they see to it that no
　one is set free.
Daughter: Why?
Poet: Because—No, that's not the *Dutch-
　man!* That's an ordinary ship in dis-
　tress. Why doesn't the buoy sing out
　now? Look how the sea is rising . . .
　how high the waves are . . . we'll
　soon be trapped in the cave! Now
　the ship's bell is clanging. There'll
　soon be another figurehead in here.
　Cry out, buoy! Do your duty, watch-
　man!
　　[The buoy sounds a four-part
　　chord in fifths and sixths, like a
　　foghorn.]
The crew is beckoning to us . . . but
　we're doomed ourselves .
Daughter: Don't you want to be set free?
Poet: Yes, of course . . . of course I want
　to—but not now . . . and not in water.
The Crew: [Sings in quartet.] Christ
　Kyrie!
Poet: Now they're roaring . . . and the
　sea is roaring. But no one hears.
The Crew: [As before.] Christ Kyrie!
Daughter: Who's that coming there?
Poet: Walking on the water? There's
　only one who walks on water—and
　it's not Peter the Rock, because he
　sank like a stone . . .
　　[In the distance, a white light
　　shines over the sea.]
The Crew: Christ Kyrie!
Daughter: Is that He?
Poet: It's He, who was crucified . . .
Daughter: Why? Now tell me, why was
　He crucified?
Poet: Because He wanted to set men
　free.

Daughter: Who was it—I've forgotten —who crucified Him?

Poet: All the right-minded!

Daughter: What a strange world!

Poet: The sea is rising. Darkness is closing in on us. The storm is getting worse.

[**The Crew** *set up an outcry.*]

Poet: The sailors are screaming with horror at the sight of their Saviour! And now . . . they're jumping overboard for fear of the Redeemer.

[**The Crew** *cry out again.*]

Poet: Now they're screaming because they must die. Screaming when they're born, and screaming when they die!

[*The rising waves threaten to engulf the two in the cave.*]

Daughter: If I knew for sure it was a ship—

Poet: To tell the truth, I don't think it's a ship. It's a two-story house with trees in front of it . . . and telephone poles—a pole reaching up to the skies. It's the modern Tower of Babel, sending up wires to communicate with those up there . . .

Daughter: My child, men's thoughts don't need wires to travel on. Prayers said with devotion make their way to the ends of the world. That's certainly no Tower of Babel. If you want to storm heaven, storm it with your prayers!

Poet: No, it's not a house . . . not a telephone pole . . . Do you see it?

Daughter: What do you see?

While the **Poet** *speaks, the scene changes back to the alleyway outside the opera house.*

Poet: I see a heath covered with snow . . . a drill ground. The winter sun is shining behind a church on a hill, and the steeple casts a long shadow on the snow. Now a troop of soldiers comes marching over the heath. They march along the steeple and up the spire. Now they've reached the cross, but I have a feeling that the first one to step on the weathercock has to die. Now they're getting near it. A corporal is leading them . . . Aha! There comes a cloud sailing over the heath and right in front of the sun, of course . . . now everything is gone . . . the water in the cloud has put out the sun's fire! The sun's light created the shadow of the steeple, but the shadow of the steeple was swallowed by the shadow of the cloud.

[**The Gatekeeper** *is at her post;* **The Daughter** *approaches her.*]

Daughter: [*To* **The Gatekeeper.**] Has the Lord Chancellor arrived yet?

Gatekeeper: No.

Daughter: Have the Deans come?

Gatekeeper: No.

Daughter: Then call them at once, because the door's going to be opened.

Gatekeeper: Is it so urgent?

Daughter: Yes, it is. Because people have the mistaken notion that the answer to the riddle of the world was put in there for safekeeping. So call the Lord Chancellor and the Deans of the Four Faculties!

[**The Gatekeeper** *blows a whistle.*]

Daughter: And don't forget the Glazier and his diamond . . . otherwise nothing can be done

[**Members of the Opera Company** *enter from the left, as in the earlier scene.*

The Officer, *in frock coat and top hat, comes through the gate, carrying a bouquet of roses and looking radiantly happy. (He is young again.)*]

Officer: [*Sings.*] Victoria!

Gatekeeper: The young lady will be down in a minute

Officer: Good! The carriage is waiting, the table is set, the champagne is on ice—Let me hug you, Madam.

[*He embraces* **The Gatekeeper,** *then sings.*] Victoria!

Woman's Voice: [*From above.*] I am here!

Officer: [*Paces up and down.*] Well, I'm waiting!

Poet: It seems to me I've been through all this before.

Daughter: I have the same feeling.

Poet: Perhaps I dreamt it.

Daughter: Or made a poem of it.

Poet: Or made a poem of it.

Daughter: Then you know what poetry is.

Poet: I know what dreaming is.

Daughter: It seems to me we were some place else and said these words before.

Poet: Then you'll soon be able to figure out what reality is!

Daughter: Or dreaming!

Poet: Or poetry!

> [**The Lord Chancellor;** *the* **Deans of Theology, Philosophy, Medicine,** *and* **Law;** *(then several of the* **Right-Minded** *and* **The Glazier**) *enter.*]

Lord Chancellor: It's a question of opening the door, of course. What does the Dean of Theology think?

Dean of Theology: I don't think. I believe. *Credo.*

Dean of Philosophy: I hold—

Dean of Medicine: I know—

Dean of Law: I doubt until I have evidence and witnesses.

Lord Chancellor: Now they're going to bicker again. Well then, first, what does Theology believe?

Theology: I believe that this door should not be opened because it conceals dangerous truths . . .

Philosophy: The truth is never dangerous.

Medicine: What is truth?

Law: Whatever can be proved by two witnesses.

Theology: Anything can be proved by two false witnesses—if you're a shyster.

Philosophy: Truth is wisdom, and wisdom—knowledge—is philosophy itself. Philosophy is the science of sciences, the knowledge of all knowledge, and all other sciences are the handmaidens of philosophy.

Medicine: Natural science is the only true science—and philosophy is no science at all. It's nothing but empty speculation.

Theology: Bravo!

Philosophy: [*To* **Theology.**] You say bravo! And what, may I ask, are you? You're the arch-enemy of all knowledge. You're the very antithesis of knowledge. You're utter ignorance and darkness.

Medicine: Bravo!

Theology: [*To* **Medicine.**] You say bravo, you who can only see as far as the end of your nose in a magnifying glass. You who believe in nothing but your own unreliable senses —in your eyes, for instance, which may be far-sighted, near-sighted, blind, purblind, cross-eyed, one-eyed, color-blind, red-blind, green-blind . . .

Medicine: Idiot!

Theology: Ass!

> [*They fight.*]

Lord Chancellor: Stop! One hawk doesn't peck out another hawk's eyes!

Philosophy: If I had to choose between those two, Theology and Medicine, I'd choose—neither.

Law: And if I had to sit in judgment over the three of you, I'd find all of you—guilty! You can't even agree on a single point, and you never could. Now back to the case on the calendar. What are the Lord Chancellor's opinions as to this door and its opening?

Lord Chancellor: Opinions? I have no opinions. I was only appointed by the government to see that you don't break each other's arms and legs during faculty meetings—while educating the young. Opinions? No, I'm very careful not to have any opinions. I once had a few but they were immediately contradicted. Opinions are always contradicted—by their opponents, of course. But can't we have the door opened now, even at the risk of finding some dangerous truths behind it?

Law: What is truth? Where is the truth?

Theology: I am the Truth and the Life . . .

Philosophy: I am the knowledge of all knowledge . . .

Law: I doubt!

[*They fight.*]

Daughter: Teachers of the young, shame on you!

Law: Lord Chancellor, as the representative of the government and head of the entire faculty, you must prosecute this woman for her misdemeanor. She said, "Shame on you!" That's an insult! And in a sneering and ironical way, she called you "teachers of the young." That's slander!

Daughter: Poor young people!

Law: She pities the young—in effect, she's accusing us. Lord Chancellor, you must prosecute the misdemeanor.

Daughter: Yes, I accuse you—all of you —of sowing doubt and dissension in the minds of the young.

Law: Listen to her—she herself is making the young question our authority, and then she accuses us of sowing doubt. Isn't that a criminal offense? I ask all the right-minded!

All The Right-Minded: Certainly, it's criminal.

Law: All the right-minded people have condemned you. Take your winnings and leave peacefully, or else—

Daughter: My winnings? Or else? Or else what?

Law: Or else you'll be stoned.

Poet: Or crucified.

Daughter: I'm going. Follow me, and you'll get the answer to the riddle.

Poet: Which riddle?

Daughter: What did he mean by "my winnings"?

Poet: Probably nothing at all. That's what we call empty talk. He was just talking.

Daughter: But he hurt me very deeply when he said that.

Poet: That's probably just why he said it. That's the way human beings are.

All The Right-Minded: Hurray! The door is open!

Lord Chancellor: What's hidden behind the door?

Glazier: I can't see anything.

Lord Chancellor: He can't see anything! No, I'm sure he can't! Deans! What's hidden behind that door?

Theology: Nothing! That's the answer to the riddle of the world. In the beginning God created heaven and earth out of nothing . . .

Philosophy: Out of nothing comes nothing.

Medicine: Rubbish! That's nothing!

Law: I doubt. And lying here before us we have a case of fraud. I appeal to all the right-minded.

Daughter: [*To **The Poet.**] Who are the right-minded?

Poet: Yes, who can tell! More often than not all the right-minded are only one person. Today it's me and mine, tomorrow it's you and yours. It's a job you're appointed to, or rather, appoint yourself to.

All The Right-Minded: We've been swindled!

Lord Chancellor: Who's swindled you?

All The Right-Minded: The Daughter!

Lord Chancellor: Will the Daughter kindly tell us what her reason was for having the door opened?

Daughter: No, my friends. If I told you, you wouldn't believe me.

Medicine: But there's nothing there.

Daughter: You say it—but you don't understand it.

Medicine: She's talking rubbish!

All: Rubbish!

Daughter: [*To **The Poet.**] They're to be pitied!

Poet: Are you serious?

Daughter: Always serious.

Poet: Do you think the right-minded are to be pitied too?

Daughter: They most of all, perhaps.

Poet: And the four Deans?

Daughter: They, too, and not the least. Four heads, four minds, and one body. Who made that monster?

All: She's not answering!

Lord Chancellor: Then stone her!

Daughter: I have answered.

Lord Chancellor: Listen, she's answering.

All: Stone her! She's answering.

Daughter: Whether she answers or doesn't answer, stone her! [To **The Poet.**] Come with me, Seer, and I'll tell you the answer to the riddle— but far away from here—out in the desert, where no one can hear us, no one can see us! Because—

[**The Lawyer** enters.]

Lawyer: [Takes **The Daughter** by the arm.] Have you forgotten your duties?

Daughter: Oh, God, no! But I have higher duties.

Lawyer: And your child?

Daughter: My child! What, again?

Lawyer: Your child is crying for you.

Daughter: My child! Alas, I'm earthbound! And this agony in my breast, this anguish . . . what is it?

Lawyer: Don't you know?

Daughter: No.

Lawyer: They're the pangs of conscience.

Daughter: These are the pangs of conscience?

Poet: Yes, they come after every neglected duty; after every pleasure, even the most innocent, if there's such a thing as an innocent pleasure, which is doubtful; and after every pain you cause another.

Daughter: Isn't there any remedy?

Lawyer: Yes, but only one—to do your duty promptly.

Daughter: You look like a devil when you say the word "duty." But what if, like me, you have two duties to do?

Lawyer: Do one first and then the other.

Daughter: The higher first! So you look after my child, and I'll do my duty.

Lawyer: Your child is suffering . . . it misses you. How can you bear to know a human being is suffering because of you?

Daughter: Now there's a struggle in my soul . . . it's being pulled two ways . . . being torn in two.

Lawyer: Those, you see, are life's little discords!

Daughter: Oh, how they tear me apart!

Poet: If you had any idea of the misery and ruin I've caused by following my vocation—notice I say *vocation*, which is the highest duty—you wouldn't even touch my hand.

Daughter: What do you mean?

Poet: I had a father who put all his hopes in me, his only son, who would carry on his business. I ran away from business school. My father grieved himself to death. My mother wanted me to be religious. I couldn't be religious. She disowned me. I had a friend who helped me through some very hard times, but that friend turned out to be an oppressor of those I was defending in my speaking and writing. I had to throw over my friend and benefactor in order to save my soul! Since then I've had no peace. I'm called dishonorable, the scum of the earth— and it doesn't help that my conscience says, "You've done right," because a minute later it says, "You've done wrong." That's the way life is!

Daughter: Come with me into the desert.

Lawyer: Your child!

Daughter: [Indicates everyone present.] Here are my children! Each one by himself is good, but when they come together they quarrel and turn into devils. Farewell!

The scene changes. It is the outside of the Growing Castle, as in the first scene of the first act, but now the ground is

*covered with such flowers as blue monks-
hood or aconite. On the roof of the castle,
at the very top of its beacon light, there
is a chrysanthemum bud on the point of
opening. The castle windows are lit with
candles. [There is a fire in the foreground.]*

[**The Daughter** *and* **The Poet**
enter.]

Daughter: It won't be long before I rise
again into the ether . . . with the
help of the fire. That's what you call
dying and approach with fear.

Poet: Fear of the unknown.

Daughter: Which you know.

Poet: Who knows it?

Daughter: All of you! Why don't you
believe your prophets?

Poet: Prophets have never been believed. Why is that? And "if God has
spoken, why will men then not believe?" His power to convince ought
to be irresistible.

Daughter: Have you always doubted?

Poet: No, I've had faith many times, but
after a while it faded away—like a
dream when you wake up.

Daughter: It's not easy to be human!

Poet: You realize that—and admit it?

Daughter: Yes.

Poet: Tell me, wasn't it Indra who once
sent His son down here to listen to
man's complaints?

Daughter: Yes, it was. And how was He
received?

Poet: How did He fulfill His mission? To
answer with a question.

Daughter: And if I may reply with another—wasn't man's condition improved after His visit to earth? Answer truthfully!

Poet: Improved? Yes, a little. Very little.
But instead of asking questions, will
you tell me the answer to the riddle?

Daughter: Yes, but what good would it
do? You know you won't believe me!

Poet: Of course, I'll believe you, because
I know who you are.

Daughter: Then I'll tell you. In the
dawn of time, before the sun gave

light, Brahma, the primal power, let
himself be seduced by Maya, the
mother of the world, so he would
multiply. This mingling of divine
force with earthly matter was the
fall of heaven into sin. And so
the world—life and mankind—are
only phantom, illusion, and dream-
image . . .

Poet: My dream!

Daughter: A dream come true! But the
offspring of Brahma try to free themselves of the earth-matter by self-
denial and suffering. There you have
suffering as a liberator. But this craving for suffering comes into conflict
with the longing for joy, for love.
Now do you understand what love
is? The greatest joy mixed with the
worst suffering, the sweetest with
the bitterest! Now do you understand what woman is? Woman,
through whom sin and death came
into life?

Poet: I understand! And the end of it all?

Daughter: You already know it: the conflict between the pain of pleasure
and the pleasure of suffering, between the agony of the penitent
and the ecstasy of the sensualist—

Poet: That means struggle!

Daughter: The struggle of opposites gen-
erates energy, just as fire and water
produce the power of steam.

Poet: But peace? Rest?

Daughter: Hush! You mustn't ask any
more questions, and I mustn't answer
any. The altar is already decorated
for the sacrifice, the flowers stand
watch, the candles are lit, white
sheets hang at the windows, the
spruce lies on the threshold.[7]

Poet: You say that so calmly—as though
suffering didn't exist for you.

Daughter: Didn't exist? I've suffered all
you've suffered, but a hundred-fold,
because my senses are keener.

Poet: Tell me your sorrows!

---

[7] White sheets and spruce are signs of mourning in Sweden.

Daughter: Could you tell me yours, Poet, without wasting a single word? Could your words ever—even once —really express your thoughts?

Poet: No, you're right! It always seemed to me I was deaf and dumb, and though the crowd listened to my song with admiration, I thought it was just a lot of noise. You see, that's why I always felt ashamed when they praised me.

Daughter: And yet you want me to— Look me in the eye!

Poet: I can't stand your glance—

Daughter: Then how could you stand my words, if I were to speak in my own tongue!

Poet: Tell me, anyway, before you go, what did you suffer from most down here?

Daughter: From—being . . . From feeling my vision weakened by an eye, my hearing impaired by an ear, and my thoughts, my bright, airy thoughts, bound down in labyrinthine coils of fat. I'm sure you've seen a brain . . . what crooked, what creeping paths . . .

Poet: Yes, and that's why all the right-minded think crookedly!

Daughter: Malicious, always malicious . . . but you're all like that!

Poet: How can we be anything else?

Daughter: Now, first of all, I shake the dust from my feet . . . the dirt and the clay . . .
[She takes off her shoes and puts them into the fire.]

Gatekeeper: *[Enters and puts her shawl into the fire.]* Perhaps I can burn my shawl too?
[Exits.]

Officer: *[Enters.]* And I my roses . . . only the thorns are left.
[Exits.]

Billposter: *[Enters.]* The posters can go, but the fish-net never.
[Exits.]

Glazier: *[Enters.]* The diamond that opened the door. Farewell!
[Exits.]

Lawyer: *[Enters.]* The minutes of that great case re the Pope's beard or the water shortage at the sources of the Ganges.
[Exits.]

Q. Master: *[Enters.]* A little contribution —the black mask that made me a blackamoor against my will!
[Exits.]

Victoria: *[Enters.]* My beauty, my sorrow!
[Exits.]

Edith: *[Enters.]* My ugliness, my sorrow!
[Exits.]

The Blind Man: *[Enters and puts his hand in the fire.]* I give my hand for my eye.
[Exits.]

*[***Don Juan,*** in his wheelchair; **The Coquette,** and **The Friend** enter.]*

Don Juan: Hurry up! Hurry up! Life is short!
[He leaves with the other two.]

Poet: I've read that when life is about to end everything and everybody rushes by in one unbroken stream . . . Is this the end?

Daughter: Yes, it's my end. Farewell!

Poet: Say a parting word!

Daughter: No, I can't. Do you think your words can express our thoughts?

Theology: *[Enters in a rage.]* I'm disowned by God and persecuted by man, deserted by the government and scorned by my colleagues! How can I believe when nobody else believes? How can I defend a God who doesn't defend his own? Rubbish, that's what it is!
[Throws a book on the fire and goes out.]

Poet: *[Snatches the book from the flames.]* Do you know what this is? A history of martyrs, a calendar with a martyr for each day of the year.

Daughter: A martyr?

Poet: Yes, someone who suffers and dies for his faith! Tell me why! Do you think everyone who's tortured suffers, and everyone who's put to death feels pain? Suffering is said to be salvation, and death a deliverance.

Kristin: *[Enters with strips of paper.]* I'm pasting . . . I'm pasting . . . till there's nothing left to paste . . .

Poet: And if heaven itself should split open, you'd try to paste it together . . . Go away!

Kristin: Aren't there any double windows up there in the castle?

Poet: No, I tell you, not there!

Kristin: Well, then I'll be going!
    [Exits.]

Daughter:
    The time to part has come, the end
        draws near;
    farewell, you child of man, you
        dreamer,
    you poet, who best knows how to
        live;
    you soar on wings above the earth
    and dive at times to touch the dust,
    to touch it lightly, not to sink.
    And now that I must go, now in the
        parting hour,
    I feel great loss for a friend and place
        I loved,
and deep regret for everything un-
    done.
Oh, now I know the pains of life,
and all the suffering men endure . . .
You feel remorse for sins you didn't
    commit;
you long to leave, but also yearn to
    stay.
And so the heart is split in two, as
    though
by horses dragged apart—the feel-
    ings torn
by conflict, discord, indecision.
Farewell! Tell your brothers and
    sisters
I'll not forget them where I'm going,
    and,
in your name, I'll carry their com-
    plaints
up to the very throne. Farewell!
    [She goes into the castle. Music is heard. The background is lit up by the burning castle and reveals a wall of human faces, questioning, grieving, despairing. As the castle burns, the flower bud on the roof opens and becomes a gigantic chrysanthemum.]

CURTAIN

THE
SEAGULL

Anton Chekhov

Konstantin (Stephen Haggard) presents the dead sea gull to Nina (Peggy Ashcroft) in the Komisarjevsky production of the play at the New Theatre, London 1936. Photograph: Houston Rogers Theatre Collection, New York Public Library.

Anton Pavlovich Chekhov

Anton Pavlovich Chekhov, an imposing figure in world literature, and Russia's greatest playwright, was born January 17, 1860, in the Ukrainian port of Taganrog on the Sea of Azov. His grandfather was a serf who, by 1841, had accumulated through hard work and frugality, 3500 rubles to buy his freedom. Chekhov's father, Pavel Yegorovich, a clerk in a counting-house, married Evgenia Yakovlovna Morozova in 1854 and scraped together enough money to open a little grocery store. Anton was the third of six children.

The difficult days of his childhood he always recalled with sadness. His father was a religious fanatic and a petty despot, who whipped the boy daily without provocation and forced him to go to church morning and evening and to extra services on Sundays and holidays. From the age of eight, Anton worked long hours in his father's grocery store, at the same time trying to keep up with his studies.

Anton's father, for all his brutality, dabbled in ikon-painting, played the violin, and had a passion for liturgical music, and organizing a church choir in which his sons had to sing. Anton's mother was an excellent story-teller. From both parents Chekhov inherited his love of the arts, but his character was formed primarily by his mother, for he took after her in kindliness, generosity, and consideration for others. His father's religious excesses drove Chekhov from organized religion. Instead, he subscribed to a sort of pantheism, believing that love of God could best be shown through love of man. This theme, which recurs in his stories and plays, was amply demonstrated in his daily life.

When it was time for Anton to go to school, he was sent first to the Greek school at the Church of St. Constantine; but when, at the end of the year, it was found that he had learned nothing, his mother insisted he be transferred to the local secondary school, from which he was graduated ten years later. As a student, Chekhov wrote sketches, poems, and essays, and saw some of them published in the school magazine. He had a special gift for mimicry, and, at home, wrote and appeared in humorous skits, which delighted his family. When he was thirteen, his mother took him to the theatre for the first time; thereafter, he took part in amateur theatricals, winning a reputation among his relatives and neighbors for the excellence of his comic characterizations.

In 1876 his father's business failed, and the penniless family moved to Moscow, leaving Anton behind to finish his schooling in Taganrog. To support himself, the sixteen-year-old boy found work as a tutor. Freed from church-going and servitude in the grocery store, he now read widely among classic and contemporary writers and went often to the local theatre, where he became acquainted with the actors and learned something of stagecraft and make-up. In his last years at school, he wrote several plays—a full-length drama called *Without Fathers,* and some short comedies, entitled *Diamond Cuts Diamond, Why the Hen Clucks,* and *Laugh It Off If You Can.* His older brother Alexander who took an interest in Anton's efforts, did not think very highly of these early pieces, and they have not been pre-served. But the jokes and humorous anecdotes that Anton dashed off, Alexander was able to place with the comic magazines in Moscow. Chekhov wrote with enormous facility, but it did not occur to him at this time to take his gift seriously. Writing seemed just an easy way to make money to send home. He had set his heart on becoming a doctor.

Chekhov completed his secondary schooling in 1879 and went to Moscow to join his family. His father had found work in a distant warehouse and lived away from home, as did his two elder brothers, Alexander and Nicholas, who were leading loose and undisciplined lives. In the household were his mother, two younger brothers, and his sister. At nineteen Anton became the head of the family, assuming a responsibility for support he was to maintain for the rest of his life.

At about the time he enrolled in the medical school at Moscow Univer-sity, he began to send his literary efforts to various comic magazines. His first piece appeared in *The Dragonfly* on March 9, 1880. Free-lance compe-tition was brutally hard, but he scribbled so persistently that by the time he completed his medical studies in 1884, he had published about three hundred short, humorous tales, some of which had been gathered together into book form. He was now ready, he felt, to write longer and more serious stories; he made an agreement with the editor of the *Petersburg Gazette,* to supply a story a week, with no limitations as to length or theme. In addition to his labors as a writer, Chekhov began to practice medicine. At twenty-four, from the strain of overwork and from an inherited predis-position to tuberculosis, Chekhov had a severe hemorrhage, the first sign of his chronic illness.

In 1885 Chekhov learned, to his surprise, that his work was held in high esteem by a number of celebrated writers in St. Petersburg, the literary capital of Russia. A well-known novelist, D. V. Grigorovich, wrote to Chekhov praising him as an artist, but urging him to write fewer stories so that he could devote more time and care to each one. Grigorovich also suggested that Chekhov dispense with the pseudonym, Antosha Chekhonte, under which all of his tales had thus far appeared. Chekhov was pleased to know that he was regarded as an artist but, in view of his need for money, was troubled by the advice that he write more slowly.

Through Grigorovich Chekhov met A. S. Suvorin, the wealthy and influential publisher of *New Times.* Chekhov became a regular contributor to that newspaper, in spite of his disapproval of its ultraconservative point of view. In his stories he rose above partisanship and tried to maintain the scientific objectivity of the physician. "Literature is called artistic," he said, "when it depicts life as it actually is. Its aim is absolute and honest truth." Later he amplified this: "The artist should not be a judge of his characters or of what they say, but only an objective observer. I heard a confused, indecisive talk by two Russians on pessimism and so must convey this conversation in the same form in which I heard it, but it is up to the jury, i.e., the readers, to give it an evaluation. My job is only to be talented, i.e., to be able to throw light upon some figures and speak their language." This was the principle he observed in writing his plays, as well as his short stories. If his characters expressed social, political, or philosophical ideas, Chekhov recorded them, without necessarily agreeing with them. Yet, because of the supreme talent with which he portrayed human beings—subtly suggesting the economic and political, as well as the psychological, causes of their suffering—he was "able to throw light" of enormous intensity upon the social evils of his time.

Chekhov began to devote more care and attention to his work. He spent the entire month of January, 1888, writing and polishing The Steppe, a very long story, which he sent to the important literary journal The Northern Herald. Publication of The Steppe brought him high praise and, later that year, the much-coveted Pushkin prize for literature.

The year 1889 marks the beginning of a dark period in Chekhov's life. In that year he attempted a full-length novel, which proved an impossible task for him; his play The Wood Demon was accounted a failure; and his brother Nicholas died of tuberculosis at the age of thirty-one. This series of events threw him into a state of frustration and despair, an emotional crisis that was to last for almost four years. It was during this time that Chekhov went on a journey of about twelve thousand miles to the notorious Russian penal colony on the island of Sakhalin, situated off the eastern coast of Siberia. There he interviewed convicts and jailers and collected material for his book Sakhalin Island, a valuable record and an intensely human document.

In 1892 Chekhov moved his family to a country house in Melikhovo, about fifty miles from Moscow. There he practiced medicine, entertained friends, and relaxed by gardening and fishing. With his move to the country, Chekhov's creative powers returned in full force, to remain unabated until the end of his life. In the twelve years left to him, he wrote almost two hundred tales of ever-deepening significance and became, for his time, the undisputed master of the short story. At Melikhovo, too, his great dramatic period began with the writing of The Seagull.

Chekhov had been interested in the theatre from childhood, but when he was ready to embark on a writing career, he discovered that no serious playwright could expect to succeed in the political and cultural climate that prevailed in Russia during the eighties and nineties. In 1881, when Chekhov was a student at Moscow University, the comparatively liberal Czar Alexander II was assasinated. His successor, Alexander III, immediately instituted a series of repressive and reactionary measures, which dealt especially severely with university students and intellectuals. An atmo-sphere of boredom, apathy, and despair engulfed the professional and upper classes, while the poverty and hopelessness of the peasants were intensified. Chekhov managed to portray the plight of these people in his short stories by so subtle a use of poetic naturalism that few readers were aware of the implied social criticism. Still, on occasion he ran afoul of the sharp-eyed censor. He had not as yet found a way to deal with serious subject matter in play form.

Standard fare in the Russian theatres of the time were plays of romance and intrigue, dealing with sentimental and superficial material and adapted mainly from French and German originals. Scenery, costumes, and lighting were crude, and the acting was artificial. The theatre had nothing to do with reality and, to make it even less attractive to Chekhov, could not provide a living for a full-time playwright. Nevertheless, Chekhov wrote plays regularly throughout his career.

His most successful efforts during the 1880s were his one-act comedies and farces, such as *The Bear, The Marriage Proposal, The Wedding,* and *The Anniversary.* These were produced throughout Russia and brought their author a small but regular income. *The Bear* was the one play of Chekhov's that Tolstoy admitted liking, while an excellent performance of *The Marriage Proposal* at the summer palace drew high praise from Alexander III. Several serious one-acters also met with public and critical approval; these included *On the Highway, On the Harmfulness of Tobacco,* and *The Swan Song.*

The fate of his three full-length plays written before he was thirty proved a great disappointment to Chekhov, but taught him many valuable lessons. *Platonov* (c., 1881) deals with an aimless individual, "a weak-willed character of contemporary life," who is in love with three women and is finally shot by one of them. The play was neither produced nor published during its author's lifetime. The central character in *Ivanov* (1887–89)—who, like Platonov, is bored and disillusioned—neglects his dying wife and turns his attentions to a naïve young girl; then, in a fit of despair, he commits suicide. This play was fairly well received at Korsh's Theatre in Moscow in 1887; but Chekhov revised it for its presentation in 1889 at the Alexandrinsky Theatre in St. Petersburg, where it made an enormous impression. In the character of Ivanov, the critics recognized a type rather than an individual, one writer remarking that there were "many weak, will-less Ivanovs in Russia, who evaded the significant problems of society." In both these early plays Chekhov managed to move away from the sentimental and the romantic. Although he was slow to eliminate the elements of melodrama or the use of a pistol to achieve a dramatic climax, he did succeed, however, in dealing realistically with ordinary, middle-class people at a time when audiences and critics clamored for larger-than-life-size heroes. In defense of his "antiheroes," Chekhov wrote:

> The demand is made that the hero and heroine should be dramatically effective. But in life people do not shoot themselves, or hang themselves, or fall in love, or deliver themselves of clever sayings every minute. They spend most of their time eating, drinking, running after women or men, talking nonsense. It is therefore necessary that this should be shown on the stage. A play ought to be written in which the people should come and go, dine, talk of the weather, or play cards, not because the author wants it but because that is what happens in real life. Life on the stage should be as it really is, and the people, too, should be as they are and not on stilts.

In *The Wood Demon,* his next full-length play, Chekhov took a significant step away from the conventional drama of his time and achieved, if only in outline, the play he wanted to write. It dealt not with a single protagonist but with the interrelationship of a group of people. How unusual the play was, Chekhov himself realized, for in a letter to Suvorin, he said: "The play is terribly queer and I'm surprised that such peculiar things can come from my pen." As in his later, and greater, plays, Chekhov dealt here with the emotional distress and confusion of the Russian intellectual, capturing at the same time the lyrical mood of the Russian countryside. He was still trying desperately to subordinate overt dramatic action to the inner reactions of his characters; he showed them in their ordinary pursuits —eating, drinking, and playing games—even while being drawn unknowingly, to disaster. Ironically, *The Wood Demon* seemed to those to whom it was submitted for production to be unreal, contrived, and melodramatic; it was turned down by the Alexandrinsky Theatre and by Korsh's. It was finally put on in December, 1889, for a brief run at the Abramova Theatre in Moscow and drew harsh comments from the critics. Thereafter, Chekhov would permit neither the production nor the publication of this play.

It was six years before Chekhov undertook to write another play. He completed *The Seagull* at the end of 1895 and, after revising it several times, saw it performed the following year at the Alexandrinsky Theatre in St. Petersburg. The day after the opening he wrote to his brother, Michael, "The play flopped with a bang. . . . The moral of the story is: I shouldn't write plays." The real reason for the catastrophe, however, was the total inability of an old-fashioned director and actors, famous though they were, to cope with a Chekhovian work. This failure led Chekhov to declare, "If I live to be seven hundred, I'll not give another play to the theatre." But *The Seagull* was soon being presented with more or less success in various provincial cities, and *The Wood Demon*, which Chekhov had revised and renamed *Uncle Vanya*, was also succeeding in the provinces. What Chekhov actually required was a theatre company that had the sensitivity and skill to interpret his complex and subtle plays.

It was only after much pleading that V. I. Nemirovich-Danchenko, a friend of Chekhov's, got the playwright's permission to produce *The Seagull* at the Moscow Art Theatre, which Nemirovich-Danchenko was planning with his collaborator, Constantin Stanislavsky. The Moscow Art Theatre opened its doors in 1898 with a spectacular production of Alexey Tolstoy's historical play, *Czar Fyodor*, which was a great success; there followed in quick succession five plays that failed. The theatre was in a precarious financial position and the success or failure of its next offering, *The Seagull*, would determine its fate. The play opened on December 17 and was received with ecstatic approval. The Moscow Art Theatre was saved. In gratitude to Chekhov, the company adopted a seagull as its official emblem, which it uses to this day. As a result of its brilliant productions of the plays of Shakespeare, Ibsen, Tolstoy, Chekhov, Gorky and Maeterlinck, the Moscow Art Theatre has won world-wide recognition; and, mainly because of the production techniques developed by Stanislavsky, it has exerted the greatest influence on world theatre of any company in modern times.

By September, 1898, Chekhov's health had deteriorated so seriously that he was forced to leave Moscow and take up residence at Yalta in the Crimea. He was thus prevented from attending the opening of *The Seagull* and of his next two plays. *Uncle Vanya*, which dealt with a group of bored and melancholy people and which Chekhov called "scenes from country life," was produced in Moscow on October 26, 1899. Olga Knipper, the company's leading actress, with whom Chekhov had fallen in love, wrote him after the opening that the play had "gripped the whole audience." *The Three Sisters*, another play dealing with deeply frustrated people, had its première on January 31, 1901. Its reception was only lukewarm, although Maxim Gorky considered it the profoundest and most effective of Chekhov's plays. It took the critics and the public several years to recognize its greatness. For this play, however, Chekhov was awarded the Griboyedov prize by the Society of Dramatic Writers.

On May 25, 1901, Chekhov married Olga Knipper. After a short honeymoon the couple went to Yalta, where the playwright's mother and sister shared his home. In August Olga left for Moscow to start rehearsing for the new season, while Chekhov remained in Yalta. They wrote to each other daily, but their meetings were infrequent. Although his health was in a precarious state, Chekhov went to Moscow for the opening of *The Cherry Orchard* on January 17, 1904, which coincided exactly with his forty-fourth birthday and his twenty-fifth anniversary as a writer. *The Cherry Orchard,* which dealt prophetically with the social, economic, and cultural changes that were soon to cause an upheaval in Russian life, has proved to be Chekhov's most popular play.

A new theatre had been provided for the Moscow Art Theatre company by Savva Morozov, a wealthy industrialist and patron of the arts. Appearing on the stage at the end of the play, Chekhov was greeted by roars of approval from the overflowing audience and the entire personnel of the Art Theatre. He was deluged with flowers, wreaths, and gifts. Looking pale, thin, and deathly ill, he stood there and listened while representatives of all the cultural organizations in Russia uttered interminable speeches of praise.

After the jubilee Chekhov returned to Yalta. In the next few months his health took a turn for the worse. Early in June he went with his wife to Germany to seek treatment for his disease; there, in Badenweiler, on the morning of July 2, 1904, Chekhov died. He was buried in the Novodevichy Cemetery in Moscow.

A few years before his death Chekhov's collected works were published in ten volumes. It was an impressive monument to the writer—particularly so because all the while he was engaged in his literary efforts, he was active in medicine and in public affairs: he doctored the peasants, took part in local government, stocked several public libraries with books, built three schools and a tuberculosis sanitorium largely at his own expense, and sponsored the construction of new roads and new housing—activities which, though ephemeral, form an awesome monument to the humanitarianism of the man.

Chekhov's great contribution to modern drama was his ability to combine reality with theatricality, to interweave the threads of comedy, tragedy, melodrama, and farce with so skillful a hand as to create the illusion of life itself. The full complexity and subtlety of his work have often escaped even his most devoted admirers. Stanislavsky, for example, was almost totally blind to the comic and farcical elements in the plays, which drew from Chekhov the constant complaint that the director was turning his characters into "cry-babies." Bernard Shaw wrote *Heartbreak House* under the impression that he was creating "in the Russian manner," including the lachrymose title, but his play is more Shavian than Chekhovian. There have been many "disciples" of Chekhov, among whom we may include Luigi Pirandello, Clifford Odets, Federico Garcia Lorca, Lillian Hellman, Tennessee Williams, and Samuel Beckett. But in the depth of his humanity, the breadth of his perception, and the unsurpassed skill of his workmanship, Chekhov remains unique among modern playwrights.

The Seagull

In a letter to his friend Alexey Suvorin, dated October 21, 1895, Chekhov said, "I'm writing a play which I probably won't finish until the end of November. I'm writing it with a great deal of pleasure, though I sin terribly against the conventions of the stage. It is a comedy with three female parts, six male, four acts, a landscape (view of a lake), lots of talk about literature, little action, and five tons of love." About a month later he informed another friend, "I've finished my play. It's called *The Seagull*. It's nothing to rave about. In general, I'd say that I'm not a very good playwright."

Both fact and fiction went into the making of *The Seagull*.[1] One important component of the plot came from *A Boring Story*, which Chekhov had written in 1889; in it a young girl, who yearns to be an actress, is seduced, has a child out of wedlock, is deserted by the man, and then loses the child. Coincidentally, not long before writing his play, Chekhov learned that two of his friends were having an illicit affair: the young Lika Mizinova, who wanted to be an opera singer, and I. N. Potapenko, an older, sophisticated man, who was a writer. Lika gave birth to a child, who died after Lika was deserted by Potapenko.

Two other elements in the play lead back to Chekhov's friend Isaac Levitan, the celebrated landscape painter and lady's man. Levitan, who enjoyed hunting—a sport Chekhov despised—one day urged the writer to go with him for a walk in the woods. On the way Levitan sighted a woodcock and shot it. The bird, in all its beautiful plumage, was still living when it fell at Chekhov's feet. Levitan, in a highly nervous state, prevailed upon Chekhov to kill it. Referring to this incident in a letter to Suvorin, Chekhov wrote: "One lovely amorous creature less in the world, and two fools returned home and sat down to supper." For the play Chekhov transformed the woodcock into a seagull. A few years later the temperamental Levitan was having an affair with a woman whose estate was not far from Chekhov's home. In a fit of depression, Levitan attempted to commit suicide but merely injured himself; Chekhov was sent for to treat him. It was a superficial scalp wound, but Chekhov stayed with his friend for several days to cheer him up. Near the house there was a marshy, misty lake; this house and lake may have served as the setting for *The Seagull*, and Konstantin's attempt at suicide very much resembles Levitan's.

Chekhov seems to have been almost obsessed by Shakespeare's *Hamlet;* quotations from it appear in many of his stories and plays. In *The Seagull* the Hamlet-Gertrude relationship is clearly reflected in that of Konstantin and Arkadina. Mother and son actually quote from *Hamlet* just before Konstantin's own play is presented. Although this play within a play is not meant to "catch the conscience of the king," Arkadina views it as an attack upon herself and says angrily, "These continual sallies at my expense— these continual pin-pricks would put anyone out of patience . . ." Konstantin, like Hamlet, is jealous of his mother's lover, but he has an additional cause for jealousy in Trigorin's success as a writer.

---

[1] For a detailed analysis of the play and its sources, see David Magarshack, *Chekhov the Dramatist*, Hill and Wang, New York, 1960, Chapters 16–17.

If the play has a theme, it is predicated upon Chekhov's belief that an artist must have an aim and must work indefatigably toward it. In a letter to Suvorin, the playwright remarked, "He who doesn't desire anything, doesn't hope for anything, and isn't afraid of anything cannot be an artist." Though Arkadina and Trigorin are far from being artists of the first rank, they work hard at their professions and are successful. Nina, too, makes dogged headway in her career as an actress. But Konstantin, a young man of undoubted talent, is weak and confused and finds no satisfaction in his writing; he has lost faith in himself, he does not know what his vocation is, and he fails.

The plot of *The Seagull* is as beautiful, complex, and intricately woven as a tapestry. Though the central thread of the story concerns two young artists—writer and actress—and their aspirations and efforts to succeed in their chosen professions, those two dazzling personalities Arkadina and Trigorin have a way in most productions of drawing attention to themselves. Konstantin, dreaming of creating new literary forms, vies desperately with Trigorin, his mother's lover, who is an established and well-known author; Nina would like to be as successful an actress as Arkadina and to replace her in Trigorin's affections. Chekhov demonstrates clearly that it is not merely the desire to succeed but the ability to work and to endure that distinguishes the genuinely creative person. Nina faces real obstacles—the hostility of her parents, her seduction by Trigorin, and the loss of her child —yet she perseveres; Konstantin's obstacles, which are in his own psyche, cripple him.

As a symbol the seagull is made to serve a double purpose. It represents Nina, who falls in with Trigorin's flight of fancy and sees herself as the shattered bird, until she is finally strong enough to deny the fiction. When she confronts Konstantin for the last time, she says in her excitement, "I am a seagull," then immediately denies the assertion, "No, that's not true. I am an actress!" The seagull also represents Konstantin, who destroys himself as willfully and pointlessly as he has destroyed the bird.

Chekhov had said that there was "little action" in the play; it is true that the most intensely dramatic encounters take place offstage, before the curtain rises or between the acts; but the internal action is enormous, and the emotional reactions of the characters reach a fever pitch of excitement. It was Maxim Gorky who pointed out that Chekhov, better than anyone else, understood "the tragic import of life's trivialities" and that in Chekhov's plays "There passes before one a long file of men and women, slaves of their love, of their stupidity and idleness, of their greed for the good things of life." Chekhov's genius lay in his ability to invest with universal significance these trivial men and women who so much resemble ourselves.

Chekhov had also said that his play contained "five tons of love." Surely he was being ironic when he used the word "love." We are, indeed, presented with five clearly defined "triangles"— Konstantin-Nina-Trigorin, Konstantin-Arkadina-Trigorin, Arkadina-Trigorin-Nina, Medvedenko-Masha-Konstantin, and Shamrayev-Polina-Dorn—yet all of this "love" is unrequited; what we are actually confronted with are five tons of unfulfilled yearning (a forerunner of the situation in Jean-Paul Sartre's play, *No Exit.*) A sexual current flows from Medvedenko to Masha to Konstantin to Arkadina to Trigorin to Nina, and from Polina to Dorn, but in each case the circuit is broken and no one achieves happiness.

Despite this state of general frustration and the fact that the play ends with a death, Chekhov insisted upon calling *The Seagull* a comedy. Stanislavsky maintained just as firmly that it was a tragedy. The two men could never agree on that point, and it has remained a moot question for modern producers. As a director Tyrone Guthrie supports Stanislavsky's view and has said that what an author hopes to write or means to write "and what he actually expresses are not always quite the same thing." While those who accept the playwright's designation point out that, like Balzac, who wrote of man's suffering under the broad title of *The Human Comedy*, and like Dante, who called the pilgrimage of man's soul *The Divine Comedy*, Chekhov was taking a cosmological view of pathetic, pretentious, ludicrous Man, who is satisfied to live in the hell and purgatory of the present while dreaming of a vague paradise in the future.

In *The Seagull* Chekhov deals with a group of people belonging to the landed gentry and professional classes. Unlike George Bernard Shaw, however, Chekhov wished his characters to be viewed not as representatives of their social classes nor as spokesmen for his own ideas but as carefully observed and differentiated individuals. Chekhov himself may be identified in part with four of the male personages. In Konstantin he depicts his own youthful artistic struggles and his persistent effort to find a new dramatic form; it is interesting to note that Konstantin's play does away with both plot and characterization and resembles our own avant-garde drama. In Trigorin Chekhov portrays the successful author, who is a slave to his writing, has an occasional affair, and finds complete relaxation in fishing (Chekhov's own favorite pastime). The levelheaded Dr. Dorn, who is slightly world-weary and freely dispenses valerian drops (a mild tranquilizer), has something in common with Chekhov the physician; Dorn felt he must give literary advice and encouragement to Konstantin, just as Chekhov generously did to innumerable young writers throughout his life. The kindly and sympathetic Sorin, who never got to do what he wanted to do, is Chekhov, old and ill before his time, unhappy but uncomplaining.

Nina, as has been mentioned, is patterned after a young friend of Chekhov's, Lika Mizinova. Arkadina is freely drawn from an actress named Lidiya Yavorskaya, whom Chekhov thought to be beautiful, intelligent, and well dressed but a poser rather than an actress, as well as a petty and jealous schemer. Medvedenko, too, was modeled in part on an actual person, of whom Chekhov wrote to Suvorin, "The teacher is paid twenty-three roubles a month, has a wife and four children, and is already gray though he is only thirty. He has been so beaten down by need that he can talk of nothing else except remuneration. In his opinion, poets and novelists ought to write only about increasing wages." Polina and Masha are commonplace women, who have no aim in life but the satisfaction of their own sensuality; and Shamrayev, the third member of the family, is an arrogant underling, a boor with pretentions to culture.

The characterization, which is astounding in its psychological truth, is matched in brilliance and subtlety by the dialogue. In their enormous compression and intensity, the speeches are anything but realistic; yet, because of Chekhov's ability to reveal the innermost feelings, the most complex thoughts of his characters, in an unfinished sentence or a few simple words, they give the impression of complete verisimilitude. "You think there is no greater misfortune than poverty," says Masha to Medvedenko, "but to my

Scene from the first act of the Stanislavsky production at the Moscow Art Theatre, 1898. In the gazebo, left, Medvedenko and Masha look out towards the lake. In the foreground, Sorin (V. V. Luzhsky) bends over the bench; Konstantin (Vsevolod Meyerhold) stands on the bench and faces the little stage; Nina (M. P. Roksanova) and Yakov listen to Konstantin, who is saying: "We'll take the curtain up at exactly half past eight, when the moon rises." Theatre Collection, New York Public Library.

mind it is a thousand times better to go in rags and be a beggar than . . ." She breaks off, but we know what she cannot bring herself to say: ". . . to be scorned by someone you love." The reference is to Konstantin, himself scorned and rejected by a mother who not only refuses to buy him much needed clothing but hurls at him the brutal insult, "You ragged beggar!"— which echoes Masha's words.

Chekhov was also an innovator in the use of oblique dialogue—the conversation of people who appear to be talking to each other but who are actually carrying on a series of semi-asides and soliloquies, which follow their own trains of thought. This device represents a lack of communication, loneliness, and even alienation. The technique was borrowed and elaborated upon by such avant-gardists as Beckett, Ionesco, Pinter, and Genet.

Much has been written about Chekhovian lyricism and mood, qualities the playwright achieved by a sustained and conscious effort. Chekhov had noticed that in conventional plays the actors talk incessantly, while in real life people pause between words and sentences, and conversations are interspersed with long moments of silence. While working on revisions of *The Seagull*, Chekhov was reading the plays of Maurice Maeterlinck, the originator of the "static" play. The Belgian playwright used interminable pauses to suggest the supervention upon life of mystical and supernatural forces; Chekhov adapted the device to the needs of poetic realism. The pauses, which vary in length according to the feelings involved, are indicated in the text by ellipses (. . .) in the dialogue or by the specific direction "(Pause)." Concerning these pauses Nemirovich-Danchenko wrote, "They were used to convey the feeling of relaxation from the tension of a previous scene, or to prepare the way for a coming emotional climax, or again to maintain a long silence charged with dramatic significance . . . a pause that was not dead, but capable of holding the audience in a state of suspense, or deepening the emotions of the characters, or accompanied by sound effects to heighten the mood."

The last point is of special importance, since in order to underscore the emotional tone of a scene, Chekhov not only filled the pauses with appropriate sound effects but also with evocative music; the pauses take on a lyrical quality when one becomes aware of the sound of a bell tolling, a dog howling, the wind whistling in the chimney, or when a song floats across the lake, someone plays the piano in a distant room, or a character hums a gay or melancholy tune. This technique accounts for many moments of great tenderness and beauty in *The Seagull*.

The words with which Arkadina flatters Trigorin may be applied in earnest to Chekhov himself: "You have so much sincerity, simplicity, freshness, healthy humor . . . With one stroke of your pen you can express all the essential characteristics of a person or a place. You bring your characters to life." It is these very qualities that are clearly exemplified in *The Seagull*.

The Production Record

The Seagull (*Chaika*, in Russian) was first offered to the public at the Alexandrinsky Theatre in St. Petersburg on October 17, 1896. This was an old imperial theatre, which upheld the conservative traditions of the Russian nobility and offered plays of the most stereotyped and conventional sort. Chekhov's friend Alexey Suvorin brought *The Seagull* to the attention of the noted comic actress at the Alexandrinsky, E. I. Levkeyeva, who accepted it for production on her benefit night, though she herself would not act in it. Chekhov's play was the first of a double bill, to be followed by a comedy called *A Happy Day*, in which Levkeyeva would appear.

The company at the Alexandrinsky was made up of stars who specialized in broad comedies, farces, and sentimental romances, under the direction of the unimaginative E. P. Karpov. *The Seagull* had only eight desultory rehearsals, but Karpov was counting on the "talent and experience" of his players to come through with finished performances. The great star and "dictator" at the Alexandrinsky, Maria Savina, refused to play the part of Nina; so the role was given to the young Vera Komisarjevskaya, who was to become one of the most celebrated actresses in Russia. She and Davydov, who played Sorin, were the only members of the company who acted their parts with understanding.

Chekhov attended a rehearsal and was appalled by the company's hackneyed conceptions of his characters. He kept saying, "Don't act so much. Do it simply." He was particularly displeased with the interpretation of the character of Arkadina. He said, "Arkadina is a foolish, mendacious, self-admiring egoist, whose moods change very quickly, but Dyuzhikova plays her as a clever, kindly, truthful woman . . . My actress Arkadina is not there at all." He made equally unflattering comments about the actors who played Dorn and Shamrayev. On opening night the performers forgot their lines, made ludicrous slips of the tongue, and added dialogue of their own. In addition to the poor acting, the scenery was a hodgepodge made up of pieces from old productions; some scenes were too "beautiful" and "luxurious" for the play, according to Chekhov, while others were shoddy. The back cloth, which depicted a forest, was touched up by the scene painter to show a view of a lake.

Because it was Levkeyeva's benefit and Levkeyeva was celebrated for comic roles, the opening-night audience was in a festive mood and ready for laughs. The most serious lines and situations in Chekhov's play were greeted with outbursts of raucous laughter, interspersed with boos, hisses, and crude comments. The play was a resounding failure. The critics took a brutal and malevolent tone in their condemnation of Chekhov's work, but were less critical of the acting and the production. The play closed after five performances.

Chekhov's friend Nemirovich-Danchenko wrote to say how sorry he was about the play's "strange lack of success," adding "that the play could not possibly have succeeded in view of such an incredibly bad performance by the cast and such an utter lack of understanding of the characters and their moods." Not long afterward, the Griboyedov prize for the best dramatic work of the season was awarded to Nemirovich-Danchenko for *The Worth of Life;* he urged that the award be given instead to Chekhov for *The Seagull,* but the committee would not honor his request. This creative and energetic man wished to establish his own theatre, in which good plays might be given the productions they deserved; he invited the actor Constantin Stanislavsky to join him in the venture. The two met on June 22, 1897, at the Slavyansky Bazaar (the very hotel, incidentally, at which Nina stayed when she followed Trigorin to Moscow), and during a meeting that lasted for eighteen hours without a break, they drew up the plans for the Moscow Art Theatre.

Nemirovich-Danchenko, who was to be in charge of administration, decided that their theatre would have to be entirely reorganized in both its business and artistic methods and that everyone, "big and small, must be inspired with the idea of their common interests; drastic changes in the system of rehearsals and production of the plays must be introduced; the audience itself must be forced to obey our regime." Stanislavsky, who was to be in charge of production, concurred in these views; as he later wrote, "We protested against the old methods of acting, especially overacting, against theatricality, false pathos, declamation, the bad conventions of production and scenery, the 'star' system which destroyed the ensemble, and the low level of the repertoire."

In short, the founders of the Moscow Art Theatre meant to introduce realism to the stage. By the intensive training of their actors and the extensive study and rehearsal of carefully selected plays, they managed eventually to achieve a "theatre of inner feeling." To Nemirovich-Danchenko and Stanislavsky every aspect of stage production,—directing, costuming, lighting, and music—was of equal importance in the creation of an integrated and

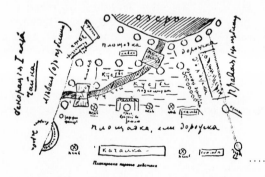

Drawing by Constantin Stanislavsky for *The Seagull,* 1896.

Arkadina (Olga Knipper, who became Chekhov's wife) and Trigorin (Constantin Stanislavsky) in the Moscow Art Theatre production, 1898. Theatre Collection, New York Public Library.

artistic experience. In addition to Stanislavsky, the acting company included such brilliant young players as Alexander Artyom, Ivan Moskvin, Vsevolod Meyerhold, Maria Lilina (Stanislavsky's wife), and Olga Knipper (who was to become Chekhov's wife); all were later to achieve world renown.

Certain that his prospective theatre would meet Chekhov's exact needs, Nemirovich-Danchenko asked the playwright for permission to produce *The Seagull*. Remembering the earlier failure of the play, Chekhov at first refused; only after a great deal of coaxing did he give his consent. Stanislavsky, who admitted that he neither liked nor understood the play at that time, went off for a month with the manuscript and drew up a "score," a detailed prompt-book, for the production.[1]

In this prompt-book each actor's every movement, gesture, and intonation was indicated by Stanislavsky, who later came to realize that each individual player would have to work from his own emotions; but even here we see intimations of Stanislavsky's famous System.

The play went into rehearsal in August and opened in Moscow on December 17, 1898. Seen in the leading roles were Olga Knipper as Arkadina, Stanislavsky as Trigorin, Meyerhold as Konstantin, and M. P. Roksanova as Nina. After the première Nemirovich-Danchenko sent a telegram to Chekhov

[1] See, *The Seagull Produced by Stanislavsky*, edited with an introduction by S. D. Balukhaty, and translated by David Magarshack, Theatre Arts Books, New York, 1952.

in Yalta, saying "All papers with astonishing unanimity talk of *The Seagull's* brilliant, immense, resounding success. The notices of the play are rapturous."

Chekhov did not have an opportunity to see the play acted until May, 1899, when a special performance (without scenery) was put on for him. In the main he was satisfied, but he objected strenuously to the actress who played Nina and to Stanislavsky's interpretation of Trigorin. In a letter to Maxim Gorky, Chekhov said, "I cannot say that I can pass an impartial judgment on the play because the Seagull herself acted so abominably, sobbing at the top of her voice all the time, and Trigorin . . . walked about and talked as though he were paralyzed; he has 'no will of his own' [one of his lines in the play], so the actor interpreted that in such a way that it made me sick to look at him . . ." Stanislavsky, who conceived of Trigorin as a dandy with exquisite manners, got himself up in an immaculate white suit, with a walking stick, and highly polished shoes—his own idea of the character's clothes about which Chekhov made a single comment, without explanation, "But he wears checked trousers and he has holes in his shoes." It took Stanislavsky a year to realize that Chekhov intended Trigorin to be a "bohemian" type, which would account in part for his special appeal to Nina.

Despite its artistic success and the part it played in putting the Moscow Art Theatre on its feet, *The Seagull* was subsequently performed less frequently than Chekhov's other great plays. It was restaged several times and recast, Maria Lilina taking over the part of Nina and the superb Kachalov playing Trigorin. The piece was removed from the repertory in 1906. By that time, however, it had been staged in a number of provincial cities, including Kiev, Taganrog, and Astrakhan.

The Seagull has been performed innumerable times in various parts of the world by amateurs as well as by stars of the first magnitude. As early as

Set for Act Four and the closing moment of the play in the 1905 revival at the Moscow Art Theatre. Kachalov, left, replaced Stanislavsky in the role of Trigorin in this production. Theatre Collection, New York Public Library.

1909, it was put on for the first time in English, in George Calderon's translation, by the Scottish Repertory Company of Glasgow. In London John Gielgud was connected with two outstanding productions of the play. In October, 1925, he appeared in the role of Konstantin, at the Little Theatre, under the direction of Philip Ridgeway. In his book *Early Stages,* Gielgud says,

> Konstantin is a very romantic character, a sort of miniature Hamlet, and a very exciting part for an ambitious young actor. [Gielgud was twenty-one at the time]. I was given very good notices on the whole, and thought at first that I was very well suited to the part. I resented the laughter of the audience when I came on in the second act holding the dead seagull, but on a very small stage it did look rather like a stuffed Christmas goose, however carefully I arranged its wings and legs beforehand. The last act used to go magnificiently, thanks to the really beautiful acting of Valerie Taylor, whose performance as Nina made her reputation overnight.
>
> In contrast to the praises I received in some quarters for my performances, I received a good deal of personal criticism from a few discriminating friends, who told me that my mannerisms were becoming extremely pronounced, my walk as bad as ever and my diction slovenly and affected. In one scene I had to quote Hamlet's 'Words, words, words.' My critics were perfectly right when they said I pronounced the line to sound like 'Wirds, wirds, wirds,' but I found it surprisingly difficult to rid myself of this habit of closed vowels. I had begun to learn something of pace and the way to build up to a climax, my emotional outbursts were sincere, and I found I could make a great effect at times with pauses carefully timed and spaced, or with a suddenly simple delivery of a line at a pathetic moment. But as soon as I made one of these momentous discoveries I could not resist showing off what a clever technician I had become. The audience was quick to notice my self-satisfaction, and my acting became alternately shamefaced and 'tricky', according to the way I felt I was failing or succeeding in that particular part of the play.

At the end of the run of this production, Philip Ridgeway introduced John Gielgud to Theodore Komisarjevsky (the brother of Vera, who had been the original Nina at the Alexandrinsky). In his second appearance in the play, Gielgud was associated with Komisarjevsky, who did a new translation, designed the scenery, and directed. This version opened at the New Theatre on May 20, 1936, with a brilliant cast, which included Gielgud as Trigorin, Edith Evans as Arkadina, Peggy Ashcroft as Nina, Stephen Haggard as Konstantin, George Devine as Shamrayev, Leon Quartermaine as Dorn, Martita Hunt as Masha, and Alec Guinness (just beginning his career) as Yakov. Of this production Gielgud says,

> It was enormously interesting to work again in *The Seagull* and to see how differently the parts came out with the new cast. . . . Peggy [Ashcroft] was exquisitely eager and womanly in the first three acts, but could not efface for me entirely the vivid impression made by Valerie Taylor in the final scene of the earlier production, when she returns to Sorin's house after Trigorin has deserted her. Nothing could have been

more different from Miriam Lewis's striking performance than the brilliantly poised, temperamental Arkadina of Edith Evans. Miriam played the part as a tragic actress. She stalked on to the stage in the first act, angry and sullen, looking rather barbaric in appearance, dressed in a strange picture frock and pacing the stage like a tigress, violent in her rages, and moody and self-accusing in her griefs. Edith, on the other hand, dressed the part like a Parisian, with a high, elegant coiffure, sweeping fashionable dresses, hats and scarves and parasols. On her first entrance she was all smiles and graciousness, but one could see from the angle of her head, as she sat with her back to the audience watching Konstantin's play, that underneath all the sweetness she was a selfish woman in a bad temper.

In describing the costume he wore as Trigorin, Gielgud mentions "his elegant hat and stick," which suggests that he, under Komisarjevsky's direction, was following Stanislavsky's interpretation of the character rather than Chekhov's. "The revival was a really big success," Gielgud recalls, "though most people thought my own performance the least satisfactory in an almost perfect ensemble . . ."

At any rate, Gielgud's 1936 production of *The Seagull* has been used by critics as the yardstick against which to measure all the more recent revivals of the play in England, revivals that have displayed the talents of such stars as Tony Richardson, Vanessa Redgrave, and Judith Anderson.

The Seagull (*La Mouette*) has had a number of productions in France. Probably the most notable were those of Georges and Ludmilla Pitoëff, who appeared in two versions of the play. The Pitoëffs staged it for the first time on October 3, 1921, and again on January 17, 1939. In the manner for which this company became famous, the scenery was stripped to the basic essentials, and the entire style of acting and production was simplified in accordance with the tastes of the French; it was the very antithesis of the excessively detailed manner of Stanislavsky. Although the critics did not at first approve of his efforts, Pitoëff's productions of *The Seagull* and of Chekhov's other plays, rendered with great feeling and imagination, eventually had a noticeable influence on the work of such playwrights as Jean-Jacques Bernard, Charles Vildrac, and Georges Duhamel.

The Seagull (*Il Gabbiano*) was done in several Italian cities as early as the 1920s; on November 24, 1948, it was mounted by the splendid company of the Piccolo Teatro (Little Theatre) in Milan, under the brilliant direction of Giorgio Strehler. It was a sensitive psychological study, in the naturalistic style of Stanislavsky but suffused with a Latin spirit. Arkadina was played by Lilla Brignone, Trigorin by Gianni Santuccio, Konstantin by Giorgio De Lullo, Nina by Anna Proclemer, and Shamrayev by the greatest Arlecchino of our time, the late Marcello Moretti. The scenery was designed by Gianni Ratto, the costumes by Ebe Colciaghi, and special music was composed by Fiorenzo Carpi.

In 1946 in the Soviet Union, Alexander Tairov, the director of the Kamerny (Chamber) Theatre and an unusual experimentalist, offered *The Seagull* in a new and remarkable interpretation. It was a concert presentation with strong symbolic overtones. Black velvet draperies provided the main setting, and the actors wore black clothes of contemporary fashion; some critics spoke of the funereal mood of the evening. Special dialogues were

The American premiere of *The Seagull* presented by the Washington Square Players (later known as the Theatre Guild) at the Bandbox Theatre, New York 1915. Konstantin (Roland Young) kneels at the feet of Nina (Mary Morris). Photograph: White. Theatre Collection, New York Public Library.

arranged between Trigorin and Konstantin, who discussed naturalism, symbolism, and other trends in the theatre; Konstantin's search for new forms was made to sound very much like an attack on the drabness of Soviet "socialist realism." In Tairov's production everything was presented symbolically; during the scene in the garden near the lake, for example, spotlights picked out apparitions, and the vague silhouettes of people and of birch trees were seen through thin layers of theatrical gauze. As if in reply to Tairov's "formalism," Yuri Zavadsky promptly mounted a production of *The Seagull* in the naturalistic style of Stanislavsky at the Moscow Soviet Theatre. Zavadsky's traditional production was extravagantly praised in the Soviet press, while Tairov's production was greeted by silence. When, shortly afterward, the great director was "liquidated," the joke went around Moscow that Tairov's seagull had proved to be his swan song.

In addition to being seen in almost every country in Europe, *The Seagull* has had some notable productions in the United States. It was done for the first time in America by the Washington Square Players (later to become the Theatre Guild) at the Bandbox Theatre on East Fifty-seventh Street in New York and ran from May 22 to June 1, 1916. Roland Young appeared as Konstantin, Helen Westley as Arkadina, and Mary Morris as Nina, in Marian Fell's translation from the Russian. Walter Prichard Eaton, a well-known critic who very much admired this group of young actors, wrote, "The production of *The Seagull,* it must be admitted, gave more practice to the players than pleasure to the audience. Frankly, it was too much for their still immature histrionic powers. . . . To make it at all impressive, certainly, a very high grade of subtle acting is required, not in one or two parts, but in all. . . . It is only necessary to point out that the abrupt transition, the shift from a strong emotion to an irrelevancy, is possibly the most difficult technical feat in the actor's art. However, this failure of the Washington Square

Program of *The Seagull* at the Bandbox Theatre, season of 1915–1916. Museum of the City of New York.

Players had no criminal element of low aim. At the worst, it merely proved that it takes longer to develop a company of competent actors out of a group of amateurs than we impatient Americans like to fancy."

On September 16, 1929, Eva Le Gallienne appeared in *The Seagull* at her Civic Repertory Theatre on Fourteenth Street in New York. Miss Le Gallienne directed the play and acted the role of Masha; Jacob Ben-Ami was Trigorin, and Josephine Hutchinson was Nina. In six seasons the play was presented sixty-four times. During the theatrical season of 1963–64, Miss Le Gallienne directed her own adaptation of the play for the National Repertory Theatre, a traveling company that performed in twenty cities all across the United States. In the cast were Miss Le Gallienne as Arkadina, Denholm Elliott as Trigorin, Farley Granger as Konstantin, and Anne Meacham as Nina. The sets were designed by Peter Larkin and the lighting by Tharon Musser.

The Theatre Guild produced *The Seagull* at the Shubert Theatre in New York on March 28, 1938, with Lynn Fontanne as Arkadina, Alfred Lunt as Trigorin, Uta Hagen as Nina, Richard Whorf as Konstantin, and Margaret Webster as Masha. The production received mixed notices. Brooks Atkinson thought that the company merely presented "the surface of an introspective play" and ended his review by saying, ". . . Margaret Webster is the only member of the cast who plays with perception of the evanescent life that is hovering under and around the written skeleton of the drama. As Masha, the lovesick one, the melancholy tippler, her acting is rich and aware. Something appreciative must be said for Robert Edmond Jones' settings and costumes that capture the somber mood of this ode to man's loneliness and indifference."

In its first New York appearance under its own management, the Association of Producing Artists (APA) presented *The Seagull,* in Alex Szogyi's translation, at the Folksbiene Playhouse on March 21, 1962. Nancy Marchand was seen as Arkadina, Paul Sparer as Trigorin, Richard Easton as Konstantin, and Rosemary Harris as Nina. The play was performed in modern dress and was directed by Ellis Rabb. Lloyd Burlingame designed the sets and Conrad Susa provided a musical score. The critic for the *New Yorker* magazine wrote,

> Clayton Corzatte [who had replaced Richard Easton] and Rosemary Harris are so good as Konstantine and Nina that they almost (not quite) throw everything off balance. Mr. Corzatte has the tougher assignment, for the young writer he plays—unstrung, often in tears, frustrated at every turn, his love for Nina hopeless and his affection for his mother rebuffed—could so easily be merely pathetic, but Mr. Corzatte makes him tragic. In his final scene with Nina (his dream has come true and here she is again—but here she isn't), he is superb as every bit of hope

Trigorin (Alfred Lunt) back to camera, and Arkadina (Lynn Fontanne) seated right, watch Nina (Uta Hagen) perform on the makeshift stage. The Theatre Guild production at the Shubert Theatre, New York 1938. Museum of the City of New York.

quietly drains out of him. Miss Harris is a lovely Nina, who grows and deepens and toughens before our eyes. The contrast between her Act I recitation, in a funny high-school voice and with declamatory gestures, of the monologue in Konstantine's play, and here repetition of it with depth and conviction, right before her final exit, when its significance and its importance to her and to Chekhov's play have become clear, is touching indeed.

For her performances during the APA repertory season at the Folksbiene Playhouse, Miss Harris won an Off-Broadway (Obie) Award.

In 1968 revivals of *The Seagull* were performed professionally on stage, television, and screen. The play was presented during the summer at the Stratford Festival in Ontario; in a production staged by Jean Gascon and designed by Brian Jackson. Dan Sullivan, who reviewed it for *The New York Times* (July 24, 1968), found little to rave about in the production aside from William Hutt's performance as Trigorin. Mr. Sullivan wrote:

> Trigorin is the quintessential Chekhov male—intelligent, good-natured, spineless, unwilling to hurt other people, and absolutely resolved not to be hurt by them. He is a weathervane that swings with the strongest wind—now his fear of Arkadina, now his desire for the innocent Nina.
>
> Mr. Hutt makes the smallest movement of his cramped soul visible to his audience. As Arkadina flatters and bullies him into going to Moscow with her, he raises his arms, drops them helplessly and gives in with a smile. "Well . . . we're going.'
>
> A moment later he finds that Nina will be in Moscow, too; again there is the same humorous yielding to circumstance, the same helpless shrug as destiny shows him his script.
>
> We ought to despise this Trigorin. In fact we understand him and sympathize. Mr. Hutt gives him a shyness and a sincerity that cannot be resisted, a fundamental innocence that is far more appealing than Arkadina's kind of powerhouse charm.
>
> There is also a certain firmness in the portrayal that makes Trigorin hard to dismiss as a mere moral slug. Mr. Hutt describes the agony of knowing yourself to be a second-rate person with bitterness and accuracy; but he does not whine about it. For all his passivity, he is a man.
>
> Mr. Hutt effortlessly, even modestly, outshines everyone else on the stage.

On November 8, the NET Playhouse, Channel 13, New York, broadcast a television version of the play, which had been made by the British Broadcasting Corporation. George Calderon's translation was used for the ninety-minute show; the producer was Cedric Messina; the director, Alan Cooke. In the cast were Pamela Brown as Arkadina, Robert Stephens as Trigorin, Robin Phillips as Kostya, and Gemma Jones as Nina. The production was not remarkable for outstanding performances or exciting moments, and minor confusions resulted from cuts in the text, but interest was maintained at a consistently high level.

On December 22, Warner Brothers-Seven Arts released its motion picture version of the play at the Plaza Theatre in New York. The picture, which had many moments of great visual beauty, was filmed entirely in Sweden, with a cast of internationally famous actors, headed by Simone Signoret as Arkadina, James Mason as Trigorin, Vanessa Redgrave as Nina, and David Warner as Kostya; also featured were Harry Andrews, Eileen Herlie, Kathleen Widdoes, Denholm Elliott, and Alfred Lynch. The picture was produced and directed by Sidney Lumet, from a script translated and adapted by Moura Budberg, with production design and costumes by Tony Walton. The deletion of several significant lines from the text and the introduction of certain action not suggested by the play (such as the love encounter between Masha and Medvedenko) did injury to Chekhov's intentions; but the major fault of the film lay in the use of stars—box-office attractions—who were not perfectly suited to their roles. Several of the individual performances were first-rate, but the noticeable lack of anything like ensemble acting drew the following remark from Vincent Canby, whose review of the film appeared in *The New York Times* (December 23, 1968):

> As a result of the variety of styles, the movie turns into a series of individual confrontations that seem as isolated as specialty acts. Without the single dominating influence that should have been provided by [Sidney] Lumet, the play is fragmented beyond repair.

Numerous semiprofessional, amateur, and college productions of *The Seagull* have been presented in the United States. Walter Kerr's comment about a professional production he had seen is appropriate: "Young and well-meaning actors are always playing Chekhov to improve themselves. It seems to me that they should first improve themselves, and then play Chekhov."

The Seagull at the Moscow
Art Theatre

Comments by Constantin Stanislavsky

I have already said that after my first acquaintance with Chekhov's "Seagull" I did not understand the essence, the aroma, the beauty of his play. I wrote the *mise en scène,* and still I did not understand, although, unknown to myself, I had apparently felt its substance. When I directed the play I still did not understand it. But some of the inner threads of the play attracted me, although I did not notice the evolution that had taken place in me.

The role of the fashionable writer Trigorin, the literary antipode of the talented Treplev who is his rival in the love of Nina Zarechnaya, the heroine of the play, a young, naive, provincial girl, was somehow beyond my powers. Yet nevertheless I was in the play, I was bound to it innerly, and together

From *My Life in Art,* New York: Theatre Arts Books, 1948, Chapter 34.

Anton Chekhov reading his play to the members of the Moscow Art Theatre company. Seated at Chekhov's right, hand to chin, is Stanislavsky; right of him, in profile, Olga Knipper; and standing far right, framed by the draperies, Nemirovich-Danchenko. Other celebrated performers present are Alexander Artyom, Ivan Moskvin, Vsevolod Meyerhold, and Maria Lilina. Theatre Collection, New York Public Library.

with the other actors sincerely gave myself up to the mood that was being created on the stage. The Chekhov mood is that cave in which are kept all the unseen and hardly palpable treasures of Chekhov's soul, so often beyond the reach of mere consciousness. This cave is that vessel in which is hidden the great riches of Chekhov. One must know how to find the place where it is hidden; one must be able to find the vessel itself, that is, the mood; one must know how to open it, in order to perceive what it is that makes Chekhov's art so unescapable. Apparently there are many ways to the hidden riches, to the entrance into the soul of the play, the rôles, and the actors who play them.

Nemirovich-Danchenko and I approached the hidden riches each in his own way, Vladimir Ivanovich by the literary road and I by the road of the actor, the road of images. Vladimir Ivanovich spoke of the feelings which he sought or foresaw in the play and the rôles. I could not speak of them and preferred to illustrate them. When I entered into a debate of words I was not understood and I was not persuasive. When I mounted the stage and showed what I was talking about, I became understandable and eloquent. True, often these varied approaches to the play interfered with the work and the rehearsals and caused long discussions which passed from debates of a detail to debates about principles, from the role to the play, from the play to art, from art to its fundamentals. There were even quarrels, but these quarrels were always of artistic origin and they were more useful than dangerous. They taught us that very essence which we seemed to foreknow in its general outlines, but not in concrete, systematic and clear rules. We seemed to be digging tunnels from two opposite sides toward one central point. Little by little we approached each other; now only a thin wall separated us; now the wall was broken and we could easily pass from the literary to the artistic and unite them for the general procession of the actors along the way that we had found. Once we found that inner line of the play, which we could not define in words at that time, everything became comprehensible of itself not only to the actors and the stage directors, but to the artist and the electrician and the *costumier* and all the other co-creators of the production. Along this line of inner action, which Chekhov has in a greater degree than any other dramatist, although until this time only actors are aware of it, there was formed a natural force of gravity towards the play itself, which pulled all of us in one direction. Much was correctly guessed by the interpreter of the play, Nemirovich-Danchenko, much by the stage directors, the *mise en scène,* the interpreters of the rôles (with the exception of myself), the scenic artist, and the properties.

Simov understood my plans and purpose of stage direction and began to help me marvelously towards the creation of the mood. On the very forestage, right near the footlights, in direct opposition to all the accepted laws and customs of the theatre of that time, almost all the persons in the play sat on a long swinging bench characteristic of Russian country estates, with their backs to the public. This bench, placed in a line with some tree stumps that remained from a destroyed forest, bordered an alley set with century-old trees that stood at a measured distance from each other. In the spaces between their trunks, which seemed mysterious in the darkness of the night, there showed something in the form of a proscenium that was closed from sight by a large white sheet. This was the open-air theatre of the unsuccessful and unacknowledged Treplev. The scenery and properties of this theatre are poor and modest. But listen to the essence of his art and you find that it is a complete grammar for the actor of today. Treplev speaks of real art in the midst of night, amidst the trees of a damp and ancient park, waiting for the rising of the moon. Meanwhile from the distance there comes the trivial racket of a fashionable and tasteless waltz that changes at times to an even more tasteless but melodious Gipsy song played by Treplev's mother, a provincial actress. The tragedy is self-evident. Can the provincial mother understand the complex longings of her talented son? It is not at all amazing that he runs away from the house to the park so often.

To the accompaniment of tasteless conversation and jokes, the domestic spectators take their places on the long bench and the tree stumps, their backs to the public, very much like sparrows on a telegraph line. The moon rises, the sheet falls, one sees the lake, its surface broken with the silver gleams of the moon. On a high eminence that resembles the base of a monument, sits a grief-stricken female figure wrapped in manifold white, but with eyes that are young and shining and cannot be grief-stricken. This is Nina Zarechnaya in the costume of World Grief, the long train of which, like the tail of a snake, is stretched over grass and undergrowth. The wide cloth was a courageous gesture on the part of the artist, a gesture of deep contents and beautiful generalized form. How talented is this Treplev with the soul of Chekhov and a true comprehension of art.

The use of the bench by the actors. Drawings by Constantin Stanislavsky, 1896.

Nina Zarechnaya is the cause of the failure of Treplev's talented play. She is not an actress, although she dreams of being one so as to earn the love of the worthless Trigorin. She does not understand what she is playing. She is too young to understand the deep gloom of the soul of Treplev. She has not yet suffered enough to perceive the eternal tragedy of the world. She must first fall in love with the scoundrelly Lovelace Trigorin and give him all that is beautiful in woman, give it to him in vain, at an accidental meeting in some low inn. The young and beautiful life is deformed and killed just as meaninglessly as the beautiful white seagull was killed by Treplev because of nothing to do. Poor Nina, before understanding the depth of what she is playing, must bear a child in secret, must suffer hunger and privation many years, dragging herself through the lower depths of all the provincial theatres, must come to know the scoundrelly attentions of merchants to a young actress, must come to know her own giftlessness, in order to be able in her last farewell meeting with Treplev in the fourth act of the play to feel at last all the eternal and tragic depth of Treplev's monologue, and perhaps for the last and only time say it like a true actress and force Treplev and the spectators in the theatre to shed holy tears called forth by the power of art.

The conditions under which we produced "The Seagull" were complex and hard. The production was necessary to us because of the material circumstances of the life of our Theatre. Business was in a bad way. The administration hurried our labors. And suddenly Anton Pavlovich fell ill in Yalta with a new attack of tuberculosis. His spiritual condition was such that if "The Seagull" should fail as it did at its first production in Petrograd, the great poet would not be able to weather the blow. His sister Maria Pavlovna warned us of this with tears in her eyes, when, on the eve of the performance, she begged us to postpone it. You can judge of the condition in which we actors played on the first night before a small but chosen audience. There were only six hundred roubles in the box office. When we were on the stage there was an inner whisper in our hearts:

"You must play well, you must play better than well; you must create not only success, but triumph, for know that if you do not, the man and writer you love will die, killed by your hands."

These inner whisperings did not aid our creative inspiration. The boards were becoming the floor of a gallows, and we actors the executioners.

I do not remember how we played. The first act was over. There was a gravelike silence. Knipper fainted on the stage. All of us could hardly keep our feet. In the throes of despair we began moving to our dressing rooms. Suddenly there was a roar in the auditorium, and a shriek of joy or fright on the stage. The curtain was lifted, fell, was lifted again, showing the whole

auditorium our amazed and astounded immovability. It fell again, it rose;
it fell, it rose, and we could not even gather sense enough to bow. Then
there were congratulations and embraces like those of Easter night, and ova-
tions to Lilina, who played Masha, and who had broken the ice with her
last words which tore themselves from her heart, moans washed with tears.
This it was that had held the audience mute for a time before it began to
roar and thunder in mad ovation.

We were no longer afraid of sending a telegram to our dear and beloved
friend and poet.

Illness prevented Anton Pavlovich Chekhov from coming to Moscow
during the season. But in the spring of 1899 he arrived with the secret hope
of seeing "The Seagull" and demanded that we show it to him.

"Listen, it is necessary for me. I am its author. How can I write anything
else until I have seen it?" he repeated at every favorable opportunity.

What were we to do? The season was over, the theatre was in the hands
of strangers for all of the summer, all our belongings had been taken away
and stored in a small barn. In order to show Chekhov a single performance,
we would have had to go through almost the same amount of preparatory
work as we did for the beginning of the whole season, that is, we would
have had to hire a theatre and stage hands to unpack the scenery, the properties, the costumes, the wigs, and to bring them to the theatre, to collect the
actors, to rehearse the play, to put in the necessary lighting system, and so
on. And as a result of all this, the special performance would be a failure.
It would be impossible to arrange it in a hurry. The inexperienced actors,
not being used to the new stage, would lose themselves completely, and that
would be the worst thing that could happen, especially in a Chekhov play.
Besides, the auditorium of a theatre hired by chance would be devoid of all
furniture, as the latter would be in the hands of cabinet makers and uphol-
sterers during all summer for renovation. The play would have no appeal in
an empty theatre. And Chekhov would be disappointed. But the words of
Chekhov were a law to us, and once he insisted, it was necessary to fulfill
his wishes.

The special performance took place in the Nikitsky Theatre. It was attended by Chekhov and about ten other spectators. The impression, as we
had expected, was only middling. After every act Chekhov ran on the stage
and his face bore no signs of any inner joy. But as soon as he saw the backstage activities, he would regain his courage and smile, for he loved the life
of the theatre behind the scenes. Some of the actors were praised by Chekhov,
others received their full meed of blame. This was true of one actress especially, with whose work Chekhov was completely dissatisfied.

"Listen," he said, "she can't act in my play. You have another actress
who could be much finer in the part, who is a much better actress."

"But how can we take away the part once the season is over?" we
defended ourselves. "That would amount to the same thing as if we threw
her out of the company. Think what a blow that would be. She won't be
able to bear it."

"Listen, I will take the play away from you," he summed up in a severe
way, almost cruelly, surprising us by his hardness and firmness. Notwithstanding his exceptional tenderness, delicacy and kindness, he was severe
and merciless in questions of art and never accepted any compromises. In
order not to anger and excite the sick man, we did not contradict him, hoping

that with time everything would be forgotten. But no. Unexpectedly, when no one even dreamt that he would say it, Chekhov would repeat:

"Listen, she can't act in my play."

At the special performance he seemed to be trying to avoid me. I waited for him in my dressing room, but he did not come. That was a bad sign. I went to him myself.

"Scold me, Anton Pavlovich," I begged him.

"Wonderful! Listen, it was wonderful! Only you need torn shoes and checked trousers."

He would tell me no more. What did it mean? Did he wish not to express his opinion? Was it a jest to get rid of me? Was he laughing at me? Trigorin in "The Seagull" was a young writer, a favorite of the women—and suddenly he was to wear torn shoes and checked trousers! I played the part in the most elegant of costumes—white trousers, white vest, white hat, slippers, and a handsome make-up.

A year or more passed. Again I played the part of Trigorin in "The Seagull"—and during one of the performances I suddenly understood what Chekhov had meant.

Of course, the shoes must be torn and the trousers checked, and Trigorin must not be handsome. In this lies the salt of the part: for young, inexperienced girls it is important that a man should be a writer and print touching and sentimental romances, and the Nina Zarechnayas, one after the other, will throw themselves on his neck, without noticing that he is not talented, that he is not handsome, that he wears checked trousers and torn shoes. Only afterwards, when the love affair with such "seagulls" is over, do they begin to understand that it was girlish imagination which created the great genius in their heads, instead of a simple mediocrity. Again, the depth and the richness of Chekhov's laconic remarks struck me. It was very typical and characteristic of him.

A Letter to Chekhov

From V. I. Nemirovich-Danchenko

Dear Anton Pavlovitch!

From my telegrams you already know of the general success of "The Seagull." In order to paint for you a picture of the first performance, I must tell you that after the third act there reigned behind the wings a kind of drunken atmosphere. As some one has aptly said, it was just as on Easter Day. They all kissed one another, flung themselves on one another's neck; all were excited with the mood of the supreme triumph of truth and honest labour. Just consider the reasons for such joy: the actors are in

From Nemirovich-Danchenko's *My Life in the Russian Theatre.* Boston: Little, Brown and Co., 1936, pp. 189–192.

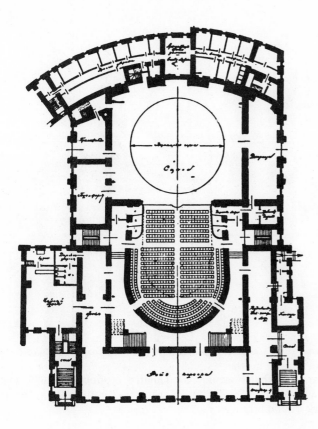

The ground plan of the famous Moscow Art playhouse shows the stage area larger than the auditorium. The revolving section was divided into three transverse parts that could be separated, raised, and lowered. Theatre Collection, New York Public Library.

love with the play, with every rehearsal they discovered in it more and more new pearls of art. At the same time they trembled because the public was so unliterary, so poorly developed, spoiled by cheap stage effects, and unready for a higher artistic simplicity, and would therefore be unable to appreciate the beauty of "The Seagull." We gave up our whole soul to the play, and we risked everything on this one card. We *regisseurs*, i.e. Alekseiev [Stanislavsky] and I, bent all our efforts and capabilities so that the astonishing moods of the play might be intensified. We had three dress rehearsals, we examined every corner of the stage, we tested every electric-light bulb. For two weeks I lived in the theatre with the decorations, the properties; I made trips to the antique shops, seeking out objects which would give the necessary touches of colour. But why dwell on this? I am speaking of a theatre in which not a single nail has been overlooked. . . .

At the first performance, I, as at a jury trial, "challenged" the jury, so that the public should consist of persons capable of valuing the beauty of truth on the stage. But I, true to myself, did not do a thing to prepare a spurious success.

From the first dress rehearsal there prevailed a spirit in the company that promised success. Nevertheless, my dreams *never* went that far. In any event, I anticipated that at best success would be one of serious

Scene from Act Three of the Moscow Art Theatre production, 1898. Olga Knipper and V. V. Luzhsky as Arkadina and Sorin, sister and brother. Theatre Collection, New York Public Library.

attention. Then suddenly—I cannot convey to you the whole sum of my impressions—not a single word, not a single sound escaped me. Not only the general mood reached the public, not only the *legend,* which in this play it was so hard to stress with a red line, but each separate thought, everything indeed that makes you what you are, both as an artist and as a thinker, everything, everything—well, in a word, every psychological movement—everything reached the public and possessed it. And all my fears that only a few would understand the play vanished. There could not have been more than a dozen persons who failed to grasp something in it. Then I thought that the general success would express itself merely in a few friendly curtain calls after the third act. Actually, what happened was this: after the first act the audience demanded no less than six curtain calls (we do not respond promptly to such demands). The auditorium was enthralled and excited; while after the third act not a single auditor left the theatre, but remained standing, and the calls became an endless uproarious ovation. There were calls for the author, and I informed the audience that you were not present. Then came voices: "Send him a telegram!" . . .

You can see how busy I've been. I began this letter on Friday morning, and until Monday I couldn't snatch a single hour to finish it! And you tell me: "Come to Yalta." On the 23rd I'll make my escape to Chernigovskaya, just in order to get a good sleep!

But to continue. . . . So I asked the public: "You authorize me to send a telegram?" At this there was loud applause and cries of "Yes!" "Yes!"

After the fourth act the ovation was renewed. You have probably seen the papers. Thus far, the most favourable reaction to the play has appeared in the *Moskauer Deutsche Zeitung,* which I will send you today together with a fairly intelligent article in the *Courier*—"The Diary of a Nervous Man." The *Russkiye Viedomosti* has, of course, been rather in a fix. Poor Ignatov—he's always at a loss when a play happens to be even a trifle above the ordinary.

We played . . . in this order: Knipper is an astonishing, an ideal Arkadina. To such a degree has she merged with the rôle that you cannot tear away from her either her elegance as an actress, or her bewitching triviality, *stinginess,* jealousy, etc. Both scenes in the third act—with Treplev and Trigorin, the first in particular—had a tremendous success. And the departure which concluded the act was an unusual piece of staging, without superfluous people. After Knipper comes Alekseieva [Stanislavsky's wife]—Masha. A marvellous image! Very characteristic and remarkably touching. She was a great success. Then Luzhsky—Sorin. He played like a major artist. Then Meyerhold [as Treplev]. He was tender, touching and definitely a decadent. Then Alekseiev. He used a successfully mild, will-less tone. He spoke the monologues of the second act, excellently, marvellously. He was a bit sugary in the third act. Roxanova [the actress to whose performance Chekhov later objected] was not so good; Alekseiev disconcerted her, forcing her to play the rôle [Nina] of a little fool. I was angry and demanded a return to the previous lyrical tone. The poor woman got all mixed up. Vishnevsky has not yet quite merged with his rôle of the tender-hearted, shrewd, observing and all-experiencing Dorn, who was however very well made up in the style of Alexey Tolstoy and superbly ended the play. The remainder of the cast maintained a harmonious ensemble. The general tone was restrained and highly literary.

The public listened to the play with such absorbed attention as I have rarely witnessed. Moscow is in an uproar over it. In the Small Theatre they are ready to tear us to pieces.

The play is sure of a run. You'd have enjoyed the first act—and, in my opinion, the fourth, in particular.

I am infinitely happy.

I embrace you.

Yours,
Vladimir Nemirovitch-Dantchenko.

What about letting us have "Uncle Vanya"?

The stylized representation of a sea gull adopted as the emblem of the Moscow Art Theatre after the success of Chekhov's play. This design appeared on the theatre curtain, the programs, and all advertising.

Philip Ridgeway's production at the Little Theatre, London, 1925. Inset, John Gielgud, age 21, as Konstantin. Scene from Act One (left to right): Trigorin (Randolph McLeod), Arkadina (Miriam Lewis), Nina onstage (Valerie Taylor), Konstantin (John Gielgud) with his script, Masha (Margaret Swallow), and Medvedenko (James Whale). Theatre Collection, New York Public Library.

Two Versions of *The Seagull*

Interview with John Gielgud

John Gielgud, one of the greatest actors in the English-speaking theatre today, has appeared in two noteworthy productions of *The Seagull*. He was twenty-one years old when he played Konstantin, thirty when he acted Trigorin. Gielgud, who has thought and written a good deal about the art of acting and his own development, has said:

"When I was young I was not a good actor. My earliest ambition was to design scenery—to follow in the footsteps of my cousin, Gordon Craig, and try to create ideal physical settings for an ideal theatre. I loved the pictorial magic of the stage, but I was too lazy to learn the technical requirements necessary for a stage designer—arithmetic, blueprints, accuracy of drawing, and so on.

"Having been lucky enough to be born into a great theatrical family, . . . I was still very young when I first came to feel the satisfaction that is the actor's reward, and I responded to it immediately with all the egotism at my command. I posed, I gestured, I made what I thought were beautiful noises, and thoroughly enjoyed the attention and admiration of any audience that was willing to allow me the opportunity to display what I took to be my talents at that time.

"I don't suppose there was anything unusual in this. In the case of a young actor one must always expect a greater exhibitionism and self-interest than in other mortals. But I was to suffer a rude awakening when, after a few years, I suddenly became aware of the difficulties and responsibilities of the profession I had so lightly chosen."

Gielgud was delighted when Philip Ridgeway, an imaginative producer who planned to put on several of Chekhov's plays, engaged him for the role of Konstantin in *The Seagull,* which opened at the Little Theatre in London, on October 19, 1925. Among the excellent players in the company were Miriam Lewis, Valerie Taylor, James Ware, and Margaret Swallow; but A. E. Philmer, of the Birmingham Repertory Theatre, who directed the play, was not especially gifted.

"I loved playing Konstantin," said Gielgud, "because it was such a romantic and showy part, but I was probably too young at the time to understand either the play or the character. All creative art can be studied, of course. When one is young one imitates the players one most admires, as young painters copy great pictures in the galleries. But one cannot copy acting, or even what seems to be 'the method' of acting. One has to experiment and discover one's own way of expression for one's self, and one never ceases to be dissatisfied. There are so many lessons to be learned. Application, concentration, self-discipline, the use of the voice and the body, imagination, observation, simplification, self-criticism."

At the end of the run at the Little Theatre, Gielgud was introduced to the Russian director-designer Theodore Komisarjevsky, who had seen the Ridgeway production. He thought it was "most un-Russian and very 'funny,'" and said that "it demonstrated the ridiculousness of all English productions of Chekhov." Gielgud began to work and study with Komisarjevsky, whom he found fascinating and contradictory—an often inspired director, a talented designer, and a brilliant teacher. The Russian was bitter and cynical about the English stage and the English public, was often pessimistic and destructive, and sometimes perverse and cruel. He took delight in shocking, ridiculing, and criticizing people, and seemed to try to fool the public with his own theories. But Gielgud asserts that he owes a terrific debt to this man: "He taught me everything I know about acting."

In 1936, when Gielgud was well on his way to becoming a star, and was putting on plays under the aegis of Howard Wyndham and Bronson Albery, he planned to revive *The Seagull* at the New Theatre, in the West End, for a limited run. He was to leave in eight weeks for New York, where his playing of Hamlet would establish his reputation in America. For his production of *The Seagull,* in which Gielgud acted Trigorin, there was Edith Evans as Arkadina, Peggy Ashcroft as Nina, Stephen Haggard as Konstantin, with strong support from Leon Quartermaine, Martita Hunt, and George Devine. Komisarjevsky was brought in to direct; he also designed the scenery, and supplied a new translation of the text. For the Ridgeway production Constance Garnett's translation was used.

Before starting rehearsals, Komisarjevsky gathered the company together and delivered a long harangue on everything that was wrong with the English theatre, English audiences, all productions of Russian plays done in England, and particularly the last one of *The Seagull*. Edith Evans was terribly annoyed by this, but Gielgud, who stood in awe of Komisarjevsky's talent, was willing to forgive him.

Generally, actors liked to work with Komisarjevsky. He would let them find their own way, watch, keep silent, then arrange the timing carefully. Occasionally, he would make some short but immensely illuminating comment. He always sneered at stars, preferring to work with young people and unknowns. (Years later, when Edith Evans and John Gielgud became famous, Komisarjevsky said they were "no longer any good because they were stars and refused to take direction.") But even toward young actors his attitude was inconsistent; he could be very cruel. If he did not like an actor, he would completely ignore him, give him no direction whatsoever, or even put him in positions in which he would look awkward. He treated Peggy Ashcroft so ruthlessly during rehearsals that she was in tears nearly all the time; his behavior toward her almost ruined her as an actress. Later on he married her, but, as might be expected, the marriage did not last very long. He was particularly brutal to members of the cast who were of German or Jewish origin. Another of his weaknesses was to introduce his mistresses into all his productions, whether they could act or not.

Despite his failings Komisarjevsky accomplished wonders on the stage. "It seems that his theory about directing Chekhov," said Gielgud, "was pause—pause—pause. During the first act, Edith Evans paused 'to listen to music' and the pause lasted a full ten minutes, but it was so brilliantly done that it held."

Gielgud was not very happy in the part of Trigorin although he himself chose to play it. When casting began, Komisarjevsky was under the impression that Gielgud would act Konstantin, as he had done in the earlier production. But Gielgud now considered himself too old for that part despite the fact that he was only thirty and looked much younger. Trigorin is a man of about forty-five and Gielgud thought it would stretch his talents, as well as demonstrate his versatility, to play an older person. Soon after the play opened, however, Gielgud began to have misgivings about his choice. He actually was too young, and the part was far less showy than Konstantin's. Furthermore, Komisarjevsky's conception of Trigorin was more like Stanislavsky's than Chekhov's: he did not want the character to be played as a bohemian who wore "checked trousers and had holes in his shoes," but as a dandy, who put a silver streak in his hair, sported dapper clothes, and even went so far as to appear (in the last act) in a purple suit. The critics thought Gielgud "too soft and too shallow," and in his own estimation, he played the part very stiffly and without verve. His general dissatisfaction at the time led Gielgud to think that Stephen Haggard and Peggy Ashcroft were not as good in the parts of the boy and the girl as he and Valerie Taylor had been. This opinion, Gielgud later realized, was probably the result "of pique and jealousy." He also concluded that if he were to play Trigorin again, he would do it entirely differently; he would be "a loose sort of person," warm, informal, and undoubtedly more interesting.

"It is easy to think one is working hard when one is acting," said Gielgud, "to substitute physical energy and noisy exhibitionism, or even

Scene from Act Four of the Komisarjevsky production, London 1936. From the left, Masha, in black, seated (Martita Hunt), Arkadina (Edith Evans), Trigorin (John Gielgud), Sorin, in wheelchair (Frederick Lloyd), Shamrayev (George Devine). Komisarjevsky designed as well as directed this production. Act Three took place in the dining-room, and the living-room could be seen through the wide doorway; for Act Four he reversed the sets. Theatre Collection, New York Public Library.

self-assured intensity, for subtlety and self-control. . . . Selectiveness is, for me, the most valuable lesson I have tried to learn over the years, and the one I most admire in the finest of my contemporaries. The truest test an actor must pass in sustaining a role over a long period of consecutive performances is that he is continually discarding every unnecessary gesture, simplifying every movement and inflection, so that he may eventually achieve the most truthful expression of his role at every moment of his creation, however often he has to repeat it."

Selectiveness and simplification also apply to a play's scenic investiture. Chekhov sets the first act of *The Seagull* in "a part of the park on Sorin's estate" and the second act on "the croquet lawn of Sorin's house." Gielgud was surprised to find Komisarjevsky putting both acts into the same setting, however beautiful it was, with its paths and pillars and banks of flowers. Gielgud would have done it differently: "The first act in the park should be cold and bleak, with a 'tattered' mood, despairing and gloomy, like a painting by Chagall; not orderly and charming but squally, because Kostya is antitheatre and would have selected a wet, damp, mournful spot. No wonder Arkadina shivers in her thin dress and shoes! The second act, on the croquet lawn, should have an entirely different mood because it is Arkadina's own territory. It is orderly, bourgeois, with a neat bed of geraniums, sunlight, Arkadina in a Paris dress, Trigorin flaunting his bohemianism, and Kostya ill-at-ease in his shabby suit. Some realistic details are essential because Chekhov does not play well on an entirely bare stage.

"The scenery for the last two acts of Komisarjevsky's production," said Gielgud, "was brilliantly conceived. In the third act, when the members of the family were in the dining-room, the audience could see into the drawing-room; and in the fourth act, when the drawing-room was in the foreground, the audience could look into the dining-room. In presenting the two rooms from opposite viewpoints, Komisarjevsky made the spectator feel that he knew the whole of the rest of the house. The lighting, which the director did himself, was very beautiful, as was his control of mood and atmosphere, tone and pace, and the grouping of the characters. Komisarjevsky achieved a genuine ensemble and proved a master of orchestration; he also helped to take the oppressive gloom out of Chekhov productions in England."

Gielgud recalled that the young actor who played Yakov (he had just one or two lines in the first act, and pulled the curtain of Kostya's homemade theatre) was so completely unknown at the time that the program did not even list his name. He was Alec Guinness.

"There was so much to admire in Komisarjevsky's production," said Gielgud, "that I am not surprised that many people still recall it with pleasure."

A Memory of Two Productions

Notes by Phyllis Hartnoll

> *The following are Miss Hartnoll's notes on John Gielgud's two appearances in* The Seagull.

1. At the Little Theatre, October 19, 1925, when he played Konstantin. . . . I enjoyed it at the time, but looking back I think it was not a very good production. Gielgud was rather awkward (it was a very small stage) but did manage to give the impression of someone with great potentialities who is not quite sure in which direction he is going. He wasn't quite young and appealing enough, and he didn't manage the petulance in the first act very well, though the anger later on and the sarcasm was most effective. He says in his book *[Early Stages]* that people laughed when he came on with the seagull in Act II. I don't remember that, but I do remember the sort of shudder that went over most people when he said, "I shall kill myself in the same way." The changing of the bandage was not well done, but it is a terrible scene. The only person I ever saw do it well was [Stephen] Haggard in the 1936 production, and he had Edith Evans as Mme. Arkadina! In this production (1925) one had the impression that both participants dreaded the scene and wanted to get it over as soon as possible. The transitions from tenderness to anger and back to tenderness were too staccato, too forced. In the last act, when he was telling the story of Nina, he was not personally involved enough, so that it took one a moment to get adjusted to the love-scene later, but once it got going it was good, though Gielgud was still a little wooden. But he is never very good in straightforward love scenes. He was better once he had realized that

Trigorin (John Gielgud), Nina (Peggy Ashcroft), and seated, Arkadina (Edith Evans), all in street clothes, in Gielgud's dressing room, during the run of the play in 1936. Photograph: Angus McBean.

Nina still loved Trigorin. But, taking it all round, it was a good performance in a difficult part in a difficult production. England had not quite got around to Chekhov, even then. He certainly looked the part—I remember him as dark, romantic, haggard, all nose and eyes, with more talent than technique, with a fumbling for something which, when it came off, was first-rate.

2. At the New Theatre, May 20, 1936, when he played Trigorin. The play was produced by Komisarjevsky, and had a brilliant cast. As for Gielgud, I have always thought that his Trigorin was one of his finest parts. I don't agree with what he says about people thinking his performance the least satisfactory. On the contrary, what I think some people thought of as imperfections were really the things that made other actors [look] better—I mean that where he was unsympathetic (to an audience which was used to him in romantic parts) or seemed to hold back in making an effect, it was so that the person playing opposite him could make a greater effect. Of course, the part suited him to perfection. The finest moments were (apart from his first line, "Everyone writes as he likes (a pause) and (though I would swear he said "or") as he can," which came as a deep slow note after Nina's light voice and Mme. Arkadina's petulance, and seemed to sum up all Trigorin's melancholy and disillusionment with himself)—the finest bits were when he sat frozen at the lunch table and Mme. Arkadina knelt by his chair and threw her arms round him, begging for his love. He was frozen with the horror of it—the horror of a man who feels himself trapped by a love he neither wants nor understands. There is a photograph of this moment [in the London *Play Pictorial,* for May, 1936] on p. 12, but it is absolutely wrong; it was obviously not taken during a performance. There he looks sad and mournful, but on stage it was quite different. One felt in every tense muscle of his head and shoulders the

repulsion he felt for this soft feminine body so close to his own, which he refused to touch or look at. As I remember it, he certainly did not put his arm round Mme. Arkadina, but sat with his hands tightly clasped, resting on the table, his gaze fixed, as if he were willing himself not to yield to his impulse to throw her off. One felt humiliated for the woman's sake, his hatred of her was so evident. The other moment was when he came back from looking up the quotation, and read it "If ever my life can be of use to you, come and take it." He read it first somewhat mechanically, and then it sank in, and he looked up from the book and repeated it, with such agony of longing that one felt: "This may be a cold-hearted, second-rate writer, but just for a moment he is experiencing a pure, selfless emotion, a real love for the child who is giving her life into his hands." It seemed, at that moment, as if Nina might be happy with him, and he with her. It was a wonderful glimpse of something buried so deep in the man that he hardly knew himself that it was there—and it certainly made the later scene with Mme. Arkadina even more poignant, because one felt that he could love, given the right person, and she was not right; she could never evoke such pure affection. And also it seemed as if the scene with Arkadina spoiled his love for Nina, so that in spite of that moment of self-revelation one knew the end would be tragic.

The whole picture was of a man who has achieved success, but not the success he wanted, who knows he is second-rate, who has become bitter and self-seeking because there is nothing in life he really values. He has thrown away his integrity as a writer for facile popularity, and now he has to keep on writing, writing, to keep up with himself. The scene where he describes his life to Nina was painful in its revelation of inadequacy. The noting of little things to put into stories, the search for something new, a plot, a phrase, the flatness of repetition, all that gave the scene extraordinary poignancy. One suffered with the man, even while despising him. That, I think, was what Gielgud showed so clearly all through—that Trigorin, from the beginning, is a despicable person, and the worst moment of all was when he described, in the tale of the seagull and the girl, exactly what would happen to Nina, how he would treat her, so that the whole tragedy, of her and of Konstantin and of Trigorin himself, is implicit in those few hasty lines. He certainly seemed to be speaking the bitter truth when he said, "I dislike my own work." The tragedy of the second-rate artist who is clear-sighted enough to judge his own mediocrity.

The *Seagull* in Summer Stock

Interview with Jack Witikka

In the spring of 1964, Jack Witikka, Deputy Director of the Finnish National Theatre and Chairman of its Theatre School in Helsinki, was asked by Kenneth Ireland, manager of the Pitlochry Theatre Festival in Scotland, to direct a play by Chekhov for the summer season. Witikka had directed several of the one-act plays of Chekhov, among them *The Marriage Proposal* and *The Bear.* He had established his reputation in Finland on the strength of his productions of the plays of Samuel Beckett, which also resulted in his going to Germany as a guest-director. Witikka believes that his work was called to the attention of Mr. Ireland by Harold Hobson, the drama critic for the London *Sunday Times.*

When Witikka expressed a wish to mount a production of his favorite Chekhov play, *The Three Sisters,* at Pitlochry, he was advised that it could not be done with the actors available. The company at Pitlochry is hired for the entire season, and the plays produced are chosen on the basis of the special talents of its members. Because there were two players in the company who were especially suitable for the roles of Arkadina and Trigorin, *The Seagull* was Witikka's obvious alternative.

The English translation to be used was David Magarshack's. Witikka thought it slightly stiff. He remarked that the Finnish translations of Chekhov, which were done in the East Karelian dialect, produced a rhythmical, musical, poetic effect, and were the most successful. Witikka also objected to the simplification of the character's names—Konstantin for Konstantin Gavrilovitch, for example—because it diminished the formality and flavor of the Russian. He restored to the text the full Russian names with their patronyms and, over Mr. Ireland's objections, made several minor alterations in the lines.

The design for the play's scenery was simple and "neutral," not only because of the limitation of the budget but because the director wished to emphasize the characters and their conflicts rather than the period or the locale. The set was not smothered in Russian detail: no huge paintings or heavy draperies, no samovars ("We couldn't find a samovar, in any case"). For the outdoor set of the first act, the backdrop showed an impressionistic view of a lake; the gauze curtain in front of it produced, when lighted, the effect of mist or fog, and shadows of trees and bushes were cast against the gauze. The stage at Pitlochry was difficult to work on because it was very wide and shallow, and scenery could not be flown; the director felt that the sets, unpretentious as they were, worked satisfactorily.

Regarding the emotional tone of *The Seagull,* the director said that although the play is full of comic invention, it is not a comedy; though it ends with a suicide, it is not a tragedy. It is always difficult to pin a label on a Chekhov play; like life *The Seagull* has varying and conflicting moods. Masha's drunkenness at the breakfast table, for example, is very funny and very moving at the same time. The actress must play it seriously, but it is the director's business to make the audience react with both pity and laughter.

When Witikka arrived at Pitlochry, he found that members of the stock company had already been assigned roles in *The Seagull.* He was generally pleased with the casting but regarded as unsatisfactory the actress who had been cast in the role of Nina. That part he gave to the assistant stage manager, who was an apprentice actress with the company.

Witikka felt that the more vividly he could present the characters as human beings, with their emotional problems and frustrations, the more validity the play would have for modern audiences. He wanted to avoid at all costs the atmosphere of a period piece.

Witikka spoke of how he would cast *The Seagull* under ideal conditions. He would probably select his Nina first because she had the most difficult part. In her first scene she must be pathetic in her amateurishness, reciting in a singsong voice that reveals a complete lack of understanding of Kostya's text; but when she returns in the last act, she speaks the lines with a wonderful irony that can come only from experience. Chekhov requires a young performer to demonstrate development as an actress as well as growing maturity as a person. Witikka volunteered the comment that he probably would cast Konstantin before Arkadina, whereas he would select his Gertrude before his Hamlet; he did not elaborate on this statement.

Witikka has seen Trigorin played very often as a Don Juan, but he does not believe for a minute that Trigorin is an insatiable lover. Trigorin is a competent and successful writer, though not a great one, and he recognizes this himself. He is sexually passive; Arkadina, who is getting on in years, is the aggressor and has to conquer him again and again. Nina, too, is the pursuer; Trigorin merely succumbs to a brief infatuation with her. When Trigorin is introduced to Nina in the first scene, he is almost rude to her; he does not actually become aware of her, "see" her, until the seagull scene. Then he is functioning as a writer; he jots in his notebook a comment about Masha, who has caught his attention; by the end of the scene with Nina he has made up a prophetic short story in which she figures as the heroine.

Functioning as the observer and commentator is Dr. Dorn, a former Don Juan, and an urbane and objective man. His importance to the play lies in his balanced, clear-eyed view of the other characters.

Masha is Witikka's favorite character. He feels that Chekhov has given her very Slavic qualities: sensuousness and grace, the latter attractive, the former repellent. Masha is difficult to cast because she must display a mordant sense of comedy underneath her bitterness and frustration, must be earthy rather than sophisticated, and must have a rich voice with a full range. Masha accepts her humiliation and rejection with dignity, knowing from the beginning that she will fail with Konstantin. Like Nina she suffers greatly and pays for her errors, but unlike Nina she has no reward, having no personal goal.

Witikka tried to depict the Arkadina-Trigorin and the Konstantin-Nina relationships as paralleling each other, in an attempt to give them equal importance, while pointing up the similarities and differences.

Jack Witikka feels that actors need special training to play Chekhov, which involves much more than learning lines and stage business and carrying out a director's concept. The actor himself must be able to analyze the text and work into his role. Each character has a well-defined personality and past, which Witikka spoke of as "the breadth or narrowness of his reality," as well as a definite goal toward which he strives. The actor must carry the text rather than the text carrying the actor. Movement grows organically out of the drives of the character; and thought and dialogue must be dynamically integrated when expressed.

To be convincing, the actor must be trained to give the impression that he is actually living inside the skin of the character. He must seem to be the intellectual and emotional double of the person he portrays. For that reason it is not enough to train young actors in theatrical techniques; they must also be subjected to strenuous intellectual, emotional, and physical discipline. Such discipline should be put to the test during the rehearsal period. At the National Theatre in Finland, six weeks of rehearsal are allotted for a new play. At Pitlochry only three were scheduled; the director asked for, and was granted, an extra week.

Mr. Witikka, who runs the government-supported theatre school in Helsinki, described the procedures followed by his students. They are first presented with three principles derived from the Roumanian school of acting: (1) Think. (2) Think independently. (3) Think creatively. Students do not act during the first semester. At the beginning of the term, they are asked to bring in clippings from the newspapers, which they analyze and discuss from the point of view of emotional and intellectual content. They then advance to the short story; the stories are reduced to their basic elements—plot, characterization, dialogue, theme—and students are encouraged to alter the stories, adding dialogue, changing motivations, and so on. They do the same with poetry and, finally, with one-act plays and with scenes from full-length plays. At this point they co-ordinate their reading and analysis with improvisations. They call on sense memory for internal acting, and wear masks for external acting. They are trained in acrobatics and mime.

Witikka entered upon this digression concerning the teaching of acting because the company he directed in *The Seagull,* though competent and highly experienced, had been trained according to various techniques and methods and did not play as an ensemble, which he feels is of the utmost importance in the full realization of a Chekhov play. The speech of the actors particularly troubled the director; it was beautiful British stage diction, which sounded elegant and high-toned but completely un-Russian. Witikka feels that American English—which has fewer set expressions and tends toward the colloquial—is less indicative of social class and works better for Chekhov in translation.

At rehearsals of *The Seagull,* Witikka listened carefully as the cast read through the play three or four times; occasionally he interjected comments. He does not attempt to establish any hard and fast ideas too early in the production. He even keeps the blocking loose and undetermined for as long as possible since he does not wish to tie the actor down. He likes the actors to find themselves through a certain amount of improvisation, then they gradually move on to "fixing" the scenes. He strongly believes in the German way of rehearsing: When the actor gets on his feet for the first time, he has already memorized the first scene or two (at least thirty pages); they work on the scenes they know by heart, while they learn the next thirty pages or so. Each scene is then set, and the production takes shape as they move ahead; but the actor never has the script in his hand. This method helps the actor to concentrate on and co-ordinate dialogue and movement as they proceed. Though he knows in advance what he wishes to achieve in each scene, the director tries to help the actor find his own way to that end.

Witikka has never worked easily with actors he does not know well, which was the case with the stock company at Pitlochry. When asked to appraise his production of *The Seagull,* he replied, "I would have succeeded better with a Noel Coward comedy." While working in Scotland, Mr. Witikka received several lucrative offers as "visiting director," in various foreign countries, but the Pitlochry experience led him to decide against accepting them. He realized that he was better suited to work with a permanent company and chose to stay on at the Finnish National Theatre, with which he has been connected since 1953.

Witikka recalled that Chekhov had said, "Talent alone is not enough; it is the will to fight that counts." But "if each production is to mean a 'fight' with new personalities, it is wiser to devote your talent to a group with which you have an established rapport."

Acting Trigorin in "Rep"

Interview with Dennis Holmes

As a boy in Coventry, Dennis Holmes had a decided Midlands accent. His older sister, who, as an amateur actress, was extremely speech-conscious, considered a regional accent a drawback for a young man who hoped to "get on in the world" and urged him to take voice and elocution lessons, for which she agreed to pay. Dennis preferred to play ball with his friends, but badgered by his sister, he finally consented to attend a local speech class. The teacher one day assigned W. S. Gilbert's "The Stranger," a poem about an actor, which was to be read aloud in class the following week by each student in turn. When he was called on, Dennis gave a complete performance—jumped up on the desk, stabbed himself, and fell to the floor. At the end of the hour, the teacher asked him if he would like to join her private acting class, which met in a neighboring town. Dennis said he could not afford the high fee and was promptly accepted free of charge. For two years he cycled back and forth between Coventry and Leamington Spa, where the class met; it was this teacher who gave him a letter of recommendation to the London Academy of Music and Dramatic Arts.

Holmes applied for admission and, as a result of his audition, was awarded one of the three scholarships offered by the Academy. When he completed the course a year later, he had won a bronze, a silver, and a gold medal. At the Academy, Holmes was tutored in the playing of Shakespeare by Beatrice Forbes-Robertson, an experienced actress who had appeared in England and America in many Shakespearean roles in the company of her celebrated uncle, Sir Johnston Forbes-Robertson. Her interpretations of Shakespeare had a long tradition, having come to her from her uncle, who had been coached by Samuel Phelps; they had been handed down to Phelps from David Garrick through Mrs. Siddons and William Charles Macready. It was from Miss Forbes-Robertson that Holmes inherited his dedication to, and respect for, the theatre, as well as his acting techniques and understanding of Shakespeare. This woman, who was about seventy years old at the time, had an amazing involvement with character. When she played Juliet to a student's Romeo, her whole being lit up with youth and innocence. Although her approach to acting had a nineteenth-century flavor, Holmes and most of her students were able to adapt her methods to suit twentieth-century tastes.

After leaving the Academy, Holmes got his first professional job as juvenile lead with the Liverpool Repertory Company under the direction of John Fernald. Two years later he moved to the Sheffield Repertory Company as leading man. He joined the Old Vic in 1955 and the following year came to America with that company; one of his roles was Aeneas in Tyrone Guthrie's production of *Troilus and Cressida*. On his return to London, he appeared in half a dozen West End plays and then began a career in television, which lasted for seven years.

In 1963 when he was appearing in Terence Rattigan's *The Sleeping Prince* at Newcastle-on-Tyne, he was seen by Kenneth Ireland and Brian Shelton, who were scouting for actors for the 1964 season of the Pitlochry Theatre Festival in Scotland. It was a summer-stock company, which presented six plays in repertory; the theatre's motto is "Stay Six Days and See Six Plays." Since repertory is an established tradition in the English theatre, it is not especially difficult for actors, directors, and technicians to adjust to this system in summer stock. At Pitlochry, which has been in operation from April to September each year since 1952, the plays and productions have been of high quality. During the summer of 1964, the program consisted of Shakespeare's *Twelfth Night*, Anouilh's *Ring Round the Moon* (in Christopher Fry's adaptation), Noel Coward's *Present Laughter*, James Bridie's *Daphne Laureola*, Mrs. Henry Wood's *East Lynne*, and Chekhov's *The Seagull* (in David Magarshack's translation). Dennis Holmes was hired and assigned three important roles: Malvolio (*Twelfth Night*), Sir Joseph Pitts (*Daphne Laureola*), and Trigorin (*The Seagull*), as well as two minor roles: Joshua (*Ring Round the Moon*) and Hugo Lippiatt (*Present Laughter*); he did not appear in *East Lynne*. The two greatest financial successes of the season were *Present Laughter* and *Ring Round the Moon*, modern sophisticated comedies both. The roles Holmes found most rewarding, because they made the heaviest demands upon his talent and broadened the scope of his experience, were Malvolio and Trigorin.

The company rehearsed for six weeks before the season opened in Pitlochry, working simultaneously on the first three plays for four weeks in London and two weeks at the theatre in Scotland. When the curtain went up in April, 1964, three plays were presented within five days, and the season was under way. This feat could only have been accomplished with good artistic results by experienced performers and highly competent technicians.

Jack Witikka, who directed *The Seagull*, was allowed four weeks of rehearsal time for the play. According to Holmes, Witikka is a gentle, quiet man, very sensitive and imaginative, but with strong ideas and a special gift for adding comedic touches to characters and scenes. Before casting the Chekhov play (the last to be produced that season), Witikka carefully observed the actors in the company and evaluated their strengths and weaknesses in the light of his conception of the characters in *The Seagull*. He felt very strongly that the clipped and affected upper-class English speech, which was perfect for *Ring Round the Moon* and *Present Laughter*, was all wrong for the Chekhov play, and he helped the actors to ameliorate it. He never gave an actor a line-reading, however, but being an excellent performer himself, would get up on the stage and move through the part in such a way as to communicate the essence of what he wanted. Witikka and Holmes made slight alterations in Trigorin's lines in an effort to achieve a more realistic effect; the character's asides, for instance, were eliminated, which is the practice in Witikka's native Finland. Trigorin's long speech about the life of a writer was trimmed slightly. No other character's lines were altered as much, yet these minor revisions, Holmes felt, made it possible for him to play the part more smoothly and naturally.

Trigorin, in Holmes's view, is not only a second-rate writer but a second-rate human being; his relations with people—especially with women —are opportunistic; he uses others constantly. Weak and easily swayed, he needs impetus from without. This is not only true of his relations with Arkadina but also with Nina. She is the aggressor in their affair, but his interest in her lasts only as long as she can do something for him—satisfy his ego, perhaps—then he forgets her. When, in the last act, he is shown the stuffed and mounted seagull, which has been prepared at his request, and he says he cannot recall it, he is being perfectly honest. He has wiped Nina from his memory.

Because of his own personality, Holmes had some difficulty at first in assuming the role of Trigorin; he was too warm and too sympathetic toward Nina. He worked hard, with the director and by himself, all through the rehearsal period trying to achieve the proper coolness and distance, but it was not until the last week of rehearsal, actually during a scene with Masha, that Holmes suddenly got the feeling of detachment he wanted. He was then able to sustain the feeling throughout the play. While playing Trigorin, Holmes also came to understand how an older man must feel when he is idolized by a young girl; this was a revelation to the actor.

By the end of the season, Holmes also realized that it was possible for his interpretation of a character to be affected by another character he was playing during the same period. Trigorin and Malvolio took on subtle colorations from each other, and it required a constant effort to keep them sharply delineated. Trigorin has often been played as a dandy, but in the Pitlochry production he was casually dressed in summer clothing, a comfortable old suit, with a colorful scarf-tie. Malvolio, who is usually played as a fop, with elegant clothes and exaggerated speech, was here more subdued. The lives and characters of Trigorin and Malvolio seemed to Holmes to have certain elements in common: both were born poor; Trigorin became well known and well-to-do by the exercise of his creative ability; Malvolio rose to a position of trust and importance in a great household through his administrative talents. Both men remained weak and vacillating, took their work very seriously—too seriously perhaps—and because of their fears, insecurity, and lack of self-awareness, eventually made fools of themselves. Malvolio, the more complex of the two was, in addition, pedantic and puritanical, unloved and unable to love. A strong intermixture of pathos and comedy—Chekhov's hallmark—consequently found its way into the actor's interpretation of Malvolio; the mutation of Trigorin into a Shakespearean character was more subtle and harder to define. Such artificial coloration of character, new and interesting though the resulting interpretation may be, is, Holmes feels, one of the pitfalls of the repertory system.

And yet Holmes much prefers to appear in repertory than in long-run productions, finding it refreshing and challenging to switch from role to role. The actor's problem during a long run is to discover ways to keep from going stale in his part. His effort in repertory, as already mentioned, is to realize each of his roles fully and to keep it sharply delineated and distinct from the others.

To do this, Holmes has his own method. He arrives at the theatre an hour or more before curtain time and gets into his make-up and costume very slowly. While doing so, he goes through his lines. This procedure, which, he feels, allows the mood and essence of the character to sink in along with the make-up, calls for tremendous concentration. He cannot stand much noise or distraction before going on. In one sense, working at Pitlochry was ideal. The theatre was beautifully situated in the highlands, and Holmes had his own little cottage beside a burn (brook) just a few minutes away from the playhouse. In another way, however, Pitlochry was far from ideal: the dressing-room facilities at the theatre were limited, so that there was a good deal of hurly-burly before and during the performance. It is absolutely essential, Holmes feels, for the actor to be self-disciplined, to take his work seriously as an art, and to have reverence for the people who labor to perfect that art. If the actor approaches his work with dedication, he can usually manage to find his way into his role even under unfavorable conditions, but seriousness of purpose is absolutely necessary. Good working habits, once learned, can be of great value to the actor throughout his career.

"I think the season at Pitlochry was very valuable for me from an artistic point of view," said Holmes, "because of the wide variety of parts I was able to play. I loved the character of Trigorin but I haven't read, seen, or even thought of it or of Chekhov's play since I appeared in it in Scotland. I've put the production out of my mind, consciously, because I hope to play the part again and I'd like to approach it from a fresh angle. If I do it again, I'll have a new director, new supporting players, and I myself will have grown and matured, hopefully, which would mean bringing new perceptions to the part. I have no desire to repeat anything I've already done. I had some very 'good battles' (from which I learned something) with Jack Witikka, and some very 'bad battles' (from which I learned nothing) with other directors—mainly over the interpretation of the characters I've been called on to play. I expect, of course, to have many more battles."

His experience at Pitlochry made Holmes realize that he was much happier in the theatre than in any other medium. In the summer of 1967, he appeared on Broadway in the Royal Shakespeare Company's production of Harold Pinter's play, *The Homecoming,* and, in the fall of that year, toured the United States in it before returning to the theatre in London.

The Seagull in America

Interview with Eva Le Gallienne

Eva Le Gallienne—actress, director, producer, translator, and teacher—is the most notable exponent of repertory theatre in the United States.

Miss Le Gallienne has directed two separate productions of *The Seagull* and acted in both. In the first she appeared as Masha at the Civic Repertory

Trigorin (Jacob Ben-Ami) and Masha (Eva Le Gallienne) share a moment of understanding in the Civic Repertory Theatre production, 1929. Museum of the City of New York.

Theatre during the seasons 1929–1932; in the second, she played Madame Arkadina with the National Repertory Theatre in the 1963–64 season.

"My first production was rather somber," said Miss Le Gallienne. "I was quite young and probably felt, as almost everyone else did then, that Chekhov's plays should be saturated with 'Russian mood,' which meant deep shadows, tortured souls, and very little humor. When I did the play for the NRT, my experience both with life and with the theatre had grown considerably. I understood more clearly what Chekhov meant when he called the play a comedy. It is full of wit and irony and if skillfully done can produce a great deal of laughter."

For the NRT production Miss Le Gallienne used her own translation of the play. It was arranged in two parts, two scenes to each part, with just one intermission. Acts I and II were played in the same set, which represented a part of the park on Sorin's estate; for the second scene, there was a complete change of lighting and a rearrangement of props and furniture. "The benches on which we sat to watch Kostya's play," said Miss Le Gallienne, "were replaced with rather shabby, outdoor, wicker furniture, and the little stage was used in the second scene as a place to put picnic baskets, etc." Making one basic set serve for both scenes, Miss Le Gallienne explained, simplified the transportation problem, as the production traveled from coast to coast; and the single intermission made it easier to sustain the complex yet delicate mood of the play.

In Miss Le Gallienne's opinion, all of Chekhov's plays are difficult to do, but *The Seagull* presents special problems. First, there is the need to establish the proper mood—an intermixture of humor and pathos—from the very beginning. But Masha announces in her opening line that she wears black "in mourning for her life," which appears to sound a "tragic" note. It is not until later that we discover that Masha's statement should be viewed with a certain amount of amusement since she dramatizes herself constantly! Another Masha in *Three Sisters* and Varya in *The Cherry Orchard* also wear only black. Working in the manner of a modern painter, Chekhov puts this touch of black on a canvas full of brilliant colors in order to focus attention and to heighten dramatic contrast.

Another problem the director faces at the beginning of this play is to find a way of communicating a sense of stillness and relaxation when the audience has barely had time to quiet down. After the curtain rises, Masha and Medvedenko, who have been strolling about the estate, simply wander into view. To seize the attention of an audience and arouse its interest in what seems to be a desultory conversation is extremely difficult. "During rehearsals of the NRT production," said Miss Le Gallienne, "I tried in several ways to get a sense of casualness into the opening conversation. I even brought the curtain down to cut the actors off from the house in order to increase the feeling of intimacy. I began the actual performance with Yakov working on the little stage, adjusting its curtain, and so on, until the house settled down. Then Masha and Medvedenko strolled on; it was not the usual 'entrance and first lines,' but as if they were in the midst of a fitful conversation."

The character of Masha is one of the most complex in the play; her soul is full of dark corners. Her emotions are so complicated that one sees hints of neuroticism, the faint beginnings of a "case." Though a very young woman, she is frustrated, and a self-devouring ego makes her an intolerable, extraordinary, and pitiable figure. When she drinks with Trigorin, she becomes more communicative and expresses herself with more vehemence than usual, but she does not show physically that she is drunk. She is sometimes played that way. Under the influence of liquor, Masha should lose her usual tenseness, should relax and slow down, but her "mellowness" should perhaps exaggerate her eccentricities. "It is difficult to find a young actress who can play Masha," said Miss Le Gallienne. "The role has many nuances and requires great intensity, but the tendency among young players today is to give a more surface portrayal, or else to make her so neurotic that she becomes unreal."

The part of Kostya is as difficult as that of Masha and for many of the same reasons. Kostya, too, is frustrated and unhappy because he is rejected in love—not only by Nina but by his mother—and, in addition, he has artistic yearnings, which he does not seem able to fulfill. The part is difficult to cast because it calls for a young actor who can play with "cerebral passion." By that Miss Le Gallienne means that the actor must be able to display a passionate conviction for an idea or ideal, that he must be able to drive toward his goal with intense emotion. Such passion, which was a notable characteristic in the Russia of the period of the play, is hard for a young American actor either to understand or to achieve. It is clearly present in the manner in which Kostya pours out his heart to his uncle, rebukes his mother, and finally kills himself because of his complete disillusionment with life—its vulgarity, coarseness, and cheapness. He is reacting, of course, to the people around him and to their behavior toward him. Miss Le Gallienne thought that Marlon Brando, as a young actor, could have played Kostya to perfection. She had seen him in *Truckline Cafe* and as Marchbanks in *Candida* and felt that he had "a spark of true genius." She invited him to join the American Repertory Company, which she helped to found after World War II, and planned to give him the opportunity of appearing in a variety of challenging roles; but Brando chose to pursue the more immediate success and prosperity of a career in motion pictures.

In Miss Le Gallienne's estimation, Trigorin is not a seducer or "*homme fatal.*" He is modest, shy, and withdrawn. Denholm Elliott, who played this part in Miss Le Gallienne's NRT production, happened to possess these very characteristics and brought great credibility to the part. There is, however, a normal amount of male vanity in Trigorin; when a charming young girl swoons at his feet, pursues, and practically seduces him, he cannot help taking advantage of her. But he is a weak man and very much in need of Arkadina's strength. Though he complains about the writer's life and feels overworked, Trigorin is dedicated to his profession. He is not a great artist, and he knows it, but he is a popular and successful author, an excellent craftsman, and an indefatigable worker. Kostya, on the other hand, has a more subjective approach to writing, is more serious, more experimental, and gives the impression that he is more gifted than Trigorin; but he lacks self-confidence and self-discipline and envies the older man his literary, as well as his sexual, conquests. It is interesting to note that Chekhov speaks to us in the guise of Kostya, the serious young writer; of Trigorin the lionized author of best sellers; and of Dr. Dorn, the levelheaded confidant of the others.

According to Miss Le Gallienne, Arkadina is usually played too seriously and is actually a comic part. Chekhov modeled her on a performer who, he said, "posed rather than acted." Although Arkadina appears in second-rate plays, she delights her audiences and is successful in her profession. A spoiled darling, she insists upon being the center of attention at home as well as on the stage. She is vain, domineering, miserly, and terrified of growing old. She is furious with Shamrayev for reminding her of "antediluvian" actors and resents her son not only because his father was a merchant and because she must support him, but because his age gives hers away. Afraid that Trigorin will desert her for Nina, Arkadina, in a passionate scene, clings to his knees and tearfully begs him to go away with her. Trigorin finally capitulates. Then follows a long silence which the actress must fill and sustain—a very difficult thing to do—before speaking her next line, which should top and give point to the scene that

A. TOURING FACTS   '63-'64

    Weeks on Tour................   23
                         Broadway...   5

    Miles Traveled   6,642

    Tour Attendance   145,660
        Average per week.............   6,330
        Average per city   10,404
        Student attendance.............   44,351
        Average per week.............   1,494
    Broadway Attendance.............   23,056

    Average Top Price................ $5.76

    Number of Cities Played...........   15
        Average run.................   1.8 weeks

B. THE COSTS

    Production (3 plays).............. $144,501.46

    Tour Operation $639,667.20
        Average per week............. $ 27,811.61

    Total Tour Cost $784,168.66

    Broadway Operation.............. $128,662.41

    Office and Administration.......... $ 55,662.60

    TOTAL YEAR'S COST............. $968,493.67

C. INCOME

    Tour Admissions $455,876.43
        Average per week $ 19,820.71

    Broadway Admissions .... $ 75,242.19

    Gifts, Grants and Misc. $221,503.11

    TOTAL YEAR'S INCOME $752,621.73

D. THE DEFICIT

    For the Year $215,871.94

    CUMULATIVE................... $331,897.06

Budget of The National Repertory Theatre, March 27, 1965.

has just been played. Miss Le Gallienne described the manner in which she performed it: "After Trigorin agreed to leave with me, and I knew I had won, I rose from my knees, turned away from him, went to the mirror, blew my nose, wiped away my tears, repaired my make-up with a powder puff, arranged my hair, put on my hat, and slowly stuck two hatpins through it—taking all the time in the world to do this. Then with the utmost casualness, as if it made no difference whatsoever to me, I said rather blithely, 'But, of course, you may stay if you like . . .' If the line got a resounding laugh, I knew that the scene had been successful." According to Howard Taubman, then drama critic for *The New York Times*, Miss Le Gallienne accomplished this feat "with the neat, calm poise of the performer who has made a scene count."

Probably no role in a modern play provides so great a challenge for a young actress as does that of Nina. During the first three acts she is innocent and inexperienced, romantic and hopeful. She returns in the last act after a passage of two years, during which she has had an affair with Trigorin, been deserted, lost her child, and struggled doggedly through the provinces to learn her craft as an actress. Though still in love with Trigorin, she has suffered and matured, and her bitter experiences have only served to reinforce her determination to succeed. To be believable as both the innocent and the battered Nina is almost too much to expect of a young actress.

Miss Le Gallienne spoke of four Ninas—Josephine Hutchinson, Anne Meacham, Uta Hagen, and Rosemary Harris—and of what each had brought to the part. "Josephine Hutchinson, who played Nina in the Civic Repertory

Konstantin (Farley Granger) confronts Nina (Anne Meacham) who cradles the dead sea gull in her arms. National Repertory Theatre production directed by Eva Le Gallienne, season of 1963–1964. Compare this scene with those on pages 204 and 221. Photograph: Van Williams. Courtesy ANTA Collection, The Players.

production, was youthful and lovely. Her adoration of Trigorin was very touching; she was such an easy seagull to shoot. But she did not have Anne's strength or maturity for the Nina who returns. Anne, who played the part in the NRT production, was older and had more experience of life to begin with. Perhaps Anne did not create the aura of innocence which Jo did, but she performed the long, difficult speech in Kostya's play with great skill. It was the later Nina that Anne acted brilliantly, with enormous intensity and anguish. The character's harassment and hysteria came through, but one felt she had conquered. It was an extremely moving performance.

"In 1937, when I was preparing to play Nina myself at Westport, Connecticut, Uta Hagen, then just a beginner, studied the role along with me. The production did not come off, but early in 1938, Uta appeared in *The Seagull* with Lynn Fontanne and Alfred Lunt; Nina was her first part on Broadway. I remember how well she expressed the loveliness and longing of youth, but I don't have any strong impression of the final scene. She was very young, perhaps not yet ready for the part.

"Rosemary Harris played Nina with the APA company and was entrancing in the first scene, but she did not move me in her last scene. In the performance I saw, she seemed too cool, too reserved." It is interesting to note that Chekhov strongly disapproved of, and never ceased to criticize, the performance of Roksanova, the talented young actress who created the role of Nina in the original Moscow Art Theatre production, which gives some idea of the enormous range and skill required of the actress who undertakes the part.

"It is almost as difficult to end *The Seagull* as it is to begin it. The lotto game requires careful preparation if it is to be convincing; the playing of the game and the action of the play must be completely interwoven." In working up this scene, Miss Le Gallienne had the actors engage in endless games of lotto while they spoke the lines of the play to accustom them to do both at the same time. The actors did not make use of the numerals mentioned in the text; as they were actually playing the game, they called out the numbers they picked out of the box, and these differed naturally from performance to performance. For even greater verisimilitude, a "period" lotto game was supplied for the NRT production by Parker Brothers. As the scene emerged, the sense of reality was impressive; audiences noticed it and commented on it.

For the very last moment of the play, Miss Le Gallienne arranged a contrapuntal effect: at one side of the stage were the two grave figures discussing Kostya's suicide, while at the other side Shamrayev lifted the stuffed seagull overhead and made an unheard joke, which drew a burst of laughter from the lotto players. Frivolity and tragedy occurring side by side at the final curtain provided the exciting contrast that characterizes real life.

"Ilya Ehrenburg, the Russian writer, compared Chekhov to Mozart," said Miss Le Gallienne. "He saw a similarity in the texture of their work, in their astonishing and impeccable craftsmanship, in the gleaming froth of the surface beneath which flows a current of profound seriousness. For all its brightness, *The Seagull* is a deeply felt play that makes a direct appeal to the emotions. It is the haunting and beautiful work of a younger writer, and in it Chekhov does what Kostya talks of doing—he breaks the mold of conventional writing and acting."

The Seagull on BBC-Radio

Interview with Charles Lefeaux

Early in October, 1967, Charles Lefeaux, a director of dramatic programs for the British Broadcasting Corporation, prepared a radio version of The Seagull for presentation on the Third Programme, the channel reserved for artistic and cultural offerings.

Lefeaux was particularly concerned about the translation he would use, because, as he pointed out, radio drama depends almost entirely on just one thing—the language of the play. Lefeaux studied eleven English versions of The Seagull, including a list of suggestions offered him by Martin Esslin, head of radio drama at the BBC. The director was able to limit the possibilities to five translations, which he evaluated further, finally selecting the work of David Magarshack, which was particularly faithful to the original. "A translation with 'period' but archaic flavor is as bad as one using slangy, modern idioms which jar," said Lefeaux. "I was looking for a style which would sound timeless, and yet do justice to Chekhov." Constance Garnett's version, according to Lefeaux, though good in other respects, is bowdlerized; Magarshack's lines, on the other hand, catch the attention, suggest the atmosphere of the time, render the meaning, and are reasonably speakable.

A second kind of translation takes place when a stage play is adapted for radio presentation—the translation of the visual effects for the ear of the listener. The Seagull creates few difficulties in that respect, for most of the action is vividly evoked by the dialogue. There are not even many ensemble scenes in which several characters appear together, a situation that can confuse the listener. To make identification of characters clearer, "sound perspective" is used: important speakers in the scene being placed closer to the microphones, less important ones, farther away. Evocative sound effects help to create visual images: birdcalls and crickets suggest the woods and meadows; frogs and lapping water, the lake; and so on. Chekhov had complained that Stanislavsky, in the Moscow Art Theatre production, used too many sound effects; this was avoided in the BBC radio production. Chekhov made frequent use of silences in his plays, and pauses always have special significance in radio. According to Lefeaux, "Pauses are a major tool in the creation of suspense in radio drama, whose primary appeal is to the ear." Only very minor cuts and alterations, solely for clarity, were made in the text of The Seagull. Its presentation on the air consumed a full two hours.

Radio drama in the United States is practically defunct, but in Great Britain it is very much alive—and popular. Its performers are drawn from among the greatest talents in the theatre. Lefeaux had just produced a radio version of the life of the operatic tenor Enrico Caruso, based on Dorothy Caruso's biography of her husband, with Irene Worth in the role of Mrs. Caruso. The production had been so well received that the director wished to do another play starring Miss Worth and suggested that she should play Mrs. Alving in Ibsen's Ghosts. Miss Worth, however, expressed a preference for Mme. Arkadina in The Seagull, a role she had never had the opportunity to play on the stage. That is one of the compelling motivations for well-known players to accept radio work: a chance to create characters that especially interest them, particularly in the classics.

Radio, admittedly, does not pay as well as other forms of entertainment. "It is difficult, therefore," Lefeaux said, "to get top stars to commit themselves long in advance of a program, because there is always the chance that something more lucrative will turn up! This adds to the uncertainty of radio production."

Lefeaux went along with Miss Worth's choice of play, recognizing its greatness, but feeling that it lacked the maturity of Chekhov's later work in *The Three Sisters* and *The Cherry Orchard*. He proceeded with the production and surrounded the star with an excellent cast: Zena Walker as Nina, Ian McKellen as Konstantin, Hugh Burden as Trigorin, and Jack May as Dr. Dorn.

The official BBC rehearsal and editing schedule read as follows:

The Seagull

Rehearsal:		Studio
10:30–6:00	Monday 2nd October	Rm. 253, Langham
10:30–6:00	Tuesday 3rd "	Rm. B10, Broadcasting House
10:30–6:00	Wednesday 4th "	"
10:30–6:00	Thursday 5th "	"
10:00–onwards	Friday 6th "	"
Pre-recording:		
2:30–5:30	Friday 6th October 1967	"
Editing:		
9:30–5:30	Tuesday 10th October	"

Devoting five days to rehearsal, Lefeaux spends the whole of the first day sitting at a table with the actors, their scripts in their hands. He talks for some time about Chekhov's relationship to society and to the theatre, about his work as a whole, and then superficially about the play they will be doing—its creation, its production at the Alexandrinsky and then at the Moscow Art Theatre, and Chekhov's reactions and comments. The actors begin to read while Lefeaux takes note of the interpretation each brings to his part; he interrupts them after every three or four pages or at the ends of scenes. If he likes the actor's reading—if it is not at variance with the text, even though it may differ from his own conception—he permits the actor to retain it. If, however, the actor has misread the part or seems to be heading in the wrong direction, he sets him right. In addition to working on individual characterization and the relation of one character to another, Lefeaux explores the emotional climate of each scene. In the first act, for instance, Konstantin's nervousness and excitement in anticipation of the presentation of his play give his voice a special tension, bordering at times on hysteria. The director comments particularly on those lines that are of crucial importance to characterization and plot. By the end of the first day, having gone in this way through the whole play, the director and actors have a "road map" for the production.

On the second day the actors begin to use the microphones, and the technical details are worked out; these details include the placing of the actors in relation to the mikes, the level of the voices and of the sound effects (rain, opening of doors, music across the lake). Interiors and exteriors are differentiated by the use of special acoustic screens around the microphones, which are numbered, the actors noting by number in their scripts the mikes to be used for each scene. Green light-cues are used for the beginnings of scenes and for dialogue following certain of the effects played into the production from tape or disc in the control room and not heard by the actors.

On the third day the company goes through the play in a sort of dress rehearsal, while the director listens unseen and unseeing in another room as if the program were coming over the air. He takes notes on the line-readings, character interpretations, volume, tempo, effects, and so on, for the play must be not only well interpreted and well performed but also entirely clear and comprehensible through sound alone. After the run-through the director gives his notes to the actors and technicians, and any lines, scenes, or effects that have been unsatisfactory are rehearsed once more.

On the fourth day the whole play is run through for the last time and the finer details polished. At this point the actors often make their own contributions by adding subtleties of expression and timing. On the fifth day the play is recorded on tape in continuous performance, as if it were being done in the theatre with all the tension and excitement of a first night. "Some producers," said Lefeaux, "rehearse a scene until they are satisfied and then tape it, then another scene and so on, finally piecing the whole thing together like a film. But I was trained in the theatre and worked for many years as an actor and believe that actors should be allowed to 'build' their performances, to vary in mood and tempo from scene to scene, until a final climax is achieved. The pace, too, is quicker and sharper when a play is done without interruption; when it is put together piece by piece there is no accumulation of tempo." The completed tape, regardless of the method used to produce it, is edited for slips of the tongue, unwanted pauses, and so on; then there is a playback, and possibly more editing, before the show is ready to be broadcast.

Charles Lefeaux's production of *The Seagull* had its première on Tuesday, February 13, 1968, at 8:10 P.M. A review by David Wade in *The Times* (London), headed "Magnificent Chekhov" praised the director and the leading actors. Mr. Wade said, in part: ". . . Miss Walker's unaffected readings sounded entirely in key, the perfect counterpart to some very exciting . . . acting from Ian McKellen and Irene Worth. As Konstantin Mr. McKellen was quite magnificent; he possesses the ideal voice for this part and he used it with immense skill to suggest a nervous energy always verging on hysteria. I wish I could actually have seen him tearing up his papers, for at this point radio could do little even to suggest the climax of anguish to which Mr. McKellen had led us.

"As Irina, Miss Worth almost completely overcame the somewhat fragmentary nature of her part; her Act III encounter with her son was especially impressive. Here the emotions of both careered out of control from love to hate and back again in a frenzy of mutual torture. It would be hard to imagine a more deadly interpretation of this corroding relationship. . . ."

Scene from the Warner Brothers-Seven Arts film version of *The Seagull* designed by Tony Walton and directed by Sidney Lumet, 1968. On the lawn before Sorin's house are Masha, in black (Kathleen Widdoes), Nina, seated in the hammock (Vanessa Redgrave), Arkadina reclining (Simone Signoret), and Sorin in his wheelchair (Harry Andrews). Courtesy Warner Brothers-Seven Arts, Inc.

THE
SEAGULL   *A Comedy in Four Acts*

ANTON CHEKHOV
English Version by Randolph Goodman

Characters

Irina Nikolayevna Arkadina (Madame Trepleva), an actress
Konstantin Gavrilovich Treplev, her son, a young man
Pyotr Nikolayevich Sorin, her brother
Nina Mikhailovna Zarechnaya, a young girl, daughter of a wealthy landowner
Ilya Afanasyevich Shamrayev, a retired lieutenant, manager of Sorin's estate
Polina Andreyevna, his wife
Masha, his daughter
Boris Alexeyevich Trigorin, a writer
Yevgeny Sergeyevich Dorn, a doctor
Semyon Semyonovich Medvedenko, a schoolteacher
Yakov, a workman
A Cook (Male)
A Maid

The action takes place on Sorin's estate. Between the third and fourth acts there is an interval of two years.

Act One

A lawn on Sorin's estate. A wide avenue, leading away from the spectators toward a lake, is obstructed by a small stage which is being hurriedly put together for amateur theatricals, so that the lake is not visible. To the right and left of the little stage there are bushes. A few chairs and a small table.

*[The sun has just set. **Yakov** and other workmen are on the small stage behind the curtain; there are sounds of hammering and coughing. **Masha** and **Medvedenko** enter from the left, returning from a walk.]*

Medvedenko: Why do you always go around in black?

Masha: I'm in mourning for my life. I'm unhappy.

Medvedenko: Why? *[Thoughtfully.]* I can't understand it ... Your health's good ... and even if your father's not rich, he's pretty well off. My life is much harder than yours. I only get twenty-three roubles a month, and they take something out of that for the pension fund, but I don't wear mourning.

[They sit down.]

Masha: Money isn't everything. Even a beggar can be happy.

Medvedenko: Yes, in theory, but in practice it's altogether different. I have to support myself and my mother, my two sisters and my little brother, and all on a salary of twenty-three roubles. We must eat and drink, mustn't we? We must have tea and sugar. And what about tobacco? I tell you, it's not easy.

Masha: *[Glances toward the stage.]* The play'll be starting soon.

Medvedenko: Yes, Nina's going to act in Konstantin's play. They're in love, and tonight when they create a work of art together their souls will be united. But your soul and mine are far apart. I'm in love with you. I walk four miles here and four miles back home every day, and all I get from you is coldness and indifference. But I can understand that! I'm poor and I have a large family to support. Who wants to marry a man who can hardly feed himself?

Masha: That's ridiculous! *[Takes a pinch of snuff.]* I'm touched by your love but I can't return it, that's all. *[Holds out the snuff box to him.]* Help yourself.

Medvedenko: I don't feel like it.

[A pause.]

Masha: There's not a breath of air! We'll probably have a storm tonight . . . All you ever do is philosophize or talk about money. You think poverty is the worst thing in the world; the way I feel, it's a thousand times better to go around in rags and be a beggar than to—But you wouldn't understand that . . .

[Sorin and Treplev enter from the right.]

Sorin: *[Walks with a cane.]* For some reason the country doesn't seem to agree with me, my boy, and I don't think I'll ever get used to it. Last night I went to bed at ten and this morning I woke up at nine feeling as if my brains were glued to my skull from too much sleep, and so on . . . *[Laughs.]* And after dinner I actually dozed off again and now I'm all broken up and feel as if I were in a nightmare, and so forth . . .

Treplev: Yes, Uncle, you really ought to live in town. *[Catches sight of Masha and Medvedenko.]* Look, my friends, we'll call you when we're ready to start the play. You shouldn't be here now. Please go away.

Sorin: *[To Masha.]* Marya Ilyinishna, will you kindly ask your father to have that dog taken off the chain—it never stops howling. It kept my sister awake again all last night.

Masha: Speak to my father yourself. I won't do it, so please don't ask me to. *[To Medvedenko.]* Let's go.

Medvedenko: *[To Treplev.]* You won't forget to call us before the play starts, will you?

[Masha and Medvedenko go out.]

Sorin: I suppose that means the dog'll howl again all night long. It's a strange thing, but I've never really done what I've wanted to in the country. I used to get a month's vacation and come down here for a rest and so on, but I hardly had my foot in the door when they began to pester me so with all sorts of nonsense, I wanted to turn around and leave. *[Laughs.]* I couldn't wait to get away from here. But now I'm retired and I have no place else to go. So, you see—I've got to live here whether I like it or not.

Yakov: *[To Treplev.]* We're going for a swim, Konstantin Gavrilich.

Treplev: All right, but don't take more than ten minutes. *[Looks at his watch.]* We're going to begin soon.

Yakov: Right.

[Goes out.]

Treplev: *[Looking at the little stage.]* Now, there's a theater for you! The curtain, two wings, and beyond that —open space! No scenery at all. There's a clear view of the lake and the horizon. We'll raise the curtain at exactly half past eight, just as the moon is rising.

Sorin: Marvelous!

Treplev: But if Nina is late, the whole effect will be ruined. She should've been here by now. Her father and her stepmother watch her like a hawk. It's harder for her to get out of that house than to break out of a prison.

[Straightens his uncle's necktie.] Your hair and your beard are a mess. You ought to have them trimmed or something—

Sorin: *[Combs his beard.]* It's the tragedy of my life. Even when I was young I always looked as if I'd been on a drunk, and all that.

[He sits down.]

Why is your mother in such a bad mood?

Treplev: Why? Because she's bored.

[Sits down beside **Sorin**.*]*

And she's jealous. She's set against me, and against the performance, and even against my play because Nina is acting in it, and she isn't. She's never read my play, but she hates it.

Sorin: *[Laughs.]* What put that in your head!

Treplev: It kills her to think it'll be Nina's success and not hers—even on this little stage. *[Looks at his watch.]* My mother is a psychological freak. Of course, she's talented and intelligent, but she can shed bitter tears over a novel and reel off all of Nekrassov's poetry by heart. When you're sick she'll nurse you like an angel, but just try praising Duse in her presence. Then, look out! You mustn't praise anyone but her . . . just write about her, make a fuss over her, rave about her brilliant acting in *Camille* and *The Fumes of Life*. But here in the country she can't get those drugs, so she's bored and cranky, and we're all her enemies—we're all to blame. She's superstitious, too—she's afraid of three candles, and the number thirteen! And she's a miser. She's got seventy thousand roubles in a bank in Odessa—I know that for a fact—but just ask her to lend you some money and she'll burst out crying.

Sorin: You think your mother doesn't like your play, so now you're upset and all that. Don't worry—your mother adores you.

Treplev: *[Pulls the petals of a flower.]* She loves me—she loves me not; she loves me—she loves me not; she loves me—she loves me not . . . *[Laughs.]* You see, my mother doesn't love me. And why should she! She wants to live, to have love affairs, to wear girlish clothes. And I'm twenty-five, and keep reminding her she's not young any more. When I'm not around she's only thirty-two, when I am, she's forty-three, and she hates me for that. And she knows I despise the theater. She loves the stage . . . she thinks she's serving humanity and the Sacred Cause of Art . . . but the way I look at it, the modern theater is nothing but a lot of clichés and worn-out conventions. When the curtain goes up you see a room with three walls, lit by artificial light, and then those great geniuses—the High Priests of the Sacred Art—show you how people eat, drink, make love, walk around, and wear their clothes. Then they try to fish a moral out of those commonplace lines and scenes —a nice little moral that's easy to understand and useful in the home. When I see the same thing over and over again in a thousand variations, I feel exactly like Maupassant, who ran away from the Eiffel Tower, which almost drove him mad with its vulgarity.

Sorin: But we can't do without the theater.

Treplev: We need new forms of expression. We need them desperately, and if we can't have new forms, we'd better have nothing. *[He looks at his watch.]* I love my mother—I love her very much—but she leads such a stupid sort of life, running around with that writer of hers, her name always turning up in the papers—it bores me stiff. And sometimes, being a simple, self-centered person makes me resent the fact that my mother is a famous actress, and I imagine I'd be a lot happier if she were just an ordinary woman. Uncle, can there be anything more hopeless and depressing than the position I'm in? She often used to have visitors, all celebrities— actors and writers—and I was the only nobody among them. They only tolerated me because I was her son. Who am I? What am I? I left college in my junior year, "owing," as the editors say, "to circumstances beyond our control." I have no talent, not a penny to my name, and my passport describes me as a shopkeeper from Kiev, because my father was a shopkeeper from Kiev, even though he became a famous actor. So when all those actors and authors in her drawing-room were kind enough to acknowledge my existence, I imagined from the way they looked at me they were measuring my insignificance—I could read their thoughts and was tortured with humiliation . . .

Sorin: By the way, will you please tell me what sort of person this author of hers is? I can't figure him out. He never opens his mouth.

Treplev: He's intelligent, simple, a bit on the melancholy side. A very decent fellow. He's still a long way from forty, but he's already famous and very well off. So far as his books are concerned . . . what shall I say? They're charming, full of talent, but after Tolstoy or Zola . . . you don't care to read Trigorin.

Sorin: Well, my boy, I happen to like writers. There was a time when I passionately wanted two things: I wanted to get married and I wanted to be an author, but I didn't manage to do either. Well, it must be nice to be even a second-rate writer, and so on.

Treplev: *[Listens.]* I think someone's coming . . . *[Hugs his uncle.]* I can't live without her . . . Even the sound of her footsteps is beautiful . . . I'm insanely happy . . .

    *[**Nina Zarechnaya** enters and **Treplev** goes quickly to meet her.]*
My enchantress . . . my dream . . .

Nina: *[Upset.]* I'm not late . . . surely, I'm not late . . .

Treplev: *[Kisses her hands.]* No, no, no . . .

Nina: I've been nervous all day. I was so frightened. I was afraid father wouldn't let me come. But he's just gone out with my stepmother. The sky is red . . . the moon is just rising . . . and I made the horse run faster and faster . . . *[Laughs.]* Oh, I'm so happy!

    *[Shakes **Sorin's** hand warmly.]*

Sorin: *[Laughs.]* Your pretty eyes look as if they've been crying. Now, now! That's not right!

Nina: Oh, it's nothing . . . I'm so out of breath! I have to leave in half an hour. We must hurry. I can't stay, I really can't! For God's sake don't keep me too late! My father doesn't know I'm here.

Treplev: It's time to begin, anyhow. I'll go and call everybody.

Sorin: I'll go, and so forth. I'll go right away.

    [He starts off right singing "The Two Grenadiers" then stops and turns.]
Once I started to sing like that and the Assistant Prosecutor said to me, "You have a powerful voice, Your Honor," then he thought for a minute and added, "but it's not a very pleasant one."

    [He laughs and goes out.]

Nina: My father and his wife don't want me to come here. They say it's too bohemian . . . They're afraid I'll go on the stage. But I'm drawn here to the lake, like a seagull . . . My heart is full of you . . . *[She glances around.]*

Treplev: We're alone.

Nina: I thought I heard someone there . . .

Treplev: There's no one . . . *[He kisses her.]*

Nina: What kind of tree is this?

Treplev: An elm.

Nina: Why is it so dark?

Treplev: Because it's evening . . . and everything looks darker. Don't leave early, please don't!

Nina: I must.

Treplev: And if I follow you home, Nina, I'll stand in the garden all night and look up at your window.

Nina: No, you mustn't. The watchman would see you. And Trésor isn't used to you. He'd bark.

Treplev: I love you.

Nina: Shh . . .

Treplev: [Hears footsteps.] Who's there? You, Yakov?

Yakov: [From behind the curtain of the little stage.] Yes, sir.

Treplev: Get ready. It's time to begin. Is the moon rising?

Yakov: Yes, sir.

Treplev: Have you got the alcohol? Have you got the sulphur? When the red eyes appear there must be a smell of sulphur.

[To **Nina.**]

You'd better go backstage now. Everything's ready. Are you nervous?

Nina: Yes, terribly! It's not your mother . . . I'm not afraid of her . . . But there's Trigorin . . . that terrifies me . . . I'm ashamed of acting in front of him . . . a famous writer . . . Is he young?

Treplev: Yes.

Nina: His stories are so wonderful!

Treplev: [Coldly.] I don't know. I haven't read them.

Nina: It's very hard to act in your play. There are no real people in it.

Treplev: Real people! One mustn't depict life as it is or even as it ought to be, but as we see it in our dreams.

Nina: There's very little action in your play—nothing but speeches. And I really think a play ought to have some love in it . . .

[**Nina** and **Treplev** go behind the curtain.]

[Enter **Polina Andreyevna** and **Dorn.**]

Polina: It's getting damp. Go back and put on your galoshes.

Dorn: I'm hot.

Polina: You don't take care of yourself. You're just stubborn. You're a doctor, and you know perfectly well the damp air is bad for you, but you want to make me worry. You sat out on the veranda all last night on purpose . . .

Dorn: [Sings softly.] "Do not say my youth was wasted . . ."

Polina: You were so absorbed in your conversation with Irina Nikolayevna . . . you didn't even notice the cold. Tell the truth, you find her attractive, don't you?

Dorn: I'm fifty-five.

Polina: Nonsense! That's not old for a man. You look very young for your age and you're still attractive to women.

Dorn: Well, what do you want me to do about it?

Polina: All you men are ready to get down on your knees in front of an actress. Every one of you!

Dorn: [Sings softly.] "Once again I stand before you . . ." If people like artists and treat them better than shopkeepers, for example, that's the way things are. It's idealism!

Polina: Women have always been mad about you and thrown themselves at you. Is that idealism, too?

Dorn: [Shrugs.] Well, there was a great deal of good in the way women have treated me. What they really loved in me was a first-rate doctor. You know, ten or fifteen years ago I was the only decent obstetrician in the whole district. And what's more, I've always been honest.

Polina: [Seizes his hand.] My dearest!

Dorn: Shh! They're coming.

[Enter **Madame Arkadina,** on **Sorin's** arm, followed by **Trigorin, Shamrayev, Medvedenko,** and **Masha.**]

Shamrayev: In 1873 I saw her at the Poltava Fair. What a terrific actress! It was a pleasure! A terrific actress! Do you happen to know, Madame, where Chadin is now? Pavel Semyonich Chadin, the comedian? His Rasplyuyev was unbeatable, even better than Sadovsky's, I assure you, my dear lady. Where is he now?

Arkadina: You keep asking me about those antediluvians. How should I know?

[She sits down.]

Shamrayev: [Sighs.] Pashka Chadin! We

don't have actors like that any more. No, my dear lady, the stage is going down. In the old days there were mighty oaks, and now we have nothing but stumps.

Dorn: That's true, we don't have many brilliant actors nowadays, but the general level of acting is much higher than it used to be.

Shamrayev: I can't agree with you there, but that's a matter of taste. *De gustibus aut bene, aut nihil.*

[**Treplev** *comes out from behind the stage.*]

Arkadina: [*To* **Treplev.**] My dear son, when's it going to start?

Treplev: In a minute. Please be patient.

Arkadina: My son!

[*Recites from* Hamlet.]

"Thou turn'st mine eyes into my very soul;

And there I see such black and grainéd spots

As will not leave their tinct."

Treplev: [*Paraphrases* Hamlet.]

Nay, but to live

in evil, to seek love

in the depths of sin . . .

[*A horn is sounded behind the curtain.*]

Treplev: Ladies and gentlemen, we're ready to start. Please pay attention . . .

[*Pause.*]

I begin—

[*He taps with a stick and recites in a loud voice.*]

Oh, you ancient, venerable shades that float at night above this lake, lull us to sleep, and allow us to dream of what is to be in two hundred thousand years!

Sorin: There'll be nothing in two hundred thousand years!

Treplev: Then let them show us that nothing.

Arkadina: Yes, let them. We're asleep.

[*The curtain rises; the lake is now visible, with the moon above the horizon and its reflection in the water.* **Nina Zarechnaya,** *all in white, is seated on a large rock.*]

Nina: Men, lions, eagles, and partridges, horned deer, geese, spiders, silent fish that dwell in the deep, starfishes and creatures invisible to the eye—all living things, all living things, all living things, having completed their cycle of sorrow, are now extinct . . . For thousands of years no living creature has been born on the earth, and this poor moon now lights its lamp in vain. The cranes in the meadow no longer waken with a cry, and the drone of the May-beetles is heard no more in the lime trees. It is cold, cold, cold! Empty, empty, empty! Fearful, fearful, fearful!

[*Pause.*]

The bodies of living creatures have disappeared in dust, and eternal matter has turned them into rocks, into water, into clouds, while the souls of all have merged into one. I am that world-soul, I— In me is the soul of Alexander the Great, of Caesar, of Shakespeare, of Napoleon, and of the lowest worm. In me the consciousness of men is blended with the instincts of the animals, and I remember all, all, all! And I live every life over again in myself!

[*Will-of-the-wisps appear.*]

Arkadina: [*Whispers.*] Decadent, isn't it!

Treplev: [*Imploringly and reproachfully.*] Mama!

Nina: I am alone. Once in a hundred years I open my lips to speak but my voice echoes mournfully in the void, no one hears . . . And you, pale fires, hear me not . . . You are born before daybreak in the putrid marsh and you wander until dawn, but without thought, without will, without the pulse-beat of life. Afraid that life will spring up in you, the devil, father of eternal matter, keeps the atoms in you in continual flux, and you, like the stones and the water, change perpetually. For in all the world nothing remains permanent and un-altered but the spirit . . .

[*Pause.*]

Like a prisoner cast into a deep and empty well, I know not where I am nor what awaits me. One thing alone is clear to me: In the cruel, persistent struggle with the devil, I am destined to conquer the forces of matter, and then matter and spirit will blend in glorious harmony, and the Kingdom of the Cosmic Will shall come. But it will come only little by little, through long, long thousands of years when the moon, and bright Sirius, and the earth have turned to dust . . . Until then . . . terror, terror . . .

[Pause. Two red spots appear against the background of the lake.]

And now, the devil, my powerful enemy, approaches. I see his frightful, bloodshot eyes . . .[1]

Arkadina: There's a smell of sulphur! Is there supposed to be?

Treplev: Yes.

Arkadina: [Laughs.] Oh, it's a stage effect!

Treplev: Mama!

Nina: [Attempts to continue.] He is lost without Man—

Polina: [To **Dorn**.] You're taking your hat off. Put it on or you'll catch cold.

Arkadina: The doctor is taking his hat off to the devil, the father of eternal matter.

Treplev: [Furious, shouts.] The play is over! Enough! Curtain!

Arkadina: Why are you angry?

Treplev: Enough! Curtain! Bring down the curtain!

[He stamps his foot.]

Curtain!

[The curtain falls.]

I'm sorry! I forgot only a few special people are allowed to write plays and act in them. I've infringed on the monopoly. I . . . I . . .

[Tries to speak, but with a wave of the hand, rushes out left.]

Arkadina: What's the matter with him?

Sorin: Irina, my dear, you really ought to have more respect for a young man's pride!

Arkadina: What did I say to him?

Sorin: You hurt his feelings.

Arkadina: He told us the play was only going to be a joke, and that's the way I took it!

Sorin: All the same—

Arkadina: Now, it seems, he's written a masterpiece! What next! So he gets up this performance and smothers us with sulphur not as a joke but as a protest . . . He wants to show us how to write and how to act! He's going too far with his everlasting attacks at my expense. His cutting remarks would make anyone lose patience. I don't care what you say, he's a conceited, arrogant boy!

Sorin: He only wanted to please you.

Arkadina: Really? Then why didn't he choose an ordinary play instead of making us listen to this decadent drivel? I don't mind listening to drivel for the sake of a joke, but all this pretentiousness about new forms and a new view of art! I don't think it has anything to do with new forms, it's just bad temper.

Trigorin: Everyone writes as he likes and as he can.

Arkadina: Well, let him write as he likes and as he can, only let him leave me in peace.

Dorn: You are angry, Jupiter—

Arkadina: I'm not Jupiter—I'm a woman. [Lights a cigarette.] And I'm not angry —only annoyed that a young man should waste his time like that. I didn't mean to hurt his feelings.

Medvedenko: There's no proof that spirit

---

[1] In Treplev's play, Chekhov was satirizing the concept of the World Soul preached by Vladimir Solovyov, mystic, philosopher, and poet, who had a strong influence on the avant-garde writers in Russia at the end of the nineteenth and beginning of the twentieth century. Chekhov disposed of Solovyov's ideas with a whiff of sulphur. For this information I am indebted to David Magarshack.—R. G.

can be separated from matter, because spirit itself may be a combination of material atoms. *[Excitedly, to Trigorin.]* But, you know, someone ought to write about how poor teachers live, and put that on the stage. We have a very hard life.

Arkadina: That's true, but let's not talk any more about plays or atoms. It's such a glorious evening! Listen! They're singing!

[All listen.]

It's so lovely!

Polina: It's on the other side of the lake.

[A pause.]

Arkadina: *[To Trigorin.]* Sit here beside me. Ten or fifteen years ago there was always music or singing on the lake ... almost every night. There are six houses around the lake. And I can remember the laughter, the noise, the shooting, and the endless love affairs ... the young hero, in those days, the idol in all six houses, was our friend here— *[Motions with her head toward Dorn.]* Yevgeny Sergeyich. He's still charming, but in those days he was irresistible! My conscience is beginning to bother me. Why did I hurt my poor boy's feelings? It upsets me.

[Calls.]

Kostya! Kostya, dear!

Masha: I'll go look for him.

Arkadina: Would you, my dear?

Masha: *[Starts out left.]* Yoo-hoo! Konstantin Gavrilovich! Yoo-hoo!

[She goes out.]

Nina: *[Comes out from behind the curtain.]* I suppose the play's over, so I can come out now. Good evening!

[She kisses Arkadina and Polina Andreyevna.]

Sorin: Bravo! Bravo!

Arkadina: Bravo! Bravo! We loved you. With your looks and your lovely voice, you really mustn't stay in the country—it's a sin! I'm sure you have talent. Do you hear? You've simply got to go on the stage.

Nina: Oh, that's my dream. *[Sighs.]* But it'll never come true.

Arkadina: Who knows? Here, let me introduce Boris Alexeyevich Trigorin.

Nina: Oh, I'm so glad to—

[She is overcome with embarrassment.]

I'm always reading your—

Arkadina: *[Draws Nina down beside them.]* Don't be shy, my dear. He's a celebrity, but he has a simple heart. You see, he's shy himself.

Dorn: I suppose we can raise the curtain now. It looks rather frightening.

Shamrayev: *[Calls.]* Yakov, pull up the curtain, my boy.

[The curtain goes up.]

Nina: *[To Trigorin.]* It's a queer play, isn't it?

Trigorin: I didn't understand a word of it. But I liked it. You acted so sincerely. And the scenery was delightful—

[Pause.]

There must be a lot of fish in that lake.

Nina: Oh, yes.

Trigorin: I love fishing. There's nothing I enjoy more than to sit on the bank of a river in the evening and watch the float.

Nina: And I'd have thought a great artist couldn't enjoy anything but creating.

Arkadina: *[Laughs.]* Don't talk like that. When people say nice things to him he's utterly floored.

Shamrayev: I remember one evening at the opera in Moscow the great Silva hit low C. It so happened that the bass from our church choir was sitting in the gallery, and all of a sudden —you can imagine our surprise—we heard from the gallery, "Bravo, Silva!" a whole octave lower—like this: *[In a deep bass.]* "Bravo, Silva!" The audience was thunderstruck!

[A pause.]

Dorn: The angel of silence has flown over us.

Nina: It's time for me to go. Goodbye.

Arkadina: Where are you off to? Why so early? We won't let you go.

Nine: My father expects me.

Arkadina: What a man, really . . .

[Kisses her.]

Well, if you must—but I'm sorry to let you go.

Nina: If you only knew how I hate to go.

Arkadina: Someone ought to see you home, my little pet.

Nina: [Frightened.] Oh, no, no!

Sorin: [Imploringly.] Please stay!

Nina: I can't, Pyotr Nikolayevich.

Sorin: Just stay for an hour, and so on. Come now, really . . .

Nina: [Hesitates for a moment, speaks tearfully.] I can't!

[Shakes hands and goes out hurriedly.]

Arkadina: Poor, unfortunate girl. They say her mother left an enormous estate to her father—every penny of it—and she gets nothing because her father's already made a will leaving everything to his second wife. It's absolutely shocking!

Dorn: Yes, her father is a perfect beast, to give him his due.

Sorin: [Rubs his hands.] Let's go in, too. It's getting damp. My legs are beginning to ache.

Arkadina: They're like wooden legs. You can hardly walk. Yes, let's go in, you poor old man!

[She takes his arm.]

Shamrayev: [Offers his arm to his wife.] Madame?

Sorin: I hear that dog howling again. [To **Shamrayev**.] Ilya Afanasyevich, will you kindly have him taken off the chain.

Shamrayev: That's impossible, Pyotr Nikolayevich! I'm afraid of thieves breaking into the barn. I've got the millet in there.

[To **Medvedenko**, who is walking beside him.]

Imagine, a whole octave lower: "Bravo, Silva!" And not even a real singer, just a member of the church choir!

Medvedenko: And how much do you get paid to sing in the choir?

[All go out except **Dorn**.]

Dorn: [Alone.] I don't know. I suppose I don't know anything about it, or maybe I'm going out of my mind, but I liked the play. It's got something. When that girl talked about loneliness . . . and when the devil's red eyes appeared, I got so excited I felt my hands trembling. It was really fresh and naive . . . I think he's coming back. I must say something nice to him . . .

Treplev: [Enters.] They've all gone.

Dorn: I'm here.

Treplev: Masha's been hunting all over the place for me. She's a damned nuisance!

Dorn: Konstantin Gavrilovich, I liked your play very much. It's rather strange, and I haven't heard the end of it, but it made a great impression on me. You have talent . . . you must go on.

[**Treplev** presses his hand warmly and embraces him impulsively.]

Dorn: My, but you're emotional! Tears in your eyes . . . Now, what did I want to say? You took a subject from the realm of abstract ideas, and that's right! A work of art ought to express a great idea. A thing is only worth while when it's serious. You're so pale!

Treplev: So you think I ought to go on?

Dorn: Of course I do. But only write about what's important and lasting. I've had a lot of experiences in my life, you know, and enjoyed them. I'm satisfied. But if I could have felt the joy of artistic creation, I'm sure I would've despised my body and all its pleasures. I'd've tried to rise above all physical things.

Treplev: Excuse me . . . where's Nina?

Dorn: She went home.

Treplev: [In despair.] What shall I do? I want to see her . . . I must see her . . . I'm going . . .

[Enter **Masha**.]

Dorn: [To **Treplev.**] You must calm down, my friend.

Treplev: But I'm going. I must go.

Masha: Come inside, Konstantin Gavrilovich. Your mother wants you. She's worried.

Treplev: Tell her I went away. And please leave me alone, all of you! Just leave me alone! Don't follow me around!

Dorn: Come, come, my boy. Don't carry on like that. It's not right.

Treplev: [In tears.] Goodbye, doctor. Thank you . . .

[He goes out.]

Dorn: [Sighs.] Youth! Youth!

Masha: When people have nothing better to say, they say, "Youth, youth!" [She takes a pinch of snuff.]

Dorn: [Takes the snuff-box from her and flings it into the bushes.] That's a disgusting habit!

[Pause.]

They're playing the piano in there. We'd better go in.

Masha: Wait a minute.

Dorn: What is it?

Masha: I'd like to talk to you again . . . I must talk . . . [Excitedly.] I don't like my father . . . but I like you. For some reason, I feel very close to you . . . Help me, help me, or I'll do something foolish, I'll make a mess of my life, I'll ruin it . . . I can't go on like this . . .

Dorn: What is it? Help you . . . how?

Masha: Oh, I'm so miserable. No one, no one knows how I'm suffering!

[Lays her head on his chest, softly.]

I love Konstantin!

Dorn: You're all so emotional! So emotional! And there's so much love . . . It's the witchery of the lake! [Tenderly.] But what can I do, my child? What? What?

CURTAIN

Act Two

A croquet lawn, with flowerbeds. In the background, on the right, the house with a large veranda; on the left, a view of the lake with the blazing sun reflected in it. It is noon and hot.

[At one side of the croquet lawn, **Arkadina, Dorn,** and **Masha** are sitting on a garden bench in the shade of an old lime tree. **Dorn** has an open book on his lap.]

Arkadina: [To **Masha.**] Come on, let's stand up.

[Both get up.]

Side by side. You're twenty-two and I'm nearly twice that. Yevgeny Sergeyich, who looks younger?

Dorn: You do, of course.

Arkadina: There, you see? And why? Because I work, I'm alive, I'm always on the go, but you just stick in the mud . . . you're not living . . . And I make it a rule not to worry about the future. I never think about old age or death. What will be, will be!

Masha: And I feel about a hundred years old; I drag my life behind me like an endless train. Sometimes I don't even want to go on living.

[She sits down.]

Of course, that's a lot of nonsense. I've got to get hold of myself and throw it all off.

Dorn: [Sings softly.] "Tell me, pretty flowers . . ."

Arkadina: And what's more, I'm as neat as an Englishman, I take good care of myself, as they say, my clothes and my hair always comme il faut. Would I allow myself to leave the house, even to come out here in the garden, in a dressing-gown, or without my hair being done? Never! And that's what's kept me young! I've never been slovenly, I've never let myself go, as some women do . . .

[Walks up and down the lawn, with her hands on her hips.]

Here I am—lively as a bird. I could play a girl of fifteen.

Dorn: Anyway, I'll continue . . .

[He takes up the book.]

We got to the part about the grain-dealer and the rats . . .

Arkadina: And the rats. Go ahead.

[She sits down.]

No, give it to me. I'll read. It's my turn, anyhow.

[She takes the book and looks for the place.]

And the rats . . . Here it is . . .

[She reads.]

"And it goes without saying it's as dangerous for society people to surround themselves with novelists and to lionize them as it is for a grain-dealer to raise rats in his barn. And so, when a woman has picked out an author she wants to capture, she lays siege to him with compliments, flattery, and favors . . ." Well, that may be the way the French go about it, but we don't do anything like that, we don't put on a regular campaign. Here, if you please, before a woman sets out to capture an author she's usually head over heels in love herself. Take Trigorin and me, for example—

*[Enter **Sorin**, leaning on his cane, with **Nina** beside him; **Medvedenko** follows them, pushing a wheel-chair.]*

Sorin: *[To **Nina**, in a caressing tone, as one speaks to a child.]* Yes, we're delighted, aren't we? We're happy today and so on? *[To his sister.]* We're delighted! Father and step-mother have gone to Tver, and now we're free for three whole days.

Nina: *[Sits down beside **Arkadina** and embraces her.]* I'm so happy! Now I belong to you.

Sorin: *[Sits down in the wheel-chair.]* She looks lovely today.

Arkadina: Beautifully dressed and interesting . . . There's a clever girl!

*[Kisses **Nina**.]*

But we mustn't praise you too much. It's bad luck. Where's Boris Alexeyevich?

Nina: He's down at the bath-house, fishing.

Arkadina: You'd think he'd be sick of it!

[Is about to go on reading.]

Nina: What's that?

Arkadina: Maupassant's "On the Water," my dear.

[Reads a few lines to herself.]

Well, the rest isn't interesting or true.

[Shuts the book.]

I'm awfully worried. Tell me, what's the matter with my son? He's so moody and withdrawn. He's out on that lake day after day, and I hardly ever see him.

Masha: He's unhappy. *[To **Nina**, timidly.]* Please recite something from his play.

Nina: You really want me to? It's so dull!

Masha: *[Trying to restrain her enthusiasm.]* When he recites anything himself, his eyes shine and his face gets pale. He has a beautiful, sad voice, and he looks like a poet.

*[**Sorin** begins to snore.]*

Dorn: Good night!

Arkadina: *[To **Sorin**.]* Petrusha!

Sorin: Ah?

Arkadina: Are you asleep?

Sorin: Of course not.

Arkadina: You're not looking after your health, and that's not right, dear.

Sorin: I'd be glad to take some kind of treatment, but the doctor there doesn't want me to.

Dorn: Start treatments at sixty!

Sorin: Even at sixty a man wants to live!

Dorn: *[Impatiently.]* Oh, all right, then, take some valerian drops!

Arkadina: I think it would do him a lot of good to go to some mineral springs for a cure.

Dorn: Well, it might and it might not.

Arkadina: Try to figure that out!

Dorn: There's nothing to figure out. It's very clear.

[A pause.]

Medvedenko: Pyotr Nikolayevich ought to give up smoking.

Sorin: Rubbish!

Dorn: No, it's not rubbish. Wine and tobacco affect your personality. After a cigar or a glass of vodka, you're not Pyotr Nikolayevich any more, you're

Pyotr Nikolayevich plus somebody else; your ego begins to blur, you see yourself as a third person—as he.

Sorin: [Laughs.] You're a fine one to talk! You've lived a full life, but what about me? I served in the Department of Justice for twenty-eight years, but I haven't lived yet, haven't seen or done a thing and so on; naturally I feel very much like living. You've had your fill and you don't care any more, so you can afford to be philosophical, but I want to live—that's why I drink sherry at dinner and smoke cigars and so forth. And that's all there is to it!

Dorn: We must take life seriously, but when you go in for cures at sixty and regrets over the lost pleasures of your youth it seems a bit silly, if you'll forgive my saying so.

Masha: [Gets up.] It must be time for lunch.
[She walks slowly and with a limp.]
My leg's gone to sleep . . .
[She goes out.]

Dorn: She'll go in and have a couple of drinks before lunch.

Sorin: She's very unhappy, poor thing.

Dorn: Oh, nonsense, Your Honor.

Sorin: You talk like a man who's had his fill.

Arkadina: Oh, what could be more boring than this sweet country boredom! Hot, quiet, nobody does anything, everybody philosophizes . . . It's nice being with you, my friends, delightful to listen to you, but . . . sitting in some hotel room and learning a part would be so much better.

Nina: [Enthusiastically.] Oh, yes! I know just what you mean!

Sorin: Of course, it's better in town. You sit in your study, the doorman lets no one in without announcing him, there's a telephone, cabs in the street, and so on . . .

Dorn: [Sings softly.] "Tell her, my flowers . . ."

[Enter **Shamrayev,** followed by **Polina Andreyevna.**]

Shamrayev: Here they are! Good morning!
[Kisses **Arkadina's** hand and then **Nina's.**]
Very glad to see you looking so well. [To **Arkadina.**] My wife tells me you're planning on driving into town with her today. Is that so?

Arkadina: Yes, we're thinking of it.

Shamrayev: Hm! That's fine, but how are you going to get there, my dear lady? They're bringing in the rye today and all the men are busy. And what horses will you use, may I ask?

Arkadina: What horses? How should I know—what horses!

Sorin: We've got carriage horses.

Shamrayev: [Flares up.] Carriage horses! And where'll I get the harness for them? Where'll I get the harness? It's amazing! It's incredible! My dear lady, excuse me, I worship you for your talent. I'd give ten years of my life for you, but I can't let you have the horses!

Arkadina: But what if I have to go? It's the queerest thing!

Shamrayev: My dear lady, you don't know what farming means.

Arkadina: [Flares up.] It's the same old story! In that case, I'll go back to Moscow today. You'll hire some horses for me in the village, or I'll walk to the station.

Shamrayev: [Furious.] In that case, I resign! Find yourself another manager.
[He goes out.]

Arkadina: It's like this every summer . . . every summer I'm insulted here! I'll never set foot in this place again.
[She goes out in the direction of the bath-house. A moment later she is seen entering the house, followed by **Trigorin,** who is carrying fishing rods, tackle, and a pail.]

Sorin: [Furious.] What insolence! It beats everything! I'm sick of it and so forth.

Bring all the horses here this minute!

Nina: [To **Polina Andreyevna**.] To refuse Irina Nikolayevna, the famous actress! Any wish of hers, any whim, is more important than all your farming. It's absolutely unbelievable!

Polina: [In despair.] What can I do? Put yourself in my place, what can I do?

Sorin: [To **Nina**.] Let's go to my sister. We'll all beg her not to go. Won't we? [Looks in the direction **Shamrayev** went.] Unbearable man! Tyrant!

Nina: [Prevents him from getting up.] Sit still, sit still. We'll wheel you in. [She and **Medvedenko** push the wheel-chair.] Oh, how awful it is!

Sorin: Yes, yes, it's awful ... but he won't leave. I'll talk to him in a little while. [They go out. **Dorn** and **Polina** are left alone.]

Dorn: People make me sick. They simply ought to kick your husband out of here once and for all, but in the end that old woman Pyotr Nikolayevich and his sister will be begging him to forgive them. You'll see.

Polina: He sent the carriage horses into the fields, too! There are quarrels like this every day. If you only knew how it upsets me! It makes me ill. You can see how I'm trembling. I can't bear his coarseness. [Imploringly.] Yevgeny, my dearest, my darling, take me away with you. Our time is passing, we're not young any more, and if only we could stop hiding and stop lying for the little time we have left, at least ... [A pause.]

Dorn: I'm fifty-five. It's too late to change my way of life.

Polina: I know why you refuse me—because there are other women who mean as much to you as I do. Of course, you can't take them all with you. I understand. I'm sorry, you're tired of me. [**Nina** appears near the house; she is picking flowers.]

Dorn: No, not at all.

Polina: I'm eaten up with jealousy. Of course, you're a doctor, you can't avoid women. I understand.

Dorn: [To **Nina**, who comes up to them.] How are things going in there?

Nina: Irina Nikolayevna is crying and Pyotr Nikolayevich is having an attack of asthma.

Dorn: [Gets up.] I'd better go in and give them both some valerian drops.

Nina: [Gives him the flowers.] These are for you.

Dorn: Merci bien. [He goes toward the house.]

Polina: [Goes with him.] What pretty flowers! [As they near the house, in an intense undertone.] Give me those flowers! Give me those flowers! [He gives them to her; she tears them to pieces and throws them away; both go into the house.]

Nina: [Alone.] It's so strange to see a famous actress cry, and for such a little thing! But it's even stranger for a great writer to spend the whole day fishing. The public adores him, he's written up in all the papers, they sell his picture everywhere, and translate his books into foreign languages, and he's in seventh heaven if he catches two minnows. I thought famous people were proud and standoffish; I was sure they hated the crowd and used their fame and glory to get revenge on the people who put money and position above everything else. But here they are crying, fishing, playing cards, laughing, and losing their tempers like everybody else! [**Treplev** enters, bareheaded, carrying a gun and a dead seagull.]

Treplev: Are you alone here?

Nina: Yes. [**Treplev** lays the seagull at her feet.]

Nina: What's that for?

Treplev: I was mean enough today to kill this seagull. I lay it at your feet.

Nina: What's the matter with you?

[She picks up the bird and looks at it.]

Treplev: *[After a pause.]* I'll kill myself in the same way soon.

Nina: I hardly know you any more.

Treplev: Yes, and ever since that day I feel I hardly know you. You've changed toward me, your eyes are cold, and I seem to be in your way.

Nina: You're so irritable lately, and I can't understand you, you seem to be talking in symbols. And this seagull is a symbol, too, I suppose, but forgive me, I don't get it . . .

[Lays the seagull on the bench.]

I'm too simple to understand you.

Treplev: All this began that evening when my play was such a terrible disaster. Women never forgive failure. I've burnt it all, every scrap of it. If only you knew how I'm suffering! Your coldness to me is awful, unbelievable, it's as if I suddenly woke up and found this lake dried up or sunk into the earth. You say you're too simple to understand me. What is there to understand? They didn't like my play, so you despise my talent, and now you think I'm ordinary and insignificant, like all the rest of them . . .

[Stamps his foot.]

Oh, I understand it very well, and how I understand it! It's like a spike in my brain, damn it! And damn my pride that's sucking my blood, sucking it like a snake . . .

*[He sees **Trigorin,** who enters reading a book.]*

Here comes the real genius, he walks like Hamlet, and with a book too. *[Mimics.]* "Words, words, words . . ." The sun has hardly reached you and you're smiling already, your glance is melting in its rays. I won't stand in your way . . .

[He goes out quickly.]

Trigorin: *[Writing in his notebook.]* Takes snuff and drinks vodka. Always in black. The schoolteacher is in love with her . . .

Nina: Good-morning, Boris Alexeyevich!

Trigorin: Good-morning. Things have taken an unexpected turn and it seems we're leaving today. We probably won't meet again. I'm sorry. I don't often get a chance to meet young and interesting girls. I've forgotten what it feels like to be eighteen or nineteen; I can't even imagine it. That's why the young girls in my novels and stories are usually unconvincing. I'd like to be in your shoes just for one hour to find out how you think and what sort of person you are.

Nina: And I'd like to be in your shoes!

Trigorin: Why?

Nina: To know what it feels like to be a famous and talented writer. How does it feel to be famous? How does it affect you?

Trigorin: How? I'd say not at all. I've never thought about it.

[After a moment's thought.]

It's one of two things: either you're exaggerating my fame, or it's never affected me.

Nina: But when you read about yourself in the newspapers?

Trigorin: When they praise me I'm pleased; when they attack me I'm in a bad humor for a couple of days.

Nina: You live in a wonderful world! If you only knew how I envy you! People's lives are so different! Some can hardly get through their dull, meaningless days, all alike and all miserable; while others, like you, for instance—you're one in a million—lead exciting, interesting lives that mean something. You're happy.

Trigorin: I? *[Shrugs.]* H'm . . . You talk of fame and happiness, of an exciting, interesting life, but to me all those fine words, if you'll forgive my saying so, are just like marmalade, which I never eat. You're very young and very kind.

Nina: Your life is beautiful!

Trigorin: What's so good about it? *[Looks at his watch.]* I must get back to my writing. Excuse me, I'm busy ... [Laughs.] You've stepped on my pet corn, as they say, and I'm beginning to get excited and a little annoyed. But let's talk. We'll talk about my beautiful, fascinating life ... Well, where'll we start?

[After a moment's thought.]

There are such things as fixed ideas, when a man keeps thinking day and night about nothing, let's say, but the moon. Well, I have a moon like that! I'm haunted day and night by just one idea: I must write, I must write, I must ... I scarcely finish one book when, for some reason, I've got to start writing another, then a third, and a fourth. I write continually, at top speed; it's the only way I can write! What's so beautiful and exciting about that, I ask you? It's a ridiculous life! Here I am talking to you and I find it really exciting, but I can't forget for a minute that my unfinished novel is waiting for me. I see a cloud up there that looks like a grand piano. Immediately I think: remember to put that in a story—a cloud that looked like a grand piano went sailing by. There's a scent of heliotrope in the air. I quickly make a note: sickly-sweet smell—widow's color—mention in description of a summer evening. I snatch at every sentence and every word I say and you say, and put them in my literary storeroom—they might come in handy! When I finish my work, I rush off to the theatre or go fishing; I try to rest and forget myself. But no, a new idea starts rolling around in my head like a heavy iron cannonball, and I have to dash back to my desk and go on writing and writing again like mad. And it's always like that, always! I don't give myself a minute's rest, I eat myself up alive; and for the sake of giving honey to people I don't even know, I strip the pollen from my best flowers, then tear up the flowers, and trample on their roots. Do you think I'm crazy? Do my friends and relatives treat me as if I'm sane? "What are you writing now?" "What are you giving us next?" It's the same thing over and over again, until I begin to think all this attention from my friends—their praise and their admiration—is nothing but deceit, like humoring an invalid, and it won't be long before they sneak up behind me and cart me off to the asylum. And in those years, the best years of my youth, when I was just starting out, writing was pure torture for me. A minor writer, especially if he has no luck, feels clumsy, awkward, and unwanted; his nerves are on edge and he's overwrought. He can't resist hanging around people connected with literature and the arts; he's unrecognized, unnoticed, afraid to look anyone straight in the eye—exactly like a man with a passion for gambling, but no money. I never met my readers, but for some reason I always imagined them to be unfriendly and critical. I was afraid of the public, they terrified me, and when my first play was produced, it seemed to me that all the dark-haired people in the audience were hostile and all the fair-haired ones were cold and indifferent. It was awful! Perfect agony!

Nina: But when you're really inspired and you're actually creating something, don't you feel tremendously happy, even for a moment?

Trigorin: Yes. When I'm writing, I enjoy it, and I enjoy reading my proofs, but as soon as it's published, I detest it. I see that it's all wrong, a mistake, and should never have been written at all, and I feel unhappy and sick about it ...

[He laughs.]

Then the public reads it: "Yes, it's charming, clever ... very charming, but a far cry from Tolstoy," or, "It's a fine thing, but Turgenev's *Fathers and Sons* is better." And that's the way it'll be till the day I die—charming and clever, charming and clever—nothing more. And after I'm dead my friends will pass my grave and say, "Here lies Trigorin. He was a good writer, but not as good as Turgenev."

Nina: Forgive me, but I just can't understand you. You're simply spoiled by success.

Trigorin: What success? I've never been satisfied with anything I've written; I don't like it. The worst of it is I'm in a sort of daze and don't know what I'm writing about. I love the water here, the trees, the sky. I'm passionately fond of nature, it arouses an irresistible desire in me to write. But I'm not just a landscape painter. I'm a citizen, too. I love my country and the people, and I feel if I'm really a writer it's my duty to write about them and their sufferings and their future, and about science, and the rights of man, and so on. So I write about everything, and I'm hurried and flustered. People attack me on all sides and get angry at me, and I dash back and forth like a fox at the mercy of hounds. I see that life and science keep moving further and further ahead while I fall further and further behind, like the peasant who ran after the train. And the upshot is I feel I can only describe landscapes and in everything else I'm false—false to the marrow of my bones.

Nina: You work too hard and have no time or desire to appreciate your own importance. You may not think much of yourself, but other people think you're great and wonderful! If I were a writer like you, I'd dedicate my life to the people, but I'd know they could only be happy if they rose to my level, and they'd harness themselves to my chariot.

Trigorin: What, to my chariot? Who am I, Agamemnon?

[They both smile.]

Nina: For the pleasure of being an author or an actress, I'd be willing to endure poverty, disillusionment, and the disapproval of everyone around me. I'd live in a garret and eat nothing but black bread, and I'd suffer because I was dissatisfied with myself and recognized my own shortcomings, but in return I'd ask for fame—real, resounding fame!

[She covers her face with her hands.]

My head is spinning . . . oh!

Arkadina: *[Calls from within the house.]* Boris Alexeyevich!

Trigorin: They're calling me . . . to pack, I suppose. But I don't want to leave here.

[Looks round at the lake.]

Just look, what a heavenly spot! It's glorious!

Nina: Do you see the house and the garden on the other side of the lake?

Trigorin: Yes.

Nina: That was my mother's house. I was born there. I've spent all my life by this lake and I know every little island on it.

Trigorin: It's marvellous here!

[Sees the seagull.]

And what's this?

Nina: A seagull. Konstantin Gavrilich shot it.

Trigorin: It's a beautiful bird! I really don't want to leave. Try to persuade Irina Nikolayevna to stay.

[Writes in his notebook.]

Nina: What are you writing? . .

Trigorin: Just making a note . . . I got an idea . . .

[Puts the notebook away.]

An idea for a short story: a young girl, like you, has lived beside a lake all her life; she loves the lake like a seagull and she's as happy and free as a seagull. But a man comes along by chance, sees her, and having nothing better to do, destroys her like the seagull here.

*[A pause. **Arkadina** appears at the window.]*

Arkadina: Boris Alexeyevich, where are you?

Trigorin: Coming!

[*Goes toward the house, and looks back at* **Nina**. *To* **Arkadina**, *at the window.*]

What is it?

Arkadina: We're staying.

[**Trigorin** *goes into the house.*]

Nina: [*Comes down to the footlights, and stands lost in thought.*] It's a dream!

CURTAIN

Act Three

The dining-room in **Sorin's** house. Doors on the right and left. A sideboard. A medicine chest. A table in the middle of the room. A suitcase and hat-boxes; signs of preparations for leaving.

[**Trigorin** *is having lunch;* **Masha** *is standing beside the table.*]

Masha: I'm telling you all this because you're a writer. You can use it if you want to. I'm telling you the truth— if he had wounded himself seriously, I couldn't have gone on living another minute. Anyway, I'm getting braver. I've just made up my mind I'm going to tear this love out of my heart— tear it out by the roots.

Trigorin: How are you going to do that?

Masha: I'm going to get married. To Medvedenko.

Trigorin: That's the schoolteacher?

Masha: Yes.

Trigorin: I don't see why you have to do that.

Masha: To go on loving without hope and waiting year after year for something . . . Once I'm married there won't be any time for love, new worries will crowd out the old ones. Anyway, it'll be a change, you know. Shall we have another?

Trigorin: Haven't you had enough?

Masha: Now, really!

[*Fills two glasses.*]

Don't look at me like that! Women drink a lot more than you think. A few of them drink openly like me, but most of them do it in secret. Yes, and it's always vodka or brandy.

[*They clink glasses.*]

Well, here's to you! You're a nice man, I'm sorry you're going.

[*They drink.*]

Trigorin: I don't want to leave here my-self.

Masha: You ought to ask her to stay.

Trigorin: No, she'd never stay now. Her son is behaving very tactlessly. First, he tries to shoot himself, and now they say he's going to challenge me to a duel. And what for? He sulks, he sneers, he preaches new art forms . . . But there's room for all—the new and the old—why shove one another?

Masha: Well, it's jealousy, too. But that's none of my business.

[*A pause.* **Yakov** *crosses from right to left with a suitcase.* **Nina** *enters and stands by the window.*]

Masha: My schoolteacher isn't very bright, and he's poor, but he's a good man and he's very much in love with me. I'm sorry for him and I'm sorry for his old mother. Well, I want to wish you all the best. Don't think badly of me.

[*She shakes hands with him warmly.*]

Thank you for your kindness and your sympathy. Send me your books and be sure to autograph them. But don't say, "To a dear friend." Just say, "To Marya, who doesn't know where she comes from or why she's living." Goodbye!

[*She goes out.*]

Nina: [*Holds out her hand toward* **Trigorin**, *with her fist clenched.*] Odd or even?

Trigorin: Even.

Nina: [*Sighs.*] Wrong. I only have one pea in my hand. I was trying to tell my fortune—whether to go on the stage or not. I wish somebody would tell me what to do.

Trigorin: Nobody can tell you what to do about that.

[A pause.]

Nina: You're going . . . and I may never see you again. I'd like to give you this little medallion to remember me by. I had your initials engraved on one side of it . . . and on the other side the title of your book, *Days and Nights*.

Trigorin: How charming!

[Kisses the medallion.]

What a lovely gift!

Nina: Think of me sometimes.

Trigorin: Of course, I'll think of you. I'll think of you as you were on that beautiful day—do you remember?—a week ago, when you were wearing that pretty dress . . . we were talking . . . and there was a white seagull lying on the bench.

Nina: *[Thoughtfully.]* Yes, the seagull . . .

[A pause.]

We can't talk any more, someone's coming . . . Let me see you for two minutes before you go, won't you . . . ?

[She goes out, left.]

*[At the same moment, enter from the right, **Arkadina, Sorin** in a dress suit with a star of some order on it, then **Yakov** with some luggage.]*

Arkadina: Stay home, old man. Don't go gallivanting around with your rheumatism. *[To **Trigorin**.]* Who was that who just went out? Nina?

Trigorin: Yes.

Arkadina: So sorry we disturbed you . . .

[She sits down.]

I think I've packed everything. I'm worn out.

Trigorin: *[Reads the inscription on the medallion.]* Days and Nights, page 121, lines 11 and 12.

Yakov: Shall I pack the fishing rods too?

Trigorin: Yes, I'll be wanting them again. But you can give the books away.

Yakov: Right.

Trigorin: *[To himself.]* Page 121, lines 11 and 12. What's in those lines? *[To **Arkadina**.]* Are there copies of my books in the house?

Arkadina: Yes, in my brother's study, in the corner bookcase.

Trigorin: Page 121 . . .

[He goes out.]

Arkadina: Really, Petrusha, you'd better stay home.

Sorin: You're going away. It's boring for me here without you.

Arkadina: And what's there in town?

Sorin: Nothing special, but all the same . . . *[He laughs.]* They'll be laying the corner-stone for the town hall, and all that sort of thing. I hate to be stuck in the mud, I'd like to get out even if it's only for an hour or two. I've been on the shelf too long, like some old cigarette holder. I've ordered the horses for one o'clock; we'll leave together.

Arkadina: *[After a pause.]* Oh, stay here, don't be bored, and don't catch cold. Look after my son. Take care of him. Give him a talking to. *[A pause.]* Here I am going away and I'll never know why Konstantin tried to shoot himself. I have an idea the main reason was jealousy, and the sooner I take Trigorin away from here the better.

Sorin: How shall I put it? There were other reasons too. It's not hard to understand. Here's an intelligent young man stuck out in the country, in the woods, with no money, no position, no future. He has nothing to do. He's ashamed of his idleness and he's afraid of it. I'm really very fond of him and he's attached to me, but even so he feels as if he's unnecessary, like a poor relation, a parasite . . . So it's not hard to understand, it's his pride . . .

Arkadina: I'm so worried about him! *[Thoughtfully.]* Maybe he ought to get himself a job . . .

Sorin: *[Whistles, then hesitatingly.]* It seems to me the best thing would be if you could . . . give him a little money. In the first place he ought to be able to dress like other people, and all that. Just look at him, he's been going around in the same old jacket for the last three years, and he has no overcoat ... [*He laughs.*] And it wouldn't do him any harm to have a little fun ... to go abroad or something ... It wouldn't cost much.

Arkadina: Well ... maybe I can manage the suit, but as for going abroad ... No, right now I can't even manage the suit. [*Firmly.*] I haven't any money!

[**Sorin** *laughs.*]

No, I haven't!

Sorin: [*Whistles.*] I see. Forgive me, my dear, don't be angry. I believe you ... You're a generous, kind-hearted woman.

Arkadina: [*Crying.*] I haven't any money.

Sorin: Of course, if I had any money, I'd give him some myself, but I haven't got any, not a penny. [*Laughs.*] My manager takes my entire pension and spends it on the farm, raising cattle, keeping bees, and all my money is wasted. The bees die, the cows die, and he never lets me have any horses ...

Arkadina: Yes, I have some money, but I'm an actress. My costumes alone are enough to ruin me.

Sorin: You're good and kind ... I respect you ... Yes ... But I'm afraid ... I'm not feeling well again ...

[*He staggers.*]

I'm dizzy ...

[*Holds on to the table.*]

I feel sick and all that ...

Arkadina: [*Alarmed.*] Petrusha!

[*Tries to support him.*]

Petrusha, my dear!

[*Cries out.*]

Help me! Help!

[*Enter* **Treplev,** *with a bandage around his head; followed by* **Medvedenko.***]*

Arkadina: He doesn't feel well!

Sorin: It's nothing ... it's nothing ... [*Smiles and drinks some water.*] It's gone already ... and so on ...

Treplev: [*To his mother.*] Don't be fright-

ened, mama, it's not serious. Uncle often has these attacks now. [*To his uncle.*] Uncle, you must lie down.

Sorin: For a little while, yes ... But I'm going to town, anyway ... I'll lie down ... then I'm going ... you understand?

[*He goes out leaning on his cane.*]

Medvedenko: [*Offers his arm.*] There's a riddle: in the morning on four legs, at noon on two, in the evening on three ...

Sorin: [*Laughs.*] That's right. And at night on the back. Thank you, I can manage alone ...

Medvedenko: Come, come, why stand on ceremony!

[**Medvedenko** *and* **Sorin** *go out.*]

Arkadina: He frightened the life out of me!

Treplev: It's not good for him to live in the country. He gets depressed. If you'd be generous for once, mama, and lend him fifteen hundred or two thousand, he could spend a whole year in town.

Arkadina: I have no money. I'm an actress, not a banker.

Treplev: Mama, change my bandage. You're so good at it.

Arkadina: [*Takes a bottle of iodoform and a box of bandages out of the medicine chest.*] The doctor is late.

Treplev: He promised to be here at ten, and it's twelve already.

Arkadina: Sit down.

[*Takes the bandage off his head.*] You look as if you're wearing a turban. Some man who was in the kitchen yesterday asked what nationality you were. It's almost healed; just a little scar left.

[*Kisses him on the head.*]

And no playing with guns while I'm away?

Treplev: No, mama, for a minute I went out of my head with despair, and I couldn't control myself. It won't happen again.

[*Kisses her hand.*]

You have such clever fingers. I

remember, long ago, when you were still acting at the Imperial Theater—I was a little boy then—there was a fight in our yard and a washerwoman, who lived in the house, was beaten up. Remember? She was picked up unconscious ... you took care of her, gave her medicine, and bathed her children in a tub. Don't you remember?

Arkadina: No.

[Puts on a clean bandage.]

Treplev: And two ballet dancers lived in that house then, too ... They used to come in and have coffee with you ...

Arkadina: I remember that.

Treplev: They were very religious. [A pause.] Lately, these last few days, I've loved you as I did when I was a little boy, tenderly and completely. I have no one left but you now. But why, why are you under the influence of that man?

Arkadina: You don't understand him, Konstantin. He's a very honorable person.

Treplev: But when he heard I was going to challenge him to a duel, his honor didn't keep him from turning tail. He's running away. Ignominious retreat!

Arkadina: That's nonsense! I myself asked him to leave.

Treplev: Honorable person! Here we are —you and I—nearly quarreling over him, and right now he's probably out in the drawing-room or the garden laughing at us ... cultivating Nina and trying to convince her he's an absolute genius.

Arkadina: You seem to enjoy saying disagreeable things to me. I respect that man and I don't want you to criticize him in my presence.

Treplev: Well, I don't respect him. You want me to think he's a genius too, but I won't lie to you, his books turn my stomach.

Arkadina: You're jealous! People with big ideas and no talent have nothing better to do than attack those with real talent. It's a fine consolation, I must say!

Treplev: [Sarcastically.] Real talent! [Angrily.] I have more talent than both of you put together, if it comes to that!

[He tears the bandage off his head.]

You, with your stale ideas, have taken over the top places in the arts and you think only what you yourselves do is real and legitimate. You stifle and suppress everything else. I don't believe in you! I don't believe in you or in him!

Arkadina: You decadent upstart!

Treplev: Go back to your charming theater and act in your stupid, trashy plays!

Arkadina: I've never acted in such plays. Leave me alone! You couldn't even write a cheap vaudeville act. You Kiev shopkeeper! You sponger!

Treplev: You miser!

Arkadina: Beggar!

[He sits down and cries quietly.] Nonentity!

[After walking back and forth excitedly.]

Don't cry ... You mustn't cry ...

[She begins to cry.]

Don't ...

[She kisses him on the forehead, the cheeks, the head.]

My dear child, forgive me ... Forgive your sinful mother ... Forgive me, I'm so unhappy ...

Treplev: [Puts his arms around her.] Oh, if only you knew! I've lost everything. She doesn't love me, and now I can't write any more ... There's no hope for me ...

Arkadina: Don't give up ... Everything'll be all right ... He's going away today, she'll love you again ... [Wipes away his tears.] That's enough. We've made it up now.

Treplev: [Kisses her hands.] Yes, mama.

Arkadina: [Tenderly.] Make it up with him, too. There's no need for a duel ... Is there, really?

Treplev: All right, mama, but don't make me see him. It's too painful . . . it's more than I can stand.

[**Trigorin** comes in.]

There he is . . . I'm going . . .

[He quickly puts the dressings in the medicine chest.]

The doctor will take care of the bandage.

Trigorin: [Leafing through a book.] Page 121 . . . lines 11 and 12. Here it is. [Reads.] "If ever my life can be of use to you, come and take it."

[**Treplev** picks up the bandage from the floor and goes out.]

Arkadina: [Looks at her watch.] The carriage will be here soon.

Trigorin: [To himself.] "If ever my life can be of use to you, come and take it."

Arkadina: I hope you're all packed.

Trigorin: [Impatiently.] Yes, yes . . . [In deep thought.] Why does that appeal from a pure soul make me feel so sad? Why does my heart ache with pity? "If ever my life can be of use to you, come and take it." [To **Arkadina**.] Let's stay just one more day.

[**Arkadina** shakes her head.]

Let's stay!

Arkadina: Darling, I know what attracts you here. But have a little self-control. You're slightly intoxicated, try to sober up.

Trigorin: You sober up, too . . . be understanding and reasonable . . . please. Look at it as a true friend should . . .

[He presses her hand.]

You know how to be generous. Be my friend, let me go . . .

Arkadina: [Very upset.] Are you so infatuated with her?

Trigorin: I'm strongly attracted to her. Maybe it's just what I need.

Arkadina: The love of a country girl? Oh, how little you know yourself!

Trigorin: Sometimes people talk in their sleep . . . That's what it's like now, I'm talking to you but I'm asleep and dreaming of her . . . such a sweet, wonderful dream . . . Let me go . . .

Arkadina: [Trembles.] No, no! I'm an ordinary woman, you can't talk to me like that. Stop torturing me, Boris. It frightens me.

Trigorin: If you wanted to, you could be extraordinary. A love that's young, beautiful, and full of poetry, can carry us away into a world of dreams; that's the only thing on earth can make us happy. I've never known such love. When I was young, I had no time, I was always hanging around some editor's office, fighting off starvation. Now that love is here at last, it's calling to me. What's the sense of running away from it?

Arkadina: [Angrily.] You're going mad!

Trigorin: Well, let me!

Arkadina: You're all in a plot to torture me today!

[She weeps.]

Trigorin: [Clutches his heart.] She doesn't understand! She doesn't want to understand!

Arkadina: Am I so old and ugly you don't mind talking to me about other women?

[Puts her arms around him and kisses him.]

Oh, you madman! My beautiful, wonderful . . . You're the last chapter of my life!

[Falls to her knees.]

My joy, my pride, my happiness!

[Embraces his knees.]

If you leave me even for an hour, I won't survive, I'll go out of my mind, my marvelous, magnificent darling, my master!

Trigorin: Somebody might come in.

[He helps her to get up.]

Arkadina: Let them, I'm not ashamed of my love for you. [She kisses his hands.] My darling, reckless boy, you want to do something mad, but I won't let you, I won't let you . . . [Laughs.] You're mine . . . you're mine . . . and this forehead is mine, and these eyes are mine, and this lovely silky hair is mine, too . . . you're all mine. You're so talented, so clever, the best of all modern writers, you're the one and only hope of Russia... You have such sincerity, simplicity, freshness, healthy humor... With one stroke you give the very essence of a character or a scene, your people are alive. It's a delight to read you! You think I'm exaggerating? Flattering you? Just look into my eyes... look... Do I look like a liar? You see, I'm the only one who really appreciates you, I'm the only one who tells you the truth, my precious darling... You'll come with me? Yes? You won't leave me?

Trigorin: I have no will of my own—I've never had a will of my own. Flabby, weak, always giving in—how can a woman like such a man? Take me, take me away, but don't ever let me out of your sight...

Arkadina: *[To herself.]* Now he's mine. *[In a casual tone, as if nothing had happened.]* But, of course, you can stay if you like. I'll go by myself, and you can come later, in a week. After all, what's your hurry?

Trigorin: No, we may as well go together.

Arkadina: Just as you say. Together, yes, together...

*[A pause. **Trigorin** writes in his notebook.]*

Arkadina: What are you writing?

Trigorin: This morning I heard that old expression, "Virgin forest." I might be able to use it. *[He stretches.]* So we're leaving, eh? Oh, those trains and stations, snack bars, refreshments, conversations...

Shamrayev: *[Enters.]* I have the honor to announce with deep regret that the horses are ready. It's time, my dear lady, to leave for the station. The train comes in at five minutes past two. And please do me a favor, Irina Nikolayevna, don't forget to find out what's become of the actor Suzdaltsev. Is he alive and well? We used to drink together once upon a time. In *The Mail Robbery* he was terrific

...and I remember the tragedian Izmaïlov, another terrific actor, who appeared with him in Elisavetograd ...Don't hurry, dear lady, you still have another five minutes. Once they were playing two conspirators in some melodrama and when they were suddenly discovered Ismaïlov was supposed to say, "We're caught in a trap," instead he said, "We're traught in a cap!" *[Laughs.]* A cap!

*[During **Shamrayev's** speech, **Yakov** is busy looking after the luggage; the **Maid** brings **Arkadina** her hat, coat, umbrella, and gloves; they all help **Arkadina** to put her things on. The **Chef** looks in at the door on the left and after some hesitation comes in. Enter **Polina Andreyevna**.]*

Polina: *[With a small basket.]* Here's some fruit for the trip... nice sweet plums. You might feel like having something refreshing...

Arkadina: You're very kind, Polina Andreyevna.

Polina: Goodbye, my dear. If anything wasn't quite to your liking, forgive it. *[She weeps.]*

Arkadina: *[Embraces her.]* Everything was lovely, just lovely. But you mustn't cry.

Polina: Our time goes by so fast!

Arkadina: There's nothing we can do about that!

*[**Sorin,** in an overcoat with a cape to it, wearing his hat and carrying his cane, enters through the door on the left, followed by **Medvedenko**.]*

Sorin: *[As he crosses the room.]* Sister, you'd better start if you don't want to miss the train. I'm going to get into the carriage.

[He goes out.]

Medvedenko: And I'll walk to the station ... to see you off. I'll be there in no time...

[He goes out.]

Arkadina: Goodbye, my friends... if

we're alive and well, we'll meet again next summer.

[The **Maid,** the **Chef,** and **Yakov** kiss her hand in turn.]

Don't forget me.

[She gives the **Chef** a rouble.]

Here's a rouble for the three of you.

Chef: We humbly thank you, madam. A pleasant journey to you. Thank you for your kindness.

Yakov: God bless you!

Shamrayev: You'd make us happy if you wrote us a letter! Goodbye, Boris Alexeyevich!

Arkadina: Where's Konstantin? Tell him I'm leaving. I must say goodbye to him. Well, think kindly of me. [To **Yakov.**] I gave the cook a rouble. It's for the three of you.

[All go out to the right. The stage is empty. From off-stage come the voices of people saying goodbyes. The **Maid** comes back, takes the basket of plums from the table, and goes out again. **Trigorin** returns.]

Trigorin: I forgot my stick. I think I left it out there on the veranda.

[He starts toward the door on the left and meets **Nina** who is coming in.]

Is that you? We're just going ...

Nina: I knew we'd meet each other again. [Excitedly.] Boris Alexeyevich, I've made up my mind, the die is cast. I'm going on the stage. I won't be here tomorrow. I'm leaving my father, I'm leaving everything, I'm starting a new life. Like you, I'm going to ... Moscow. We'll meet there.

Trigorin: [Glances behind him.] Stay at the Slavyansky Bazaar ... let me know as soon as you get there ... Molchanovka, Groholsky House ... I must run ...

[A pause.]

Nina: Just another minute ...

Trigorin: [In a whisper.] You're so beautiful ... Oh, it makes me so happy to think we'll be meeting soon.

[She rests her head on his chest.]

I'll see these lovely eyes again, this inexpressibly beautiful and tender smile, this sweet face, with its look of angelic purity ... My darling ...

[A long kiss.]

CURTAIN

Act Four

One of the drawing-rooms in **Sorin's** house, which has been turned into a study by **Konstantin Treplev.** There are doors on the right and left leading to other parts of the house. Besides the usual drawing-room furniture, there is a writing table in the corner on the right; a sofa near the door on the left; also a bookcase, and books in the windows and on the chairs. Two years have passed since Act Three. It is evening. A lamp with a shade is lighted; but the room is in semi-darkness. From outside comes the sound of trees rustling, and the wind howls in the chimney. A night watchman is heard tapping.

[Enter **Medvedenko** and **Masha.**]

Masha: [Calls.] Konstantin Gavrilich! Konstantin Gavrilich! [She looks around.] No, no one's here! Every minute the old man keeps asking, where's Kostya, where's Kostya? He can't live without him ...

Medvedenko: He's afraid to be alone. [Listens.] What terrible weather ... for two days now!

Masha: [Turns up the lamp.] There are waves on the lake. Great big ones.

Medvedenko: The garden is pitch dark. We should've told them to take that stage off the lawn. It stands there like a skeleton ... it's so bare and ugly ... and the curtain flaps in the wind. When I passed it last night, I thought I heard someone crying there.

Masha: Well, really ...

[A pause.]

Medvedenko: Let's go home, Masha.

Masha: [Shakes her head.] I'm going to stay here tonight.

Medvedenko: [Imploringly.] Please,

Masha, let's go! The baby must be hungry!

Masha: Nonsense. Matryona will feed him.

[A pause.]

Medvedenko: It's a shame! Three nights now without his mother.

Masha: You're getting to be an awful bore! There was a time you used to spout philosophy at least, now it's nothing but baby and home, baby and home—that's all you keep harping on.

Medvedenko: Come on, Masha!

Masha: Go by yourself.

Medvedenko: Your father won't give me a horse.

Masha: Yes, he will. Just ask him.

Medvedenko: All right, I'll ask him. Then will you come home tomorrow?

Masha: [Takes a pinch of snuff.] All right, tomorrow. Stop pestering me!
[Enter **Treplev** and **Polina Andreyevna**; **Treplev** carries pillows and a blanket, **Polina Andreyevna**, sheets and pillowcases; they lay them on the sofa, then **Treplev** goes to his desk and sits down.]

Masha: What're you doing, mama?

Polina: Pyotr Nikolayevich wants to sleep in Kostya's room.

Masha: Let me do it. [She makes the bed.]

Polina: [Sighs.] Old people are like children . . .
[**Polina** goes to the desk, leans on her elbow, and looks at a manuscript. A pause.]

Medvedenko: Well, I'd better be going. Goodbye, Masha.
[He kisses her hand.]
Goodbye, mother.
[Tries to kiss her hand.]

Polina: [Annoyed.] Well, if you're going, go.

Medvedenko: Goodbye, Konstantin Gavrilich.
[**Treplev** shakes hands with him without speaking; **Medvedenko** goes out.]

Polina: [Gazes at the manuscript.] Who'd have thought, or even dreamed, that you would turn out to be a real writer, Kostya! And now, thank God, the magazines are sending you money for your stories.
[Passes her hand over his hair.]
And you've gotten so handsome . . . Kostya dear, you're so good, try to be a little nicer to my Mashenka.

Masha: [As she makes the bed.] Oh, leave him alone, mama.

Polina: [To **Treplev**.] She's a sweet little thing.
[A pause.]
A woman doesn't want anything, Kostya, only a kind look. Believe me, I know.
[**Treplev** gets up from the desk and goes out without speaking.]

Masha: Now you've made him angry. Why do you have to pester him like that!

Polina: I feel sorry for you, Mashenka.

Masha: A lot of good that does me!

Polina: My heart aches for you. I see what's going on, you know I understand.

Masha: It's a lot of nonsense. Hopeless love—that's only in novels. So what! The only thing is you've got to stop hoping and waiting for things to change . . . When love starts growing in your heart, you have to weed it out. Anyway, they promised to transfer my husband to another district. Once we're there, I'll forget all about it—I'll tear it out of my heart by the roots.
[Two rooms away a melancholy waltz is being played.]

Polina: Kostya's playing. That means he's depressed.

Masha: [Quietly dances a few waltz steps.] The main thing, mama, is not to have him in front of me all the time. If only they give Semyon his transfer, believe me, I'll forget Kostya in a month. The whole thing's so ridiculous!
[The door on the left opens. **Dorn** and **Medvedenko** bring **Sorin** in in his wheelchair.]

Medvedenko: I've got six people to take care of now, and flour's two kopecks a pound.

Dorn: It's tough going.

Medvedenko: It's easy for you to smile. You've got more money than you know what to do with.

Dorn: Money? After thirty years of practice, and back-breaking practice, my friend, when I couldn't call my soul my own day or night, I managed to save up a measly two thousand roubles, and I've just spent it all on a trip abroad. I'm broke.

Masha: [To her husband.] Haven't you gone yet?

Medvedenko: [Apologetically.] How can I go, when they won't give me a horse!

Masha: [Bitterly, in an undertone.] I can't bear the sight of you!

[**Sorin** is in the wheelchair, on the left side of the room; **Polina Andreyevna,** and **Dorn** sit down near him; **Medvedenko** moves sadly away.]

Dorn: You've certainly made a lot of changes here! You've turned this drawing-room into a study.

Masha: It's more convenient for Konstantin Gavrilich to work in here. He can go into the garden when he feels like it and do his thinking there.

[A watchman is heard tapping.]

Sorin: Where's my sister?

Dorn: She went to the station to meet Trigorin. She'll be back soon.

Sorin: If you had to send for my sister, I must be very sick. [Pause.] It's a funny thing, I'm very sick and nobody gives me any medicine around here.

Dorn: Well, what kind would you like? Valerian drops? Soda? Quinine?

Sorin: There he goes again with his ideas! Oh, what an affliction! [Nods in the direction of the sofa.] Was that bed made up for me?

Polina: For you, Pyotr Nikolayevich.

Sorin: Thank you.

Dorn: [Sings softly.] "The moon is floating in the midnight sky . . ."

Sorin: Listen, I want to give Kostya an idea for a story. It would be called "The Man Who Wanted to"— L'homme qui a voulu. When I was young I wanted to be a writer—but I never was; I wanted to be a good speaker—and I spoke miserably—
[Mimics himself.]
"and all the rest of it, and all that, and so on, and so forth" . . . and summing up a case I would drag on and on until I broke out in a sweat. I wanted to get married—and I never did; I always wanted to live in town—and here I am ending my life in the country, and so on and so forth.

Dorn: Wanted to become a district attorney—and did.

Sorin: [Laughs.] That's one thing I never wanted. It just happened.

Dorn: To start complaining about life at sixty-two is pretty useless, you know.

Sorin: How pig-headed can you be! Can't you understand—I want to live?

Dorn: That's just foolish. Every life has to end—it's the law of nature.

Sorin: You talk like a man who's had his fill. You're satisfied so you don't care about living, it makes no difference to you. But you'll be afraid to die, too, when your time comes.

Dorn: The fear of death is just an animal fear. We've got to overcome it. The only ones with a real reason to fear death are those who believe in an afterlife and are afraid of being punished for their sins. But, in the first place, you're an atheist, and in the second place—what sins did you ever commit? You served in the law courts for twenty-five years—that's all.

Sorin: [Laughs.] Twenty-eight . . .
[**Treplev** comes in and sits down on a stool at **Sorin's** feet. **Masha** never takes her eyes off him.]

Dorn: We're keeping Konstantin Gavrilich from his work.

Treplev: No, it's nothing.

[A pause.]

Medvedenko: Excuse me, Doctor, but when you were on your trip what city did you like best?

Dorn: Genoa.

Treplev: Why Genoa?

Dorn: Because the streets are so full of life there. When you go out of your hotel in the evening, the whole street is just packed with people. You wander up and down, here and there, and actually get lost in the crowd ... psychologically, it seems, you're all living the same life, and you begin to feel there really is such a thing as a world soul, like the one Nina Zarechnaya acted in your play. By the way, where is she now? How is she getting along?

Treplev: All right, I suppose.

Dorn: I've heard she's been leading a rather strange life. What does that mean?

Treplev: Well, it's a long story, Doctor.

Dorn: Then make it short.

[A pause.]

Treplev: She ran away from home and went to live with Trigorin. Do you know about that?

Dorn: Yes, I know.

Treplev: She had a child, but the child died. Trigorin got tired of her and went back to his old love, as you might expect. Of course, he never broke with the old but in his spineless way he manged to keep both going at the same time. As far as I can make out from what I've heard, Nina's private life was a complete mess.

Dorn: And her acting career?

Treplev: Even worse, I imagine. She made her debut in a summer theater near Moscow, then she went on tour in the provinces. At that time I never let her out of my sight, I followed her wherever she went. Somehow she managed to get big parts, but her acting was crude and awkward, she waved her hands and screamed. But there were moments that were very moving—when she cried or played a death scene—but they were only moments.

Dorn: Then she really has some talent?

Treplev: It's hard to tell. I suppose she has. I saw her but she didn't want to see me; they wouldn't let me go up at the hotel. I understood how she felt, so I didn't insist on seeing her. *[Pause.]* What else can I tell you? Later on, after I got back here, she wrote me some letters. They were very friendly and clever and interesting. She didn't complain, but I knew she was very unhappy. Every line told me she was sick, and nervous, and tense. And her mind seemed a little unbalanced. She always signed herself "The Seagull." In Pushkin's play, "The Mermaid," the miller calls himself a raven, and in all her letters she kept calling herself a seagull. Now she's here.

Dorn: What do you mean—here?

Treplev: In town, staying at the inn. I thought of going to see her, but Masha's been there and she won't see anyone. Semyon Semyonovich says he met her yesterday afternoon walking across the fields a mile and a half from here.

Medvedenko: Yes, I saw her. She was going away from here, towards the town. I said hello and asked her why she didn't come to see us. She said she would.

Treplev: She won't come. *[Pause.]* Her father and stepmother don't want to have anything to do with her. They've got watchmen all around, so she can't even get near the house. *[He and **Dorn** move toward the desk.]* Let me tell you, Doctor, it's very easy to be a philosopher on paper, but it's very hard in real life!

Sorin: She was a charming girl.

Dorn: What's that?

Sorin: I said she was a charming girl. District Attorney Sorin was madly in love with her for a while.

Dorn: You old rake.

*[**Shamrayev's** laugh is heard off-stage.]*

Polina: They must have come back from the station . . .

Treplev: Yes, I can hear mama.

*[Enter **Arkadina, Trigorin,** and **Shamrayev.**]*

Shamrayev: *[As he comes in.]* We're all growing old and weather-beaten like autumn leaves, but you, my dear lady, are as young as ever . . . a light dress . . . lively and graceful . . .

Arkadina: You want to bring me bad luck again, you awful man!

Trigorin: How are you, Pyotr Nikolaye-vich? Not feeling any better? That's too bad! *[Pleased at seeing **Masha.**]* Marya Ilyinishna!

Masha: You remember me? *[She shakes hands with him.]*

Trigorin: Married?

Masha: Long ago.

Trigorin: Happy?

*[He bows to **Dorn** and **Medve-denko,** then approaches **Treplev** hesitantly.]*

Your mother tells me you've forgotten the past and aren't angry with me any more.

*[**Treplev** offers **Trigorin** his hand.]*

Arkadina: *[To her son.]* Look, Boris Alexeyevich has brought you the magazine with your new story in it.

Treplev: *[Takes the magazine; to **Trig-orin.**]* Thanks, that was very kind of you.

[They sit down.]

Trigorin: Your admirers send you their greetings . . . In Petersburg and Moscow there's a great deal of interest in your work, and they always ask me all sorts of questions about you. They want to know: what is he like, how old is he, dark hair or blond? For some strange reason, they all seem to think you're an old man. And no one knows your real name, of course, because you always write under a pseudonym. You're as mysterious as the Man in the Iron Mask.

Treplev: Will you be staying here long?

Trigorin: No, I think I'll be going back tomorrow. I really have to. I'm in a hurry to finish my novel, and besides, I promised to write a story for a new collection that's being published. In other words, it's the same old grind.

*[**Arkadina** and **Polina** have been setting up a card table in the middle of the room. **Shamrayev** lights candles and puts chairs around. A game of lotto is brought out of the cupboard.]*

Trigorin: The weather hasn't given me a very friendly welcome. There's a cruel wind. If it dies down by tomorrow morning, I'll go fishing on the lake. And I want to look around the garden and that place—do you remember?—where your play was put on. I've got an idea for a story, but I just want to refresh my memory of the place in which it's laid.

Masha: *[To her father.]* Papa, please let my husband have a horse! He's got to get home.

Shamrayev: *[Mimics her.]* Got to get home—a horse! *[Sternly.]* You can see for yourself—they've just come back from the station. I won't send them out again.

Masha: But there are other horses . . .

[She waits for an answer, gets none, and waves her hand impatiently.]

Oh, what's the use of talking to you . . .

Medvedenko: I can walk, Masha. Really . . .

Polina: *[With a sigh.]* Walk, in such weather!

[Sits down at the card table.]

If you don't mind, ladies and gentlemen . . .

Medvedenko: It's only four miles. Goodbye. *[He kisses his wife's hand.]* Goodbye, mama.

*[**Polina** reluctantly holds out her hand for him to kiss.]*

I wouldn't have bothered you if it weren't for the baby . . . *[He bows to* the company.] Goodbye. [He goes out guiltily.]

Shamrayev: He can walk all right. He's not a general.

Polina: [Taps on the table.] Please, ladies and gentlemen, let's not waste time. They'll be calling us to supper soon.

[**Shamrayev, Masha,** and **Dorn** sit down at the table.]

Arkadina: [To **Trigorin**.] We always play lotto here in the long autumn evenings. And look: it's the same old set we had when we were children and my mother used to play with us. Don't you want to have a game before supper?

[She and **Trigorin** sit down at the table.]

It's a dull game, really, but it's not so bad when you get used to it.

[She deals three cards to each one.]

Treplev: [Turns the pages of the magazine.] He's read his own story, but he hasn't even cut the pages of mine.

[He puts the magazine down on the desk, then goes towards the door left; as he passes his mother he kisses her on the head.]

Arkadina: And what about you, Kostya?

Treplev: Sorry, I don't feel like it . . . I'm going for a walk.

[He goes out.]

Arkadina: The stake is ten kopecks. Put it down for me, Doctor, will you?

Dorn: Right.

Masha: Everyone put his money in? I'll start . . . Twenty-two!

Arkadina: I've got it.

Masha: Three!

Dorn: That's it!

Masha: Did you put down three? Eight! Eighty-one! Ten!

Shamrayev: Don't be in such a hurry!

Arkadina: What a wonderful reception they gave me in Kharkov! My goodness, it makes me dizzy just to think of it!

Masha: Thirty-four!

[A melancholy waltz is being played in another part of the house.]

Arkadina: The students gave me an ovation . . . Three baskets of flowers, two wreaths, and this—look—

[She takes off a brooch and puts it on the table.]

Shamrayev: That's really something.

Masha: Fifty.

Dorn: Did you say fifty?

Arkadina: I wore a beautiful gown . . . You can say what you like, I really know how to dress.

Polina: Kostya's playing the piano. He's depressed, poor boy.

Shamrayev: The critics are always attacking him.

Masha: Seventy-seven!

Arkadina: Why should that bother him?

Trigorin: He has no luck. He hasn't found his own style yet. There's always something queer and vague in his writing, at times it almost sounds like delirium. Not one of his characters comes to life.

Masha: Eleven!

Arkadina: [Glances at **Sorin**.] Petrusha, are you bored? [A pause.] He's asleep.

Dorn: The district attorney is asleep.

Masha: Seven! Ninety!

Trigorin: If I lived in a place like this, near a lake, do you think I'd ever write? I'd get over that insanity and do nothing but fish.

Masha: Twenty-eight!

Trigorin: To catch a perch or a bass— that's my idea of heaven!

Dorn: Well, I have faith in Konstantin Gavrilich. He has something! Yes, he has something! He thinks in images . . . his stories are very vivid and full of color . . . and they really move me. Only it's a pity he doesn't have anything definite to say. He creates an impression, but you can't get very far with nothing but an impression. Irina Nikolayevna, are you glad your son is a writer?

Arkadina: Would you believe it, I haven't read a single thing he's written. I've never found the time.

Masha: Twenty-six!

[**Treplev** *comes in quietly and sits down at his desk.*]

Shamrayev: [*To* **Trigorin.**] Boris Alexeyevich . . . we still have something here belonging to you.

Trigorin: What's that?

Shamrayev: That seagull Konstantin Gavrilich shot; you asked me to have it stuffed for you.

Trigorin: I don't remember that! [*Thinks.*] No, I don't remember!

Masha: Sixty-six! One!

Treplev: [*Throws open the window, and stands listening.*] It's very dark out there! I don't know why I feel so restless.

Arkadina: Kostya, shut the window, there's a draught.

[**Treplev** *shuts the window.*]

Masha: Eighty-eight!

Trigorin: I win, ladies and gentlemen!

Arkadina: [*Happily.*] Bravo, bravo!

Shamrayev: Bravo!

Arkadina: That man is always lucky in everything.

[*She gets up.*]

And now let's go and have a bite to eat. Our celebrated author missed his dinner today. We'll go on playing after supper. [*To her son.*] Kostya, stop writing and come and eat.

Treplev: I don't want to, mama. I'm not hungry.

Arkadina: All right.

[*Wakes* **Sorin.**]

Petrusha, supper.

[*She takes* **Shamrayev's** *arm.*]

I must tell you about my triumph in Kharkov . . .

[**Polina Andreyevna** *puts out the candles on the table, then she and* **Dorn** *wheel* **Sorin** *out through the door on the left; all the others follow.*]

[**Treplev,** *left alone, sits at his desk; he settles down to write, and reads through what he has already written.*]

Treplev: I used to talk a lot about new forms, and now more and more I seem to be using the same old clichés myself.

[*Reads.*]

"The poster on the fence announced . . ." "A pale face framed by dark hair." Announced, framed . . . they're so trite!

[*He crosses out what he has written.*]

I'll begin where the hero is awakened by the sound of rain, and throw out all the rest. The description of the moonlit night is too long and involved. Trigorin's worked out his own way of doing it, and it's easy for him . . . He just says the broken bottle neck glitters on the dam and the mill-wheel casts a black shadow—and there you have a moonlit night; but I go on and on about the shimmering light, the soft twinkling of the stars, and the far-off strains of a piano dying away in the still, sweet-scented air . . . It's torture!

[*A pause.*]

Little by little I'm coming to believe it's not a question of old or new forms . . . the important thing is to write without thinking of forms at all . . . to write what pours out of your heart.

[*There is a tap at the window nearest the desk.*]

What's that?

[*He looks out.*]

I can't see anything . . .

[*He opens the door and looks out into the garden.*]

Someone ran down the steps.

[*Calls.*]

Who's there?

[*He goes out and can be heard running across the veranda; a moment later he returns with* **Nina Zarechnaya.**]

Nina, Nina!

[**Nina** *lays her head on his chest and sobs softly.*]

Treplev: [*Moved.*] Nina! Nina! It's you . . . It's you . . . I had a feeling you'd come ... All day my heart's been aching ...

[He takes off her hat and cape.]

Oh, my darling, my precious, you've come at last. Let's not cry, let's not cry!

Nina: There's someone here.

Treplev: No there isn't.

Nina: Lock the doors, someone might come in.

Treplev: Nobody's coming in.

Nina: I know Irina Nikolayevna is here. Lock the doors.

Treplev: *[Locks the door on the right; goes to the door on the left.]* There's no lock on this one. I'll put a chair against it.

[He puts an armchair against the door.]

Don't be afraid, no one will come in.

Nina: *[Stares into his face.]* Let me look at you. *[Then glances around.]* It's warm and nice ... This used to be the drawing-room. Have I changed a lot?

Treplev: Yes ... You're thinner and your eyes seem bigger. Nina, it's so strange, your being here. Why wouldn't you let me see you? Why haven't you come here sooner? I know you've been in town almost a week now. I went to the inn several times every day and stood under your window like a beggar.

Nina: I was afraid you hated me. I dream every night that you look at me and don't recognize me. Oh, if you only knew! Ever since I came back I've been walking around ... by the lake. I've been near this house many times, but I was afraid to come in. Let's sit down.

[They sit down.]

Let's just sit here and talk and talk. Oh, it's so nice here, so warm and cozy ... Do you hear ... the wind? Somewhere Turgenev says, "Lucky is the man who on a night like this has a roof over his head and a warm corner of his own ..." I'm ... a seagull ... No, not that ... *[Rubs her forehead.]* What was I saying? Yes ...

Turgenev ... "And may the Lord help all homeless wanderers!" Oh, it doesn't matter.

[She sobs.]

Treplev: Nina, you're crying again ... Nina!

Nina: Never mind, it makes me feel better ... I haven't cried for two years. Last night I went into the garden to see if our stage was still there, and it was, and I cried for the first time in two years; it took a weight off my heart and I felt better. You see, I'm not crying any more.

[She takes his hand.]

So you're an author now ... You're an author—I'm an actress ... Both of us have been sucked into the whirlpool. I used to be as happy as a child ... I'd wake up in the morning singing. I loved you and dreamt of being famous, and now? Tomorrow, early in the morning, I must go to Yelets, third class ... with the peasants, and in Yelets the businessmen, interested in culture, will pester me with their attentions. It's a rotten life!

Treplev: Why to Yelets?

Nina: I've been signed up for the whole winter. It's time for me to go now.

Treplev: Nina, I cursed you and hated you, I tore up all your letters and photographs, but I knew every minute that my heart belonged to you and it always would. I can't stop loving you, Nina. After I lost you, my stories began to be published, but my life has been unbearable ... I'm miserable ... All of a sudden I was robbed of my youth, and I feel as if I've been living for ninety years. I cry out to you, I kiss the ground you walked on; wherever I look I see your face and the tender smile that brightened the best years of my life ...

Nina: *[Distractedly.]* Why does he talk like that? Why does he talk like that?

Treplev: I'm all alone. I have no one's love to warm me. I'm so cold ... it's like living in a dungeon ... and everything I write is dry and harsh and gloomy. Stay here, Nina, I beg you, or let me go with you!

[**Nina** *quickly begins to put on her hat and cape.*]

Treplev: Nina, why? For God's sake . . .

[*He watches her as she puts her things on. A pause.*]

Nina: A carriage is waiting for me at the gate. Don't come with me, I'll go alone . . .

[*Sobbing.*]

Give me some water . . .

Treplev: [*As he hands her a glass of water.*] Where are you going now?

Nina: Back to town. [*A pause.*] Is Irina Nikolayevna here?

Treplev: Yes . . . My uncle had an attack last Thursday, so we wired her to come.

Nina: Why do you say you kiss the ground I walked on? I ought to be killed!

[*She leans on the table for support.*]

Oh, I'm so tired! If only I could rest— just rest!

[*She raises her head.*]

I'm a seagull . . . No, that's not so. I'm an actress. Well, what of it!

[*She hears **Arkadina** and **Trigorin** laughing off-stage; she stops and listens, then runs to the door at the left, and looks through the keyhole.*]

So he's here, too . . .

[*Turns back to **Treplev**.*]

Well, yes . . . Never mind . . . Yes . . . He didn't believe in the theater, he laughed at all my dreams, and little by little I stopped believing in them myself and lost heart. And then there was the strain of love and jealousy and the constant worry about my baby . . . I got to be petty and mean and it showed in my acting. I didn't know what to do with my hands, how to move on the stage, or control my voice. You can't imagine what it feels like when you know your acting is atrocious. I'm—a seagull. No, that's

not so. Do you remember, you shot a seagull? A man came along by chance, saw it, and destroyed it, just to pass the time . . . A subject for a short story. That's not so . . .

[*She rubs her forehead.*]

What was I saying? . . . I was talking about the stage. I'm entirely different now . . . I'm a real actress. I enjoy acting, I revel in it. I feel intoxicated when I'm on the stage and know I'm acting beautifully. And since I've come back here, I've been walking around and thinking, thinking and feeling that my spirit is growing stronger every day. I know now, Kostya, I've come to understand, that in our work, whether it's acting or writing, what matters most is not fame and glory, nor any of the things I used to dream about, but how to be patient, and bear your cross, and have faith in yourself. I have faith, so I can stand the pain; when I think of my calling, I'm not afraid of life.

Treplev: [*Sadly.*] You've found your way, you know where you're going, but I'm still floundering in a chaos of dreams and images, and I don't know why or for whom. I have no faith and don't even know what my calling is.

Nina: [*Listens.*] Sssh! . . . I'm going now. Goodbye. When I become a great actress, you must come and see me act. Promise? And now . . .

[*She presses his hand.*]

It's late. I can hardly stand on my feet. I'm exhausted and I'm hungry . . .

Treplev: Stay, and I'll get you something to eat . . .

Nina: No, no . . . Don't come with me . . . I'll go by myself . . . My carriage is outside . . . So she brought him with her? Well, what's the difference. When you see Trigorin, don't say anything to him . . . I love him! I love him even more than before . . . An idea for a short story . . . I love him, I love him passionately, I love him to despair. It was so nice in the old days, Kostya! Do you remember? Life was so bright and warm, so full of joy and so pure, and the feelings we had . . . our feelings were like tender, beautiful flowers . . . Do you remember?

[She recites.]

"Men, lions, eagles, and partridges, horned deer, geese, spiders, silent fish that dwell in the water, star-fishes, and creatures invisible to the eye—all living things, all living things, all living things, having completed their cycle of sorrow, are now extinct . . . For thousands of years no living creature has been born on the earth, and this poor moon now lights its lamp in vain. The cranes in the meadow no longer waken with a cry, and the drone of the May-beetles is heard no more in the lime trees . . ."

[She embraces **Treplev** *impulsively, then runs out through the door to the garden.]*

Treplev: *[After a pause.]* It'll be awful if someone sees her in the garden and tells mama. That might upset mama . . .

*[***Treplev*** *spends the next two minutes tearing up all his manuscripts and throwing them under the desk; then he unlocks the door on the right and goes out.]*

Dorn: *[Off-stage, trying to open the door on the left.]* That's funny. The door seems to be locked . . .

[Comes in and puts the armchair in its place.]

What's going on here? It's a regular obstacle race!

[Enter **Arkadina** *and* **Polina Andreyevna,** *behind them* **Yakov** *carrying a tray with bottles, then* **Masha,** *and finally* **Shamrayev** *and* **Trigorin.**]*

Arkadina: Put the red wine, and the beer for Boris Alexeyevich, here on the table. We can have our drinks while we play. Come on, everybody, let's sit down.

Polina: *[To* **Yakov**.*]* You can bring the tea in at the same time.

[She lights the candles and sits down at the card table.]

Shamrayev: *[Leads* **Trigorin** *to the cupboard.]* Here's the thing I was telling you about before . . .

[He takes the stuffed seagull out of the cupboard.]

This is what you ordered.

Trigorin: *[Looks at the seagull.]* I don't remember that!

[Thinks for a moment.]

I don't remember it at all!

[The sound of a shot comes from offstage right; everyone starts.]

Arkadina: *[Alarmed.]* What was that?

Dorn: It's nothing. Something must have gone off in my medicine case. Don't worry.

[He goes out right, and returns a moment later.]

That's what it was. A bottle of ether blew up.

[He sings softly.]

"I stand before you once again, enchanted . . ."

Arkadina: *[Sits down at the table.]* Oh, what a fright it gave me! It reminded me of the time—

[She puts her hands over her face.]

Everything went black for a minute . . .

Dorn: *[Turns the pages of the magazine, to* **Trigorin**.*]* There was an article in here a couple of months ago . . . a letter from America . . . and I wanted to ask you about it . . .

[He puts his arm around **Trigorin's** *waist and leads him down-stage, away from the others.]*

Get Irina Nikolayevna away from here somehow. The truth is . . . Konstantin Gavrilovich has shot himself . . .

CURTAIN

PYGMALION

Bernard Shaw

Mrs. Patrick Campbell, for whom Shaw created Eliza Doolittle, as she appeared in the first English production at His Majesty's Theatre, London, April 1914. Here Eliza proudly shows Freddy the cab fare that will get her home in style. Museum of the City of New York.

George Bernard Shaw

George Bernard Shaw (who, as his fame grew, came to be known simply as Bernard Shaw and then as G.B.S.) was born in Dublin, Ireland, on July 26, 1856. Shaw was the author of many volumes of art, music, and drama criticism; social, political, economic, and philosophical works of a polemic nature; novels, letters, and plays. His name seldom appeared in print without the adjective "brilliant," which displeased him, "as it suggested a glittering superficiality" he abhorred. But the adjective still adheres to his name and is always meant as a compliment.

The Shaws were Protestants in a Catholic country, so the boy began life as an outsider. His father, George Carr Shaw, was an impecunious civil servant, a failure in business, and an alcoholic. He bequeathed to his son a remarkable sense of humor, a skeptical view of life, and an abhorrence of liquor. Shaw's mother, Lucinda Elizabeth Gurly, a cultivated young woman with a beautiful mezzo-soprano voice, was sixteen years younger than her husband. When she realized that her marriage was a mistake, she began to prepare herself to support the family, which grew to include two daughters, Lucy and Agnes, and a son, George Bernard. Mrs. Shaw studied singing with George John Vandaleur Lee, a well-known teacher, who came to live in the Shaw household and whom George Bernard looked upon as a second father. Soon, under Lee's direction, Mrs. Shaw was appearing in recitals and operatic performances; later she composed and published music, and gave voice lessons herself. As Shaw's mother became more and more involved with her career, Shaw's father lost interest in the family; paid scant attention to the children. It was a cold and loveless household. The boy as a result, although endowed fortunately with enormous intelligence, wit, and creativity, became self-centered and self-directed. He found an outlet for his emotions in speaking and writing, not in human relations.

When very young, Shaw was taught by a governess to read and write and afterward was given private lessons in Latin by a relative. Perfunctorily he attended three or four elementary and secondary educational institutions, which he called "prisons," claiming that he learned nothing in them, even forgetting what he had known when he entered.

In 1871, at the age of fifteen, he left school for good and took a job as junior clerk in a real estate office. Shaw's actual education began when, in his leisure time, he turned his attention seriously to the study of music, literature, art, and drama. From childhood, he had been surrounded by music at home; he had heard and learned by heart the masterpieces of the great composers (Mozart, Haydn, Handel, Beethoven, Verdi, and many others), as well as Vandaleur Lee's theories concerning voice production and dramatic expression. He read voraciously the works of Shakespeare, Bunyan, Smollett, Dickens, Shelley, and Scott, among others. He went regularly to the Dublin National Gallery and spent hours looking at the paintings of the masters, which he learned to appreciate both technically and aesthetically. He frequented the Royal Theatre, where he saw productions of Shakespeare's plays and of the melodramas, comedies, and sentimental romances that were standard theatrical fare. He was particularly drawn to the popular performer Barry Sullivan, who awakened his interest in acting. All of these experiences were stored in his prodigious memory for future use.

In 1873 Vandaleur Lee left Dublin to seek greater opportunities in London. Mrs. Shaw believed that such a move would further her career as well; taking Agnes with her, she followed Lee. Not long afterward she sent for Lucy, leaving Shaw and his father in Dublin to fend for themselves. By 1876, though Bernard was doing well in the real estate office, having been promoted from junior clerk to cashier, he felt that he was ready to leave his job and his native city, and set out for London. Four days before he arrived in England, his sister Agnes died of tuberculosis. This was the only time Shaw was to see his mother in an obvious state of grief.

According to his own estimate, Shaw at twenty was "very awkward and self-conscious . . . ugly, uninteresting, and unpresentable." His clothing was frayed, his speech was hesitant, and he was painfully shy, but he began immediately and determinedly to correct his intellectual and physical shortcomings. He spent hours in the Reading Room of the British Museum studying the works of such philosophers and economists as Schopenhauer, Nietzsche, Mill, Ruskin, Comte, and Marx; he pored over the scores of Wagner's operas; he even devoted some attention to books of etiquette. During his first decade in London, Shaw held a few random jobs, turned out an occasional article, and tried his hand at being a novelist, but was actually being supported by his mother. With his usual bravado, he said of this period, "I did not throw myself into the struggle for life: I threw my mother into it. "

By writing assiduously—five pages a day every day—from 1879 to 1883, Shaw managed to produce five long novels. *Immaturity,* his first book, was submitted to eleven publishers and rejected by all of them; his next four novels—*The Irrational Knot, Love Among the Artists, Cashel Byron's Profession,* and *An Unsocial Socialist*—were turned down by all the book publishers in England and America to whom he sent them, but appeared serially in various magazines. Macmillan's rejection of *An Unsocial Socialist* convinced Shaw that he would never make his name as a novelist. What he did not know was that Macmillan's reader, though cool to Shaw's manuscript, had said in his report, ". . . but the writer, if he is young, is a man to keep one's eye upon."

In the early 1880s Shaw's development took on momentum, with several events and influences important to his career. In 1883 he met William Archer, a man of his own age and a working journalist, who was later to become a celebrated drama critic, playwright, and translator into English of Henrik Ibsen's plays. It was from Archer that Shaw learned of the works of the Norwegian dramatist, who immediately became Shaw's idol and an extremely important influence on him. With Archer's help, Shaw got his first regular jobs as critic for various London publications. He began his career in journalism as art critic for *The World.* He turned next to music criticism, writing for *The Star* under the pseudonym of "Corno di Bassetto"; he returned to *The World* as music critic, writing now under his own name. In 1891 he became a play reviewer. Stimulated by his contact with the theatre, he began in earnest to write plays. By 1898 he was the most celebrated drama critic in London. In that year he left the *Saturday Review,* with which he had been connected for three eyars, to devote full time to playwriting. He had already written eight plays, of which five had been performed.

In 1882 Shaw had heard an address by the American economist Henry George and his eyes were opened to the importance of economics. He began to affirm that, like Shelley, he was an "atheist, a vegetarian, and socialist." In 1884 he became a member of the newly formed Fabian Society, a moderate socialist organization, which proposed to educate people to work for their own betterment through political action (by evolution rather than revolution). The Fabian Society initiated the formation of the British Labor Party. In 1885 Shaw was elected to the Society's Executive Committee, and for the next twenty-five years he wrote and spoke regularly for the cause. He made speeches as often as three times a week, without remuneration, on street corners, at the docks, and in cultural institutions. In the process he transformed himself from an awkward, tongue-tied youth into a self-assured, dynamic man, whose sharpness of intellect and tongue brought him to the attention first of London and then of the world. His clever and persuasive arguments appeared not only in pamphlets and books but also, of course, in many of his plays.

Shaw said that he rose in the world by "the accident of possessing a lucrative talent." The theatre gave him the opportunity to display that talent; his zest to teach and to reform determined the direction his talent would take. Socialism served as a yardstick for Shaw the critic and provided Shaw the playwright with an ideological base. Like Plato Shaw thought that the function of art was to improve and enrich the spectator, finding sheer entertainment not only a waste of time but actually debasing. Applying these didactic standards to the plays he reviewed, he had lavish praise for the works of Ibsen, Strindberg, Zola, Brieux, and Becque; severe criticism for Oscar Wilde and even for Shakespeare (who, he felt, was not philosophical and had no message); and nothing but contempt for the whole tribe of commercial playwrights, including Scribe and Sardou.

Like Ibsen Shaw objected to the sentimental, romantic, conventional ideas and false ideals in the plays of the period; he had a special dislike for the "well-made play" because its contrived action gave an untrue picture of the way events occurred in real life. From the name of one of its most successful purveyors, Victorien Sardou, Shaw coined the pejorative term "Sardoodledom." Unlike Ibsen, who wrote seriously on serious themes, Shaw, whose purpose was equally serious, could not keep "funny business" out of his plays. He said, "Just when I am really rising to the height of my power that I may become really tragic and great, some absurd joke occurs and the anti-climax is irresistible . . . I have got the tragedian and I have got the clown in me; and the clown trips me up in the most dreadful way."

Between 1892 and 1947, a period of fifty-five years, Shaw wrote about fifty plays. His first, *Widowers' Houses,* had started out as a collaboration with William Archer in 1884. Archer was to supply the plot; Shaw, the dialogue. Shaw later wrote, "Laying violent hands on his [Archer's] thoroughly planned scheme for a sympathetically romantic 'well made play' of the Parisian type then in vogue, I perversely distorted it into a grotesquely realtistic exposure of slum landlordism, municipal jobbery, etc." Having completed only two acts and run out of plot, Shaw had applied to Archer for more material. Archer was displeased with the turn the play had taken, and the project was shelved. In 1892 J. T. Grein, an enterprising producer who had founded the Independent Theatre in London on the model of Antoine's *Théâtre Libre* in Paris, was looking for a play with which to follow up his production of Ibsen's *Ghosts*. Shaw offered to supply one and resurrected the script he had begun with Archer. He revised it, added a third act, and turned it over to Grein who put it on for two performances in December, 1892. *Widowers' Houses* was followed by *The Philanderer* and *Mrs. Warren's Profession* (both written in 1893). The second play dealt with the New Woman; the third, with a woman who owned a string of brothels yet proved to be more honorable than the men she had to deal with. As Shaw said in the preface to the volume in which these three "unpleasant" plays appeared, "Rich men without conviction are more dangerous in modern society than poor women without chastity." This play was Shaw's last frontal attack on capitalism.

Shaw's second volume of plays was called "pleasant"; it contained *Arms and the Man* and *Candida* (both written in 1894) and *The Man of Destiny* (1895). In these he dealt wittily with the subjects of war, marriage, and "heroes," respectively. *Arms and the Man* was first played with great success by Richard Mansfield in America; *Candida* was put on by the Independent Theatre; but *The Man of Destiny*, which treated its hero, Napoleon, realistically, had to wait two years for a production. When Shaw offered the play to Henry Irving, the celebrated Shakespearean actor rejected it in favor of Sardou's romantic *Madame Sans-Gêne*, which also had Napoleon as its hero. This led to a feud between Irving and Shaw, which lasted until Irving's death.

Written in a few weeks in 1897, *The Devil's Disciple*, a play dealing with the American Revolution, proved another perfect vehicle for Richard Mansfield in New York. It was not seen in London until nine years later.

In 1898 Shaw married Miss Charlotte Payne-Townshend, a wealthy Irish woman whom he had met in the Fabian Society and who had taken care of him when he had injured his leg bicycling. In the early days of his marriage, still on crutches and in great pain, Shaw wrote *Caesar and Cleopatra*. This play was given a spectacular production at the Neues Theater in Berlin, and other plays of his were staged in various cities in Austria and Germany. Shaw's name was coming more and more to be heard abroad.

Between 1901 and 1903 Shaw wrote *Man and Superman*, which treated sexual attraction as a working out of the "Life Force," which drove women to pursue men in order to insure the continuance of the species. (The Life Force concept was derived from Henri Bergson's *élan vital*.) *Man and Superman* was the first play to have a full-scale Shavian preface; the text of the play was followed by *The Revolutionist's Handbook*, supposed to have been written by the hero, a brilliant young man who thumbs his nose at the Establishment but cannot elude the woman who pursues him. The play is subtitled "A Comedy and a Philosophy." Act III, which is a disquisition on heaven and hell, is omitted from most productions and is occasionally presented by itself. With or without Act III *Man and Superman* has been one of Shaw's most successful and best-known plays.

Between 1904 and 1907 Harley Granville-Barker, well-known producer, director, actor, and playwright, managed the Royal Court Theatre in association with J. E. Vedrenne. They put on productions of Euripides, Shakespeare, and Shaw; 701 performances of eleven Shaw plays firmly established the Shavian theatrical reputation. In this same period, Shaw wrote two unpopular pieces, *John Bull's Other Island* and *How He Lied to Her Husband* (both in 1904), and two very popular plays, *Major Barbara* (1905) and *The Doctor's Dilemma* (1906).

In 1906 be bought the house at Ayot St. Lawrence that became his permanent home.

Shaw's next great success was written in 1911; it was *Androcles and the Lion,* an intellectual farce on the subject of religion. This was immediately followed by *Pygmalion* (1912), the playwright's most popular work and the one that brought him the largest financial returns.

Shaw's mother died in 1913, a year in which he was deeply troubled by the growing dissension among European nations. When World War I broke out in 1914, Shaw fulminated against the insanity of the conflict and reviled the superpatriots who supported it. His popularity evaporated. In *Heartbreak House,* a "Chekhovian" play which he wrote during the war years, there is a strong note of disillusionment and despair.

Mulling over the fate of man, Shaw came up with *Back to Methuselah* (1921), which he subtitled "A Metabiological Pentateuch." It was a gigantic work, comprising five plays grouped under a single title and erected around a single idea: that mankind, through creative evolution (Bergson's concept), may reach a state of longevity that resembles eternal life. By this time Shaw was back in the public's favor, and his next play, considered by some to be his greatest, raised him almost to the rank of sage or oracle. The play was *St. Joan* (1923), and the central figure was depicted as the "first Protestant," a woman who rose above self-indulgence and fear to triumph through the power and joy of spirituality.

In 1925 Shaw was awarded the Nobel Prize but he promptly handed over the prize money (about $35,000) to the Anglo-Swedish Literary Alliance for the promotion of "intercourse and understanding in literature and art between Sweden and the British Isles" and expressed the particular wish that Strindberg's plays would be done more frequently in England.

In 1927 the Malvern Festival was founded by Barry Jackson solely for the presentation of Shaw's plays. For the festival, Shaw wrote *The Apple Cart* (1929), in which he seemed to be responding to the wide movement against the confusions of parliamentary government and at the same time saying farewell to democracy and Fabian socialism. He was still shocking people, but he was well aware of the trend toward totalitarianism in Russia, Italy, and Germany. Most of the plays that followed *The Apple Cart* were extremely polemic and "talky"; they include *Too True to Be Good* (1931), *The Simpleton of the Unexpected Isles* (1934), *The Millionairess* (1935), *Geneva* (1938), and *In Good King Charles' Golden Days* (1939).

In 1943, during World War II, Shaw's wife died. Four years later, at the age of ninety-one, he wrote his last complete play, *Buoyant Billions.* He continued to write, as he had for over seventy years, though his health was fast failing. He was at work on a play, *The Lady She Would Not,* (the title suggests his still lively spirit), when, as the result of a fall in his garden at Ayot St. Lawrence, he died on November 2, 1950.

George Bernard Shaw won the attention of the world not only with his plays but with such important critical and political works as *The Quintessence of Ibsenism* (1891), *The Sanity of Art* (1895), *The Perfect Wagnerite* (1898), *The Intelligent Woman's Guide to Socialism and Capitalism* (1928), *The Adventures of the Black Girl in Her Search for God* (1932), and *Everybody's Political What's What* (1943).

By the "conservative" estimate of Professor Dan H. Laurence, Shaw wrote a quarter of a million letters and postcards in his lifetime. Two collections, his letters to the actresses Mrs. Patrick Campbell and Ellen Terry, are particularly well known. Although they were "love letters," Shaw admitted that he had only met Miss Terry on a few occasions—both times publicly in the theatre—and that his "delicious flirtation" was a work of the imagination. When critics remarked that he always wrote far more from the mind than he did from the heart or the emotions, Shaw defended his intellectual approach to life: "Let those who may complain that it was all on paper remember that only on paper has humanity yet achieved glory, beauty, truth, knowledge, virtue, and abiding love."

During his lifetime Shaw attracted wider attention to himself and his work than any other man of letters writing in English. He was a favorite subject for artists. Rodin was the first to do a bust of him, followed by Paul Troubetskoy, Jo Davidson, Sigmund Strobl, and Jacob Epstein. His portrait was painted by Augustus John, William Rothenstein, and John Collier. Shaw was often caricatured; there are cartoons by Max Beerbohm, Ruth, and many others. H. G. Wells commented with some annoyance, "His extraordinary industry in sitting to painters, photographers, and sculptors will fill the museums of the future with entire galleries of his portraits, medals, statues and busts."

At his death Shaw left one of the largest fortunes ever amassed by a writer—about $1,225,000—which is said to have more than tripled since 1950. It was his wish that the money should be used for the reformation of the English language—its spelling, writing, and speaking; but the British law court negated this section of his will, granting another provision, which directed that the money be divided equally among the Irish National Gallery, the Reading Room of the British Museum, and the Royal Academy of Dramatic Art.

Just as Ibsen had protested that he was a poet not a reformer, Shaw maintained that his plays were works of art not social documents. He was undoubtedly a dramatic artist of enormous power and originality, with a rare and special gift for comedy. In his plots his comedic sense dictated the use of reversals, surprises, and anticlimaxes; in his characters it accounted for the creation of whimsical, pathetic, and absurd types, satirical inversions, and caricatures; and in his dialogue, comedy appeared in every guise from wit, humor, and irony to parody, paradox, and pun. He cannot be faulted for contributing little to poetry or tragedy; these were outside the natural line of his vision. Yet one must not overlook the purity and elegance of his prose, which few modern writers have matched. If there is any weakness in his plays, it is an excess of eloquence, which often leads to windy disquisitions and dizzy flights of rhetoric.

Shaw's great and distinctive contribution to modern drama was the irrepressible gaiety with which he attacked the most sacrosanct social, moral, political, and religious beliefs of his day. In this he has been likened to Aristophanes and Molière. He has had a marked influence, in subject matter and style, on such playwrights as Brecht, Duerrenmatt, Frisch, Giraudoux, Adamov, and Ionesco.

Pygmalion

Pygmalion was written in 1912 and 1913, when Shaw was fifty-six years old; but the idea for the play had occurred to him at least fifteen years before, and some of the elements of the plot and characterizations may be traced back to his childhood and youth. The excessive dependence of Henry Higgins upon his mother and his lack of interest in young women reflect Shaw's own emotional and sexual constitution and inclinations. But Shaw had a romantic imagination and, as a youth, read many eighteenth- and nineteenth-century novels, among them the works of Tobias Smollett. Though Shaw said he had no recollection of ever having read Smollett's *The Adventures of Peregrine Pickle* (1751), a summary of Chapter 87 of that book will show its close connection with the plot of *Pygmalion*.

> Peregrine is accosted on the road by a beggar-woman and her daughter. The girl is young and beautiful but very coarse and dirty. Peregrine is attracted to her, has a talk with her mother, "and for a small sum of money purchased her property in the wench." Peregrine orders his man, Thomas, to take the girl away and clean her up. Despite her screams and curses the girl is bathed and scrubbed, and her clothes are burned. When Peregrine next sees her, he is amazed at the transformation. Believing that the only difference between a person of the upper class and one of the lower resides in his education, Peregrine undertakes to improve the girl's speech and behavior and to pass her off as a lady. He teaches her to quote sentences from Shakespeare, Otway, and Pope, to hum "remnants of opera tunes" between pauses in the conversation, to utter her words with "emphasis and theatrical cadence," to smile prettily and make small talk, and to play cards. The most difficult obstacle he has to overcome, however, is her "habit of swearing, which she had indulged in from infancy." The girl passes a preliminary test when she is introduced to a company of gentlemen and impresses them as "a sprightly young lady, of uncommon learning and taste." Peregrine then takes her to London, where his Swiss valet gives her lessons in French and dancing, after which she is ready to make her début at a great ball. She is accepted as a lady of fashion and invited to elegant parties; at one of these she catches another lady cheating at cards and, in her wrath, drops her mask of gentility, lets go a flood of vile language, snaps her fingers in the face of the company, and leaves the room, applying "her hand to that part which was the last of her that disappeared, inviting the company to kiss it, by one of its coarsest denominations." [For that shocking word, Shaw substituted "bloody," but in *My Fair Lady* Alan Jay Lerner actually uses the

"coarse denomination" alluded to by Smollett.] Shortly afterward, the girl elopes with the Swiss valet; Peregrine becomes angry at first, but then decides to set the young couple up in business as proprietors of a coffee-house and tavern.

Smollett's character, Peregrine Pickle, clearly contains the features of both Higgins and Pickering, while the Swiss valet is transformed into Freddy. The two interesting parents involved, Mr. Doolittle and Mrs. Higgins, are characteristically Shavian creations.

Before Shaw left Dublin, he taught himself shorthand and thereafter wrote the first drafts of his literary compositions, including *Pygmalion,* in his own version of the Pitman system. And in the Dublin lodginghouse where he lived with his father after his mother had left for London, Shaw made the acquaintance of Chichester Bell. This young man was the son of Alexander Bell (author of *The Standard Elocutionist*), nephew of Melville Bell (inventor of the phonetic script known as Visible Speech), and cousin of Alexander Graham Bell (inventor of the telephone). Shaw's chance meeting with Bell gave great impetus to his interest in speech and phonetics and led to his later contacts with many eminent phoneticians, among them Henry Sweet, who served in part as a model for Henry Higgins. Throughout his life Shaw was deeply involved with these subjects, which served as the basis for *Pygmalion.* In his will he left the major portion of his fortune for the creation of a new phonetic alphabet which would, he believed, improve both written and spoken English. That proviso in the will, however, was almost entirely invalidated by the court.

Pygmalion also presents one side of Shaw's socialist philosophy. As a Fabian he believed that the democratization of society depended upon the removal of the barriers between the classes, and the institution of economic and educational equality. This idea serves as the theme of *Pygmalion* and finds dramatic demonstration in Eliza's rehabilitation by education and Mr. Doolittle's, by a financial windfall.

In 1896, while Shaw was serving as drama critic for the *Saturday Review,* the great actor-manager, Johnston Forbes-Robertson, appeared in repertory at the Lyceum Theatre, with Mrs. Patrick Campbell as his leading lady; these stars acting in conjunction had a powerful influence upon Shaw's creativity. With them in mind, he conceived the play *Caesar and Cleopatra.* Then in February, 1896, Shaw saw them act in *For the Crown,* a romantic piece translated from the French of Francois Coppée. Forbes-Robertson played the part of a prince's son, and Mrs. Campbell was a gypsy girl who becomes his slave. When she meets her master for the first time, she tells him that she was "born upon the highway" and picks her bread "out of the mire." He wishes to free her, but she prefers to remain his slave. When she asks him for a pledge, he offers her a ring, which she refuses. Later in the play, when the prince is dejected, the girl brings him a bunch of flowers to cheer him. She admits that she is ignorant and worthless, yet offers him her love. He replies, "You move me strongly, but I know not love, and love is not for me."

Shaw called the play "balderdash," but praised the acting of the stars and was deeply moved by the relationship of the prince and the gypsy girl. It haunted him, apparently, for he was eager to cast these particular players in a similar relationship in a modern play. A year and a half later the idea was still simmering; in a letter to Ellen Terry, Shaw referred to Forbes-Robertson and Mrs. Campbell, remarking: "I would teach that rapscallionly flower girl of his something. 'Caesar and Cleopatra' has been driven clean out of my head by a play I want to write for them in which he shall be a west end gentleman and she an east end dona [ragamuffin] in an apron and three orange and red ostrich feathers." Fifteen years were to pass, however, before the play finally took shape as *Pygmalion.*

Shaw got his title from the ancient myth concerning Pygmalion, King of Cyprus, who carved in ivory a beautiful maiden with whom he fell in love. Pygmalion prayed to Aphrodite to breathe life into his statue and, when his request was granted, he married the girl. Shaw's most significant departure from the myth was his insistence that there was no romantic attachment between Higgins and Eliza. Though Shaw called the play a Romance, he considered it quite romantic enough for a flower girl to be transformed into a lady, and saw no need for her to marry the hero merely to provide sentimental playgoers with the stock happy ending. In the cause of realism, Shaw wrote a rather long epilogue to the play, in which he explained why Higgins would necessarily remain a bachelor while Eliza would marry Freddy. But actors, directors, adaptors, and audiences have done their best to circumvent Shaw's directions and to provide the play with the conventional romantic conclusion.

Pygmalion is a Cinderella story in which a girl advances from rags to riches, and passes the typical fairy-tale test. As treated by Shaw, it has all the earmarks of the "well-made" play—the coincidences, contrivances, reversals, surprises, and almost mechanical working out of the plot. Shaw, like Scribe, used a five-act structure, with the climax in the fourth act, and the denouement in the fifth; he omitted the big "ballroom scene" that was standard equipment in most Scribean dramas. Since Shaw's play hinges on a bet that a common girl can be passed off as a duchess, it would be absolutely necessary, according to the nineteenth-century French critic Francisque Sarcey, that the playwright provide visual proof of the heroine's triumph or failure. Sarcey, chief proponent of the *pièce bien faite,* would have objected violently to Shaw's omission of the so-called obligatory scene. However, Shaw was not primarily interested in preserving the structure of the "well-made" play; his chief concern lay in showing the transformation of a poor girl, not into an imitation duchess, but into a genuinely independent woman. It is that idea that gives *Pygmalion* its authentic Shavian hallmark. To be sure, Shaw had initially conceived of a ballroom scene but, as a practical man of the theatre, had omitted it from the play for reasons of economy. He once told an interviewer:

> Plays begin in all sorts of ways. I can sit down without an idea in my head except that I must write a play, and a play comes. . . . As to *Pygmalion,* the scene in which Eliza makes her successful début at the Ambassador's party was the root of the play at its inception. But when I got to work I left it to the imagination of the audience, as the theatre could not afford its expense and it made the play too long. Sir James Barrie spotted this at once and remonstrated. So when the play was screened, I added the omitted scene, as the cinema can afford practically unlimited money, and the absence of intervals [intermissions] left plenty of time to spare.

To the millions who have been entertained by the musical comedy and motion picture versions of *Pygmalion,* the ballroom scene has proved to be one of the highlights.

In its characterization *Pygmalion* differs from most of Shaw's plays in that each person depicted is carefully individualized and complexly motivated. Not one is a puppet nor a mere spokesman for the playwright, but each plays his part strongly in a clear conflict of wills. Henry Higgins is coldly cerebral, egotistical and arrogant, scornful of the established moral and social codes. A confirmed bachelor, he is concerned only with his professional skills and his creature comforts. His chief interest in Eliza is as a means of demonstrating his superiority to his fellow phoneticist Pickering. His only emotional reaction to his pupil is fury when she threatens to compete with him professionally. Eliza wants desperately to rise above her station in life and is willing to work like a slave to attain her goal. Her ambition is shored up by intelligence and sensitivity, as well as the shrewdness she has learned in the streets. She is clearly infatuated with Higgins; but when his unshakable self-centeredness is borne home to her, she is willing to do battle with him to achieve status and independence. Pickering is a generous and sympathetic human being, more "fatherly" to Eliza than her own father. It is his considerate manner toward Eliza that awakens in her an awareness of her value as a person. Pickering serves as a foil for both Higgins and Doolittle. Mr. Doolittle, a hearty buffoon with a native sharpness of mind and tongue, is the vital and earthy common man. He is a male Cinderella who passes from undeserving rags to undeserving riches but remains to the end a victim of middle-class morality. Doolittle comes closest to uttering Shaw's ideas in the form of a parody. Mrs. Higgins, the "superior" mother who, without meaning to, has crippled her son emotionally, is left to bear the burden of his bachelorhood. She "has intelligence, personal grace, dignity of character without harshness, and a cultivated sense of the best art," but she would be shocked to learn that her image stands between her son and his sexual freedom. The Eynsford Hills, a pathetic family of "downstarts," are financially and intellectually impoverished. Freddy, the young scion, is the typical romantic juvenile and the man, according to Shaw, who will eventually win Eliza's hand—let audiences complain as they will.

Dialogue was always Shaw's strongest point (also his weakest when used to excess); in *Pygmalion* he demonstrates his complete mastery of the art. His lines do everything that dialogue is meant to do: they characterize the speaker, advance the plot, define the theme, set the mood, stimulate thought, and entertain. They are sharp, witty, concise, built with impeccable logic, surprise, shock, and are hilariously funny. His use of the word "bloody" is a case in point. Today it signifies nothing more than filthy or rotten and is used without a second thought; but in 1914 it was considered shocking and not fit for decent ears. Though it had been used humorously in society and been uttered on the stage before, Shaw was able to get the last ounce of notoriety out of it. In a letter to his wife, after the first night of the play, Shaw said, ". . . When 'Not bloody likely' came, the performance was nearly wrecked. They laughed themselves into such utter abandonment and disorder that it was really doubtful for some time whether they could recover themselves and let the play go on." The critics devoted more attention to the use of this word (which they referred to only with euphemisms) than to the entire play. Shaw's triumph lay in the perfect aptness of the word to the character and situation.

Although Shaw's verbal swordplay is dazzling, it is not all glitter; deep emotions very often shine through. During World War II, the British War Office asked Shaw to select his three best plays for circulation among the troops; after re-reading all his plays very critically, he finally chose *Androcles and the Lion, Pygmalion,* and *Saint Joan,* because, he said, there was genuine feeling in them. He hoped that they might have a cathartic effect in a time of so much suffering.

Shaw's brilliant use of language, coupled with his high purpose and warmth of feeling, make his comedies humane and universal. *Pygmalion,* his most popular play, is a telling example of Shaw's remarkable gifts as a dramatist.

Concerning Shaw's Additions for the Screen

Shaw used the printed version of *Pygmalion* [which he called "the book"] as the basis for the screenplay. In red ink throughout the script, he made slight alterations in the dialogue and stage business. In addition, he wrote, in pencil, about thirty pages of script, consisting of full-length scenes as well as suggestions and comments for the director. Several of the items, the following among them, are characteristically Shavian and each is headed "Note":

1. [Referring to the Covent Garden scene:] In the book the play begins at 11:15 P.M. after the theatres close. In the film the play begins in the late afternoon, as the theatres are closing after their matinées. Consequently nobody is in evening dress.

2. [The bathroom scene, indicative of Shavian prudery:] Eliza is of course dressed from the waist to the knees; but she is masked by Mrs. Pearce during the moment between the snatching off of the bathing gown and the concealment of her bathing drawers by the side of the tub.

3. The first appearance of Doolittle should be impressive and threatening. The audience should have a good look at him as he appears in the doorway.

A strong point must be made of the change in his expression from the outraged avenging father to the irresistibly charming old rascal on the line, "Well, what *would* a man come for? Be human, governor."

After this change, Doolittle should be thoroughly *liked* by the audience.

This must be managed by close-ups. At his exit also a feature must be made of the look at Mrs. Pearce and the wink at Higgins.

Bernard Shaw, playwright, as inspiration and guardian angel for Gabriel Pascal, producer of the 1938 film version of *Pygmalion*.

The Production Record

British critics had reacted so violently to Shaw's earlier plays that Continental, especially Austrian and German, producers hesitated to put them on. Shaw decided to try a new tactic with *Pygmalion*: he permitted the play to be produced in German before it was presented in English. The première performance took place, at the Hofburgtheater in Vienna on October 16, 1913, with Higgins and Eliza played by two great stars, Max Paulsen and Lili Marberg, under the direction of the brilliant Hugo Thimig. It was an enormous success, as was the production at the Lessing Theater in Berlin on November 1 of the same year, with Tilla Durieux playing Eliza. The play was immediately translated into Swedish, Polish, Hungarian, and Czechoslovakian and was performed in Stockholm, Warsaw, Budapest, and Prague, and for the German colony in New York, before it was done in English at His Majesty's Theatre, London, on April 11, 1914. In the leading roles were Sir Herbert Beerbohm Tree as Higgins and Mrs. Patrick Campbell as Eliza. Although she was forty-nine years old at the time, Mrs. Campbell is said to have created the illusion of youth.

Directing the play himself, Shaw found it almost impossible to cope with his temperamental stars. He had always insisted that actors follow his directions to the last detail, but both Tree and Mrs. Campbell considered a play merely an outline that each might develop according to his own inspiration. Many are the stories told about the clashes of personality that took place during the rehearsals of *Pygmalion*. Tree treated Shaw as if he were a complete outsider and paid no attention to the playwright's directions. Twice, Shaw stalked out of the theatre in frustration, returning only at the request of the other members of the cast, so that the play might get going again. "On both occasions," wrote Shaw, "Tree took leave of me as if it had been very kind of me to look in as I was passing to see his rehearsals, and received me on my return as if it were still more friendly of me to come back and see how he was getting on."

Generally very cool and unruffled, Tree was twice badly upset. He was playing Higgins as a romantic lover, when Shaw, unable to suppress his

Tilla Durieux, German actress, who played Eliza at the Lessing Theater, Berlin, November 1913, prior to the presentation of the play in English. Compare this with the photograph on page 135. Museum of the City of New York.

Tea party scene from Act Three of the Russian production presented at the Maly Theatre, Moscow. Left to right: Higgins (N. L. Afanasyev, Honored Artist of the RSFSR), Mrs. Higgins (N. A. Belevtseva, People's Artist of the RSFSR), Clara Eynsford Hill (Y. I. Yelanskaya), and Eliza (L. V. Yudina.) Gabrielle Enthoven Collection, Victoria and Albert Museum, London.

distaste, punned, "Oh, Tree, must you be so treacly?" The actor stopped short, Mrs. Campbell reports, appeared to be on the verge of tears, and went to the stage door to recover himself. On another occasion, in the scene in which Eliza flings the slippers at Higgins, Mrs. Campbell, who was a dead shot, caught Tree square in the face. The actor, forgetting that the action was called for in the script, took it as an expression of personal animosity and collapsed in a chair. Mrs. Campbell apologized profusely, pointing out the directions in the script; thereafter, she was careful, however, to miss her target. Although Shaw was usually the victor in his battles with the actors, Tree triumphed in the addition of one brilliant bit of business. In the moment between the end of the play and the fall of the curtain, he threw flowers to Eliza, thus turning a rude bachelor into an eager lover and outwitting the playwright to win the hearts of the audience. In his letter to his wife, after the opening night of the play, Shaw spoke of "the raving absurdity of Tree's acting" and was especially furious about the distortion of the final scene. He wrote, "I had particularly coached him at the last rehearsal in the concluding lines, making him occupy himself affectionately with his mother, and throw Eliza the commission to buy the ham etc., over his shoulder. The last thing I saw as I left the house was Higgins shoving his mother rudely out of his way and wooing Eliza with appeals to buy a ham for his lonely home like a bereaved Romeo." Fortunately, Shaw had not stayed until the final curtain, so that he had not seen Tree fling the flowers to Eliza; the playwright had left in a rage long before the interpolation of that inspired gesture. Although *Pygmalion* was a tremendous success, it was withdrawn at the end of July, 1914, after only 119 performances—not for the reason generally given, the outbreak of World War I—but because Tree could not stand the strain of playing opposite Mrs. Campbell. The actor apparently was not the only sufferer. A stagehand once remarked to Philip Merivale, the original Colonel Pickering, "That there Patrick Campbell—'e was a lucky man!" "Why, yes," Merivale agreed, "she's still a handsome woman." "I don't mean that," said the stagehand, "I mean 'e got 'isself killed in the Boer War!"

In New York *Pygmalion* opened at the Park Theatre on October 12, 1914, with Mrs. Campbell in her original role and Philip Merivale in the part of Higgins. The play was presented by George C. Tyler, to whom, on the eve of the production, Shaw wrote a warning letter; it read, in part:

> You will find that Mrs. Pat Campbell's changes of dress will take longer than the change of scenery. The play is very hard work for her in this way; and you must arrange her dressing accommodation in such a position as to avoid running up and down stairs. If you cannot give her a room on the stage level she will agitate for a tent (she had one at His Majesty's here); and when SHE starts agitating don't argue but surrender at once, even if it involves rebuilding the theatre; you will find it cheaper in the long run.

Mona Hofland as Eliza in the Norwegian production of *My Fair Lady*. Miss Hofland, an extremely versatile actress, has also been seen in Oslo as Hedda Gabler and as Anna I in *The Seven Deadly Sins*. Courtesy Mona Hofland.

When you have fixed her up comfortably in this respect," Shaw continues, "you can then press her if necessary to keep pace with the stage staff. If she does that, the play can be got through between 8 and 11. Tree got through by 11:30; and Merivale can easily save half an hour on Tree if the others keep going. You must be firm about this; for Mrs. Campbell wants to cut the play, partly because its length hurries her dressing and interferes with the delightful léeves she holds in her dressing-room, and partly because she thinks that Mrs. Pearce and Doolittle are insufferable boors and should be cut down to two or three lines apiece. . . .

At the end of the successful run in New York, Mrs. Campbell took the play on a road tour of the United States, which lasted well into 1915 and proved a personal triumph for her. In March, 1920, she revived the play in London under Shaw's direction, with C. Aubrey Smith in the part of Higgins. Arnold Bennett, much taken by the fifty-five-year-old Eliza, noted in his journal, "Mrs. Campbell was superb. There is still nobody else to touch her." In the audience of this revival was a young schoolboy who was so deeply impressed by the actress that when, eighteen years later, he codirected the film version of *Pygmalion,* he drew heavily on his memories of her performance. This was Anthony Asquith, who recalled, among other details, that Mrs. Campbell had added two words to her speech, "But it's my belief *as how* they done the old woman in." Asquith used these words in the picture, though they do not appear in Shaw's text.

From 1927 to 1953 *Pygmalion* was revived in London about a dozen times, with such stars as Esmé Percy, Robert Morley, Basil Sidney, Alec Clunes, and John Clements as Higgins; Lewis Casson and Nicholas Hannen as Pickering; Gwen Ffrangcon-Davies, Margaret Rawlings, Diana Wynyard, Yvonne Mitchell, and Kay Hammond as Eliza. Among the directors of these revivals were Esmé Percy (four times), Tyrone Guthrie (at the Old Vic), Douglas Seale, Michael Langham, and John Clements.

In the United States the Theatre Guild, the "official" producers of Shaw in America, presented *Pygmalion* at their own theatre in New York, on November 15, 1926, with Lynn Fontanne in the role of Eliza, Reginald Mason as Higgins, and Henry Travers as Mr. Doolittle, under the direction of Dudley Digges. Dressed to resemble "The Shrimp Girl" in Hogarth's famous painting, and drawing on her memories of the coster girls in the London of her childhood, Miss Fontanne gave a performance that was unanimously praised. "What Lynn did so especially well was the cockney part of Liza," said Theresa Helburn, one of the directors of the Theatre Guild. "She made no compromise of any sort with the vulgarity of Liza. She was the dirty snot-nosed draggletail without a trace of the gloss that both Gertie Lawrence and Stella Campbell couldn't get rid of when they played Liza. I think they softened Liza. Lynn didn't. She didn't romanticize Liza Doolittle one bit." Mrs. Campbell happened to be in New York when *Pygmalion* opened and, after attending a performance of the play, went backstage to see Miss Fontanne, who was terrified at meeting the creator of the part. But, Miss Fontanne recalls, Mrs. Campbell "sat down, as politely as you please, and she did what a great actress should do for a younger actress. She told me several things Shaw had told her to do when he directed her in the original production. They were very valuable things for me to know. . . ." The play ran for 143 performances in New York and was then sent to Philadelphia and Chicago, with Alfred Lunt in the role of Henry Higgins playing opposite Lynn Fontanne. Twenty years later—early in 1946—Lunt and Fontanne appeared in *Pygmalion* on the radio program called "The Theatre Guild of the Air," which was put on by the National Broadcasting Company under the sponsorship of the United States Steel Corporation; the play was done in two one-hour installments, since Shaw would not approve any cuts in the script.

The Theatre Guild produced *Pygmalion* again on June 16, 1952, at the Westport Country Playhouse, their summer theatre in Connecticut, with Dolores Grey as Eliza, Tom Helmore as Higgins, and John C. Wilson in charge of direction. The special reason for this production was the desire of the Theatre Guild to get Alan Jay Lerner and Frederick Loewe to prepare a musical version of the play. Lerner and Loewe saw the production at Westport and proceeded with their musical adaptation called *My Fair Lady,* but they brought in another producer in place of the Theatre Guild.

Another memorable production of *Pygmalion* was done at the Barrymore Theatre in New York by Theatre Incorporated on December 26, 1945. This lavish presentation, with scenery designed by Donald Oenslager and costumes by Motley, starred Gertrude Lawrence as Eliza, Raymond Massey as Higgins, and Melville Cooper as Doolittle and was directed by Sir Cedric Hardwicke. Miss Lawrence won the praise of all the daily reviewers for the wit and humor of her performance, but the critic for *The New York Times* had some minor reservations. He wrote, "There are moments in the earlier scenes when she is not quite believable, and again there are moments in the final scene when one wishes she would get through with more pathos and tenderness. But then, perhaps, this is only carping. Miss Lawrence knows how to wring the fun from Mr. Shaw's lines. . . ." After a limited run on Broadway, ending June 1, 1946, the play went on a coast-to-coast tour of the United States with Dennis King, in the part of Higgins, playing opposite Miss Lawrence.

Pygmalion was also presented by such stars as Ruth Chatterton and Sylvia Sidney, as well as by many semiprofessional and amateur players in schools, colleges, and community theatres in various parts of the United States. It has been done frequently in foreign countries. One production worthy of note was the French version offered by Jean Marais at the Bouffes-Parisien Théâtre in Paris on January 15, 1955. Jeanne Moreau was seen as Eliza; in addition to acting Higgins, Marais designed the scenery and costumes and directed the play. Since Shakespeare and Shaw are as little appreciated in France as Racine is in English-speaking countries, Marais' production was unusual in proving to be a great popular success.

Pygmalion, like Eliza, has been transformed extravagantly—in films and musical comedy. The two earliest motion picture productions were in foreign languages: a German version made by Klagemann-Tobis-Rota appeared in 1935, and a Dutch version made by Filmex-Cinetone was released in 1937. It was in 1935 that Gabriel Pascal, a penniless Hungarian who had produced motion pictures in Italy and France, approached Shaw for permission to film *The Devil's Disciple.* Though Shaw had previously turned down many Hollywood producers, he was impressed by Pascal for some reason and agreed to let him do *Pygmalion.* Shaw insisted that the role of Eliza be given to Wendy Hiller, a then relatively unknown but tremendously gifted performer. The part of Higgins was assigned to Leslie Howard, a film star with

Pickering (Cecil Humphreys), Higgins (Raymond Massey, standing center) and Eliza (Gertrude Lawrence) in the Theatre Incorporated production at the Barrymore Theatre, New York, 1945. Museum of the City of New York.

an extremely attractive personality and superb diction. In his evaluation of this film, Parker Tyler said, "*Pygmalion* is an adventure in the English language and must be heard in order to be properly seen. [Leslie] Howard's equipment as a living model of the professor's advanced ideas was certainly insidious with charms linguistic and personal: so was Miss Hiller's. She is, in fact, just the type of natural beauty in which the permutation to a sublime state of speech and manners seems to find plausible roots. . . ." The supporting players were equally expert, among them were Wilfred Lawson as Doolittle, Marie Löhr as Mrs. Higgins, Esmé Percy as Karpathy, and Cathleen Nesbitt as A Lady. The film, which was made at the Pinewood Studios, London, was codirected by Leslie Howard and Anthony Asquith, with settings by Laurence Irving and costumes designed by Czettell and executed by Worth and Schiaparelli. Shaw inserted a great deal of additional material into the screenplay, including such scenes as the taxi driver taking Eliza home from Covent Garden, Eliza being given a bath by Mrs. Pearce, Eliza being tutored by Higgins, and the Embassy Ball, which introduced many new characters, such as Count Karpathy (the Hungarian phoneticist, who is called Nepommuck in the play). The picture opened in London on October 6 and in New York on December 21, 1938; it was immediately acclaimed by both critics and public. Shaw won an Academy Award (Oscar) for the Best Screenplay and Dialogue of 1938. Interviewed in London, the playwright, pretending to be indignant, said, "It's an insult for them to offer me any honor. They might as well send some honor to George for being King of England." Then he added, "Of course, it's a good film. It's the only film! But it wouldn't have been if Hollywood had made it."

In October, 1951, Gabriel Pascal suggested to Lawrence Langner, of the Theatre Guild, that they co-operate in producing a musical version of *Pygmalion*. Pascal had obtained the rights to produce such a version from the Shaw estate, and the Guild had already converted some of their earlier plays into such successful musical works as *Oklahoma!, Porgy and Bess,* and *Carousel.* A search began at once for writers, composers, and actors who could bring the project to fruition. Some of the people approached were Rodgers and Hammerstein, Frank Loesser, Cole Porter, Leonard Bernstein, Gian-Carlo Menotti, and Lerner and Loewe. Among the performers considered were Mary Martin, Dolores Grey, George Sanders, Noel Coward, and Rex Harrison. The complicated story of the Theatre Guild's efforts to produce the play is told in Lawrence Langner's book, *G. B. S. and the Lunatic.* Negotiations for the production had come to a standstill by July, 1954, when Gabriel Pascal died. Shortly afterward, Lerner and Loewe secured the rights to work on *Pygmalion* from the Shaw and Pascal estates.

Two years later, on March 15, 1956, *My Fair Lady* opened at the Mark Hellinger Theater on Broadway. The musical was produced by Herman Levin with capital supplied by the Columbia Broadcasting System. Alan Jay Lerner was responsible for the book and lyrics, Frederick Loewe for the music. Rex Harrison played Henry Higgins; Julie Andrews—a twenty-year-old newcomer who was not only English but very close to Eliza's actual age—played the Cockney flower girl; Stanley Holloway, an English music-hall and stage star, was Doolittle; and Cathleen Nesbitt, who had had a small part in the 1938 film, was Mrs. Higgins. The production was directed by Moss Hart, with scenery by Oliver Smith, costumes by Cecil Beaton, choreography by Hanya Holm, lighting by Feder, orchestrations by Robert Russell Bennett and Philip J. Lang, and orchestra conducted by Franz Allers.

The dramatic structure of *My Fair Lady* differs radically, of course, from that of *Pygmalion;* Shaw's traditional five-act play was transformed by Lerner into the accepted two-act musical comedy, and subdivided into eighteen short scenes. In place of the three sets used in the original play, Lerner called for ten different sets—some using the entire stage and full construction, others played on the apron in front of a painted drop. The Embassy Ball, which occurs offstage, between Acts III and IV of Shaw's play, provides the great finale of Lerner's first act. In the musical the lyrics, music, and dances replace sections of Shaw's dialogue, define situations, and heighten characterization. These productional elements, in addition to the eye-filling and fast-changing scenery and breathtaking costumes, helped to account for the show's phenomenally popular success.

My Fair Lady won six Drama Critics' Circle Awards and ten American Theater Wing Antoinette Perry (Tony) Awards. It ran for six and a half years on Broadway, five and a half years in London, two years in Stockholm. It toured professionally across the United States and was presented in twenty-one countries from Iceland to Japan, after which it was performed in summer stock and amateur theatres. Ticket sales added up to over $75 million dollars. The musical was an enormous success in Russia; but as that country does not honor foreign copyrights, there were no financial returns to the owners. Columbia Records hit a high in album sales by selling about six million copies of the original cast recording; and a spokesman for Chappell, the English company that published the sheet music, said, "It's the biggest thing we've seen since we've been in business, and that's 300 years." It is interesting to note that when Rex Harrison was approached to play the part of Higgins, he expressed doubts as to his ability to carry a heavy singing role in a musical and suggested that he listen to some of the music and lyrics and possibly record them himself before making a decision. Since Mr. Harrison receives nine cents for each record album sold, he has earned about a half a million dollars on this by-product alone.

The motion picture rights to *My Fair Lady* were sold to Warner Brothers for the record-breaking price of $5.5 million and a percentage of the profits. The cost of the film production was an astounding $17 million, as against $400,000 for the stage version of the musical. To protect his investment, Jack L. Warner bypassed Julie Andrews, who had never appeared in a film, and cast Audrey Hepburn, an established "box-office attraction," in the part of Eliza. Miss Hepburn's "singing" was done by Marni Nixon. Rex Harrison and Stanley Holloway repeated their stage roles; Wilfred Hyde-White played Pickering, and Gladys Cooper was Mrs. Higgins. The film was directed by George Cukor, with sets and costumes by Cecil Beaton, choreography by Hermes Pan, orchestrations by André Previn, and cinematography by Harry Stradling, Jr., who had been in charge of the camera for the Pascal production in 1938. Alan Jay Lerner wrote the screenplay, which ran to about 165 scenes; in film-writing each camera setup denotes another scene. All of the original material was elaborated for the film, and additional action, dialogue, and music were interpolated. The style of the production was partly realistic (Covent Garden with its flower barrows and rainstorm) and partly stylized (the races at Ascot without horses or turf).

The picture was shot in full color, on wide film, and in stereophonic sound. British critic Kenneth Tynan, who had the highest praise for the acting of Rex Harrison and the music of Frederick Loewe, noted that the clarity of the sound made one particularly aware of "a couple of *gaffes* [blunders] in Mr. Lerner's otherwise immaculate lyrics:

'She should be taken out and hung
For the cold-blooded murder of the English tongue.'

Shaw would have *hanged* Higgins for that. As for:—

'I'd be *equally as* willing
That a dentist should be drilling
Than to ever let a woman in my life'

—it is quite an achievement to make Higgins, the defender of pure English, commit two syntactical crimes (compounded by a split infinitive) within the space of three lines."

These grammatical errors in no way dampened the public's or the critics' enjoyment of the film, which opened on October 21, 1964, at the Criterion Theater in New York, and closed on June 19, 1966, after a run of eighty-two weeks. The picture promptly won several New York Film Critics'

Awards, Golden Globe Awards, Screen Producers' Guild Award, All American Press Association Awards, and seven Academy Awards. It received a prize as the Best Foreign Film in Norway, broke attendance records in France (though the stage version of the musical had not been presented there for lack of a satisfactory translation and acting company), and, "dubbed" in all important foreign languages, has been shown almost everywhere in the world.

If played exactly as Shaw originally wrote it, *Pygmalion* still provides a challenge for actors and great excitement for audiences.

The First Film Version

Interviews with Anthony Asquith and Edward Baird

"The English film version of *Pygmalion*," said Anthony Asquith, who directed the picture in 1938, "would never have been made without Gabriel Pascal. He had the imagination to see its possibilities for the screen, the cleverness to get Shaw's approval, and the initiative to raise the money for the production. But he was a difficult man to work with. Pascal was temperamental, mercurial, excitable, and sharp, and it was necessary to stand up strongly against him."

Samuel Goldwyn and other well-known Hollywood producers had made generous offers for the film rights to Shaw's plays but had been flatly turned down. It seems remarkable that Pascal, who had only seven shillings in his pocket when he went to see the playwright, managed to obtain permission to produce the picture; but with Shaw's consent in his hand, he behaved like a millionaire and hired the best available talent in the English theatre and films.

Asquith was chosen as the director, with the complete collaboration of a specially selected team of film-makers. Outstanding among them was David Lean, now a celebrated director in his own right. Lean, whose title at the time was Film Editor, worked in close cooperation with Asquith, first on the script, then in the studio during the shooting of the film, and finally in the cutting room.

The screenplay, which went through at least four revisions, was mainly an elaboration of the stage script. At the suggestion of Asquith, Pascal, and others, Shaw—sometimes reluctantly—added a number of important scenes, which gave the story greater fluidity and cinematic quality. The playwright had no objection to the introduction of a bathroom scene, showing Eliza being scrubbed, so long as it was handled decorously. And he was very much in favor of the teaching scenes, in which the improvement in Eliza's speech would be shown step by step. Lean supplied most of the ideas for the teaching scenes. A professor of phonetics, who served as advisor on the film, gave Asquith the line, "The rain in Spain stays mainly in the plain," but Asquith himself thought up, "In Hertford, Hereford, and Hampshire, hurricanes hardly ever happen." From a Dutch film version of the play, made a year before the English one, they borrowed the idea of having Higgins put marbles into Eliza's mouth as a means of teaching her to speak.

When the question arose as to whether they would include a ballroom scene in which Eliza could be shown being passed off successfully as a lady of quality, they anticipated running into opposition from the playwright. Asquith made a special visit to Shaw's home to propose the inclusion of this suspenseful and "obligatory" scene, but he did not have the courage to confront his formidable host with a direct request. Asquith chatted about music, one of Shaw's favorite subjects, until he got up the nerve to slip in the remark, "Audiences will feel cheated if we omit the ballroom scene." Shaw's immediate response was, "Out of the question!" But Mrs. Shaw, coming to Asquith's rescue, helped to sell her husband on the idea. She visualized Eliza coming up the stairs into the ballroom, with, as she said, "the frozen calm of the sleepwalker." Shaw, taken with the phrase, gave his approval.

Under Shaw's watchful eye, W. P. Lipscomb and Cecil Lewis put together the screen adaptation from which Asquith and Lean worked out a complete shooting script. Asquith then took a room at the Mayfair Hotel, which he used as an office, and there he worked with his assistant director, Edward Baird; his script-girl, Hazel Wilkinson; his editor, David Lean; his cameraman, Harry Stradling, Jr., and the other members of his staff. Using blueprints and models of the sets, Asquith rehearsed the company for ten days in the ballroom of the hotel. This was an unusual procedure in those days, when films were not rehearsed in advance and when many motion picture actors never got to meet other actors in the same picture unless they happened to play a scene together. But the *Pygmalion* company worked in the tradition of the theatre, with a camaraderie exceptional among film companies. From the hotel Asquith moved to the Pinewood Studios, where he shot the picture in less than two months. Such speed would have been out of the question if the company had not been made up of thorough professionals in every department. Though credit for adhering to his standard of providing "nothing but the best" must go to Pascal, his inclination to pass on every foot of film proved irksome. There were ten takes of the Covent Garden sequence, with which the picture opens with concertgoers caught in the rain and passers-by hurrying along the street. Asquith and Lean wanted to use Take Seven; Pascal preferred Take Six, because in it two actresses dressed as nuns could be seen briefly passing under the arches of St. Paul's Church. That, said Pascal, "would be worth £20,000 in Catholic countries." He said it with a laugh, but Take Six was the one that went into the picture

Pascal had a special talent for irritating Miss Hiller. There were differences in their interpretations of her role. Pascal wanted a cruder, earthier Eliza than Miss Hiller was willing to provide. During one scene he said to her in his heavy Hungarian accent, "I want this should be more animal." There were innumerable retakes of the tea-party scene, because Pascal did not consider it "funny" enough. Pascal wanted Miss Hiller to swing her parasol like a tart, but she refused. In this she stuck to her guns, and Asquith seconded her.

It was during the shooting of the tea-party scene that Asquith realized what a great technician Leslie Howard was. In take after take Howard's movements, gestures, and line-readings were precise and unvarying, and yet there was nothing mechanical about them. He appeared to be acting each time with enormous spontaneity and verve.

What has interested Asquith most in the making of a picture is the relationship of the actor to the audience. "People are always objecting to a

From Bernard Shaw.

The stills are wonderful; and Wendy is perfect.

But Higgins is fatally wrong. He should have a topper (cylinder hat) badly in want of brushing, stuck on the back of his head, and a professorial black frock coat and black overcoat, very unvaleted. This is the only way in which he can be made a unique figure in the crowd. And it is this rig-out which should be reproduced in the final scene.

If the scenes are shot it cannot be helped; but it starts Leslie frightfully on the wrong lines.

Letter to Pascal in which Shaw comments on scenes from the film. He was particularly disturbed by the fact that Leslie Howard, who played Higgins, would not be wearing "professorial" garb.

movie that has been made from a play. They call it a photographed play unless you buzz about from set to set and keep everybody moving. But, really, that has nothing to do with it. The important thing is what the actor does to the audience. The dialogue was changed very little from the stage version, and there was a minimum amount of movement of the camera, but what the actors did would have been invisible on the stage. It was so much more intimate and expressive. The camera can do that. It's really a kind of internal movement."

Three different endings were shot for the film. The first followed Shaw's script to the letter. Although none of the film-makers approved of such a cold and realistic conclusion, this version was filmed in case Shaw should object to any other. The second version was a compromise between Shaw's ideas and a happy ending which everyone agreed was not good. The third ending has Higgins listening to an old recording of Eliza's voice, as Eliza enters and continues where the recording leaves off, saying, "I washed my face and 'ands afore I come, I did." Higgins, in a triumphant gesture, pushes his hat over his face. This was the ending that won Shaw's approval and that found its way, along with many other details from the film, into *My Fair Lady*.

Arthur Honegger, the well-known Swiss-French composer, created for the film an original score in an extremely modern idiom. The music was played under the titles and for the montage of scenes in which Eliza was learning to speak properly. In the editing process, while they were working on the music, Pascal suddenly turned to Asquith and said, "Tell Honegger you don't like the music." Asquith replied, "If you want me to support you in your lies, you must give me advance notice." Pascal flew into a rage. "I am a man of honor," he cried, "and I will challenge you." "Swords or pistols?" asked Asquith, and everyone laughed. "You all rolled upon me," said Pascal enigmatically. When the film was released in America a number of alterations were made in it and, it is Asquith's impression, inferior music was substituted for Honegger's, though the original composer received credit for the score. Pascal's scrutiny of every detail in the film is typified by his comment on a parrot used in one scene: "The parrot is too heavy in the body."

"The enormous tension generated during the making of this film," said Asquith, "was not caused by conflicting personalities, but by the excruciatingly long hours everyone worked." In 1938 the film industry was much less highly organized and unionized than it is today; there were no strict lines of demarcation among categories of workers and no questions of rights or privileges, restricted tasks, or overtime. Working on a film in those days was like participating in a joint venture with a group of friends. The atmosphere was informal and suggestions were freely offered, discussed, tried out, and accepted or rejected.

In a brief interview with Edward Baird, the film's assistant director, it was learned that that functionary's tasks were many and varied. Baird not only sat in on script conferences, but lent a hand to actors, designers, and technicians, and even accompanied Asquith and Pascal to St. Paul's and to other sites in London in search of authentic locations and backgrounds. "The production of Pygmalion went so well from the very beginning," said Baird, "that everyone was sure the picture would be a success. A great deal of this optimism was, of course, a reflection of Shaw's remarkable personality. Just being connected in a creative effort with the great playwright lent a special aura to the venture. Shortly before Pygmalion was released, Shaw went out to the studio to be filmed making a brief speech, which would serve as a prologue to the picture. He rehearsed his walk and his talk several times but, just as the filming began, the air-raid warning sounded, and everyone was ordered to go to the shelter in the basement. Shaw refused to budge, so the crew went on and completed the job."

Anthony Asquith does not believe in making a picture slanted toward a special audience. "I believe passionately," he said, "that for a film to have a wide appeal, it must have its roots somewhere in its own native soil. Otherwise, it will appeal to no one. The intensely British character of its wit and style undoubtedly helped to account for the universal success of Pygmalion."

The Script Girl

Interview with Hazel Wilkinson

Hazel Wilkinson served as the continuity, or script, girl for the film version of Pygmalion.

"When a picture is released," said Miss Wilkinson, "everything seen on the screen looks as if it happened naturally with a camera standing by just

On the *Pygmalion* set at Pinewood Studios, London 1938. Seated far left, Gabriel Pascal, the producer; next to him, the script-girl Hazel Wilkinson; at the camera, Harry Stradling, Jr., who shot *My Fair Lady* for Warner Brothers in 1963; seated center, legs crossed, Anthony Asquith, the director, his attention focussed on Wendy Hiller (Eliza) and Leslie Howard (Higgins) in soft felt hat and tweeds. British National Film Archive.

grinding away. But the fact is that a film is not shot in absolute sequence. For various reasons, later scenes may be done before earlier ones, and close-up, medium, and long shots of the same action may be taken at different times. But when all the little pieces of film are put together in proper order, everything in the scene has to match, and it is the continuity girl's job to see that it does."

Two prime requisites for a continuity girl are an all-seeing eye and an infallible memory. When the set is ready for use, every detail of furniture, props, and lighting must be noted in the script, as well as the positions, clothing, accessories, and even the mood of the actors. Any set or scene that had been shot before would have to be scrutinized down to the last detail before work could proceed' on it. If an actor was smoking a cigarette in a long shot, the script girl would have to note the exact length of the cigarette, so that it would match up in the close-up that might be shot several days or weeks later. Or an actor, first seen going through a doorway and later coming out the other side (known as a reverse-angle shot which requires two separate camera setups), must be wearing the same clothes, carrying the same objects, and moving at the same pace. That was the way it was done in 1938; today a script girl need not rely on a photographic memory or laborious notes. She just steps in at the end of each scene with a Polaroid camera and makes visual records to which she may later refer.

The conditions under which films are made are always hectic. At every moment the actors are surrounded by a small army of shirt-sleeved technicians coping with lights, cameras, properties, hairdressing, wardrobe, and microphones. And one of the busiest workers in this crew is the script girl. To make it easier for her to get through the maze of wires, pipes, and equipment, Miss Wilkinson wore gray flannel slacks and something like a man's coverall. She was never parted from her stop-watch, pencil, and clip-board, which she needed for her endless noting and checking. Film-making is plagued with innumerable interruptions and retakes and long waits between scenes for new setups and technical checking, about which the actors complain bitterly. To Miss Wilkinson, however, these intervals were a godsend, because they gave her an opportunity to dart to her typewriter and make a record of the work just completed, to organize her notes for the coming scene, and, before it was shot, to pass on it for accuracy, according to what had gone before. Once, when everything was ready for a close-up, Miss Wilkinson recalled, she sent Leslie Howard to change his suit and later called out, "Pipe in the *left* side of your mouth, please!"

At the end of each long day at the studio, Miss Wilkinson would go home and complete the log of all that had been done in readiness for the next day's work, which began usually at eight in the morning. She earned what in pre-World War II England was considered exceedingly high pay, particularly for a woman: ten pounds (about fifty dollars) a week. She found the job itself fascinating.

Each scene, whether long shot or close-up, had a ritualistic beginning. The Assistant Director would call out, "Clear the set!" and after it was cleared of workmen, "Bell, please!" This meant silence, but just to reinforce it, "Quiet, everyone!" "Camera" and the film would start to roll, "Shot seven hundred and eight." A boy would hold up a clap-board, showing this number, and give it a loud clap, so that the number would be recorded both on the film and on the sound track. Then the Assistant Director would call out, "Action!" And possibly for the sixth time Miss Wendy Hiller would step forward through a door, so that her feet would land exactly on two small strips of wood nailed to the floor (the measured distance necessary for the camera and microphone); she would gaze up toward where Leslie Howard's voice was supposed to be coming from (actually someone else spoke his lines since they would not be heard in this scene), after which she would say, "Buy it yourself," smile, turn sharply on her heels and walk away. Anthony Asquith would call "Cut!" And that is a close-up.

At the word "cut," the utter silence during the "shooting" is immediately broken by a terriffic din—carpenters hammering on nearby sets, the dolly—the rolling platform on which the camera is mounted—being shoved about by several men, carpet-sweepers cleaning up a patch of floor for the next shot; the director's and stars' canvas chairs, each with his name painted on it, being moved wherever the next scene is, and endless electric power cables being tugged and pulled into position, where they lie tangled like pythons. The hubbub goes on more or less incessantly until the silence bell rings and

A scene from the 1938 film (shot specifically to test Eliza's make-up), Eliza (Wendy Hiller) at home in her little bedroom in Angel Court. British National Film Archive.

everyone is warned "Settle down now, please!" Even then, a girl darts forward with a comb to tweak up Miss Hiller's hair under her hat, while the make-up man touches her mouth with a brush dipped in liquid lipstick.

The set representing Mrs. Higgins' drawing room was beautifully furnished and, according to Miss Wilkinson, absolutely authentic, for all the furniture, china, pictures, and even the real Aubusson carpet, had been borrowed from a house in Portland Place. Here was shot the famous tea-party scene, with Marie Löhr, a very popular actress, playing Mrs. Higgins, the "mother" of Leslie Howard. For the film Miss Löhr wore a white wig and in this scene a lovely gray dress, copied exactly by Handley-Seymour from one they had made for her mother to wear at Marie Löhr's own wedding in 1912. So attached did she become to the dress that when she finished her part in the film, Pascal gave it to her as a souvenir, instead of sending it to the studio wardrobe with the other costumes. In the film Miss Löhr also wore her mother's lace shawl and her own jewelry and sable cape, all of which had to be insured for a very large sum.

One day during the making of the film, Miss Wilkinson recalled, someone discovered it was Leslie Howard's birthday. He was a favorite with everyone, and it was agreed they would give him a surprise party on the set. Anthony Asquith, all the members of the cast, the technicians, their crew, and the grips (stagehands) were in on the conspiracy. It was prearranged that they would shoot a close-up of Howard in a scene with Marie Löhr and that during the second retake, the silence would suddenly be broken by a violent altercation in the anteroom of the set. Everything went off as planned. When Anthony Asquith furiously shouted, "Cut!", Leslie Howard fell into the trap at once and leaped up, saying, "It's really *disgraceful,* ruining a shot like this!" He strode across to the double doors and threw them open, to confront a crowd of smiling faces, a lighted birthday cake, huge placards reading "Many Happy Returns," and, most surprising of all, a present subscribed for by the entire studio, from the call-boy up. The present was the painting by Dorothea Sharp that hung over the mantelpiece in the drawing-room set. During the making of the film, Howard had admired the picture several times. In his speech of thanks, he said that he had never worked with such a congenial group of people.

Three endings to the film were actually shot, and the "rushes" (the unedited film) were studied and discussed in the studio projection room before the final decision was made.

Scott Sunderland, the actor who played Colonel Pickering, was a friend of Bernard Shaw's and had appeared in many of his plays. *Pygmalion* was his first motion picture, and it was amusing to hear him say, "I hate being photographed and, to make it worse, they've made me grow a moustache and wear my hair long." Miss Wilkinson's eyes twinkled. "Today that would be no cause for complaint."

Eliza on the Screen

Interview with Wendy Hiller

Wendy Hiller began her career in the theatre as assistant stage manager and then as an actress with the Manchester Repertory Company in England, but first attracted attention when she appeared in the leading part in *Love on the Dole* in 1935. This play was adapted by Ronald Gow (who later married Miss Hiller) and Walter Greenwood, from the latter's novel of the same name, and proved to be a huge success in both London and New York. George Bernard Shaw attended a performance of the play in New York, was impressed by Miss Hiller's work, particularly by her expert handling of a Lancashire dialect, and invited her to appear the following season at the Malvern Festival (England). This annual drama festival had been founded several years before by Sir Barry Jackson and was devoted most notably to the works of Shaw. Miss Hiller was seen, accordingly, at Malvern in the title role in *St. Joan* and as Eliza in *Pygmalion*; for both characterizations she won high praise from the critics. In the cast of *Pygmalion,* along with the twenty-one-year-old actress, were Ernest Thesiger as Higgins, Cecil Trouncer as Pickering, and Elspeth March as Mrs. Higgins. It was 1936, and by that year the expletive "bloody" was in general use and had practically lost its force, but when Miss Hiller uttered the word on stage, the audience broke up and screamed with laughter. As a young performer, she had had no ex-

Professor Higgins (Leslie Howard) threatens a defiant Eliza (Wendy Hiller) when she suggests that she can earn a living as a teacher of speech. Scene from the 1938 film. British National Film Archive.

perience in coping with such a prolonged outburst, but kept a straight face and stayed in character until the uproar subsided.

Shaw was delighted with Wendy Hiller's acting and became her staunch supporter. He suggested to Gabriel Pascal, who was just then planning a film production of *Pygmalion,* that she be offered the part of Eliza. Reluctantly, Pascal asked her to take a screen test, for which she went to the MGM studios in London. When she arrived there, she discovered to her amazement that half the young actresses in town were in competition with her. Up to that time she had appeared in only one film, a not very distinguished one, and was virtually unknown in motion picture circles. Pascal, who was having trouble securing financial backing for the picture, hesitated to hire her because he could raise no money on the strength of her name. But Shaw insisted she be given the part. In an interview published later, Pascal claimed that he had discovered Miss Hiller at the Malvern Festival and would use her in many films; he said of her in broken English, "I have a sensation."

Very soon after they went into production, Miss Hiller and Pascal ceased to be on speaking terms; the incompatibility of their personalities was aggravated by the producer's insistence that the young actress sign a long-term, personal contract with him, which she refused to do. With Shaw, however, Miss Hiller was on ever friendlier terms. "He was the most charming man in the world," she recalled. "Of course, I was in awe of him at first. But he immediately put me at my ease—so much so that I could go to him and discuss certain scenes I had to do which I thought were unplayable. I was even bold enough to advise him to rewrite them. Imagine!" Shaw seldom appeared on the set during the filming of his plays but sent frequent letters to her and to Pascal. After one dispute Shaw wrote Pascal: "We must not quarrel with Wendy, because she has a good business head on her shoulders, or else has a good adviser. I should do the same in her place." Miss Hiller said, "He would often come to the rehearsals of his plays, though. He was the greatest conversationalist. And he had the most beautiful voice—rather high and lyric, with a soft Dublin accent he always kept."

In the film version of *Pygmalion,* there were such expert players as Leslie Howard, Wilfrid Lawson, Marie Löhr, and Esmé Percy; the company rehearsed for a week in the ballroom of the Mayfair Hotel in London and then moved to the Pinewood Studios, where the picture was shot in its entirety in eight weeks. Miss Hiller was paid £70 (about $350) a week and earned a total of $3500 for her work in the picture. Leslie Howard, who played Henry Higgins, had more film experience than anyone else connected with the venture and was billed as codirector with Anthony Asquith; but, according to Miss Hiller, Asquith actually directed the picture. Asquith did not do very much work with her on the role of Eliza, however, believing that since she had already played the part, she had mastered it. The truth of the matter was that at Malvern she had had only six regular rehearsals and the dress rehearsal, which Shaw had attended. And though her performance had been "set" for the stage, she felt at a distinct disadvantage in recreating the role on the screen because she had no film technique to draw on. She was forced to learn as she went along and do much of the work on her own. "My husband and I were living in Bloomsbury," she recalled, "and we had a Cockney servant. I copied her accent for the film."

Miss Hiller's youth and inexperience not only made her feel insecure on the set, but colored her relations with the other members of the company. She was overawed by most of her colleagues, who were expert at their jobs and well known for their work on the stage and screen. She and Leslie Howard were polite to each other during their scenes but were not on very friendly terms. She got through the film, she said, only because she knew that Shaw was behind her. He had confidence in her and that gave her confidence in herself. Yet despite this fact she worried and fretted during the making of the film and felt very much alone. She found it an unpleasant experience and was glad when it was over.

It is Miss Hiller's opinion that "it is much easier to give an excellent performance on the screen than on the stage, because in the films a scene may be done over and over until you get it just right, and there is also the help given by make-up artists, lighting and sound technicians, cameraman, cutters, and editors. On the stage the actor has much more independence and responsibility; it is his job to work for perfection in his performance, for regardless of the most blatant errors, they cannot bring the curtain down. Film-making is the director's, not the serious actor's, idea of heaven." Even after turning in many brilliant screen performances and winning an Academy Award, Miss Hiller said, "I still like the theatre best. The camera always frightens me, and it's so exhausting to be frightened all the time; but occasionally I'm willing to be frightened for a consideration."

During the filming of *Pygmalion,* Anthony Asquith was most friendly and encouraging to Miss Hiller. "He was extremely sensitive, aware of the actors' needs, and most helpful," she said. "He gave the actor every opportunity to shine. As the son of one of England's prime ministers, he knew from personal experience the world of high society which is so important in the film." Mr. Gow, Miss Hiller's husband, who often visited the studio during the making of the film, and who was present at the interview with his wife, recalled that Asquith, while directing the ballroom scene, wore long white gloves and waved his arms about like a ballet master or musical conductor.

Though the film was turned out in record time, everyone concerned with it worked with such concentration and dedication that no detail was overlooked and no effort spared. A scene showing Eliza in her sleazy, slum bedroom, for instance, was not used in the film but was shot solely to test her "gutter-snipe" make-up.

Pascal wished to add several bits of comic business to Mrs. Higgins' tea-party scene, in order to make it funnier, but Miss Hiller insisted that they play it exactly as it had been written. Having done it on the stage and heard the uproarious response of the audience, she knew that it worked and that the comedy in the scene arises not from the actions of the characters but from their reactions to Eliza's speech and behavior. The "improvements," consequently, were omitted.

The ending of the picture, as was to be expected, occasioned some difficulties. The Malvern Festival production had adhered strictly to Shaw's script: Eliza swept grandly out of the room, and Higgins announced mirthfully that she would marry Freddy. The film, as originally shot, retained that ending. But one day Miss Hiller received a phone call and was asked to come in for several days of retakes. When she got to the studio, she discovered that they had stuck up a corner of the professor's laboratory and the doorway leading into it. In this setting Higgins is sunk in a deep easy chair, listening to an early recording of Eliza's voice; Eliza enters and continues the speech from memory; seeing that she has returned, Higgins relaxes and, with a self-satisfied smile, pushes his hat over his eyes—he has won! The film was released with the new ending as a concession to the romantic tastes of the movie-going public.

Alterations are made in films for various and strange reasons. One retake involved Esmé Percy in the role of Nepommuck (Karpathy), the speech expert, who, for the purpose of getting laughs, had been made to speak with a stammer and a foreign accent. When it was realized that King George VI stammered, Percy's scenes were reshot without the speech defect, in order to avoid giving offense. The foreign accent remained.

Miss Hiller recalled still another incident that occurred during the retakes, which showed the influence on the film of "current events." She was then in the early stages of pregnancy, and they were redoing Eliza's arrival at the ball. Beautifully gowned and with enormous dignity, she entered the ballroom—the cameras grinding away—when suddenly her eyes went glassy with morning sickness, and she fainted. The faint was cut, but the glassy look of "fear" was kept in.

After the picture was released, Miss Hiller had invitations, at the rate of one a week, to go to Hollywood, but she had just had her first child, and World War II had begun. She was not to go to Hollywood for many years, but Eliza had already made her a star. In her next screen appearance she played the title role in Pascal's production of Shaw's *Major Barbara*.

Henry Higgins in Paris

Interview with Jean Marais

Jean Marais, the French film and stage star, appeared in a theatrical production of *The Infernal Machine* by Jean Cocteau in 1954; also appearing in that play, in the role of the Sphinx, was a young and little-known actress, Jeanne Moreau. "We played together with great harmony," said Marais, "and she proved to be the talented performer whom everybody has come to know.

Scene from Jean Marais' production at the Bouffes-Parisien Theatre, Paris 1955. Marais designed the scenery and costumes, directed and co-produced the play, and acted the part of Henry Higgins. Here he is shown with Jeanne Moreau, who played Eliza. Photograph: Studio Bernand. Courtesy Jean Marais.

I was very much impressed with her and suggested that we team up in another play. I asked her what part especially appealed to her and she said, 'Eliza Doolittle.' " This is not as strange as it may seem, as Miss Moreau had a French father and an English mother; her mother had been a professional dancer, and the young girl was well acquainted with British drama and theatre.

Marais, who had thought for a long time of appearing in *Pygmalion,* decided to produce the play with Miss Moreau acting opposite him. He called upon Claude-André Puget, a well-known playwright, to prepare the French script; Puget turned in an adaptation rather than a straight translation, adding material from the 1938 English film version to the original Shaw text. This, to a certain extent, is what Alan Jay Lerner was doing, at that very moment, in creating the book of *My Fair Lady.*

In addition to acting the part of Henry Higgins, Marais, who is a painter as well as a performer, created the scenery and costumes for the play. Although he had hired a director, Marais discovered, soon after they went into production, that neither he nor Miss Moreau was happy with the man's work. "I would say that directing must never be considered more important than any other aspect of a production," Marais commented, "it should serve the author and the actors and must efface itself before them."

Having completed the designs for the sets and costumes, Marais reluctantly assumed the task of directing the play himself; when blocking the scenes in which Higgins appears, he had an actor stand in for him. "It would have given me a much greater feeling of security," said Marais, "if someone like Peter Brook, Laurence Olivier, or Luchino Visconti had directed the play, but I much prefer self-direction to working with someone in whom I have no confidence. A play's success depends, in the long run, upon the script and the actors."

For the décor and costumes, Marais chose English high styles and silhouettes of the period around 1912. In his designs he strove for attractiveness, good taste, and simplicity. There was a great deal of painted, rather than built, scenery; the sets were not overloaded with realistic details, but essential furniture and properties were carefully selected and arranged. Marais did his own lighting. In the opening scene the church was offstage but the flower market was in full view of the audience. In the scene in which Eliza, Higgins, and the Colonel return from the ball, some dialogue and business from the film were introduced into the play. In the closing moments of the play, it was hinted that Mrs. Higgins would have a hand in bringing her son and Eliza together; Marais attempted to suggest that there would eventually be a romance between the two, but the matter was left largely to the audience's imagination.

Marais believes that in casting a play, the very best actors available for each part should be secured, regardless of cost, but his coproducer (who provided some of the financial backing) was not of like mind. Marais wanted Noël Roquevert for the role of Mr. Doolittle and Suzanne Dehelly for the part of Mrs. Pearce; they were strong and seasoned character actors, but their salary demands were high. Marais' partner was willing to pay only half the amounts asked, but Marais said that in order to secure these players, he was willing to pay the other half of their salaries out of his own pocket. When the play proved to be a tremendous success, Marais was not called

Jeanne Moreau as Eliza in the Marais production.

Mr. Doolittle (Noël Roquevert) puts a business proposition to Professor Higgins (Jean Marais) in the French production, 1955. Photograph: George Henri. Courtesy Jean Marais.

upon to make a personal contribution; the actors in question received full salaries out of income from the production.

In the case of Jeanne Moreau, who was not especially known as a comedienne before she appeared in *Pygmalion,* the play amounted to a personal triumph in that it brought her considerable talents to the attention of the Parisian theatre and film worlds. Marais had given much care and consideration to the actress's portrayal of Eliza, concentrating on her make-up and costumes, as well as her characterization. People thought he was very generous in favoring her at every opportunity, but he was actually trying to build her into a star for his own theatre. As it turned out, they never appeared together after that. But her acting of Eliza went a long way in accounting for the play's success.

Shaw's work has never been very well received in Paris, possibly because of inadequate translations but more likely because that writer's special brand of didacticism, with its puritanical slant, does not appeal to the French. *Pygmalion* proved to be an exception, however, for it generated continuous laughter and became an enormous hit. The actors, of course, made no attempt to be "funny" but played it straight; yet the dialogue and action were continually interrupted by the audience's response, and the players had to stop and wait until the laughter subsided before they could go on. Noël Roquevert was excruciatingly funny and got especially big laughs. These vocal reactions on the part of the audience seemed amazing to Marais—at first even a little disconcerting—because as an actor he had specialized in serious and romantic roles and was not accustomed to noisy and explosive interruptions from the house.

Just before going into production (the play opened on January 15, 1955, at the Bouffes-Parisien Théâtre), Marais happened to meet John Gielgud and mentioned that he was going to play Higgins. Gielgud said that he thought Marais was too young for the part. Marais could not agree and looked upon it as a challenge.

"I liked the role of Higgins," he said, "because of the difficulty of interpreting it. When a character is difficult, I put a lot more effort and will into mastering it, and through these efforts I am more likely to succeed than if it were easy. In the acting profession, facility is sterile and merely enables you to mark time. Higgins demands authority and irreproachable diction and voice—qualities that I lacked. I should add that this was the first role for which I did not have to use my 'sensitiveness,' which is perhaps the only true quality that I recognize in myself."

Jean Marais was extremely proud of the fact that many people called his production "very English" in tone and style. He explained the reason for this: his hobby is painting and he pays particular attention to the "national" characteristics of the scenery and costumes he designs for a play. By an interesting coincidence, Sir Johnston Forbes-Robertson, the celebrated English actor who inspired Shaw to create the part of Henry Higgins and who later appeared in *Caesar and Cleopatra* and *The Devil's Disciple,* was well known as a painter and actually preferred painting to acting. Marais, for whom painting would always remain a serious avocation, had also appeared in *Caesar and Cleopatra* and was planning a production of *The Devil's Disciple* in Jean Cocteau's adaptation.

Act I, Scene I of the original Broadway production of *My Fair Lady* with Julie Andrews as Eliza and Rex Harrison as Higgins. Mark Hellinger Theater, New York, 1956. Museum of the City of New York.

Lyrics for *My Fair Lady*

Article by Alan Jay Lerner

It seemed to me, when I graduated from college, that everything that could be said in lyrics had been said. If you were witty, how could you be wittier than Larry Hart? If you were romantic, how could you be more romantic than Oscar Hammerstein? We start off, in any art form, eclectic; but it's an acute problem—how to find an individuality.

I've been writing lyrics, professionally, since 1940. It's only within the last few years that I have begun to feel for myself, that I've come close to finding something that's pretty much my own. It isn't Hammerstein. It isn't Hart. It isn't Porter; it's my own particular vernacular and the first song in *My Fair Lady*, "Why Can't the English," I think, illustrates what I mean.

The first ten minutes of any musical offering should dictate the style of the entire evening: on what level the work is to be accepted critically and emotionally. Loewe and I wanted Professor Henry Higgins to be the first one to sing. We decided he should not be a singer; he should be an actor who sort of spoke some songs. We wanted the audience to know at the beginning of the evening, before they had heard anybody else—this was what they were in for.

Higgins was going to sing and the question was what. There was no situation, so obviously it was to be a character song; it would concern itself with the cornerstones of his personality, his frustrations, his intense interest in the English language. How do you write a comic song of that nature, which is to be spoken, and not have it sound like Coward or Gilbert? We wrote several versions until we finally discovered a key. We didn't write the song first; it was written much later, the result of having solved another problem. We found that if we could write each comedy song based on some emotion—either frustration or anger or disappointment or bitterness—on a definite emotion, we could escape from a humor that came from clever rhymes or from the author's intrusion of himself. It would come out of the antic of the character.

> Look at her—a pris'ner of the gutters;
> Condemned by ev'ry syllable she utters.
> By right she should be taken out and hung
> For the cold-blooded murder of the English tongue!

I can only speak of the second song, "Wouldn't It Be Loverly," with pain because it was obvious that the leading lady was there and she must have a song to establish her. (In a musical play, even with the dialogue of Bernard Shaw, nothing establishes a character as much as a song.) My great frustration was that I couldn't find a climax for the song without going into "someone's head resting on a knee," and there I was back in "Over the Rainbow" and "The Man I Love." I went seven weeks trying to find a solution for it. Finally, I couldn't find a creature comfort that was as climactic as someone's head resting on a knee. So the lyric stayed.

> Someone's head restin' on my knee,
> Warm and tender as he can be,
> Who takes good care of me . . .
> Oh, wouldn't it be loverly?
> Loverly! Loverly!
> Loverly! Loverly!

Every time I hear it, my skin turns a little crabby.

The next song of the play, I think, is a good example of the inter-relationship between composer and lyricist. No lyric writer can ever realize himself or his talents alone; I don't think it's possible for a lyric writer ever to reach his full expression without continuing collaboration with a composer. The knowledge of how a composer thinks and how he creates and how he feels about work is simply of incalculable influence upon a lyric writer and upon his ideas. "With a Little Bit of Luck" was the introduction of the father, Doolittle, and we wanted a character song to establish him.

> The Lord above made liquor for temptation,
> To see if man could turn away from sin.
> The Lord above made liquor for temptation—but
> With a little bit of luck,
> With a little bit of luck,
> When temptation comes you'll give right in!

We decided the type was to be an English music hall song. The reason is indicative of what I mean by knowing the abilities and inclinations of a composer: Loewe does not write jazz. He's Viennese by birth and is more at home in tempo than rhythm.

The song, "I'm an Ordinary Man," went through many, many stages of development. We had a problem with that song; we had a man who was not a singer. How do you write a climax for a man who doesn't sing? Usually a baritone can go up to an F or G—and you're home theatrically. So we inserted his turning on the phonographs, the noise gets louder and louder; we had machines give us the climax which he, with his vocal limitations, could not give us.

The song, "Just You Wait," wherein Eliza Doolittle gives vent to her hatred of and anger at Higgins, was the song that told us how to write the show.

> Just you wait, 'enry 'iggins, just you wait!
> You'll be sorry but your tears'll be too late!
> You'll be broke and I'll have money;
> Will I help you? Don't be funny!
> Just you wait, 'enry 'iggins, just you wait!

We had written eight songs before we wrote that one, and none of them seemed right. It was after writing "Just You Wait" that we threw out all the others and started over, because it was there that we suddenly saw the value, the whole kind of freshness that seemed to nail down an emotional attitude, an emotional point of view.

I don't know how to talk about "The Rain in Spain" because we had no idea what its effect would be. We wrote it in about ten minutes. We're very slow workers; I don't know what happened. I said one day, "We'd better write something where they scream with joy about the Rain in Spain." Fritz sat down and wrote it in a very few minutes.

> By George, she's got it!
> By George, she's got it!
> Now once again, where does it rain?

We thought it would be amusing if Higgins did a little Spanish fandango—and that was the end of it. I think it's quite obvious to any student that it's not a great piece of music, nor a great lyric. It's just a pure, simple piece of business that seems to come out of Eliza's longing. Certainly it's nothing anybody should examine twice.

"I Could Have Danced All Night" was an unsolvable problem; the reasons were manifold. One was a dramatic one. It was impossible for

Julie Andrews and Rex Harrison dance a tango to "The Rain in Spain" (Act I, Scene 5) in the New York production, 1956. Museum of the City of New York.

Higgins to love Eliza; for them to admit to themselves that they felt anything emotional about each other. At the same time, you have to have a ballad in a musical and it seemed like the place for it; but every song we wrote—we wrote seven—said too much. Somehow they seemed to indicate that Eliza was in love with Higgins or that she felt something for him. Finally, we were only able to write the song when we were near the end of the whole work itself and we had written "I've Grown Accustomed to Her

Face." We said, "There's the ballad. We don't have to worry about a ballad. We'll just go back and write a happy song."

> I could have danced all night!
> I could have danced all night!
> And still have begged for more.
> I could have spread my wings
> And done a thousand things
> I've never done before.

Writing happy songs is the thing I care least about doing. I'm embarrassed by that lyric. Although I think the first half of it is very good, it's not something I'm proud of. It's not a lyric I enjoy listening to in the theatre. I said to Loewe, "Can't we make it look a little more interesting? We'll put the servants in and give it some kind of life other than a girl being ecstatically happy."

The "Ascot Gavotte" is a first-rate example of how a humorous song is impossible without humorous music.

> Ev'ry duke and earl and peer is here.
> Ev'ry one who should be here is here.
> What a smashing, positively dashing
> Spectacle: the Ascot op'ning day.

It's not enough to be able to write a charming little gavotte. It has to be a very good gavotte; it has to be very good music. An inconsequential piece of music will detract from a song as a whole, no matter how good the lyric may be. It's very hard—to the point of impossibility—for a lyric writer ever to reach any sort of self-fruition without a working knowledge of music. It might be an intuitive knowledge of music. It might be a trained knowledge. I've never known a great lyric writer who wasn't intensely musical, who didn't have decided ideas about form—not only in terms of lyrics, but of music as well.

[One of the most popular songs in the show, "On the Street Where You Live," a ballad sung by Freddy, followed the Ascot Gavotte scene.]

I said to Fritz one day, "Let's write a sort of Hyde Park *Fledermaus*." He went right to the piano and wrote "You Did It."

> Tonight, old man, you did it!
> You did it! You did it!
> You said that you would do it,
> And indeed you did.

Not one of the people on stage could really sing, so we tried to write it in such a way that when you were about to throw something at one for not being able to sing, you were distracted by another who couldn't sing either. As a matter of fact, when we were on the road we discovered that Pickering was singing too long and you couldn't stand it any more. So we increased the number of servants. The whole thing is a sort of ruse to prevent the audience from realizing that a lot of very bad singing is going on.

The next song, "Show Me," is a clear example of searching high and low for an emotional attitude in order to avoid saying something that has been said before. We have the obvious place where girl and boy have broken up, the obvious place for a song that always appears in the second act of a musical—glad to be unhappy. We wrote a song called "Over Your Head." No matter how we approached the music and lyrics, it came out full of self-pity and seemed wrong for the character. It bore to me no indication of a proud Cockney girl. We examined the emotion very carefully; we examined it from every conceivable side. We finally arrived at the idea of her turning her bitterness and heartbreak into anger against Freddy.

> Never do I ever want to hear another word.
> There isn't one I haven't heard.
> Here we are together in what ought to be a dream;
> Say one more word and I'll scream!

"Get Me to the Church on Time" was needed for many reasons. When you have thirty people standing in the wings, somewhere in the middle of the second act—they ought to come on stage and sing; after two intimate scenes, we felt the need for splash and color; we felt the need for Doolittle underscoring his getting married. The best way by which Fritz could capture that kind of gaiety was the music hall song.

> I'm getting married in the morning!
> Ding dong! The bells are gonna chime.
> Pull out the stopper!
> Let's have a whopper!
> But get me to the church on time!

It has no modern rhythm but it has real vitality. From my point of view, it's too heavily rhymed and nothing of which to be proud.

We discovered one day that Higgins became lost in the second act; there was so much music in which he did not participate. I got the idea of "Why Can't a Woman Be More Like a Man" ["A Hymn to Him."] and went home to work on it. It became obvious that what Higgins really wanted was a friend. He wanted Eliza, but he wanted her to behave as a friend because he didn't understand the emotional pressure of an intimate relationship.

> Yes. Why can't a woman be more like a man?
> Men are so honest, so thoroughly square;
> Eternally noble, historically fair;
> Who when you win will always give your back a pat.
> Why can't a woman be like that?

It was a bore. It didn't express anything. It wasn't amusing. Finally, the idea emerged of doing it in $\frac{6}{8}$ tempo, a "manly" tempo; the whole song came to life and the exact same lyrics became effective.

[Next came the song in which Eliza defies Higgins and asserts her independence: "Without You."]

The last song, "I've Grown Accustomed to Her Face," is my favorite. Years ago, Maxwell Anderson wrote a book called *Off Broadway* and for those students interested in writing for the musical theatre, I certainly recommend it. He discusses what he calls the "recognition scene," that scene wherein the hero or heroine recognizes the nature of his problem, be it external or internal, and either conquers it or is conquered by it. We felt that Higgins must have a recognition scene in which he recognizes the nature of his problem, albeit obliquely and slightly astigmatically.

> Damn! Damn! Damn! Damn!
> I've grown accustomed to her face!
> She almost makes the day begin.
> I've grown accustomed to the tune
> She whistles night and noon.
> Her smiles, her frowns,
> Her ups, her downs
> Are second nature to me now;
> Like breathing out and breathing in.
> I was serenely independent and content before we met;
> Surely I could always be that way again—and yet
> I've grown accustomed to her looks,
> Accustomed to her voice,
> Accustomed to her face.

The only difference is—he neither conquers it nor is conquered by it.
"Eliza? Where the devil are my slippers?"

Orchestrating Frederick Loewe's Music

Interview with Philip J. Lang

Philip J. Lang, who with Robert Russell Bennett orchestrated Frederick Loewe's music for *My Fair Lady,* considers the orchestrator's task a highly specialized and complex one and of great importance to the success of a musical show. It is the orchestrator's job to adapt and arrange the composer's music for each instrument in the orchestra and for the voices of the singers, according to the particular style of the play and the special vocal requirements of the performer. A serious composer prepares his own orchestrations when he writes for the concert hall, but if he should compose the music for a Broadway show, as Leonard Bernstein did for *West Side Story,* he may delegate that complicated and time-consuming process to a professional orchestrator.

The orchestrator is engaged by the producer of the show, usually with the advice and consent of the composer, with whom he will work very closely. A rapport must be established between the orchestrator and the composer very early in their association; their musical ideas must mesh, and they must be able to work agreeably together under the pressures generated during the preparation of the play.

The orchestrator's job begins when the composer gives him a "piano copy" of the music, which indicates melodies and harmonies, and the lyrics

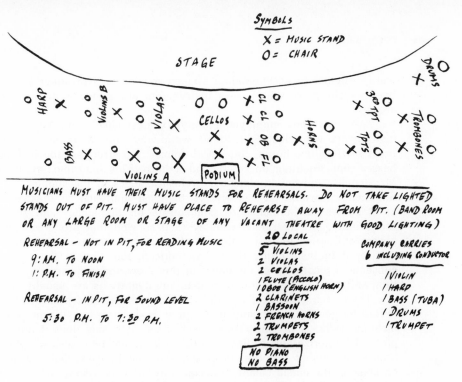

Seating arrangement for members of the *My Fair Lady* orchestra; directions to the players; rehearsal schedule; and two lists of musicians required: six travel with the show, twenty are hired in the city where the play is performed. Theatre Collection, New York Public Library.

to the songs. Very soon a meeting takes place between the orchestrator, the composer, the lyricist, the book writer, and the dance arranger; at this meeting musical plans are developed in detail. The composer usually plays the music and sings the songs while the book writer or lyricist (Alan Jay Lerner served in both capacities for *My Fair Lady*) gives the orchestrator a synopsis of each scene in which music or a song is to be used. They discuss such things as the over-all style of the music, the mood, and the general tempo. It is possible to do something gimmicky like setting an Elizabethan story to rock-and-roll music, but if the composer wants to achieve a feeling of authenticity, the locale of the story and the period in which it is set must be taken into consideration. For *My Fair Lady*, Frederick Loewe wanted to recreate the musical sound heard in London in the opening years of the twentieth century. It was necessary, therefore, to determine the number and kind of instruments in the orchestra that would produce the desired sound. The specific period and place in Shaw's play seemed to demand classical instrumentation. That meant that the orchestra would not include such identifiably modern instruments as saxophones, electronic organ or guitar, or a large brass section. It would be, in effect, a reduced symphony orchestra. The size of the orchestra, of course, sets certain limitations on the work of the orchestrator. In New York City, according to the rules of the musicians' union, a musical show may not employ fewer than twenty-five players; it may, however, employ more. Most of the theatres in New York that house musicals were built by the Shuberts for the presentation of their operettas, and most orchestra pits were designed to accommodate sixteen musicians. Nowadays as many as twenty-eight players and their instruments are crowded into these small areas.

"*My Fair Lady* employed twenty-six musicians," said Mr. Lang. "The instruments we selected included woodwinds (no doubling), a moderate brass section, two horns, and one drummer; the string section included two basses (one doubling on tuba), and a harp. This instrumentation enabled Mr. Bennett and me to state our orchestral ideas in the simplest of terms. Simplicity, I would say, is always the best approach to theatre scoring, as it allows the audience to concentrate on the singer and the action. Incidentally, our instrumentation worked so well that producers and composers still refer to it as "the *My Fair Lady* orchestra" and quite often ask for it in their productions. I've noticed, too, that in the innumerable subsequent recordings of the music of this show, the basic style of orchestration, and even many of the accompanying figurations are usually retained."

There is a great deal of other information that the orchestrator needs before he goes to work, and much of it is discussed at the preproduction meeting. What is the purpose of each piece of music: does it advance the plot, characterize, or supply a bridge between two scenes? During an orchestral number (for the Ascot scene or the Embassy ball), what action on stage is the music meant to accompany? If it is a song, who sings it—a man, a woman, a trio, the chorus? Concerning the songs, there is a particularly detailed discussion as to how each is to be introduced and how each is to end; that is, how the singer will work into the song and how it will connect with what follows. What is avoided at all costs is to stop the story dead in its tracks and allow the singer or chorus to start the song cold.

"Mr. Bennett provided a remarkably brilliant beginning for 'The Rain in Spain,'" said Mr. Lang. "It was so subtle that the audience was hardly aware that Eliza had begun to sing. The opening bars of the song were hesitant and tentative, a perfect meld of music and dramatic action. It began as an unobtrusive underscoring of the dialogue and built up into the number as if on a wave of emotion. The value of the underscoring is that it gives the singer the key. Another type of opening is the 'talk start,' in which the first line of the song is spoken as part of the dialogue and then is repeated and sung.

"The way a song ends is just as important as the way it begins. Sometimes it is orchestrated for an 'applause ending'—it builds to a crescendo that compels a response from the audience. The other extreme is the 'down, or quiet ending,' which allows the play to continue without the interruption of applause; this type of ending helps to preserve the mood and the tension of the story. The 'applause' ending is often used to bring a scene to a close, or to bring the curtain down; the 'down' ending serves to tie one scene to the next in conjunction with a musical or visual 'bridge.' Between these two extreme types of endings, there are many variations; the composer and the play's director make the basic decisions as to how each number is to begin and end."

It was during the preproduction meetings that the score for *My Fair Lady* was divided between the two orchestrators. Philip Lang was to do the arrangements for the following numbers: "With a Little Bit of Luck" (for Doolittle and his Friends), "The Ascot Gavotte" (for chorus and orches-

Scene at Ascot in the revival of *My Fair Lady* at the New York City Center Theatre, June 1968. Courtesy New York City Center.

tra), "On the Street Where You Live" (for Freddy), "The Embassy Waltz" (for the orchestra), "Get Me to the Church on Time" (for Doolittle, Friends, and chorus), and "Without You" (for Higgins and Eliza); Robert Russell Bennett scored the other numbers.

Certain numbers in the play are specially adapted by a dance arranger for the use of the choreographer; these arrangements are then incorporated into the score by the orchestrator. The music for the opening number of *My Fair Lady,* a dance routine done by the Three Buskers, was set by Trude Rittman, the dance arranger for the show. It should be noted that the musical conductor often makes valuable suggestions concerning the orchestrations.

There is a five-week rehearsal period for New York musicals. "The rehearsals for *My Fair Lady* were exciting," said Lang, "because there was an unusually high degree of support in the music department. Frederick Loewe and Alan Lerner were always present, explicit, and co-operative.

Franz Allers, our musical conductor; Trude Rittman, who arranged the dance and incidental music; and Robert Russell Bennett and I quickly reached an understanding and eagerly attacked our respective assignments."

During rehearsals the music is played on the piano, and the performers learn their songs from the piano parts. At this time the performer becomes another element of concern to the orchestrator: What is the singer's best key? This will establish the key for the arrangement of his particular songs. What is the quality of the singer's voice? The orchestration of the song must be tailored to the personal vocal style and range of a Julie Andrews, a Rex Harrison, or a Stanley Holloway. What sort of character does the singer represent, what will he be wearing, what will he be doing, and so on. "The suggestion of bawdiness in the music of 'Get Me to the Church on Time,'" said Mr. Lang, "was produced by the use of the tuba, with street band figurations in the woodwind and brass. That setting helped to give the number the earthiness and coarseness the composer desired. On the other hand, Freddy's ballad, 'On the Street Where You Live,' had a very warm and romantic flavor achieved largely with strings and a slow and languorous tempo."

The book writer and the director assume a greater command over the production during the rehearsal period when they work out the routine for each scene, that is, the form each musical number will take in performance. Although a song usually has thirty-two bars in the chorus (plus a verse, or introduction), the director may wish to elaborate it by interjecting some action and additional music. Moss Hart and the writers decided to develop the song "I Could Have Danced All Night" into an authentic "production number" by having Julie Andrews sing five choruses interspersed with dramatic action and musical interludes sung by the servants.

While the rehearsals are in progress, the orchestrator works at home on two or three numbers at a time. He manages, however, to attend the practice sessions several times a week; he listens, watches carefully, asks questions—particularly about the numbers he is working on—and his observations and reactions help to spark the musical ideas that find expression in the score. The actual writing is done on a large sheet of music paper, perhaps 12 by 16 inches in size, which will fit on the conductor's stand. Down the left side of the paper are listed the various instruments in the orchestra (flute, trombone, 1st violin, etc.), and beside each is a musical staff on which the orchestrator writes the part for that instrument. This is called an orchestral score. The score, when completed, is turned over to a copyist, who transcribes the separate parts for each musician.

At the end of its five weeks of rehearsal, the show goes out of town— to Boston, let us say—for its tryout. On the final Sunday of the rehearsal period, the cast usually remains in New York and continues to work, while the orchestrator and some of the musicians leave for Boston; other musicians, to make up the full complement of the orchestra, are hired locally. On Monday morning, in a rehearsal hall in Boston, the members of the orchestra gather and have a reading (playing) of the entire orchestral score. By Tuesday afternoon the entire company has arrived, and another reading takes place, with everyone present. From this point on, the performers work with the full orchestra.

"Orchestrations sometimes undergo extensive changes during the tryout period," said Mr. Lang, "but as I recall we did very little rewriting on the orchestrations for *My Fair Lady*. A piece of underscoring was added to highlight Eliza's appearance in her ball gown at the top of the stairs in Higgins' study. The ball music was altered, mostly cut, and the original entr'acte music expanded. So little rewriting was necessary partly because of the care we took in the preparation of the orchestrations but mainly because of the close co-operation of the authors and producer during the preproduction planning stage."

Philip Lang studied orchestration at Ithaca College, where he received his advanced musical education. After serving in the United States Army during World War II, he began his career in the musical theatre by doing the orchestrations for *Billion Dollar Baby*, a play which was not a success but which brought his work to the attention of Rodgers and Hammerstein, who were just then producing Irving Berlin's *Annie Get Your Gun* (1946). Lang was invited to provide the orchestrations for that show, which proved to be a tremendous hit. Since collaborating on *My Fair Lady*, he has by himself done the orchestrations for *Mame, Hello, Dolly!*, and *George M,* among other plays; and for several films, including *The Night They Raided Minsky's, The Molly Maguires*, and *Hello, Dolly!* with Barbra Streisand.

In discussing his own training, Lang remarked in passing that there is a dearth of orchestrators as well as of musical comedy directors, "possibly because young people do not have the opportunity to gain the necessary experience and possibly because they lack an all-around knowledge of music. These fields can be exciting and lucrative for the person who is adequately prepared."

Designing *My Fair Lady*

by Cecil Beaton

[In 1955 Cecil Beaton, British designer, photographer, and artist, was asked to create the costumes for the stage production of My Fair Lady. He kept a detailed record of the work he did for the stage and screen versions; it was published as a book called Cecil Beaton's 'Fair Lady,' Holt, Rinehart and Winston, Inc., 1964. The following excerpts are published by permission of the author and publisher.]

[London, 1955]

. . . When Fritz Loewe, at Claridge's played and sang to me the first songs he had composed for his musical *Pygmalion* I was immediately under the spell of his extraordinary talent. By this time he was, with hair flying, eyes popping, and whole frame jerking in a state of euphoria, thumping out the rhumba rhythm and singing Alan Lerner's lyrics for 'The Rain in Spain,' I knew nothing in the world would prevent me from working on this show.

At first the producer, Herman Levin, and the Director, Moss Hart, had considered that our venture should be costumed in the period around 1904.

Covent Garden dance scene choreographed by Hanya Holm. One of the exciting production numbers in the first act of *My Fair Lady*. Scenery by Oliver Smith, costumes by Cecil Beaton. Mark Hellinger Theatre, New York 1956. Courtesy ANTA Collection, The Players.

This was the epoch in which all recent musicals had automatically been costumed, no doubt because of the similarity with the present fashion in up-swept hairstyles and tight-fitting bodices which, it was considered, would ingratiate audiences, and portray that 'never never land' with less of a jolt than some less familiar look. But so frantic was my appeal for the re-creation of the world I knew before it disappeared in the first World War, that I was given the reins. 'Just so long as you're sure the girls will look attractive and sexy,' said my friend Herman. When I told Moss of my intention to make Ascot entirely black and white—an idea that had originated with the famous Black Ascot after King Edward's death—he was worried, 'You're sure it won't look like a comic strip?' But, luckily, further fears were kept from me, so that I went to work with the greatest fervour. Never had any theatre assignment given me so much pleasure. Suddenly, a myriad childhood's impressions were paying dividends: haphazard pieces of the jig-saw puzzle of memory suddenly started sorting themselves into place. Remembered, for example, was that, when I was about five years old, Miss Elfie Perry, 'the first actress I had ever met,' had come to dinner wearing a frock of striped silk. Of course that would be perfect for Eliza's last appearance. Madame Triana, an enormous elephant of a woman, had eaten an ice-cream in a marquee at a garden party given by my Aunt Jessie, wearing a dress of grey and apricot: this colour combination I would certainly use. Mrs. Higgins must wear the Malmaison, with circular pink cardboard back-reinforcement, that my mother wore with her grey satin and ostrich feathers at Ascot. Shades of my mother, my Aunt Jessie, shades of my first theatre goddesses—Lily Elsie, Gaby Deslys, and Mrs. Vernon Castle!

[Warner Brothers bought the motion picture rights to *My Fair Lady,* which was filmed in 1963, with Cecil Beaton "in charge of the costumes, sets and the whole of the visual production."]

Friday, 14 September [1962, London]

George Cukor [who directed the film] and Gene Allen [his assistant] were waiting at the main entrance of the Savoy Hotel when I arrived six minutes late for an expedition to hunt for locations. We were to be accompanied by a reasearch photographer, but the photographer was missing.

Without him we started off to prospect in Wimpole Street ('On the Street Where You Live') where my own physician Dr Gottfried lives, at number 75. Many of these houses, with their decorative windows of frosted glass and individual doorways of no accepted style, could certainly have belonged to Professor Higgins. . . . Cukor asked, couldn't we ring any front-door bell and ask if we might come and have a look at their fire-irons?

I decided that Dr Gottfried, who, in the days before he left Vienna, had dealings with theatre and opera artists, would be sympathetic to this sudden intrusion. He was amused and intrigued as he showed us around. . . . So entirely suitable for our purposes did this house appear that we decided to copy it in almost all essentials. Permission was granted to photograph and measure every detail from the servants' basement to attic bedrooms.

Monday, 18 February [1963, Hollywood]

. . . It was difficult to realize that any work was being done as George, Gene and I, lolling around, feet up, talked in a desultory manner. But, in fact, we were going through the script, scene by scene, deciding how to do the ballroom scene, or how to differentiate the houses of Mrs Higgins and her son. 'How would you react to my doing the ballroom in trellis? It was very fashionable in 1912 and would be a welcome relief from the usual gold and cream "Grace Kelly" sets.' Books arrived forthwith from Research, showing Elsie de Wolfe salons and lobbies done in 1910 in the fashionable lattice work. Gene, enthusiastic, produced a ravishing *treillage* room from Schönbrunn.

Wednesday, 20 February

To me it is still quite a shock to watch a movie at ten in the morning; somehow it gives a feeling of guilt to sit in the dark, oblivious of the sun outside. I feel the best part of the day is being squandered; this is so even when I tell myself that this is 'work.' . . . We were watching the old *Pygmalion,* which I'd loved when I saw it twenty years ago. Wendy Hiller's truth and honesty still shine through the years. George was of the opinion that Leslie Howard's performance was too vindictive, alarming and even cruel; Rex Harrison would give the role a sweep of grandeur and the impression of being extraordinarily aristocratic in his attitude to everyone.

Friday, 15 March

With Gene, I went through all the details of the various architectural elements to be incorporated in the Higgins' households: picking cornices, details of panellings, mouldings, balustrades and typical pieces of English *art nouveau* 1910.

It has taken us a month to collect our thoughts in trying to find a style to present Shaw as a film-musical, for this style must be consistent. We must romanticize the exteriors. The buildings will be imperceptibly elongated and painted in exaggerated light-contrasts to create a slightly-heightened effect to the ordinary.

Tuesday, 19 March

The time had now come for Cukor to see the rough drawings from which I will take my designs. After an enormous amount of research the sketches fill a fat book. . . .

When, at last, George thumbed through to the last page he screwed up his face. 'I didn't care for "The Rain in Spain" costume you did for Julie Andrews. We must make Audrey look slightly . . . comic in that scene, as if Mrs Pearce had been out and bought her a dress. . . . She should look clean but not *chic*. . . . Also, at Ascot she should seem somewhat . . . over-powered by her finery. She shouldn't be quite able to . . . carry it off. Try and devise a costume that will work dramatically to accentuate the comic content of the scene.'

Monday, 25 March

In the workrooms, a row of *toiles* of the Ascot costumes were on stands for my inspection and criticism. They left nothing to be desired. Hundreds of yards of materials and trimmings were chosen, and forthwith ordered. . . . When creating the original production in New York, it was impossible to discover a shoemaker who could provide us with ladies' slippers with pointed toes. Likewise, it was difficult to explain that bodices of evening dresses should not necessarily look like jewelled brassieres. Fashion and the Empire line have caught up with us, and make life here much easier.

Thursday, 11 April

I showed George the designs for Gladys Cooper's costumes. We have decided not to make Mrs Higgins into the conventional . . . dowager, but into quite an 'original,' a Fabian, rather an aesthetic intellectual (for, after all, she is the mother of the young Bernard Shaw). To suggest the character is quite a tricky technical problem.

This is, from a costume point of view, a play about three women—Eliza, Mrs Higgins and Mrs Eynsford-Hill. They are surrounded by people who are all dressed as important characters. In this production there are virtually no 'extras' and, with the exception of the tails at the Ball, and the grey frock-coats at Ascot, there are no 'repeats.' Even the men in the cockney scenes are being created as individual characters, whose prototypes are to be found in Phil May, Belcher or photographs of the period. Among the four hundred women at the Ball and at Ascot, there is not one costume that has not been specially designed, or recreated from museum sources, with the care and attention given to a principal's clothes.

The sets, however, seem to take forever. The drawings for the builders are now being made in the Art Department from the two models that were finished two weeks ago. The amount of detail is prodigious, and I am impatient, for one always has the feeling of the ever-oncoming typhoon [when the cameras begin to roll]. We must finish as many sets as possible before the roar starts. . . .

Stanley Holloway, celebrated English music-hall performer, created the role of Alfred Doolittle in both the Broadway production and the film version of *My Fair Lady*. Courtesy Warner Brothers.

Monday, 6 May

Most of the laughs are to be found in the millinery corner. One hat looks like a weather-vane on which half a dozen crows are trying to alight; another is a large chauffeur's cap made of most unsuitable materials, while yet another is just an upturned bucket with a cascade of ostrich feathers. The work girls take off their spectacles and pose in the most outrageous millinery. But this is not merely a fun-fair. These are great artisans whose craft is apparent in so many delicate nuances of understanding and experience. If these hats were made by a heavy hand, they would be vulgar, ugly and impractical.

On Stage 2, Higgins' house is being built. It is a most intricate and ingenious arrangement with the three floors and their staircases built side by side on the sound stage instead of one above the other as in a real house. In spite of the difficulty of the staircases being cut off sharp, half-way up- or downstairs, it now begins to take shape. Many aspects of the transplanted house—the nodes and crannies—are so familiar to me that I feel that Dr Gottfried will materialize at any minute to give me an injection.

Friday, 17 May

Work this morning was to take place in Cukor's garden, where Alan [Lerner] would give us an outline for the new beginning of the picture. . . .

Scenes were juggled about, but in the new form everything seemed to fit better. There was great improvement on the former treatment for introducing Doolittle, and for doing away with a reprise of 'With a Little Bit of Luck.' 'What do we have during the overture, and for the titles?' asked Cukor. Looking at the garden bed in front of him, Alan said: 'I'd like flowers.' I saw myself enthusiastically planning a long panning shot of flowers in baskets, as in the market: thickly-packed country flowers, and spring flowers, peonies, lilacs, daisies. These would gradually melt into the vivid patterns of the ladies' cloaks as they are leaving the foyer of the Opera, and over all these effects the 'credits' will be written.

Tuesday, 11 June

I started to design Audrey's last act dress, but when George saw the sketch he suggested something more waspish and stylish. I thought a lyric note was needed. Now I must think again. *Later:* I can't think of anything that suits the mood.

Tuesday, 25 June

. . . Half-a-dozen people wanted me at the same time. . . . Gene appeared with a rough draft of a portrait of Gladys Cooper, done in pre-Raphaelite style, for correction. 'Make the dove, a lily. Make the hair fuller. Paint the whole thing more meticulously—less impressionistic.' He showed me some blueprints for the Embassy staircase. 'Make the tops of the panels semicircular—not squashed.' Bob Richards arrived from Men's Wardrobe with samples for Rex's dressing-gown and pyjamas. He said: 'Do you think, as Rex sweats so much, two pyjamas are enough?' Jim [inquired] about more doorknobs, and Robbie about a prop handkerchief for wiping Audrey's nose. A decision: 'no' to the swans on Eliza's bedpost, but 'yes' to having cretonne curtains of the same design as the wallpaper behind the bedhead.

Wednesday, 3 July

Geoff Allan, a burly, somewhat top-heavy-looking youth from the out-skirts of London, has become an expert at 'ageing' clothes. Today he was breaking down Eliza's little jacket in which she first visits Higgins' house. Everyone who had seen the coat in a test agreed that the black velveteen appeared too elegant and rich-looking. In an effort to save the garment, Geoff decided to take drastic measures. . . . Geoff put the coat in a boiling vat. After a few hours the black velvet had become a cream colour. Geoff now started to make the coat darker. Putting a spoon in dye, he smeared its surface, leaving light patches where the sun might have faded the collar and shoulders. He purposely left paler the material at the edges and in the creases. The coat was then dried out in a furnace . . . it was as hard and brittle and brown as poppadum. . . . Geoff then brought out a wire brush and gave the garment a few deft strokes, saying, 'This bit of pile will soon disappear.' It did. Later Geoff said, . . . 'I'll take the thing home tonight and sew frogs on it again—coarsely, with black thread. . . . Of course, the collar [lapels] will have to be stained a bit as if Eliza had spilled coffee on it (no, she would drink tea . . . it will have to be tea stains), and there must be greasy marks on the haunches where she wipes her dirty hands. Naturally the skirt will have to be made muddy around the hem, because, you see, she sits when she sells her violets, and the skirt, and petticoats also, would seep up the wet.'

Friday, 9 August

Shooting is scheduled to begin next Tuesday, but already Stage 7 [the Covent Garden set] is in an uproar. . . .

Tuesday, 13 August

. . . Sixty-four photographers from all over the world were there to catch the first shot of the first scene. Now our preparations were at an end. We were in Production.

Monday, 30 September

Joe Hiatt said euphemistically, 'This week's going to be tough for you. We have to dress four hundred people in ten days, and we will send 'em in to you in relays of ten.'

A posse of young women were already entrenched in my rooms on my arrival, and once again the game was played of fitting human bodies into the outer shells that had already been made. The hat belonging to one cos-tume would not look its best on a certain woman so the whole outfit must be changed. A grey-haired dowager mustn't wear a chinchilla hat as the camera will confuse where hat and hair begin, so another switch. Among those who appeared was one glorious young English girl from Sandy in Bedfordshire. . . . Unlike most Americans, who seem to have given up the habit, this stupid girl spoilt the effect of her calm, Canova marble serenity, by chewing gum.

Tuesday, 15 October

Went to see the tests of the Ascot scene, and glad to think that they are only tests. The camera somehow had reduced everything to a degree of banality. It is as if our opalescent setting had been reproduced by some cheap, coloured picture-postcard process. In spite of all previous tests, the men's coats came out blue, Rex Harrison's face Red Indian, and the subtle gradations of cream and white, over which we had deliberated like philosophers, suddenly became olive drab and beige. 'Oh, this is not a rectified print,' I was told when I moaned in despair.

Tuesday, 22 October

Today was the 'Big Push.' All the women for whom we have made Ascot dresses were called in, over a hundred and fifty of them. Hairdressers had to start at dawn, but . . . each woman has already been 'established' (has had her photograph taken showing every angle of her hair style, the angle of the hat, her jewellery and her props). . . .

Wednesday, 23 October

Another 'Big Push'—one hundred and fifty women to be hairdressed, made up, bejewelled, clothed and cloaked for the arrival at the Embassy. . . . I got busy wrecking and re-making hair styles, pulling at wigs, pulling at real hair. A few of the hairdressers aghast, but that could not be helped.

Thursday, 31 October

Hopkins came in to show me upholstery materials for the Mrs Higgins set which is now being built and, this complete, my work on the sets will be finished.

. . . Intending to show off to a visitor from outside the various sets for which I have acquired the same affection as for an old friend I discovered that already the ballroom, ante-room and Embassy staircase had been denuded of their light fittings, furniture and 'props' before being dismantled and stored away in pieces. But the glorious white *treillage* world of Ascot had not only been torn down but (so I had been informed) somewhat ghoulishly taken away and burned.

Three weeks to go before my contract is up. . . . I realized the end of my visit was in sight when Stanley Fleischer of the Art Department came to say he had heard I was leaving, and would I return to him any of the 'artists' materials' I had not used.

Friday [22 November 1963]

My contract is up. . . .

I went to pay my bill and collect my diaries from the hotel safe, (seven notebooks have been filled since my arrival). . . .

Now, my contribution made, the work has passed into the hands of tried experts who, for almost another year, will be working on cutting, scoring, polishing and refining the finished product. . . .

Eliza (Audrey Hepburn) at the Ascot races in the motion picture version of *My Fair Lady*. Freddy (Jeremy Brett), Professor Higgins (Rex Harrison) and Colonel Pickering (Wilfrid Hyde-White) stand beside her. Miss Hepburn is wearing one of Cecil Beaton's remarkable costume creations. Courtesy Warner Brothers.

PYGMALION   *A Romance in Five Acts*

BERNARD SHAW

Characters

Henry Higgins
Colonel Pickering
Freddy Eynsford Hill
Alfred Doolittle
A Bystander
Another Bystander
Eliza Doolittle
Mrs. Eynsford Hill
Miss Eynsford Hill
Mrs. Higgins
Mrs. Pearce
Parlormaid

[For the films many characters were added: **Karpathy [Nepommuck], A Taxi-man, A Vicar, A Grand Duchess, Guests at the Ball,** *etc. etc.]*

ACT ONE: The portico at Covent Garden
ACT TWO: Henry Higgins' laboratory in Wimpole Street. The next day.
ACT THREE: Mrs. Higgins' drawing-room. Some months later.
ACT FOUR: Henry Higgins' laboratory. Several months later.
ACT FIVE: Mrs. Higgins' drawing-room. The next day.

PREFACE TO PYGMALION

A Professor of Phonetics

As will be seen later on, Pygmalion needs, not a preface, but a sequel, which I have supplied in its due place.

The English have no respect for their language, and will not teach their children to speak it. They cannot spell it because they have nothing to spell it with but an old foreign alphabet of which only the consonants—and not all of them—have any agreed speech value. Consequently no man can teach himself what it should sound like from reading it; and it is impossible for an Englishman to open his mouth without making some other Englishman despise him. Most European languages are now accessible in black and white to foreigners: English and French are not thus accessible even to Englishmen and Frenchmen. The reformer we need most today is an energetic enthusiast: that is why I have made such a one the hero of a popular play.

There have been heroes of that kind crying in the wilderness for many years past. When I became interested in the subject towards the end of the eighteen-seventies, the illustrious Alexander Melville Bell, the inventor of Visible Speech, had emigrated to Canada, where his son invented the telephone; but Alexander J. Ellis was still a London Patriarch, with an impressive head always covered by a velvet skull cap, for which he would apologize to public meetings in a very courtly manner. He and Tito Pagliardini, another phonetic veteran, were men whom it was impossible to dislike. Henry Sweet, then a young man, lacked their sweetness of character: he was about as conciliatory to conventional mortals as Ibsen or Samuel Butler. His great ability as a phonetician (he was, I think, the best of them all at his job) would have entitled him to high official recognition, and perhaps enabled him to popularize his subject, but for his Satanic contempt for all academic dignitaries and persons in general who thought more of Greek than of phonetics. Once, in the days when the Imperial Institute rose in South Kensington, and Joseph Chamberlain was booming the Empire, I induced the editor of a leading monthly review to commission an article from Sweet on the imperial importance of his subject. When it arrived, it contained nothing but a savagely derisive attack on a professor of language and literature whose chair Sweet regarded as proper to a phonetic expert only. The article, being libellous, had to be returned as impossible; and I had to renounce my dream of dragging its author into the limelight. When I met him afterwards, for the first time for many years, I found to my astonishment that he, who had been a quite tolerably presentable young man, had actually managed by sheer scorn to alter his personal appearance until he had become a sort of walking repudiation of Oxford and all its traditions. It must have been largely in his own despite that he was squeezed into something called a Readership of phonetics there. The future of phonetics rests probably with his pupils, who all swore by him; but nothing could bring the man himself into any sort of compliance with the university to which he nevertheless clung by divine right in an intensely Oxonian way. I daresay his papers, if he has left any, include some satires that may be published without too destructive results fifty years hence. He was, I believe, not in the least an ill-natured man: very much the opposite, I should say; but he would not suffer fools gladly; and to him all scholars who were not rabid phoneticians were fools.

Those who knew him will recognize in my third act the allusion to the Current Shorthand in which he used to write postcards. It may be acquired from a four and sixpenny manual published by the Clarendon Press. The postcards which Mrs Higgins describes are such as I have received from Sweet. I would decipher a sound which a cockney would represent by *zerr,* and a Frenchman by *seu,* and then write demanding with some heat what on earth it meant. Sweet, with boundless contempt for my stupidity, would reply that it not only meant but obviously was the word Result, as no other word containing that sound, and capable of making sense with the context, existed in any language spoken on earth. That less expert mortals should require fuller indications was beyond Sweet's patience. Therefore, though the whole point of his Current Shorthand is that it can express every sound in the language perfectly, vowels as well as consonants, and that your hand has to make no stroke except the easy and current ones with which you write m, n, and u, l, p, and q, scribbling them at whatever angle comes easiest to you, his unfortunate determination to make this remarkable and quite legible script serve also as a shorthand reduced it in his own practice to the most inscrutable of cryptograms. His true objective was the provision of a full, accurate, legible script for our language; but he was led past that by his contempt for the popular Pitman system of shorthand, which he called the Pitfall system. The triumph of Pitman was a triumph of business organization: there was a weekly paper to persuade you to learn Pitman: there were cheap textbooks and exercise books and transcripts of speeches for you to copy, and schools where experienced teachers coached you up to the necessary proficiency. Sweet could not organize his market in that fashion. He might as well have been the Sybil who tore up the leaves of prophecy that nobody would attend to. The four and sixpenny manual, mostly in his lithographed handwriting, that was never vulgarly advertized, may perhaps some day be taken up by a syndicate and pushed upon the public as The Times pushed the Encyclopaedia Britannica; but until then it will certainly not prevail against Pitman. I have bought three copies of it during my lifetime; and I am informed by the publishers that its cloistered existence is still a steady and healthy one. I actually learned the system two several times; and yet the shorthand in which I am writing these lines is Pitman's. And the reason is, that my secretary cannot transcribe Sweet, having been perforce taught in the schools of Pitman. In America I could use the commercially organized Gregg shorthand, which has taken a hint from Sweet by making its letters writable (current, Sweet would have called them) instead of having to be geometrically drawn like Pitman's; but all these systems, including Sweet's, are spoilt by making them available for verbatim reporting, in which complete and exact spelling and word division are impossible. A complete and exact phonetic script is neither practicable nor necessary for ordinary use; but if we enlarge our alphabet to the Russian size, and make our spelling as phonetic as Spanish, the advance will be prodigious.

Pygmalion Higgins is not a portrait of Sweet, to whom the adventure of Eliza Doolittle would have been impossible; still, as will be seen, there are touches of Sweet in the play. With Higgins's physique and temperament Sweet might have set the Thames on fire. As it was, he impressed himself professionally on Europe to an extent that made his comparative personal obscurity, and the failure of Oxford to do justice to his eminence, a puzzle to foreign specialists in his subject. I do not blame Oxford, because I think Oxford is quite right in demanding a certain social amenity from its nurslings (heaven knows it is not exorbitant in its requirement!); for although I well know how hard it is for a man of genius with a seriously underrated subject to maintain serene and kindly relations with the men who underrate it, and who keep all the best places for less important subjects which they profess without originality and sometimes without much capacity for them, still, if he overwhelms them with wrath and disdain, he cannot expect them to heap honors on him.

Of the later generations of phoneticians I know little. Among them towered Robert Bridges, to whom perhaps Higgins may owe his Miltonic sympathies, though here again I must disclaim all portraiture. But if the play makes the public aware that there are such people as phoneticians, and that they are among the most important people in England at present, it will serve its turn.

I wish to boast that Pygmalion has been an extremely successful play, both on stage and screen, all over Europe and North America as well as at home. It is so intensely and deliberately didactic, and its subject is esteemed so dry, that I delight in throwing it at the heads of the wiseacres who repeat the parrot cry that art should never be didactic. It goes to prove my contention that great art can never be anything else.

Finally, and for the encouragement of people troubled with accents that cut them off from all high employment, I may add that the change wrought by Professor Higgins in the flower-girl is neither impossible nor uncommon. The modern concierge's daughter who fulfills her ambition by playing the Queen of Spain in Ruy Blas at the Théâtre Français is only one of many thousands of men and women who have sloughed off their native dialects and acquired a new tongue. Our West End shop assistants and domestic servants are bilingual. But the thing has to be done scientifically, or the last state of the aspirant may be worse than the first. An honest slum dialect is more tolerable than the attempts of phonetically untaught persons to imitate the plutocracy. Ambitious flower-girls who read this play must not imagine that they can pass themselves off as fine ladies by untutored imitation. They must learn their alphabet over again, and differently, from a phonetic expert. Imitation will only make them ridiculous.

Note for Technicians. A complete representation of the play as printed in this edition is technically possible only on the cinema screen or on stages furnished with exceptionally elaborate machinery. For ordinary theatrical use the scenes separated by rows of asterisks are to be omitted.

In the dialogue an e upside down indicates the indefinite vowel, sometimes called obscure or neutral, for which, though it is one of the commonest sounds in English speech, our wretched alphabet has no letter.

Act One

London at 11:15 p.m. Torrents of heavy summer rain. Cab whistles blowing frantically in all directions. Pedestrians running for shelter into the portico of St. Paul's church (not Wren's cathedral but Inigo Jones's church in Covent Garden vegetable market), among them a lady and her daughter in evening dress. All are peering out gloomily at the rain, except one man with his back turned to the rest, wholly preoccupied with a notebook in which he is writing.

The church clock strikes the first quarter.

The Daughter: [In the space between the central pillars, close to the one on her left.] I'm getting chilled to the bone. What can Freddy be doing all this time? He's been gone twenty minutes.

The Mother: [On her daughter's right.] Not so long. But he ought to have got us a cab by this.

A Bystander: [On the lady's right.] He wont get no cab not until half-past eleven, missus, when they come back after dropping their theatre fares.

The Mother: But we must have a cab. We cant stand here until half-past eleven. It's too bad.

The Bystander: Well, it ain't my fault, missus.

The Daughter: If Freddy had a bit of gumption, he would have got one at the theatre door.

The Mother: What could he have done, poor boy?

The Daughter: Other people got cabs. Why couldnt he?

[**Freddy** rushes in out of the rain from the Southampton Street side, and comes between them closing a dripping umbrella. He is a young man of twenty, in evening dress, very wet around the ankles.]

The Daughter: Well, havnt you got a cab?

Freddy: Theres not one to be had for love or money.

The Mother: Oh, Freddy, there must be one. You cant have tried.

The Daughter: It's too tiresome. Do you expect us to go and get one ourselves?

Freddy: I tell you theyre all engaged. The rain was so sudden: nobody was prepared; and everybody had to take a cab. Ive been to Charing Cross one way and nearly to Ludgate Circus the other; and they were all engaged.

The Mother: Did you try Trafalgar Square?

Freddy: There wasn't one at Trafalgar Square.

The Daughter: Did you try?

Freddy: I tried as far as Charing Cross Station. Did you expect me to walk to Hammersmith?

The Daughter: You havnt tried at all.

The Mother: You really are very helpless, Freddy. Go again; and dont come back until you have found a cab.

Freddy: I shall simply get soaked for nothing.

The Daughter: And what about us? Are we to stay here all night in this draught, with next to nothing on? You selfish pig—

Freddy: Oh, very well: I'll go. [He opens his umbrella and dashes off Strandwards, but comes into collision with a flower girl who is hurrying in for shelter, knocking her basket out of her hands. A blinding flash of lightning, followed instantly by a rattling peal of thunder, orchestrates the incident].

The Flower Girl: Nah then, Freddy: look wh'y' gowin, deah.

Freddy: Sorry
[He rushes off.]

The Flower Girl: [Picking up her scattered flowers and replacing them in the basket.] Theres menners f' yer! Tə-oo banches o voylets trod into the mad. [She sits down on the plinth of the column, sorting her flowers, on the lady's right. She is not at all a romantic figure. She is perhaps eighteen, perhaps twenty, hardly older. She wears a little sailor hat of black straw that has long been exposed to the dust and soot of London and has seldom if ever been brushed. Her hair needs washing rather badly: its mousy color can hardly be natural. She wears a shoddy black coat that reaches nearly to her knees and is shaped to her waist. She has a brown skirt with a coarse apron. Her boots are much the worse for wear. She is no doubt as clean as she can afford to be; but compared to the ladies she is very dirty. Her features are no worse than theirs; but their condition leaves something to be desired; and she needs the services of a dentist.]

The Mother: How do you know that my son's name is Freddy, pray?

The Flower Girl: Ow, eez yə-ooa san, is

e? Wal, fewd dan y'də-ooty bawmz a mather should, eed now bettern to spawl a pore gel's flahrzn than ran awy athaht pyin. Will yə-oo py me f'them? *[Here, with apologies, this desperate attempt to represent her dialect without a phonetic alphabet must be abandoned as unintelligible outside London.]*

The Daughter: Do nothing of the sort, mother. The idea!

The Mother: Please allow me, Clara. Have you any pennies?

The Daughter: No. Ive nothing smaller than sixpence.

The Flower Girl: *[Hopefully.]* I can give you change for a tanner, kind lady.

The Mother: *[To Clara.]* Give it to me. *[Clara parts reluctantly.]* Now *[To the girl.]* This is for your flowers.

The Flower Girl: Thank you kindly, lady.

The Daughter: Make her give you the change. These things are only a penny a bunch.

The Mother: Do hold your tongue, Clara. *[To the girl.]* You can keep the change.

The Flower Girl: Oh, thank you, lady.

The Mother: Now tell me how you know that young gentleman's name.

The Flower Girl: I didnt.

The Mother: I heard you call him by it. Dont try to deceive me.

The Flower Girl: *[Protesting.]* Who's trying to deceive you? I called him Freddy or Charlie same as you might yourself if you was talking to a stranger and wished to be pleasant.

The Daughter: Sixpence thrown away! Really, mamma, you might have spared Freddy that. *[She retreats in disgust behind the pillar.]*

> *An elderly* **Gentleman** *of the amiable military type rushes into the shelter, and closes a dripping umbrella. He is in the same plight as Freddy, very wet about the ankles. He is in evening dress, with a light overcoat. He takes the place left vacant by the daughter*

The Gentleman: Phew!

The Mother: *[To* **The Gentleman.***]* Oh, sir, is there any sign of its stopping?

The Gentleman: I'm afraid not. It started worse than ever about two minutes ago *[He goes to the plinth beside the* **Flower Girl**; *puts his foot on it; and stoops to turn down his trouser ends.]*

The Mother: Oh dear! *[She retires sadly and joins her daughter.]*

The Flower Girl: *[Taking advantage of the military gentleman's proximity to establish friendly relations with him.]* If it's worse, it's a sign it's nearly over. So cheer up, Captain; and buy a flower off a poor girl.

The Gentleman: I'm sorry. I havnt any change.

The Flower Girl: I can give you change, Captain.

The Gentleman: For a sovereign? Ive nothing less.

The Flower Girl: Garn! Oh do buy a flower off me, Captain. I can change half-a-crown. Take this for tuppence.

The Gentleman: Now dont be troublesome: theres a good girl. *[Trying his pockets]* I really havnt any change— Stop: heres three hapence, if thats any use to you *[He retreats to the other pillar.]*

The Flower Girl: *[Disappointed, but thinking three halfpence better than nothing.]* Thank you sir.

The Bystander: *[To the girl.]* You be careful: give him a flower for it. Theres a bloke here behind taking down every blessed word youre saying. *[All turn to the man who is taking notes.]*

The Flower Girl: *[Springing up terrified.]* I aint done nothing wrong by speaking to the gentleman. Ive a right to sell flowers if I keep off the kerb. *[Hysterically.]* I'm a respectable girl: so help me, I never spoke to him except to ask him to buy a flower off me.

> *[General hubbub, mostly sympathetic to the flower girl, but deprecating her excessive sensibility. Cries of* Dont start hollerin. Who's hurting you? Nobody's going to touch you. Whats the good of*

fussing? Steady on. Easy easy, etc., *come from the elderly staid spectators, who pat her comfortingly. Less patient ones bid her shut her head, or ask her roughly what is wrong with her. A remoter group, not knowing what the matter is, crowd in and increase the noise with question and answer:* Whats the row? What-she do? Where is he? A tec taking her down. What! him? Yes: him over there: Took money off the gentleman, etc.]

The Flower Girl: [*Breaking through them to* **The Gentleman,** *crying wildly.*] Oh, sir, dont let him charge me. You dunno what it means to me. Theyll take away my character and drive me on the streets for speaking to gentlemen. They—

The Note Taker: [*Coming forward on her right, the rest crowding after him.*] There! there! there! there! who's hurting you, you silly girl? What do you take me for?

The Bystander: It's aw rawt: e's a genleman: look at his bə-oots: [*Explaining to* **The Note Taker**] She thought you was a copper's nark, sir.

The Note Taker: [*With quick interest.*] Whats a copper's nark?

The Bystander: [*Inapt at definition.*] It's a—well, it's a copper's nark, as you might say. What else would you call it? A sort of informer.

The Flower Girl: [*Still hysterical.*] I take my Bible oath I never said a word—

The Note Taker: [*Overbearing but good-humored.*] Oh, shut up, shut up. Do I look like a policeman?

The Flower Girl: [*Far from reassured.*] Then what did you take down my words for? How do I know whether you took me down right? You just shew me what youve wrote about me: [**The Note Taker** *opens his book and holds it steadily under her nose, though the pressure of the mob trying to read it over his shoulders would upset a weaker man.*] Whats that?

That aint proper writing. I cant read that.

The Note Taker: I can. [*Reads, reproducing her pronunciation exactly.*] "Cheer ap, Keptin; n' baw ya flahr orf a pore gel."

The Flower Girl: [*Much distressed.*] It's because I called him Captain. I meant no harm. [*To* **The Gentleman.**] Oh, sir, dont let him lay a charge agen me for a word like that. You—

The Gentleman: Charge! I make no charge. [*To* **The Note Taker.**] Really, sir, if you are a detective, you need not begin protecting me against molestation by young women until I ask you. Anybody could see that the girl meant no harm.

The Bystanders Generally: [*Demonstrating against police espionage.*] Course they could. What business is it of yours? You mind your own affairs. He wants promotion, he does. Taking down people's words! Girl never said a word to him. What harm if she did? Nice thing a girl cant shelter from the rain without being insulted, etc., etc., etc. [*She is conducted by the more sympathetic demonstrators back to her plinth, where she resumes her seat and struggles with her emotion.*]

The Bystander: He aint a tec. He's a bloming busybody: thats what he is. I tell you, look at his bə-oots.

The Note Taker: [*Turning on him genially.*] And how are all your people down at Selsey?

The Bystander: [*Suspiciously.*] Who told you my people come from Selsey?

The Note Taker: Never you mind. They did. [*To the girl.*] How do you come to be up so far east? You were born in Lisson Grove.

The Flower Girl: [*Appalled.*] Oh, what harm is there in my leaving Lisson Grove? It wasnt fit for a pig to live in; and I had to pay four-and-six a week. [*In tears*] Oh, boo—hoo—oo—

The Note Taker: Live where you like; but stop that noise.

The Gentleman: *[To the girl.]* Come, come! he cant touch you: you have a right to live where you please.

A Sarcastic Bystander: *[Thrusting himself between* **The Note Taker** *and* **The Gentleman.***]* Park Lane, for instance. I'd like to go into the Housing Question with you, I would.

The Flower Girl: *[Subsiding into a brooding melancholy over her basket, and talking very low-spiritedly to herself.]* I'm a good girl, I am.

The Sarcastic Bystander: *[Not attending to her.]* Do you know where I come from?

The Note Taker: *[Promptly.]* Hoxton.
> *[Titterings. Popular interest in* **The Note Taker's** *performance increases.]*

The Sarcastic One: *[Amazed]* Well, who said I didnt? Bly me! you know everything, you do.

The Flower Girl: *[Still nursing her sense of injury.]* Aint no call to meddle with me, he aint.

The Bystander: *[To her.]* Of course he aint. Dont you stand it from him. *[To* **The Note Taker.***]* See here: what call have you to know about people what never offered to meddle with you?

The Flower Girl: Let him say what he likes. I dont want to have no truck with him.

The Bystander: You take us for dirt under your feet, dont you? Catch you taking liberties with a gentleman!

The Sarcastic Bystander: Yes: tell him where he come from if you want to go fortune-telling.

The Note Taker: Cheltenham, Harrow, Cambridge, and India.

The Gentleman: Quite right.
> *[Great laughter. Reaction in* **The Note Taker's** *favor. Exclamations of* He knows all about it. Told him proper. Hear him tell the toff where he come from? *etc.]*

The Gentleman: May I ask, sir, do you do this for your living at a music hall?

The Note Taker: I've thought of that. Perhaps I shall some day.
> *[The rain has stopped; and the persons on the outside of the crowd begin to drop off.]*

The Flower Girl: *[Resenting the reaction.]* He's no gentleman, he aint, to interfere with a poor girl.

The Daughter: *[Out of patience, pushing her way rudely to the front and displacing* **The Gentleman,** *who politely retires to the other side of the pillar.]* What on earth is Freddy doing? I shall get pneumownia if I stay in this draught any longer.

The Note Taker: *[To himself, hastily making a note of her pronunciation of "monia."]* Earlscourt.

The Daughter: *[Violently.]* Will you please keep your impertinent remarks to yourself.

The Note Taker: Did I say that out loud? I didn't mean to. I beg your pardon. Your mother's Epsom, unmistakeably.

The Mother: *[Advancing between* **The Daughter** *and* **The Note Taker.***]* How very curious! I was brought up in Largelady Park, near Epsom.

The Note Taker: *[Uproariously amused.]* Ha! ha! What a devil of a name! Excuse me. *[To* **The Daughter***]* You want a cab, do you?

The Daughter: Dont dare speak to me.

The Mother: Oh please, please, Clara. *[Her* **Daughter** *repudiates her with an angry shrug and retires haughtily]* We should be so grateful to you sir, if you found us a cab. *[***The Note Taker** *produces a whistle.]* Oh, thank you. *[She joins her* **Daughter.***]*
> *[***The Note Taker** *blows a piercing blast.]*

The Sarcastic Bystander: There! I knowed he was a plainclothes copper.

The Bystander: That aint a police whistle: thats a sporting whistle.

The Flower Girl: *[Still preoccupied with her wounded feelings.]* He's no right to take away my character. My character is the same to me as any lady's.

The Note Taker: I dont know whether

youve noticed it; but the rain stopped about two minutes ago.

The Bystander: So it has. Why didn't you say so before? and us losing our time listening to your silliness! [*He walks off towards the Strand.*]

The Sarcastic Bystander: I can tell where you come from. You come from An- well. Go back there.

The Note Taker: [*Helpfully.*] Hanwell.

The Sarcastic Bystander: [*Affecting great distinction of speech.*] Thenk you, teacher. Haw haw! So long [*He touches his hat with mock respect and strolls off.*]

The Flower Girl: Frightening people like that! How would he like it himself?

The Mother: It's quite fine now, Clara. We can walk to a motor bus. Come. [*She gathers her skirts above her ankles and hurries off towards the Strand.*]

The Daughter: But the cab—[*Her* **Mother** *is out of hearing.*] Oh, how tiresome! [*She follows angrily.*]

[*All the rest have gone except* **The Note Taker, The Gentleman,** *and* **The Flower Girl,** *who sits arranging her basket, and still pitying herself in murmurs.*]

The Flower Girl: Poor girl! Hard enough for her to live without being worrited and chivied.

The Gentleman: [*Returning to his former place on* **The Note Taker's** *left.*] How do you do it, if I may ask?

The Note Taker: Simply phonetics. The science of speech. That's my profession: also my hobby. Happy is the man who can make a living by his hobby! You can spot an Irishman or a Yorkshireman by his brogue. *I* can place any man within six miles. I can place him within two miles in London. Sometimes within two streets.

The Flower Girl: Ought to be ashamed of himself, unmanly coward!

The Gentleman: But is there a living in that?

The Note Taker: Oh yes. Quite a fat one.

This is an age of upstarts. Men begin in Kentish Town with £80 a year, and end in Park Lane with a hundred thousand. They want to drop Kentish Town; but they give themselves away every time they open their mouths. Now I can teach them—

The Flower Girl: Let him mind his own business and leave a poor girl—

The Note Taker: [*Explosively.*] Woman: cease this detestable boohooing instantly; or else seek the shelter of some other place of worship.

The Flower Girl: [*With feeble defiance.*] Ive a right to be here if I like, same as you.

The Note Taker: A woman who utters such depressing and disgusting sounds has no right to be anywhere— no right to live. Remember that you are a human being with a soul and the divine gift of articulate speech: that your native language is the language of Shakespear and Milton and The Bible; and dont sit there crooning like a bilious pigeon.

The Flower Girl: [*Quite overwhelmed, looking up at him in mingled wonder and deprecation without daring to raise her head.*] Ah-ah-ah-ow-ow-ow-oo!

The Note Taker: [*Whipping out his book.*] Heavens! what a sound! [*He writes; then holds out the book and reads, reproducing her vowels exactly.*] Ah-ah-ah-ow-ow-ow-oo!

The Flower Girl: [*Tickled by the performance, and laughing in spite of herself.*] Garn!

The Note Taker: You see this creature with her kerbstone English: the English that will keep her in the gutter to the end of her days. Well, sir, in three months I could pass that girl off as a duchess at an ambassador's garden party. I could even get her a place as lady's maid or shop assistant, which requires better English.

The Flower Girl: What's that you say?

The Note Taker: Yes, you squashed cabbage leaf, you disgrace to the noble architecture of these columns, you incarnate insult to the English language: I could pass you off as the Queen of Sheba. [*To* **The Gentleman.**] Can you believe that?

The Gentleman: Of course I can. I am myself a student of Indian dialects; and—

The Note Taker: [*Eagerly.*] Are you? Do you know Colonel Pickering, the author of Spoken Sanscrit?

The Gentleman: I am Colonel Pickering. Who are you?

The Note Taker: Henry Higgins, author of Higgins's Universal Alphabet.

Pickering: [*With enthusiasm.*] I came from India to meet you.

Higgins: I was going to India to meet you.

Pickering: Where do you live?

Higgins: 27A Wimpole Street. Come and see me tomorrow.

Pickering: I'm at the Carlton. Come with me now and lets have a jaw over some supper.

Higgins: Right you are.

The Flower Girl: [*To* **Pickering,** *as he passes her.*] Buy a flower, kind gentleman. I'm short for my lodging.

Pickering: I really havnt any change. I'm sorry. [*He goes away.*]

Higgins: [*Shocked at the girl's mendacity.*] Liar. You said you could change half-a-crown.

The Flower Girl: [*Rising in desperation.*] You ought to be stuffed with nails, you ought. [*Flinging the basket at his feet.*] Take the whole blooming basket for sixpence.

[*The church clock strikes the second quarter.*]

Higgins: [*Hearing in it the voice of God, rebuking him for his Pharisaic want of charity to the poor girl.*] A reminder. [*He raises his hat solemnly; then throws a handful of money into the basket and follows* **Pickering.**]

The Flower Girl: [*Picking up a half-crown.*] Ah-ow-ooh! [*Picking up a couple of florins.*] Aaah-ow-ooh! [*Picking up several coins.*] Aaaaah-ow-ooh! [*Picking up a half-sovereign.*] Aaaaaaaaaaaah-ow-ooh!!!

Freddy: [*Springing out of a taxicab.*] Got one at last. Hallo! [*To the girl.*] Where are the two ladies that were here?

The Flower Girl: They walked to the bus when the rain stopped.

Freddy: And left me with a cab on my hands! Damnation!

The Flower Girl: [*With grandeur.*] Never mind, young man. I'm going home in a taxi. [*She sails off to the cab. The driver puts his hand behind him and holds the door firmly shut against her. Quite understanding his mistrust, she shews him her handful of money.*] A taxi fare aint no object to me, Charlie. [*He grins and opens the door.*] Here. What about the basket?

The Taximan: Give it here. Tuppence extra.

Liza: No: I dont want nobody to see it. [*She crushes it into the cab and gets in, continuing the conversation through the window.*] Goodbye, Freddy.

Freddy: [*Dazedly raising his hat.*] Goodbye.

Taximan: Where to?

Liza: Bucknam Pellis [Buckingham Palace].

Taximan: What d'ye mean—Bucknam Pellis?

Liza: Dont you know where it is? In the Green Park, where the King lives. Goodbye, Freddy. Dont let me keep you standing there. Goodbye.

Freddy: Goodbye.

[*He goes.*]

Taximan: Here? Whats this about Bucknam Pellis? What business have you at Bucknam Pellis?

Liza: Of course I havnt none. But I wasn't going to let him know that. You drive me home.

Taximan: And wheres home?

Liza: Angel Court, Drury Lane, next Meiklejohn's oil shop.

Taximan: That sounds more like it, Judy.

[*He drives off.*]

*   *   *

Let us follow the taxi to the entrance to Angel Court, a narrow little archway between two shops, one of them Meiklejohn's oil shop. When it stops there, **Eliza** gets out, dragging her basket with her.

Liza: How much?

Taximan: [Indicating the taximeter.] Cant you read? A shilling.

Liza: A shilling for two minutes!!

Taximan: Two minutes or ten: it's all the same.

Liza: Well, I dont call it right.

Taximan: Ever been in a taxi before?

Liza: [With dignity.] Hundreds and thousands of times, young man.

Taximan: [Laughing at her.] Good for you, Judy. Keep the shilling, darling, with best love from all at home. Good luck! [He drives off.]

Liza: [Humiliated.] Impidence!

She picks up the basket and trudges up the alley with it to her lodging: a small room with very old wall paper hanging loose in the damp places. A broken pane in the window is mended with paper. A portrait of a popular actor and a fashion plate of ladies' dresses, all wildly beyond poor Eliza's means, both torn from newspapers, are pinned up on the wall. A birdcage hangs in the window; but its tenant died long ago: it remains as a memorial only.

These are the only visible luxuries: the rest is the irreducible minimum of poverty's needs: a wretched bed heaped with all sorts of coverings that have any warmth in them, a draped packing case with a basin and jug on it and a little looking glass over it, a chair and table, the refuse of some suburban kitchen, and an American alarum clock on the shelf above the unused fireplace: the whole lighted with a gas lamp with a penny in the slot meter. Rent: four shillings a week.

Here Eliza, chronically weary, but too excited to go to bed, sits, counting her new riches and dreaming and planning what to do with them, until the gas goes out, when she enjoys for the first time the sensation of being able to put in another penny without grudging it. This prodigal mood does not extinguish her gnawing sense of the need for economy sufficiently to prevent her from calculating that she can dream and plan in bed more cheaply and warmly than sitting up without a fire. So she takes off her shawl and skirt and adds them to the miscellaneous bedclothes. Then she kicks off her shoes and gets into bed without any further change.

Act Two

Next day at 11 a.m. **Higgins's** laboratory in Wimpole Street. It is a room on the first floor, looking on the street, and was meant for the drawing room. The double doors are in the middle of the back wall; and persons entering find in the corner to their right two tall file cabinets at right angles to one another against the walls. In this corner stands a flat writing-table, on which are a phonograph, a laryngoscope, a row of tiny organ pipes with a bellows, a set of lamp chimneys for singing flames with burners attached to a gas plug in the wall by an indiarubber tube, several tuning-forks of different sizes, a life-size image of half a human head, shewing in section the vocal organs, and a box containing a supply of wax cylinders for the phonograph.

Further down the room, on the same side, is a fireplace, with a comfortable leather-covered easy-chair at the side of the hearth nearest the door, and a coal-scuttle. There is a clock on the mantle-piece. Between the fireplace and the phonograph table is a stand for newspapers.

On the other side of the central door, to the left of the visitor, is a cabinet of shallow drawers. On it is a telephone and the telephone directory. The corner beyond, and most of the side wall, is occupied by a grand piano, with the keyboard at the end furthest from the door, and a bench for the players extending the full length of the keyboard. On the piano is a dessert dish heaped with fruit and sweets, mostly chocolates.

The middle of the room is clear. Besides the easy-chair, the piano bench, and two chairs at the phonograph table, there is one stray chair. It stands near the fireplace. On the walls, engravings: mostly Piranesis and mezzotint portraits. No paintings.

Pickering *is seated at the table, putting down some cards and a tuning-fork which he has been using.* Higgins *is standing up near him, closing two or three file drawers which are hanging out. He appears in the morning light as a robust, vital, appetizing sort of man of forty or thereabouts, dressed in a professional-looking black frock-coat with a white linen collar and black silk tie. He is of energetic, scientific type, heartily, even violently interested in everything that can be studied as a scientific subject, and careless about himself and other people, including their feelings. He is, in fact, but for his years and size, rather like a very impetuous baby "taking notice" eagerly and loudly, and requiring almost as much watching to keep him out of unintended mischief. His manner varies from genial bullying when he is in a good humor to stormy petulance when anything goes wrong; but he is so entirely frank and void of malice that he remains likeable even in his least reasonable moments.*

Higgins: [*As he shuts the last drawer.*] Well, I think thats the whole show.

Pickering: It's really amazing. I havnt taken half of it in, you know.

Higgins: Would you like to go over any of it again?

Pickering: [*Rising and coming to the fireplace, where he plants himself with his back to the fire.*] No. thank you: not now. I'm quite done up for this morning.

Higgins: [*Following him, and standing beside him on his left.*] Tired of listening to sounds?

Pickering: Yes. It's a fearful strain. I rather fancied myself because I can pronounce twenty-four distinct vowel sounds; but your hundred and thirty beat me. I cant hear a bit of difference between most of them.

Higgins: [*Chuckling, and going over to the piano to eat sweets.*] Oh, that comes with practice. You hear no difference at first; but you keep on listening, and presently you find theyre all as different as A from B.

[**Mrs Pearce** *looks in: she is* **Higgins's** *housekeeper.*] Whats the matter?

Mrs Pearce: [*Hesitating, evidently perplexed.*] A young woman asks to see you, sir.

Higgins: A young woman! What does she want?

Mrs Pearce: Well, sir, she says youll be glad to see her when you know what she's come about. She's quite a common girl, sir. Very common indeed. I should have sent her away, only I thought perhaps you wanted her to talk into your machines. I hope Ive not done wrong; but really you see such queer people sometimes—youll excuse me, I'm sure, sir—

Higgins: Oh, thats all right, Mrs Pearce. Has she an interesting accent?

Mrs Pearce: Oh, something dreadful, sir, really. I dont know how you can take an interest in it.

Higgins: [*To* **Pickering**] Lets have her up. Shew her up, Mrs Pearce [*He rushes across to his working table and picks out a cylinder to use on the phonograph.*]

Mrs Pearce: [*Only half resigned to it.*] Very well, sir. It's for you to say. [*She goes downstairs.*]

Higgins: This is rather a bit of luck. I'll shew you how I make records. We'll set her talking; and I'll take it down first in Bell's Visible Speech; then in broad Romic; and then we'll get her on the phonograph so that you can turn her on as often as you like with the written transcript before you.

Mrs Pearce: [*Returning.*] This is the young woman, sir.

[**The Flower Girl** *enters in state. She has a hat with three ostrich feathers, orange, sky-blue, and red. She has a nearly clean apron, and the shoddy coat has been tidied a little. The pathos of this deporable figure, with its innocent vanity and consequential air, touches* **Pickering,** *who has already straightened himself in the presence of* **Mrs Pearce.** *But as to*

Higgins, *the only distinction he makes between men and women is that when he is neither bullying nor exclaiming to the heavens against some feather-weight cross, he coaxes women as a child coaxes its nurse when it wants to get anything out of her.]*

Higgins: *[Brusquely, recognizing her with unconcealed disappointment, and at once, babylike, making an intolerable grievance of it.]* Why, this is the girl I jotted down last night. She's no use: I've got all the records I want of the Lisson Grove lingo; and I'm not going to waste another cylinder on it. *[To* **The Girl.***]* Be off with you: I dont want you.

The Flower Girl: Dont be so saucy. You aint heard what I come for yet. *[To* **Mrs Pearce,** *who is waiting at the door for further instructions.]* Did you tell him I come in a taxi?

Mrs Pearce: Nonsense, girl! what do you think a gentleman like Mr Higgins cares what you came in?

The Flower Girl: Oh, we are proud! He aint above giving lessons, not him: I heard him say so. Well, I aint come here to ask for any compliment; and if my money's not good enough I can go elsewhere.

Higgins: Good enough for what?

The Flower Girl: Good enough for yǝ-oo. Now you know, dont you? I've come to have lessons, I am. And to pay for em tǝ-oo: make no mistake.

Higgins: *[Stupent.]* Well!!! *[Recovering his breath with a gasp.]* What do you expect me to say to you?

The Flower Girl: Well, if you was a gentleman, you might ask me to sit down, I think. Dont I tell you I'm bringing you business?

Higgins: Pickering: shall we ask this baggage to sit down, or shall we throw her out of the window?

The Flower Girl: *[Running away in terror to the piano, where she turns at bay.]* Ah-ah-oh-ow-ow-ow-oo! *[Wounded and whimpering.]* I wont be called a baggage when Ive offered to pay like any lady.

[Motionless, the two men stare at her from the other side of the room, amazed.]

Pickering: *[Gently.]* But what is it you want?

The Flower Girl: I want to be a lady in a flower shop stead of sellin at the corner of Tottenham Court Road. But they wont take me unless I can talk more genteel. He said he could teach me. Well, here I am ready to pay him —not asking for any favor—and he treats me zif I was dirt.

Mrs Pearce: How can you be such a foolish ignorant girl as to think you could afford to pay Mr Higgins?

The Flower Girl: Why shouldnt I? I know what lessons cost as well as you do; and I'm ready to pay.

Higgins: How much?

The Flower Girl: *[Coming back to him, triumphant.]* Now youre talking! I thought youd come off it when you saw a chance of getting back a bit of what you chucked at me last night. *[Confidentially.]* Youd had a drop in, hadnt you?

Higgins: *[Peremptorily.]* Sit down.

The Flower Girl: Oh, if youre going to make a compliment of it—

Higgins: *[Thundering at her.]* Sit down.

Mrs Pearce: *[Severely.]* Sit down, girl. Do as youre told.

The Flower Girl: Ah-ah-ah-ow-ow-oo! *[She stands, half rebellious, half bewildered.]*

Pickering: *[Very courteous.]* Wont you sit down? *[He places the stray chair near the hearthrug between himself and* **Higgins.***]*

Liza: *[Coyly.]* Dont mind if I do. *[She sits down.* **Pickering** *returns to the hearthrug.]*

Higgins: Whats your name?

The Flower Girl: Liza Doolittle.

Higgins: *[Declaiming gravely.]*
Eliza, Elizabeth, Betsy and Bess,
They went to the woods to get a bird's nes':

Pickering: They found a nest with four eggs in it:

Higgins: They took one apiece, and left three in it.

> [They laugh heartily at their own fun.]

Liza: Oh, dont be silly.

Mrs Pearce: [Placing herself behind Eliza's chair.] You mustnt speak to the gentleman like that.

Liza: Well, why wont he speak sensible to me?

Higgins: Come back to business. How much do you propose to pay me for the lessons?

Liza: Oh, I know whats right. A lady friend of mine gets French lessons for eighteenpence an hour from a real French gentleman. Well, you wouldnt have the face to ask me the same for teaching me my own language as you would for French; so I wont give more than a shilling. Take it or leave it.

Higgins: [Walking up and down the room, rattling his keys and his cash in his pockets.] You know, Pickering, if you consider a shilling, not as a simple shilling, but as a percentage of this girl's income, it works out as fully equivalent to sixty or seventy guineas from a millionaire.

Pickering: How so?

Higgins: Figure it out. A millionaire has about £150 a day. She earns about half-a-crown.

Liza: [Haughtily.] Who told you I only—

Higgins: [Continuing.] She offers me two-fifths of her day's income for a lesson. Two-fifths of a millionaire's income for a day would be somewhere about £60. It's handsome. By George, it's enormous! it's the biggest offer I ever had.

Liza: [Rising, terrified.] Sixty pounds! What are you talking about? I never offered you sixty pounds. Where would I get—

Higgins: Hold your tongue.

Liza: [Weeping.] But I aint got sixty pounds. Oh—

Mrs Pearce: Dont cry, you silly girl. Sit down. Nobody is going to touch your money.

Higgins: Somebody is going to touch you, with a broomstick, if you dont stop snivelling. Sit down.

Liza: [Obeying slowly.] Ah-ah-ah-ow-oo-o! One would think you was my father.

Higgins: If I decide to teach you, I'll be worse than two fathers to you. Here! [He offers her his silk handkerchief.]

Liza: Whats this for?

Higgins: To wipe your eyes. To wipe any part of your face that feels moist. Remember: thats your handkerchief; and thats your sleeve. Dont mistake the one for the other if you wish to become a lady in a shop.

> [Liza, utterly bewildrered, stares helplessly at him.]

Mrs Pearce: It's no use talking to her like that, Mr Higgins: she doesnt understand you. Besides, youre quite wrong: she doesnt do it that way at all [She takes the handkerchief.]

Liza: [Snatching it.] Here! You give me that handkerchief. He gev it to me, not you.

Pickering: [Laughing.] He did. I think it must be regarded as her property, Mrs Pearce.

Mrs Pearce: [Resigning herself.] Serve you right, Mr Higgins.

Pickering: Higgins: I'm interested. What about the ambassador's garden party? I'll say youre the greatest teacher alive if you make that good. I'll bet you all the expenses of the experiment you cant do it. And I'll pay for the lessons.

Liza: Oh, you are real good. Thank you Captain.

Higgins: [Tempted, looking at her.] It's almost irresistible. She's so deliciously low—so horribly dirty—

Liza: [Protesting extremely.] Ah-ah-ah-ah-ow-ow-oo-oo!!! I aint dirty: I washed my face and hands afore I come, I did.

Pickering: Youre certainly not going to

turn her head with flattery, Higgins.

Mrs Pearce: *[Uneasy.]* Oh, dont say that, sir: theres more ways than one of turning a girl's head; and nobody can do it better than Mr Higgins, though he may not always mean it. I do hope, sir, you wont encourage him to do anything foolish.

Higgins: *[Becoming excited as the idea grows on him.]* What is life but a series of inspired follies? The difficulty is to find them to do. Never lose a chance: it doesnt come every day. I shall make a duchess of this draggletailed guttersnipe.

Liza: *[Strongly deprecating this view of her.]* Ah-ah-ah-ow-ow-oo!

Higgins: *[Carried away.]* Yes: in six months—in three if she has a good ear and a quick tongue—I'll take her anywhere and pass her off as anything. We'll start today: now! this moment! Take her away and clean her, Mrs Pearce. Monkey Brand, if it wont come off any other way. Is there a good fire in the kitchen?

Mrs Pearce: *[Protesting.]* Yes; but—

Higgins: *[Storming on.]* Take all her clothes off and burn them. Ring up Whitely or somebody for new ones. Wrap her up in brown paper til they come.

Liza: Youre no gentleman, youre not, to talk of such things. I'm a good girl, I am; and I know what the like of you are, I do.

Higgins: We want none of your Lisson Grove prudery here, young woman. Youve got to learn to behave like a duchess. Take her away, Mrs Pearce. If she gives you any trouble, wallop her.

Liza: *[Springing up and running between* **Pickering** *and* **Mrs Pearce** *for protection.]* No! I'll call the police, I will.

Mrs Pearce: But Ive no place to put her.

Higgins: Put her in the dustbin.

Liza: Ah-ah-ah-ow-ow-oo!

Pickering: Oh come, Higgins! be reasonable.

Mrs Pearce: *[Resolutely.]* You must be reasonable, Mr Higgins: really you must. You cant walk over everybody like this.

*[***Higgins,*** *thus scolded, subsides. The hurricane is succeeded by a zephyr of amiable surprise.]*

Higgins: *[With professional exquisiteness of modulation.]* I walk over everybody! My dear Mrs Pearce, my dear Pickering, I never had the slightest intention of walking over anyone. All I propose is that we should be kind to this poor girl. We must help her to prepare and fit herself for her new station in life. If I did not express myself clearly it was because I did not wish to hurt her delicacy, or yours.

*[***Liza,*** *reassured, steals back to her chair.]*

Mrs Pearce: *[to* **Pickering***]* Well, did you ever hear anything like that, sir?

Pickering: *[Laughing heartily.]* Never, Mrs Pearce: never.

Higgins: *[Patiently.]* Whats the matter?

Mrs Pearce: Well, the matter is, sir, that you cant take a girl up like that as if you were picking up a pebble on the beach.

Higgins: Why not?

Mrs Pearce: Why not! But you dont know anything about her. What about her parents? She may be married.

Liza: Garn!

Higgins: There! As the girl very properly says, Garn! Married indeed! Dont you know that a woman of that class looks a worn out drudge of fifty a year after she's married?

Liza: Whood marry me?

Higgins: *[Suddenly resorting to the most thrillingly beautiful low tones in his best elocutionary style.]* By George, Eliza, the streets will be strewn with the bodies of men shooting themselves for your sake before Ive done with you.

Mrs Pearce: Nonsense, sir. You mustnt talk like that to her.

Liza: *[Rising and squaring herself de-*

terminedly.] I'm going away. He's off his chump, he is. I dont want no balmies teaching me.

Higgins: *[Wounded in his tenderest point by her insensibility to his elocution.]* Oh, indeed! I'm mad, am I? Very well, Mrs Pearce: you neednt order the new clothes for her. Throw her out.

Liza: *[Whimpering.]* Nah-ow. You got no right to touch me.

Mrs Pearce: You see what comes of being saucy. *[Indicating the door.]* This way, please.

Liza: *[Almost in tears.]* I didnt want no clothes. I wouldnt have taken them *[She throws away the handkerchief.]* I can buy my own clothes.

Higgins: *[Deftly retrieving the handkerchief and intercepting her on her reluctant way to the door.]* Youre an ungrateful wicked girl. This is my return for offering to take you out of the gutter and dress you beautifully and make a lady of you.

Mrs Pearce: Stop, Mr Higgins. I wont allow it. It's you that are wicked. Go home to your parents, girl; and tell them to take better care of you.

Liza: I aint got no parents. They told me I was big enough to earn my own living and turned me out.

Mrs Pearce: Wheres your mother?

Liza: I aint got no mother. Her that turned me out was my sixth stepmother. But I done without them. And I'm a good girl, I am.

Higgins: Very well, then, what on earth is all this fuss about? The girl doesnt belong to anybody—is no use to anybody but me. *[He goes to **Mrs Pearce** and begins coaxing.]* You can adopt her, Mrs Pearce: I'm sure a daughter would be a great amusement to you. Now dont make any more fuss. Take her downstairs; and—

Mrs Pearce: But whats to become of her? Is she to be paid anything? Do be sensible, sir.

Higgins: Oh, pay her whatever is necessary: put it down in the housekeeping book. *[Impatiently.]* What on earth will she want with money? She'll have her food and her clothes. She'll only drink if you give her money.

Liza: *[Turning on him.]* Oh you are a brute. It's a lie: nobody ever saw the sign of liquor on me. *[To **Pickering**]* Oh, sir: youre a gentleman: dont let him speak to me like that.

Pickering: *[In good-humored remonstrance.]* Does it occur to you, Higgins, that the girl has some feelings?

Higgins: *[Looking critically at her.]* Oh no, I dont think so. Not any feelings that we need bother about. *[Cheerily.]* Have you, Eliza?

Liza: I got my feelings same as anyone else.

Higgins: *[To **Pickering**, reflectively.]* You see the difficulty?

Pickering: Eh? What difficulty?

Higgins: To get her to talk grammar. The mere pronunciation is easy enough.

Liza: I dont want to talk grammar. I want to talk like a lady in a flower-shop.

Mrs Pearce: Will you please keep to the point, Mr Higgins. I want to know on what terms the girl is to be here. Is she to have any wages? And what is to become of her when youve finished your teaching? You must look ahead a little.

Higgins: *[Impatiently.]* Whats to become of her if I leave her in the gutter? Tell me that, Mrs Pearce.

Mrs Pearce: Thats her own business, not yours, Mr Higgins.

Higgins: Well, when Ive done with her, we can throw her back into the gutter; and then it will be her own business again; so thats all right.

Liza: Oh, youve no feeling heart in you: you dont care for nothing but yourself. *[She rises and takes the floor resolutely.]* Here! Ive had enough of this. I'm going *[Making for the door.]* You ought to be ashamed of yourself, you ought.

Higgins: *[Snatching a chocolate cream from the piano, his eyes suddenly* *beginning to twinkle with mischief.]* Have some chocolates, Eliza.

Liza: *[Halting, tempted.]* How do I know what might be in them? Ive heard of girls being drugged by the like of you.

[Higgins whips out his penknife; cuts a chocolate in two; puts one half into his mouth and bolts it; and offers her the other half.]

Higgins: Pledge of good faith, Eliza. I eat one half: you eat the other. *[Liza opens her mouth to retort: he pops the half chocolate into it.]* You shall have boxes of them, barrels of them, every day. You shall live on them. Eh?

Liza: *[Who has disposed of the chocolate after being nearly choked by it.]* I wouldnt have ate it, only I'm too ladylike to take it out of my mouth.

Higgins: Listen, Eliza. I think you said you came in a taxi.

Liza: Well, what if I did? Ive as good a right to take a taxi as anyone else.

Higgins: You have, Eliza; and in future you shall have as many taxis as you want. You shall go up and down and round the town in a taxi every day. Think of that, Eliza.

Mrs Pearce: Mr Higgins: youre tempting the girl. It's not right. She should think of the future.

Higgins: At her age! Nonsense! Time enough to think of the future when you havnt any future to think of. No, Eliza: do as this lady does: think of other people's futures; but never think of your own. Think of chocolates, and taxis, and gold, and diamonds.

Liza: No: I dont want no gold and no diamonds. I'm a good girl, I am. *[She sits down again, with an attempt at dignity.]*

Higgins: You shall remain so, Eliza, under the care of Mrs Pearce. And you shall marry an officer in the Guards, with a beautiful moustache: the son of a marquis, who will disinherit him for marrying you, but will relent when he sees your beauty and goodness—

Pickering: Excuse me, Higgins; but I really must interfere. Mrs Pearce is quite right. If this girl is to put herself in your hands for six months for an experiment in teaching, she must understand thoroughly what she's doing.

Higgins: How can she? She's incapable of understanding anything. Besides, do any of us understand what we are doing? If we did, would we ever do it?

Pickering: Very clever, Higgins; but not to the present point. *[To Eliza.]* Miss Doolittle—

Liza: *[Overwhelmed.]* Ah-ah-ow-oo!

Higgins: There! Thats all youll get out of Eliza. Ah-ah-ow-oo! No use explaining. As a military man you ought to know that. Give her her orders: thats enough for her. Eliza: you are to live here for the next six months, learning how to speak beautifully, like a lady in a florist's shop. If youre good and do whatever youre told, you shall sleep in a proper bedroom, and have lots to eat, and money to buy chocolates and take rides in taxis. If youre naughty and idle you will sleep in the back kitchen among the black beetles, and be walloped by Mrs Pearce with a broomstick. At the end of six months you shall go to Buckingham Palace in a carriage, beautifully dressed. If the King finds out youre not a lady, you will be taken by the police to the Tower of London, where your head will be cut off as a warning to other presumptuous flower girls. If you are not found out, you shall have a present of seven-and-sixpence to start life with as a lady in a shop. If you refuse this offer you will be a most ungrateful wicked girl; and the angels will weep for you. *[To Pickering.]* Now are you satisfied, Pickering? *[To Mrs Pearce]* Can I put it more plainly and fairly, Mrs Pearce?

Mrs Pearce: [*Patiently.*] I think youd better let me speak to the girl properly in private. I dont know that I can take charge of her or consent to the arrangement at all. Of course I know you dont mean her any harm; but when you get what you call interested in people's accents, you never think or care what may happen to them or you. Come with me, Eliza.

Higgins: Thats all right. Thank you, Mrs Pearce. Bundle her off to the bathroom.

Liza: [*Rising reluctantly and suspiciously.*] Youre a great bully, you are. I wont stay here if I dont like. I wont let nobody wallop me. I never asked to go to Bucknam Palace, I didnt. I was never in trouble with the police, not me. I'm a good girl—

Mrs Pearce: Dont answer back, girl. You dont understand the gentleman. Come with me. [*She leads the way to the door, and holds it open for* **Eliza.**]

Liza: [*As she goes out.*] Well, what I say is right. I wont go near the King, not if I'm going to have my head cut off. If I'd known what I was letting myself in for, I wouldnt have come here. I always been a good girl; and I never offered to say a word to him; and I dont owe him nothing; and I dont care; and I wont be put upon; and I have my feelings the same as anyone else—

[**Mrs Pearce** *shuts the door; and* **Eliza's** *plaints are no longer audible.*]

*   *   *

Eliza is taken upstairs to the third floor greatly to her surprise; for she expected to be taken down to the scullery. There **Mrs. Pearce** *opens a door and takes her into a spare bedroom.*

Mrs Pearce: I will have to put you here. This will be your bedroom.

Liza: O-h, I couldnt sleep here, missus. It's too good for the likes of me. I should be afraid to touch anything. I aint a duchess yet, you know.

Mrs Pearce: You have got to make your-self as clean as the room: then you wont be afraid of it. And you must call me Mrs Pearce, not missus. [*She throws open the door of the dressing-room, now modernized as a bathroom.*]

Liza: Gawd! whats this? Is this where you wash clothes? Funny sort of copper I call it.

Mrs Pearce: It is not a copper. This is where we wash ourselves, Eliza, and where I am going to wash you.

Liza: You expect me to get into that and wet myself all over! Not me. I should catch my death. I knew a woman did it every Saturday night; and she died of it.

Mrs Pearce: Mr Higgins has the gentlemen's bathroom downstairs; and he has a bath every morning, in cold water.

Liza: Ugh! He's made of iron, that man.

Mrs Pearce: If you are to sit with him and the Colonel and be taught you will have to do the same. They wont like the smell of you if you dont. But you can have the water as hot as you like. There are two taps: hot and cold.

Liza: [*Weeping.*] I couldnt. I dursnt. Its not natural: it would kill me. Ive never had a bath in my life: not what youd call a proper one.

Mrs Pearce: Well, dont you want to be clean and sweet and decent, like a lady? You know you cant be a nice girl inside if youre a dirty slut outside.

Liza: Boohoo!!!!

Mrs Pearce: Now stop crying and go back into your room and take off all your clothes. Then wrap yourself in this [*Taking down a gown from its peg and handing it to her*] and come back to me. I will get the bath ready.

Liza: [*All tears.*] I cant. I wont. I'm not used to it. Ive never took off all my clothes before. It's not right: it's not decent.

Mrs Pearce: Nonsense, child. Dont you take off all your clothes every night when you go to bed?

Liza: [Amazed.] No. Why should I? I should catch my death. Of course I take off my skirt.

Mrs Pearce: Do you mean that you sleep in the underclothes you wear in the daytime?

Liza: What else have I to sleep in?

Mrs Pearce: You will never do that again as long as you live here. I will get you a proper nightdress.

Liza: Do you mean change into cold things and lie awake shivering half the night? You want to kill me, you do.

Mrs Pearce: I want to change you from a frowzy slut to a clean respectable girl fit to sit with the gentlemen in the study. Are you going to trust me and do what I tell you or be thrown out and sent back to your flower basket?

Liza: But you dont know what the cold is to me. You dont know how I dread it.

Mrs Pearce: Your bed won't be cold here: I will put a hot water bottle in it. [Pushing her into the bedroom.] Off with you and undress.

Liza: Oh, if only I'd known what a dreadful thing it is to be clean I'd never have come. I didnt know when I was well off. I—[**Mrs Pearce** pushes her through the door, but leaves it partly open lest her prisoner should take to flight.]

[**Mrs Pearce** puts on a pair of white rubber sleeves, and fills the bath, mixing hot and cold and testing the result with the bath thermometer. She perfumes it with a handful of bath salts and adds a palmful of mustard. She then takes a formidable looking long handled scrubbing brush and soaps it profusely with a ball of scented soap.

Eliza comes back with nothing on but the bath gown huddled tightly round her, a piteous spectacle of abject terror.]

Mrs Pearce: Now come along. Take that thing off.

Liza: Oh I couldnt, Mrs Pearce: I reely couldnt. I never done such a thing.

Mrs Pearce: Nonsense. Here: step in and tell me whether its hot enough for you.

Liza: Ah-oo! Ah-oo! It's too hot.

Mrs Pearce: [Deftly snatching the gown away and throwing **Eliza** down on her back.] It wont hurt you. [She sets to work with the scrubbing brush.]

[**Eliza's** screams are heartrending.]

*   *   *

Meanwhile the **Colonel** has been having it out with **Higgins** about **Eliza**. **Pickering** has come from the hearth to the chair and seated himself astride of it with his arms on the back to cross-examine him.

Pickering: Excuse the straight question, Higgins. Are you a man of good character where women are concerned?

Higgins: [Moodily.] Have you ever met a man of good character where women are concerned?

Pickering: Yes: very frequently.

Higgins: [Dogmatically, lifting himself on his hands to the level of the piano, and sitting on it with a bounce.] Well, I havnt. I find that the moment I let a woman make friends with me, she becomes jealous, exacting, suspicious, and a damned nuisance. I find that the moment I let myself make friends with a woman, I become selfish and tyrannical. Women upset everything. When you let them into your life, you find that the woman is driving at one thing and youre driving at another.

Pickering: At what, for example?

Higgins: [Coming off the piano restlessly.] Oh, Lord knows! I suppose the woman wants to live her own life; and the man wants to live his; and each tries to drag the other on to the wrong track. One wants to go north and the other south; and the result is that both have to go east, though they both hate the east wind. [He sits down on the bench at the keyboard.] So here I am, a confirmed old bachelor, and likely to remain so.

Pickering: [Rising and standing over him gravely.] Come, Higgins! You know what I mean. If I'm to be in this business I shall feel responsible for that girl. I hope it's understood that no advantage is to be taken of her position.

Higgins: What! That thing! Sacred, I assure you. [Rising to explain.] You see, she'll be a pupil; and teaching would be impossible unless pupils were sacred. Ive taught scores of American millionairesses how to speak English: the best looking women in the world. I'm seasoned. They might as well be blocks of wood. I might as well be a block of wood. It's—

[Mrs Pearce opens the door. She has Eliza's hat in her hand. Pickering retires to the easy-chair at the hearth and sits down.]

Higgins: [Eagerly.] Well, Mrs Pearce: is it all right?

Mrs Pearce: [At the door.] I just wish to trouble you with a word, if I may, Mr Higgins.

Higgins: Yes, certainly. Come in. [She comes forward.] Dont burn that, Mrs Pearce. I'll keep it as a curiosity. [He takes the hat.]

Mrs Pearce: Handle it carefully, sir, please. I had to promise her not to burn it; but I had better put it in the oven for a while.

Higgins: [Putting it down hastily on the piano.] Oh! thank you. Well, what have you to say to me?

Pickering: Am I in the way?

Mrs Pearce: Not in the least, sir. Mr Higgins: will you please be very particular what you say before the girl?

Higgins: [Sternly.] Of course. I'm always particular about what I say. Why do you say this to me?

Mrs Pearce: [Unmoved.] No, sir: youre not at all particular when youve mislaid anything or when you get a little impatient. Now it doesnt matter before me: I'm used to it. But you really must not swear before the girl.

Higgins: [Indignantly.] I swear! [Most emphatically.] I never swear. I detest the habit. What the devil do you mean?

Mrs Pearce [Stolidly.] Thats what I mean, sir. You swear a great deal too much. I dont mind your damning and blasting, and what the devil and where the devil and who the devil—

Higgins: Mrs Pearce: this language from your lips! Really!

Mrs Pearce: [Not to be put off.]—but there is a certain word I must ask you not to use. The girl used it herself when she began to enjoy the bath. It begins with the same letter as bath. She knows no better: she learnt it at her mother's knee. But she must not hear it from your lips.

Higgins: [Loftily.] I cannot charge myself with having ever uttered it, Mrs Pearce. [She looks at him steadfastly. He adds, hiding an uneasy conscience with a judicial air.] Except perhaps in a moment of extreme and justifiable excitement.

Mrs Pearce: Only this morning, sir, you applied it to your boots, to the butter, and to the brown bread.

Higgins: Oh, that! Mere alliteration, Mrs Pearce, natural to a poet.

Mrs Pearce: Well, sir, whatever you choose to call it, I beg you not to let the girl hear you repeat it.

Higgins: Oh, very well, very well. Is that all?

Mrs Pearce: No, sir. We shall have to be very particular with this girl as to personal cleanliness.

Higgins: Certainly. Quite right. Most important.

Mrs Pearce: I mean not to be slovenly about her dress or untidy in leaving things about.

Higgins: [Going to her solemnly.] Just so. I intended to call your attention to that. [He passes on to Pickering, who is enjoying the conversation immensely.] It is these little things that matter, Pickering. Take care of the pence and the pounds will take care of themselves is as true of personal habits as of money. [He comes to anchor on the hearthrug, with the air of a man in an unassailable position.]

Mrs Pearce: Yes, sir. Then might I ask you not to come down to breakfast in your dressing-gown, or at any rate not to use it as a napkin to the extent you do, sir. And if you would be so good as not to eat everything off the same plate, and to remember not to put the porridge saucepan out of your hand on the clean tablecloth, it would be a better example to the girl. You know you nearly choked yourself with a fishbone in a jam only last week.

Higgins: [Routed from the hearthrug and drifting back to the piano.] I may do these things sometimes in absence of mind; but surely I dont do them habitually. [Angrily.] By the way: my dressing-gown smells most damnably of benzine.

Mrs Pearce: No doubt it does, Mr Higgins. But if you will wipe your fingers—

Higgins: [Yelling.] Oh very well, very well: I'll wipe them in my hair in future.

Mrs Pearce: I hope youre not offended, Mr Higgins.

Higgins: [Shocked at finding himself thought capable of an unamiable sentiment.] Not at all, not at all. Youre quite right, Mrs Pearce: I shall be particularly careful before the girl. Is that all?

Mrs Pearce: No, sir. Might she use some of those Japanese dresses you brought from abroad? I really cant put her back into her old things.

Higgins: Certainly. Anything you like. Is that all?

Mrs Pearce: Thank you, sir. Thats all.
[She goes out.]

Higgins: You know, Pickering, that woman has the most extraordinary ideas about me. Here I am, a shy, diffident sort of man. Ive never been able to feel really grown-up and tremendous, like other chaps. And

yet she's firmly persuaded that I'm an arbitrary overbearing bossing kind of person. I cant account for it.
[Mrs Pearce returns.]

Mrs Pearce: If you please, sir, the trouble's beginning already. Theres a dustman downstairs, Alfred Doolittle, wants to see you. He says you have his daughter here.

Pickering: [Rising.] Phew! I say!

Higgins: [Promptly.] Send the blackguard up.

Mrs Pearce: Oh, very well, sir.
[She goes out.]

Pickering: He may not be a blackguard, Higgins.

Higgins: Nonsense. Of course he's a blackguard.

Pickering: Whether he is or not, I'm afraid we shall have some trouble with him.

Higgins: [Confidently.] Oh no: I think not. If theres any trouble he shall have it with me, not I with him. And we are sure to get something interesting out of him.

Pickering: About the girl?

Higgins: No. I mean his dialect.

Pickering: Oh!

Mrs Pearce: [At the door.] Doolittle, sir.
[She admits Doolittle and retires. **Alfred** is an elderly but vigorous dustman, clad in the costume of his profession, including a hat with a back brim covering his neck and shoulders. He has well marked and rather interesting features, and seems equally free from fear and conscience. He has a remarkably expressive voice, the result of a habit of giving vent to his feelings without reserve. His present pose is that of wounded honor and stern resolution.]

Doolittle: [At the door, uncertain which of the two gentlemen is his man.] Professor Iggins?

Higgins: Here. Good morning. Sit down.

Doolittle: Morning, Governor. [He sits down magisterially.] I come about a very serious matter, Governor.

Higgins: [To **Pickering.**] Brought up in Hounslow. Mother Welsh, I should think. [**Doolittle** *opens his mouth, amazed.* **Higgins** *continues.*] What do you want, Doolittle?

Doolittle: [*Menacingly.*] I want my daughter: thats what I want. See?

Higgins: Of course you do. Youre her father, arnt you? You dont suppose anyone else wants her, do you? I'm glad to see you have some spark of family feeling left. She's upstairs. Take her away at once.

Doolittle: [*Rising, fearfully taken aback.*] What!

Higgins: Take her away. Do you suppose I'm going to keep your daughter for you?

Doolittle: [*Remonstrating.*] Now, now, look here, Governor. Is this reasonable? Is it fairity to take advantage of a man like this? The girl belongs to me. You got her. Where do I come in? [*He sits down again.*]

Higgins: Your daughter had the audacity to come to my house and ask me to teach her how to speak properly so that she could get a place in a flower-shop. This gentleman and my house-keeper have been here all the time. [*Bullying him.*] How dare you come here and attempt to blackmail me? You sent her here on purpose.

Doolittle: [*Protesting.*] No, Governor.

Higgins: You must have. How else could you possibly know that she is here?

Doolittle: Don't take a man up like that, Governor.

Higgins: The police shall take you up. This is a plant—a plot to extort money by threats. I shall telephone for the police. [*He goes resolutely to the telephone and opens the directory.*]

Doolittle: Have I asked you for a brass farthing? I leave it to the gentleman here: have I said a word about money?

Higgins: [*Throwing the book aside and marching down on* **Doolittle** *with a poser.*] What else did you come for?

Doolittle: [*Sweetly.*] Well, what would a man come for? Be human, Governor.

Higgins: [*Disarmed.*] Alfred: did you put her up to it?

Doolittle: So help me, Governor, I never did. I take my Bible oath I aint seen the girl these two months past.

Higgins: Then how did you know she was here?

Doolittle: [*"Most musical, most melancholy."*] I'll tell you, Governor, if youll only let me get a word in. I'm willing to tell you. I'm wanting to tell you. I'm waiting to tell you.

Higgins: Pickering: this chap has a certain natural gift of rhetoric. Observe the rhythm of his native woodnotes wild. "I'm willing to tell you: I'm wanting to tell you: I'm waiting to tell you." Sentimental rhetoric! thats the Welsh strain in him. It also accounts for his mendacity and dishonesty.

Pickering: Oh, please, Higgins: I'm west country myself. [*To* **Doolittle.**] How did you know the girl was here if you didnt send her?

Doolittle: It was like this, Governor. The girl took a boy in the taxi to give him a jaunt. Son of her landlady, he is. He hung about on the chance of her giving him another ride home. Well, she sent him back for her luggage when she heard you was willing for her to stop here. I met the boy at the corner of Long Acre and Endell Street.

Higgins: Public house. Yes?

Doolittle: The poor man's club, Governor: why shouldnt I?

Pickering: Do let him tell his story, Higgins.

Doolittle: He told me what was up. And I ask you, what was my feelings and my duty as a father? I says to the boy, "You bring me the luggage," I says—

Pickering: Why didnt you go for it yourself?

Doolittle: Landlady wouldnt have trusted me with it, Governor. She's that kind of woman: you know. I had to give the boy a penny afore he trusted me with it, the little swine. I brought it to her just to oblige you like, and make myself agreeable. Thats all.

Higgins: How much luggage?

Doolittle: Musical instrument, Governor. A few pictures, a trifle of jewelry, and a bird-cage. She said she didnt want no clothes. What was I to think from that, Governor? I ask you as a parent what was I to think?

Higgins: So you came to rescue her from worse than death, eh?

Doolittle: [Appreciatively: relieved at being so well understood.] Just so, Governor. Thats right.

Pickering: But why did you bring her luggage if you intended to take her away?

Doolittle: Have I said a word about taking her away? Have I now?

Higgins: [Determinedly.] Youre going to take her away, double quick. [He crosses to the hearth and rings the bell.]

Doolittle: [Rising.] No, Governor. Dont say that. I'm not the man to stand in my girl's light. Heres a career opening for her, as you might say; and—
[Mrs Pearce opens the door and awaits orders.]

Higgins: Mrs Pearce: this is Eliza's father. He has come to take her away. Give her to him. [He goes back to the piano, with an air of washing his hands of the whole affair.]

Doolittle: No. This is a misunderstanding. Listen here—

Mrs Pearce: He cant take her away, Mr Higgins: how can he? You told me to burn her clothes.

Doolittle: Thats right. I cant carry the girl through the streets like a blooming monkey, can I? I put it to you.

Higgins: You have put it to me that you want your daughter. Take your daughter. If she has no clothes go out and buy her some.

Doolittle: [Desperate.] Wheres the clothes she come in? Did I burn them or did your missus here?

Mrs Pearce: I am the housekeeper, if you please. I have sent for some clothes for your girl. When they come you can take her away. You can wait in the kitchen. This way, please.
[Doolittle, much troubled, accompanies her to the door; then hesitates; finally turns confidentially to Higgins.]

Doolittle: Listen here, Governor. You and me is men of the world, aint we?

Higgins: Oh! Men of the world, are we? Youd better go, Mrs Pearce.

Mrs Pearce: I think so, indeed, sir. [She goes, with dignity.]

Pickering: The floor is yours, Mr Doolittle.

Doolittle: [To Pickering.] I thank you, Governor. [To Higgins, who takes refuge on the piano bench, a little overwhelmed by the proximity of his visitor; for Doolittle has a professional flavour of dust about him.] Well, the truth is, I've taken a sort of fancy to you, Governor; and if you want the girl, I'm not so set on having her back home again but what I might be open to an arrangement. Regarded in the light of a young woman, she's a fine handsome girl. As a daughter she's not worth her keep; and so I tell you straight. All I ask is my rights as a father; and youre the last man alive to expect me to let her go for nothing; for I can see youre one of the straight sort, Governor. Well, whats a five-pound note to you? and whats Eliza to me? [He turns to his chair and sits down judicially.]

Pickering: I think you ought to know, Doolittle, that Mr Higgins's intentions are entirely honorable.

Doolittle: Course they are, Governor. If I thought they wasn't, I'd ask fifty.

Higgins: [Revolted.] Do you mean to say that you would sell your daughter for £50?

Doolittle: Not in a general way I would; but to oblige a gentleman like you I'd do a good deal, I do assure you.

Pickering: Have you no morals, man?

Doolittle: [*Unabashed.*] Cant afford them, Governor. Neither could you if you was as poor as me. Not that I mean any harm, you know. But if Liza is going to have a bit out of this, why not me too?

Higgins: [*Troubled.*] I dont know what to do, Pickering. There can be no question that as a matter of morals it's a positive crime to give this chap a farthing. And yet I feel a sort of rough justice in his claim.

Doolittle: Thats it, Governor. Thats all I say. A father's heart, as it were.

Pickering: Well, I know the feeling; but really it seems hardly right—

Doolittle: Dont say that, Governor. Dont look at it that way. What am I, Governors both? I ask you, what am I? I'm one of the undeserving poor: thats what I am. Think of what that means to a man. It means that he's up agen middle class morality all the time. If theres anything going, and I put in for a bit of it, it's always the same story: "Youre undeserving; so you cant have it." But my needs is as great as the most deserving widow's that ever got money out of six different charities in one week for the death of the same husband. I dont need less than a deserving man: I need more. I dont eat less hearty than him; and I drink a lot more. I want a bit of amusement, cause I'm a thinking man. I want cheerfulness and a song and a band when I feel low. Well, they charge me just the same for everything as they charge the deserving. What is middle class morality? Just an excuse for never giving me anything. Therefore, I ask you, as two gentlemen, not to play that game on me. I'm playing straight with you. I aint pretending to be deserving. I'm undeserving; and I mean to go on being undeserving. I like it; and thats the truth. Will you take advantage of a man's nature to do him out of the price of his own daughter what he's brought up and fed and clothed by the sweat of his brow until she's growed big enough to be interesting to you two gentlemen? Is five pounds unreasonable? I put it to you; and I leave it to you.

Higgins: [*Rising, and going over to* **Pickering**.] Pickering: if we were to take this man in hand for three months, he could choose between a seat in the Cabinet and a popular pulpit in Wales.

Pickering: What do you say to that, Doolittle?

Doolittle: Not me, Governor, thank you kindly. Ive heard all the preachers and all the prime ministers—for I'm a thinking man and game for politics or religion or social reform same as all the other amusements—and I tell you it's a dog's life any way you look at it. Undeserving poverty is my line. Taking one station in society with another, it's—it's—well, it's the only one that has any ginger in it, to my taste.

Higgins: I suppose we must give him a fiver.

Pickering: He'll make a bad use of it, I'm afraid.

Doolittle: Not me, Governor, so help me I wont. Dont you be afraid that I'll save it and spare it and live idle on it. There wont be a penny of it left by Monday: I'll have to go to work same as if I'd never had it. It wont pauperize me, you bet. Just one good spree for myself and the missus, giving pleasure to ourselves and employment to others, and satisfaction to you to think it's not been throwed away. You couldnt spend it better.

Higgins: [*Taking out his pocket book and coming between* **Doolittle** *and the piano.*] This is irresistible. Lets give him ten. [*He offers two notes to the dustman.*]

Doolittle: No, Governor. She wouldnt have the heart to spend ten; and perhaps I shouldnt neither. Ten pounds is a lot of money: it makes a man feel prudent like; and then goodbye to happiness. You give me what I ask you, Governor: not a penny more, and not a penny less.

Pickering: Why dont you marry that missus of yours? I rather draw the line at encouraging that sort of immorality.

Doolittle: Tell her so, Governor: tell her so. I'm willing. It's me that suffers by it. Ive no hold on her. I got to be agreeable to her. I got to give her presents. I got to buy her clothes something sinful. I'm a slave to that woman, Governor, just because I'm not her lawful husband. And she knows it too. Catch her marrying me! Take my advice, Governor: marry Eliza while she's young and dont know no better. If you dont you'll be sorry for it after. If you do, she'll be sorry for it after; but better her than you, because youre a man, and she's only a woman and dont know how to be happy anyhow.

Higgins: Pickering: if we listen to this man another minute, we shall have no convictions left. [To **Doolittle.**] Five pounds I think you said.

Doolittle: Thank you kindly, Governor.

Higgins: Youre sure you wont take ten?

Doolittle: Not now. Another time, Governor.

Higgins: [Handing him a five-pound note.] Here you are.

Doolittle: Thank you, Governor. Good morning. [He hurries to the door, anxious to get away with his booty. When he opens it he is confronted with a dainty and exquisitely clean young Japanese lady in a simple blue cotton kimono printed cunningly with small white jasmine blossoms. **Mrs Pearce** is with her. He gets out of her way deferentially and apologizes.] Beg pardon, miss.

The Japanese Lady: Garn! Dont you know your own daughter?

Doolittle: [Exclaiming] Bly me! it's Eliza!
Higgins: { simul- } Whats that? This!
Pickering: [taneously.] By Jove!

Liza: Dont I look silly?

Higgins: Silly?

Mrs Pearce: [At the door.] Now, Mr Higgins, please dont say anything to make the girl conceited about herself.

Higgins: [Conscientiously.] Oh! Quite right, Mrs Pearce. [To **Eliza.**] Yes: damned silly.

Mrs Pearce: Please, sir.

Higgins: [Correcting himself.] I mean extremely silly.

Liza: I should look all right with my hat on. [She takes up her hat; puts it on; and walks across the room to the fireplace with a fashionable air.]

Higgins: A new fashion, by George! And it ought to look horrible!

Doolittle: [With fatherly pride.] Well, I never thought she'd clean up as good looking as that, Governor. She's a credit to me, aint she?

Liza: I tell you, it's easy to clean up here. Hot and cold water on tap, just as much as you like, there is. Woolly towels, there is; and a towel horse so hot, it burns your fingers. Soft brushes to scrub yourself, and a wooden bowl of soap smelling like primroses. Now I know why ladies is so clean. Washing's a treat for them. Wish they could see what it is for the like of me!

Higgins: I'm glad the bathroom met with your approval.

Liza: It didnt: not all of it; and I dont care who hears me say it. Mrs Pearce knows.

Higgins: What was wrong, Mrs. Pearce?

Mrs Pearce: [Blandly.] Oh, nothing, sir. It doesnt matter.

Liza: I had a good mind to break it. I didnt know which way to look. But I hung a towel over it, I did.

Higgins: Over what?

Mrs Pearce: Over the looking-glass, sir.

Higgins: Doolittle: you have brought your daughter up too strictly.

Doolittle: Me! I never brought her up at all, except to give her a lick of a strap now and again. Dont put it on me, Governor. She aint accustomed to it, you see: thats all. But she'll soon pick up your free-and-easy ways.

Liza: I'm a good girl, I am; and I wont pick up no free-and-easy ways.

Higgins: Eliza: if you say again that youre a good girl, your father shall take you home.

Liza: Not him. You dont know my father. All he come here for was to touch you for some money to get drunk on.

Doolittle: Well, what else would I want money for? To put into the plate in church, I suppose. *[She puts out her tongue at him. He is so incensed by this that* **Pickering** *presently finds it necessary to step between them.]* Dont you give me none of your lip; and dont let me hear you giving this gentleman any of it neither, or youll hear from me about it. See?

Higgins: Have you any further advice to give her before you go, Doolittle? Your blessing, for instance.

Doolittle: No, Governor: I aint such a mug as to put up my children to all I know myself. Hard enough to hold them in without that. If you want Eliza's mind improved, Governor, you do it yourself with a strap. So long, gentlemen. *[He turns to go.]*

Higgins: *[Impressively.]* Stop. Youll come regularly to see your daughter. It's your duty, you know. My brother is a clergyman; and he could help you in your talks with her.

Doolittle: *[Evasively.]* Certainly, I'll come, Governor. Not just this week, because I have a job at a distance. But later on you may depend on me. Afternoon, gentlemen. Afternoon, maam.

[He touches his hat to **Mrs Pearce***, who disdains the salutation and goes out. He winks at* **Higgins***, thinking him probably a fellow-sufferer from Mrs Pearce's difficult disposition, and follows her.]*

Liza: Dont you believe the old liar. He'd as soon you set a bulldog on him as a clergyman. You wont see him again in a hurry.

Higgins: I dont want to, Eliza. Do you?

Liza: Not me. I dont want never to see him again, I dont. He's a disgrace to me, he is, collecting dust, instead of working at his trade.

Pickering: What is his trade, Eliza?

Liza: Talking money out of other people's pockets into his own. His proper trade's a navvy; and he works at it sometimes too—for exercise—and earns good money at it. Aint you going to call me Miss Doolittle any more?

Pickering: I beg your pardon, Miss Doolittle. It was a slip of the tongue.

Liza: Oh, I dont mind; only it sounded so genteel. I should just like to take a taxi to the corner of Tottenham Court Road and get out there and tell it to wait for me, just to put the girls in their place a bit. I wouldnt speak to them, you know.

Pickering: Better wait til we get you something really fashionable.

Higgins: Besides, you shouldnt cut your old friends now that you have risen in the world. Thats what we call snobbery.

Liza: You dont call the like of them my friends now, I should hope. Theyve took it out of me often enough with their ridicule when they had the chance; and now I mean to get a bit of my own back. But if I'm to have fashionable clothes, I'll wait. I should like to have some. Mrs Pearce says youre going to give me some to wear in bed at night different to what I wear in the daytime; but it do seem a waste of money when you could get something to shew. Besides, I never could fancy changing into cold things on a winter night.

Mrs Pearce: *[Coming back.]* Now, Eliza. The new things have come for you to try on.

Liza: Ah-ow-oo-ooh!

[She rushes out.]

Mrs Pearce: *[Following her.]* Oh, dont

rush about like that, girl. *[She shuts the door behind her.]*

Higgins: Pickering: we have taken on a stiff job.

Pickering: *[With conviction.]* Higgins: we have.

*   *   *

There seems to be some curiosity as to what **Higgins's** *lessons to* **Eliza** *were like. Well, here is a sample: the first one.*

Picture **Eliza,** *in her new clothes, and feeling her inside put out of step by a lunch, dinner, and breakfast of a kind to which it is unaccustomed, seated with* **Higgins** *and the* **Colonel** *in the study, feeling like a hospital out-patient at a first encounter with the doctors.*

*[***Higgins,*** constitutionally unable to sit still, discomposes her still more by striding restlessly about. But for the reassuring presence and quietude of her friend the* **Colonel** *she would run for her life, even back to Drury Lane.]*

Higgins: Say your alphabet.

Liza: I know my alphabet. Do you think I know nothing? I dont need to be taught like a child.

Higgins: *[Thundering.]* Say your alphabet.

Pickering: Say it, Miss Doolittle. You will understand presently. Do what he tells you; and let him teach you in his own way.

Liza: Oh well, if you put it like that— Ahyee, bəyee, cəyee, dəyee—

Higgins: *[With the roar of a wounded lion.]* Stop. Listen to this, Pickering. This is what we pay for as elementary education. This unfortunate animal has been locked up for nine years in school at our expense to teach her to speak and read the language of Shakespear and Milton. And the result is Ahyee, Bə-yee, Cə-yee, Dəyee. *[To* **Eliza.]** Say A, B, C, D.

Liza: *[Almost in tears.]* But I'm sayin it. Ahyee, Bəyee, Cəyee—

Higgins: Stop. Say a cup of tea.

Liza: A cappətə-ee.

Higgins: Put your tongue forward until it squeezes against the top of your lower teeth. Now say cup.

Liza: C-c-c—I cant. C-Cup.

Pickering: Good. Splendid, Miss Doolittle.

Higgins: By Jupiter, she's done it the first shot. Pickering: we shall make a duchess of her. *[To* **Eliza.]** Now do you think you could possibly say tea? Not tə-yee, mind: if you ever say bə-yee cə-yee də-yee again you shall be dragged round the room three times by the hair of your head. *[Fortissimo.]* T, T, T, T.

Liza: *[Weeping.]* I cant hear no difference cep that it sounds more genteel-like when you say it.

Higgins: Well, if you can hear that difference, what the devil are you crying for? Pickering: give her a chocolate.

Pickering: No, no. Never mind crying a little, Miss Doolittle: you are doing very well; and the lessons wont hurt. I promise you I wont let him drag you round the room by your hair.

Higgins: Be off with you to Mrs Pearce and tell her about it. Think about it. Try to do it by yourself: and keep your tongue well forward in your mouth instead of trying to roll it up and swallow it. Another lesson at half-past four this afternoon. Away with you.

[Eliza, still sobbing, rushes from the room.]

And that is the sort of ordeal poor **Eliza** *has to go through for months before we meet her again on her first appearance in London society of the professional class.*

Act Three

It is **Mrs Higgins's** *at-home day. Nobody has yet arrived. Her drawing room, in a flat on Chelsea Embankment, has three windows looking on the river; and the ceiling is not so lofty as it would be in an older house of the same pretension. The windows are open, giving access to a balcony with flowers in pots. If you* stand with your face to the windows, you have the fireplace on your left and the door in the right-hand wall close to the corner nearest the windows.

Mrs Higgins *was brought up on Morris and Burne Jones; and her room, which is very unlike her son's room in Wimpole Street, is not crowded with furniture and little tables and nicknacks. In the middle of the room there is a big ottoman; and this, with the carpet, the Morris wall-papers, and the Morris chintz window curtains and brocade covers of the ottoman and its cushions, supply all the ornament, and are much too handsome to be hidden by odds and ends of useless things. A few good oil-paintings from the exhibitions in the Grosvenor Gallery thirty years ago (the Burne Jones, not the Whistler side of them) are on the walls. The only landscape is a Cecil Lawson on the scale of a Rubens. There is a portrait of* **Mrs Higgins** *as she was when she defied the fashion in her youth in one of the beautiful Rossettian costumes which, when caricatured by people who did not understand, led to the absurdities of popular estheticism in the eighteen-seventies.*

In the corner diagonally opposite the door **Mrs Higgins,** *now over sixty and long past taking the trouble to dress out of the fashion, sits writing at an elegantly simple writing-table with a bell button within reach of her hand. There is a Chippendale chair further back in the room between her and the window nearest her side. At the other side of the room, further forward, is an Elizabethan chair roughly carved in the taste of Inigo Jones. On the same side a piano in a decorated case. The corner between the fireplace and the window is occupied by a divan cushioned in Morris chintz.*

It is between four and five in the afternoon.

[The door is opened violently; and **Higgins** *enters with his hat on.]*

Mrs Higgins: *[Dismayed.]* Henry! *[Scolding him.]* What are you doing here today? It is my at-home day: you promised not to come. *[As he bends* to kiss her, she takes his hat off, and presents it to him.]*

Higgins: Oh bother! *[He throws the hat down on the table.]*

Mrs Higgins: Go home at once.

Higgins: *[Kissing her.]* I know, mother. I came on purpose.

Mrs Higgins: But you mustnt. I'm serious, Henry. You offend all my friends: they stop coming whenever they meet you.

Higgins: Nonsense! I know I have no small talk; but people dont mind. *[He sits on the settee.]*

Mrs Higgins: Oh! dont they? Small talk indeed! What about your large talk? Really, dear, you mustnt stay.

Higgins: I must. Ive a job for you. A phonetic job.

Mrs Higgins: No use, dear. I'm sorry; but I cant get round your vowels; and though I like to get pretty postcards in your patent shorthand, I always have to read the copies in ordinary writing you so thoughtfully send me.

Higgins: Well, this isnt a phonetic job.

Mrs Higgins: You said it was.

Higgins: Not your part of it. Ive picked up a girl.

Mrs Higgins: Does that mean that some girl has picked you up?

Higgins: Not at all. I dont mean a love affair.

Mrs Higgins: What a pity!

Higgins: Why?

Mrs Higgins: Well, you never fall in love with anyone under forty-five. When will you discover that there are some rather nice-looking young women about?

Higgins: Oh, I cant be bothered with young women. My idea of a lovable woman is somebody as like you as possible. I shall never get into the way of seriously liking young women: some habits lie too deep to be changed. *[Rising abruptly and walking about, jingling his money and his keys in his trouser pockets.]* Besides, theyre all idiots.

Mrs Higgins: Do you know what you

would do if you really loved me, Henry?

Higgins: Oh bother! What? Marry, I suppose.

Mrs Higgins: No. Stop fidgeting and take your hands out of your pockets. *[With a gesture of despair, he obeys and sits down again.]* Thats a good boy. Now tell me about the girl.

Higgins: She's coming to see you.

Mrs Higgins: I dont remember asking her.

Higgins: You didnt. *I* asked her. If youd known her you wouldnt have asked her.

Mrs Higgins: Indeed! Why?

Higgins: Well, it's like this. She's a common flower girl. I picked her off the kerbstone.

Mrs. Higgins: And invited her to my at-home!

Higgins: *[Rising and coming to her to coax her.]* Oh, thatll be all right. Ive taught her to speak properly; and she has strict orders as to her behavior. She's to keep to two subjects: the weather and everybody's health— Fine day and How do you do, you know—and not to let herself go on things in general. That will be safe.

Mrs Higgins: Safe! To talk about our health! about our insides! perhaps about our outsides! How could you be so silly, Henry?

Higgins: *[Impatiently.]* Well, she must talk about something. *[He controls himself and sits down again.]* Oh, she'll be all right: dont you fuss. Pickering is in it with me. Ive a sort of bet on that I'll pass her off as a duchess in six months. I started on her some months ago; and she's getting on like a house on fire. I shall win my bet. She has a quick ear; and she's easier to teach than my middle-class pupils because she's had to learn a complete new language. She talks English almost as you talk French.

Mrs Higgins: Thats satisfactory, at all events.

Higgins: Well, it is and it isnt.

Mrs Higgins: What does that mean?

Higgins: You see, Ive got her pronunciation all right; but you have to consider not only how a girl pronounces, but what she pronounces; and that's where—

[They are interrupted by the parlor-maid, announcing guests.]

The Parlormaid: Mrs and Miss Eynsford Hill. *[She withdraws.]*

Higgins: Oh Lord! *[He rises; snatches his hat from the table; and makes for the door; but before he reaches it his mother introduces him.]*

[Mrs and Miss Eynsford Hill are the mother and daughter who sheltered from the rain in Covent Garden. The mother is well bred, quiet, and has the habitual anxiety of straitened means. The daughter has acquired a gay air of being very much at home in society: the bravado of genteel poverty.]

Mrs Eynsford Hill: *[To **Mrs Higgins.**]* How do you do? *[They shake hands.]*

Miss Eynsford Hill: How d'you do? *[She shakes.]*

Mrs Higgins: *[Introducing.]* My son Henry.

Mrs Eynsford Hill: Your celebrated son! I have so longed to meet you, Professor Higgins.

Higgins: *[Glumly, making no movement in her direction.]* Delighted. *[He backs against the piano and bows brusquely.]*

Miss Eynsford Hill: *[Going to him with confident familiarity.]* How do you do?

Higgins: *[Staring at her.]* Ive seen you before somewhere. I havnt the ghost of a notion where; but Ive heard your voice. *[Drearily.]* It doesnt matter. Youd better sit down.

Mrs Higgins: I'm sorry to say that my celebrated son has no manners. You mustnt mind him.

Miss Eynsford Hill: *[Gaily.]* I don't. *[She sits in the Elizabethan chair.]*

Mrs Eynsford Hill: *[A little bewildered.]*

Not at all. *[She sits on the ottoman between her daughter and* **Mrs. Higgins***, who has turned her chair away from the writing-table.]*

Higgins: Oh, have I been rude? I didnt mean to be.

[He goes to the central window, through which, with his back to the company, he contemplates the river and the flowers in Battersea Park on the opposite bank as if they were a frozen desert.

The Parlormaid *returns, ushering in* **Pickering***.]*

The Parlormaid: Colonel Pickering. *[She withdraws.]*

Pickering: How do you do, Mrs Higgins?

Mrs Higgins: So glad youve come. Do you know Mrs Eynsford Hill—Miss Eynsford Hill? *[Exchange of bows. The* **Colonel** *brings the Chippendale chair a little forward between* **Mrs Hill** *and* **Mrs Higgins***, and sits down.]*

Pickering: Has Henry told you what weve come for?

Higgins *[Over his shoulder.]* We were interrupted: damn it!

Mrs Higgins: Oh Henry, Henry, really!

Mrs Eynsford Hill: *[Half rising.]* Are we in the way?

Mrs Higgins: *[Rising and making her sit down again.]* No, no. You couldnt have come more fortunately: we want you to meet a friend of ours.

Higgins: *[Turning hopefully.]* Yes, by George! We want two or three people. You'll do as well as anybody else.

[The **Parlor-Maid** *returns, ushering* **Freddy***.]*

The Parlormaid: Mr Eynsford Hill.

Higgins: *[Almost audibly, past endurance.]* God of Heaven! another of them.

Freddy: *[Shaking hands with* **Mrs Higgins***.]* Ahdedo?

Mrs Higgins: Very good of you to come. *[Introducing.]* Colonel Pickering.

Freddy: *[Bowing.]* Ahdedo?

Mrs Higgins: I dont think you know my son, Professor Higgins.

Freddy: *[Going to* **Higgins***.]* Ahdedo?

Higgins: *[Looking at him much as if he were a pickpocket.]* I'll take my oath I've met you before somewhere. Where was it?

Freddy: I don't think so.

Higgins: *[Resignedly.]* It dont matter, anyhow. Sit down.

[He shakes **Freddy's** *hand, and almost slings him on to the ottoman with his face to the window; then comes round to the other side of it.]*

Higgins: Well, here we are, anyhow! *[He sits down on the ottoman next to* **Mrs Eynsford Hill***, on her left.]* And now, what the devil are we going to talk about until Eliza comes?

Mrs Higgins: Henry: you are the life and soul of the Royal Society's soirées; but really youre rather trying on more commonplace occasions.

Higgins: Am I? Very sorry. *[Beaming suddenly.]* I suppose I am, you know. *[Uproariously.]* Ha, ha!

Miss Eynsford Hill: *[Who considers* **Higgins** *quite eligible matrimonially.]* I sympathize. I havnt any small talk. If people would only be frank and say what they really think!

Higgins: *[Relapsing into gloom.]* Lord forbid!

Mrs Eynsford Hill: *[Taking up her daughter's cue.]* But why?

Higgins: What they think they ought to think is bad enough, Lord knows; but what they really think would break up the whole show. Do you suppose it would be really agreeable if I were to come out now with what I really think?

Miss Eynsford Hill: *[Gaily.]* Is it so very cynical?

Higgins: Cynical! Who the dickens said it was cynical? I mean it wouldnt be decent.

Mrs Eynsford Hill *[Seriously.]* Oh! I'm sure you dont mean that, Mr. Higgins.

Higgins: You see, we're all savages, more or less. We're supposed to be civilized and cultured—to know all about poetry and philosophy and art and science, and so on; but how many of us know even the meanings of these names? [*To* **Miss Hill.**] What do you know of poetry? [*To* **Mrs Hill.**] What do you know of science? [*Indicating* **Freddy.**] What does he know of art or science or anything else? What the devil do you imagine I know of philosophy?

Mrs Higgins: [*Warningly.*] Or of manners, Henry?

The Parlor-Maid: [*Opening the door.*] Miss Doolittle. [*She withdraws.*]

Higgins: [*Rising hastily and running to* **Mrs Higgins.**] Here she is, mother. [*He stands on tiptoe and makes signs over his mother's head to* **Eliza** *to indicate to her which lady is her hostess.*]

> [**Eliza**, *who is exquisitely dressed, produces an impression of such remarkable distinction and beauty as she enters that they all rise, quite fluttered. Guided by* **Higgins's** *signals, she comes to* **Mrs Higgins** *with studied grace.*]

Liza: [*Speaking with pedantic correctness of pronunciation and great beauty of tone.*] How do you do, Mrs. Higgins? [*She gasps slightly in making sure of the H in Higgins, but is quite successful.*] Mr. Higgins told me I might come.

Mrs. Higgins: [*Cordially.*] Quite right: I'm very glad indeed to see you.

Pickering: How do you do, Miss Doolittle?

Liza: [*Shaking hands with him.*] Colonel Pickering, is it not?

Mrs Eynsford Hill: I feel sure we have met before, Miss Doolittle. I remember your eyes.

Liza: How do you do? [*She sits down on the ottoman gracefully in the place just left vacant by Higgins.*]

Mrs Eynsford Hill: [*Introducing.*] My daughter Clara.

Liza: How do you do?

Clara: [*Impulsively.*] How do you do? [*She sits down on the ottoman beside* **Eliza,** *devouring her with her eyes.*]

Freddy: [*Coming to their side of the ottoman.*] Ive certainly had the pleasure.

Mrs Eynsford Hill: [*Introducing.*] My son Freddy.

Liza: How do you do?

> [**Freddy** *bows and sits down in the Elizabethan chair, infatuated.*]

Higgins: [*Suddenly.*] By George, yes: it all comes back to me! [*They stare at him.*] Covent Garden! [*Lamentably.*] What a damned thing!

Mrs. Higgins: Henry, please! [*He is about to sit on the edge of the table.*] Dont sit on my writing-table: youll break it.

Higgins: [*Sulkily.*] Sorry.

> [*He goes to the divan, stumbling into the fender and over the fire-irons on his way; extricating himself with muttered imprecations; and finishing his disastrous journey by throwing himself so impatiently on the divan that he almost breaks it.* **Mrs Higgins** *looks at him, but controls herself and says nothing.*
>
> *A long and painful pause ensues.*]

Mrs Higgins: [*At last, conversationally.*] Will it rain, do you think?

Liza: The shallow depression in the west of these islands is likely to move slowly in an easterly direction. There are no indications of any great change in the barometrical situation.

Freddy: Ha! ha! how awfully funny!

Liza: What is wrong with that, young man? I bet I got it right.

Freddy: Killing!

Mrs Eynsford Hill: I'm sure I hope it wont turn cold. Theres so much influenza about. It runs right through our whole family regularly every spring.

Liza: [*Darkly.*] My aunt died of influenza: so they said.

Mrs Eynsford Hill: [*Clicks her tongue sympathetically.*]!!!

Liza: [*In the same tragic tone.*] But it's my belief they done the old woman in.

Mrs Higgins: [*Puzzled.*] Done her in?

Liza: Y-e-e-e-es, Lord love you! Why should she die of influenza? She come through diphtheria right enough the year before. I saw her with my own eyes. Fairly blue with it, she was. They all thought she was dead; but my father he kept ladling gin down her throat til she came to so sudden that she bit the bowl off the spoon.

Mrs Eynsford Hill: *[Startled.]* Dear me!

Liza: *[Piling up the indictment.]* What call would a woman with that strength in her have to die of influenza? What become of her new straw hat that should have come to me? Somebody pinched it; and what I say is, them as pinched it done her in.

Mrs Eynsford Hill: What does doing her in mean?

Higgins: *[Hastily.]* Oh, thats the new small talk. To do a person in means to kill them.

Mrs Eynsford Hill: *[To Eliza, horrified.]* You surely dont believe that your aunt was killed?

Liza: Do I not! Them she lived with would have killed her for a hat-pin, let alone a hat.

Mrs Eynsford Hill: But it cant have been right for your father to pour spirits down her throat like that. It might have killed her.

Liza: Not her. Gin was mother's milk to her. Besides, he'd poured so much down his own throat that he knew the good of it.

Mrs Eynsford Hill: Do you mean that he drank?

Liza: Drank! My word! Something chronic.

Mrs Eynsford Hill: How dreadful for you!

Liza: Not a bit. It never did him no harm what I could see. But then he did not keep it up regular. *[Cheerfully.]* On the burst, as you might say, from time to time. And always more agreeable when he had a drop in. When he was out of work, my mother used to give him fourpence and tell him to go out and not come back until

he'd drunk himself cheerful and loving-like. Theres lots of women has to make their husbands drunk to make them fit to live with. *[Now quite at her ease.]* You see, it's like this. If a man has a bit of conscience, it always takes him when he's sober; and then it makes him low-spirited. A drop of booze just takes that off and makes him happy. *[To **Freddy,** who is in convulsions of suppressed laughter.]* Here! what are you sniggering at?

Freddy: The new small talk. You do it so awfully well.

Liza: If I was doing it proper, what was you laughing at? *[To **Higgins.**]* Have I said anything I oughtnt?

Mrs Higgins: *[Interposing.]* Not at all, Miss Doolittle.

Liza: Well, thats a mercy, anyhow. *[Expansively.]* What I always say is—

Higgins: *[Rising and looking at his watch.]* Ahem!

Liza: *[Looking round at him; taking the hint; and rising.]* Well: I must go. *[They all rise. **Freddy** goes to the door.]* So pleased to have met you. Goodbye. *[She shakes hands with **Mrs Higgins.**]*

Mrs Higgins: Goodbye.

Liza: Goodbye, Colonel Pickering.

Pickering: Goodbye, Miss Doolittle. *[They shake hands.]*

Liza: *[Nodding to the others.]* Goodbye, all.

Freddy: *[Opening the door for her.]* Are you walking across the Park, Miss Doolittle? If so—

Liza: *[With perfectly elegant diction.]* Walk! Not bloody likely. *[Sensation.]* I am going in a taxi.

*[She goes out. **Pickering** gasps and sits down. **Freddy** goes out on the balcony to catch another glimpse of **Eliza.**]*

Mrs Eynsford Hill: *[Suffering from shock.]* Well, I really cant get used to the new ways.

Clara: *[Throwing herself discontentedly into the Elizabethan chair.]* Oh, it's all right, mamma, quite right. People will think we never go anywhere or see anybody if you are so old-fashioned.

Mrs Eynsford Hill: I daresay I am very old-fashioned; but I do hope you wont begin using that expression, Clara. I have got accustomed to hear you talking about men as rotters, and calling everything filthy and beastly; though I do think it horrible and unlady like. But this last is really too much. Dont you think so, Colonel Pickering?

Pickering: Dont ask me. Ive been away in India for several years; and manners have changed so much that I sometimes dont know whether I'm at a respectable dinnertable or in a ship's forecastle.

Clara: It's all a matter of habit. Theres no right or wrong in it. Nobody means anything by it. And it's so quaint, and gives such a smart emphasis to things that are not in themselves very witty. I find the new small talk delightful and quite innocent.

Mrs Eynsford Hill: [Rising.] Well, after that, I think it's time for us to go.

[Pickering and Higgins rise.]

Clara: [Rising.] Oh yes: we have three at-homes to go to still. Goodbye, Mrs Higgins. Goodbye, Colonel Pickering. Goodbye, Professor Higgins.

Higgins: [Coming grimly at her from the divan, and accompanying her to the door.] Goodbye. Be sure you try on that small talk at the three at-homes. Dont be nervous about it. Pitch it in strong.

Clara: [All smiles.] I will. Goodbye. Such nonsense, all this early Victorian prudery!

Higgins: [Tempting her.] Such damned nonsense!

Clara: Such bloody nonsense!

Mrs Eynsford Hill: [Convulsively.] Clara!

Clara: Ha! ha! [She goes out radiant, conscious of being thoroughly up to date, and is heard descending the stairs in a stream of silvery laughter.]

Freddy: [To the heavens at large.] Well,

I ask you—[He gives it up, and comes to **Mrs Higgins.**] Goodbye.

Mrs Higgins: [Shaking hands.] Goodbye. would you like to meet Miss Doolittle again?

Freddy: [Eagerly.] Yes, I should, most awfully.

Mrs Higgins: Well, you know my days.

Freddy: Yes, Thanks awfully. Goodbye.

[He goes out.]

Mrs Eynsford Hill: Goodbye, Mr Higgins.

Higgins: Goodbye. Goodbye.

Mrs Eynsford Hill: [To **Pickering.**] It's no use. I shall never be able to bring myself to use that word.

Pickering: Dont. It's not compulsory, you know. Youll get on quite well without it.

Mrs Eynsford Hill: Only, Clara is so down on me if I am not positively reeking with the latest slang. Goodbye.

Pickering: Goodbye [They shake hands.]

Mrs Eynsford Hill: [To **Mrs Higgins.**] You mustnt mind Clara.

[**Pickering,** catching from her lowered tone that this is not meant for him to hear, discreetly joins **Higgins** at the window.]

We're so poor! and she gets so few parties, poor child! She doesnt quite know.

[**Mrs Higgins,** seeing that her eyes are moist, takes her hand sympathetically and goes with her to the door.]

But the boy is nice. Dont you think so?

Mrs Higgins: Oh, quite nice. I shall always be delighted to see him.

Mrs Eynsford Hill: Thank you, dear. Goodbye.

[She goes out.]

Higgins: [Eagerly.] Well? Is Eliza presentable? [He swoops on his mother and drags her to the ottoman, where she sits down in **Eliza's** place with her son on her left.]

[**Pickering** returns to his chair on her right.]

Mrs Higgins: You silly boy, of course she's not presentable. She's a triumph of your art and of her dressmaker's; but if you suppose for a moment that she doesn't give herself away in every sentence she utters, you must be perfectly cracked about her.

Pickering: But dont you think something might be done? I mean something to eliminate the sanguinary element from her conversation.

Mrs Higgins: Not as long as she is in Henry's hands.

Higgins: [Aggrieved.] Do you mean that my language is improper?

Mrs Higgins: No, dearest: it would be quite proper—say on a canal barge; but it would not be proper for her at a garden party.

Higgins: [Deeply injured.] Well I must say—

Pickering: [Interupting him.] Come, Higgins: you must learn to know yourself. I havent heard such language as yours since we used to review the volunteers in Hyde Park twenty years ago.

Higgins: [Sulkily.] Oh, well, if you say so, I suppose I dont always talk like a bishop.

Mrs Higgins: [Quieting **Henry** with a touch.] Colonel Pickering: will you tell me what is the exact state of things in Wimpole Street?

Pickering: [Cheerfully: as if this completely changed the subject.] Well, I have come to live there with Henry. We work together at my Indian Dialects; and we think it more convenient—

Mrs Higgins: Quite so. I know all about that: it's an excellent arrangement. But where does this girl live?

Higgins: With us, of course. Where should she live?

Mrs Higgins: But on what terms? Is she a servant? If not, what is she?

Pickering: [Slowly.] I think I know what you mean, Mrs Higgins.

Higgins: Well, dash me if I do! Ive had to work at the girl every day for months to get her to her present pitch. Besides, she's useful. She knows where my things are, and remembers my appointments and so forth.

Mrs Higgins: How does your housekeeper get on with her?

Higgins: Mrs Pearce? Oh, she's jolly glad to get so much taken off her hands; for before Eliza came, she used to have to find things and remind me of my appointments. But she's got some silly bee in her bonnet about Eliza. She keeps saying "You dont think, sir": doesnt she, Pick?

Pickering: Yes: thats the formula. "You dont think, sir." Thats the end of every conversation about Eliza.

Higgins: As if I ever stop thinking about the girl and her confounded vowels and consonants. I'm worn out, thinking about her, and watching her lips and her teeth and her tongue, not to mention her soul, which is the quaintest of the lot.

Mrs Higgins: You certainly are a pretty pair of babies, playing with your live doll.

Higgins: Playing! The hardest job I ever tackled: make no mistake about that, mother. But you have no idea how frightfully interesting it is to take a human being and change her into a quite different human being by creating a new speech for her. It's filling up the deepest gulf that separates class from class and soul from soul.

Pickering: [Drawing his chair closer to **Mrs Higgins** and bending over to her eagerly.] Yes: it's enormously interesting. I assure you, Mrs Higgins, we take Eliza very seriously. Every week —every day almost—there is some new change. [Closer again.] We keep records of every stage—dozens of gramophone disks and photographs—

Higgins: [Assailing her at the other ear.] Yes, by George: it's the most absorbing experiment I ever tackled. She regularly fills our lives up: doesnt she, Pick?

Pickering: We're always talking Eliza.

Higgins: Teaching Eliza.

Pickering: Dressing Eliza.

Mrs Higgins: What!

Higgins: Inventing new Elizas.

Higgins: *[Speaking together.]* You know, she has the most extraordinary quickness of ear:

Pickering: I assure you, my dear Mrs Higgins, that girl

Higgins: just like a parrot. Ive tried her with every

Pickering: is a genius. She can play the piano quite beautifully.

Higgins: possible sort of sound that a human being can make—

Pickering: We have taken her to classical concerts and to music

Higgins: Continental dialects, African dialects, Hottentot

Pickering: halls; and it's all the same to her: she plays everything

Higgins: clicks, things it took me years to get hold of; and

Pickering: she hears right off when she comes home, whether it's

Higgins: she picks them up like a shot, right away, as if she had

Pickering: Beethoven and Brahms or Lehar and Lionel Monckton;

Higgins: *[Speaking together.]* been at it all her life.

Pickering: though six months ago, she'd never as much as touched a piano—

Mrs Higgins: *[Putting her fingers in her ears, as they are by this time shouting one another down with an intolerable noise.]* Sh-sh-sh—sh! *[They stop.]*

Pickering: I beg your pardon. *[He draws his chair back apologetically.]*

Higgins: Sorry. When Pickering starts shouting nobody can get a word in edgeways.

Mrs Higgins: Be quiet, Henry. Colonel Pickering: dont you realize that when Eliza walked in Wimpole Street, something walked in with her?

Pickering: Her father did. But Henry soon got rid of him.

Mrs Higgins: It would have been more to the point if her mother had. But as her mother didnt something else did.

Pickering: But what?

Mrs Higgins: *[Unconsciously dating herself by the word.]* A problem.

Pickering: Oh, I see. The problem of how to pass her off as a lady.

Higgins: I'll solve that problem. Ive half solved it already.

Mrs Higgins: No, you two infinitely stupid male creatures: the problem of what is to be done with her afterwards.

Higgins: I dont see anything in that. She can go her own way, with all the advantages I have given her.

Mrs Higgins: The advantages of that poor woman who was here just now! The manners and habits that disqualify a fine lady from earning her own living without giving her a fine lady's income! Is that what you mean?

Pickering: *[Indulgently, being rather bored.]* Oh, that will be all right, Mrs Higgins. *[He rises to go.]*

Higgins: [*Rising also.*] We'll find her some light employment.

Pickering: She's happy enough. Dont you worry about her. Goodbye. [*He shakes hands as if he were consoling a frightened child, and makes for the door.*]

Higgins: Anyhow, theres no good bothering now. The thing's done. Goodbye, mother. [*He kisses her, and follows* **Pickering**.]

Pickering: [*Turning for a final consolation.*] There are plenty of openings. We'll do whats right. Goodbye.

Higgins: [*To* **Pickering** *as they go out together.*] Lets take her to the Shakespear exhibition at Earls Court.

Pickering: Yes: lets. Her remarks will be delicious.

Higgins: She'll mimic all the people for us when we get home.

Pickering: Ripping.

[*Both are heard laughing as they go downstairs.*]

Mrs Higgins: [*Rises with an impatient bounce, and returns to her work at the writing-table. She sweeps a litter of disarranged papers out of the way; snatches a sheet of paper from her stationary case; and tries resolutely to write. At the third time she gives it up; flings down her pen; grips the table angrily and exclaims.*] Oh, men! men!! men!!!

* * *

Clearly **Eliza** will not pass as a duchess yet; and **Higgins's** bet remains unwon. But the six months are not yet exhausted and just in time **Eliza** does actually pass as a princess. For a glimpse of how she did it imagine an Embassy in London one summer evening after dark. The hall door has an awning and a carpet across the sidewalk to the kerb, because a grand reception is in progress. A small crowd is lined up to see the guests arrive.

A Rolls-Royce car drives up. **Pickering** in evening dress, with medals and orders, alights, and hands out **Eliza,** in opera cloak, evening dress, diamonds, fan, flowers and all accessories. **Higgins** follows. The car drives off; and the three

go up the steps and into the house, the door opening for them as they approach.

Inside the house they find themselves in a spacious hall from which the grand staircase rises.

[On the left are the arrangements for the gentlemen's cloaks. The male guests are depositing their hats and wraps there. On the right is a door leading to the ladies' cloakroom. Ladies are going in cloaked and coming out in splendor. **Pickering** whispers to **Eliza** and points out the ladies' room. She goes into it. **Higgins** and **Pickering** take off their overcoats and take tickets for them from the attendant.

One of the guests, occupied in the same way, has his back turned. Having taken his ticket, he turns round and reveals himself as an important looking young man with an astonishingly hairy face. He has an enormous moustache, flowing out into luxuriant whiskers. Waves of hair cluster on his brow. His hair is cropped closely at the back, and glows with oil. Otherwise he is very smart. He wears several worthless orders. He is evidently a foreigner, guessable as a whiskered Pandour from Hungary; but in spite of the ferocity of his moustache he is amiable and genially voluble.

Recognizing **Higgins,** he flings his arms wide apart and approaches him enthusiastically.]

Whiskers: Maestro, maestro [He embraces **Higgins** and kisses him on both cheeks.] You remember me?

Higgins: No I dont. Who the devil are you?

Whiskers: I am your pupil: your first pupil, your best and greatest pupil. I am little Nepommuck, the marvellous boy. I have made your name famous throughout Europe. You teach me phonetic. You cannot forget ME.

Higgins: Why dont you shave?

Nepommuck: I have not your imposing appearance, your chin, your brow. Nobody notice me when I shave. Now I am famous: they call me Hairy Faced Dick.

Higgins: And what are you doing here among all these swells?

Nepommuck: I am interpreter. I speak 32 languages. I am indispensable at these international parties. You are great cockney specialist: you place a man anywhere in London the moment he open his mouth. I place any man in Europe.

[A **Footman** hurries down the grand staircase and comes to **Nepommuck.**]

Footman: You are wanted upstairs. Her Excellency cannot understand the Greek gentleman.

Nepommuck: Thank you, yes, immediately.

[The **Footman** goes and is lost in the crowd.]

Nepommuck: [To **Higgins.**] This Greek diplomatist pretends he cannot speak nor understand English. He cannot deceive me. He is the son of a Clerkenwell watchmaker. He speaks English so villainously that he dare not utter a word of it without betraying his origin. I help him to pretend; but I make him pay through the nose. I make them all pay. Ha ha! [He hurries upstairs.]

Pickering: Is this fellow really an expert? Can he find out Eliza and blackmail her?

Higgins: We shall see. If he finds her out I lose my bet.

[**Eliza** comes from the cloakroom and joins them.]

Pickering: Well, Eliza, now for it. Are you ready?

Liza: Are you nervous, Colonel?

Pickering: Frightfully. I feel exactly as I felt before my first battle. It's the first time that frightens.

Liza: It is not the first time for me, Colonel. I have done this fifty times—hundreds of times—in my little pig-gery in Angel Court in my daydreams. I am in a dream now. Promise me not to let Professor Higgins wake me; for if he does I shall forget everything and talk as I used to in Drury Lane.

Pickering: Not a word, Higgins. [To **Eliza.**] Now, ready?

Liza: Ready.

Pickering: Go.

[They mount the stairs, **Higgins** last. **Pickering** whispers to the **Footman** on the first landing.]

First Landing Footman: Miss Doolittle, Colonel Pickering, Professor Higgins.

Second Landing Footman: Miss Doolittle, Colonel Pickering, Professor Higgins.

[At the top of the staircase the **Ambassador** and his wife, with **Nepommuck** at her elbow, are receiving.]

Hostess: [Taking **Eliza's** hand] How d'ye do?

Host: [Same play.] How d'ye do? How d'ye do, Pickering?

Liza: [With a beautiful gravity that awes her hostess.] How do you do? [She passes on to the drawingroom.]

Hostess: Is that your adopted daughter, Colonel Pickering? She will make a sensation.

Pickering: Most kind of you to invite her for me. [He passes on.]

Hostess: [To **Nepommuck**] Find out all about her.

Nepommuck: [Bowing.] Excellency—[He goes into the crowd.]

Host: How d'ye do, Higgins? You have a rival here tonight. He introduced himself as your pupil. Is he any good?

Higgins: He can learn a language in a fortnight—knows dozens of them. A sure mark of a fool. As a phonetician, no good whatever.

Hostess: How d'ye do, Professor?

Higgins: How do you do? Fearful bore for you this sort of thing. Forgive my part in it. [He passes on.]

In the drawingroom and its suite of salons the reception is in full swing. **Eliza** passes through. She is so intent on *her ordeal that she walks like a somnambulist in a desert instead of a débutante in a fashionable crowd. They stop talking to look at her, admiring her dress, her jewels, and her strangely attractive self. Some of the younger ones at the back stand on their chairs to see.*

*[The **Host** and **Hostess** come in from the staircase and mingle with their guests. **Higgins,** gloomy and contemptuous of the whole business, comes into the group where they are chatting.]*

Hostess: Ah, here is Professor Higgins: he will tell us. Tell us all about the wonderful young lady, Professor.

Higgins: *[Almost morosely.]* What wonderful young lady?

Hostess: You know very well. They tell me there has been nothing like her in London since people stood on their chairs to look at Mrs Langtry.

*[**Nepommuck** joins the group, full of news.]*

Hostess: Ah, here you are at last, Nepommuck. Have you found out all about the Doolittle lady?

Nepommuck: I have found out all about her. She is a fraud.

Hostess: A fraud! Oh no.

Nepommuck: YES, yes. She cannot deceive me. Her name cannot be Doolittle.

Higgins: Why?

Nepommuck: Because Doolittle is an English name. And she is not English.

Hostess: Oh, nonsense! She speaks English perfectly.

Nepommuck: Too perfectly. Can you shew me any English woman who speaks English as it should be spoken? Only foreigners who have been taught to speak it speak it well.

Hostess: Certainly she terrified me by the way she said How d'ye do. I had a schoolmistress who talked like that; and I was mortally afraid of her. But if she is not English what is she?

Nepommuck: Hungarian.

All The Rest: Hungarian!

Nepommuck: Hungarian. And of royal blood. I am Hungarian. My blood is royal.

Higgins: Did you speak to her in Hungarian?

Nepommuck: I did. She was very clever. She said "Please speak to me in English: I do not understand French." French! She pretend not to know the difference between Hungarian and French. Impossible: she knows both.

Higgins: And the blood royal? How did you find that out?

Nepommuck: Instinct, maestro, instinct. Only the Magyar races can produce that air of the divine right, those resolute eyes. She is a princess.

Host: What do you say, Professor?

Higgins: I say an ordinary London girl out of the gutter and taught to speak by an expert. I place her in Drury Lane.

Nepommuck: Ha ha ha! Oh, maestro, maestro, you are mad on the subject of cockney dialects. The London gutter is the whole world for you.

Higgins: *[To the **Hostess.**]* What does your Excellency say?

Hostess: Oh, of course I agree with Nepommuck. She must be a princess at at least.

Host: Not necessarily legitimate, of course. Morganatic perhaps. But that is undoubtedly her class.

Higgins: I stick to my opinion.

Hostess: Oh, you are incorrigible.

*[The group breaks up, leaving **Higgins** isolated. **Pickering** joins him.]*

Pickering: Where is Eliza? We must keep an eye on her.

*[**Eliza** joins them.]*

Liza: I dont think I can bear much more. The people all stare so at me. An old lady has just told me that I speak exactly like Queen Victoria. I am sorry if I have lost your bet. I have done my best; but nothing can make me the same as these people.

Pickering: You have not lost it, my dear. You have won it ten times over.

Higgins: Let us get out of this. I have

had enough of chattering to these fools.

Pickering: Eliza is tired; and I am hungry. Let us clear out and have supper somewhere.

Act Four

The Wimpole Street laboratory. Midnight. Nobody in the room. The clock on the mantelpiece strikes twelve. The fire is not alight: it is a summer night.

[*Presently* **Higgins** *and* **Pickering** *are heard on the stairs.*]

Higgins: [*Calling down to* **Pickering.**] I say, Pick: lock up, will you? I shant be going out again.

Pickering: Right. Can Mrs Pearce go to bed? We dont want anything more, do we?

Higgins: Lord, no!

[**Eliza** *opens the door and is seen on the lighted landing in all the finery in which she has just won* **Higgins's** *bet for him. She comes to the hearth, and switches on the electric lights there. She is tired: her pallor contrasts strongly with her dark eyes and hair; and her expression is almost tragic. She takes off her cloak; puts her fan and gloves on the piano; and sits down on the bench, brooding and silent.* **Higgins,** *in evening dress, with overcoat and hat, comes in, carrying a smoking jacket which he has picked up downstairs. He takes off the hat and overcoat; throws them carelessly on the newspaper stand; disposes of his coat in the same way; puts on the smoking jacket; and throws himself wearily into the easy-chair at the hearth.* **Pickering,** *similarly attired, comes in. He also takes off his hat and overcoat, and is about to throw them on* **Higgins's** *when he hesitates.*]

Pickering: I say: Mrs Pearce will row if we leave these things lying about in the drawing room.

Higgins: Oh, chuck them over the bannisters into the hall. She'll find them there in the morning and put them away all right. She'll think we were drunk.

Pickering: We are, slightly. Are there any letters?

Higgins: I didnt look. [**Pickering** *takes the overcoats and hats and goes downstairs.* **Higgins** *begins half singing half yawning an air from La Fanciulla del Golden West. Suddenly he stops and exclaims.*] I wonder where the devil my slippers are!

[**Eliza** *looks at him darkly; then rises suddenly and leaves the room.* **Higgins** *yawns again, and resumes his song.* **Pickering** *returns, with the contents of the letter-box in his hand.*]

Pickering: Only circulars, and this coroneted billet-doux for you. [*He throws the circulars into the fender, and posts himself on the hearth-rug, with his back to the grate.*]

Higgins: [*Glancing at the billet-doux.*] Money-lender. [*He throws the letter after the circulars.*]

[**Eliza** *returns with a pair of large down-at-heel slippers. She places them on the carpet before* **Higgins,** *and sits as before without a word.*]

Higgins: [*Yawning again.*] Oh Lord! What an evening! What a crew! What a silly tomfoolery! [*He raises his shoe to unlace it, and catches sight of the slippers. He stops unlacing and looks at them as if they had appeared there of their own accord.*] Oh! theyre there, are they?

Pickering: [*Stretching himself.*] Well, I feel a bit tired. It's been a long day. The garden party, a dinner party, and the reception! Rather too much of a good thing. But youve won your bet, Higgins. Eliza did the trick, and something to spare, eh?

Higgins: [*Fervently.*] Thank God its over! [**Eliza** *flinches violently; but they take no notice of her; and she recovers herself and sits stonily as before.*]

Pickering: Were you nervous at the garden party? *I* was. Eliza didnt seem a bit nervous.

Higgins: Oh, she wasnt nervous. I knew she'd be all right. No: it's the strain of putting the job through all these months that has told on me. It was interesting enough at first, while we were at the phonetics; but after that I got deadly sick of it. If I hadnt backed myself to do it I should have chucked the whole thing up two months ago. It was a silly notion: the whole thing has been a bore.

Pickering: Oh come! the garden party was frightfully exciting. My heart began beating like anything.

Higgins: Yes, for the first three minutes. But when I saw we were going to win hands down, I felt like a bear in a cage, hanging about doing nothing. The dinner was worse: sitting gorging there for over an hour, with nobody but a damned fool of a fashionable woman to talk to! I tell you, Pickering, never again for me. No more artificial duchesses. The whole thing has been simple purgatory.

Pickering: Youve never been broken in properly to the social routine. *[Strolling over to the piano.]* I rather enjoy dipping into it occasionally myself: it makes me feel young again. Anyhow, it was a great success: an immense success. I was quite frightened once or twice because Eliza was doing it so well. You see, lots of the real people cant do it at all: theyre such fools that they think style comes by nature to people in their position; and so they never learn. Theres always something professional about doing a thing superlatively well.

Higgins: Yes: thats what drives me mad: the silly people dont know their own silly business. *[Rising.]* However, it's over and done with; and now I can go to bed at last without dreading tomorrow.

[Eliza's beauty becomes murderous.]

Pickering: I think I shall turn in too. Still, it's been a great occasion: a triumph for you. Goodnight. *[He goes.]*

Higgins: *[Following him.]* Goodnight. *[Over his shoulder, at the door.]* Put out the lights, Eliza; and tell Mrs Pearce not to make coffee for me in the morning: I'll take tea. *[He goes out.]*

[Eliza tries to control herself and feel indifferent as she rises and walks across to the hearth to switch off the lights. By the time she gets there she is on the point of screaming. She sits down in Higgins's chair and holds on hard to the arms. Finally she gives way and flings herself furiously on the floor, raging.]

Higgins: *[In despairing wrath outside.]* What the devil have I done with my slippers? *[He appears at the door.]*

Liza: *[Snatching up the slippers, and hurling them at him one after the other with all her force.]* There are your slippers. And there. Take your slippers; and may you never have a day's luck with them!

Higgins: *[Astounded.]* What on earth—! *[He comes to her.]* Whats the matter? Get up. *[He pulls her up.]* Anything wrong?

Liza: *[Breathless.]* Nothing wrong—with you. Ive won your bet for you, havnt I? Thats enough for you. *I* dont matter, I suppose.

Higgins: You won my bet! You! Presumptuous insect! *I* won it. What did you throw those slippers at me for?

Liza: Because I wanted to smash your face. I'd like to kill you, you selfish brute. Why didnt you leave me where you picked me out of—in the gutter? You thank God it's all over, and that now you can throw me back again there, do you? *[She crisps her fingers frantically.]*

Higgins: *[Looking at her in cool wonder.]* The creature is nervous, after all.

Liza: *[Gives a suffocated scream of fury,*

and instinctively darts her nails at his face.]!!

Higgins: *[Catching her wrists.]* Ah! would you? Claws in, you cat. How dare you shew your temper to me? Sit down and be quiet. *[He throws her roughly into the easy-chair.]*

Liza: *[Crushed by superior strength and weight.]* Whats to become of me? Whats to become of me?

Higgins: How the devil do I know whats to become of you? What does it matter what becomes of you?

Liza: You dont care. I know you dont care. You wouldnt care if I was dead. I'm nothing to you—not so much as them slippers.

Higgins: *[Thundering.]* Those slippers.

Liza: *[With bitter submission.]* Those slippers. I didnt think it made any difference now.

> *[A pause.* **Eliza** *hopeless and crushed.* **Higgins** *a little uneasy.]*

Higgins: *[In his loftiest manner.]* Why have you begun going on like this? May I ask whether you complain of your treatment here?

Liza: No.

Higgins: Has anybody behaved badly to you? Colonel Pickering? Mrs Pearce? Any of the servants?

Liza: No.

Higgins: I presume you dont pretend that *I* have treated you badly?

Liza: No.

Higgins: I am glad to hear it. *[He moderates his tone.]* Perhaps youre tired after the strain of the day. Will you have a glass of champagne? *[He moves towards the door.]*

Liza: No. *[Recollecting her manners.]* Thank you.

Higgins: *[Good-humored again.]* This has been coming on you for some days. I suppose it was natural for you to be anxious about the garden party. But thats all over now. *[He pats her kindly on the shoulder. She writhes.]* Theres nothing more to worry about.

Liza: No. Nothing more for you to worry about. *[She suddenly rises and gets away from him by going to the piano bench, where she sits and hides her face.]* Oh God! I wish I was dead.

Higgins: *[Staring after her in sincere surprise.]* Why? In heaven's name, why? *[Reasonably, going to her.]* Listen to me, Eliza. All this irritation is purely subjective.

Liza: I dont understand. I'm too ignorant.

Higgins: It's only imagination. Low spirits and nothing else. Nobody's hurting you. Nothing's wrong. You go to bed like a good girl and sleep it off. Have a little cry and say your prayers: that will make you comfortable.

Liza: I heard your prayers. "Thank God it's all over!"

Higgins: *[Impatiently.]* Well, dont you thank God it's all over? Now you are free and can do what you like.

Liza: *[Pulling herself together in desperation.]* What am I fit for? What have you left me fit for? Where am I to go? What am I to do? Whats to become of me?

Higgins: *[Enlightened, but not at all impressed.]* Oh, thats whats worrying you, is it? *[He thrust his hands into his pockets, and walks about in his usual manner, rattling the contents of his pockets, as if condescending to a trivial subject out of pure kindness.]* I shouldnt bother about it if I were you. I should imagine you wont have much difficulty in settling yourself somewhere or other, though I hadnt quite realized that you were going away. *[She looks quickly at him: he does not look at her, but examines the dessert stand on the piano and decides that he will eat an apple.]* You might marry, you know. *[He bites a large piece out of the apple and munches it noisily.]* You see, Eliza, all men are not confirmed old bachelors like me and the Colonel. Most men are the marrying sort (poor devils!); and youre not bad-looking: it's quite a pleasure to look at you sometimes—not now, of course, because youre crying and looking as ugly as the very devil; but when youre all right and quite yourself, youre what I should call attractive. That is, to the people in the marrying line, you understand. You go to bed and have a good nice rest; and then get up and look at yourself in the glass; and you wont feel so cheap.

[*Eliza again looks at him, speechless, and does not stir.*

The look is quite lost on him: he eats his apple with a dreamy expression of happiness, as it is quite a good one.]

Higgins: [*A genial afterthought occurring to him.*] I daresay my mother could find some chap or other who would do very well.

Liza: We were above that at the corner of Tottenham Court Road.

Higgins: [*Waking up.*] What do you mean?

Liza: I sold flowers. I didnt sell myself. Now youve made a lady of me I'm not fit to sell anything else. I wish youd left me where you found me.

Higgins: [*Slinging the core of the apple decisively into the grate.*] Tosh, Eliza. Dont you insult human relations by dragging all this cant about buying and selling into it. You neednt marry the fellow if you dont like him.

Liza: What else am I to do?

Higgins: Oh, lots of thing. What about your old idea of a florist's shop? Pickering could set up you in one: he has lots of money. [*Chuckling.*] He'll have to pay for all those togs you have been wearing today; and that, with the hire of the jewellery, will make a big hole in two hundred pounds. Why, six months ago you would have thought it the millennium to have a flower shop of your own. Come! youll be all right. I must clear off to bed: I'm devilish sleepy. By the way, I came down for something: I forget what it was.

Liza: Your slippers.

Higgins: Oh yes, of course. You shied them at me. [*He picks them up, and is going out when she rises and speaks to him.*]

Liza: Before you go, sir—

Higgins: [*Dropping the slippers in his surprise at her calling him Sir.*] Eh?

Liza: Do my clothes belong to me or to Colonel Pickering?

Higgins: [*Coming back into the room as if her question were the very climax of unreason.*] What the devil use would they be to Pickering?

Liza: He might want them for the next girl you pick up to experiment on.

Higgins: [*Shocked and hurt.*] Is that the way you feel towards us?

Liza: I dont want to hear anything more about that. All I want to know is whether anything belongs to me. My own clothes were burnt.

Higgins: But what does it matter? Why need you start bothering about that in the middle of the night?

Liza: I want to know what I may take away with me. I dont want to be accused of stealing.

Higgins: [*Now deeply wounded.*] Stealing! You shouldnt have said that, Eliza. That shews a want of feeling.

Liza: I'm sorry. I'm only a common ignorant girl; and in my station I have to be careful. There cant be any feelings between the like of you and the like of me. Please will you tell me what belongs to me and what doesnt?

Higgins: [*Very sulky.*] You may take the whole damned houseful if you like. Except the jewels. Theyre hired. Will that satisfy you? [*He turns on his heel and is about to go in extreme dudgeon.*]

Liza: [*Drinking in his emotion like nectar, and nagging him to provoke a further supply.*] Stop, please. [*She takes off her jewels.*] Will you take these to your room and keep them safe? I dont want to run the risk of their being missing.

Higgins: [*Furious.*] Hand them over. [*She puts them into his hands.*] If these belonged to me instead of to the jeweller, I'd ram them down your ungrateful throat. [*He perfunctorily thrusts them into his pockets, unconsciously decorating himself with the protruding ends of the chains.*]

Liza: [*Taking a ring off.*] This ring isnt the jeweller's: it's the one you bought me in Brighton. I dont want it now. [*Higgins dashes the ring violently into the fireplace, and turns on her so threateningly that she crouches over the piano with her hands over her face, and exclaims.*] Dont you hit me.

Higgins: Hit you! You infamous creature, how dare you accuse me of such a thing? It is you who have hit me. You have wounded me to the heart.

Liza: [*Thrilling with hidden joy.*] I'm glad. Ive got a little of my own back, anyhow.

Higgins: [*With dignity, in his finest professional style.*] You have caused me to lose my temper: a thing that has hardly ever happened to me before. I prefer to say nothing more tonight. I am going to bed.

Liza: [*Pertly.*] Youd better leave a note for Mrs Pearce about the coffee; for she wont be told by me.

Higgins: [*Formally.*] Damn Mrs Pearce; and damn the coffee; and damn you; and [*wildly*] damn my own folly in having lavished my hard-earned knowledge and the treasure of my regard and intimacy on a heartless guttersnipe. [*He goes out with impressive decorum, and spoils it by slamming the door savagely.*]

[*Eliza goes down on her knees on the hearthrug to look for the ring. When she finds it she considers for a moment what to do with it. Finally she flings it down on the dessert stand and goes upstairs in a tearing rage.*]

*   *   *

The furniture of **Eliza's** room has been increased by a big wardrobe and a sumptuous dressing-table. She comes in and switches on the electric light. She goes to the wardrobe; opens it; and pulls out a walking dress, a hat, and a pair of shoes, which she throws on the bed. She takes off her evening dress and shoes; then takes a padded hanger from the wardrobe; adjusts it carefully in the evening dress; and hangs it in the wardrobe, which she shuts with a slam. She puts on her walking shoes, her walking dress, and hat. She takes her wrist watch from the dressing-table and fastens it on. She pulls on her gloves; takes her vanity bag; and looks into it to see that her purse is there before hanging it on her wrist. She makes for the door. Every movement expresses her furious resolution.

She takes a last look at herself in the glass.

She suddenly puts out her tongue at herself; then leaves the room, switching off the electric light at the door.

[*Meanwhile, in the street outside,* **Freddy Eynsford Hill,** *lovelorn, is gazing up at the second floor, in which one of the windows is still lighted.*

The light goes out.]

Freddy: Goodnight, darling, darling, darling.

[**Eliza** *comes out, giving the door a considerable bang behind her.*]

Liza: Whatever are you doing here?

Freddy: Nothing. I spend most of my nights here. It's the only place where I'm happy. Dont laugh at me, Miss Doolittle.

Liza: Dont you call me Miss Doolittle, do you hear? Liza's good enough for me. [*She breaks down and grabs him by the shoulders.*] Freddy: you dont think I'm a heartless guttersnipe, do you?

Freddy: Oh no, no, darling: how can you imagine such a thing? You are the loveliest, dearest—

[*He loses all self-control and smothers her with kisses. She, hungry for comfort, responds. They stand there in one another's arms.*

An elderly police constable arrives.]

Constable: *[Scandalized.]* Now then! Now then!! Now then!!!

[They release one another hastily.]

Freddy: Sorry, constable. Weve only just become engaged.

[They run away.]

The **Constable** shakes his head, reflecting on his own courtship and on the vanity of human hopes. He moves off in the opposite direction with slow professional steps.

The flight of the lovers takes them to Cavendish Square. There they halt to consider their next move.

Liza: *[Out of breath.]* He didnt half give me a fright, that copper. But you answered him proper.

Freddy: I hope I havent taken you out of your way. Where were you going?

Liza: To the river.

Freddy: What for?

Liza: To make a hole in it.

Freddy: *[Horrified.]* Eliza, darling. What do you mean? What's the matter?

Liza: Never mind. It doesnt matter now. There's nobody in the world now but you and me, is there?

Freddy: Not a soul.

[They indulge in another embrace, and are again surprised by a much younger constable.]

Second Constable: Now then, you two! What's this? Where do you think you are? Move along here, double quick.

Freddy: As you say, sir, double quick.

[They run away again, and are in Hanover Square before they stop for another conference.]

Freddy: I had no idea the police were so devilishly prudish.

Liza: It's their business to hunt girls off the streets.

Freddy: We must go somewhere. We cant wander about the streets all night.

Liza: Cant we? I think it'd be lovely to wander about for ever.

Freddy: Oh, darling.

[They embrace again, oblivious of the arrival of a crawling taxi. It stops.]

Taximan: Can I drive you and the lady anywhere, sir?

[They start asunder.]

Liza: Oh, Freddy, a taxi. The very thing.

Freddy: But, damn it, I've no money.

Liza: I have plenty. The Colonel thinks you should never go out without ten pounds in your pocket. Listen. We'll drive about all night; and in the morning I'll call on old Mrs Higgins and ask her what I ought to do. I'll tell you all about it in the cab. And the police wont touch us there.

Freddy: Righto! Ripping. *[To the **Taximan.**]* Wimbledon Common.

[They drive off.]

Act Five

Mrs Higgins's drawing room. She is at her writing-table as before. **The Parlormaid** comes in.

The Parlormaid: *[At the door.]* Mr Henry, maam, is downstairs with Colonel Pickering.

Mrs Higgins: Well, shew them up.

The Parlormaid: Theyre using the telephone, maam. Telephoning to the police, I think.

Mrs Higgins: What!

The Parlormaid: *[Coming further in and lowering her voice.]* Mr Henry is in a state, maam. I thought I'd better tell you.

Mrs Higgins: If you had told me that Mr Henry was not in a state it would have been more surprising. Tell them to come up when theyve finished with the police. I suppose he's lost something.

The Parlormaid: Yes, maam *[Going.]*

Mrs Higgins: Go upstairs and tell Miss Doolittle that Mr Henry and the Colonel are here. Ask her not to come down til I send for her.

The Parlormaid: Yes, maam.

*[**Higgins** bursts in. He is, as the parlormaid has said, in a state.]*

Higgins: Look here, mother: heres a confounded thing!

Mrs Higgins: Yes, dear. Good morning. *[He checks his impatience and kisses*

her, whilst **The Parlormaid** goes out.]
What is it?

Higgins: Eliza's bolted.

Mrs Higgins: [Calmly continuing her writing.] You must have frightened her.

Higgins: Frightened her! nonsense! She was left last night, as usual, to turn out the lights and all that; and instead of going to bed she changed her clothes and went right off: her bed wasnt slept in. She came in a cab for her things before seven this morning; and that fool Mrs Pearce let her have them without telling me a word about it. What am I to do?

Mrs Higgins: Do without, I'm afraid, Henry. The girl has a perfect right to leave if she chooses.

Higgins: [Wandering distractedly across the room.] But I cant find anything. I dont know what appointments Ive got. I'm—

[Pickering comes in. **Mrs Higgins** puts down her pen and turns away from the writing-table.]

Pickering: [Shaking hands.] Good morning, Mrs Higgins. Has Henry told you? [He sits down on the ottoman.]

Higgins: What does that ass of an inspector say? Have you offered a reward?

Mrs Higgins: [Rising in indignant amazement.] You dont mean to say you have set the police after Eliza.

Higgins: Of course. What are the police for? What else could we do? [He sits in the Elizabethan chair.]

Pickering: The inspector made a lot of difficulties. I really think he suspected us of some improper purpose.

Mrs Higgins: Well, of course he did. What right have you to go to the police and give the girl's name as if she were a thief, or a lost umbrella, or something? Really! [She sits down again, deeply vexed.]

Higgins: But we want to find her.

Pickering: We cant let her go like this, you know, Mrs Higgins. What were we to do?

Mrs Higgins: You have no more sense, either of you, than two children. Why—

[**The Parlormaid** comes in and breaks off the conversation.]

The Parlormaid: Mr Henry: a gentleman wants to see you very particular. He's been sent on from Wimpole Street.

Higgins: Oh, bother! I cant see anyone now. Who is it?

The Parlormaid: A Mr Doolittle, sir.

Pickering: Doolittle! Do you mean the dustman?

The Parlormaid: Dustman! Oh no, sir: a gentleman.

Higgins: [Springing up excitedly.] By George, Pick, it's some relative of hers that she's gone to. Somebody we know nothing about. [To **The Parlormaid**.] Send him up, quick.

The Parlormaid: Yes, sir. [She goes.]

Higgins: [Eagerly, going to his mother.] Genteel relatives! now we shall hear something. [He sits down in the Chippendale chair.]

Mrs Higgins: Do you know any of her people?

Pickering: Only her father: the fellow we told you about.

The Parlormaid: [Announcing.] Mr. Doolittle. [She withdraws.]

[**Doolittle** enters. He is resplendently dressed as for a fashionable wedding, and might, in fact, be the bridegroom. A flower in his buttonhole, a dazzling silk hat, and patent leather shoes complete the effect. He is too concerned with the business he has come on to notice **Mrs Higgins**. He walks straight to **Higgins**, and accosts him with vehement reproach.]

Doolittle: [Indicating his own person.] See here! Do you see this? You done this.

Higgins: Done what, man?

Doolittle: This, I tell you. Look at it. Look at this hat. Look at this coat.

Pickering: Has Eliza been buying you clothes?

Doolittle: Eliza! not she. Why would she buy me clothes?

Mrs Higgins: Good morning, Mr Doolittle. Wont you sit down?

Doolittle *[Taken aback as he becomes conscious that he has forgotten his hostess.]* Asking your pardon, maam. *[He approaches her and shakes her proffered hand.]* Thank you. *[He sits down on the ottoman, on* **Pickering's** *right.]* I am that full of what has happened to me that I cant think of anything else.

Higgins: What the dickens has happened to you?

Doolittle: I shouldnt mind if it had only happened to me: anything might happen to anybody and nobody to blame but Providence, as you might say. But this is something that you done to me: yes, you, Enry Iggins.

Higgins: Have you found Eliza?

Doolittle: Have you lost her?

Higgins: Yes.

Doolittle: You have all the luck, you have. I aint found her; but she'll find me quick enough now after what you done to me.

Mrs Higgins: But what has my son done to you, Mr Doolittle?

Doolittle: Done to me! Ruined me. Destroyed my happiness. Tied me up and delivered me into the hands of middle class morality.

Higgins: *[Rising intolerantly and standing over* **Doolittle.***]* Youre raving. Youre drunk. Youre mad. I gave you five pounds. After that I had two conversations with you, at half-a-crown an hour. Ive never seen you since.

Doolittle: Oh! Drunk am I? Mad am I? Tell me this. Did you or did you not write a letter to an old blighter in America that was giving five millions to found Moral Reform Societies all over the world, and that wanted you to invent a universal language for him?

Higgins: What! Ezra D. Wannafeller! He's dead. *[He sits down again carelessly.]*

Doolittle: Yes: he's dead; and I'm done for. Now did you or did you not write a letter to him to say that the most original moralist at present in England, to the best of your knowledge, was Alfred Doolittle, a common dustman?

Higgins: Oh, after your first visit I remember making some silly joke of the kind.

Doolittle: Ah! you may well call it a silly joke. It put the lid on me right enough. Just give him the chance he wanted to shew that Americans is not like us: that they reckonize and respect merit in every class of life, however humble. Them words is in his blooming will, in which, Henry Higgins, thanks to your silly joking, he leaves me a share in his Pre-digested Cheese Trust worth four thousand a year on condition that I lecture for his Wannafeller Moral Reform World League as often as they ask me up to six times a year.

Higgins: The devil he does! Whew! *[Brightening suddenly.]* What a lark!

Pickering: A safe thing for you, Doolittle. They wont ask you twice.

Doolittle: It aint the lecturing I mind. I'll lecture them blue in the face, I will, and not turn a hair. It's making a gentleman of me that I object to. Who asked him to make a gentleman of me? I was happy. I was free. I touched pretty nigh everybody for money when I wanted it, same as I touched you, Enry Iggins. Now I am worrited; tied neck and heels; and everybody touches me for money. It's a fine thing for you, says my solicitor. Is it? says I. You mean it's a good thing for you, I says. When I was a poor man and had a solicitor once when they found a pram in the dust cart, he got me off, and got shut of me and got me shut of him as quick as he could. Same with the doctors: used to shove me out of the hospital before I could hardly stand on my legs, and nothing to pay. Now they finds out that I'm not a healthy man and cant live unless they looks after me twice a day. In the house I'm not let do a hand's turn for myself: somebody else must do it and touch me for it. A year ago I hadnt a relative in the world except two or three that wouldnt speak to me. Now Ive fifty, and not a decent week's wages among the lot of them. I have to live for others and not for myself: thats middle class morality. You talk of losing Eliza. Dont you be anxious: I bet she's on my doorstep by this: she that could support herself easy by selling flowers if I wasnt respectable. And the next one to touch me will be you, Enry Iggins. I'll have to learn to speak middle class language from you, instead of speaking proper English. Thats where youll come in; and I daresay thats what you done it for.

Mrs Higgins: But, my dear Mr Doolittle, you need not suffer all ᵗhis if you are really in earnest. Nobody can force you to accept this bequest. You can repudiate it. Isnt that so, Colonel Pickering?

Pickering: I believe so.

Doolittle: [Softening his manner in deference to her sex.] Thats the tragedy of it, maam. It's easy to say chuck it; but I havnt the nerve. Which of us has? We're all intimidated. Intimidated, maam: thats what we are. What is there for me if I chuck it but the workhouse in my old age? I have to dye my hair already to keep my job as a dustman. If I was one of the deserving poor, and had put by a bit, I could chuck it; but then why should I, acause the deserving poor might as well be millionaires for all the happiness they ever has. They dont know what happiness is. But I, as one of the undeserving poor, have nothing between me and the pauper's uniform but this here blasted four thousand a year that shoves me into the middle class. (Excuse the expression, maam; youd use it yourself if you had my provocation.) Theyve got you every way you turn: it's a choice between the Skilly of the workhouse and the Char Bydis of the middle class; and I havnt the nerve for the workhouse. Intimidated: thats what I am. Broke. Bought up. Happier men than me will call for my dust, and touch me for their tip; and I'll look on helpless, and envy them. And thats what your son has brought me to. [He is overcome by emotion.]

Mrs Higgins: Well, I'm very glad youre not going to do anything foolish, Mr Doolittle. For this solves the problem of Eliza's future. You can provide for her now.

Doolittle: [With melancholy resignation.] Yes, maam: I'm expected to provide for everyone now, out of four thousand a year.

Higgins: [Jumping up.] Nonsense! he cant provide for her. He shant provide for her. She doesnt belong to him. I paid him five pounds for her. Doolittle: either youre an honest man or a rogue.

Doolittle: [Tolerantly.] A little of both, Henry, like the rest of us: a little of both.

Higgins: Well, you took that money for the girl; and you have no right to take her as well.

Mrs Higgins: Henry: dont be absurd. If you want to know where Eliza is, she is upstairs.

Higgins: [Amazed.] Upstairs!!! Then I shall jolly soon fetch her downstairs. [He makes resolutely for the door.]

Mrs Higgins: [Rising and following him.] Be quiet, Henry. Sit down.

Higgins: I—

Mrs Higgins: Sit down, dear; and listen to me.

Higgins: Oh very well, very well, very well. [He throws himself ungraciously on the ottoman, with his face towards the windows.] But I think you might have told us ᵗhis half an hour ago.

Mrs Higgins: Eliza came to me this morning. She told me of the brutal way you two treated her.

Higgins: [*Bounding up again.*] What!

Pickering: [*Rising also.*] My dear Mrs. Higgins, she's been telling you stories. We didnt treat her brutally. We hardly said a word to her; and we parted on particularly good terms. [*Turning on* **Higgins.**] Higgins: did you bully her after I went to bed?

Higgins: Just the other way about. She threw my slippers in my face. She behaved in the most outrageous way. I never gave her the slightest provocation. The slippers came bang into my face the moment I entered the room—before I had uttered a word. And used perfectly awful language.

Pickering: [*Astonished.*] But why? What did we do to her?

Mrs Higgins: I think I know pretty well what you did. The girl is naturally rather affectionate, I think. Isnt she, Mr Doolittle?

Doolittle: Very tender-hearted, maam. Takes after me.

Mrs Higgins: Just so. She had become attached to you both. She worked very hard for you, Henry. I dont think you quite realize what anything in the nature of brain work means to a girl of her class. Well, it seems that when the great day of trial came, and she did this wonderful thing for you without making a single mistake, you two sat there and never said a word to her, but talked together of how glad you were that it was all over and how you had been bored with the whole thing. And then you were surprised because she threw your slippers at you! *I* should have thrown the fire-irons at you.

Higgins: We said nothing except that we were tired and wanted to go to bed. Did we, Pick?

Pickering: [*Shrugging his shoulders.*] That was all.

Mrs Higgins: [*Ironically.*] Quite sure?

Pickering: Absolutely. Really, that was all.

Mrs Higgins: You didnt thank her, or pet her, or admire her, or tell her how splendid she'd been.

Higgins: [*Impatiently.*] But she knew all about that. We didnt make speeches to her, if thats what you mean.

Pickering: [*Conscience stricken.*] Perhaps we were a little inconsiderate. Is she very angry?

Mrs Higgins: [*Returning to her place at the writing-table.*] Well, I'm afraid she wont go back to Wimpole Street, especially now that Mr Doolittle is able to keep up the position you have thrust on her; but she says she is quite willing to meet you on friendly terms and to let bygones be bygones.

Higgins: [*Furious.*] Is she, by George? Ho!

Mrs Higgins: If you promise to behave yourself, Henry, I'll ask her to come down. If not, go home; for you have taken up quite enough of my time.

Higgins: Oh, all right. Very well. Pick: you behave yourself. Let us put on our best Sunday manners for this creature that we picked out of the mud. [*He flings himself sulkily into the Elizabethan chair.*]

Doolittle: [*Remonstrating.*] Now, now, Enry Iggins! Have some consideration for my feelings as a middle class man.

Mrs Higgins: Remember your promise, Henry. [*She presses the bell-button on the writing-table.*] Mr Doolittle: will you be so good as to step out on the balcony for a moment. I dont want Eliza to have the shock of your news until she has made it up with these two gentlemen. Would you mind?

Doolittle: As you wish, lady. Anything to help Henry to keep her off my hands. [*He disappears through the window.*]

　　[**The Parlormaid** *answers the bell.* **Pickering** *sits down in Doolittle's place.*]

Mrs Higgins: Ask Miss Doolittle to come down, please.

The Parlormaid: Yes, maam. *[She goes out.]*

Mrs Higgins: Now, Henry: be good.

Higgins: I am behaving myself perfectly.

Pickering: He is doing his best, Mrs Higgins.

> *[A pause.* **Higgins** *throws back his head; stretches out his legs; and begins to whistle.]*

Mrs Higgins: Henry, dearest, you dont look at all nice in that attitude.

Higgins: *[Pulling himself together.]* I was not trying to look nice, mother.

Mrs Higgins: It doesnt matter, dear. I only wanted to make you speak.

Higgins: Why?

Mrs Higgins: Because you cant speak and whistle at the same time.

> *[***Higgins*** *groans. Another very trying pause.]*

Higgins: *[Springing up, out of patience.]* Where the devil is that girl? Are we to wait here all day?

> *[***Eliza*** *enters, sunny, self-possessed, and giving a staggeringly convincing exhibition of ease of manner. She carries a little workbasket, and is very much at home.* **Pickering** *is too much taken aback to rise.]*

Liza: How do you do, Professor Higgins? Are you quite well?

Higgins: *[Choking.]* Am I— *[He can say no more.]*

Liza: But of course you are: you are never ill. So glad to see you again, Colonel Pickering. *[He rises hastily; and they shake hands.]* Quite chilly this morning, isn't it? *[She sits down on his left. He sits beside her.]*

Higgins: Dont you dare try this game on me. I taught it to you; and it doesnt take me in. Get up and come home; and dont be a fool.

> *[***Eliza*** *takes a piece of needlework from her basket, and begins to stitch at it, without taking the least notice of his outburst.]*

Mrs Higgins: Very nicely put, indeed, Henry. No woman could resist such an invitation.

Higgins: You let her alone, mother. Let her speak for herself. You will jolly soon see whether she has an idea that I havnt put into her head or a word that I havnt put into her mouth. I tell you I have created this thing out of the squashed cabbage leaves of Covent Gardens; and now she pretends to play the fine lady with me.

Mrs Higgins: *[Placidly.]* Yes, dear; but youll sit down, wont you?

> *[***Higgins*** *sits down again, savagely.]*

Liza: *[To* **Pickering**, *taking no apparent notice of Higgins, and working away deftly.]* Will you drop me altogether now that the experiment is over, Colonel Pickering?

Pickering: Oh dont. You mustnt think of it as an experiment. It shocks me, somehow.

Liza: Oh, I'm only a squashed cabbage leaf—

Pickering: *[Impulsively.]* No.

Liza: *[Continuing quietly.]* —but I owe so much to you that I should be very unhappy if you forgot me.

Pickering: It's very kind of you to say so, Miss Doolittle.

Liza: It's not because you paid for my dresses. I know you are generous to everybody with money. But it was from you that I learnt really nice manners; and that is what makes one a lady, isnt it? You see it was so very difficult for me with the example of Professor Higgins always before me. I was brought up to be just like him, unable to control myself, and using bad language on the slightest provocation. And I should never have known that ladies and gentlemen didnt behave like that if you hadnt been there.

Higgins: Well!!

Pickering: Oh, thats only his way, you know. He doesnt mean it.

Liza: Oh, *I* didnt mean it either, when I was a flower girl. It was only my way. But you see I did it; and thats what makes the difference after all.

Pickering: No doubt. Still, he taught you to speak; and I couldnt have done that, you know.

Liza: [*Trivially.*] Of course: that is his profession.

Higgins: Damnation!

Liza: [*Continuing.*] It was just like learning to dance in the fashionable way: there was nothing more than that in it. But do you know what began my real education?

Pickering: What?

Liza: [*Stopping her work for a moment.*] Your calling me Miss Doolittle that day when I first came to Wimpole Street. That was the beginning of self-respect for me. [*She resumes her stitching.*] And there were a hundred little things you never noticed, because they came naturally to you. Things about standing up and taking off your hat and opening doors—

Pickering: Oh, that was nothing.

Liza: Yes: things that shewed you thought and felt about me as if I were something better than a scullery-maid; though of course I know you would have been just the same to a scullery-maid if she had been let into the drawing room. You never took off your boots in the dining room when I was there.

Pickering: You mustnt mind that. Higgins takes off his boots all over the place.

Liza: I know. I am not blaming him. It is his way, isnt it? But it made such a difference to me that you didnt do it. You see, really and truly, apart from the things anyone can pick up (the dressing and the proper way of speaking, and so on), the difference between a lady and a flower girl is not how she behaves, but how she's treated. I shall always be a flower girl to Professor Higgins, because he always treats me as a flower girl, and always will; but I know I can be a lady to you, because you always treat me as a lady, and always will.

Mrs Higgins: Please dont grind your teeth, Henry.

Pickering: Well, this is really very nice of you, Miss Doolittle.

Liza: I should like you to call me Eliza, now, if you would.

Pickering: Thank you. Eliza, of course.

Liza: And I should like Professor Higgins to call me Miss Doolittle.

Higgins: I'll see you damned first.

Mrs Higgins: Henry! Henry!

Pickering: [*Laughing.*] Why dont you slang back at him? Dont stand it. It would do him a lot of good.

Liza: I cant. I could have done it once; but now I cant go back to it. You told me, you know, that when a child is brought to a foreign country, it picks up the language in a few weeks, and forgets its own. Well, I am a child in your country. I have forgotten my own language, and can speak nothing but yours. Thats the real break-off with the corner of Tottenham Court Road. Leaving Wimpole Street finishes it.

Pickering: [*Much alarmed.*] Oh! but youre coming back to Wimpole Street, arnt you? Youll forgive Higgins?

Higgins: [*Rising.*] Forgive! Will she, by George! Let her go. Let her find out how she can get on without us. She will relapse into the gutter in three weeks without me at her elbow.

[**Doolittle** *appears at the centre window. With a look of dignified reproach at* **Higgins,** *he comes slowly and silently to his daughter, who, with her back to the window, is unconscious of his approach.*]

Pickering: He's incorrigible, Eliza. You wont relapse, will you?

Liza: No: not now. Never again. I have learnt my lesson. I dont believe I could utter one of the old sounds if I tried. [**Doolittle** *touches her on the left shoulder. She drops her work, losing her self-possession utterly at* *the spectacle of her father's splendor.]* A-a-a-a-ah-ow-ooh!

Higgins: *[With a crow of triumph.]* Aha! Just so. A-a-a-a-ahowooh! A-a-a-a-ahowooh! A-a-a-a-ahowooh! Victory! Victory! *[He throws himself on the divan, folding his arms, and spraddling arrogantly.]*

Doolittle: Can you blame the girl? Dont look at me like that, Eliza. It aint my fault. Ive come into some money.

Liza: You must have touched a millionaire this time, dad.

Doolittle: I have. But I'm dressed something special today. I'm going to St George's, Hanover Square. Your stepmother is going to marry me.

Liza: *[Angrily.]* Youre going to let yourself down to marry that low common woman!

Pickering: *[Quietly.]* He ought to, Eliza. *[To* **Doolittle.***]* Why has she changed her mind?

Doolittle: *[Sadly.]* Intimidated, Governor. Intimidated. Middle class morality claims its victim. Wont you put on your hat, Liza, and come and see me turned off?

Liza: If the Colonel says I must, I—I'll *[Almost sobbing.]* I'll demean myself. And get insulted for my pains, like enough.

Doolittle: Dont be afraid: she never comes to words with anyone now, poor woman! respectability has broke all the spirit out of her.

Pickering: *[Squeezing* **Eliza's** *elbow gently.]* Be kind to them, Eliza. Make the best of it.

Liza: *[Forcing a little smile for him through her vexation.]* Oh well, just to shew theres no ill feeling. I'll be back in a moment.
[She goes out.]

Doolittle: *[Sitting down beside* **Pickering.***]* I feel uncommon nervous about the ceremony, Colonel. I wish youd come and see me through it.

Pickering: But youve been through it before, man. You were married to Eliza's mother.

Doolittle: Who told you that, Colonel?

Pickering: Well, nobody told me. But I concluded—naturally—

Doolittle: No: that aint the natural way, Colonel: it's only the middle class way. My way was always the undeserving way. But dont say nothing to Eliza. She dont know: I always had a delicacy about telling her.

Pickering: Quite right. We'll leave it so, if you dont mind.

Doolittle: And youll come to the church, Colonel, and put me through straight?

Pickering: With pleasure. As far as a bachelor can.

Mrs Higgins: May I come, Mr Doolittle? I should be very sorry to miss your wedding.

Doolittle: I should indeed be honored by your condescension, maam; and my poor old woman would take it as a tremenjous compliment. She's been very low, thinking of the happy days that are no more.

Mrs Higgins: *[Rising.]* I'll order the carriage and get ready. *[The men rise, except* **Higgins.***]* I shant be more than fifteen minutes. *[As she goes to the door Eliza comes in, hatted and buttoning her gloves.]* I'm going to the church to see your father married, Eliza. You had better come in the brougham with me. Colonel Pickering can go on with the bridegroom.
*[*Mrs **Higgins** *goes out.* **Eliza** *comes to the middle of the room between the centre window and the ottoman.* **Pickering** *joins her.]*

Doolittle: Bridegroom. What a word! It makes a man realize his position, somehow. *[He takes up his hat and goes towards the door.]*

Pickering: Before I go, Eliza, do forgive Higgins and come back to us.

Liza: I dont think dad would allow me. Would you, dad?

Doolittle: *[Sad but magnanimous.]* They played you off very cunning, Eliza, them two sportsmen. If it had been only one of them, you could have nailed him. But you see, there was two; and one of them chaperoned the other, as you might say. [To **Pickering.**] It was artful of you, Colonel; but I bear no malice: I should have done the same myself. I been the victim of one woman after another all my life, and I dont grudge you two getting the better of Liza. I shant interfere. It's time for us to go, Colonel. So long, Henry. See you in St George's, Eliza.

[He goes out.]

Pickering: [Coaxing.] Do stay with us, Eliza. [He follows **Doolittle.**]

[**Eliza** goes out on the balcony to avoid being alone with **Higgins.** He rises and joins her there. She immediately comes back into the room and makes for the door; but he goes along the balcony and gets his back to the door before she reaches it.]

Higgins: Well, Eliza, youve had a bit of your own back, as you call it. Have you had enough? and are you going to be reasonable? Or do you want any more?

Liza: You want me back only to pick up your slippers and put up with your tempers and fetch and carry for you.

Higgins: I havnt said I wanted you back at all.

Liza: Oh, indeed. Then what are we talking about?

Higgins: About you, not about me. If you come back I shall treat you just as I have always treated you. I cant change my nature; and I dont intend to change my manners. My manners are exactly the same as Colonel Pickering's.

Liza: Thats not true. He treats a flower girl as if she was a duchess.

Higgins: And I treat a duchess as if she was a flower girl.

Liza: I see. [She turns away composedly, and sits on the ottoman, facing the window.] The same to everybody.

Higgins: Just so.

Liza: Like father.

Higgins: [Grinning, a little taken down.] Without accepting the comparison at all points, Eliza, it's quite true that your father is not a snob, and that he will be quite at home in any station of life to which his eccentric destiny may call him. [Seriously.] The great secret, Eliza, is not having bad manners or good manners or any other particular sort of manners, but having the same manner for all human souls: in short, behaving as if you were in Heaven, where there are no third-class carriages, and one soul is as good as another.

Liza: Amen. You are a born preacher.

Higgins: [Irritated.] The question is not whether I treat you rudely, but whether you ever heard me treat anyone else better.

Liza: [With sudden sincerity.] I dont care how you treat me. I dont mind your swearing at me. I shouldnt mind a black eye: Ive had one before this. But [Standing up and facing him.] I wont be passed over.

Higgins: Then get out of my way; for I wont stop for you. You talk about me as if I were a motor bus.

Liza: So you are a motor bus: all bounce and go, and no consideration for anyone. But I can do without you: dont think I cant.

Higgins: I know you can. I told you you could.

Liza: [Wounded, getting away from him to the other side of the ottoman with her face to the hearth.] I know you did, you brute. You wanted to get rid of me.

Higgins: Liar.

Liza: Thank you. [She sits down with dignity.]

Higgins: You never asked yourself, I suppose, whether I could do without you.

Liza: [Earnestly.] Dont you try to get round me. Youll have to do without me.

Higgins: [Arrogant.] I can do without anybody. I have my own soul: my own spark of divine fire. But [*With sudden humility.*] I shall miss you, Eliza. [*He sits down near her on the ottoman.*] I have learnt something from your idiotic notions: I confess that humbly and gratefully. And I have grown accustomed to your voice and appearance. I like them, rather.

Liza: Well, you have both of them on your gramophone and in your book of photographs. When you feel lonely without me, you can turn the machine on. It's got no feelings to hurt.

Higgins: I cant turn your soul on. Leave me those feelings; and you can take away the voice and the face. They are not you.

Liza: Oh, you are a devil. You can twist the heart in a girl as easy as some could twist her arms to hurt her. Mrs Pearce warned me. Time and again she has wanted to leave you; and you always got round her at the last minute. And you dont care a bit for her. And you dont care a bit for me.

Higgins: I care for life, for humanity; and you are a part of it that has come my way and been built into my house. What more can you or anyone ask?

Liza: I wont care for anybody that doesnt care for me.

Higgins: Commercial principles, Eliza. Like [*Reproducing her Covent Garden pronunciation with professional exactness.*] s'yollin voylets [selling violets], isnt it?

Liza: Dont sneer at me. It's mean to sneer at me.

Higgins: I have never sneered in my life. Sneering doesnt become either the human face or the human soul. I am expressing my righteous contempt for Commercialism. I dont and wont trade in affection. You call me a brute because you couldnt buy a claim on me by fetching my slippers and finding my spectacles. You were a fool: I think a woman fetching a man's slippers is a disgusting sight: did I ever fetch your slippers? I think a

good deal more of you for throwing them in my face. No use slaving for me and then saying you want to be cared for: who cares for a slave? If you come back, come back for the sake of good fellowship; for youll get nothing else. Youve had a thousand times as much out of me as I have out of you; and if you dare to set up your little dog's tricks of fetching and carrying slippers against my creation of a Duchess Eliza, I'll slam the door in your silly face.

Liza: What did you do it for if you didnt care for me?

Higgins: [*Heartily.*] Why, because it was my job.

Liza: You never thought of the trouble it would make for me.

Higgins: Would the world ever have been made if its maker had been afraid of making trouble? Making life means making trouble. Theres only one way of escaping trouble; and thats killing things. Cowards, you notice, are always shrieking to have troublesome people killed.

Liza: I'm no preacher: I dont notice things like that. I notice that you dont notice me.

Higgins: [*Jumping up and walking about intolerantly.*] Eliza: youre an idiot. I waste the treasures of my Miltonic mind by spreading them before you. Once for all, understand that I go my way and do my work without caring twopence what happens to either of us. I am not intimidated, like your father and your stepmother. So you can come back or go to the devil: which you please.

Liza: What am I to come back for?

Higgins: [*Bouncing up on his knees on the ottoman and leaning over it to her.*] For the fun of it. Thats why I took you on.

Liza: [*With averted face.*] And you may throw me out tomorrow if I dont do everything you want me to?

Higgins: Yes; and you may walk out

tomorrow if I dont do everything you want me to.

Liza: And live with my stepmother?

Higgins: Yes, or sell flowers.

Liza: Oh! if I only could go back to my flower basket! I should be independent of both you and father and all the world! Why did you take my independence from me? Why did I give it up? I'm a slave now, for all my fine clothes.

Higgins: Not a bit. I'll adopt you as my daughter and settle money on you if you like. Or would you rather marry Pickering?

Liza: [Looking fiercely round at him.] I wouldnt marry you if you asked me; and youre nearer my age than what he is.

Higgins: [Gently.] Than he is: not "than what he is."

Liza: [Losing her temper and rising.] I'll talk as I like. Youre not my teacher now.

Higgins: [Reflectively.] I dont suppose Pickering would, though. He's as confirmed an old bachelor as I am.

Liza: Thats not what I want; and dont you think it. I've always had chaps enough wanting me that way. Freddy Hill writes to me twice and three times a day, sheets and sheets.

Higgins: [Disagreeably surprised.] Damn his impudence! [He recoils and finds himself sitting on his heels.]

Liza: He has a right to if he likes, poor lad. And he does love me.

Higgins: [Getting off the ottoman.] You have no right to encourage him.

Liza: Every girl has a right to be loved.

Higgins: What! By fools like that?

Liza: Freddy's not a fool. And if he's weak and poor and wants me, may be he'd make me happier than my betters that bully me and dont want me.

Higgins: Can he make anything of you? Thats the point.

Liza: Perhaps I could make something of him. But I never thought of us making anything of one another; and you never think of anything else. I only want to be natural.

Higgins: In short, you want me to be as infatuated about you as Freddy? Is that it?

Liza: No I dont. Thats not the sort of feeling I want from you. And dont you be too sure of yourself or of me. I could have been a bad girl if I'd liked. Ive seen more of some things than you, for all your learning. Girls like me can drag gentlemen down to make love to them easy enough. And they wish each other dead the next minute.

Higgins: Of course they do. Then what in thunder are we quarrelling about?

Liza: [Much troubled.] I want a little kindness. I know I'm a common ignorant girl, and you a book-learned gentleman; but I'm not dirt under your feet. What I done [Correcting herself.] what I did was not for the dresses and the taxis: I did it because we were pleasant together and I come —came—to care for you; not to want you to make love to me, and not forgetting tht difference between us, but more friendly like.

Higgins: Well, of course. Thats just how I feel. And how Pickering feels. Eliza: youre a fool.

Liza: Thats not a proper answer to give me. [She sinks on the chair at the writing-table in tears.]

Higgins: It's all youll get until you stop being a common idiot. If youre going to be a lady, youll have to give up feeling neglected if the men you know dont spend half their time snivelling over you and the other half giving you black eyes. If you cant stand the coldness of my sort of life, and the strain of it, go back to the gutter. Work til youre more a brute than a human being; and then cuddle and squabble and drink til you fall asleep. Oh, it's a fine life, the life of the gutter. It's real: it's warm: it's violent: you can feel it through the thickest skin: you can taste it and smell it without any training or any work. Not like Science and Literature and Classical Music and Philosophy and Art. You find me cold, unfeeling, selfish, dont you? Very well: be off with you to the sort of people you like. Marry some sentimental hog or other with lots of money, and a thick pair of lips to kiss you with and a thick pair of boots to kick you with. If you cant appreciate what youve got, youd better get what you can appreciate.

Liza: [Desperate.] Oh, you are a cruel tyrant. I cant talk to you: you turn everything against me: I'm always in the wrong. But you know very well all the time that youre nothing but a bully. You know I cant go back to the gutter, as you call it, and that I have no real friends in the world but you and the Colonel. You know well I couldnt bear to live with a low common man after you two; and it's wicked and cruel of you to insult me by pretending I could. You think I must go back to Wimpole Street because I have nowhere else to go but father's. But dont you be too sure that you have me under your feet to be trampled on and talked down. I'll marry Freddy, I will, as soon as I'm able to support him.

Higgins: [Thunderstruck.] Freddy!!! that young fool! That poor devil who couldnt get a job as an errand boy even if he had the guts to try for it! Woman: do you not understand that I have made you a consort for a king?

Liza: Freddy loves me: that makes him king enough for me. I dont want him to work: he wasnt brought up to it as I was. I'll go and be a teacher.

Higgins: Whatll you teach, in heaven's name?

Liza: What you taught me. I'll teach phonetics.

Higgins: Ha! ha! ha!

Liza: I'll offer myself as an assistant to that hairyfaced Hungarian.

Higgins: [Rising in a fury.] What! That imposter! that humbug! that toadying ignoramus! Teach him my methods! my discoveries! You take one step in his direction and I'll wring your neck. [He lays hands on her.] Do you hear?

Liza: [Defiantly non-resistant.] Wring away. What do I care? I knew youd strike me some day. [He lets her go, stamping with rage at having forgotten himself, and recoils so hastily that he stumbles back into his seat on the ottoman.] Aha! Now I know how to deal with you. What a fool I was not to think of it before! You cant take away the knowledge you gave me. You said I had a finer ear than you. And I can be civil and kind to people, which is more than you can. Aha! [Purposely dropping her aitches to annoy him.] Thats done you, Enry Iggins, it az. Now I dont care that [Snapping her fingers.] for your bullying and your big talk. I'll advertize it in the papers that your duchess is only a flower girl that you taught, and that she'll teach anybody to be a duchess just the same in six months for a thousand guineas. Oh, when I think of myself crawling under your feet and being trampled on and called names, when all the time I had only to lift up my finger to be as good as you, I could just kick myself.

Higgins: [Wondering at her.] You damned impudent slut, you! But it's better than snivelling; better than fetching slippers and finding spectacles, isnt it? [Rising.] By George, Eliza, I said I'd make a woman of you; and I have. I like you like this.

Liza: Yes: you turn round and make up to me now that I'm not afraid of you, and can do without you.

Higgins: Of course I do, you little fool. Five minutes ago you were like a millstone round my neck. Now youre a tower of strength: a consort battleship. You and I and Pickering will be three old bachelors instead of only two men and a silly girl.

[*Mrs Higgins* returns, dressed for the wedding. **Eliza** instantly becomes cool and elegant.]

Mrs Higgins: The carriage is waiting, Eliza. Are you ready?

Liza: Quite. Is the Professor coming?

Mrs Higgins: Certainly not. He cant behave himself in church. He makes remarks out loud all the time on the clergyman's pronunciation.

Liza: Than I shall not see you again, Professor. Goodbye. [*She goes to the door.*]

Mrs Higgins: [*Coming to* **Higgins.**] Goodbye, dear.

Higgins: Goodbye, mother. [*He is about to kiss her, when he recollects something.*] Oh, by the way, Eliza, order a ham and a Stilton cheese, will you? And buy me a pair of reindeer gloves, number eights, and a tie to match that new suit of mine. You can choose the color. [*His cheerful, careless, vigorous voice shews that he is incorrigible.*]

Liza: [*Disdainfully.*] Number eights are too small for you if you want them lined with lamb's wool. You have three new ties that you have forgotten in the drawer of your washstand. Colonel Pickering prefers double Gloucester to Stilton; and you dont notice the difference. I telephoned Mrs Pearce this morning not to forget the ham. What you are to do without me I cannot imagine.

[*She sweeps out.*]

Mrs Higgins: I'm afraid youve spoilt that girl, Henry. I should be uneasy about you and her if she were less fond of Colonel Pickering.

Higgins: Pickering! Nonsense: she's going to marry Freddy. Ha ha! Freddy! Freddy!! Ha ha ha ha ha ! ! ! ! [*He roars with laughter as the play ends.*]

The rest of the story need not be shewn in action, and indeed, would hardly need telling if our imaginations were not so enfeebled by their lazy dependence on the ready-mades and reach-me-downs of the ragshop in which Romance keeps its stock of "happy endings" to misfit all stories. Now, the history of Eliza Doolittle, though called a romance because the transfiguration it records seems exceedingly improbable, is common enough. Such transfigurations have been achieved by hundreds of resolutely ambitious young women since Nell Gwynne set them the example by playing queens and fascinating kings in the theatre in which she began by selling oranges. Nevertheless, people in all directions have assumed, for no other reason than that she became the heroine of a romance, that she must have married the hero of it. This is unbearable, not only because her little drama, if acted on such a thoughtless assumption, must be spoiled, but because the true sequel is patent to anyone with a sense of human nature in general, and of feminine instinct in particular.

Eliza, in telling Higgins she would not marry him if he asked her, was not coquetting: she was announcing a well-considered decision. When a bachelor interests, and dominates, and teaches, and becomes important to a spinster, as Higgins with Eliza, she always, if she has character enough to be capable of it, considers very seriously indeed whether she will play for becoming that bachelor's wife, especially if he is so little interested in marriage that a determined and devoted woman might capture him if she set herself resolutely to do it. Her decision will depend a good deal on whether she is really free to choose; and that, again, will depend on her age and income. If she is at the end of her youth, and has no security for her livelihood, she will marry him because she must marry anybody who will provide for her. But at Eliza's age a good-looking girl does not feel that pressure: she feels free to pick and choose. She is therefore guided by her instinct in the matter. Eliza's instinct tells her not to marry Higgins. It does not tell her to give him up. It is not in the slightest doubt as to his remaining one of the strongest personal interests in her life. It would be very sorely strained if there was another woman likely to supplant her with him. But as she feels sure of him on that last point, she has no doubt at all as to her course, and would not have any, even if the difference of twenty years in age, which seems so great to youth, did not exist between them.

As our own instincts are not appealed to by her conclusion, let us see whether we cannot discover some reason in it. When Higgins excused his indifference to young women on the ground that they had an irresistible rival in his mother, he gave the clue to his inveterate old-bachelordom. The case is uncommon only to the extent that remarkable mothers are uncommon. If an imaginative boy has a sufficiently rich mother who has intelligence, personal grace, dignity of character without harshness, and a cultivated sense of the best art of her time to enable her to make her house beautiful, she sets a standard for him against which very few women can struggle, besides effecting for him a disengagement of his affections, his sense of beauty, and his idealism from his specifically sexual impulses. This makes him a standing puzzle to the huge number of uncultivated people who have been brought up in tasteless homes by commonplace or disagreeable parents, and to whom, consequently, literature, painting, sculpture, music, and affectionate personal relations come as modes of sex if they come at all. The word passion means nothing else to them; and that Higgins could have a passion for phonetics and idealize his mother instead of Eliza, would seem to them absurd and unnatural. Nevertheless, when we look round and see that hardly anyone is too ugly or disagreeable to find a wife or a husband if he or she wants one, whilst many old maids and bachelors are above the average in quality and culture, we cannot help suspecting that the disentanglement of sex from the associations with which it is so commonly confused, a disentanglement which persons of genius achieve by sheer intellectual analysis, is sometimes produced or aided by parental fascination.

Now, though Eliza was incapable of thus explaining to herself Higgins's formidable powers of resistance to the charm that prostrated Freddy at the first glance, she was instinctively aware that she could never obtain a complete grip of him, or come between him and his mother (the first necessity of the married woman). To put it shortly, she knew that for some mysterious reason he had not the makings of a married man in him, according to her conception of a husband as one to whom she would be his nearest and fondest and warmest interest. Even had there been no mother-rival, she would still have refused to accept an interest in herself that was secondary to philosophic interests. Had Mrs. Higgins died, there would still have been Milton and the Universal Alphabet. Landor's remark that to those who have the greatest power of loving, love is a secondary affair, would not have recommended Landor to Eliza. Put that along with her resentment of Higgins's domineering superiority, and her mistrust of his coaxing cleverness in getting round her and evading her wrath when he had gone too far with his impetuous bullying, and you will see that Eliza's instinct had good grounds for warning her not to marry her Pygmalion.

And now, whom did Eliza marry? For if Higgins was a predestinate old bachelor, she was most certainly not a predestinate old maid. Well, that can be told very shortly to those who have not guessed it from the indications she has herself given them.

Almost immediately after Eliza is stung into proclaiming her considered determination not to marry Higgins, she mentions the fact that young Mr. Frederick Eynsford Hill is pouring out his love for her daily through the post. Now Freddy is young, practically twenty years younger than Higgins: he is a gentleman (or, as Eliza would qualify him, a toff), and speaks like one. He is nicely dressed, is treated by the Colonel as an equal, loves her unaffectedly, and is not her master, nor ever likely to dominate her in spite of his advantage of social standing. Eliza has no use for the foolish romantic tradition that all women love to be mastered, if not actually bullied and beaten. "When you go to women" says Nietzsche "take your whip with you." Sensible despots have never confined that precaution to women: they have taken their whips with them when they have dealt with men, and been slavishly idealized by the men over whom they have flourished the whip much more than by women. No doubt there are slavish women as well as slavish men; and women, like men, admire those that are stronger than themselves. But to admire a strong person and to live under that strong person's thumb are two different things. The weak may not be admired and hero-worshipped; but they are by no means disliked or shunned; and they never seem to have the least difficulty in marrying people who are too good for them. They may fail in emergencies; but life is not one long emergency: it is mostly a string of situations for which no exceptional strength is needed, and with which even rather weak people can cope if they have a stronger partner to help them out. Accordingly, it is a truth everywhere in evidence that strong people, masculine or feminine, not only do not marry stronger people, but do not shew any preference for them in selecting their friends. When a lion meets another with a louder roar "the first lion thinks the last a bore." The man or woman who feels strong enough for two, seeks for every other quality in a partner than strength.

The converse is also true. Weak people want to marry strong people who do not frighten them too much; and this often leads them to make the mistake we describe metaphorically as "biting off more than they can chew." They want too much for too little; and when the bargain is unreasonable beyond all bearing, the union becomes impossible: it ends in the weaker party being either discarded or borne as a cross, which is worse. People who are not only weak, but silly or obtuse as well, are often in these difficulties.

This being the state of human affairs, what is Eliza fairly sure to do when she is placed between Freddy and Higgins? Will she look forward to a lifetime of fetching Higgins's slippers or to a lifetime of Freddy fetching hers? There can be no doubt about the answer. Unless Freddy is biologically repulsive to her, and Higgins biologically attractive to a degree that overwhelms all her other instincts, she will, if she marries either of them, marry Freddy.

And that is just what Eliza did.

Complications ensued; but they were economic, not romantic. Freddy had no money and no occupation. His mother's jointure, a last relic of the opulence of Largelady Park, had enabled her to struggle along in Earlscourt with an air of gentility, but not to procure any serious secondary education for her children, much less give the boy a profession. A clerkship at thirty shillings a week was beneath Freddy's dignity, and extremely distasteful to him besides. His prospects consisted of a hope

that if he kept up appearances somebody would do something for him. The something appeared vaguely to his imagination as a private secretaryship or a sinecure of some sort. To his mother it perhaps appeared as a marriage to some lady of means who could not resist her boy's niceness. Fancy her feelings when he married a flower girl who had become disclassed under extraordinary circumstances which were now notorious!

It is true that Eliza's situation did not seem wholly ineligible. Her father, though formerly a dustman, and now fantastically disclassed, had become extremely popular in the smartest society by a social talent which triumphed over every prejudice and every disadvantage. Rejected by the middle class, which he loathed, he had shot up at once into the highest circles by his wit, his dustmanship (which he carried like a banner), and his Nietzschean transcendence of good and evil. At intimate ducal dinners he sat on the right hand of the Duchess; and in country houses he smoked in the pantry and was made much of by the butler when he was not feeding in the dining room and being consulted by cabinet ministers. But he found it almost as hard to do all this on four thousand a year as Mrs Eynsford Hill to live in Earlscourt on an income so pitiably smaller that I have not the heart to disclose its exact figure. He absolutely refused to add the last straw to his burden by contributing to Eliza's support.

Thus Freddy and Eliza, now Mr and Mrs Eynsford Hill, would have spent a penniless honeymoon but for a wedding present of £500 from the Colonel to Eliza. It lasted a long time because Freddy did not know how to spend money, never having had any to spend, and Eliza, socially trained by a pair of old bachelors, wore her clothes as long as they held together and looked pretty, without the least regard to their being many months out of fashion. Still, £500 will not last two young people for ever; and they both knew, and Eliza felt as well, that they must shift for themselves in the end. She could quarter herself on Wimpole Street because it had come to be her home; but she was quite aware that she ought not to quarter Freddy there, and that it would not be good for his character if she did.

Not that the Wimpole Street bachelors

objected. When she consulted them, Higgins declined to be bothered about her housing problem when that solution was so simple. Eliza's desire to have Freddy in the house with her seemed of no more importance than if she had wanted an extra piece of bedroom furniture. Pleas as to Freddy's character, and the moral obligation on him to earn his own living, were lost on Higgins. He denied that Freddy had any character, and declared that if he tried to do any useful work some competent person would have the trouble of undoing it: a procedure involving a net loss to the community, and great unhappiness to Freddy himself, who was obviously intended by Nature for such light work as amusing Eliza, which, Higgins declared, was a much more useful and honorable occupation than working in the city. When Eliza referred again to her project of teaching phonetics, Higgins abated not a jot of his violent opposition to it. He said she was not within ten years of being qualified to meddle with his pet subject; and as it was evident that the Colonel agreed with him, she felt she could not go against them in this grave matter, and that she had no right, without Higgins's consent, to exploit the knowledge he had given her; for his knowledge seemed to her as much his private property as his watch: Eliza was no communist. Besides, she was superstitiously devoted to them both, more entirely and frankly after her marriage than before it.

It was the Colonel who finally solved the problem, which had cost him much perplexed cogitation. He one day asked Eliza, rather shyly, whether she had quite given up her notion of keeping a flower shop. She replied that she had thought of it, but had put it out of her head, because the Colonel had said, that day at Mrs Higgins's, that it would never do. The Colonel confessed that when he said that, he had not quite recovered from the dazzling impression of the day before. They broke the matter to Higgins that evening. The sole comment vouchsafed by him very nearly led to a serious quarrel with Eliza. It was to the effect that she would have in Freddy an ideal errand boy.

Freddy himself was next sounded on the subject. He said he had been thinking of a shop himself; though it had presented itself to his pennilessness as a small place in which Eliza should sell tobacco at one counter whilst he sold newspapers at the opposite one. But he agreed that it would be extraordinarily jolly to go early every morning with Eliza to Covent Garden and buy flowers on the scene of their first meeting: a sentiment which earned him many kisses from his wife. He added that he had always been afraid to propose anything of the sort, because Clara would make an awful row about a step that must damage her matrimonial chances, and his mother could not be expected to like it after clinging for so many years to that step of the social ladder on which retail trade is impossible.

This difficulty was removed by an event highly unexpected by Freddy's mother. Clara, in the course of her incursions into those artistic circles which were the highest within her reach, discovered that her conversational qualifications were expected to include a grounding in the novels of Mr H. G. Wells. She borrowed them in various directions so energetically that she swallowed them all within two months. The result was a conversion of a kind quite common today. A modern Acts of the Apostles would fill fifty whole Bibles if anyone were capable of writing it.

Poor Clara, who appeared to Higgins and his mother as a disagreeable and ridiculous person, and to her own mother as in some inexplicable way a social failure, had never seen herself in either light; for, though to some extent ridiculed and mimicked in West Kensington like everybody else there, she was accepted as a rational and normal—or shall we say inevitable?—sort of human being. At worst they called her The Pusher; but to them no more than to herself had it ever occurred that she was pushing the air, and pushing it in a wrong direction. Still, she was not happy. She was growing desperate. Her one asset, the fact that her mother was what the Epsom greengrocer called a carriage lady, had no exchange value, apparently. It had prevented her from getting educated, because the only education she could have afforded was education with the Earlscourt greengrocer's daughter. It had led her to seek the society of her mother's class; and that class simply would not have her, because she was much poorer than the greengrocer, and, far from being able to afford a maid, could not afford even a housemaid, and had to scrape along at home with an illiberally treated general servant. Under such circumstances nothing could give her an air of being a genuine product of Largelady Park. And yet its tradition made her regard a marriage with anyone within her reach as an unbearable humiliation. Commercial people and professional people in a small way were odious to her. She ran after painters and novelists; but she did not charm them; and her bold attempts to pick up and practise artistic and literary talk irritated them. She was, in short, an utter failure, an ignorant, incompetent, pretentious, unwelcome, penniless, useless little snob; and though she did not admit these disqualifications (for nobody ever faces unpleasant truths of this kind until the possibility of a way out dawns on them) she felt their effects too keenly to be satisfied with her position.

Clara had a startling eyeopener when, on being suddenly wakened to enthusiasm by a girl of her own age who dazzled her and produced in her a gushing desire to take her for a model, and gain her friendship, she discovered that this exquisite apparition had graduated from the gutter in a few months time. It shook her so violently, that when Mr H. G. Wells lifted her on the point of his puissant pen, and placed her at the angle of view from which the life she was leading and the society to which she clung appeared in its true relation to real human needs and worthy social structure, he effected a conversion and a conviction of sin comparable to the most sensational feats of General Booth or Gypsy Smith. Clara's snobbery went bang. Life suddenly began to move with her. Without knowing how or why, she began to make friends and enemies. Some of the acquaintances to whom she had been a tedious or indifferent or ridiculous affliction, dropped her: others became cordial. To her amazement she found that some "quite nice" people were saturated with Wells, and that this accessibility to ideas was the secret of their niceness. People she had thought deeply religious, and had tried to conciliate on that tack with disastrous results, suddenly took an interest in her, and revealed a hostility to conventional religion which she had never conceived possible except among the most desperate characters. They made her read Galsworthy; and Galsworthy exposed the vanity of Largelady Park and finished her. It exasperated her to think that

the dungeon in which she had languished for so many unhappy years had been unlocked all the time, and that the impulses she had so carefully struggled with and stifled for the sake of keeping well with society, were precisely those by which alone she could have come into any sort of sincere human contact. In the radiance of these discoveries, and the tumult of their reaction, she made a fool of herself as freely and conspicuously as when she so rashly adopted Eliza's expletive in Mrs Higgins's drawing room; for the new-born Wellsian had to find her bearings almost as ridiculously as a baby; but nobody hates a baby for its ineptitudes, or thinks the worse of it for trying to eat the matches; and Clara lost no friends by her follies. They laughed at her to her face this time; and she had to defend herself and fight it out as best she could.

When Freddy paid a visit to Earlscourt (which he never did when he could possibly help it) to make the desolating announcement that he and his Eliza were thinking of blackening the Largelady scutcheon by opening a shop, he found the little household already convulsed by a prior announcement from Clara that she also was going to work in an old furniture shop in Dover Street, which had been started by a fellow Wellsian. This appointment Clara owed, after all, to her old social accomplishment of Push. She had made up her mind that, cost what it might, she would see Mr Wells in the flesh; and she had achieved her end at a garden party. She had better luck than so rash an enterprise deserved. Mr Wells came up to her expectations. Age had not withered him, nor could custom stale his infinite variety in half an hour. His pleasant neatness and compactness, his small hands and feet, his teeming ready brain, his unaffected accessibility, and a certain fine apprehensiveness which stamped him as susceptible from his topmost hair to his tipmost toe, proved irresistible. Clara talked of nothing else for weeks and weeks afterwards. And as she happened to talk to the lady of the furniture shop, and that lady also desired above all things to know Mr Wells and sell pretty things to him, she offered Clara a job on the chance of achieving that end through her.

And so it came about that Eliza's luck held, and the expected opposition to the flower shop melted away. The shop is in the arcade of a railway station not very far from the Victoria and Albert Museum; and if you live in that neighbourhood you may go there any day and buy a buttonhole from Eliza.

Now here is a last opportunity for romance. Would you not like to be assured that the shop was an immense success, thanks to Eliza's charms and her early business experience in Covent Garden? Alas! the truth is the truth: the shop did not pay for a long time, simply because Eliza and her Freddy did not know how to keep it. True, Eliza had not to begin at the very beginning: she knew the names and prices of the cheaper flowers; and her elation was unbounded when she found that Freddy, like all youths educated at cheap, pretentious, and thoroughly inefficient schools, knew a little Latin. It was very little, but enough to make him appear to her a Porson or Bentley, and to put him at his ease with botanical nomenclature. Unfortunately he knew nothing else; and Eliza, though she could count money up to eighteen shillings or so, and had acquired a certain familiarity with the language of Milton from her struggles to qualify herself for winning Higgins's bet, could not write out a bill without utterly disgracing the establishment. Freddy's power of stating in Latin that Balbus built a wall and that Gaul was divided into three parts did not carry with it the slightest knowledge of accounts or business: Colonel Pickering had to explain to him what a cheque book and a bank account meant. And the pair were by no means easily teachable. Freddy backed up Eliza in her obstinate refusal to believe that they could save money by engaging a bookkeeper with some knowledge of the business. How, they argued, could you possibly save money by going to extra expense when you already could not make both ends meet? But the Colonel, after making the ends meet over and over again, at last gently insisted; and Eliza, humbled to the dust by having to beg from him so often, and stung by the uproarious derision of Higgins, to whom the notion of Freddy succeeding at anything was a joke that never palled, grasped the fact that business, like phonetics, has to be learned.

On the piteous spectacle of the pair spending their evenings in shorthand schools and polytechnic classes, learning bookkeeping and typewriting with incipient junior clerks, male and female, from the elementary schools, let me not dwell. There were even classes at the London School of Economics, and a humble personal appeal to the director of that institution to recommend a course bearing on the flower business. He, being a humorist, explained to them the method of the celebrated Dickensian essay on Chinese Metaphysics by the gentleman who read an article on China and an article on Metaphysics and combined the information. He suggested that they should combine the London School with Kew Gardens. Eliza, to whom the procedure of the Dickensian gentleman seemed perfectly correct (as in fact it was) and not in the least funny (which was only her ignorance), took the advice with entire gravity. But the effort that cost her the deepest humiliation was a request to Higgins, whose pet artistic fancy, next to Milton's verse, was caligraphy, and who himself wrote a most beautiful Italian hand, that he would teach her to write. He declared that she was congenitally incapable of forming a single letter worthy of the least of Milton's words; but she persisted; and again he suddenly threw himself into the task of teaching her with a combination of stormy intensity, concentrated patience, and occasional bursts of interesting disquisition on the beauty and nobility, the august mission and destiny, of human handwriting. Eliza ended by acquiring an extremely uncommercial script which was a positive extension of her personal beauty, and spending three times as much on stationery as anyone else because certain qualities and shapes on paper became indispensable to her. She could not even address an envelope in the usual way because it made the margins all wrong.

Their commercial schooldays were a period of disgrace and despair for the young couple. They seemed to be learning nothing about flower shops. At last they gave it up as hopeless, and shook the dust of the shorthand schools, and the polytechnics, and the London School of Economics from their feet for ever. Besides, the business was in some mysterious way beginning to take care of itself. They had somehow forgotten their objections to employing other people. They came to the conclusion that their own way was the best, and that they had really a remarkable talent for business. The Colonel, who had been compelled for some years to keep a sufficient sum on current account at his bankers to make up their deficits, found that the provision was unnecessary: the young people were prospering. It is true that there was not quite fair play between them and their competitors in trade. Their week-ends in the country cost them nothing, and saved them the price of their Sunday dinners; for the motor car was the Colonel's; and he and Higgins paid the hotel bills. Mr F. Hill, florist and green-grocer (they soon discovered that there was money in asparagus; and asparagus led to other vegetables), had an air which stamped the business as classy; and in private life he was still Frederick Eynsford Hill, Esquire. Not that there was any swank about him: nobody but Eliza knew that he had been christened Frederick Challoner. Eliza herself swanked like anything.

That is all. That is how it has turned out. It is astonishing how much Eliza still manages to meddle in the housekeeping at Wimpole Street in spite of the shop and her own family. And it is notable that though she never nags her husband, and frankly loves the Colonel as if she were his favorite daughter, she has never got out of the habit of nagging Higgins that was established on the fatal night when she won his bet for him. She snaps his head off on the faintest provocation, or on none. He no longer dares to tease her by assuming an abysmal inferiority of Freddy's mind to his own. He storms and bullies and derides; but

she stands up to him so ruthlessly that the Colonel has to ask her from time to time to be kinder to Higgins; and it is the only request of his that brings a mulish expression into her face. Nothing but some emergency or calamity great enough to break down all likes and dislikes, and throw them both back on their common humanity—and may they be spared any such trial!—will ever alter this. She knows that Higgins does not need her, just as her father did not need her. The very scrupulousness with which he told her that day that he had become used to having her there, and dependent on her for all sorts of little services, and that he should miss her if she went away (it would never have occurred to Freddy or the Colonel to say anything of the sort) deepens her inner certainty that she is "no more to him than them slippers"; yet she has a sense, too, that his indifference is deeper than the infatuation of commoner souls. She is immensely interested in him. She has even secret mischievous moments in which she wishes she could get him alone, on a desert island, away from all ties and with nobody else in the world to consider, and just drag him off his pedestal and see him making love like any common man. We all have private imaginations of that sort. But when it comes to business, to the life that she really leads as distinguished from the life of dreams and fancies, she likes Freddy and she likes the Colonel; and she does not like Higgins and Mr Doolittle. Galatea never does quite like Pygmalion: his relation to her is too godlike to be altogether agreeable.

DESIRE UNDER THE ELMS

Eugene O'Neill

Set for the original production of *Desire Under the Elms* showing simultaneous action in exterior and interior portions. Ephraim Cabot (Walter Huston)
leans against the house, below; Eben (Charles Ellis) and Abbie Putnam (Mary
Morris) in their bedrooms, yearn for each other but are separated by a wall.
Greenwich Village Theatre, New York 1924. Museum of the City of New York.

Eugene O'Neill

Eugene Gladstone O'Neill, America's foremost playwright, was born on October 16, 1888, at the Barrett House, a hotel located at the corner of Broadway and Forty-third Street in New York City. He was the second son of James O'Neill and Ella Quinlan; his elder brother, James, Jr., had been born ten years before him. Their parents were devout Catholics. James O'Neill, a celebrated actor, was a tall, handsome man, who performed in the romantic, elocutionary style of the nineteenth century and became famous for his portrayal of Edmond Dantes in a dramatization of *The Count of Monte Cristo.* In this play he toured back and forth across the United States, year after year, until he was known in every city and town from coast to coast. The endless repetition of this role, which made him extremely wealthy, ruined him as a serious artist and caused him to have bitter regrets in later years.

Until he was seven years old, Eugene knew no regular home but traveled with his family and spent his time playing in the wings and the dressing rooms of the theatres in which his father appeared. He thus began life as a trouper, his earliest experiences connected with actors and the stage. From the age of eight, he attended various Catholic and nonsectarian boarding schools, but these were temporary stops, and failed to give him the sense of belonging he apparently needed. In 1906, after graduation from the Betts Academy in Stamford, Connecticut, he entered Princeton University. He was suspended the following June for failure in most of his courses and for "general hell-raising."

Eugene then went to work in New York as corresponding secretary for a mail-order jewelry firm in which his father had a financial interest. This occupation was as little to his liking as studying, so that he was not too unhappy when the business failed and he lost his job. He never returned to Princeton and had no further formal education.

In 1909 he married Kathleen Jenkins of New York, but by the following year, when his son Eugene, Jr., was born, he had already left his wife and child and set out for Honduras in search of gold and exotic adventures. He acquired a case of malaria and the following year was back in the United States serving as assistant manager for *The White Sister,* a play in which his father was appearing with Viola Allen. At the end of the theatrical season, he made his first sea voyage, a trip of sixty-five days on a Norwegian freighter to Buenos Aires. There he found work in the branch offices of several American corporations, but either quit or was fired from each job; he finally wound up living among the sailors, stevedores, and outcasts along the docks.

From these men, with whom he was most at ease, he heard amazing yarns and acquired intimate insights into human nature, which he stored in his memory for future use. Then he shipped out on a cattle steamer, tending mules from Buenos Aires to Durban, South Africa, but was not permitted to land because he was destitute. Returning to Buenos Aires, he lived for months as a beachcomber.

In 1911 O'Neill worked his way back to the United States as an ordinary seaman on a British tramp steamer, which later served as the model for the "S.S. Glencairn," of his one-act sea plays. In New York he went to live in a water-front dive run by a character known as "Jimmy the Priest." He paid $3 a month for a vermin-infested room, which he shared with an assortment of derelicts, one of whom committed suicide by jumping out of the window. This disreputable flophouse and bar provided the locale for The Iceman Cometh, for the first act of Anna Christie, and for several of the one-act plays. One day O'Neill won a large sum of money at gambling, celebrated by getting drunk, and woke up on a train headed for New Orleans; when he got there, he discovered that his father was in New Orleans, performing in the old favorite, Monte Cristo. He went around to the theatre, hoping to borrow money for a return ticket to New York, but his father refused to give him a handout; he insisted that his son work his way back North, assigned him an unimportant role in the play, and put him on the payroll as an actor.

At the end of the season, the O'Neill family went to their summer home in New London, Connecticut. The year was 1912. Eugene's divorce from Kathleen Jenkins came through. He was twenty-four and had no idea of what he was going to do with his life. That summer he got a job as cub reporter on the New London Telegraph, for which he wrote highly colored news items and some very immature poems; but both Frederick P. Latimer, the publisher of the paper, and Malcolm Mollan, the city editor, recognized his gift for words as well as his sensitivity and his understanding of human nature. These men were the first to encourage O'Neill and to suggest that he consider writing as a career.

The conflicts and tensions in O'Neill's personal life came to a head during that summer of 1912; O'Neill was later to deal fully with this difficult period of his life in his play Long Day's Journey into Night. His father's authoritarian attitude, his mother's unfortunate drug addiction, and his brother Jim's alcoholism all took their toll on Eugene. Jim had done his best to initiate his younger brother into his own ways of dissipation with liquor and women. Before Eugene could achieve some measure of self-discipline and control, his health broke down. During the winter of 1912 and the spring of 1913, he was a patient at Gaylord Farm, a tuberculosis sanitarium at Wallingford, Connecticut. An account of his experiences at the sanitarium appears in the early part of his play The Straw. At Gaylord Farm O'Neill took stock of his life, and he determined to become a writer. After his discharge from the sanitarium as an arrested case, he went to live with an English family who had a home overlooking Long Island Sound. There he read voluminously in the dramatists, from the Greeks to his own time; he exercised regularly, rested, and began to write. In a little over a year, he completed two full-length plays, eleven one-acters, and some verse.

At twenty-six he had had wide and varied experiences with people in all walks of life, as well as a first-hand knowledge of the American theatre, with all its romantic ideas and conventions; he did not like what he saw either in life or in the theatre. His own thinking and feeling had been deeply dyed in the philosophy of Nietzsche and the psychology of Strindberg. But before he could adequately express his own point of view, he felt that he needed training in the technical aspects of playwriting. In the fall of 1914, he enrolled in George Pierce Baker's "47 Workshop" at Harvard; as a student he wrote a long play and a one-acter, neither of which had any significance. When he showed Professor Baker the manuscript of *Bound East for Cardiff,* a short play he had written before entering the class, Baker's reaction was negative. He said that it was no play at all but that it indicated promise. Though O'Neill was later to express gratitude for Baker's encouragement, he left the class at the end of the school year.

In 1914 O'Neill submitted five of his plays to several commercial publishers, all of whom rejected the manuscript. Then the young dramatist prevailed on his father to pay the publishing costs and the volume called *Thirst and Other One-act Plays* appeared. With this little book and a trunkful of unproduced and unpublished plays, O'Neill went to live in Greenwich Village, where he mixed congenially with bohemians and with all shades of liberals, progressives, radicals, and anarchists. In the summer of 1916, he moved into a shack in Provincetown on Cape Cod, Massachusetts. There he ran into a group of writers from Greenwich Village, which included Susan Glaspell, Mary Heaton Vorse, Edna St. Vincent Millay, and Wilbur Daniel Steele. This group was attempting to establish in America the sort of art theatre that such men as Stanislavsky, Antoine, Otto Brahm, and J. T. Grein had initiated in Europe. The young Americans had produced some one-acters during the summer of 1915, and in 1916 they had formed an organization called the Provincetown Players, with headquarters at the Wharf Theatre. Just when they were looking for scripts, O'Neill turned up with *Bound East for Cardiff,* which the group put on and followed with a production of *Thirst.* In each of these, O'Neill acted a small part. When spectators reacted to the plays as original and profound, the group was encouraged to continue.

In the fall the Provincetown Players returned to New York and took over a stable at 133 Macdougal Street. This they converted into a a theatre, which became their permanent home and served for O'Neill as a laboratory where he was free to perform his experiments in dramatic form. He wrote with great speed and intensity and the sea plays began to make their appearance: *In the Zone, The Long Voyage Home,* and *'Ile* were all performed in 1917; *Where the Cross Is Made* and *The Moon of the Caribbees* were produced in 1918. At the same time several of these plays were published in *The Smart Set,* a magazine edited by George Jean Nathan and H. L. Mencken, two astute critics who recognized O'Neill's talent. It was Nathan who introduced the dramatist's work to the producer John D. Williams.

On April 12, 1918, O'Neill married Agnes Boulton, a professional writer he had met in Greenwich Village the previous year; they had two children— a son, Shane, born in 1919, and a daughter, Oona, born in 1925. With his family he spent his summers in Provincetown, his winters in Ridgefield, Connecticut, and in a house in New Jersey which his wife owned. His writing went on uninterruptedly, but he gave up the one-act form to concentrate on full-length dramas.

His first Broadway production, *Beyond the Horizon,* opened at the Morosco Theatre in February, 1920, under the management of John D. Williams. The play won the Pulitzer prize and established O'Neill as

America's outstanding dramatist. The unpredictability of fate, the disillusionment of the characters, and the deep gloom of the atmosphere—which were to become well-known O'Neill trade-marks—were very much in evidence in this play. James O'Neill went to the opening night and is said to have wept during the performance; but the old actor was so steeped in the romantic tradition that he could not understand his son's outspokenness and asked him if he was "trying to send the audience home to commit suicide."

The Emperor Jones, Diff'rent, Gold, and *Anna Christie* were all produced within one year—November 3, 1920 to November 2, 1921. O'Neill was proclaimed the theatre's most daring and inveterate experimenter and recognized as a full-fledged rebel, impatient with and critical of religion, politics, social customs and conventions, and, above all, dramatic form. *The Emperor Jones,* a play in eight brief scenes, is the psychological study of a Negro; it was one of the first plays in recent times to use an actual Negro instead of a white actor in blackface. O'Neill, who had very little faith in actors, said that except for Charles Gilpin, the Negro performer who played the title role in *The Emperor Jones,* no actor ever portrayed "every notion of a character I had in mind. . . . It is for that reason that I always attend the rehearsals of my plays. While I do not want to change the personalities of the artists acting in them, I want to make it clear to them what was in my mind when I wrote the play." *The Emperor Jones* was an enormous success. *Diff'rent* and *Gold,* which dealt with frustration, suicide, and insanity, both failed in the theatre. *Anna Christie* was a resounding hit, brought its author his second Pulitzer prize, has been revived many times, was filmed twice, and served as the basis for a Broadway musical called *New Girl in Town* (1957).

Yank, the central character in O'Neill's next major play, *The Hairy Ape* (1922), symbolized modern man, who wanted to belong but could neither rise to a spiritual level nor return to the level of the animals, and was destroyed in the conflict.

In 1924 O'Neill stirred up "a storm of unwelcome notoriety" with *All God's Chillun Got Wings,* a play that attempted to deal honestly with the problems arising out of the intermarriage of a Negro boy and a white girl. The subject did not appeal to audiences and aroused the ire of New York district attorney Banton. In the fall of the same year, *Desire Under the Elms,* which many consider one of the playwright's finest works, aroused even louder protests and more violent reactions. The district attorney attempted to close the play, and a jury was set up to investigate its moral fitness to be shown. It was eventually given a clean bill of health, ran for a year in New York, and was played throughout the country by two road companies.

During 1925, 1926, and 1927 O'Neill lived in Bermuda for a good part of each year. The plays produced during this period were unconventional in both subject matter and form. *The Fountain* (1925) dealt with Ponce de Leon's vain search for the elixir of youth; it was a play that cried out for poetic treatment, but unfortunately the dramatist could not provide the requisite language. *The Great God Brown* (1926) was an elaborate symbolic exposition of the conflict between paganism and Christianity in modern man; the players wore masks to signify the difference between a man's real face and the one he showed the world. *Marco Millions* (1928), a satirical attack on American big business and the American businessman, came close to being a comedy, a form in which the playwright never felt comfortable. The three plays just mentioned all failed in the theatre. The next play, *Strange Interlude*

(1928), a "novelistic" work, which probed the psyche of a woman who was all things to all men, was performed each day from 5:30 to 11 P.M., with an eighty-minute break for dinner. In addition to its extreme length, the play was radically unconventional in that the characters spoke their innermost thoughts aloud, the dramatist utilizing the old-fashioned aside to achieve a modern effect of psychological depth. This play brought O'Neill his greatest financial returns, won a Pulitzer prize, and was made into a successful film.

The next two experiments, *Lazarus Laughed* (1928) and *Dynamo* (1929), were dismal failures. The latter play was intended as the first in a trilogy dealing with modern man's worship of science and materialism, but the public's rejection of the work led O'Neill to abandon the project.

Agnes Boulton divorced O'Neill in 1928, and the following year he married Carlotta Monterey, who had played the female lead in *The Hairy Ape*. There were no children of this marriage. From 1931 to 1936, O'Neill and his wife lived at Casa Genotta, a house on Sea Island, Georgia.

Mourning Becomes Electra was produced by the Theatre Guild in October, 1931, and won the unanimous praise of the critics as well as the intense interest of audiences. This trilogy, which took some four and one-half hours to perform, was loosely based on the Oresteian trilogy of Aeschylus. The love and hate of a New England family was played out against the background of the Civil War, and for the ancient "belief in gods and supernatural retribution," O'Neill attempted to substitute a "modern psychological approximation of the Greek sense of fate." In its total effect, however, the play was not Greek but Gothic; it never rose to true tragic heights, mainly because of its prosaic language.

O'Neill's only acknowledged comedy, *Ah, Wilderness!*, a nostalgic, auto-biographical work, was presented in 1933; brilliantly acted by George M. Cohan, it became a great popular success. The following year he had a re-sounding "flop," with a philosophical treatment of a religious theme in *Days Without End;* in this work the leading character was played by two different actors to suggest the conflicting sides of his personality. The drama-tist was still seeking an answer to man's quest for spiritual certainty, and the play's failure proved a great disappointment to him. In 1937 O'Neill became seriously ill and retired temporarily from the theatre. He and his wife moved to Contra Costa County, near Berkeley, California, where they built a home called Tao House.

In 1946 the Theatre Guild presented *The Iceman Cometh,* the last play to be produced during O'Neill's lifetime. The playwright came out of retire-ment to attend rehearsals although he was a partial invalid, suffering from the nervous disorder to which he finally succumbed. This play's action was laid in Harry Hope's water-front dive, which was closely modeled on Jimmy the Priest's and was somewhat reminiscent of Gorky's *Lower Depths*. The play has astonishing profundities and nuances, scarcely realized in its initial production. Critics expressed conflicting views of the play's merits, and it closed after 136 performances.

O'Neill died in Boston on November 27, 1953, at the age of sixty-five. He was buried without religious rites in Forest Hills Cemetery on the out-skirts of that city.

During his long illness O'Neill had continued to work on an enormous cycle of plays known as *A Tale of Possessors Self-Dispossessed,* which was meant to be an ironic comment on the rise and fall of an American family through the whole span of American history. Before his death he destroyed all of these plays but two, *A Touch of the Poet* and *More Stately Mansions*. From another cycle entitled *By Way of Obit,* on which he was also at work, only a single, long one-act play called *Hughie* remained. The previously unproduced plays had their première performances, by the explicit request of the author, at the Royal Dramatic Theatre in Stockholm; they were later mounted elsewhere.

The following is a list of the plays produced posthumously in New York:

The Iceman Cometh was revived on May 8, 1956, at an off-Broadway theatre called the Circle in the Square, located in Greenwich Village a few blocks away from the old Provincetown Playhouse, where the playwright's first successful efforts were produced. Under the brilliant direction of José Quintero, the pipe-dreaming habitués of Harry Hope's barroom emerged with new meaning, pathos, and humor. The play had a record-breaking run of 565 performances. This production established Quintero as a director of importance, and Jason Robards, Jr., as a dramatic star; it also initiated a renaissance of O'Neill's work in the United States.

Long Day's Journey into Night opened on Broadway, November 7, 1956, under Quintero's direction, with Frederic March, Florence Eldridge, and Jason Robards, Jr., in the leading roles; the play won a Pulitzer prize (O'Neill's fourth) and received the Drama Critics Circle Award, as well as every other major trophy of the year. It deals with the events of the summer of 1912, which were crucial in the dramatist's life, and is generally accounted one of O'Neill's greatest plays.

A Moon for the Misbegotten opened on May 2, 1957, directed by Carmen Capalbo and starring Wendy Hiller, Franchot Tone, and Cyril Cusack. This play carries on, in thin disguise, O'Neill's family history and traces the final disintegration of his brother, James. The play closed after a very short run.

A Touch of the Poet opened on October 2, 1958, with a cast headed by Helen Hayes, Kim Stanley, and Eric Portman, under the direction of Harold Clurman. An early episode in the American family cycle, the play seemed incomplete and met with mixed critical notices. It ran for 284 performances and was called by *Variety* a "financial success."

Hughie, a long one-act play, which is actually a monologue carried on by a lonely, worn-out traveling salesman, was brilliantly enacted by Jason Robards, Jr., under the direction of José Quintero. The play ran from December 22, 1964, to January 30, 1965, at the Royale Theatre on Broadway.

More Stately Mansions, another play in the family cycle, would require about ten and a half hours for its performance if it were done as O'Neill left it. For its American production the script was "trimmed and finished" by José Quintero, who directed it, with Ingrid Bergman, Colleen Dewhurst, and Arthur Hill in the leading parts. The play opened at the Ahmanson Theatre in Los Angeles in September, 1967, and moved to the Broadhurst Theatre in New York on October 31; it closed on March 2, 1968.

No recent playwright except George Bernard Shaw has been more widely produced than Eugene O'Neill. It may safely be estimated that he wrote about one hundred plays, half of which, in line with his rigorous standards, he destroyed; of the fifty left to us, only half have been successful in the theatre. But all the plays that remain have an exceptional interest because of their author's unceasing experimentation in form and content, mood and style. O'Neill has been found to be deficient in two areas: His plays are said to be humorless, and his language is not as elevated as his ideas. It is true that he wrote only one play he called a comedy, but all of his work is shot through with bitter, wry, ironic shafts of wit and humor, and if the lines are delivered with skill they have a convulsing and telling effect. Of his language Barrett H. Clark has said: "His gift for poetry lies not in written speeches, but in his conceptions, in scenes and situations, and occasionally in separate lines that illuminate not by their intrinsic verbal values but by their implications."

By nature O'Neill was serious, brooding, and rebellious. In searching men's hearts to discover the mystery of their unrest, he found terror, disillusionment, and frustration driving them to run the gamut of crimes and aberrations from alcoholism to zombiism. Yet the total effect of his work is neither depraved nor pessimistic, because love, security, and faith—though unattainable—are everywhere in evidence in his characters' hopes and dreams. His profound sincerity and penetrating insights into human relationships have evoked a universal response.

In addition to being a four-time recipient of the Pulitzer prize, O'Neill was awarded a medal for artistic achievement by the American Academy of Arts and Letters in 1923, was granted the degree of Doctor of Literature at Yale University in 1926, and won the Nobel prize in 1936. In 1965 the Eugene O'Neill Memorial Theatre Foundation was established in Waterford, Connecticut, under the direction of George C. White. A museum and library, devoted to O'Neill's life and work, and a workshop for the development of new playwrights are special features of the foundation. On October 16, 1967, the United States government issued, in its Prominent Americans Series, a one-dollar postage stamp bearing the portrait of the playwright; O'Neill is the only dramatist this country has produced to have been honored in this way.

But the greatest tribute to O'Neill is the vitality that the reading and theatregoing publics still find in his work; new editions and revivals of his plays continue to make their appearance not only in the United States but throughout the world.

Desire Under the Elms

In *Desire Under the Elms* O'Neill deals, as he does in many of his plays, with the love-hate relationships between husband and wife and between parent and child, and with the frustration of human desires. His basic material is autobiographical, unconsciously so, but identifiable nevertheless. Eben represents the playwright himself; Ephraim, James O'Neill, as his son conceived him to be; and Abbie, his mother, upon whom the dramatist projected his ambivalent emotions as son and lover[1].

It is interesting to note that many of O'Neill's ideas for his plays came to him in dreams, and he once told Walter Huston that he had dreamed most

---

[1] See, Philip Weissman, *Creativity in the Theater* (New York: Basic Books, 1965), for psychoanalytical studies, in Chap. 8, of *Desire Under the Elms*, and in Chap. 9, of Shaw's *Pygmalion*.

of *Desire Under the Elms.* He objected, however, when he was accused of being a Freudian. He remarked to a correspondent, "Playwrights are either intuitively keen analytical psychologists—or they aren't good playwrights. . . . Whatever Freudianism [there] is in 'Desire' must have walked right in 'through my unconscious.'"

Regardless of the source of the material, the playwright had to find an acceptable form in which to present it. O'Neill had been studying the plays of the great Greek dramatists and felt, with his characteristically somber outlook on life, that people of every era have been tortured in their souls and have inevitably been destructive of each other. But if he was to achieve the powerful effect of Greek tragedy, he would have to seek out the elements parallel to those of the ancients in subject matter—time, place, people, and events—and in structure.

He set the action of *Desire Under the Elms* and *Mourning Becomes Electra,* the two plays for which he obviously used classical models, in nineteenth-century New England. The former age would lend a mythic quality to the story, and the hard and unyielding earth of New England reminded him of the rocky soil of Greece. The people who attempted to wrest a living from such recalcitrant land were bound to have many characteristics in common: they were stern, hard-working, stubborn, and ingrown; their passions, like their minds, were held in check by the terrifying image of a wrathful, thunder-hurling God.

For the plot of *Mourning Becomes Electra,* O'Neill drew heavily upon Aeschylus's Oresteian trilogy; while for *Desire Under the Elms* he appears to have taken ideas from Sophocles' *Oedipus Rex* and from Euripides' *Hippolytus.* The *Oedipus* concerns a headstrong young man who is fated to kill his father and to have children by his mother. In *Desire Under the Elms* Eben Cabot is in deep and mortal conflict with his father; he wishes him dead, without actually killing him. There is no doubt, however, that the young man's incestuous relationship with his stepmother, and what follows from it, is the cause of his father's spiritual death.

The play bears an even closer resemblance to the *Hippolytus.* In Euripides' drama Theseus, a powerful and hard-hearted man, is thrice married: he has deserted his first wife, killed his second, and then married Phaedra, a young and passionate woman. Hippolytus, his son by his second wife, hates and resents his father and the new bride. But Phaedra falls madly in love with the boy, and when he fails to return her feeling, she falsely accuses him to his father and then commits suicide. O'Neill was highly original in his adaptation of this material, but the source remains clear. Ephraim Cabot was thrice wed, worked his second wife to death, and then married a passionate woman less than half his age. His son by his second wife, hating and resenting his father, uses the third wife as the instrument of his revenge. In the original story Phaedra actually writes a letter to Hippolytus, suggesting that he revenge himself on his father "by paying homage to Aphrodite in my company." And in the O'Neill play Abbie (Phaedra), furious at being spurned by Eben (Hippolytus), falsely accuses him to his father, who offers to blow the boy's brains out or to horsewhip him off the place.

There are many other resemblances in the O'Neill dramas to their Greek counterparts, but the playwright has assimilated the material so brilliantly that his stories seem completely indigenous to New England. This is especially true of *Desire Under the Elms* and accounts for the great power

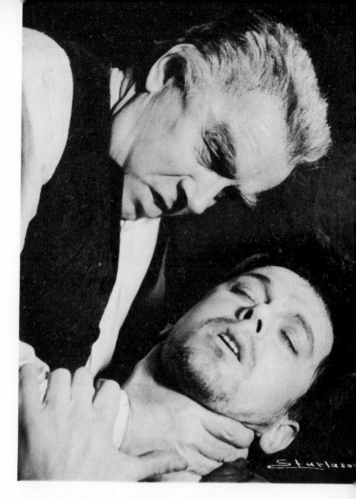

Alfred and Toralv Maurstad (father and son), celebrated Norwegian performers who often appeared together, here seen as Ephraim and Eben Cabot in a moment of violence between parent and child. National Theatre, Oslo 1962. Photograph: Sturlason.

of the play. With its frustrated protagonists, its weighty sense of the past haunting the present, and its hard and primitive God, working both as an active and as an immanent force in the lives of the characters, *Desire Under the Elms* is the closest thing we have to Greek tragedy in the modern theatre.

Visually, too, the play was made to resemble a Greek tragedy. The set, as conceived by O'Neill and designed for the stage by Robert Edmond Jones, presents a single side view of a New England farmhouse. Although the audience was able to see into the various rooms when sections of the outer wall were removed, the house itself remained on stage throughout, like the façade of the *skene* in the Greek theatre. The area downstage of the farmhouse represented, as did the *orchestron,* an adjoining road, field, or lawn, as called for by the action.

In addition, *Desire Under the Elms* has the structure of a Greek play; it is a trilogy in that it consists of three parts—O'Neill used the word "parts," not "acts." Although there is a time lapse of two months between Parts I and II and of one year between Parts II and III, each part consumes but a single day, from the afternoon or evening to dawn. The playwright was apparently attempting to observe the neoclassical unities: unity of place— the farmhouse; unity of time—the single day; unity of action—the single plot line involving the three protagonists; and, in addition, an overwhelming unity of mood.

The play's central characters, Ephraim, Eben, and Abbie, are drawn with remarkable credibility and exhibit all the human complexities of emotion

Abbie (Urda Arneberg) and Eben (Toralv Maurstad) in a tender moment from the Norwegian production of *Desire Under the Elms*. National Theatre, Oslo 1962. Photograph: Sturlason.

and motivation. Ephraim Cabot, the hard-fisted and stony-hearted owner of the old farm, often confuses himself with the Old Testament God; he has triumphed over his environment by the power of his body and his will and is the controlling figure in his family as he is in the action of the play. In her struggle for physical satisfaction, financial security, and sexual domination, Abbie's weapons are her physical attractiveness, her sensuality, and her possessiveness; but in arousing Eben's repressed passions, she unleashes a force she does not understand and cannot control in herself or in him, a force that is finally responsible for the general doom. Eben yearns to be free of his father's control but, confounded by his infatuation with Abbie, becomes more and more hopelessly entangled. Eben's mental and emotional confusion have an almost paralyzing effect upon him; yet it is only through Abbie's love for him, which he reciprocates, that he finally achieves a measure of insight into his guilty thoughts and behavior and comes to realize that he must suffer the consequences of them. It is difficult to understand why this play was hounded by the censors and banned as obscene and immoral, in view of the obvious conclusion to be drawn from the fate of its characters: The wages of sin is death!

Humor—bitter, wry, and mordant—characteristic of the people of New England, runs through the play. We find it in the coarse playfulness of the brothers, Simeon and Peter; in the sarcastic jibes of Ephraim, Eben, and Abbie; and in the sly innuendoes of the townspeople; but the over-all impression left by the work is of somber and deep seriousness.

Only in his dialogue—in the studied reproduction of a Down East dialect—does the playwright leave something to be desired. Occasionally, he achieves an incisive force in the laconic remarks of the farmers, but at those moments of emotional climax when we expect the language to soar, we are treated instead to an effusion of one of the more unpleasant and awkward of our regional folk idioms.

In its projection of raw feelings upon the stage, in its terrifying intensity and fiercely emotional impact, *Desire Under the Elms* stands as one of the most memorable plays in the entire range of O'Neill's work.

The Production Record

Desire Under the Elms, written during the winter and spring of 1923–24, had its première performance at the Greenwich Village Theatre in New York on November 11, 1924. It was produced at a cost of $6,000 by the Provincetown Players, an organization then under the direction of Kenneth Macgowan (a former drama critic), Robert Edmond Jones, Eugene O'Neill, and James Light. The cast was headed by Walter Huston as Ephraim Cabot, Charles Ellis as Eben, and Mary Morris as Abbie—all of whom gave notable performances. In addition to being one of its coproducers, Robert Edmond Jones designed and directed the play. Jones had grown up in Milton, New Hampshire, in a grim and lonely farmhouse not unlike the one that served as the play's setting. Jones felt, to use his own words, that New England was "violent, passionate, sensual, sadistic, lifted, heated, frozen, transcendental, Poesque," and these were the moods and emotions he tried for in the production. It was realism played with a brooding austerity.

Set for *Desire Under the Elms* lighted for the first and third acts, Norwegian production, Oslo 1962. Photograph: Sturlason.

Alexander Tairov's production at the Kamerny Theatre in Moscow c. 1929. O'Neill saw it in Paris in 1930 and praised it highly. Tairov turned the stage into a house with the elm trees as beams, thus making an architectural unit of the whole. Alice Koonen, Tairov's wife and star of the Kamerny, played Abbie. She is seen center. Theatre Collection, New York Public Library.

The play was an immediate success and caught the interest of the commercial producers A. L. Jones (no relation to Robert Edmond) and Morris Green, who moved it from the Greenwich Village Theatre to the Earl Carroll Theatre on Broadway on January 10, 1925. As soon as it was installed uptown, a number of people complained that the play was "obscene"; District Attorney Joab Banton branded it "thoroughly bad" and ordered it closed, under threat of grand jury investigation. Most of the New York newspapers came to the play's defense editorially; it was also defended by a group of prominent citizens, including the Reverend John Haynes Holmes, Rachel Crothers, and Brander Matthews. The district attorney's jury of specially selected citizens, which was set up to pass judgment on *Desire Under the Elms,* found nothing objectionable in the play. All through 1925 people formed lines at the box office. On June 1 the play was moved from the Earl Carroll Theatre to the George M. Cohan Theatre. The original cast remained intact until June 13, when Mary Morris was replaced by Mary Blair; during the week of September 12, Walter Huston's role was taken over by Frank McGlynn; Charles Ellis continued in the part of Eben for the entire run of the play. On September 28 *Desire* moved again, this time to Daly's Sixty-third Street Theatre, where it ended its run on October 17, 1925, after chalking up more than 350 performances.

During 1925 and 1926 two road companies toured the play from coast to coast, and in a number of cities they ran into trouble with the law. In Boston the censor read a copy of the script and demanded that extensive revisions be made before he would grant permission for the play to be performed there; when both author and producers refused to comply, the play was banned. After a few performances in Los Angeles, police arrested the entire cast. A long court trial followed, while the play continued its run; when the jury could not agree on a verdict, a retrial was ordered, but by that time the show had closed, and the matter was dropped.

Shortly after its American production, the play was translated into many languages, including Japanese, Turkish, Russian and the Scandinavian languages. It has been produced all over the world. In Russia, particularly during the 1920s and 1930s, *Desire Under the Elms* played frequently to enthusiastic audiences. Alexander Tairov, a great theatrical innovator, staged the play at the Kamerny (Chamber) Theatre in Moscow in the winter of 1926, with his wife Alice Koonen in the role of Abbie. Stylized realism marked both the acting and the décor. An architect rather than a scene designer provided the setting. The entire stage was turned into a two-story house with the front removed and with the heavy branches of the elms serving as structural beams and making an architectural unit of the whole. Called "constructivist" and "abstract," it was a highly dynamic set and much imitated by later directors, designers, and producers. In the summer of 1930, O'Neill saw the Tairov production in Paris and, in his enthusiasm for it, wrote the Russian director a letter, in which he said,

> . . . My feeling is one of amazement—and most profound gratitude! Let me humbly confess I came to the theatre with secret misgivings. Not that I doubted your presentation would be a splendid thing in itself, artistically conceived and executed. I know the reputation of the Kamerny as one of the finest theatres in Europe too well for that. But I did have an author's fear that in the difficult process of transition and transformation into another language and milieu the inner spirit—that indefinable essential quality so dear to the creator as being for him the soul of his work!—might be excusably, considering the obstacles, distorted or lost. . . . A theatre of creative imagination has always been my ideal! To see my plays given by such a theatre has always been my dream! The Kamerny Theatre has realized this dream for me! . . ."

In 1933, thinking to sell *Desire Under the Elms* to the movies, O'Neill prepared his own screen treatment of the play. Aware of the strictures placed upon motion pictures by the various state censorship boards, he toned down the language, altered some of the situations, and turned Abbie into a Portuguese woman whose husband fished out of New England harbors. The playwright felt that screen audiences would more readily accept unreasoning passion in a woman from southern Europe than in a native American. He sent the script to Kenneth Macgowan, who was a Hollywood producer at the time, but no film company could be induced to make the picture.

In October, 1933, *Desire Under the Elms,* directed by Alf Sjöberg, with Lars Hanson and Tora Teje in the leading roles, was produced at the Royal Dramatic Theatre in Stockholm. Twenty years later this theatre, under the direction of Karl Ragnar Gierow, was to present the world premières of O'Neill's last plays; it was to Dr. Gierow that Mrs. O'Neill entrusted the initial cutting and editing of *More Stately Mansions.*

Desire Under the Elms had been banned in London at the time that Boston and Los Angeles refused to allow it to be played. But by 1940 the restrictions had been removed, and in January of that year, the London Mask Company produced its version of the play at the Westminster Theatre, later touring with it through the British provinces. The set resembled Tairov's, but the acting was realistic rather than stylized. The leading roles were performed by actors of great skill: Ephraim was played by Mark Dignam, Eben by Stephen Murray; Abbie was played by Beatrix Lehmann, whom several critics thought superb. One critic, W. A. Darlington, wrote of Miss Lehmann's

Anders Henrikson as Eben and Tora Teje as Abbie in the Royal Dramatic Theatre production directed by Alf Sjöberg, Stockholm 1933. Photograph: Almberg and Preinitz. Courtesy Royal Dramatic Theatre.

performance: "She is not the least what O'Neill meant the part to be, but she is forceful in her own quiet way."

On November 21, 1951, The Craftsmen, an off-Broadway group, produced the play at the Barbizon Plaza Playhouse. It was staged by Edward Ludlum, with setting and lighting by Robert L. Ramsey. The set, which represented the farmhouse, was constructed of iron piping and was seen only in skeleton form. It conveyed a very stark, modern, and constructivist feeling, suggesting abstractly and symbolically the unyielding natures of the protagonists. The set completely filled the tiny stage, the very tightness of the playing areas heightening the audience's awareness of the cramped lives of the characters. The acting and the directing were electrifying in their effect. Brooks Atkinson, in his enthusiasm, wrote: "The heartening thing about the performance which Edward Ludlum has directed is the fact that it catches the elemental fury of the drama. Carl Low's harsh, braggart, gnarled Ephraim, Priscilla Amidon's passionate, ruthless, defiant Abbie, and Paul Stevens' bewildered and boyish Eben are all clearly defined and acted with burning conviction." So great was the impression that this production made upon Atkinson that he went on to say: "And what a play it is! From every point of view it is one of our greatest treasures. As craftsmanship it is vivid and inventive. As a piece of writing it is compact and forceful. As a portrait of greed, lust, hatred, wrath, horror, and the primitive basis of civilization, it is unerring and remorseless, and it comes out of the convictions of a great dramatist." Another production of the play, at the Brattle Theatre, Cambridge, Massachusetts, in May, 1952, had Paul Stevens and Priscilla Amidon repeating their roles, with Larry Gates as Ephraim, and with direction by Henry Weinstein.

On January 16, 1952, the American National Theater and Academy sponsored Robert Whitehead's production of the play, which was presented at the ANTA Theatre on Broadway for a run of forty-six performances. The director was Harold Clurman, the costumes were by Ben Edwards, and the set—the outstanding feature of the production—was designed by Mordecai Gorelik. The leading roles were played by Karl Malden as Ephraim, Douglas Watson as Eben, and Carol Stone as Abbie. In November of the same year, the play was done in the round at the Arena Stage, Washington, D.C., under Alan Schneider's direction.

In 1955 the work was mounted at the Cleveland Playhouse by Benno D. Frank, who presented it in two parts with a single intermission. This two-part arrangement obviously destroyed the concept of the Greek trilogy that O'Neill had taken such pains to achieve.

Foreign countries had begun to show an increasing interest in the work of O'Neill. A production of the play, called in French *Le Désir sous les ormes,* was put on at the Comédie des Champs-Elysées in Paris in 1954, with settings by Claude Sainval and impassioned performances by Françoise Christophe as Abbie and François Perrot as Eben. In Zurich, Switzerland, in the fall of 1956, a two-year cycle of the plays of O'Neill was begun with a production of *Desire Under the Elms.*

Since the mid-1950s the play has been produced frequently by college and community theatres in various parts of the United States. In the summer of 1957, a group of students, who had been studying drama at Boston University, started a stock company at Buzzards Bay, Massachusetts. Their theatre was a tent, and their productions were presented in arena style, wtih the audience entirely surrounding the stage. As the last play of the season, they offered *Desire Under the Elms,* which opened on Tuesday evening, August 27, and ran for six performances. The group's director was Jordan Hott; the leading parts were played by John Heffernan as Ephraim, Jacques André as Eben, and Olympia Dukakis as Abbie. Sets and costumes were designed by Esther Small, with lighting by H. Philbrick. Done in the round, with the audience as close as eavesdropping neighbors, the play had a greater immediacy and impact than is usually achieved on the "picture frame" stage.

Abbie (Carol Stone) seated extreme left; Eben (Douglas Watson) seated center; and Ephraim (Karl Malden) in shirtsleeves, standing. ANTA Playhouse production, 1952. Photograph: Vic Shifreen. ANTA Collection, The Players.

Abbie (Sophia Loren) and Ephraim (Burl Ives) in a scene from the film version of *Desire Under the Elms* produced by Paramount Pictures and released in 1958. Courtesy Paramount Pictures Corporation.

Between 1933 and 1958, a great change apparently took place in the intellectual and moral climate of America, for in the latter year it was possible to present a film version of the play complete with seduction, adultery, incest, and infanticide, without a word of complaint from the public or the censors. On March 13, 1958, the picture opened simultaneously at the Odeon and Sutton Theatres in New York; the profits from the première performances at both houses, amounting to about $5,700, were turned over to the Yale Drama School for the benefit of the Eugene O'Neill Scholarship Fund, which grants aid to young playwrights. The picture was produced by Don Hartman for Paramount, was directed by Delbert Mann, had a screenplay by Irwin Shaw, and a musical score by Elmer Bernstein.

Several minor alterations were made in the script. Following O'Neill's suggestion for the film version, Abbie became a woman of southern European origin, but as played by Sophia Loren she was transformed into an Italian immigrant girl and called Anna. The brothers, Simeon and Peter, who leave for the goldfields of California early in the play, return at the end of the film to help work the farm. Eben and his mother appear at the beginning of the picture in order to establish the boy's claim to the farm and to give the mother an opportunity to show Eben where his father's money is hidden. Supporting Miss Loren in the leading parts were Burl Ives as Ephraim and Anthony Perkins as Eben.

The film did not succeed, artistically or financially. Audiences were not pleased; critics expressed contradictory opinions, largely negative. They did not like the casting, they felt that the film lacked the emotional power of the play, and they thought that the scenery was false and looked studio-made, as indeed it was. A rather harsh but typical review appeared in *Time Magazine* (March 17, 1958), and ran as follows: "The stark images of the play are softened on the screen to glossy blowups. . . . The actors play in a welter of styles. . . . O'Neill's characters are not people; they are symbols. And the camera has a cynical eye that cannot seem to help reducing whatever tries to be larger than life to very small potatoes."

On January 8, 1963, *Desire Under the Elms* was presented in quasi-arena style at the Circle in the Square, in New York, featuring Colleen Dewhurst as Abbie, George C. Scott as Ephraim, and Rip Torn as Eben; these actors were replaced during the run by Salome Jens, Carl Low, and Alan Mixon. This production was directed by José Quintero, with set and lighting by David Hays, costumes by Noel Taylor, and choreography by Leonora Landau.

The Original Playbill

DESIRE UNDER THE ELMS
A Play in Three Parts
by Eugene O'Neill

Directed by Robert Edmond Jones
Settings by Mr. Jones

Eben Cabot	Charles Ellis
Simeon Cabot	Allen Nagle
Peter Cabot	Perry Ivins
Ephraim Cabot, their father	Walter Huston
Abbie Putnam	Mary Morris
A Young Girl	Hume Derr
Farmers	Harold Bates, R. B. Eaton, William Stahl, Clement Wilenchick
A Fiddler	Arthur Mack
An Old Woman	Mary True
A Sheriff	William Stahl
Deputies	Harold Bates, Clement Wilenchick

Other folks from the surrounding farms–
Albert Brush, Lucy Mustard, Donald Oenslager, Alma O'Neill, Lucy Shreve, Ruza Wenclawska

The action of the entire play takes place in and immediately outside the Cabot farmhouse in New England, in the year 1850.

Part 1—The beginning of summer. Sunset. Twilight.
   Just before dawn. Sunrise.
Part 2—A Sunday two months later. Afternoon. Evening.
   A little later. Dawn the next day.
Part 3—Late spring of the following year. Evening.
   Half an hour later. Just before dawn. Sunrise.

General Stage Manager: **Harold McGee**
Stage Manager: **Arthur Mack**

Despite the awkwardness of the physical setting, which provided no metaphor for the play's meaning and seemed a hindrance rather than a help to the actors, this production was a resounding success; it ran for 380 performances, a record for the play, and closed on December 8, 1963. Miss Dewhurst and Mr. Scott won Off-Broadway (Obie) Awards as Best Actress and Actor of the year.

Because the power and vitality of *Desire Under the Elms* remain undiminished, there will undoubtedly continue to be revivals of the play as well as adaptations for television, ballet, and even opera.

The First Abbie Putnam

Interview with Mary Morris

In 1924 the Provincetown Players, revived under the auspices of Kenneth Macgowan, Robert Edmond Jones, and Eugene O'Neill, were planning the production of *Desire Under the Elms*. Jones, who was to direct the play, had Mary Morris in mind for the part of Abbie, and gave the actress a copy of the script to read. "I immediately fell in love with it," said Miss Morris, "I felt particularly close to Abbie because I myself had been born and raised in New England, but I was competing for the part with an excellent actress by the name of Clare Eames." Jones asked Miss Morris to go to Provincetown, Massachusetts, to discuss the role with O'Neill. During the twenty-four hours she spent with the dramatist and his family, not a word was said about the play. When it was time for her to go, Miss Morris hinted that it would be interesting to know if she would play the part. O'Neill said, "Of course you will play Abbie; I knew it the minute you walked in here."

"This play was one of the greatest experiences of my life," Miss Morris remarked, "because it meant rehearsing eight hours a day under a superlative director and using every scrap of acting technique I had managed to acquire. An actress seldom has the opportunity of appearing in a play in which just three people carry the burden of the drama, and of working all the time at the top of the emotions. Furthermore, I had a sympathetic understanding of Abbie's problem and I identified wholly with her."

Under Jones's direction the company did not sit around a table for very long, but worked on its feet. Jones actually ran two sorts of rehearsals. The first were those in which he would permit the actors to go straight through the play without interruption; in the second, which he called "working rehearsals," he would interrupt at will, even stopping an actor at the crux of an emotion and then asking the actor to carry on from that same point. "It was an exasperating experience," said Miss Morris, "but nothing ever seemed difficult to me after that. We were all absorbed in the play and worked in absolute harmony, because each one respected the other and all of us had the greatest admiration for Bobby Jones."

Concerning Jones's special gifts as a director, Miss Morris had the following to say: "I have worked with no other director who could see through

From O'Neill's sketches, Robert Edmond Jones developed this drawing of the exterior of the house when he directed the play in 1924. From the *Greenwich Village Theatre Playbill.* New York Public Library Theatre Collection.

to the essence of the actor as a creative artist and an instrument for his creative imagination. Not for one moment was he put off by the superficial appearance of the outer being as generally interpreted, the cliché of the physical being, as it were, so often wrong, so often unimportant. When a man of his comprehension and image of the theatre sits down to talk to a company of actors in regard to a play which they are all about to rehearse and do creative work on, that experience can be a tremendous, at times, an overwhelming one. Bobby Jones was as articulate verbally as he was with the pen. He spoke in flashing images, in moving figures, with an expansive understanding and a vivid passion for life with all its tragedy and beauty. Those first days of talk about the play, whatever it might be, about the characters, about what a true "incarnation" of them might mean, are unforgettable. Life took on another dimension and man's stature was enhanced.

"Jones needed to work with trained and experienced actors, who were technically equipped to carry out his enormously creative ideas. He had had no experience with, no actual knowledge of the technical skills which the actor must have. He knew what these should be; he knew nothing of how to arrive at them. If the actor could not help himself in these ways, Jones could not help him. He valued skill highly; he never ceased to talk of the importance of the training received in their craft by all the old-time vaudevillians. This skill, this craftsmanship, he admired so intensely in Walter Huston, who had been for years a leading vaudeville performer. Bobby Jones always went to vaudeville and to burlesque shows, another medium where so many of the great comedians learned their technique. Being a true artist, Jones did not, like so many of the present generation, either fear or underestimate the necessity for form.

"While I was rehearsing with Bobby Jones in *Desire Under the Elms,* I discovered many of the fruits of my previous years of experience of playing in stock companies, discovered all the many things I had been learning, which were there in me and were called into use of necessity to carry out what Jones was getting at in his direction, in his remarkable unfolding of Abbie's character in the play. This is one of the true experiences of any artist, I am sure, to know that he has developed enough means within himself to fulfill his inner concept, to change the expression of that concept from day to day where necessary as the rehearsals progress and the director indicates.

"The character of Abbie, as written by Mr. O'Neill, is clear and unmistakable in its strength, its passion, and its terribly powerful dynamics. We were all completely in accord as to what Abbie should be when we started to rehearse. But between the conception of a characterization and its execution lies a yawning gulf! What I first did, what came out in the early rehearsals as I started to work on the part, was not this woman of New England, this passionate creature reared among the rocks and the pine trees and the repressions of Puritanism. 'You are much too Latin in what you are conveying,' Bobby said. 'You are too free, too warm, not Anglo-Saxon enough. It's in the voice, the way you move, everything. Hold back more in all the first part of the play. Then the passion when it sweeps her away past all the moorings will mean that much more.'

"To be able to take this in, to go home with it, come back the next day, feel the change happening within you, know it was happening outwardly also, that the person who had made you realize this was right, all this is good and sound artistic experience. And for the development and the recognition of this objectivity, so essential to the actor in relation to his own also so essential subjectivity, I am again grateful to Robert Edmond Jones.

"He could say the word that illumines, plant the seed that bears fruit, instill the confidence born of his faith in you. His belief that you 'had what it takes,' that you knew instinctively what it was all about, was one of his greatest gifts. He never made you feel that anything critical he said was because of him and his ideas, because they were his. It was always because of the thing itself, the play, the part, the line. He believed that the director, like the actor, exists to 'reveal' and never, never, to 'exhibit' himself.

"Jone's direction was full of rare and original images. If you understood them, you entered into a deep experience in trying as an actor to make them come true. There was always a worship of beauty, a reverence and passion for life in all its manifestations, even the most tragic, in Jones's whole approach. That is why he was so right to direct an O'Neill play."

O'Neill attended all the rehearsals; sitting at the back of the theatre, he never spoke to the actors, never interfered in any way. Any suggestions he had he conveyed to Jones. O'Neill did alter one scene, because the actors requested it. It was the scene in the parlor between Abbie and Eben. Mary Morris and Charles Ellis tried playing it several different ways but found that it contained so much repetition that the climax was always spoiled. The actors discussed the problem with Jones, who agreed that they were right; Jones then spoke to O'Neill about it. The playwright watched the scene carefully for several days and then cut a number of lines out of it. The lines were not restored in the printed version.

One day O'Neill watched a scene involving Walter Huston, Charles Ellis, and Mary Morris. After the rehearsal, as the actors were leaving the theatre, they passed O'Neill and Jones, who were deep in conversation at the rear of the house. The playwright turned to the actors and said, "Thank you for what you did today. I didn't know there was as much in that scene as you got out of it."

Although O'Neill had a reputation for never attending opening nights of his plays, Jones told the company that the playwright had been present at the première of *Desire Under the Elms*.

"What O'Neill was trying to convey in the play," said Miss Morris, "was the redemption of two people, growing out of their profound passion. They achieved complete affirmation as a result of their exalted love. O'Neill was of the opinion that great physical love could give rise to great spiritual love, but very few people understood this." After seeing the play, the Reverend John Haynes Holmes, a well-known minister of religion and himself a play-

Abbie (Mary Morris) comes to the aid of Eben (Charles Ellis) who has been knocked down by Ephraim (Walter Huston). Greenwich Village Theatre production, New York 1924. Museum of the City of New York.

wright, wrote Miss Morris a letter, in which he said that Abbie should have been doing some household chores because she was a woman who was capable of it and because the characterization would have been enriched if Abbie had had some earthy connection with the simple, practical things of everyday life. Apparently, Dr. Holmes was among those who concentrated on the physical rather than on the spiritual aspects of the story.

Two road companies went on tour with the play; Miss Morris was a member of one of them, and as such she had an excellent opportunity to observe the operation of censorship in the United States at close range. The play was banned in Boston. In Philadelphia, the authorities agreed to let it be shown if several changes were made in the dialogue, one of these being the substitution of the word "hussy" for "slut." It was the custom of the company to pick up extras for the party scene in the various cities in which the play was performed; a minister of the church, who was a member of the censorship board in Philadelphia, was invited to be one of the revelers, and he gladly accepted.

After the trouble with the censors in New York, the caliber of the audience changed. People came to the theatre looking for filth; and invariably laughed in the wrong places. This proved a great annoyance to the actors. One night, during the scene in which Abbie appears in her nightgown and Eben comes round the corner of the house, some girls in the balcony burst into fits of hysterical giggles. A man in evening clothes, a well-known lawyer, who was sitting in the front row of the orchestra, rose in his place, turned round, and called out in stentorian tones, "Usher, throw those women out!" Charles Ellis bowed to the man and said, "Thank you, sir"; then the play went on.

On Some of the Old Actors

Article by Walter Prichard Eaton

In common with most dramatic critics, I have many times been puzzled not alone to put into words the effect of acting, but even to say definitely and satisfactorily to myself (the critic who tries to satisfy anybody but himself is a fool) whether the acting was good or bad, still more to say *why* it was good or bad. Most critics—to be precise—know very little about acting, which is why they keep so largely to the safer ground of the play: and that, again, possibly accounts for the mystery cast about the actor's art. I have often wondered, certainly, whether it *is* such a mystery: whether four or five years of actual stage experience would not resolve it for the critic; whether, at any rate, such mystery as it may possess is not the eternal and unresolvable mystery of the human personality, and for the rest the secret is but the secret of how to use one's tools. Acting is the projection of situation and character, through a personality. The tools employed are that personality—which is unique and highly variable; and the voice, face, hands, etc., of that personality—which, as hands, voice, feet, etc., are not unique and may be called the invariable tools of the actor's art. If the personality of the actor is not pleasant, and if it does not suggest emotional sensitiveness in high degree, that actor will leave his audience cold and will probably fail. But if he possesses an agreeable personality and a sensitiveness obviously greater, more subtly attuned than that of the majority of his audiences, his power to move such audiences will only be limited by his command over the invariable tools of his trade. It must be admitted at once that the charm or lack of charm in a personality is not to be explained, and that something of mystery attaches to the peculiar emotional and imaginative sensitiveness which characterizes the true actor. But no mystery at all ought to attach to his use of his invariable tools; nor, without a proper use of those tools, can the most pleasing and most sensitive actor ever achieve a genuine success in the theatre. . . .

In the O'Neill play, *Desire Under the Elms,* I have seen the work of Walter Huston as the father highly praised. To me it was distinctly mediocre. His impersonation, in fact, seemed to me hardly more than a glorified Chick Sales [a vaudeville actor who specialized in "hick" roles] performance, getting what impressed some as its emotional effectiveness almost entirely from the situations devised by the dramatist. And the reason I felt so about it was because Huston lacked so largely the technical

From *Theatre Arts,* March, 1925, pp. 154–164 passim.

resources required for the impersonation of this character. This old farmer, before his entrance, is constantly held up to us as a man of granite, beneath whose will grown sons bow obedient. Yet, when Huston enters there is no effect of granite in the man, no sense of greater stature or more powerful will. The eyes, the face, the commanding bodily assurance, the tone that brooks no controversy, were not there. Especially in scenes of great stress (such as the mad dance) was the lack felt, for here Huston gave all he had of vocal power, becoming husky and perilously suggesting imminent vocal breakdown. Now, any old-timer knows that one of the very major canons of his art is to possess full vocal control at all times, never to suggest a possible breakdown, always to suggest reserve power. The more reserve power he can suggest, the greater his effect over an audience. Acting is not life, and only the silly overemphasis on realism in modern times has ever suggested that it can be or should be. Actually, under stress, a person's voice may grow shrill and break, or grow hoarse and fail. But on the stage, if that happens, it instantly suggests to the audience (even if they are quite unconscious of it) a weakness in the player, and instead of being increasingly moved by him they increasingly withdraw from his spell. I myself, in my time, have seen Salvini lift an audience from their seats, I have heard Booth, as Richelieu, launch the curse of Rome, I have seen Mrs. Fiske, in *Tess*, wring the hearts of 2,000 people, I have seen Mansfield blow Cassius clear out of his tent with his "Away, slight man!", I have heard Duse's terrible cry at the end of *La Città Morta*, but never once, in any moment of mastering emotion in the theatre, when audiences were profoundly stirred or thrilled, have I seen the actor so moving them fail to have his voice in full control, with unmistakable suggestion of reserve powers yet untapped. Without that suggestion, the audience has no confidence, and without their confidence the actor cannot deeply stir them. All this is but A B C to an old-timer, but it seems nowadays to be pretty generally forgotten. . . .

There has always been for me a peculiar fascination in the actor's art, quite as great as in the dramatist's. I fear I am not, save in rare instances, one of those who look upon the drama as of profound significance. It is vivid, immediate and delightful, but it actually leaves life much as it found it. Not one play in twenty has, or ever has had, anything to say about life. The drama, rather, is one of those artifices which make life endurable! On the whole, I remember far more impersonations by actors than I do plays, in which they acted. That may, of course, be because my eyes are better than my head! At any rate, these impersonations have roused my emotions and plowed my memory, in almost all cases, far less because the actor had a dominant personality than because he employed this personality and his technical tools alike skillfully to create illusion and wake response in me. I remember him for a good job done, for the ease, the precision, the power of his workmanship. And as no good chair was ever made or statue modeled by a workman who bungled his tools, who had not been trained to their full, free use, so no acting achievements remain in my memory that are not those of players technically proficient in the use of their voices, their faces, their hands, their feet, every part of them. Not all of them have been old-timers, by any means, but perhaps a majority of them have, because the old-timers had a wider and sounder training, and were not confined to the deadly banality of "realistic" drama. Or is it, perhaps, because I, too, am an old-timer?

"Doubling" in *Desire*

Interview with Donald Oenslager

When Donald Oenslager returned from a trip to Europe, which followed upon his graduation from college in the early 1920s, he went to work as a costume assistant for Robert Edmond Jones. Oenslager was interested in becoming a full-fledged scene designer, but he realized that it was important to take any sort of work in the theatre, including odd jobs, in order to get started. The Provincetown Players paid very small salaries, but most of the people connected with the group were dedicated souls and enormously talented. One day Jones, who was directing as well as designing *Desire Under the Elms,* asked Oenslager if, in addition to his duties as costume assistant, he would like to work as an extra—one of the guests at the party—in Part III of the play. The fledgling designer jumped at the opportunity, not because he had the least interest in acting but because "doubling" would bolster his income and his knowledge of the theatre.

Oenslager kept busy all day running around town, gathering various items needed for the costumes. He spent a great deal of time in Daniel's Department Store, which was in the neighborhood of Wanamaker's, and in Hearn's basement on Fourteenth Street, picking out buttons, ornaments, and trimmings or looking for samples of materials. These great finds he would take back to the costume shop, which was located above Cleon Throckmorton's old studio on the lower West Side. There Milia Davenport, another of Jones's assistants who helped out with the designing, made all the costumes. The building was unheated, and the elevated train passed by just outside the window, so that what Oenslager remembers most vividly about the days he spent in the costume shop is that it was fearfully cold and noisy.

Oenslager remembers very clearly O'Neill's sketches for the set, which Jones turned into workable scenery for the production. On the tiny stage of the Greenwich Village Theatre was revealed a rear view of a two-story New England farmhouse of white clapboard, with four windows marked by dilapidated green blinds. The four rooms into which these windows opened were further revealed by the removal of sections of the wall. This design gave the director many more acting areas than the stage space would ordinarily accommodate and was especially advantageous in a linear narrative play such as *Desire*. Jones used his perpendicular stage with great skill. The party scene in Part III, in which a dozen or more people were gathered to make merry in the living room and actually gave the perspective of a Virginia reel, was a marvel of economy of space. And in the scene between husband and wife, the exposure of the adjacent room with the figure of the listening boy enlarged not only the area but its emotional content as well.

Oenslager recalls that Jones, as a director, used a strange combination of techniques from the ultrarealistic to the symbolic. One day the actors arrived in the theatre to find that Jones had brought in a large pile of rocks and some wooden posts and, downstage at the apron, had erected a low stone wall and a wooden fence. The amazing thing is that, in spite of this excessive degree of realism, Jones was able to achieve a mood that was much more than realistic. Jones's personality was extremely versatile and

O'Neill's sketches for the New England farm house inside and outside of which the action of his play was to take place. From the *Provincetown Playbill*. New York Public Library Theatre Collection.

dynamic; during rehearsals he would often take Arthur Mack's fiddle and play the tunes for the dancers.

Oenslager was one of the dancers. Evaluating himself as a performer, Oenslager feels that he was less than great. The Moscow Art Theatre had visited New York in 1923 and had created a great stir in theatre circles here; two of the members of the Russian company, Richard Boleslavsky and Maria Ouspenskaya, had actually stayed on in New York and opened their own acting studios. Oenslager was a great believer in Stanislavsky, and for his performance in *Desire Under the Elms,* he tried to make use of what little he knew of the Master's system; each time he got up to dance, he adopted a different step and assumed a different facial expression, pretending that he was a different character and hoping that the audience would take note of his subtle interpretations.

Oenslager does not recall seeing O'Neill at rehearsals very often; on one or two occasions the author was to be found in the basement, whittling on a piece of wood while the play proceeded on stage.

Oenslager has never been able to understand why audiences were shocked or startled at the play or why there was so much talk of its being closed. He does remember that after the play had moved uptown to the Earl Carroll Theatre, it was performed one Saturday morning for a special audience of clergymen and educators, who gave it a clean bill of health. It nevertheless continued to attract the wrong sort of patrons and to elicit the wrong sort of reactions.

Los Angeles Must Be Kept Pure

Article by Conrad Seiler*

Lewdness and immorality must not escape punishment in this City of the Angels.

On February 18 at the Orange Grove Theatre seventeen actors in the employ of Mr. Thomas Wilkes, theatrical producer, were presenting Eugene O'Neill's somber tragedy, *Desire Under the Elms.* Little did they know of the awful Nemesis of the Law, lurking within the very portals of the theatre.

*This article originally appeared in *The Nation* for May 19, 1926.

Members of the City Vice Squad, acting upon the instructions of Sergeant Sidney Sweetnam, were there to see the performance and to ferret out any possible obscenities. As the curtains closed on the last act all the actors were placed under arrest and taken to the Central Police Station. They were accused of having presented a lewd, obscene, and immoral play.

In the Vice Squad Room of the station, where dipsomaniacs, dope addicts, prostitutes, and perverts are sent before their final consignment either to jail or liberty, as the case may be, these seventeen sons and daughters of Thespis were herded together and their finger-prints taken, like ordinary criminals.

The management of the play made vehement protest. It was absurd to arrest the actors; they could not be held to account. The management itself assumed all responsibility. But all that did not make the slightest impression on the law. The actors were kept under arrest until 4:30 the following morning, when they were set at liberty under $50 bail each—$850 in all. Later, through the solicitation of Attorney Arthur W. Green, the bail was returned, and the actors were released on their own recognizance.

Sergeant Sweetnam, whom one ungracious reporter called "Key-hole Sweetnam," or "the Chemically Pure Cop," asserted that the Parent Teachers' Association and the Board of Education were behind the arrest, and that it was a serious affair. No member, however, of either the Parent Teachers' Association or the Board of Education ever appeared in the court.

After several words in Mr. O'Neill's work were modified to suit the moral sensibilities of the police, particularly Sergeant Sweetnam—that is, after "whore," which was used twice in the play, was changed to "harlot," and "gone a-whoring" to "gone to get himself a woman"—the performances were permitted to continue, pending the final decision of the court.

A jury trial was demanded. On April 18 the case opened in Judge William Fredrickson's court. Twelve men and women—housewives, salesmen, retired farmers—were asked to pass judgment on the morality of a work of art. Such obviously vulgar aphrodisiacs as *Artists and Models, Weak Sisters, Lady Be Good, The Demi-Virgin, The Gold-Fish,* and scores upon scores of cheap burlesque shows had been produced without interference in Los Angeles. Their intrinsic decency or indecency had never even been questioned.

Le Roy Reams—small in body, large in head, pugnacious, irascible, "the fearless boy prosecutor," as one paper described him—called Officer Taylor to the witness stand. Officer Taylor solemnly testified that he "had went" to the play, *Desire Under the Elms,* on the night of February 18; that he had heard such horrible instances of profanity as "damn," "hell," and "whore" used on innumerable occasions during the evening—he couldn't say how many; that, although as a police officer in pursuance of his onerous duties he had gone to the performance "steeled against" anything obscene, he had really been shocked, yes, shocked. When he left the play he felt "like he couldn't look the world in the face again"; he had to walk up dark alleys to hide his shame. Ephraim Cabot (Mr. Frank McGlynn) at the end of the first act had said: "If I catch ye, I'll break your bones!" Officer Taylor swore that on the night of the 18th he had heard: "If I catch ye, I'll bust your——!" The dash indicates a word which even the prosecutor pronounced with reluctance. On cross-examination Officer Taylor said that he had not been able to find any good in the play, but he was certain it was very bad, very bad indeed.

Sergeant Sweetnam, City Mother Gilbert, a salesman, and an elevator operator were the principal witnesses for the prosecution. They testified also that they had heard "damns," "hells," and "certain Biblical words galore." The play was unquestionably immoral—a seducing woman in a nightgown, several beds, and so forth. . . . No, the play had not had an immoral effect on them personally, of course not; they had not left the theatre with impure thoughts, or with the intention of committing any abomination, but that was because they had gone "prepared."

The prosecutor stressed the fact that it was not so much the individual lines and expressions—filthy though they were—as the play itself that was in question. Why, the mere idea of a woman seducing her own stepson —think of it, ladies and gentlemen, *her own stepson!*—was lewd and immoral and had no place in any respectable God-fearing community. Would they, the jurors, care to tell that story in their front parlors to their sons and daughters?

Eminent clubwomen, students of the drama, the wife of the dean of the University of Southern California, several producers, all the dramatic critics of the Los Angeles newspapers, and a girl and boy testified in behalf of the defense. To them the play was not immoral—far from it. It was a literary and dramatic *tour de force*. It taught a strong, wholesome, moral lesson: the wages of sin is death. When they came from the theatre they felt cleansed, morally elevated. The chairwoman of the drama committee of the Friday Morning Club said that, after seeing the play, she felt as though she wanted to rise from her seat and say with utmost reverence: "Now let us pray." The repetition of hard, perhaps ugly words, did not embarrass or shock any of the defense's witnesses. Such words impressed each of them as being very natural and necessary expressions in the mouths of O'Neill's crude, pathetic characters.

On the afternoon of April 15, at two o'clock, the entire court, including the judge, jury, prosecutor, attorney for the defense, attachés, and witnesses, and also a few reporters, were given a special performance of *Desire Under the Elms* at the Orange Grove Theatre. No one else was admitted in the audience. The actors were the seventeen persons under indictment.

Before the play began all the players were summoned before the curtain, and the clerk of the court, B. O. Kersey, asked them: "Do each of you solemnly swear that the performance you will give here today is the play *Desire Under the Elms*, word for word, action for action, identically as it was presented in this theatre on the night of February the 18th?" The actors took the oath. And then began the most unusual performance in the annals of the theatre. The actors, with a possible jail sentence staring them in the face, and playing before the most critical audience ever assembled in any theatre, surpassed themselves. Frank McGlynn as Ephraim Cabot gave a magnificent interpretation; Jessie Arnold as Abbie caused even Bailiff Cummings to say: "She's the greatest actress I've ever seen." Women jurors wept copiously; Sergeant Sweetnam and Judge Fredrickson applauded along with the witnesses and reporters. Four curtain calls were demanded at the conclusion of the play.

On Friday morning, April 16, came the final argument. The court allotted one hour to each side. Frank McGlynn—tall, gaunt, dramatic—attorney in his own right as well as leading actor in the play, was granted half of the defense's time. McGlynn appealed to the jury as liberal-minded men and women. He hoped they were not prudes. Surely they were not shocked when life was stripped of its veneer. Surely they felt no embarassment when he told the story of *Desire Under the Elms*. Sex had its place in life; everyone knew that. There was nothing essentially obscene about it. If persons came to see O'Neill's play and smirked and giggled over the poignant lives of Eben, Ephraim Cabot and Abbie—as the prosecutor said they had—it was a reflection upon *their* morality, not the actors' or the play's. The jury was not called upon to decide whether *Desire Under the Elms* contained a moral lesson. It didn't have to have one. The question was whether the defendants were guilty of presenting an obscene play.

Attorney Green, of the defense, mentioned the classics of literature, the plays of Sophocles, Euripides, Aeschylus, Racine, Schiller (particularly Schiller's *Don Carlos*, Racine's *Phédre*, and Euripides' *Phaedra*, in which women are enamoured of their stepsons) and the tragedies of a certain well-known playwright, William Shakespeare. Most of them are not only read and studied in the classrooms of our high schools and colleges, but are actually performed by thousands of students every year. . . . Eugene O'Neill is one of the few significant figures in the American drama. He is a famous author; his works are read, played, and admired throughout the civilized world. . . . Many of the words which Officer Taylor and Sergeant Sweetnam testified that they had heard on that memorable night of the 18th were never in the play. The prosecution had not proved its case; there was absolutely nothing obscene in the play and consequently the defendants must be pronounced innocent.

The prosecutor, in his rebuttal, took occasion to castigate "those Greek and French degenerates" who are sullying the minds of our children. *Desire Under the Elms* was mere "smut and filth." There was no justification for such a play. O'Neill a famous author! He was infamous—morbid, lewd, obscene. . . . The play was not true to life. Had any member of the jury heard of a mother seducing her own stepson in real life? Of course not. Were the lives of O'Neill's characters similar to the lives of any people in New England or elsewhere that they had ever known or heard about? What a question! But they did know of thousands of clean, patient, hard-working farmer folks, didn't they? O'Neill knew nothing of such people; he only knew about morons, adultresses, infanticides, seducing stepmothers. . . . Suppose it were true to life. So are sewers. But that is no reason for putting them on the stage. . . . *Desire Under the Elms* should be suppressed. The defendants were guilty of presenting a lewd, obscene, and immoral play.

The jury retired at three o'clock that afternoon. It deliberated for almost nine hours. Shortly after midnight the verdict was announced: eight for conviction and four for acquittal.

The jury was dismissed.

At the time of writing Judge Fredrickson has voiced his intention of proceeding immediately with a new trial. In the meantime the play, which, normally, would have had a run of two, or at the most, three weeks, is doing capacity business the tenth week, and will soon go to San Francisco to commence its sinister demoralizing work there. But—

Los Angeles must be purified.

Lewdness and immorality must not escape punishment in this City of the Angels.

[Note: The case was closed after the play left town.—Ed.]

Desire in Swedish

Interview with Alf Sjöberg

Desire Under the Elms (*Blodet ropar under almarna*) was produced at the Royal Dramatic Theatre in Stockholm, on October 19, 1933, under the direction of Alf Sjöberg. The leading roles were filled by outstanding performers; Lars Hanson was seen as Ephraim, Tore Teje as Abbie, and Anders Henrikson as Eben.

Sjöberg approached the play as though it were a classical drama, a bloody family affair, in which a young man is haunted by the memory of his mother and is in open revolt not only against his father but also against the traditional structure of the family and the state. "As in all of O'Neill's plays," said Sjöberg, "the mind of the youth is opposed to the accepted formulas and conventions of the society in which he finds himself. He rebels against the cold rationalistic laws which are based on the old battle of incestuous tendencies for one thing, as well as rebelling against the stultifying atmosphere of Puritanism in general. The play, in that sense, is a cry for freedom."

The play is also concerned with the hopeless loneliness of life on an isloated New England farm. O'Neill's genius enabled him to project the whole classical constellation in terms of American culture and to transplant the ancient blood-feud to fresh American earth. This quality of the play—the conflict in human life amid the stench of cattle, blood, tears, and soil–is what Sjöberg tried particularly to get into his production.

The set, which was designed by Sven-Erik Scawonius, was patterned on the one used for the original New York production; it showed the outside of a New England clapboard farmhouse of two stories, with four windows and walls that could be removed when it was necessary to disclose the interiors of the rooms. The front entrance of the house faced left (as viewed by the audience), and exterior scenes could be played on the front steps and the lawn. Stylized elm trees, resembling hands outstretched over the house, were seen in silhouette, mainly to the left of the house. Between the trunks of the trees and the side of the house, a section of sky was visible, and upon it varying cloud effects were projected. The set had been so constructed that the section of wall that separated the parlor from the kitchen could be pushed back to the right in order to provide a larger acting area during the party scene. Many of the critics remarked upon the effectiveness of the set, praising it for its variety and interest.

The lighting throughout the production was in a low and moody key; Sjöberg was attempting to suggest that the house was a prison from which the characters were struggling to escape—yearning, in a metaphysical sense, to get out into the light. The sets were done with precise and realistic details, few but significant; the scenes were not separated by the lowering of the curtain, but by the dimming of the lights. The scenes faded into one another in a dreamlike way. The idea was to show the characters, lost in the gloom, suddenly seeing a ray of light and trying to come out of the dark. "Another image that I kept in mind while directing the play," said Sjöberg, "was that these characters were caught in a net and were thrashing about in an effort to disentangle themselves without realizing the hopelessness of their struggle. This pattern is absolutely classical in structure as well as in its philosophical determinism, for the characters find themselves in situations where Fate has placed them and they are doomed. The greatness of this play lies in the fact that though it depicts life in a genuinely American setting, it is able to recreate the grandeur and terror of ancient drama."

The authentic note of tragedy in the play is that a man desires love and freedom and has an important dream of liberty, but in its pursuit he cannot avoid destroying himself and those around him. Even today, when people seem to prefer comedies and plays of escape, nothing can be more effective in the theatre, or more stimulating to an audience, Sjöberg believes, than tragic action. True tragedy is not didactic, as so many of our current serious plays are, but contains the regenerative power of religion and therapy, which audiences continue to need and to which they respond; *catharsis* in our day should be understood as the untying of psychological knots.

Alf Sjöberg would like very much to do another production of *Desire Under the Elms,* when three excellent actors are available for the leading roles. He will not mount the play in the "naturalistic and classical" style he used before but will attempt an "idealistic and classical" style which, he believes, will provide a better means for conveying the subtleties and profundities of the script. Sjöberg has another reason for wanting to direct *Desire Under the Elms* again. He is optimistic about its reception by present-day Swedish theatregoers, as compared with those of the 1930s. Audiences were none too happy about the play in 1933. At that time Hitler was on the rise, people were particularly nervous and tense, and the brutality and suffering in the play reminded playgoers too much of the things that were going on in real life. Today Sweden is prosperous, and there is a more hopeful feeling in the air. Sjöberg is sure that under such different economic, social, and political conditions the play's reception would be more enthusiastic.

Designing *Desire*

Interview with Mordecai Gorelik

Mr. Gorelik, who designed the ANTA production of *Desire Under the Elms* in 1952, has his own particular way of approaching a playscript. He completely ignores what the author has to say about the setting until he himself has read the play through carefully; the characters, moods, and actions stimulate his imagination, and he envisions in detail the environment in which the characters live. He then compares his own ideas with the author's and, merging the two, achieves what he considers to be a more imaginative result than might have emerged from a slavish adherence to the playwright's concept. He has found that authors generally approve of this method of attack.

Mordecai Gorelik's design for the revival of the play at the ANTA Playhouse, New York, 1952. The dominant image, according to the designer, is "under the elms," expressed by a house overshadowed by two great trees, all in silhouette. "While the design has a superficial air of naturalism," said Gorelik, "it is in fact basically theatricalist in style. The silhouette of the house is established by means of a roof line and chimney, plus the eaves and porch; its interior is influenced by cubism in the relationship of the rooms and by constructivism in the partly curved cross-sectioning of the floors. In general the "house" is merely an elaborate screen enclosing a lower and an upper ledge.

The designer also works in close co-operation with the director, who is responsible for determining the style of the production. Harold Clurman had decided that he wanted to treat *Desire* as a legend with epic proportions; this called for a certain amount of stylization. The brothers, Simeon and Peter, for instance, did not relate to each other in the opening scene, but frankly addressed their speeches to the audience. This style gave the designer the license to be more theatrical in his treatment of the setting, and so Gorelik created a token house rather than a real one.

Gorelik was well acquainted with the set that Robert Edmond Jones had designed for the original production. He thought that it communicated genuine feeling for a New England farmhouse, that it had great lyrical simplicity, and that it provided an enormous novelty in the use of the shutters to close off the rooms that were not being acted in. But it also had its disadvantages: the house had a boxlike look, possibly because Jones followed O'Neill's sketches too carefully; the set's straight, uninteresting lines offered no visual variety to the audience; it had a symmetrical and static form and was placed flat on the stage parallel to the spectator; its style displayed the impressionism of an earlier period and gave no hint of the newer trends in modern art—it even made use of an old-fashioned border of leaves to represent the elms. From a practical point of view, as distinct from the aesthetic, the acting areas were more cramped than they needed to be, and it was very difficult to light the interiors of the rooms adequately.

Gorelik feels that all scenery should have four basic attributes: first, it should be *documentary*, embodying the history and geography of the play's locale; second, it should be a *machine-for-theatre*, so functional that it "acts with the actors"; third, it should contain a *metaphor*, which pinpoints poetically the relationship of set to play as, for instance, overshadowing elms; and fourth, it should be *audience-oriented*, not merely seem beautiful to the spectators but have an active influence on their thoughts and feelings.

"Under the Elms" was the metaphor Gorelik chose for his set. He expressed it in the silhouette of a house overshadowed by the silhouettes of two great trees. While the design had a superficial air of naturalism, it was, in fact, basically theatricalist in style. The silhouette of the house was established by means of a roof-line and chimney, plus the eaves and porch; its interior was influenced by cubism in the relationship of the rooms and by constructivism in the partly curved cross-sectioning of the floors. In general, the house was merely an elaborate screen enclosing a lower and an upper ledge. Such a set, with its symbolic elements and collage, would have been impossible without the influences of modern art, as seen in the work of Braque and Picasso.

In Gorelik's set all the action was clearly visible, and the possibilities of lighting the acting areas were enormously increased.

The trees were a cut-out drop, treated as semisilhouette. The drop was bordered by a curved line, which emphasized its frank theatricalism and offset any impression of a shabby foliage border. A dark-green curtain, abstract in quality, masked the parlor, whose window faced the porch. For the parlor scene, which was used only once, the green curtain opened, revealing one or two pieces of Victorian décor, and for this scene a sofa was placed downstage. When the parlor was not in use, its floor became unlocalized and could then be added to the floor space of the kitchen; the kitchen table and chairs were placed partly downstage, in front of the parlor curtain.

The design mastered an unusually difficult problem in sight lines, especially in regard to the porch. Thus the gate, downstage right, was carefully angled in order not to cut off a view of the porch from the first rows of the left side of the audience; the porch itself was angled so that the action there was fully visible even to the first rows of the right side of the audience. The upper platform was cut well back of the lower one and was low enough (6 feet, 8 inches) not to subject the first rows of the orchestra to the strain of looking up. The two-story set provided a special problem for the designer, who had to take measures to prevent the actors from falling over the edge of the upper story in the dark or semidark intervals. Gorelik solved this problem by putting a heavy molding and a strip of luminiscent tape, neither of which could be seen by the audience, along the edge of the upper floor to warn the actors. The arrangement of acting areas represented a very close collaboration of designer and director, with literally every square inch of playing space accounted for.

With its emphatic outline, its dark tones, and its spotted lighting, the "house" effectively dominated the details of furniture, which might otherwise have suggested a furniture warehouse rather than a home. The design responded well to the complex light plot required by the time sequences of the script and the constant shifting of attention from room to room and from interior to exterior. Incidentally, the ceiling of the lower floor contained special light units masked from the view of the audience.

A very important consideration for the scene designer is the amount of money available in the budget for his special use and needs. In doing *Desire* for ANTA Gorelik had very little money to work with. He originally intended the wall of "stones" that goes around the back of the house to be 5 feet high, but he had to lower it to 3 feet in order to save $40; the trees were to be made of profile board (thin laminated wood), but as an economy measure canvas was used instead. The arch connecting the trees was added to prevent the leaves from looking like the shoddy border that was in general use during the nineteenth century; this effected a saving of several hundred dollars. For reasons of economy, too, the chimney could not be built up solidly to look as if it had been constructed of stones; instead the designer had to use a single thickness of profile board, painted to create an approximate effect. The scenery was also designed to save money in shifting, and very few changes were made in the set from act to act. Three important shifts were made, however: 1. When a scene was to be played in the upper-right bedroom, the window ledge above the porch was removed in order to improve sight lines. 2. When the parlor was to be used, the green curtain was drawn back, and a sofa was pushed downstage. 3. When the kitchen was used for the dance scene, the table and chairs were placed upstage, in order to leave a large, clear space for the dancers.

Every production has a property man who is responsible for buying, making, and taking care of most of the props for the play; but the scene designer often has his own prop list, which contains those items he considers scenically important because of their appearance in relation to the set. The kitchen stove was one such prop; it was made of canvas and wood, except for the iron lids, which had to have a metallic clang when they were put in place. A more elaborate designer's prop was the front gate of the house, which was flanked by two small sections of wall made of actual stones and kept in place by chicken wire. The designer himself piled and arranged the stones, which then had to be toned in with paint so that they would match the rest of the set. This task took hours of labor, but the results proved to be extremely effective. Gorelik had originally planned to use two piles of papier-mâché "stones," but since nothing he did to them could make them look less unreal, he discarded them.

The following is the *designer's* property list for *Desire Under the Elms:*

KITCHEN

Sink
Pump
4 chairs
Stove
Table
Tablecloth
Firewood
Dish rack
Some pots and dishes (not all)
Loose boards in floor under stove
Extra chairs
Benches

LEFT BEDROOM

Bed
Blanket
Chair
Washstand
Rag rug

RIGHT BEDROOM

Bed
Washstand
Blanket
Soap dish
Rag rug
Whale-oil lamp
Chair
Cradle
Cradle-clothes

PARLOR

Organ
Sofa
2 sconces for candles
Table for candlestick
Candlestick
Pictures
Tieback for curtains
Bell jar

PORCH

Rocker
Gate

Gorelik pointed out that neither the scenery nor the properties may be used during the play's rehearsals unless a full stage crew is present, and this requires the payment of extra salaries; these are union regulations. Since very few producers are willing to take on this expense, the actors naturally do not get to work with scenery and props until the final rehearsals. This subjects the director, the designer, and the members of the cast to considerable hardship.

Not all difficulties, however, arise *before* opening night; Gorelik remembers one bad moment he had early in the run of the play. After a scene in which Eben had a violent argument with Abbie, the young man flung himself out of the house, raced down the path toward the gate and, as he was going through it, impetuously lifted the gate from its hinges and carried it offstage with him. The startled designer, watching the play from the balcony, heard a young playgoer in front of him inquire wonderingly, "Why did he take the gate with him?" To which his female companion replied, "Because she gave him the gate, of course!"

Directing *Desire*

Interview with José Quintero

José Quintero, the American stage director, must be credited with having rescued the plays of Eugene O'Neill from the comparative limbo into which they had fallen at the time of the playwright's death in 1953. Quintero had been artistic director at the Circle in the Square since its foundation in 1950; in 1955, never having directed a play by O'Neill, he thought it was time to present one. He decided he would like to do *The Iceman Cometh,* possibly because the play's entire action was set in a saloon, which could be perfectly reproduced at the Circle, a former night club where productions were mounted in arena style.

Applying to Miss Jane Rubin, the playwright's agent, for permission to present *Iceman,* Quintero was informed that O'Neill's plays were not being released for production at that time. "So I forgot about it," said the director, "but not long afterwards Miss Rubin phoned me and said that Mrs. O'Neill, the playwright's widow, wished to meet me. I was terribly nervous and excited, but I went to see her and we had a long talk, mainly about *Iceman.* She said that the Theatre Guild's production of this play in 1946, the last of his plays O'Neill lived to see, was a great disappointment to him. He regarded it as a failure, along with his other plays, and believed that his work would be relegated to the library. He died with the idea that his time had passed and that he would no longer be considered a vital writer for the living theatre which he loved."

After Quintero had expressed his feelings about *Iceman* and his ideas for its presentation, Mrs. O'Neill gave him permission to do the play. It opened in May, 1956, and its resounding success—a run of 565 performances—testified to Quintero's remarkable directorial skill. This production aroused a lively interest in O'Neill's work and led to Quintero's appointment as the authorized director, so to speak, of other plays by the dramatist. Mrs. O'Neill trusted him; she told him: "I know you, your subtlety, the way you know what O'Neill says, and nobody else I know of in this business does." In 1958 Quintero mounted his second O'Neill play, *A Moon for the Misbegotten,* at the Festival of the Two Worlds in Spoleto, Italy, with Colleen Dewhurst, one of his favorite actresses, playing Josie.

When in 1962 he decided to present *Desire Under the Elms* at the Circle in the Square, Quintero immediately thought of Colleen Dewhurst and her husband, George C. Scott, for the roles of Abbie and Ephraim. These actors had first met at the Circle when they appeared in *Children of Darkness* under Quintero's direction. Stardom had followed for both, then marriage, and *Desire Under the Elms* would mark their return to the Circle as an acting team. But Scott had television commitments and could not accept the role. Franchot Tone was then cast as Ephraim, and rehearsals got under way; but after two weeks Tone withdrew because of "artistic differences" with the director. "It is through casting that the director controls his over-all conception of the play," said Quintero; "and it is this total view of every word, gesture, or piece of furniture that is the director's primary job." Rehearsals were put off until Scott was available,

Ephraim (George C. Scott) dancing wildly at the party to prove his virility. Circle in the Square production, 1963. Photograph: Ed Rooney, ANTA Collection, The Players.

and the opening of the play was delayed until January 8, 1963. "That two such highly paid stars should be willing to work for Equity minimum salaries, which was all the Circle could afford," said Quintero, "not only speaks well for Dewhurst and Scott but also for O'Neill whose plays are able to entice and challenge fine actors."

Quintero starts the directorial process with a detailed analysis of the play and of the characters, in discussion with the cast. Although he pays strict attention to the stage directions in the script, he does not necessarily carry them out to the letter. As an example of his procedure, Quintero described the alteration in the set made for his staging of *Desire Under the Elms*. The script calls for a production on a proscenium stage, with almost all action confined to the interior of a two-story house; this set could easily have been constructed at the Circle in the Square, although the layout there is meant for arena-style presentation. The theatre is U-shaped, the audience sits around three sides, while the acting area runs down the center from the open end. The entire farmhouse might have been erected at the open end, but Quintero and his set designer David Hays worked out another arrangement. Only the facade of the house was set up, in the manner of the *skene* in the Greek theatre, and extending below it into the acting area, as in the *orchestron*, were the various rooms: first the bedrooms, below it the kitchen, then the parlor, and finally the porch and front yard, almost to the bottom of the U. Quintero knew that O'Neill had put his passionate characters inside a small house—as though clamping a lid on a teakettle—to increase the pressure; but the director felt that since the entire playing area at the Circle is rather limited, he could use all of it and still obtain a "cramped effect." Taking the action out of the house, in fact, seemed to heighten the suggestion of Greek tragedy, which had such a strong influence on the writing of the play.

O'Neill called for one effect, however, that Quintero was not able to achieve to his satisfaction in an arena-style production. That was the use of the overhanging elm trees, by which the dramatist symbolized the influence of the mother, the peace of nature contrasted with the passions of human beings, the changing seasons, and life renewing itself. Quintero had to settle for leafy patterns thrown by spotlights onto the house and front lawn, but they were rather weak and ineffective. The director now feels that the trees represent such basic symbolism—even referred to in the play's title—that he would be sure to emphasize them if he were to do another production of this play. He would not necessarily show complete trees, but would use overhanging leaves or more effective projections, variously lighted to indicate the passing seasons and the lives lived in shadow, in line with the playwright's intention.

Discussing the characters in the play, Quintero said that O'Neill not only made use of autobiographical material but also of universal archetypes. The dramatist frequently presented conflicting images of wife and mother— one attempting to displace the other or to act the other's role. This occurs in many of O'Neill's dramas, and quite clearly in *Desire Under the Elms*. At the beginning of the play, the mother's spirit permeates the house; when Abbie arrives, Eben looks upon her as a usurper of his mother's place, but in the parlor scene wife and mother merge. The conflict continues to the end of the play, however, and partially motivates Eben's hatred of Abbie's child, who would not only steal the farm but also Abbie's mother-love from him.

For Colleen Dewhurst, in the role of Abbie, Quintero had nothing but praise. He envisioned this character entering the Cabot household like a waif, bringing nothing with her but her sensuality. If her primary motive in marrying the old man was to get possession of the farm and a measure of security, she was totally unaware that such a plan might fail. As it turned out, she had actually walked into a trap, in which she was awakened as lover and mother, with dire consequences. Prostitutes figure prominently in many of O'Neill's plays, but Min, the town whore in *Desire Under the Elms,* though mentioned, does not put in an appearance; she serves merely as a foil for Abbie. Abbie, it should be noted, has much in common with Anna Christie: she is a "slightly damaged virgin" (Quintero's phrase), a woman who has suffered and been misused, but who is purified by love. "The transformation of a woman in the process of purification," according to Quintero, "is what gives the character a 'dramatic curve.' It is very much like the transformation of the Daughter of Indra in Strindberg's *Dream Play,* but in reverse, since the Daughter goes from pure goddess to soiled human being. Abbie is the quintessence of the feminine, and in the parlor scene Colleen wore a long, white, extremely simple gown, her hair loose about her shoulders. She seemed perfectly able to absorb the ghost of Eben's mother. The gowns for her other scenes were equally simple and subdued."

The character of Ephraim seems to have come fully developed out of the Old Testament. Ephraim is a hard man who defies God and mankind; he also embodies O'Neill's feelings about his father and, in a sense, represents the tragedy of old age, for he is lonely and unloved and at odds with his son. His conflict with Eben is a fight to the death; demonstrating and flaunting his strength and virility, he challenges the younger man.

"Scott did a fine job with the part," said Quintero. "He emanates strong will and he is an intuitive actor. Just give him the key words to a characterization and he fleshes it out at once. In the birth-celebration scene, for instance, I said, 'You are trying to prove to your neighbors and to yourself that you were strong enough to beget a child in Abbie's womb. Dance till you drop.' Scott merely asked, 'Where do you want me to dance—in what area?' I said, 'Anywhere—all over the place.' He began to dance, to caper, to cavort, wilder and more furiously until, at one rehearsal, he actually dropped in exhaustion—then he knew how far he had to go in performance. This is what dramatized his competition with his son."

Like many other young men in O'Neill's plays, Eben bears an identifiable resemblance to the dramatist himself. These young men are invariably torn between purity and desire, adventure and security, mother-love and conjugal love, and obedience to their own wills or to their fathers'. Eben eventually recognizes how like his father he is and is finally able to accept his share of the responsibility for Abbie's act—but he is destroyed in the process of maturing. "If an actor had the courage to play such a character fully and passionately," said Quintero, "he would understand himself better." But the character of Eben was never completely realized in the Circle production because the actors who played the part [first Rip Torn, later Alan Mixon] could not or would not entirely expose their emotions. Rip Torn, for instance, found it difficult to express total and violent hatred for the father, and also thought that being a virgin, as Eben was, made him less of a man.

Ephraim (George C. Scott) embraces Abbie (Colleen Dewhurst) possessively while she appears to be thinking her own thoughts. Circle in the Square production, New York 1963, directed by Jose Quintero. Photograph: Ed Rooney. ANTA Collection, The Players.

In the main, José Quintero was happy with his production of *Desire Under the Elms.* He had certain reservations, as he always has; he would like to do the play again and make specific changes. First of all, he would try to find an actor who could do emotional justice to Eben. Then, he would alter Abbie's characterization at the beginning of the play: "I would show her as a more shoddy and scheming person when she enters, so that she would have a longer way to go in her transformation to purity. My Abbie was already half subdued and in search of love when she came in. But Ephraim had practically rescued her from a life of drudgery; she was a desperate creature looking for some sort of security, and consented to go to the farm because one day it would be hers. Why else would she have married such a flinty old man? Colleen Dewhurst could easily have played the wider range, from toughness to tenderness, but I was at fault, I muffed it somehow. I would not do anything essentially different with Ephraim. He is a tough old bird who wants a son—one made in his own image. It is true that Scott was too young for the part, but who could have played Ephraim with more power?"

Asked to comment on O'Neill's use of language in the play, particularly his attempt to transcribe the New England dialect, Quintero replied heatedly that critics have always accused O'Neill of lacking poetry and humor, and that neither accusation is true. "If the lines are spoken properly, they have the flavor and rhythm of regional speech and the staccato quality of modern verse. Characters, situations, and mood can also be poetic, but critics insist upon setting up hard and fast rules—poetry in this column, prose in that. There is a great deal of poetry in O'Neill but it is not entirely confined to the language."

When asked why he thought the film version of *Desire Under the Elms* had failed, Quintero ventured the suggestion that the picture was too soft. Ephraim should be lean, strong, and hard, but Burl Ives, who acted the part, did not suggest these qualities. Even Sophia Loren, who is a great favorite of Quintero's, seemed miscast. All in all, the film, with its beautiful, picture postcard views, in no way communicated the passion inherent in the play.

José Quintero's production at the Circle in the Square chalked up 380 consecutive performances, the longest run in the play's history, and won almost unanimous praise from the critics.

DESIRE UNDER THE ELMS
A Play in Three Parts

EUGENE O'NEILL

Characters

Ephraim Cabot
Simeon
Peter } his sons
Eben
Abbie Putnam
Young Girl, Two Farmers, The **Fiddler,** A **Sheriff,** and other folk from the neighboring farms.

Part 1—The beginning of summer. Sunset. Twilight. Just before dawn. Sunrise.
Part 2—A Sunday two months later. Afternoon. Evening. A little later. Dawn the next day.
Part 3—Late spring of the following year. Evening. Half an hour later. Just before dawn. Sunrise.

The action of the entire play takes place in, and immediately outside of, the Cabot farmhouse in New England, in the year 1850. The south end of the house faces front to a stone wall with a wooden gate at center opening on a country road. The house is in good condition but in need of paint. Its walls are a sickly grayish, the green of the shutters faded. Two enormous elms are on each side of the house. They bend their trailing branches down over the roof. They appear to protect and at the same time subdue. There is a sinister maternity in their aspect, a crushing, jealous absorption. They have developed from their intimate contact with the life of man in the house an appalling humaneness. They brood oppressively over the house. They are like exhausted women resting their sagging breasts and hands and hair on its roof, and when it rains their tears trickle down monotonously and rot on the shingles.

There is a path running from the gate around the right corner of the house to the front door. A narrow porch is on this side. The end wall facing us has two windows in its upper story, two larger ones on the floor below. The two upper are those of the father's bedroom and that of the brothers. On the left, ground floor, is the kitchen—on the right, the parlor, the shades of which are always drawn down.

Part One

Scene I

Exterior of the farmhouse. It is sunset of a day at the beginning of summer in the year 1850. There is no wind and everything is still. The sky above the roof is suffused with deep colors, the green of the elms glows, but the house is in shadow, seeming pale and washed out by contrast.

[*A door opens and* **Eben Cabot** *comes to the end of the porch and stands looking down the road to the right. He has a large bell in his hand and this he swings mechanically, awakening a deafening clangor. Then he puts his hands on his hips and stares up at the sky. He sighs with a puzzled awe and blurts out with halting appreciation.*]

451

Eben: God! Purty! [*His eyes fall and he stares about him frowningly. He is twenty-five, tall and sinewy. His face is well-formed, good-looking, but its expression is resentful and defensive. His defiant, dark eyes remind one of a wild animal's in captivity. Each day is a cage in which he finds himself trapped but inwardly unsubdued. There is a fierce repressed vitality about him. He has black hair, mustache, a thin curly trace of beard. He is dressed in rough farm clothes.*

He spits on the ground with intense disgust, turns and goes back into the house.]

Simeon and **Peter** come in from their work in the fields. They are tall men, much older than their half-brother [**Simeon** is thirty-nine and **Peter** thirty-seven], built on a squarer, simpler model, fleshier in body, more bovine and homelier in face, shrewder and more practical. Their shoulders stoop a bit from years of farm work. They clump heavily along in their clumsy thick-soled boots caked with earth. Their clothes, their faces, hands, bare arms and throats are earth-stained. They smell of earth. They stand together for a moment in front of the house and, as if with the one impulse, stare dumbly up at the sky, leaning on their hoes. Their faces have a compressed, unresigned expression. As they look upward, this softens.]

Simeon: [*Grudgingly.*] Purty.
Peter: Ay-eh.
Simeon: [*Suddenly.*] Eighteen year ago.
Peter: What?
Simeon: Jenn. My woman. She died
Peter: I'd fergot.
Simeon: I rec'lect—now an' agin. Makes it lonesome. She'd hair long's a hoss' tail—an' yaller like gold!
Peter: Waal—she's gone. [*This with indifferent finality—then after a pause.*] They's gold in the West, Sim.

Simeon: [*Still under the influence of sunset—vaguely.*] In the sky?
Peter: Waal—in a manner o' speakin'—thar's the promise. [*Growing excited.*] Gold in the sky—in the West—Golden Gate—Californi-a!—Goldest West!—fields o' gold!
Simeon: [*Excited in his turn.*] Fortunes layin' just atop o' the ground waitin' t' be picked! Solomon's mines, they says! [*For a moment they continue loking up at the sky—then their eyes drop.*]
Peter: [*With sardonic bitterness.*] Here—it's stones atop o' the ground—stones atop o' stones—makin' stone walls—year atop o' year—him 'n' yew'n' me 'n' then Eben—makin' stone walls fur him to fence us in!
Simeon: We've wuked. Give our strength. Give our years. Plowed 'em under in the ground—[*He stamps rebelliously.*]—rottin'—makin' soil for his crops! [*A pause.*] Waal—the farm pays good for hereabouts.
Peter: If we plowed in Californi-a, they'd be lumps o' gold in the furrow!
Simeon: Californi-a's t'other side o' earth, a'most. We got t' calc'late—
Peter: [*After a pause.*] 'Twould be hard fur me, too, to give up what we've 'arned here by our sweat. [*A pause,* **Eben** *sticks his head out of the dining-room window, listening.*]
Simeon: Ay-eh. [*A pause.*] Mebbe—he'll die soon.
Peter: [*Doubtfully.*] Mebbe.
Simeon: Mebbe—fur all we knows—he's dead now.
Peter: Ye'd need proof.
Simeon: He's been gone two months—with no word.
Peter: Left us in the fields an evenin' like this. Hitched up an' druv off into the West. That's plum onnateral. He hain't never been off this farm 'ceptin' t' the village in thirty year or more not since he married Eben's maw. [*A pause. Shrewdly.*] I calc'late we might git him declared crazy by the court.

Simeon: He skinned 'em too slick. He got the best o' all on 'em. They'd never b'lieve him crazy. *[A pause.]* We got t' wait—till he's under ground.

Eben: *[With a sardonic chuckle.]* Honor thy father! *[They turn, startled, and stare at him. He grins, then scowls.]* I pray he's died. *[They stare at him. He continues matter-of-factly.]* Supper's ready.

Simeon and **Peter:** *[Together.]* Ay-eh.

Eben: *[Gazing up at the sky.]* Sun's downin' purty.

Simeon and **Peter:** *[Together.]* Ay-eh. They's gold in the West.

Eben: Ay-eh. *[Pointing.]* Yonder atop o' the hill pasture, ye mean?

Simeon and **Peter:** *[Together.]* In Californi-a!

Eben: *[Stares at them indifferently for a second, then drawls.]* Waal—supper's gittin' cold. *[He turns back into kitchen.]*

Simeon: *[Startled—smacks his lips.]* I air hungry!

Peter: *[Sniffing.]* I smells bacon!

Simeon: *[With hungry appreciation.]* Bacon's good!

Peter: *[In same tone.]* Bacon's bacon! *[They turn, shouldering each other, their bodies bumping and rubbing together as they hurry clumsily to their food, like two friendly oxen toward their evening meal. They disappear around the right corner of house and can be heard entering the door.]*

CURTAIN

Scene II

The color fades from the sky. Twilight begins. The interior of the kitchen is now visible. A pine table is at center, a cook-stove in the right rear corner, four rough wooden chairs, a tallow candle on the table. In the middle of the rear wall is fastened a big advertising poster with a ship in full sail and the word "California" in big letters. Kitchen utensils hang from nails. Everything is neat and in order but the atmosphere is of a men's camp kitchen rather than that of a home.

*[Places for three are laid. **Eben** takes boiled potatoes and bacon from the stove and puts them on the table, also a loaf of bread and a crock of water. **Simeon** and **Peter** shoulder in, slump down in their chairs without a word. **Eben** joins them. The three eat in silence for a moment, the two elder as naturally unrestrained as beasts of the field, **Eben** picking at his food without appetite, glancing at them with a tolerant dislike.]*

Simeon: *[Suddenly turns to **Eben**.]* Looky here! Ye'd oughtn't t' said that, Eben.

Peter: 'Twa'n't righteous.

Eben: What!

Simeon: Ye prayed he'd died.

Eben: Waal—don't yew pray it? *[A pause.]*

Peter: He's our Paw.

Eben: *[Violently.]* Not mine!

Simeon: *[Dryly.]* Ye'd not let no one else say that about yer Maw! Ha! *[He gives one abrupt sardonic guffaw. **Peter** grins.]*

Eben: *[Very pale.]* I meant—I hain't his'n—I hain't like him—he hain't me!

Peter: *[Dryly.]* Wait till ye've growed his age!

Eben: *[Intensely.]* I'm Maw—every drop o' blood! *[A pause. They stare at him with indifferent curiosity.]*

Peter: *[Reminiscently.]* She was good t' Sim 'n' me. A good Stepmaw's scurse.

Simeon: She was good t' everyone.

Eben: *[Greatly moved, gets to his feet and makes an awkward bow to each of them—stammering.]* I be thankful t'ye. I'm her—her heir. *[He sits down in confusion.]*

Peter: *[After a pause—judicially.]* She was good even t' him.

Eben: *[Fiercely.]* An' fur thanks he killed her!

Simeon: *[After a pause.]* No one never kills nobody. It's allus somethin'. That's the murderer.

Eben: Didn't he slave Maw t' death?

Peter: He slaved himself t' death. He's

slaved Sim 'n' me 'n' yew t' death—
on'y none o' us hain't died—yit.

Simeon: It's somethin'—drivin' him—t'
drive us!

Eben: [Vengefully.] Waal—I hold him t'
jedgment! [Then scornfully.] Somethin'! What's somethin'?

Simeon: Dunno.

Eben: [Sardonically.] What's drivin' yew
to Californi-a, mebbe? [They look at
him in surprise.] Oh, I've heerd ye!
[Then, after a pause.] But ye'll never
go t' the gold fields!

Peter: [Assertively.] Mebbe!

Eben: Whar'll ye git the money?

Peter: We kin walk. It's an a'mighty
ways—Californi-a—but if yew was t'
put all the steps we've walked on
this farm end t' end we'd be in the
moon!

Eben: The Injuns'll skulp ye on the
plains.

Simeon: [With grim humor.] We'll mebbe
make 'em pay a hair fur a hair!

Eben: [Decisively.] But t'ain't that. Ye
won't never go because ye'll wait
here fur yer share o' the farm,
thinkin' allus he'll die soon.

Simeon: [After a pause.] We've a right.

Peter: Two-thirds belongs t' us.

Eben: [Jumping to his feet.] Ye've no
right! She wa'n't yewr Maw! It was
her farm! Didn't he steal it from her?
She's dead. It's my farm.

Simeon: [Sardonically.] Tell that t' Paw
—when he comes! I'll bet ye a dollar
he'll laugh—fur once in his life.
Ha! [He laughs himself in one single
mirthless bark.]

Peter: [Amused in turn, echoes his
brother.] Ha!

Simeon: [After a pause.] What've ye got
held agin us, Eben? Year after year
it's skulked in yer eye—somethin'.

Peter: Ay-eh.

Eben: Ay-eh. They's somethin'. [Sud-
denly exploding.] Why didn't ye
never stand between him 'n' my Maw
when he was slavin' her to her grave
—t' pay her back fur the kindness
she done t' yew? [There is a long

pause. They stare at him in surprise.]

Simeon: Waal—the stock'd got t' be
watered.

Peter: 'R they was woodin' t' do.

Simeon: 'R plowin'.

Peter: 'R hayin.'

Simeon: 'R spreadin' manure.

Peter: 'R weedin'.

Simeon: 'R prunin'.

Peter: 'R milkin'.

Eben: [Breaking in harshly.] An' makin'
walls—stone atop o' stone—makin'
walls till yer heart's a stone ye heft
up out o' the way o' growth onto a
stone wall t' wall in yer heart!

Simeon: [Matter-of-factly.] We never
had no time t' meddle.

Peter: [To Eben.] Yew was fifteen afore
yer Maw died—an' big fur yer age.
Why didn't ye never do nothin'?

Eben: [Harshly.] They was chores t' do,
wa'n't they? [A pause—then slowly.]
It was on'y arter she died I come to
think o' it. Me cookin'—doin' her
work—that made me know her,
suffer her sufferin'—she'd come back
t' help—come back t' bile potatoes—
come back t' fry bacon—come back t'
bake biscuits—come back all cramped
up t' shake the fire, an' carry ashes,
her eyes weepin' an' bloody with
smoke an' cinders same's they used
t' be. She still comes back—stands by
the stove thar in the evenin'—she
can't find it nateral sleepin' an' restin'
in peace. She can't git used t' bein'
free—even in her grave.

Simeon: She never complained none.

Eben: She'd got too tired. She'd got too
used t' bein' too tired. That was what
he done. [With vengeful passion.] An'
sooner'r later, I'll meddle. I'll say the
thin's I didn't say then t' him! I'll yell
'em at the top o' my lungs. I'll see
it my Maw gits some rest an' sleep in
her grave! [He sits down again,
relapsing into a brooding silence.
They look at him with a queer
indifferent curiosity.]

Peter: [After a pause.] Whar in tarnation
d'ye s'pose he went, Sim?

Simeon: Dunno. He druv off in the buggy, all spick an' span, with the mare all breshed an' shiny, druv off clackin' his tongue an' wavin' his whip. I remember it right well. I was finishin' plowin', it was spring an' May an' sunset, an' gold in the West, an' he druv off into it. I yells "Whar ye goin', Paw?" an' he hauls up by the stone wall a jiffy. His old snake's eyes was glitterin' in the sun like he'd been drinkin' a jugful an' he says with a mule's grin: "Don't ye run away till I come back!"

Peter: Wonder if he knowed we was wantin' fur Californi-a?

Simeon: Mebbe. I didn't say nothin' and he says, lookin' kinder queer an' sick: "I been hearin' the hens cluckin' an' the roosters crowin' all the durn day. I been listenin' t' the cows lowin' an' everythin' else kickin' up till I can't stand it no more. It's spring an' I'm feelin' damned," he says. "Damned like an old bare hickory tree fit on'y fur burnin'," he says. An' then I calc'late I must've looked a mite hopeful, fur he adds real spry and vicious: "But don't git no fool idee I'm dead. I've sworn t' live a hundred an' I'll do it, if on'y t' spite yer sinful greed! An' now I'm ridin' out t' learn God's message t' me in the spring, like the prophets done. An' yew git back t' yer plowin'," he says. An' he druv off singin' a hymn. I thought he was drunk—'r I'd stopped him goin'.

Eben: [Scornfully.] No, ye wouldn't! Ye're scared o' him. He's stronger—inside—than both o' ye put together!

Peter: [Sardonically.] An' yew—be yew Samson?

Eben: I'm gittin' stronger. I kin feel it growin' in me—growin' an' growin'—till it'll bust out—! [He gets up and puts on his coat and a hat. They watch him, gradually breaking into grins. Eben avoids their eyes sheepishly.] I'm goin' out fur a spell—up the road.

Peter: T' the village?

Simeon: T' see Minnie?

Eben: [Defiantly.] Ay-eh!

Peter: [Jeeringly.] The Scarlet Woman!

Simeon: Lust—that's what's growin' in ye!

Eben: Waal—she's purty!

Peter: She's been purty fur twenty year!

Simeon: A new coat o' paint'll make a heifer out of forty.

Eben: She hain't forty!

Peter: If she hain't, she's teeterin' on the edge.

Eben: [Desperately.] What d'yew know—

Peter: All they is . . . Sim knew her—an' then me arter—

Simeon: An' Paw kin tell yew somethin' too! He was fust!

Eben: D'ye mean t' say he . . . ?

Simeon: [With a grin.] Ay-eh! We air his heirs in everythin'!

Eben: [Intensely.] That's more to it! That grows on it! It'll bust soon! [Then violently.] I'll go smash my fist in her face! [He pulls open the door in rear violently.]

Simeon: [With a wink at **Peter**—drawlingly.] Mebbe—but the night's wa'm—purty—by the time ye git thar mebbe ye'll kiss her instead!

Peter: Sart'n he will! [They both roar with coarse laughter. **Eben** rushes out and slams the door—then the outside front door—comes around the corner of the house and stands still by the gate, staring up at the sky.]

Simeon: [Looking after him.] Like his Paw.

Peter: Dead spit an' image!

Simeon: Dog'll eat dog!

Peter: Ay-eh. [Pause. With yearning.] Mebbe a year from now we'll be in Californi-a.

Simeon: Ay-eh. [A pause. Both yawn.] Let's git t'bed. [He blows out the candle. They go out door in rear. **Eben** stretches his arms up to the sky—rebelliously.]

Eben: Waal—thar's a star, an' somewhar's they's him, an' here's me, an' thar's Min up the road—in the same night. What if I does kiss her? She's like t'night, she's soft 'n' wa'm, her eyes kin wink like a star, her mouth's wa'm, her arms're wa'm, she smells like a wa'm plowed field, she's purty ... Ay-eh! By God A'mighty she's purty, an' I don't give a damn how many sins she's sinned afore mine or who's she's sinned 'em with, my sin's as purty as any one on 'em!

[He strides off down the road to the left.]

Scene III

It is the pitch darkness just before dawn. **Eben** comes in from the left and goes around to the porch, feeling his way, chuckling bitterly and cursing half-aloud to himself.

Eben: The cussed old miser! [He can be heard going in the front door. There is a pause as he goes upstairs, then a loud knock on the bedroom door of the brothers.] Wake up!
Simeon: [Startledly.] Who's thar?
Eben: [Pushing open the door and coming in, a lighted candle in his hand. The bedroom of the brothers is revealed. Its ceiling is the sloping roof. They can stand upright only close to the center dividing wall of the upstairs. **Simeon** and **Peter** are in a double bed, front. **Eben's** cot is to the rear. **Eben** has a mixture of silly grin and vicious scowl on his face.] I be!
Peter: [Angrily.] What in hell's-fire ... ?
Eben: I got news fur ye! Ha! [He gives one abrupt sardonic guffaw.]
Simeon: [Angrily.] Couldn't ye hold it 'til we'd got our sleep?
Eben: It's nigh sunup. [Then explosively.] He's gone an' married agen!
Simeon and **Peter:** [Explosively.] Paw?
Eben: Got himself hitched to a female 'bout thirty-five—an' purty, they says ...
Simeon: [Aghast.] It's a durn lie!
Peter: Who says?
Simeon: They been stringin' ye!
Eben: Think I'm a dunce, do ye? The hull village says. The preacher from New

Dover, he brung the news—told it t'our preacher—New Dover, that's whar the old loon got himself hitched —that's whar the woman lived—
Peter: [No longer doubting—stunned.] Waal ... !
Simeon: [The same.] Waal ... !
Eben: [Sitting down on a bed—with vicious hatred.] Ain't he a devil out o' hell? It's jest t' spite us—the damned old mule!
Peter: [After a pause.] Everythin'll go t' her now.
Simeon: Ay-eh. [A pause—dully.] Waal —if it's done—
Peter: It's done us. [Pause—then persuasively.] They's gold in the fields o' Californi-a, Sim. No good a-stayin' here now.
Simeon: Jest what I was a-thinkin'. [Then with decision.] S'well fust's last! Let's light out and git this mornin'.
Peter: Suits me.
Eben: Ye must like walkin'.
Simeon: [Sardonically.] If ye'd grow wings on us we'd fly thar!
Eben: Ye'd like ridin' better—on a boat, wouldn't ye? [Fumbles in his pocket and takes out a crumpled sheet of foolscap.] Waal, if ye sign this ye kin ride on a boat. I've had it writ out an' ready in case ye'd ever go. It says fur three hundred dollars t' each ye agree yewr shares o' the farm is sold t' me. [They look suspiciously at the paper. A pause.]
Simeon: [Wonderingly.] But if he's hitched agen—
Peter: An' whar'd yew git that sum o' money, anyways?
Eben: [Cunningly.] I know whar it's hid. I been waitin'—Maw told me. She knew whar it lay fur years, but she was waitin' ... It's her'n—the money he hoarded from her farm an' hid from Maw. It's my money by rights now.
Peter: Whar's it hid?
Eben: [Cunningly.] Whar yew won't never find it without me. Maw spied on him—'r she'd never knowed. [A pause. They look at him suspiciously,

and he at them.] Waal, is it fa'r trade?

Simeon: Dunno.

Peter: Dunno.

Simeon: *[Looking at window.]* Sky's grayin'.

Peter: Ye better start the fire, Eben.

Simeon: An' fix some vittles.

Eben: Ay-eh. *[Then with a forced jocular heartiness.]* I'll git ye a good one. If ye're startin' t' hoof it t' Californi-a ye'll need somethin' that'll stick t' yer ribs. *[He turns to the door, adding meaningly.]* But ye kin ride on a boat if ye'll swap. *[He stops at the door and pauses. They stare at him.]*

Simeon: *[Suspiciously.]* Whar was ye all night?

Eben: *[Defiantly.]* Up t' Min's. *[Then slowly.]* Walkin' thar, fust I felt 's if I'd kiss her; then I got a-thinkin' o' what ye'd said o' him an' her an' I says, I'll bust her nose fur that! Then I got t' the village an' heerd the news an' I got madder'n hell an' run all the way t' Min's not knowin' what I'd do — *[He pauses—then sheepishly but more defiantly.]* Waal—when I seen her, I didn't hit her—nor I didn't kiss her nuther—I begun t' beller like a calf an' cuss at the same time, I was so durn mad—an' she got scared—an' I jest grabbed holt an' tuk her! *[Proudly.]* Yes, sirree! I tuk her. She may've been his'n—an' your'n, too— but she's mine now!

Simeon: *[Dryly.]* In love, air yew?

Eben: *[With lofty scorn.]* Love! I don't take no stock in sech slop!

Peter: *[Winking at **Simeon**.]* Mebbe Eben's aimin' t' marry, too.

Simeon: Min'd make a true faithful he'pmeet! *[They snicker.]*

Eben: What do I care fur her—'ceptin' she's round an' wa'm? The p'int is she was his'n—an' now she belongs t' me! *[He goes to the door—then turns —rebelliously.]* An' Min hain't sech a bad un. They's worse'n Min in the world, I'll bet ye! Wait'll we see this cow the Old Man's hitched t'! She'll beat Min, I got a notion! *[He starts to go out.]*

Simeon: *[Suddenly.]* Mebbe ye'll try t' make her your'n, too?

Peter: Ha! *[He gives a sardonic laugh of relish at this idea.]*

Eben: *[Spitting with disgust.]* Her—here —sleepin' with him—stealin' my Maw's farm! I'd as soon pet a skunk 'r kiss a snake! *[He goes out. The two stare after him suspiciously. A pause. They listen to his steps receding.]*

Peter: He's startin' the fire.

Simeon: I'd like t' ride t' Californi-a— but—

Peter: Min might o' put some scheme in his head.

Simeon: Mebbe it's all a lie 'bout Paw marryin'. We'd best wait an' see the bride.

Peter: An' don't sign nothin' till we does!

Simeon: Nor till we've tested it's good money! *[Then with a grin.]* But if Paw's hitched we'd be sellin' Eben somethin' we'd never git nohow!

Peter: We'll wait an' see. *[Then with sudden vindictive anger.]* An' till he comes, let's yew 'n' me not wuk a lick, let Eben tend to thin's if he's a mind t', let's us jest sleep an' eat an' drink likker, an' let the hull damned farm go t' blazes!

Simeon: *[Excitedly.]* By God, we've 'arned a rest! We'll play rich fur a change. I hain't a-goin' to stir outa bed till breakfast's ready.

Peter: An' on the table!

Simeon: *[After a pause—thoughtfully.]* What d' ye calc'late she'll be like— our new Maw? Like Eben thinks?

Peter: More'n likely.

Simeon: *[Vindictively.]* Waal—I hope she's a she-devil that'll make him wish he was dead an' livin' in the pit o' hell fur comfort!

Peter: *[Fervently.]* Amen!

Simeon: *[Imitating his father's voice.]* "I'm ridin' out t' learn God's message t' me in the spring like the prophets done," he says. I'll bet right then an' thar he knew plumb well he was goin' whorin', the stinkin' old hypocrite!

Scene IV

*Same as Scene II—shows the interior of
the kitchen with a lighted candle on
table. It is gray dawn outside.* **Simeon**
and **Peter** *are just finishing their breakfast.* **Eben** *sits before his plate of un-
touched food, brooding frowningly.*

Peter: *[Glancing at him rather irritably.]*
Lookin' glum don't help none.

Simeon: *[Sarcastically.]* Sorrowin' over
his lust o' the flesh!

Peter: *[With a grin.]* Was she yer fust?

Eben: *[Angrily.]* None o' yer business. *[A
pause.]* I was thinkin' o' him. I got a
notion he's gittin' near—I kin feel
him comin' on like yew kin feel
malaria chill afore it takes ye.

Peter: It's too early yet.

Simeon: Dunno. He'd like t' catch us
nappin'—jest t' have somethin' t' hoss
us 'round over.

Peter: *[Mechanically gets to his feet.*
Simeon *does the same.]* Waal—let's
git t' wuk.

> *[They both plod mechanically
> toward the door before they
> realize. Then they stop short.]*

Simeon: *[Grinning.]* Ye're a cussed fool,
Pete—and I be wuss! Let him see we
hain't wukin'! We don't give a durn!

Peter: *[As they go back to the table.]* Not
a damned durn! It'll serve t' show
him we're done with him. *[They sit
down again.* **Eben** *stares from one to
the other with surprise.]*

Simeon: *[Grins at him.]* We're aimin' t'
start bein' lilies o' the field.

Peter: Nary a toil 'r spin 'r lick o' wuk do
we put in!

Simeon: Ye're sole owner—till he comes
—that's what ye wanted. Waal, ye
got t' be sole hand, too.

Peter: The cows air bellerin'. Ye better
hustle at the milkin'.

Eben: *[With excited joy.]* Ye mean ye'll
sign the paper?

Simeon: *[Dryly.]* Mebbe.

Peter: Mebbe.

Simeon: We're considerin'. *[Peremptor-
ily.]* Ye better git t' wuk.

Eben: *[With queer excitement.]* It's
Maw's farm agen! It's my farm!
Them's my cows! I'll milk my durn
fingers off fur cows o' mine! *[He
goes out door in rear, they stare after
him indifferently.]*

Simeon: Like his Paw.

Peter: Dead spit 'n' image!

Simeon: Waal—let dog eat dog!

> *[**Eben** comes out of front door and
> around the corner of the house.
> The sky is beginning to grow
> flushed with sunrise.* **Eben** *stops
> by the gate and stares around him
> with glowing, possessive eyes. He
> takes in the whole farm with his
> embracing glance of desire.]*

Eben: It's purty! It's damned purty! It's
mine! *[He suddenly throws his head
back boldly and glares with hard,
defiant eye at the sky.]* Mine, d'ye
hear? Mine! *[He turns and walks
quickly off left, rear, toward the
barn. The two brothers light their
pipes.]*

Simeon: *[Putting his muddy boots up on
the table, tilting back his chair, and
puffing defiantly.]* Waal—this air
solid comfort—fur once.

Peter: Ay-eh. *[He follows suit. A pause.
Unconsciously they both sigh.]*

Simeon: *[Suddenly.]* He never was much
o' a hand at milkin', Eben wa'n't.

Peter: *[With a snort.]* His hands air like
hoofs! *[A pause.]*

Simeon: Reach down the jug thar! Let's
take a swaller. I'm feelin' kind of
low.

Peter: Good idee! *[He does so—gets two
glasses—they pour out drinks of
whisky.]* Here's t' the gold in Californi-a!

Simeon: An' luck t' find it! *[They drink
—puff resolutely—sigh—take their
feet down from the table.]*

Peter: Likker don't 'pear t' sot right.

Simeon: We hain't used t' it this early.
*[A pause. They become very rest-
less.]*

Peter: Gittin' close in this kitchen.

Simeon: *[With immense relief.]* Let's git

a breath o' air. [*They arise briskly and go out rear—appear around house and stop by the gate. They stare up at the sky with a numbed appreciation.*]

Peter: Purty!

Simeon: Ay-eh. Gold's t' the East now.

Peter: Sun's startin' with us fur the Golden West.

Simeon: [*Staring around the farm, his compressed face tightened, unable to conceal his emotion.*] Waal—it's our last mornin'—mebbe.

Peter: [*The same.*] Ay-eh.

Simeon: [*Stamps his foot on the earth and addresses it desperately.*] Waal—ye've thirty year o' me buried in ye—spread out over ye—blood an' bone an' sweat—rotted away—fertilizin' ye—richin' yer soul—prime manure, by God, that's what I been t' ye!

Peter: Ay-eh! An' me.

Simeon: An' yew, Peter. [*He sighs—then spits.*] Waal—no use'n cryin' over spilt milk.

Peter: They's gold in the West—an' free-dom, mebbe. We been slaves t' stone walls here.

Simeon: [*Defiantly.*] We hain't nobody's slaves from this out—nor no thin's slaves nuther. [*A pause—restlessly.*] Speakin' o' milk, wonder how Eben's managin'?

Peter: I s'pose he's managin'.

Simeon: Mebbe we'd ought t' help—this once.

Peter: Mebbe. The cows knows us.

Simeon: An' likes us. They don't know him much.

Peter: An' the hosses, an' pigs, an' chickens. They don't know him much.

Simeon: They knows us like brothers—an' likes us! [*Proudly.*] Hain't we raised 'em t' be fust-rate, number one prize stock?

Peter: We hain't—not no more.

Simeon: [*Dully.*] I was fergittin'. [*Then resignedly.*] Waal, let's go help Eben a spell an' git waked up.

Peter: Suits me. [*They are starting off down left, rear, for the barn when* **Eben** *appears from there hurrying toward them, his face excited.*]

Eben: [*Breathlessly.*] Waal—har they be! The old mule an' the bride! I seen 'em from the barn down below at the turnin'.

Peter: How could ye tell that far?

Eben: Hain't I as far-sight as he's near-sight? Don't I know the mare 'n' buggy, an' two people settin' in it? Who else . . . ? An' I tell ye I kin feel 'em a-comin', too! [*He squirms as if he had the itch.*]

Peter: [*Beginning to be angry.*] Waal—let him do his own unhitchin'!

Simeon: [*Angry in his turn.*] Let's hustle in an' git our bundles an' be a-goin' as he's a-comin'. I don't want never t' step inside the door agen arter he's back. [*They both start back around the corner of the house.* **Eben** *follows them.*]

Eben: [*Anxiously.*] Will ye sign it afore ye go?

Peter: Let's see the color o' the old skin-flint's money an' we'll sign.

[*They disappear left. The two brothers clump upstairs to get their bundles.* **Eben** *appears in the kitchen, runs to the window, peers out, comes back and pulls up a strip of flooring in under stove, takes out a canvas bag and puts it on table, then sets the floorboard back in place. The two brothers appear a moment after. They carry old carpet bags.*]

Eben: [*Puts his hand on bag guardingly.*] Have ye signed?

Simeon: [*Shows paper in his hand.*] Ay-eh. [*Greedily.*] Be that the money?

Eben: [*Opens bag and pours out pile of twenty-dollar gold pieces.*] Twenty-dollar pieces—thirty on 'em. Count 'em. [**Peter** *does so, arranging them in stacks of five, biting one or two to test them.*]

Peter: Six hundred. [*He puts them in bag and puts it inside his shirt carefully.*]

Simeon: [Handing paper to **Eben**.] Har ye be.

Eben: [After a glance, folds it carefully and hides it under his shirt—gratefully.] Thank yew.

Peter: Thank yew fur the ride.

Simeon: We'll send ye a lump o' gold fur Christmas. [A pause. **Eben** stares at them and they at him.]

Peter: [Awkwardly.] Waal—we're a-goin'.

Simeon: Comin' out t' the yard?

Eben: No. I'm waitin' in here a spell. [Another silence. The brothers edge awkwardly to the door in rear—then turn and stand.]

Simeon: Waal—good-by.

Peter: Good-by.

Eben: Good-by. [They go out. He sits down at the table, faces the stove and pulls out the paper. He looks from it to the stove. His face, lighted up by the shaft of sunlight from the window, has an expression of trance. His lips move. The two brothers come out to the gate.]

Peter: [Looking off toward barn.] Thar he be—unhitchin'.

Simeon: [With a chuckle.] I'll bet ye he's riled!

Peter: An' thar she be.

Simeon: Let's wait 'n' see what our new Maw looks like.

Peter: [With a grin.] An' give him our partin' cuss!

Simeon: [Grinning.] I feel like raisin' fun. I feel light in my head an' feet.

Peter: Me, too. I feel like laffin' till I'd split up the middle.

Simeon: Reckon it's the likker?

Peter: No. My feet feel itchin' t' walk an' walk—an' jump high over thin's—an'. . . .

Simeon: Dance? [A pause.]

Peter: [Puzzled.] It's plumb onnateral.

Simeon: [A light coming over his face.] I calc'late it's 'cause school's out. It's holiday. Fur once we're free!

Peter: [Dazedly.] Free?

Simeon: The halter's broke—the harness is busted—the fence bars is down—

the stone walls air crumblin' an' tumblin'! We'll be kickin' up an' tearin' away down the road!

Peter: [Drawing a deep breath—oratorically.] Anybody that wants this stinkin' old rock-pile of a farm kin hev it. 'Tain't our'n, no sirree!

Simeon: [Takes the gate off its hinges and puts it under his arm.] We harby 'bolishes shet gates an' open gates, an' all gates, by thunder!

Peter: We'll take it with us fur luck an' let 'er sail free down some river.

Simeon: [As a sound of voices comes from left, rear.] Har they comes!

[The two brothers congeal into two stiff, grim-visaged statues. **Ephraim Cabot** and **Abbie Putnam** come in. **Cabot** is seventy-five, tall and gaunt, with great, wiry, concentrated power, but stoop-shouldered from toil. His face is as hard as if it were hewn out of a boulder, yet there is a weakness in it, a petty pride in its own narrow strength. His eyes are small, close together, and extremely near-sighted, blinking continually in the effort to focus on objects, their stare having a straining, ingrowing quality. He is dressed in his dismal black Sunday suit. **Abbie** is thirty-five, buxom, full of vitality. Her round face is pretty but marred by its rather gross sensuality. There is strength and obstinacy in her jaw, a hard determination in her eyes, and about her whole personality the same unsettled, untamed, desperate quality which is so apparent in **Eben**.]

Cabot: [As they enter—a queer strangled emotion in his dry cracking voice.] Har we be t' hum, Abbie.

Abbie: [With lust for the word.] Hum! [Her eyes gloating on the house without seeming to see the two stiff figures at the gate.] It's purty—purty! I can't b'lieve it's r'ally mine.

Cabot: [Sharply.] Yewr'n? Mine! [He

stares at her penetratingly. She stares back. He adds relentingly.] Our'n—mebbe! It was lonesome too long. I was growin' old in the spring. A hum's got t' hev a woman.

Abbie: [Her voice taking possession.] A woman's got t' hev a hum!

Cabot: [Nodding uncertainly.] Ay-eh. [Then irritably.] Whar be they? Ain't thar nobody about—'r wukin'—r' nothin'?

Abbie: [Sees the brothers. She returns their stare of cold appraising contempt with interest—slowly.] Thar's two men loafin' at the gate an' starin' at me like a couple o' strayed hogs.

Cabot: [Straining his eyes.] I kin see 'em—but I can't make out. . . .

Simeon: It's Simeon.

Peter: It's Peter.

Cabot: [Exploding.] Why hain't ye wukin'?

Simeon: [Dryly.] We're waitin' t' welcome ye hum—yew an' the bride!

Cabot: [Confusedly.] Huh? Waal—this be yer new Maw, boys. [She stares at them and they at her.]

Simeon: [Turns away and spits contemptuously.] I see her!

Peter: [Spits also.] An' I see her!

Abbie: [With the conqueror's conscious superiority.] I'll go in an' look at my house. [She goes slowly around to porch.]

Simeon: [With a snort.] Her house!

Peter: [Calls after her.] Ye'll find Eben inside. Ye better not tell him it's yewr house.

Abbie: [Mouthing the name.] Eben. [Then quietly.] I'll tell Eben.

Cabot: [With a contemptuous sneer.] Ye needn't heed Eben. Eben's a dumb fool—like his Maw—soft an' simple!

Simeon: [With his sardonic burst of laughter.] Ha! Eben's a chip o' yew—spit 'n' image—hard 'n' bitter's a hickory tree! Dog'll eat dog. He'll eat ye yet, old man!

Cabot: [Commandingly.] Ye git t' wuk!

Simeon: [As **Abbie** disappears in house—winks at **Peter** and says tauntingly.] So that thar's our new Maw, be it? Whar in hell did ye dig her up? [He and **Peter** laugh.]

Peter: Ha! Ye'd better turn her in the pen with the other sows. [They laugh uproariously, slapping their thighs.]

Cabot: [So amazed at their effrontery that he stutters in confusion.] Simeon! Peter! What's come over ye? Air ye drunk?

Simeon: We're free, old man—free o' yew an' the hull damned farm! [They grow more and more hilarious and excited.]

Peter: An' we're startin' out fur the gold fields o' Californi-a!

Simeon: Ye kin take this place an' burn it!

Peter: An' bury it—fur all we cares!

Simeon: We're free, old man! [He cuts a caper.]

Peter: Free! [He gives a kick in the air.]

Simeon: [In a frenzy.] Whoop!

Peter: Whoop! [They do an absurd Indian war dance about the old man who is petrified between rage and the fear that they are insane.]

Simeon: We're free as Injuns! Lucky we don't sculp ye!

Peter: An' burn yer barn an' kill the stock!

Simeon: An' rape yer new woman! Whoop! [He and **Peter** stop their dance, holding their sides, rocking with wild laughter.]

Cabot: [Edging away.] Lust fur gold—fur the sinful, easy gold o' Californi-a! It's made ye mad!

Simeon: [Tauntingly.] Wouldn't ye like us to send ye back some sinful gold, ye old sinner?

Peter: They's gold besides what's in Californi-a! [He retreats back beyond the vision of the old man and takes the bag of money and flaunts it in the air above his head, laughing.]

Simeon: And sinfuller, too!

Peter: We'll be voyagin' on the sea! Whoop! [He leaps up and down.]

Simeon: Livin' free! Whoop! [He leaps in turn.]

Cabot: [*Suddenly roaring with rage.*] My cuss on ye!

Simeon: Take our'n in trade fur it! Whoop!

Cabot: I'll hev ye both chained up in the asylum!

Peter: Ye old skinflint! Good-by!

Simeon: Ye old blood sucker! Good-by!

Cabot: Go afore I . . . !

Peter: Whoop! [*He picks a stone from the road.* **Simeon** *does the same.*]

Simeon: Maw'll be in the parlor.

Peter: Ay-eh! One! Two!

Cabot: [*Frightened.*] What air ye . . . ?

Peter: Three! [*They both throw, the stones hitting the parlor window with a crash of glass, tearing the shade.*]

Simeon: Whoop!

Peter: Whoop!

Cabot: [*In a fury now, rushing toward them.*] If I kin lay hands on ye—I'll break yer bones fur ye!

[*But they beat a capering retreat before him,* **Simeon** *with the gate still under his arm.* **Cabot** *comes back, panting with impotent rage. Their voices as they go off take up the song of the gold-seekers to the old tune of "Oh, Susannah!"*]

"I jumped aboard the Liza ship,
And traveled on the sea,
And every time I thought of home
I wished it wasn't me!
Oh! Californi-a,
That's the land fur me!
I'm off to Californi-a!
With my wash bowl on my knee."

[*In the meantime, the window of the upper bedroom on right is raised and* **Abbie** *sticks her head out. She looks down at* **Cabot**—*with a sigh of relief.*]

Abbie: Waal—that's the last o' them two, hain't it? [*He doesn't answer. Then in possessive tones.*] This here's a nice bedroom, Ephraim. It's a r'al nice bed. Is it my room, Ephraim?

Cabot: [*Grimly—without looking up.*] Our'n! [*She cannot control a grimace of aversion and pulls back her head slowly and shuts the window. A sudden horrible thought seems to enter* **Cabot's** *head.*] They been up to somethin'! Mebbe—mebbe they've pizened the stock—'r somethin'!

[*He almost runs off down toward the barn. A moment later the kitchen door is slowly pushed open and* **Abbie** *enters. For a moment she stands looking at* **Eben.** *He does not notice her at first. Her eyes take him in penetratingly with a calculating appraisal of his strength as against hers. But under this her desire is dimly awakened by his youth and good looks. Suddenly he becomes conscious of her presence and looks up. Their eyes meet. He leaps to his feet, glowering at her speechlessly.*]

Abbie: [*In her most seductive tones which she uses all through this scene.*] Be you—Eben? I'm Abbie— [*She laughs.*] I mean, I'm yer new Maw.

Eben: [*Viciously.*] No, damn ye!

Abbie: [*As if she hadn't heard—with a queer smile.*] Yer Paw's spoke a lot o' yew. . . .

Eben: Ha!

Abbie: Ye mustn't mind him. He's an old man. [*A long pause. They stare at each other.*] I don't want t' pretend playin' Maw t' ye, Eben. [*Admiringly.*] Ye're too big an' too strong fur that. I want t' be frens with ye. Mebbe with me fur a fren ye'd find ye'd like livin' here better. I kin make it easy fur ye with him, mebbe. [*With a scornful sense of power.*] I calc'late I kin git him t' do most anythin' fur me.

Eben: [*With bitter scorn.*] Ha! [*They stare again,* **Eben** *obscurely moved, physically attracted to her—in forced stilted tones.*] Yew kin go t' the devil.

Abbie: [*Calmly.*] If cussin' me does ye good, cuss all ye've a mind t'. I'm all prepared t' have ye agin me—at fust. I don't blame ye nuther. I'd feel the same at any stranger comin' t' take my Maw's place. [*He shudders. She is watching him carefully.*] Yew must've cared a lot fur yewr Maw, didn't ye? My Maw died afore I'd growed. I don't remember her none. [*A pause.*] But yew won't hate me long, Eben. I'm not the wust in the world—an' yew an' me've got a lot in common. I kin tell that by lookin' at ye. Waal—I've had a hard life, too—oceans o' trouble an' nuthin' but wuk fur reward. I was a orphan early an' had t' wuk fur others in other folks' hums. Then I married an' he turned out a drunken spreer an' so he had to wuk fur others an' me too agen in other folks' hums, an' the baby died, an' my husband got sick an' died too, an' I was glad sayin' now I'm free fur once, on'y I diskivered right away all I was free fur was t' wuk agen in other folks' hums, doin' other folks' wuk till I'd most give up hope o' ever doin' my own wuk in my own hum, an' then your Paw come. . . .

[**Cabot** *appears returning from the barn. He comes to the gate and looks down the road the brothers have gone. A faint strain of their retreating voices is heard:* "Oh, Californi-a! That's the place for me." *He stands glowering, his fist clenched, his face grim with rage.*]

Eben: [*Fighting against his growing attraction and sympathy—harshly.*] An' bought yew—like a harlot! [*She is stung and flushes angrily. She has been sincerely moved by the recital of her troubles. He adds furiously.*] An' the price he's payin' ye—this farm—was my Maw's, damn ye!—an' mine now!

Abbie: [*With a cool laugh of confidence.*] Yewr'n? We'll see 'bout that! [*Then strongly.*] Waal—what if I did need a hum? What else'd I marry an old man like him fur?

Eben: [*Maliciously.*] I'll tell him ye said that!

Abbie: [*Smiling.*] I'll say ye're lyin' a-

purpose—an' he'll drive ye off the place!

Eben: Ye devil!

Abbie: [*Defying him.*] This be my farm—this be my hum—this be my kitchen—!

Eben: [*Furiously, as if he were going to attack her.*] Shut up, damn ye!

Abbie: [*Walks up to him—a queer coarse expression of desire in her face and body—slowly.*] An' upstairs—that be my bedroom—an' my bed! [*He stares into her eyes, terribly confused and torn. She adds softly:*] I hain't bad nor mean—'ceptin' fur an enemy—but I got t' fight fur what's due me out o' life, if I ever 'spect t' git it. [*Then putting her hand on his arm—seductively.*] Let's yew 'n' me be frens, Eben.

Eben: [*Stupidly—as if hypnotized.*] Ay-eh. [*Then furiously flinging off her arm.*] No, ye durned old witch! I hate ye!

[*He rushes out the door.*]

Abbie: [*Looks after him smiling satisfiedly—then half to herself, mouthing the word.*] Eben's nice. [*She looks at the table, proudly.*] I'll wash up my dishes now.

[**Eben** *appears outside, slamming the door behind him. He comes around corner, stops on seeing his father, and stands staring at him with hate.*]

Cabot: [*Raising his arms to heaven in the fury he can no longer control.*] Lord God o' Hosts, smite the undutiful sons with Thy wust cuss!

Eben: [*Breaking in violently.*] Yew 'n' yewr God! Allus cussin' folks—allus naggin' 'em!

Cabot: [*Oblivious to him—summoningly.*] God o' the old! God o' the lonesome!

Eben: [*Mockingly.*] Naggin' His sheep t' sin! T' hell with yewr God!

[**Cabot** *turns. He and* **Eben** *glower at each other.*]

Cabot: [*Harshly.*] So it's yew. I might've knowed it. [*Shaking his finger threat-*

eningly at him.] Blasphemin' fool! [Then quickly.] Why hain't ye t' wuk?

Eben: Why hain't yew? They've went. I can't wuk it all alone.

Cabot: [Contemptuously.] Nor noways! I'm wuth ten o' ye yit, old's I be! Ye'll never be more'n half a man! [Then, matter-of-factly.] Waal—let's git t' the barn.

[They go. A last faint note of the "Californi-a" song is heard from the distance. **Abbie** is washing her dishes.]

CURTAIN

Part Two

Scene I

The exterior of the farmhouse, as in Part One—a hot Sunday afternoon two months later. **Abbie,** dressed in her best, is discovered sitting in a rocker at the end of the porch. She rocks listlessly, enervated by the heat, staring in front of her with bored, half-closed eyes.

[**Eben** sticks his head out of his bedroom window. He looks around furtively and tries to see —or hear—if anyone is on the porch, but although he has been careful to make no noise, **Abbie** has sensed his movement. She stops rocking, her face grows animated and eager, she waits attentively. **Eben** seems to feel her presence, he scowls back his thoughts of her and spits with exaggerated disdain—then withdraws back into the room. **Abbie** waits, holding her breath as she listens with passionate eagerness for every sound within the house.

Eben comes out. Their eyes meet. His falter, he is confused, he turns away and slams the door resentfully. At this gesture, **Abbie** laughs tantalizingly, amused but at the same time piqued and irritated. He scowls, strides off the porch to the path and starts to

walk past her to the road with a grand swagger of ignoring her existence. He is dressed in his store suit, spruced up, his face shines from soap and water. **Abbie** leans forward on her chair, her eyes hard and angry now, and, as he passes her, gives a sneering, taunting chuckle.]

Eben: [Stung—turns on her furiously.] What air yew cacklin' 'bout?

Abbie: [Triumphant.] Yew!

Eben: What about me?

Abbie: Ye look all slicked up like a prize bull.

Eben: [With a sneer.] Waal—ye hain't so durned purty yerself, be ye? [They stare into each other's eyes, his held by hers in spite of himself, hers glowingly possessive. Their physical attraction becomes a palpable force quivering in the hot air.]

Abbie: [Softly.] Ye don't mean that, Eben. Ye may think ye mean it, mebbe, but ye don't. Ye can't. It's agin nature, Eben. Ye been fightin' yer nature ever since the day I come— tryin' t' tell yerself I hain't purty t'ye. [She laughs a low humid laugh without taking her eyes from his. A pause —her body squirms desirously—she murmurs languorously.] Hain't the sun strong an' hot? Ye kin feel it burnin' into the earth—Nature— makin' thin's grow—bigger 'n' bigger —burnin' inside ye—makin' ye want t' grow—into somethin' else—till ye're jined with it—an' it's yourn— but it owns ye, too—an' makes ye grow bigger—like a tree—like them elums— [She laughs again softly, holding his eyes. He takes a step toward her, compelled against his will.] Nature'll beat ye, Eben. Ye might's well own up t' it fust 's last.

Eben: [Trying to break from her spell— confusedly.] If Paw'd hear ye goin' on ... [Resentfully.] But ye've made such a damned idjit out o' the old devil ... !

[**Abbie** laughs.]

Abbie: Waal—hain't it easier fur yew with him changed softer?

Eben: [*Defiantly.*] No. I'm fightin' him—fightin' yew—fightin' fur Maw's rights t' her hum! [*This breaks her spell for him. He glowers at her.*] An' I'm onto ye. Ye hain't foolin' me a mite. Ye're aimin' t' swaller up everythin' an' make it your'n. Waal, you'll find I'm a heap sight bigger hunk nor yew kin chew! [*He turns from her with a sneer.*]

Abbie: [*Trying to regain her ascendancy —seductively.*] Eben!

Eben: Leave me be! [*He starts to walk away.*]

Abbie: [*More commandingly.*] Eben!

Eben: [*Stops—resentfully.*] What d'ye want?

Abbie: [*Trying to conceal a growing excitement.*] Whar air ye goin'?

Eben: [*With malicious nonchalance.*] Oh —up the road a spell.

Abbie: T' the village?

Eben: [*Airily.*] Mebbe.

Abbie: [*Excitedly.*] T' see that Min, I s'pose?

Eben: Mebbe.

Abbie: [*Weakly.*] What d'ye want t' waste time on her fur?

Eben: [*Revenging himself now—grinning at her.*] Ye can't beat Nature, didn't ye say? [*He laughs and again starts to walk away.*]

Abbie: [*Bursting out.*] An ugly old hake!

Eben: [*With a tantalizing sneer.*] She's purtier'n yew be!

Abbie: That every wuthless drunk in the country has. . . .

Eben: [*Tauntingly.*] Mebbe—but she's better'n yew. She owns up fa'r 'n' squar' t' her doin's.

Abbie: [*Furiously.*] Don't ye dare compare. . . .

Eben: She don't go sneakin' an' stealin'—what's mine.

Abbie: [*Savagely seizing on his weak point.*] Your'n? Yew mean—my farm?

Eben: I mean the farm yew sold yerself fur like any other old whore—my farm!

Abbie: [*Stung—fiercely.*] Ye'll never live t' see the day when even a stinkin' weed on it'll belong t' ye! [*Then in a scream.*] Git out o' my sight! Go on t' yer slut—disgracin' yer Paw 'n' me! I'll git yer Paw t' horsewhip ye off the place if I want t'! Ye're only livin' here 'cause I tolerate ye! Git along! I hate the sight o' ye! [*She stops, panting and glaring at him.*]

Eben: [*Returning her glance in kind.*] An' I hate the sight o' yew!

[*He turns and strides off up the road. She follows his retreating figure with concentrated hate. Old* **Cabot** *appears coming up from the barn. The hard, grim expression of his face has changed. He seems in some queer way softened, mellowed. His eyes have taken on a strange, incongruous dreamy quality. Yet there is no hint of physical weakness about him—rather he looks more robust and younger.* **Abbie** *sees him and turns away quickly with unconcealed aversion. He comes slowly up to her.*]

Cabot: [*Mildly.*] War yew an' Eben quarrelin' agen?

Abbie: [*Shortly.*] No.

Cabot: Ye was talkin' a'mighty loud. [*He sits down on the edge of porch.*]

Abbie: [*Snappishly.*] If ye heered us they hain't no need askin' questions.

Cabot: I didn't hear what ye said.

Abbie: [*Relieved.*] Waal—it wa'nt nothin' t' speak on.

Cabot: [*After a pause.*] Eben's queer.

Abbie: [*Bitterly.*] He's the dead spit 'n' image o' yew!

Cabot: [*Queerly interested.*] D'ye think so, Abbie? [*After a pause, ruminatingly.*] Me 'n' Eben's allus fit 'n' fit. I never could b'ar him noways. He's so thunderin' soft—like his Maw.

Abbie: [*Scornfully.*] Ay-eh! 'Bout as soft as yew be!

Cabot: [*As if he hadn't heard.*] Mebbe I been too hard on him.

Abbie: [*Jeeringly.*] Waal—ye're gettin'

soft now— soft as slop! That's what Eben was sayin'.

Cabot: [*His face instantly grim and ominous.*] Eben was sayin'? Waal, he'd best not do nothin' t' try me 'r he'll soon diskiver. . . . [*A pause. She keeps her face turned away. His gradually softens. He stares up at the sky.*] Purty, hain't it?

Abbie: [*Crossly.*] I don't see nothin' purty.

Cabot: The sky. Feels like a wa'm field up thar.

Abbie: [*Sarcastically.*] Air yew aimin' t' buy up over the farm too? [*She snickers contemptuously.*]

Cabot: [*Strangely.*] I'd like t' own my place up thar. [*A pause.*] I'm gittin' old, Abbie, I'm gittin' ripe on the bough. [*A pause. She stares at him mystified. He goes on.*] It's allus lonesome cold in the house—even when it's bilin' hot outside. Hain't yew noticed?

Abbie: No.

Cabot: It's wa'm down t' the barn—nice smellin' an' warm—with the cows. [*A pause.*] Cows is queer.

Abbie: Like yew?

Cabot: Like Eben. [*A pause.*] I'm gittin' t' feel resigned t' Eben—jest as I got t' feel 'bout his Maw. I'm gittin' t' learn to b'ar his softness—jest like her'n. I calc'late I c'd a'most take t' him—jf he wa'nt sech a dumb fool! [*A pause.*] I s'pose it's old age a-creepin' in my bones.

Abbie: [*Indifferently.*] Waal—ye hain't dead yet.

Cabot: [*Roused.*] No, I hain't, yew bet—not by a hell of a sight—I'm sound 'n' tough as hickory! [*Then moodily.*] But arter three score and ten the Lord warns ye t' prepare. [*A pause.*] That's why Eben's come in my head. Now that his cussed sinful brothers is gone their path t' hell, they's no one left but Eben.

Abbie: [*Resentfully.*] They's me, hain't they? [*Agitatedly.*] What's all this sudden likin' ye tuk to Eben? Why don't ye say nothin' 'bout me? Hain't I yer lawful wife?

Cabot: [*Simply.*] Ay-eh. Ye be. [*A pause —he stares at her desirously—his eyes grow avid—then with a sudden movement he seizes her hands and squeezes them, declaiming in a queer camp-meeting preacher's tempo.*] Yew air my Rose o' Sharon! Behold, yew air fair; yer eyes air doves; yer lips air like scarlet; yer two breasts air like two fawns; yer navel be like a round goblet; yer belly be like a heap o' wheat. . . . [*He covers her hand with kisses. She does not seem to notice. She stares before her with hard angry eyes.*]

Abbie: [*Jerking her hands away— harshly.*] So ye're plannin' t' leave the farm t' Eben, air ye?

Cabot: [*Dazedly.*] Leave. . . ? [*Then with resentful obstinacy.*] I hain't a-givin' it t' no one!

Abbie: [*Remorselessly.*] Ye can't take it with ye.

Cabot: [*Thinks a moment—then reluctantly.*] No, I calc'late not. [*After a pause—with a strange passion.*] But if I could, I would, by the Etarnal! 'R if I could, in my dyin' hour, I'd set it afire an' watch it burn—this house an' every ear o' corn an' every tree down t' the last blade o' hay! I'd sit an' know it was all a-dying with me an' no one else'd ever own what was mine, what I'd made out o' nothin' with my own sweat 'n' blood! [*A pause—then he adds with a queer affection.*] 'Ceptin' the cows. Them I'd turn free.

Abbie: [*Harshly.*] An' me?

Cabot: [*With a queer smile.*] Ye'd be turned free, too.

Abbie: [*Furiously.*] So that's the thanks I git fur marryin' ye—t' have ye change kind to Eben who hates ye, an' talk o' turnin' me out in the road.

Cabot: [*Hastily.*] Abbie! Ye know I wa'n't. . . .

Abbie: [*Vengefully.*] Just let me tell ye a thing or two 'bout Eben. Whar's he gone? T' see that harlot, Min! I tried fur t' stop him. Disgracin' yew an' me—on the Sabbath, too!

Cabot: [*Rather guiltily.*] He's a sinner—nateral-born. It's lust eatin' his heart.

Abbie: [*Enraged beyond endurance—wildly vindictive.*] An' his lust fur me! Kin ye find excuses fur that?

Cabot: [*Stares at her—after a dead pause.*] Lust—fur yew?

Abbie: [*Defiantly.*] He was tryin' t' make love t' me—when ye heerd us quarrelin'.

Cabot: [*Stares at her—then a terrible expression of rage comes over his face—he springs to his feet shaking all over.*] By the A'mighty God—I'll end him!

Abbie: [*Frightened now for* **Eben.**] No! Don't ye!

Cabot: [*Violently.*] I'll git the shotgun an' blow his soft brains t' the top o' them elums!

Abbie: [*Throwing her arms around him.*] No, Ephraim!

Cabot: [*Pushing her away violently.*] I will, by God!

Abbie: [*In a quieting tone.*] Listen, Ephraim. 'Twa'nt nothin' bad—on'y a boy's foolin'—'twa'n't meant serious—jest jokin' an' teasin'. . . .

Cabot: Then why did ye say—lust?

Abbie: It must hev sounded wusser'n I meant. An' I was mad at thinkin'—ye'd leave him the farm.

Cabot: [*Quieter but still grim and cruel.*] Waal then, I'll horsewhip him off the place if that much'll content ye.

Abbie: [*Reaching out and taking his hand.*] No. Don't think o' me! Ye mustn't drive him off. 'Tain't sensible. Who'll ye get to help ye on the farm? They's no one hereabouts.

Cabot: [*Considers this—then nodding his appreciation.*] Ye got a head on ye. [*Then irritably.*] Waal, let him stay. [*He sits down on the edge of the porch. She sits beside him. He murmurs contemptuously.*] I oughn't git riled so—at that 'ere fool calf. [*A pause.*] But har's the p'int. What son

o' mine'll keep on here t' the farm—when the Lord does call me? Simeon an' Peter air gone t' hell—an' Eben's follerin' 'em.

Abbie: They's me.

Cabot: Ye're on'y a woman.

Abbie: I'm yewr wife.

Cabot: That hain't me. A son is me—my blood—mine. Mine ought t' git mine. An' then it's still mine—even though I be six foot under. D'ye see?

Abbie: [*Giving him a look of hatred.*] Ay-eh. I see. [*She becomes very thoughtful, her face growing shrewd, her eyes studying* **Cabot** *craftily.*]

Cabot: I'm gittin' old—ripe on the bough. [*Then with a sudden forced reassurance.*] Not but what I hain't a hard nut t' crack even yet—an' fur many a year t' come! By the Etarnal, I kin break most o' the young fellers' backs at any kind o' work any day o' the year!

Abbie: [*Suddenly.*] Mebbe the Lord'll give us a son.

Cabot: [*Turns and stares at her eagerly.*] Ye mean—a son—t' me 'n' yew?

Abbie: [*With a cajoling smile.*] Ye're a strong man yet, hain't ye? 'Tain't noways impossible, be it? We know that. Why d'ye stare so? Hain't ye never thought o' that afore? I been thinkin' o' it all along. Ay-eh—an' I been prayin' it'd happen, too.

Cabot: [*His face growing full of joyous pride and a sort of religious ectasy.*] Ye been prayin', Abbie?—fur a son? —t' us?

Abbie: [*With a grim resolution.*] I want a son now.

Cabot: [*Excitedly clutching both of her hands in his.*] It'd be the blessin' o' God, Abbie—the blessin' o' God A'-mighty on me—in my old age—in my lonesomeness! They hain't nothin' I wouldn't do fur ye then, Abbie. Ye'd hev on'y t' ask it—anythin' ye'd a mind t'!

Abbie: [*Interrupting.*] Would ye will the farm t' me then—t' me an' it . . . ?

Cabot: [*Vehemently.*] I'd do anythin' ye

axed, I tell ye! I swar it! May I be everlastin' damned t' hell if I wouldn't! [He sinks to his knees pulling her down with him. He trembles all over with the fervor of his hopes.] Pray t' the Lord agen, Abbie. It's the Sabbath! I'll jine ye! Two prayers air better nor one. "An' God hearkened unto Rachel"! An' God hearkened unto Abbie! Pray, Abbie! Pray fur him to hearken! [He bows his head, mumbling. She pretends to do likewise but gives him a side glance of scorn and triumph.]

Scene II

*About eight in the evening. The interior of the two bedrooms on the top floor is shown—***Eben** *is sitting on the side of his bed in the room on the left. On account of the heat he has taken off everything but his undershirt and pants. His feet are bare. He faces front, brooding moodily, his chin propped on his hands, a desperate expression on his face.*

In the other room **Cabot** *and* **Abbie** *are sitting side by side on the edge of their bed, an old four-poster with feather mattress. He is in his night shirt, she in her nightdress. He is still in the queer, excited mood into which the notion of a son has thrown him. Both rooms are lighted dimly and flickeringly by tallow candles.*

Cabot: The farm needs a son.

Abbie: I need a son.

Cabot: Ay-eh. Sometimes ye air the farm an' sometimes the farm be yew. That's why I clove t' ye in my lonesomeness. [*A pause. He pounds his knee with his fist.*] Me an' the farm has got t' beget a son!

Abbie: Ye'd best go t' sleep. Ye're gittin' thin's all mixed.

Cabot: [*With an impatient gesture.*] No, I hain't. My mind's clear's a well. Ye don't know me, that's it. [*He stares hopelessly at the floor.*]

Abbie: [*Indifferently.*] Mebbe. [*In the next room* **Eben** *gets up and paces up and down distractedly.* **Abbie** *hears him. Her eyes fasten on the interven-*ing wall with concentrated attention. **Eben** *stops and stares. Their hot glances seem to meet through the wall. Unconsciously he stretches out his arms for her and she half rises. Then aware, he mutters a curse at himself and flings himself face downward on the bed, his clenched fists above his head, his face buried in the pillow.* **Abbie** *relaxes with a faint sigh but her eyes remain fixed on the wall; she listens with all her attention for some movement from* **Eben.**]

Cabot: [*Suddenly raises his head and looks at her— scornfully.*] Will ye ever know me—'r will any man 'r woman? [*Shaking his head.*] No. I calc'late 't wa'n't t' be. [*He turns away.* **Abbie** *looks at the wall. Then, evidently unable to keep silent about his thoughts, without looking at his wife, he puts out his hand and clutches her knee. She starts violently, looks at him, sees he is not watching her, concentrates again on the wall and pays no attention to what he says.*] Listen, Abbie. When I come here fifty odd year ago— I was jest twenty an' the strongest an' hardest ye ever seen—ten times as strong an' fifty times as hard as Eben. Waal —this place was nothin' but fields o' stones. Folks laughed when I tuk it. They couldn't know what I knowed. When ye kin make corn sprout out o' stones, God's livin' in yew! They wa'n't strong enuf fur that! They reckoned God was easy. They laughed. They don't laugh no more. Some died hereabouts. Some went West an' died. They're all under ground—fur follerin' arter an easy God. God hain't easy. [*He shakes his head slowly.*] An' I growed hard. Folks kept allus sayin' he's a hard man like 'twas sinful t' be hard, so's at last I said back at 'em: Waal then, by thunder, ye'll git me hard an' see how ye like it! [*Then suddenly.*] But I give in t' weakness once. 'Twas arter I'd been here two year. I got weak—despairful—they was so many stones. They was a party leavin', givin' up, goin' West. I jined 'em. We tracked on 'n' on. We come t' broad medders, plains, whar the soil was black an' rich as gold. Nary a stone. Easy. Ye'd on'y to plow an' sow an' then set an' smoke yer pipe an' watch thin's grow. I could o' been a rich man—but somethin' in me fit me an' fit me—the voice o' God sayin': "This hain't wurth nothin' t' Me. Get ye back t' hum!" I got afeered o' that voice an' I lit out back t' hum here, leavin' my claim an' crops t' whoever'd a mind t' take 'em. Ay-eh. I actoolly give up what was rightful mine! God's hard, not easy! God's in the stones! Build my church on a rock —out o' stones an' I'll be in them! That's what He meant t' Peter! [He sighs heavily—a pause.] Stones. I picked 'em up an' piled 'em into walls. Ye kin read the years o' my life in them walls, every day a hefted stone, climbin' over the hills up and down, fencin' in the fields that was mine, whar I'd made thin's grow out o' nothin—like the will o' God, like the servant o' His hand. It wa'n't easy. It was hard an' He made me hard fur it. [He pauses.] All the time I kept gittin' lonesomer. I tuk a wife. She bore Simeon an' Peter. She was a good woman. She wuked hard. We was married twenty year. She never knowed me. She helped but she never knowed what she was helpin'. I was allus lonesome. She died. After that it wa'n't so lonesome fur a spell. [A pause.] I lost count o' the years. I had no time t' fool away countin' 'em. Sim an' Peter helped. The farm growed. It was all mine! When I thought o' that I didn't feel lonesome. [A pause.] But ye can't hitch yer mind t' one thin' day an' night. I tuk another wife—Eben's Maw. Her folks was contestin' me at law over my deeds t' the farm—my farm! That's

why Eben keeps a-talkin' his fool talk o' this bein' his Maw's farm. She bore Eben. She was purty—but soft. She tried t' be hard. She couldn't. She never knowed me nor nothin'. It was lonesomer 'n hell with her. After a matter o' sixteen odd years, she died. [A pause.] I lived with the boys. They hated me 'cause I was hard. I hated them 'cause they was soft. They coveted the farm without knowin' what it meant. It made me bitter 'n wormwood. It aged me—them coveting what I'd made fur mine. Then this spring the call come—the voice o' God cryin' in my wilderness, in my lonesomeness—t' go out an' seek an' find! [Turning to her with strange passion.] I sought ye an' I found ye! Yew air my Rose o' Sharon! Yer eyes air like. . . . [She has turned a blank face, resentful eyes to his. He stares at her for a moment—then harshly.] Air ye any the wiser fur all I've told ye?

Abbie: [Confusedly.] Mebbe.

Cabot: [Pushing her away from him—angrily.] Ye don't know nothin'—nor never will. If ye don't hev a son t' redeem ye . . . [This in a tone of cold threat.]

Abbie: [Resentfully.] I've prayed, hain't I?

Cabot: [Bitterly.] Pray agen—fur understandin'!

Abbie: [A veiled threat in her tone.] Ye'll have a son out o' me, I promise ye.

Cabot: How can ye promise?

Abbie: I got second-sight mebbe. I kin foretell. [She gives a queer smile.]

Cabot: I believe ye have. Ye give me the chills sometimes. [He shivers.] It's cold in this house. It's oneasy. They's thin's pokin' about in the dark—in the corners. [He pulls on his trousers, tucking in his night shirt, and pulls on his boots.]

Abbie: [Surprised.] Whar air ye goin'?

Cabot: [Queerly.] Down whar it's restful —whar it's warm—down t' the barn. [Bitterly.] I kin talk t' the cows. They know. They know the farm an' me. They'll give me peace. [*He turns to go out the door.*]

Abbie: [*A bit frightenedly.*] Air ye ailin' tonight, Ephraim?

Cabot: Growin'. Growin' ripe on the bough. [*He turns and goes, his boots clumping down the stairs.* **Eben** *sits up with a start, listening.* **Abbie** *is conscious of his movement and stares at the wall.* **Cabot** *comes out of the house around the corner and stands by the gate, blinking at the sky. He stretches up his hands in a tortured gesture.*] God A'mighty, call from the dark! [*He listens as if expecting an answer. Then his arms drop, he shakes his head and plods off toward the barn.*]

> **Eben** and **Abbie** *stare at each other through the wall.* **Eben** *sighs heavily and* **Abbie** *echoes it. Both become terribly nervous, uneasy. Finally* **Abbie** *gets up and listens, her ear to the wall. He acts as if he saw every move she was making, he becomes resolutely still. She seems driven into a decision —goes out the door in rear determinedly. His eyes follow her. Then as the door of his room is opened softly, he turns away, waits in an attitude of strained fixity.* **Abbie** *stands for a second staring at him, her eyes burning with desire. Then with a little cry she runs over and throws her arms about his neck, she pulls his head back and covers his mouth with kisses. At first, he submits dumbly; then he puts his arms about her neck and returns her kisses, but finally, suddenly aware of his hatred, he hurls her away from him, springing to his feet. They stand speechless and breathless, panting like two animals.*]

Abbie: [*At last—painfully.*] Ye shouldn't, Eben—ye shouldn't—I'd make ye happy!

Eben: [*Harshly.*] I don't want t' be happy —from yew!

Abbie: [*Helplessly.*] Ye do, Eben! Ye do! Why d'ye lie?

Eben: [*Viciously.*] I don't take t'ye, I tell ye! I hate the sight o' ye!

Abbie: [*With an uncertain troubled laugh.*] Waal, I kissed ye anyways— an' ye kissed back—yer lips was burnin'—ye can't lie 'bout that! [*Intensely.*] If ye don't care, why did ye kiss me back—why was yer lips burnin'?

Eben: [*Wiping his mouth.*] It was like pizen on 'em [*Then tauntingly.*] When I kissed ye back, mebbe I thought 'twas someone else.

Abbie: [*Wildly.*] Min?

Eben: Mebbe.

Abbie: [*Torturedly.*] Did ye go t' see her? Did ye r'ally go? I thought ye mightn't. Is that why ye throwed me off jest now?

Eben: [*Sneeringly.*] What if it be?

Abbie: [*Raging.*] Then ye're a dog, Eben Cabot!

Eben: [*Threateningly.*] Ye can't talk that way t' me!

Abbie: [*With a shrill laugh.*] Can't I? Did ye think I was in love with ye—a weak thin' like yew? Not much! I on'y wanted ye fur a purpose o' my own—an' I'll hev ye fur it yet 'cause I'm stronger'n yew be!

Eben: [*Resentfully.*] I knowed well it was on'y part o' yer plan t' swaller everythin'!

Abbie: [*Tauntingly.*] Mebbe!

Eben: [*Furious.*] Git out o' my room!

Abbie: This air my room an' ye're on'y hired help!

Eben: [*Threateningly.*] Git out afore I murder ye!

Abbie: [*Quite confident now.*] I hain't a mite afeerd. Ye want me, don't ye? Yes, ye do! An' yer Paw's son'll never kill what he wants! Look at yer eyes! They's lust fur me in 'em, burnin' 'em up! Look at yer lips now! They're tremblin' an' longin' t' kiss me, an' yer teeth t' bite. [*He is watching her now with a horrible fascination. She laughs a crazy triumphant laugh.] I'm a-goin' t' make all o' this hum my hum! They's one room hain't mine yet, but it's a-goin' t' be tonight. I'm a-going' down now an' light up! [She makes him a mocking bow.] Won't ye come courtin' me in the best parlor, Mister Cabot?

Eben: [Staring at her—horribly confused —dully.] Don't ye dare! It hain't been opened since Maw died an' was laid out thar! Don't ye . . . ! [But her eyes are fixed on his so burningly that his will seems to wither before hers. He stands swaying toward her helplessly.]

Abbie: [Holding his eyes and putting all her will into her words as she backs out the door.] I'll expect ye afore long, Eben.

Eben: [Stares after her for a while, walking toward the door. A light appears in the parlor window. He murmurs.] In the parlor? [This seems to arouse connotations for he comes back and puts on his white shirt, collar, half ties the tie mechanically, puts on coat, takes his hat, stands barefooted looking about him in bewilderment, mutters wonderingly.] Maw! Whar air yew? [Then goes slowly toward the door in rear.]

Scene III

A few minutes later. The interior of the parlor is shown. A grim, repressed room like a tomb in which the family has been interred alive. **Abbie** sits on the edge of the horsehair sofa. She has lighted all the candles and the room is revealed in all its preserved ugliness. A change has come over the woman. She looks awed and frightened now, ready to run away. [The door is opened and **Eben** appears. His face wears an expression of obsessed confusion. He stands staring at her, his arms hanging disjointedly from his shoulders, his feet bare, his hat in his hand.]

Abbie: [After a pause—with a nervous, formal politeness.] Won't ye set?

Eben: [Dully.] Ay-eh. [Mechanically he places his hat carefully on the floor near the door and sits stiffly beside her on the edge of the sofa. A pause. They both remain rigid, looking straight ahead with eyes full of fear.]

Abbie: When I fust come in—in the dark —they seemed somethin' here.

Eben: [Simply.] Maw.

Abbie: I kin still feel—somethin'. . . .

Eben: It's Maw.

Abbie: At fust I was feered o' it. I wanted t' yell an' run. Now—since yew come —seems like it's growin' soft an' kind t' me. [Addressing the air—queerly.] Thank yew.

Eben: Maw allus loved me.

Abbie: Mebbe it knows I love yew too. Mebbe that makes it kind t' me.

Eben: [Dully.] I dunno. I should think she'd hate ye.

Abbie: [With certainty.] No. I kin feel it don't—not no more.

Eben: Hate ye fur stealin' her place— here in her hum—settin' in her parlor whar she was laid—[He suddenly stops, staring stupidly before him.]

Abbie: What is it, Eben?

Eben: [In a whisper.] Seems like Maw didn't want me t' remind ye.

Abbie: [Excitedly.] I knowed, Eben! It's kind t' me! It don't b'ar me no grudges fur what I never knowed an' couldn't help!

Eben: Maw b'ars him a grudge.

Abbie: Waal, so does all o' us.

Eben: Ay-eh. [With passion.] I does, by God!

Abbie: [Taking one of his hands in hers and patting it.] Thar! Don't git riled thinkin' o' him. Think o' yer Maw who's kind t' us. Tell me about yer Maw, Eben.

Eben: They hain't nothin' much. She was kind. She was good.

Abbie: [Putting one arm over his shoulder. He does not seem to notice— passionately.] I'll be kind an' good t' ye!

Eben: Sometimes she used t' sing fur me.

Abbie: I'll sing fur ye!

Eben: This was her hum. This was her farm.

Abbie: This is my hum! This is my farm!

Eben: He married her t' steal 'em. She was soft an' easy. He couldn't 'preciate her.

Abbie: He can't 'preciate me!

Eben: He murdered her with his hardness.

Abbie: He's murderin' me!

Eben: She died. [A pause.] Sometimes she used to sing fur me. [He bursts into a fit of sobbing.]

Abbie: [Both her arms around him—with wild passion.] I'll sing fur ye! I'll die fur ye! [In spite of her overwhelming desire for him, there is a sincere maternal love in her manner and voice—a horribly frank mixture of lust and mother love.] Don't cry, Eben! I'll take yer Maw's place! I'll be everythin' she was t' ye! Let me kiss ye, Eben! [She pulls his head around. He makes a bewildered pretense of resistance. She is tender.] Don't be afeered! I'll kiss ye pure, Eben— same 's if I was a Maw t' ye—an' ye kin kiss me back 's if yew was my son—my boy—sayin' good-night t' me! Kiss me, Eben. [They kiss in restrained fashion. Then suddenly wild passion overcomes her. She kisses him lustfully again and again and he flings his arms about her and returns her kisses. Suddenly, as in the bedroom, he frees himself from her violently and springs to his feet. He is trembling all over, in a strange state of terror. **Abbie** strains her arms toward him with fierce pleading.] Don't ye leave me, Eben! Can't ye see it hain't enuf—lovin' ye like a Maw— can't ye see it's got t' be that an' more —much more—a hundred times more —fur me t' be happy—fur yew t' be happy?

Eben: [To the presence he feels in the room.] Maw! Maw! What d'ye want? What air ye tellin' me?

Abbie: She's tellin' ye t' love me. She knows I love ye an' I'll be good t' ye. Can't ye feel it? Don't ye know? She's tellin' ye t' love me, Eben!

Eben: Ay-eh. I feel—mebbe she—but—I can't figger out—why—when ye've stole her place—here in her hum— in the parlor whar she was—

Abbie: [Fiercely.] She knows I love ye!

Eben: [His face suddenly lighting up with a fierce triumphant grin.] I see it! I sees why. It's her vengeance on him— so's she kin rest quiet in her grave!

Abbie: [Wildly.] Vengeance o' God on the hull o' us! What d'we give a durn? I love ye, Eben! God knows I love ye! [She stretches out her arms for him.]

Eben: [Throws himself on his knees beside the sofa and grabs her in his arms—releasing all his pent-up passion.] An' I love yew, Abbie!— now I kin say it! I been dyin' fur want o' ye—every hour since ye come! I love ye! [Their lips meet in a fierce, bruising kiss.]

Scene IV

Exterior of the farmhouse. It is just dawn. The front door at right is opened and **Eben** comes out and walks around to the gate. He is dressed in his working clothes. He seems changed. His face wears a bold and confident expression, he is grinning to himself with evident satisfaction. As he gets near the gate, the window of the parlor is heard opening and the shutters are flung back and **Abbie** sticks her head out. Her hair tumbles over her shoulders in disarray, her face is flushed, she looks at **Eben** with tender, languorous eyes and calls softly.

Abbie: Eben. [As he turns—playfully.] Jest one more kiss afore ye go. I'm goin' to miss ye fearful all day.

Eben: An' me yew, ye kin bet! [He goes to her. They kiss several times. He draws away, laughingly.] Thar. That's enuf, hain't it? Ye won't hev none left fur next time.

Abbie: I got a million o' 'em left fur yew!

[*Then a bit anxiously.*] D'ye r'ally love me, Eben?

Eben: [*Emphatically.*] I like ye better'n any gal I ever knowed! That's gospel!

Abbie: Likin' hain't lovin'.

Eben: Waal then—I love ye. Now air yew satisfied?

Abbie: Ay-eh, I be. [*She smiles at him adoringly.*]

Eben: I better git t' the barn. The old critter's liable t' suspicion an' come sneakin' up.

Abbie: [*With a confident laugh.*] Let him! I kin allus pull the wool over his eyes. I'm goin' t' leave the shutters open and let in the sun 'n' air. This room's been dead long enuf. Now it's goin' t' be my room!

Eben: [*Frowning.*] Ay-eh.

Abbie: [*Hastily.*] I meant—our room.

Eben: Ay-eh.

Abbie: We made it our'n last night, didn't we? We give it life—our lovin' did. [*A pause.*]

Eben: [*With a strange look.*] Maw's gone back t' her grave. She kin sleep now.

Abbie: May she rest in peace! [*Then tenderly rebuking.*] Ye oughtn't t' talk o' sad thin's—this mornin'.

Eben: It jest come up in my mind o' itself.

Abbie: Don't let it. [*He doesn't answer. She yawns.*] Waal, I'm a-goin' t' steal a wink o' sleep. I'll tell the Old Man I hain't feelin' pert. Let him git his own vittles.

Eben: I see him comin' from the barn. Ye better look smart an' git upstairs.

Abbie: Ay-eh. Good-by. Don't fergit me. [*She throws him a kiss. He grins— then squares his shoulders and awaits his father confidently.* **Cabot** *walks slowly up from the left, staring up at the sky with a vague face.*]

Eben: [*Jovially.*] Mornin', Paw. Star-gazin' in daylight?

Cabot: Purty, hain't it?

Eben: [*Looking around him possessively.*] It's a durned purty farm.

Cabot: I mean the sky.

Eben: [*Grinning.*] How d'ye know? Them eyes o' your'n can't see that fur. [*This tickles his humor and he slaps his thigh and laughs.*] Ho-ho! That's a good un!

Cabot: [*Grimly sarcastic.*] Ye're feelin' right chipper, hain't ye? Whar'd ye steal the likker?

Eben: [*Good-naturedly.*] 'Tain't likker. Jest life. [*Suddenly holding out his hand—soberly.*] Yew 'n' me is quits. Let's shake hands.

Cabot: [*Suspiciously.*] What's come over ye?

Eben: Then don't. Mebbe it's jest as well. [*A moment's pause.*] What's come over me? [*Queerly.*] Didn't ye feel her passin'—goin' back t' her grave?

Cabot: [*Dully.*] Who?

Eben: Maw. She kin rest now an' sleep content. She's quits with ye.

Cabot: [*Confusedly.*] I rested. I slept good—down with the cows. They know how t' sleep. They're teachin' me.

Eben: [*Suddenly jovial again.*] Good fur the cows! Waal—ye better git t' work.

Cabot: [*Grimly amused.*] Air yew bossin' me, ye calf?

Eben: [*Beginning to laugh.*] Ay-eh! I'm bossin' yew! Ha-ha-ha! see how ye like it! Ha-ha-ha! I'm the prize rooster o' this roost. Ha-ha-ha! [*He goes off toward the barn laughing.*]

Cabot: [*Looks after him with scornful pity.*] Soft-headed. Like his Maw. Dead spit 'n' image. No hope in him! [*He spits with contemptuous disgust.*] A born fool! [*Then matter-of-factly.*] Waal—I'm gittin' peckish. [*He goes toward door.*]

CURTAIN

Part Three

Scene I

A night in late spring the following year. The kitchen and the two bedrooms up-stairs are shown. The two bedrooms are dimly lighted by a tallow candle in each. **Eben** *is sitting on the side of the bed in* his room, his chin propped on his fists, his face a study of the struggle he is making to understand his conflicting emotions. The noisy laughter and music from below where a kitchen dance is in progress annoy and distract him. He scowls at the floor.

In the next room a cradle stands beside the double bed.

In the kitchen all is festivity. The stove has been taken down to give more room to the dancers. The chairs, with wooden benches added, have been pushed back against the walls. On these are seated, squeezed in tight against one another, farmers and their wives and their young folks of both sexes from the neighboring farms. They are all chattering and laughing loudly. They evidently have some secret joke in common. There is no end of winking, of nudging, of meaning nods of the head toward **Cabot** who, in a state of extreme hilarious excitement increased by the amount he has drunk, is standing near the rear door where there is a small keg of whisky and serving drinks to all the men. In the left corner, front, dividing the attention with her husband, **Abbie** is sitting in a rocking chair, a shawl wrapped about her shoulders. She is very pale, her face is thin and drawn, her eyes are fixed anxiously on the open door in rear as if waiting for someone.

The Musician is tuning up his fiddle, seated in the far right corner. He is a lanky young fellow with a long, weak face. His pale eyes blink incessantly and he grins about him slyly with a greedy malice.

Abbie: [Suddenly turning to a young girl on her right.] Whar's Eben?

Young Girl: [Eyeing her scornfully.] I dunno, Mrs. Cabot. I hain't seen Eben in ages. [Meaningly.] Seems like he's spent most o' his time t' hum since yew come.

Abbie: [Vaguely.] I tuk his Maw's place.

Young Girl: Ay-eh. So I heerd. [She turns away to retail this bit of gossip to her mother sitting next to her. **Abbie** turns to her left to a big stoutish middle-aged man whose flushed face

and staring eyes show the amount of "likker" he has consumed.]

Abbie: Ye hain't seen Eben, hev ye?

Man: No, I hain't. [Then he adds with a wink.] If yew hain't, who would?

Abbie: He's the best dancer in the county. He'd ought t' come an' dance.

Man: [With a wink.] Mebbe he's doin' the dutiful an' walkin' the kid t' sleep. It's a boy, hain't it?

Abbie: [Nodding vaguely.] Ay-eh—born two weeks back—purty's a picter.

Man: They all is—t' their Maws. [Then in a whisper, with a nudge and a leer.] Listen, Abbie—if ye ever git tired o' Eben, remember me! Don't fergit now! [He looks at her uncomprehending face for a second—then grunts disgustedly.] Waal—guess I'll likker agin. [He goes over and joins **Cabot** who is arguing noisily with an old farmer over cows. They all drink.]

Abbie: [This time appealing to nobody in particular.] Wonder what Eben's a-doin'? [Her remark is repeated down the line with many a guffaw and titter until it reaches **The Fiddler**. He fastens his blinking eyes on **Abbie**.]

Fiddler: [Raising his voice.] Bet I kin tell ye, Abbie, what Eben's doin'! He's down t' the church offerin' up prayers o' thanksgivin.'

[They all titter expectantly.]

Man: What fur?

[Another titter.]

Fiddler: 'Cause unto him a—[He hesitates just long enough.]—brother is born! [A roar of laughter. They all look from **Abbie** to **Cabot**. She is oblivious, staring at the door. **Cabot**, although he hasn't heard the words, is irritated by the laughter and steps forward, glaring about him. There is an immediate silence.]

Cabot: What're ye all bleatin' about— like a flock o' goats? Why don't ye dance, damn ye? I axed ye here t' dance—t' eat, drink an' be merry— an' thar ye set cacklin' like a lot o' wet hens with the pip! Ye've swilled my likker an' guzzled my vittles like hogs, hain't ye? Then dance fur me, can't ye? That's fa'r an' squar', hain't it?

[A grumble of resentment goes around but they are all evidently in too much awe of him to express it openly.]

Fiddler: [Slyly.] We're waitin' fur Eben. [A suppressed laugh.]

Cabot: [With a fierce exultation.] T'hell with Eben! Eben's done fur now! I got a new son! [His mood switching with drunken suddenness.] But ye needn't t' laugh at Eben, none o' ye! He's my blood, if he be a dumb fool. He's better nor any o' yew! He kin do a day's work a'most up t' what I kin —an' that'd put any o' yew pore critters t' shame!

Fiddler: An' he kin do a good night's work, too! [A roar of laughter.]

Cabot: Laugh, ye damn fools! Ye're right jist the same, Fiddler. He kin work day an' night too, like I kin, if need be!

Old Farmer: [From behind the keg where he is weaving drunkenly back and forth—with great simplicity.] They hain't many t' touch ye, Ephraim—a son at seventy-six. That's a hard man fur ye! I be on'y sixty-eight an' I couldn't do it. [A roar of laughter in which **Cabot** joins uproariously.]

Cabot: [Slapping him on the back.] I'm sorry fur ye, Hi. I'd never suspicion sech weakness from a boy like yew!

Old Farmer: An' I never reckoned yew had it in ye nuther, Ephraim.

[There is another laugh.]

Cabot: [Suddenly grim.] I got a lot in me —a hell of a lot—folks don't know on. [Turning to **The Fiddler**.] Fiddle 'er up, durn ye! Give 'em somethin' t' dance t'! What air ye, an ornament? Hain't this a celebration? Then grease yer elbow an' go it!

Fiddler: [Seizes a drink which the **Old Farmer** holds out to him and downs it.] Here goes!

[He starts to fiddle "Lady of the Lake." Four young fellows and four girls form in two lines and dance a square dance. **The Fiddler** shouts directions for the different movements, keeping his words in the rhythm of the music and interspersing them with jocular personal remarks to the dancers themselves. The people seated along the walls stamp their feet and clap their hands in unison. **Cabot** is especially active in this respect. Only **Abbie** remains apathetic, staring at the door as if she were alone in a silent room.]

Fiddler: Swing your partner t' the right! That's it, Jim! Give her a b'ar hug! Her Maw hain't lookin'. [Laughter.] Change partners! That suits ye, don't it, Essie, now ye got Reub afore ye? Look at her redden up, will ye! Waal, life is short an' so's love, as the feller says.

[Laughter.]

Cabot: [Excitedly, stamping his foot.] Go it, boys! Go it, gals!

Fiddler: [With a wink at the others.] Ye're the spryest seventy-six ever I sees, Ephraim! Now if ye'd on'y good eye-sight ...! [Suppressed laughter. He gives **Cabot** no chance to retort but roars.] Promenade! Ye're walkin' like a bride down the aisle, Sarah! Waal, while they's life they's allus hope. I've heerd tell. Swing your partner to the left! Gosh A'mighty, look at Johnny Cook high-steppin'! They hain't goin' t' be much strength left fur howin' in the corn lot t'morrow. [Laughter.]

Cabot: Go it! Go it! [Then suddenly, unable to restrain himself any longer, he prances into the midst of the dancers, scattering them, waving his arms about wildly.] Ye're all hoofs! Git out o' my road! Give me room! I'll show ye dancin'. Ye're all too soft! [He pushes them roughly away. They crowd back toward the walls, muttering, looking at him resentfully.]

Fiddler: [Jeeringly.] Go it, Ephraim! Go it! [He starts "Pop Goes the Weasel," increasing the tempo with every verse until at the end he is fiddling crazily as fast as he can go.]

Cabot: [Starts to dance, which he does very well and with tremendous vigor. Then he begins to improvise, cuts incredibly grotesque capers, leaping up and cracking his heels together, prancing around in a circle with body bent in an Indian war dance, then suddenly straightening up and kicking as high as he can with both legs. He is like a monkey on a string. And all the while he intersperses his antics with shouts and derisive comments.] Whoop! Here's dancin' fur ye! Whoop! See that! Seventy-six, if I'm a day! Hard as iron yet! Beatin' the young 'uns like I allus done! Look at me! I'd invite ye t' dance on my hundredth birthday on'y ye'll all be dead by then. Ye're a sickly generation! Yer hearts air pink, not red! Yer veins is full o' mud an' water! I be the on'y man in the county! Whoop! See that! I'm a Injun! I've killed Injuns in the West afore ye was born —an' skulped 'em too! They's a arrer wound on my backside I c'd show ye! The hull tribe chased me. I outrun 'em all—with the arrer stuck in me! An' I tuk vengeance on 'em. Ten eyes fur an eye, that was my motter! Whoop! Look at me! I kin kick the ceilin' off the room! Whoop!

Fiddler: [Stops playing—exhaustedly.] God A'mighty, I got enuf. Ye got the devil's strength in ye.

Cabot: [Delightedly.] Did I beat yew, too? Wa'al, ye played smart. Hev a swig. [He pours whisky for himself and **Fiddler**. They drink. The others watch **Cabot** silently with cold, hostile eyes. There is a dead pause. **The Fiddler** rests. **Cabot** leans against the keg, panting, glaring around him confusedly. In the room above, **Eben** gets to his feet and tiptoes out the door in rear, appearing a moment later in the other bedroom. He moves silently, even frightenedly, toward the cradle

and stands there looking down at the baby. His face is as vague as his reactions are confused, but there is a trace of tenderness, of interested discovery. At the same moment that he reaches the cradle, **Abbie** seems to sense something. She gets up weakly and goes to **Cabot**.]

Abbie: I'm goin' up t' the baby.

Cabot: [With real solicitude.] Air ye able fur the stairs? D'ye want me t' help ye, Abbie?

Abbie: No. I'm able. I'll be down agen soon.

Cabot: Don't ye git wore out! He needs ye, remember—our son does! [He grins affectionately, patting her on the back. She shrinks from his touch.]

Abbie: [Dully.] Don't—tech me. I'm goin' —up. [She goes. **Cabot** looks after her. A whisper goes around the room. **Cabot** turns. It ceases. He wipes his forehead streaming with sweat. He is breathing pantingly.]

Cabot: I'm a-goin' out t' git fresh air. I'm feelin' a mite dizzy. Fiddle up thar! Dance, all o' ye! Here's likker fur them as wants it. Enjoy yerselves. I'll be back. [He goes, closing the door behind him.]

Fiddler: [Sarcastically.] Don't hurry none on our account! [A suppressed laugh. He imitates **Abbie**.] Whar's Eben? [More laughter.]

A Woman: [Loudly.] What's happened in this house is plain as the nose on yer face! [**Abbie** appears in the doorway upstairs and stands looking in surprise and adoration at **Eben** who does not see her.]

A Man: Ssshh! He's li'ble t' be listenin' at the door. That'd be like him.

[Their voices die to an intensive whispering. Their faces are concentrated on this gossip. A noise as of dead leaves in the wind comes from the room. **Cabot** has come out from the porch and stands by the gate, leaning on it, staring at the sky blinkingly. **Abbie** comes across the room silently. **Eben** does not notice her until quite near.]

Eben: [Starting.] Abbie!

Abbie: Ssshh! [She throws her arms around him. They kiss—then bend over the cradle together.] Ain't he purty?—dead spit 'n' image o' yew!

Eben: [Pleased.] Air he? I can't tell none.

Abbie: E-zactly like!

Eben: [Frowningly.] I don't like this. I don't like lettin' on what's mine's his'n. I been doin' that all my life. I'm gittin' t' the end o' b'arin' it!

Abbie: [Putting her finger on his lips.] We're doin' the best we kin. We got t' wait. Somethin's bound t' happen. [She puts her arms around him.] I got t' go back.

Eben: I'm goin' out. I can't b'ar it with the fiddle playin' an' the laughin'.

Abbie: Don't git feelin' low. I love ye, Eben. Kiss me. [He kisses her. They remain in each other's arms.]

Cabot: [At the gate, confusedly.] Even the music can't drive it out—somethin'. Ye kin feel it droppin' off the elums, climbin' up the roof, sneakin' down the chimney, pokin' in the corners! They's no peace in houses, they's no rest livin' with folks. Somethin's always livin' with ye. [With a deep sigh.] I'll go t' the barn an' rest a spell. [He goes wearily toward the barn.]

Fiddler: [Tuning up.] Let's celebrate the old skunk gittin' fooled! We kin have some fun now he's went. [He starts to fiddle "Turkey in the Straw." There is real merriment now. The young folks get up to dance.]

Scene II

A half hour later—exterior—**Eben** is standing by the gate looking up at the sky, an expression of dumb pain bewildered by itself on his face. **Cabot** appears, returning from the barn, walking wearily, his eyes on the ground. He sees **Eben** and his whole mood immediately changes. He becomes excited, a cruel,

triumphant grin comes to his lips, he strides up and slaps **Eben** on the back. From within comes the whining of the fiddle and the noise of stamping feet and laughing voices.

Cabot: So har ye be!

Eben: [Startled, stares at him with hatred for a moment—then dully.] Ay-eh.

Cabot: [Surveying him jeeringly.] Why hain't ye been in t' dance? They was all axin' fur ye.

Eben: Let 'em ax!

Cabot: They's a hull passel o' purty gals.

Eben: T' hell with 'em!

Cabot: Ye'd ought t' be marryin' one o' 'em soon.

Eben: I hain't marryin' no one.

Cabot: Ye might 'arn a share o' a farm that way.

Eben: [With a sneer.] Like yew did, ye mean? I hain't that kind.

Cabot: [Stung.] Ye lie! 'Twas yer Maw's folks aimed t' steal my farm from me.

Eben: Other folks don't say so. [After a pause—defiantly.] An' I got a farm, anyways!

Cabot: [Derisively.] Whar?

Eben: [Stamps a foot on the ground.] Har!

Cabot: [Throws his head back and laughs coarsely.] Ho-ho! Ye hev, hev ye? Waal, that's a good un!

Eben: [Controlling himself—grimly.] Ye'll see!

Cabot: [Stares at him suspiciously, trying to make him out—a pause—then with scornful confidence.] Ay-eh. I'll see. So'll ye. It's ye that's blind—blind as a mole underground. [**Eben** suddenly laughs, one short sardonic bark: "Ha." A pause. **Cabot** peers at him with renewed suspicion.] Whar air ye hawin' 'bout? [**Eben** turns away without answering. **Cabot** grows angry.] God A'mighty, yew air a dumb dunce! They's nothin' in that thick skull o' your'n but noise—like a empty keg it be! [**Eben** doesn't seem to hear—**Cabot's** rage grows.] Yewr farm! God A'mighty! If ye wa'n't a born donkey ye'd know ye'll never own stick nor stone on it, specially now arter him bein' born. It's his'n, I tell ye—his'n arter I die—but I'll live a hundred jest t' fool ye all—an' he'll be growed then—yewr age a'most! [**Eben** *laughs again his sardonic "Ha." This drives* **Cabot** *into a fury.*] Ha? Ye think ye kin git 'round that someways, do ye? Waal, it'll be her'n, too—Abbie's—ye won't git 'round her—she knows yer tricks—she'll be too much fur ye— she wants the farm her'n—she was afeerd o' ye—she told me ye was sneakin' 'round tryin' t' make love t' her 't git her on yer side . . . ye . . . ye mad fool, ye! [*He raises his clenched fists threateningly.*]

Eben: [*Is confronting him choking with rage.*] Ye lie, ye old skunk! Abbie never said no sech thing!

Cabot: [*Suddenly triumphant when he sees how shaken* **Eben** *is.*] She did. An' I says, I'll blow his brains t' the top o' them elums—an' she says no, that hain't sense, who'll ye git t' help ye on the farm in his place—an' then she says yew'n me ought t' have a son—I know we kin, she says—an' I says, if we do, ye kin have anythin' I've got ye've a mind t'. An' she says, I wants Eben cut off so's this farm'll be mine when ye die! [*With terrible gloating.*] An' that's what's happened, hain't it? An' the farm's her'n! An' the dust o' the road—that's you'rn! Ha! Now who's hawin'?

Eben: [*Has been listening, petrified with grief and rage—suddenly laughs wildly and brokenly.*] Ha-ha-ha! So that's her sneakin' game—all along!— like I suspicioned at fust—t' swaller it all—an' me, too . . . ! [*Madly.*] I'll murder her! [*He springs toward the porch but* **Cabot** *is quicker and gets in between.*]

Cabot: No, ye don't!

Eben: Git out o' my road! [*He tries to throw* **Cabot** *aside. They grapple in what becomes immediately a murderous struggle. The old man's concentrated strength is too much for* **Eben.**

Cabot *gets one hand on his throat and presses him back across the stone wall. At the same moment,* **Abbie** *comes out on the porch. With a stifled cry she runs toward them.*]

Abbie: Eben! Ephraim! [*She tugs at the hand on* **Eben's** *throat.*] Let go, Ephraim! Ye're chokin' him!

Cabot: [*Removes his hand and flings* **Eben** *sideways full length on the grass, gasping and choking. With a cry,* **Abbie** *kneels beside him, trying to take his head on her lap, but he pushes her away.* **Cabot** *stands looking down with fierce triumph.*] Ye needn't t've fret, Abbie, I wa'n't aimin' t' kill him. He hain't wuth hangin' fur—not by a hell of a sight! [*More and more triumphantly.*] Seventy-six an' him not thirty yit— an' look whar he be fur thinkin' his Paw was easy! No, by God, I hain't easy! An' him upstairs, I'll raise him t' be like me! [*He turns to leave them.*] I'm goin' in an' dance!—sing an' celebrate! [*He walks to the porch—then turns with a great grin.*] I don't calc'late it's left in him, but if he gits pesky, Abbie, ye jest sing out. I'll come a-runnin' an' by the Etarnal, I'll put him across my knee and birch him! Ha-ha-ha! [*He goes into the house laughing. A moment later his loud "whoop" is heard.*]

Abbie: [*Tenderly.*] Eben. Air ye hurt? [*She tries to kiss him but he pushes her violently away and struggles to a sitting position.*]

Eben: [*Gaspingly.*] T'hell—with ye!

Abbie: [*Not believing her ears.*] It's me, Eben—Abbie—don't ye know me?

Eben: [*Glowering at her with hatred.*] Ay-eh—I know ye—now! [*He suddenly breaks down, sobbing weakly.*]

Abbie: [*Fearfully.*] Eben—what's happened t' ye—why did ye look at me 's if ye hated me?

Eben: [*Violently, between sobs and gasps.*] I do hate ye! Ye're a whore—a damn trickin' whore!

Abbie: [Shrinking back horrified.] Eben! Ye don't know what ye're sayin'!

Eben: [Scrambling to his feet and following her—accusingly.] Ye're nothin' but a stinkin' passel o' lies! Ye've been lyin' t' me every word ye spoke, day an' night, since we fust—done it. Ye've kept sayin' ye loved me. . . .

Abbie: [Frantically.] I do love ye! [She takes his hand but he flings hers away.]

Eben: [Unheeding.] Ye've made a fool o' me—a sick, dumb fool—a-purpose! Ye've been on'y playin' yer sneakin', stealin' game all along—gittin' me t' lie with ye so's ye'd hev a son he'd think was his'n, an' makin' him promise he'd give ye the farm and let me eat dust, if ye did git him a son! [Staring at her with anguished, bewildered eyes.] They must be a devil livin' in ye! 'Tain't human t' be as bad as that be!

Abbie: [Stunned—dully.] He told yew . . . ?

Eben: Hain't it true? It hain't no good in yew lyin'.

Abbie: [Pleadingly.] Eben, listen—ye must listen—it was long ago—afore we done nothin'—yew was scornin' me—goin' t' see Min—when I was lovin' ye—an' I said it t' him t' git vengeance on ye!

Eben: [Unheedingly. With tortured passion.] I wish ye was dead! I wish I was dead along with ye afore this come! [Ragingly.] But I'll git my vengeance too! I'll pray Maw t' come back t' help me—t' put her cuss on yew an' him!

Abbie: [Brokenly.] Don't ye, Eben! Don't ye! [She throws herself on her knees before him, weeping.] I didn't mean t' do bad t'ye! Fergive me, won't ye?

Eben: [Not seeming to hear her—fiercely.] I'll git squar' with the old skunk —an' yew! I'll tell him the truth 'bout the son he's so proud o'! Then I'll leave ye here t' pizen each other— with Maw comin' out o' her grave at nights—an' I'll go t' the gold fields o' Californi-a whar Sim an' Peter be!

Abbie: [Terrified.] Ye won't—leave me? Ye can't!

Eben: [With fierce determination.] I'm a-goin', I tell ye! I'll git rich thar an' come back an' fight him fur the farm he stole—an' I'll kick ye both out in the road—t' beg an' sleep in the woods—an' yer son along with ye—t' starve an' die! [He is hysterical at the end.]

Abbie: [With a shudder—humbly.] He's yewr son, too, Eben.

Eben: [Torturedly.] I wish he never was born! I wish he'd die this minit! I wish I'd never sot eyes on him! It's him— yew havin' him—a-purpose t' steal— that's changed everythin'!

Abbie: [Gently.] Did ye believe I loved ye—afore he come?

Eben: Ay-eh—like a dumb ox!

Abbie: An' ye don't believe no more?

Eben: B'lieve a lyin' thief! Ha!

Abbie: [Shudders—then humbly.] An did ye r'ally love me afore?

Eben: [Brokenly.] Ay-eh—an' ye was trickin' me!

Abbie: An' ye don't love me now!

Eben: [Violently.] I hate ye, I tell ye!

Abbie: An' ye're truly goin' West—goin' t' leave me—all account o' him being born?

Eben: I'm a-goin' in the mornin'—or may God strike me t' hell!

Abbie: [After a pause—with a dreadful cold intensity—slowly.] If that's what his comin's done t' me—killin' yewr love—takin' yew away—my on'y joy —the on'y joy I've ever knowed—like heaven t' me—purtier'n heaven— then I hate him, too, even if I be his Maw!

Eben: [Bitterly.] Lies! Ye love him! He'll steal the farm fur ye! [Brokenly.] But 'tain't the farm so much—not no more—it's yew foolin' me—gittin' me t' love ye—lyin' yew loved me—jest t' git a son t' steal!

Abbie: [Distractedly.] He won't steal! I'd kill him fust! I do love ye! I'll prove t' ye . . . !

Eben: [*Harshly.*] 'Tain't no use lyin' no more. I'm deaf t' ye! [*He turns away.*] I hain't seein' ye agen. Good-by!

Abbie: [*Pale with anguish.*] Hain't ye even goin' t' kiss me—not once—arter all we loved?

Eben: [*In a hard voice.*] I hain't wantin' t' kiss ye never agen! I'm wantin'' t' forget I ever sot eyes on ye!

Abbie: Eben!—ye mustn't—wait a spell —I want t' tell ye. . . .

Eben: I'm a-goin' in t' git drunk. I'm a-goin' t' dance.

Abbie: [*Clinging to his arm—with passionate earnestness.*] If I could make it—'s if he'd never come up between us—if I could prove t' ye I wa'n't schemin' t' steal from ye—so's everythin' could be jest the same with us, lovin' each other jest the same, kissin' an' happy the same's we've been happy afore he come—if I could do it —ye'd love me agen, wouldn't ye? Ye'd kiss me agen? Ye wouldn't never leave me, would ye?

Eben: [*Moved.*] I calc'late not. [*Then shaking her hand off his arm—with a bitter smile.*] But ye hain't God, be ye?

Abbie: [*Exultantly.*] Remember ye've promised! [*Then with strange intensity.*] Mebbe I kin take back one thin' God does!

Eben: [*Peering at her.*] Ye're gittin' cracked, hain't ye? [*Then going towards door.*] I'm a-goin' t' dance.

Abbie: [*Calls after him intensely.*] I'll prove t' ye! I'll prove I love ye better'n. . . . [*He goes in the door, not seeming to hear. She remains standing where she is, looking after him— then she finishes desperately.*] Better'n everythin' else in the world!

Scene III

Just before dawn in the morning—shows the kitchen and **Cabot's** *bedroom. In the kitchen, by the light of a tallow candle on the table,* **Eben** *is sitting, his chin* propped on his hands, his drawn face blank and expressionless. His carpetbag is on the floor beside him. In the bedroom, dimly lighted by a small whale-oil lamp, **Cabot** lies asleep. **Abbie** is bending over the cradle, listening, her face full of terror yet with an undercurrent of desperate triumph. Suddenly, she breaks down and sobs, appears about to throw herself on her knees beside the cradle; but the old man turns restlessly, groaning in his sleep, and she controls herself, and shrinking away from the cradle with a gesture of horror, backs swiftly toward the door in rear and goes out. A moment later she comes into the kitchen and, running to **Eben,** flings her arms about his neck and kisses him wildly. He hardens himself, he remains unmoved and cold, he keeps his eyes straight ahead.

Abbie: [*Hysterically.*] I done it, Eben! I told ye I'd do it! I've proved I love ye —better'n everythin'—so's ye can't never doubt me no more!

Eben: [*Dully.*] Whatever ye done, it hain't no good now.

Abbie: [*Wildly.*] Don't ye say that! Kiss me, Eben, won't ye? I need ye t' kiss me arter what I done! I need ye t' say ye love me!

Eben: [*Kisses her without emotion— dully.*] That's fur good-by. I'm a-goin' soon.

Abbie: No! No! Ye won't go—not now!

Eben: [*Going on with his own thoughts.*] I been a-thinkin'—an' I hain't goin' t' tell Paw nothin'. I'll leave Maw t' take vengeance on ye. If I told him, the old skunk'd jest be stinkin' mean enuf to take it out on that baby. [*His voice showing emotion in spite of him.*] An' I don't want nothin' bad t' happen t' him. He hain't t' blame fur yew. [*He adds with a certain queer pride.*] An' he looks like me! An' by God, he's mine! An' some day I'll be a-comin' back an' . . . !

Abbie: [*Too absorbed in her own thoughts to listen to him—pleadingly.*] They's no cause fur ye t' go now —they's no sense—it's all the same's it was—they's nothin' come b'tween us now—arter what I done!

Eben: [*Something in her voice arouses him. He stares at her a bit frightenedly.*] Ye look mad, Abbie. What did ye do?

Abbie: I—I killed him, Eben.

Eben: [*Amazed.*] Ye killed him?

Abbie: [*Dully.*] Ay-eh.

Eben: [*Recovering from his astonishment—savagely.*] An' serves him right! But we got t' do somethin' quick t' make it look s'if the old skunk'd killed himself when he was drunk. We kin prove by 'em all how drunk he got.

Abbie: [*Wildly.*] No! No! Not him! [*Laughing distractedly.*] But that's what I ought t' done, hain't it? I oughter killed him instead! Why didn't ye tell me?

Eben: [*Appalled.*] Instead? What d'ye mean?

Abbie: Not him.

Eben: [*His face grown ghastly.*] Not—not that baby!

Abbie: [*Dully.*] Ay-eh!

Eben: [*Falls to his knees as if he'd been struck—his voice trembling with horror.*] Oh, God A'mighty! A'mighty God! Maw, whar was ye, why didn't ye stop her?

Abbie: [*Simply.*] She went back t' her grave that night we fust done it, remember? I hain't felt her about since. [*A pause. **Eben** hides his head in his hands, trembling all over as if he had the ague. She goes on dully.*] I left the piller over his little face. Then he killed himself. He stopped breathin'. [*She begins to weep softly.*]

Eben: [*Rage beginning to mingle with grief.*] He looked like me. He was mine, damn ye!

Abbie: [*Slowly and brokenly.*] I didn't want t' do it. I hated myself fur doin' it. I loved him. He was so purty—dead spit 'n' image o' yew. But I loved yew more—an' yew was goin' away—far off whar I'd never see ye agen, never kiss ye, never feel ye pressed agin me agen—an' ye said ye

hated me fur havin' him—ye said ye hated him an' wished he was dead—ye said if it hadn't been fur him comin' it'd be the same's afore between us.

Eben: [*Unable to endure this, springs to his feet in a fury, threatening her, his twitching fingers seeming to reach out for her throat.*] Ye lie! I never said—I never dreamd y'd—I'd cut off my head afore I'd hurt his finger!

Abbie: [*Piteously, sinking on her knees.*] Eben, don't ye look at me like that—hatin' me—not arter what I done fur ye—fur us—so's we could be happy agen—

Eben: [*Furiously now.*] Shut up, or I'll kill ye! I see yer game now—the same old sneakin' trick—ye're aimin' t' blame me fur the murder ye done!

Abbie: [*Moaning—putting her hands over her ears.*] Don't ye, Eben! Don't ye! [*She grasps his legs.*]

Eben: [*His mood suddenly changing to horror, shrinks away from her.*] Don't ye tech me! Ye're pizen! How could ye—t' murder a pore little critter—Ye must've swapped yer soul t' hell! [*Sudden raging.*] Ha! I kin see why ye done it! Not the lies ye jest told—but 'cause ye wanted t' steal agen—steal the last thin' ye'd left me—my part o' him—no, the hull o' him—ye saw he looked like me—ye knowed he was all mine—an' ye couldn't b'ar it—I know ye! Ye killed him fur bein' mine! [*All this has driven him almost insane. He makes a rush past her for the door—then turns—shaking both fists at her, violently.*] But I'll take vengeance now! I'll git the Sheriff! I'll tell him everythin'! Then I'll sing "I'm off to Californi-a!" an' go—gold—Golden Gate—gold sun—fields o' gold in the West! [*This last he half shouts, half croons incoherently, suddenly breaking off passionately.*] I'm a-goin' fur the Sheriff t' come an' git ye! I want ye tuk away, locked up from me! I can't stand t' luk at ye! Murderer an' thief 'r not, ye still tempt me! I'll give ye up t' the Sheriff! *[He turns and runs out, around the corner of house, panting and sobbing, and breaks into a swerving sprint down the road.]*

Abbie: *[Struggling to her feet, runs to the door, calling after him.]* I love ye, Eben! I love ye! *[She stops at the door weakly, swaying, about to fall.]* I don't care what ye do—if ye'll only love me agen— *[She falls limply to the floor in a faint.]*

Scene IV

About an hour later. Same as Scene III. Shows the kitchen and **Cabot's** *bedroom. It is after dawn. The sky is brilliant with the sunrise. In the kitchen,* **Abbie** *sits at the table, her body limp and exhausted, her head bowed down over her arms, her face hidden. Upstairs,* **Cabot** *is still asleep but awakens with a start. He looks toward the window and gives a snort of surprise and irritation—throws back the covers and begins hurriedly pulling on his clothes. Without looking behind him, he begins talking to* **Abbie** *who he supposes beside him.*

Cabot: Thunder 'n' lightnin', Abbie! I hain't slept this late in fifty year! Looks 's if the sun was full riz a'most. Must've been the dancin' an' likker. Must be gittin' old. I hope Eben's t' wuk. Ye might've tuk the trouble t' rouse me, Abbie. *[He turns—sees no one there—surprised.]* Waal—whar air she? Gittin' vittles, I calc'late. *[He tiptoes to the cradle and peers down —proudly.]* Mornin', sonny. Purty's a picter! Sleepin' sound. He don't beller all night like most o' 'em. *[He goes quietly out the door in rear—a few moments later enters kitchen—sees* **Abbie**—*with satisfaction.]* So thar ye be. Ye got any vittles cooked?

Abbie: *[Without moving.]* No.

Cabot: *[Coming to her, almost sympathetically.]* Ye feelin' sick?

Abbie: No.

Cabot: *[Pats her on shoulder. She shudders.]* Ye'd best lie down a spell. *[Half* *jocularly.]* Yer son'll be needin' ye soon. He'd ought t' wake up with a gnashin' appetite, the sound way he's sleepin'.

Abbie: *[Shudders—then in a dead voice.]* He ain't never goin' to wake up.

Cabot: *[Jokingly.]* Takes after me this mornin'. I ain't slept so late in . . .

Abbie: He's dead.

Cabot: *[Stares at her—bewilderedly.]* What . . .

Abbie: I killed him.

Cabot: *[Stepping back from her—aghast.]* Air ye drunk—'r crazy—'r . . . !

Abbie: *[Suddenly lifts her head and turns on him—wildly.]* I killed him, I tell ye! I smothered him. Go up an' see if ye don't b'lieve me!

> *[***Cabot** *stares at her a second, then bolts out the rear door, can be heard bounding up the stairs, and rushes into the bedroom and over to the cradle.* **Abbie** *has sunk back lifelessly into her former position.* **Cabot** *puts his hand down on the body in the crib. An expression of fear and horror comes over his face.]*

Cabot: *[Shrinking away—tremblingly.]* God A'mighty! God A'mighty. *[He stumbles out the door—in a short while returns to the kitchen—comes to* **Abbie,** *the stunned expression still on his face—hoarsely.]* Why did ye do it? Why? *[As she doesn't answer, he grabs her violently by the shoulder and shakes her.]* I ax ye why ye done it! Ye'd better tell me 'r . . . !

Abbie: *[Gives him a furious push which sends him staggering back and springs to her feet—with wild rage and hatred.]* Don't ye dare tech me! What right hev ye t' question me 'bout him? He wa'n't yewr son! Think I'd have a son by yew? I'd die fust! I hate the sight o' ye an' allus did! It's yew I should've murdered, if I'd had good sense! I hate ye! I love Eben. I did from the fust. An' he was Eben's son —mine an' Eben's—not your'n.

Cabot: *[Stands looking at her dazedly—a*

pause—*finding his words with an effort—dully.]* That was it—what I felt—pokin' round the corners— while ye lied—holdin' yerself from me—sayin' ye'd a'ready conceived— *[He lapses into crushed silence—then with a strange emotion.]* He's dead, sart'n. I felt his heart. Pore little critter! *[He blinks back one tear, wiping his sleeve across his nose.]*

Abbie: *[Hysterically.]* Don't ye! Don't ye! *[She sobs unrestrainedly.]*

Cabot: *[With a concentrated effort that stiffens his body into a rigid line and hardens his face into a stony mask— through his teeth to himself.]* I got t' be—like a stone—a rock o' jedgment! *[A pause. He gets complete control over himself—harshly.]* If he was Eben's, I be glad he air gone! An' mebbe I suspicioned it all along. I felt they was somethin' onnateral—some- whars—the house got so lonesome— an' cold—drivin' me down t' the barn —t' the beasts o' the field. . . . Ay-eh. I must've suspicioned—somethin'. Ye didn't fool me—not altogether, least- ways—I'm too old a bird—growin' ripe on the bough. . . . *[He becomes aware he is wandering, straightens again, looks at **Abbie** with a cruel grin.]* So ye'd liked t' hev murdered me 'stead o' him, would ye? Waal, I'll live to a hundred! I'll live t' see ye hung! I'll deliver ye up t' the jedg- ment o' God an' the law! I'll git the Sheriff now. *[Starts for the door.]*

Abbie: *[Dully.]* Ye needn't. Eben's gone fur him.

Cabot: *[Amazed.]* Eben—gone fur the Sheriff?

Abbie: Ay-eh.

Cabot: T' inform agen ye?

Abbie: Ay-eh.

Cabot: *[Considers this—a pause—then in a hard voice.]* Waal, I'm thankful fur him savin' me the trouble. I'll git t' wuk. *[He goes to the door—then turns in a voice full of strange emotion.]* He'd ought t' been my son, Abbie. Ye'd ought t' loved me. I'm a man. If

ye'd loved me, I'd never told no Sheriff on ye no matter what ye did, if they was t' brile me alive!

Abbie: *[Defensively.]* They's more to it nor yew know, makes him tell.

Cabot: *[Dryly.]* Fur yewr sake, I hope they be. *[He goes out—comes around to the gate—stares up at the sky. His control relaxes. For a moment he is old and weary. He murmurs despair- ingly.]* God A'mighty, I be lone- somer'n ever! *[He hears running foot- steps from the left, immediately is himself again. **Eben** runs in, panting exhaustedly, wild-eyed and mad look- ing. He lurches through the gate. **Cabot** grabs him by the shoulder. **Eben** stares at him dumbly.]* Did ye tell the Sheriff?

Eben: *[Nodding stupidly.]* Ay-eh.

Cabot: *[Gives him a push away that sends him sprawling—laughing with withering contempt.]* Good fur ye! A prime chip o' yer Maw ye be. *[He goes toward the barn, laughing harsh- ly. **Eben** scrambles to his feet. Sud- denly **Cabot** turns—grimly threaten- ing.]* Git off this farm when the Sheriff takes her—or, by God, he'll have t' come back an' git me fur murder, too!

*[He stalks off. **Eben** does not appear to have heard him. He runs to the door and comes into the kitchen. **Abbie** looks up with a cry of anguished joy. **Eben** stumbles over and throws himself on his knees beside her—sobbing brokenly.]*

Eben: Fergive me!

Abbie: *[Happily.]* Eben! *[She kisses him and pulls his head over against her breast.]*

Eben: I love ye! Fergive me!

Abbie: *[Ecstatically.]* I'd fergive ye all the sins in hell fur sayin' that! *[She kisses his head, pressing it to her with a fierce passion of possession.]*

Eben: *[Brokenly.]* But I told the Sheriff. He's comin' fur ye!

Abbie: I kin b'ar what happens t' me— now!

Eben: I woke him up. I told him. He says, wait 'til I git dressed. I was waiting. I got to thinkin' o' yew. I got to thinkin' how I'd loved ye. It hurt like somethin' was bustin' in my chest an' head. I got t' cryin'. I knowed sudden I loved ye yet, an' allus would love ye!

Abbie: [Caressing his hair—tenderly.] My boy, hain't ye?

Eben: I begun t' run back. I cut across the fields an' through the woods. I thought ye might have time t' run away—with me—an' . . .

Abbie: [Shaking her head.] I got t' take my punishment—t' pay fur my sin.

Eben: Then I want t' share it with ye.

Abbie: Ye didn't do nothin'.

Eben: I put it in yer head. I wisht he was dead! I as much as urged ye t' do it!

Abbie: No. It was me alone!

Eben: I'm as guilty as yew be! He was the child o' our sin.

Abbie: [Lifting her head as if defying God.] I don't repent that sin! I hain't askin' God t' fergive that!

Eben: Nor me—but it led up t' the other —an' the murder ye did, ye did 'count o' me—an' it's my murder, too, I'll tell the Sheriff—an' if ye deny it, I'll say we planned it t'gether—an' they'll all b'lieve me, fur they suspicion everythin' we've done, an' it'll seem likely an' true to 'em. An' it is true— way down. I did help ye—somehow.

Abbie: [Laying her head on his—sobbing.] No! I don't want yew t' suffer!

Eben: I got t' pay fur my part o' the sin! An' I'd suffer wuss leavin' ye, goin' West, thinkin' o' ye day an' night, bein' out when yew was in— [Lowering his voice.] —'r bein' alive when yew was dead. [A pause.] I want t' share with ye, Abbie—prison 'r death 'r hell 'r anythin'! [He looks into her eyes and forces a trembling smile.] If I'm sharin' with ye, I won't feel lonesome, leastways.

Abbie: [Weakly.] Eben! I won't let ye! I can't let ye!

Eben: [Kissing her—tenderly.] Ye can't he'p yerself. I got ye beat fur once!

Abbie: [Forcing a smile—adoringly.] I hain't beat—s'long's I got ye!

Eben: [Hears the sound of feet outside.] Ssshh! Listen! They've come t' take us!

Abbie: No, it's him. Don't give him no chance to fight ye, Eben. Don't say nothin'—no matter what he says. An' I won't neither.

[It is **Cabot**. He comes up from the barn in a great state of excitement and strides into the house and then into the kitchen. **Eben** is kneeling beside **Abbie,** his arm around her, hers around him. They stare straight ahead.]

Cabot: [Stares at them, his face hard. A long pause—vindictively.] Ye make a slick pair o' murderin' turtle doves! Ye'd ought t' be both hung on the same limb an' left thar t' swing in the breeze an' rot—a warnin' t' old fools like me t' b'ar their lonesomeness alone—an' fur young fools like ye t' hobble their lust. [A pause. The excitement returns to his face, his eyes snap, he looks a bit crazy.] I couldn't work today. I couldn't take no interest. T' hell with the farm! I'm leavin' it! I've turned the cows an' other stock loose! I've druv 'em into the woods whar they kin be free! By freein' 'em, I'm freein' myself! I'm quittin' here today! I'll set fire t' house an' barn an' watch 'em burn, an' I'll leave yer Maw t' haunt the ashes, an' I'll will the fields back t' God, so that nothin' human kin never touch 'em! I'll be a-goin' to Californi-a —t' jine Simeon an' Peter—true sons o' mine if they be dumb fools—an' the Cabots'll find Solomon's Mines t'gether! [He suddenly cuts a mad caper.] Whoop! What was the song they sung? "Oh, Californi-a! That's the land fur me." [He sings this—then gets on his knees by the floorboard under which the money was hid.] An' I'll sail thar on one o' the finest clippers I kin find! I've got the money! Pity ye didn't know whar this was hidden so's ye could steal . . . [He has pulled up the board. He stares—feels —stares again. A pause of dead silence. He slowly turns, slumping into a sitting position on the floor, his eyes like those of a dead fish, his face the sickly green of an attack of nausea. He swallows painfully several times—forces a weak smile at last.] So—ye did steal it!

Eben: [Emotionlessly.] I swapped it t' Sim an' Peter fur their share o' the farm—t' pay their passage t' Californi-a.

Cabot: [With one sardonic.] Ha! [He begins to recover. Gets slowly to his feet—strangely.] I calc'late God give it to 'em—not yew! God's hard, not easy! Mebbe they's easy gold in the West but it hain't God's gold. It hain't fur me. I kin hear His voice warnin' me agen t' be hard an' stay on my farm. I kin see his hand usin' Eben t' steal t' keep me from weakness. I kin feel I be in the palm o' His hand, His fingers guidin' me. [A pause—then he mutters sadly.] It's a-goin' t' be lonesomer now than ever it war afore— an' I'm gittin' old, Lord—ripe on the bough. . . . [Then stiffening.] Waal— what d'ye want? God's lonesome, hain't He? God's hard an' lonesome!
[A pause. **The Sheriff** with two men comes up the road from the left. They move cautiously to the door. **The Sheriff** knocks on it with the butt of his pistol.]

Sheriff: Open in the name o' the law. [They start.]

Cabot: They've come fur ye. [He goes to the rear door.] Come in, Jim! [The three men enter. **Cabot** meets them in doorway.] Jest a minit, Jim. I got 'em safe here. [**The Sheriff** nods. He and his companions remain in the doorway.]

Eben: [Suddenly calls.] I lied this mornin', Jim. I helped her to do it. Ye kin take me, too.

Abbie: [Brokenly.] No!

Cabot: Take 'em both. [He comes forward—stares at **Eben** with a trace of grudging admiration.] Purty good— fur yew! Waal, I got t' round up the stock. Good-by.

Eben: Good-by.

Abbie: Good-by. [**Cabot** turns and strides past the men—comes out and around the corner of the house, his shoulders squared, his face stony, and stalks grimly toward the barn. In the meantime **The Sheriff** and men have come into the room.]

Sheriff: [Embarrassedly.] Waal—we'd best start.

Abbie: Wait. [Turns to **Eben**.] I love ye, Eben.

Eben: I love ye, Abbie. [They kiss. The three men grin and shuffle embarrassedly. **Eben** takes **Abbie's** hand. They go out the door in rear, the men following, and come from the house, walking hand in hand to the gate. **Eben** stops there and points to the sunrise sky.] Sun's a-rizin'. Purty, hain't it?

Abbie: Ay-eh. [They both stand for a moment looking up raptly in attitudes strangely aloof and devout.]

Sheriff: [Looking around at the farm enviously—to his companion.] It's a jim-dandy farm, no denyin'. Wished I owned it!

CURTAIN

THE SEVEN DEADLY SINS OF THE LOWER MIDDLE CLASS

Bertolt Brecht

Caspar Neher's design for the cabaret scene in the original production of *The Seven Deadly Sins* at the Théâtre des Champs-Elysées, Paris, 1933. Anna II entertains the customers. New York Public Library Theatre Collection.

Bertolt Brecht

Bertolt Brecht, one of the most gifted playwrights of the twentieth century, was born in the city of Augsburg in Bavaria, on February 10, 1898. He was the son of a well-to-do businessman, the director of a paper mill. Bertolt's younger brother, Walther, shared his father's interest in paper-making, but Bertolt, a sensitive and rebellious boy with a sharp and penetrating intelligence, had no taste for anything so "bourgeois" as business; he preferred to indulge in sports and to cover sheets of paper with his poems. Later he would use up many reams for his political and theatrical essays, his short stories, novels, and plays.

Brecht's father was Catholic, his mother Protestant; the boy was very close to his mother and was brought up in her faith. The influence of Luther's Bible is evident in the beauty and fervor of the language of his plays and in the strong strain of the moralist and reformer in his character.

Brecht attended elementary school and high school in Augsburg. One of his schoolmates, Caspar Neher, who later became a celebrated painter and scene designer, was to work closely with the playwright throughout his career. When World War I broke out, Brecht was sixteen and writing poems and book reviews for the local newspaper. He had already been in trouble with the authorities over his pacifistic views. At eighteen he left Augsburg for Munich, where he began to study medicine at the university. His studies were interrupted, however, when he was drafted into the army and assigned to serve as an orderly in a military hospital. The suffering of the soldiers, and the callousness of the officers and doctors, whose only interest was in patching the men up and getting them back to the battlefields as soon as possible, shocked Brecht and further crystalized his hatred of war. This experience strengthened his conviction that radical changes were needed in the organization of society and marked the beginning of his interest in left-wing socialism.

When the war was over, Brecht gave up the idea of practicing medicine and began to frequent the political and artistic circles in Munich. He lived and dressed like a bohemian—neglected to bathe and shave, affected workman's clothes and a cap, was never seen without a cigar in his hand, pursued a free sexual life, and played the guitar and sang satirical and "folk" ballads of his own composition. His serious interest in the theatre dates from this time, when he became deeply impressed by the work of Strindberg, Wedekind, and Shaw.

Brecht began to write plays at the age of twenty. His earliest works exhibit a dark view of life and an emotional state approaching anarchy. His first play, *Baal* (1918), was named for the Phoenician god of drunkards, gluttons, and fornicators. His second play, *Drums in the Night* (1918)—his first play to be staged—concerned a soldier who returns from the war to find his girl pregnant by another man, but marries her anyway, saying, "I am a swine and the swine goes home." This play was produced by the Munich Chamber Theater on September 29, 1922, and was well received by the audience. More important for Brecht was the reaction of a celebrated critic, Herbert Ihering, who went to the opening at the dramatist's invitation and became the young man's staunchest defender. Ihering's review hailed the new playwright and announced that "a new tone, a new melody, a new vision has entered our time." Recognizing the power of Brecht's language, Ihering said in his review, "It is brutally sensuous, tender, and melancholy. It contains malice and bottomless sadness, grim wit and plaintive lyricism. . . ." Through Ihering's influence Brecht was awarded the Kleist prize as the most promising young playwright for the year 1922; this marked the beginning of his reputation as a dramatist. In the same year he married Marianne Zoff, who bore his daughter Hanne. The marriage lasted until 1927.

Two other early plays of special significance are *In the Jungle of Cities* (1921–1923) and *Edward II* (1923–1924). The first play takes place in Chicago and deals with a strange conflict between two men: it is a "motiveless malignity," with homosexual overtones. In their hostility and their inability to communicate, these men are the forerunners of characters in Beckett, Ionesco, and Pinter. *Edward II* (written in collaboration with Lion Feuchtwanger) is a free adaptation of Christopher Marlowe's play; it, too, has a homosexual aspect, but its importance lies in its being the first product of Brecht's interest in reworking historical material.

Brecht's early plays reflect the intellectual and emotional upheaval in postwar German society as well as the chaos in the writer's own life and thoughts. His frank expression of nihilism, and his vivid presentation of coarseness, brutality, and perversion, provided the writer with a much-needed outlet for his feelings and gave him a measure of personal control. But these early efforts, like Ibsen's realistic plays, were generally greeted with such comments as "vile," "disgraceful," and "a mud bath."

When, after Hitler's beer-hall *Putsch* in November, 1923, the riotous activities of the Brownshirts became more virulent in Munich, Brecht decided to leave that city for Berlin. In the German capital, between 1924 and 1933, Brecht espoused the political and dramatic theories that would inform his life and work and bring him world-wide fame.

When Brecht arrived in Berlin, the theatre was booming, although it offered little besides arid examples of photographic realism and tired versions of the classics. The three most original and serious directors were Max Reinhardt, who presented traditional romantic and realistic fare in very intimate or enormously spectacular productions; Leopold Jessner, who specialized in the expressionistic treatment of classical plays acted on a series of platforms, which came to be known as "Jessner steps"; and Erwin Piscator, the most experimental and revolutionary of the three, who dealt with topical and historical material in such a way as to emphasize its social and political significance for working-class audiences.

Piscator was five years older than Brecht; like Brecht he had come from a well-to-do Protestant home and was thoroughly disillusioned by World War I. He saw the solution to man's ills in communism and helped to found the Proletarian Theater in Berlin in 1919, drawing for inspiration on Soviet theatrical techniques. Piscator rejected the realism of Stanislavsky with its presentation of characters as unique individuals who would arouse the empathy of the audience; he adopted instead the methods of the younger Russian directors Meyerhold and Tairov, exponents of the styles known as "biomechanics" and "constructivism," which turned the actors into puppets and acrobats and the scenery into bare scaffolds, the better to portray collective man in a mechanistic age. To these principles Piscator added the ideas of the Soviet "agit-prop" (agitation and propaganda) theatres, which presented plays in documentary form, in order to indoctrinate the masses as well as entertain them. What Piscator wound up with was "Epic Theatre," the name he gave to the historical plays he produced by mixing live actors with films, charts and graphs, slides, music, song, dance, and narrators. By these methods Piscator achieved an "alienation effect," which constantly reminded the audience that it was watching a play and not reality, and thus prevented the spectators from *feeling* for the characters and started them *thinking* about their social, economic, and political problems.

Piscator had just taken over the direction of the Folk Theater in Berlin when Brecht arrived there in 1924. Fascinated by Piscator's "total theatre with a message" the young playwright immediately allied himself with the producer. Piscator welcomed writing talent because his plays were "built" to his specifications, often by several writers working in collaboration, and even the classics were "adapted" to fit his ideology and production schemes.

The association with Piscator had a tremendous effect upon Brecht. He began to elaborate the theory of Epic Theatre, to read the works of Marx, Engels, and Lenin, to attend the Karl Marx Workers' School, and to see in communism a solution to man's emotional, as well as his economic, problems. His plays ceased to be nihilistic and became didactic; he succeeded brilliantly in depicting man's confusion, suffering, and despair, but wrote with less conviction when suggesting a hopeful future. From the beginning, the Soviet critics took him to task for being "negative" and "formalist." Audiences, however, were not put off by Brecht's confusing unorthodox ideology; they were much more interested in his remarkable dramatic and theatrical effects.

Although he was not to visit the United States until 1941, Brecht very early was fascinated by the country that represented to him the citadel of capitalism, where the jungle of cities flourished. Avidly he read the works of Sherwood Anderson, Theodore Dreiser, Upton Sinclair, and others, and became a devotee of jazz. Reflecting this fascination, many of his plays were set in American cities and showed an increasing use of modern music and song. Early in the 1920s Brecht had met Kurt Weill, a brilliant and serious composer, whose progressive social outlook and special treatment of the jazz idiom appealed to the playwright. The two men collaborated on half a dozen works. Their first, *The Threepenny Opera* (1928), proved to be Brecht's most famous play and his greatest financial success; their final joint effort, *The Seven Deadly Sins of the Lower Middle Class* (1933), was created after both men had left Germany and were living in exile. A failure while Brecht and Weill were alive, *The Seven Deadly Sins* has recently had several brilliant and highly successful productions.

Kurt Weill was not the only composer to supply music for Brecht's plays; in addition, there were Paul Hindemith, Hanns Eisler, and Paul Dessau. Other important works of the period ending in 1933 are: *A Man Is a Man*

(1924–1925), *St. Joan of the Stockyards* (1929–1930), *The Measures Taken* (1930), and *The Exception and the Rule* (1930).

Attempting to apply the principles of Epic Theatre to the opera, Brecht collaborated with Kurt Weill on the *Rise and Fall of the City of Mahagonny* (1928–1929), a vicious attack on the middle-class worship of money. The work was a brilliant experiment, but it caused riots in the theatres where it was performed. When the play was published in 1930, Brecht appended to the text a table showing the difference between dramatic and Epic Theatre. Although the two are not mutually exclusive, the table indicates that dramatic theatre places its emphasis on the emotional involvement of the audience, Epic Theatre on presenting a rational argument. The following are some of the salient items:

Dramatic Theatre	*Epic Theatre*
plot	narrative
one scene makes another	each scene for itself
growth	montage
eyes on the finish	eyes on the course
involves the spectator in a vicarious experience	makes the spectator a thoughtful observer at a distance
wears down his capacity for action	arouses his capacity for action
provides him with sensations	forces him to make decisions
human nature is unalterable	human nature is alterable
man as a fixed point	man as a process
feeling	reason

On February 28, 1933, the day after the Reichstag fire, as the storm troopers were beginning to round up Communists and intellectuals, Brecht went into exile with his family. In 1928 he had married one of the outstanding actresses in Piscator's company, Helene Weigel, who remained his artistic collaborator to the end of his life. They had two children, Stephen and Barbara. When Brecht left Germany, the Nazis deprived him of his citizenship, burned his books, and listed him as an enemy of the state. Brecht was fortunate in being able to take his family with him, but, because he was proficient in no language but his own, his life as a writer-in-exile was precarious and humiliating. In Germany he had been rich and famous and could always find a market for his work; abroad he was poor and unknown and had to depend upon translations, which are inadequate at best, particularly for poetry.

Brecht went first to Austria, then to Switzerland, and finally settled in Denmark. The hospitality accorded him in Copenhagen enabled him to go on with his writing. During a short trip to Paris, he completed *The Seven Deadly Sins* (1933), but a more ambitious work, *The Roundheads and the Peakheads,* which he had begun in 1932, was finished in 1934 and presented by Danish working-class actors in 1936. When Hitler's invasions of foreign lands made life in Denmark dangerous for Brecht, he moved to Sweden in 1939, and then to Finland in 1940. During this unsettled time he wrote some of his finest plays: *Galileo* (1938), *Mother Courage and Her Children* (1939), *The Good Woman of Setzuan* (1938–1940), and *Mr. Puntila and His Hired Man, Matti* (1940–1941).

These plays spoke from Brecht's heart but contradicted his head. They depart almost completely from one of the main tenets of Epic Theatre—the alienation effect—since audiences respond with strong empathy to the characters and situations. Brecht considered Galileo reprehensible because, as a scientist who had discovered the truth, he did not have the courage to defy the authorities who persecuted him (Brecht himself, it should be remembered, was running away); audiences, however, clearly appreciated Galileo's desire to remain alive. To Brecht, Mother Courage was a contemptible person who lived on the profits of war, but audiences were more sympathetic and wept over the hardships the poor woman had to endure in order to survive. Brecht could never understand such reactions on the part of the audience and often rewrote his plays in order to clarify his point of view, without succeeding in altering the audiences' responses. The same paradoxes and confusions arose in connection with *The Good Woman, Mr. Puntila,* and *The Caucasian Chalk Circle.* Brecht's inflexible adherence to Marxism was an intellectual stance at complete variance with his psychological insight into human character and his natural genius as a dramatist.

In May, 1941, Brecht obtained a visa for entry into the United States. He crossed the Soviet Union from Finland and sailed from Vladivostok to San Pedro, California. Many of his friends and associates had gone to Russia and had come to grief, but Brecht, with a better sense of self-preservation, settled down in a colony of Austrian and German refugee writers and artists in Santa Monica, California. During his stay in America, Brecht wrote several plays of special interest: *The Resistible Rise of Arturo Ui* (1941), which depicts Hitler as a Chicago gangster; *The Visions of Simone Machard* (1941–1943, in collaboration with Lion Feuchtwanger), about a modern Joan of Arc; *The Caucasian Chalk Circle* (1944–1945), one of the playwright's undisputed masterpieces, with the theme, "Things should belong to the people who use them best"; and a revised version of *Galileo* (1945–1946), written especially for Charles Laughton and with the actor's collaboration.

Brecht tried desperately to arrange for professional productions of his plays in the United States, but the closest he came to one was the presentation by the Experimental Theatre of ANTA in December, 1947, of *Galileo,* with Laughton in the title role. American colleges and universities had begun to do Brecht's plays, but these productions brought small financial returns. In October, 1947, Brecht had been summoned to appear before the Un-American Activities Committee in Washington, D.C., which was investigating "subversives" in the United States. He was asked if he was then, or had ever been, a member of the Communist Party. He denied it vehemently and apparently satisfied his interrogators, who thanked him for being a cooperative witness and dismissed him. A few days later he left America.

Brecht settled temporarily in Zurich, Switzerland, where his plays were being given excellent productions at the Schauspielhaus. He wanted time to observe and evaluate the postwar social and political conditions in his native land before making definite plans to return to Germany. In Zurich, Brecht wrote *The Little Organon for the Theatre,* the most complete exposition of his dramatic theories; he no longer spoke of Epic Theatre but of "dialectical theatre," a theatre which would reflect social situations as they changed with the times.

Late in 1948 Brecht was invited to East Berlin, in the Soviet Zone, to put on a production of *Mother Courage;* he gathered together a company headed by Helene Weigel, and he himself directed the play at the Deutsches Theater. It was a great success and laid the foundation for the Berliner Ensemble, the permanent company he was to form. Brecht was promised a theatre of his own and the financial backing of the government, if he would remain in East Berlin; it sounded like a tempting offer, feeling as he then did that Western Europe and America had rejected him. Brecht went back to Zurich and made plans for the move, but was perspicacious enough to arrange for escape routes from the Communist world: he became an Austrian citizen and traveled on an Austrian passport; he put full control of his copyrights into the hands of his friend and publisher, Peter Suhrkamp, in West Berlin; and he deposited his money in a Swiss bank.

The Berliner Ensemble, which was the name of Brecht's theatrical organization, was, and still is, under the management of Helene Weigel. It put on its first production late in 1949, using the Deutsches Theater temporarily, and touring widely in East and West Germany. It was not until 1954 that the Berliner Ensemble was given its own home, the Theater am Schiffbauerdamm, with over two hundred and fifty personnel—actors, directors, designers, musicians, and technicians. Soon the company was taking its productions to France, Italy, and England and establishing itself as the finest repertory ensemble in the world.

Despite his fame Brecht was continually harassed by the East German authorities, who not only censored his productions but kept urging him to write propaganda plays in conformance with the latest political line. Though Brecht managed to fend them off, the pressure took a toll on his work and his life. During his seven years in East Berlin, his poetic faculty failed from day to day, and he confined his activities to revising and directing his plays and to writing adaptations, the last of which was *Trumpets and Drums* (1956), based on Farquhar's Restoration comedy, *The Recruiting Officer.* His health, too, began to fail; in 1955 he was seriously ill, but continued to work unceasingly. On August 14, 1956, while preparing a production of his adaptation of Shakespeare's *Coriolanus,* he died of a coronary thrombosis. He was buried in the Dorotheen Cemetery not far from the grave of his idol, the philosopher Hegel. It is said that when he was near death, he contemplated moving to Switzerland or to Denmark; no longer at home in Germany, he looked forward to exile.

Brecht was first and foremost a poet, and it is as poetry that his work suffers most in translation. As a playwright he theorized continually—about Epic Theatre, non-Aristotelian drama, and alienation effect—yet, when, as a director at the Berliner Ensemble, he had an opportunity to remold his actors, all of whom had been traditionally trained, he never mentioned his theories to them. Actually, he achieved his greatest effects when his story line was well developed, his characters highly individualized, and his dialogue pungent and witty; then, not even the ideological content of the play could diminish the empathy of the audience. Brecht's dedication to Marxism seems absurd in the face of his avoidance of the Communist world and of its rejection of him. Brecht and Sean O'Casey both labored under the impression that they were Communists; actually they were motivated in their battle against injustice, war, poverty, and ugliness by an innate humanitarianism and idealism. Brecht even went so far as to insist that the "good" characters in his plays appear without make-up, while the "evil" ones wear masks—when the Good Woman of Setzuan turns greedy and mean, she dons a mask!—thus affirming symbolically that man is basically good.

Side by side with Brecht's ideas concerning the class struggle and the violent transformation of society ran his deep interest in Oriental religion and philosophy, which led to his preaching nonviolence, resignation, and stoicism. It is this intellectual and emotional ambivalence that makes Brecht's plays so paradoxical and confusing, helping at the same time to explain his powerful influence upon younger playwrights as well as upon modern audiences. Since his death there has been a Brecht "explosion"—even his most controversial plays are now being performed in East Berlin and in the Soviet Union, as well as in many other countries. Brecht's work, with its militant political attitudes, appears to have a special meaning for the developing nations of the world. The elaborate seventieth birthday celebrations, which took place in both Germanies in February 1968, marked a high point in the playwright's reputation. Brecht's collected works have been brought out in about forty volumes and are now going into other editions in German and in foreign translations.

The Seven Deadly Sins

In an essay dealing with "alienation effects" in acting, written in 1935, Brecht said:

> Suppose the following is to be shown on the stage: a girl leaves home in order to take a job in a fair-sized city. . . . What! A family letting one of its members leave the nest to earn her future living independently and without help? Is she up to it? Will what she has learnt here as a member of the family help her to earn her living? Can't families keep a grip on their children any longer? Have they become a burden? Is it like that with every family? Was it always like that? . . . If so, and if it's something biological, does it always happen in the same way, for the same reasons, and with the same results? These are the questions, or a few of them, that the actors must answer if they want to show the incident as a unique, historical one: if they want to demonstrate a custom which leads to a conclusion about the entire structure of a society at a particular, though transient, time. But how is such an incident to be represented if its historic character is to be brought out? . . . When the mother, between warnings and moral injunctions, packs her daughter's bag—a very small one—how is the following to be shown: So many injunctions and so few clothes? Moral injunctions for a lifetime and bread for five hours? How is the actress to deliver the mother's line as she hands over such a very small suitcase— "There, I guess that ought to do you"—in such a way that it is understood as a historic dictum?

One might think that Brecht was here discussing the composition of his own play, *The Seven Deadly Sins of the Petit Bourgeois* (1933), when actually he was writing about the Piscator-Goldschmidt dramatization of

Theodore Dreiser's novel *An American Tragedy*. In 1927 Brecht and Piscator were closely associated in theatrical production; both men were interested in social problems and were haunted by American capitalism and culture, and both kept abreast of American economic and political conditions by reading American literature. When Dreiser's novel appeared in Germany in 1927 and 1928, Piscator saw at once the possibility of turning it into a play that would dramatize the conflict between rich and poor and show the baneful influence of economic need upon morality. With the assistance of Mrs. Lena Goldschmidt, Piscator prepared his stage version of the book and was ready to produce it in 1931, when the rise of Hitler forced him to leave the country.

Brecht was undoubtedly familiar with the Piscator-Goldschmidt manuscript, for *The Seven Deadly Sins* bears many striking resemblances to the story and theme of Dreiser's novel and to the play made from it. Helene Weigel, Brecht's wife, once remarked to an interviewer, "Brecht took from other artists plots, forms, pieces of dialogue. He was guided by them as he created new work."

The Case of Clyde Griffiths, as the Piscator adaptation was called, opens with the Speaker, a narrator who sets the scene and sometimes acts as Clyde's conscience, announcing that the play presents the Land of Poverty and the Land of Riches, with No Man's Land in between. Clyde, a poor boy, is shown with his humble, pious family—Father, Mother, two brothers, and a sister—singing a hymn to the accompaniment of a harmonium:

> Turn your eyes from earthly things
> Only in God is Truth and Salvation.

The family, having moved from city to city in the United States in search of a livelihood, has settled in the West, but Clyde leaves home and returns to the East, where he thinks he will have a better chance to succeed. In a similar manner Roberta Alden, the heroine, leaves her impoverished family and goes seeking employment. As the girl departs, her mother says, "Be careful . . . and write to us regularly." Roberta promises to send money home and to return as soon as she can.

Clyde and Roberta have their first rendezvous in a park. In their frequent meetings their talk is of work and self-denial, morality, and the difficulty of earning a living. The employers' rules are strict: No smoking, talking, or fraternizing. In one scene, several working-girls discuss their male friends and the advisability of accepting gifts of pearls from them. Roberta has been sending money regularly to her family, whom Clyde calls "crazy religious fanatics" because they even consider social dancing a sin. He asks vehemently, "Is it a sin to want to rise in the world?"

Clyde has an *alter ego* in his cousin Gilbert; there is a strong physical resemblance between the two young men, who are often mistaken for each other and who might easily be thought of as two aspects of the same personality. Between them they commit the seven deadly sins: Gilbert is guilty of sloth, pride, and wrath; Clyde, of gluttony, lust, avarice, envy, and —for good measure—murder.

Roberta too has a double; her sister Emily stands in for her in the courtroom scene. It is in this scene that many of the themes of class conflict are stated: A Rich Man says, "It never pays to let yourself be swayed by sentiment. It doesn't do to give way to your feelings. Leave that to the poor." (This credo is dramatized in Brecht's play *The Exception and the Rule*.) The Speaker, referring to Clyde, says, "He may be guilty in his thoughts and still be innocent. He may be innocent and still carry a heavier load of guilt in his heart than you are aware of." The Speaker also says, "He was so bewitched, so enslaved by his vision of the world of riches that he saw about him that he became so morally corrupted he shrank from nothing, not even murder, in his determination to become part of it!"

Clyde's mother urges him to save his soul, to beg the Lord for grace, and to pray; the Speaker blames Clyde's weakness on his family's preoccupation with religion. Clyde's only regret, as he informs his brother in a letter, is that his convictions were not strong enough, because the greatest sin is the sin of indecision.

When Kurt Weill wrote to Brecht from Paris asking for a libretto that would accommodate Lotte Lenya (an actress and singer) and Tilly Losch (a dancer), Brecht's mind turned somehow to *The Case of Clyde Griffiths*. In *The Seven Deadly Sins,* Anna I and Anna II, two aspects of the same personality, represent a single girl who leaves home and goes from city to city in the United States seeking her fortune. She has left a Father, Mother, and two brothers behind; these religious, hymn-singing people offer her pious injunctions and receive her remittances, Anna I is the narrator, the Speaker and conscience. Anna II is left to struggle with the seven deadly sins; she does not actually commit murder, but she does drive men to suicide. There are echoes, too, of the park scene (which represents Sloth), of sinful dancing (Pride), of the tyrannical employer (Gluttony), and of the gift of jewels from male friends (Lust). In Piscator the moralizing is old-fashioned, direct, and heavy-handed; in Brecht, it is subtle, ironic, and paradoxical. Brecht suggests that Anna II's vices are actually virtues, for he notes in his stage directions that the girl is slothful in committing injustice, proud of her incorruptibility, wrathful at meanness, and so on. This ambiguity, which has troubled directors, performers, critics, and audiences, is typically Brechtian.

The Piscator-Goldschmidt script, which is inconsequential, was conceived along traditional lines, with rising action, climax, and resolution. Brecht, a master dramatist, was not at all concerned with conventional structure but was more interested in making his material serve as a parable for the working out of a moral relationship between the individual and the world. It is Brecht's recognition of the ceaseless fluidity of the human personality and of society that makes his work so profoundly interesting to modern audiences. Like Brecht, Pirandello saw life as a shifting and fluctuating process, but he emphasized its philosophical and psychological, rather than its social and moral, aspects.

The means Brecht used to depict the kaleidoscopic nature of life are more expressionistic than "Epic." The simple, linear story is told episodically, with no clear transitions from scene to scene, and only meager indications of time and place. The characterizations are external and stylized: the members of the Family are caricatures, the people encountered en route are types—employers, lovers, and so on—and Anna I and Anna II are little more than personifications of Reason and Instinct. The dialogue is staccato and poetic; the theme, though unclear, has emotional appeal; and the impact of the play depends largely on music, movement, mood, and such visual devices as newspapers with pictures and headlines, and a house that is built piecemeal during the performance.

Aside from its intrinsic merit as a work of art, *The Seven Deadly Sins* deserves our attention because it contains germs of the important ideas and techniques that are characteristic of Brecht's more elaborate and better-known plays.

The Production Record

The Seven Deadly Sins was first produced on June 7, 1933, at the Théâtre des Champs-Elysées in Paris, by Edward James's "Ballet 1933." Tilly Losch, Lotte Lenya, and Roman Jasinsky headed the cast; the choreography was created by George Balanchine; the scenery and costumes by Caspar Neher; the costumes were executed by Karinska. The Orchestre Symphonique de Paris was under the direction of Maurice D'Abravanel. The work had a lukewarm reception; one critic called it "heavy and Teutonic," perhaps because it was presented in the original German.

This production was moved to the Savoy Theatre, London, on June 29, 1933, and was presented under the title of *Anna-Anna*. It was done with the original cast but in an English translation by Edward James. In the Family quartet were the singers Heinrich Gretler, Otto Pasetti, Albert Peters, and Erich Fuchs. The orchestra was conducted by Maurice D'Abravanel and Constant Lambert. The critic for *The Times* (London) said, " . . . The moral tale is worked out thoroughly and cleverly, but it leaves an uncomfortable feeling behind it." Another critic praised the work, but thought that it had a "slightly repellent flavour" and an "acrid blend of cynicism and disillusionment." The music was considered "monotonous."

While Brecht was a resident in Denmark, the play was produced at the Royal Theatre, Copenhagen, on November 12, 1936, for two performances only. The choreography was created by Harald Lander and the settings by Svend Johannsen.

The work had its American première at the City Center Theater, New York, on December 4, 1958, in an English version by W. H. Auden and Chester Kallman. Lotta Lenya and Allegra Kent headed the cast; the Family quartet was sung by Stanley Carlson, Gene Hoffman, Frank Porretta, and Grant Williams. Choreography was by George Balanchine; scenery, costumes, and lighting were by Rouben Ter-Arutunian; costumes were executed by Karinska; and the orchestra was conducted by Robert Irving. The production was enthusiastically received and remained in the repertory during the 1958–1959 season.

In April, 1960, Lotta Lenya repeated the role, this time in German, at the Opera House in Frankfurt-am-Main; Karin von Aroldingen danced Anna II. The choreography was by Tatjana Gsovsky, the sets by Hein Heckroth, and the orchestra was conducted by Wolfgang Rennert.

Early in 1961 it was announced that Lotta Lenya would play the part later that year at the Edinburgh Festival in Scotland, but when the produc-

Tilly Losch, who created the role of Anna II in the original production of the play, is here shown with a dancing partner performing one of her celebrated backbends. New York Public Library Theatre Collection.

tion opened on September 4, Cleo Laine was seen as Anna I and Anya Linden, on loan from the Royal Ballet, as Anna II. The Auden-Kallman translation was used, and Kenneth MacMillan was the choreographer. Kenneth Tynan, writing in *The Observer* (London, September 10, 1961) remarked: "Miss Laine has buckets of warmth and fills the stage with sorrow; what one misses is the irony that Lotta Lenya brings to the part, the anger and the edge, the triumphant toughness that forbids sentimentality."

In July, 1963, the play was presented in an outdoor amphitheatre under the auspices of the Park Department of the City of Stockholm. It was done in a Swedish translation by Lars Forssell; it was choreographed and directed by Birgit Cullberg, with Margareta Kjellberg, Kari Sylwan, and Bruce Marks in the leading roles; the scenery and costumes were by Sonja Carlsson, and the orchestra was conducted by Hans Wahlgren. Miss Cullberg's interpretation was highly sexual and included a satire on American puritanism, which was received with great applause by critics and audiences.

In April, 1964, Ivo Cramér created the choreography and direction for the play, which was to be broadcast on Norwegian television and also to be performed on the stage at the Bergen (Norway) Festival. André Bjerke supplied a Norwegian translation, and the cast was headed by Mona Hofland, Anne Borg, and Ronald Frazier, an American dancer and mime; Guy Krohg designed the sets and costumes. Cramér rehearsed the company for three weeks in a hall in Oslo; then, early in May, the program was taped at the television studio. The day after the taping the play was completely restaged for presentation in a theatre at the Bergen Festival on the last Sunday in May. "The orientations, of actor to actor and of actor to audience, are entirely different for television and for theater," said Cramér. "Even the sets and

Scene from the Birgit Cullberg production presented in an outdoor amphi-theatre, Stockholm, July 1963. As director and choreographer, Miss Cullberg emphasized the sexual aspects of the play. Courtesy of the Stockholm Park Department.

Ilse Hurtig as Anna II, left, and Gisela May as Anna I in the production mounted by the State Opera House in East Berlin, February, 1968, to com-memorate Brecht's birthday. Photograph: Marion Schöne. Courtesy Deutsche Staatsoper Berlin.

costumes were altered for the stage." The television program, which ran just under 37 minutes was broadcast on September 4, 1964. Brilliantly performed, it had amazing pace and spirit and was deeply moving.

In July, 1967, Bettina Jonic, Mary Hinkson, and Scott Douglas appeared in the play at the Queen Elizabeth Theatre, Vancouver, Canada. Glen Tetley was responsible for the choreography and direction, Willa Kim for the costumes, and Jackie Cassen and Rudi Stern for the décor, which was created with kinetic light; the Vancouver Symphony Orchestra was conducted by Meredith Davies. The play was put on as part of the Vancouver Festival and achieved, according to a newspaper report, "a five-curtain call, shouting, stamping success."

In February, 1968, in commemoration of Brecht's birthday, a number of his plays were presented in both East and West Germany; a production of *The Seven Deadly Sins* was offered at the State Opera House in East Berlin. The work had first been produced in that theatre on October 1, 1963, after which it was performed in Helsinki, Zagreb, Warsaw, Copenhagen, and Vienna in a highly successful tour. The memorial production of 1968, like the others before it, was enthusiastically received; the leading roles were performed by Gisela May (Anna I) and Ilse Hurtig (Anna II); direction and choreography were by Grita Krätke; scenery was by Paul Pilowski; costumes were by Christine Stromberg; and the orchestra was under the direction of Werner Stolze. The critics agreed that the production was exciting and nostalgic, and captured the authentic flavor of the Berlin of the 1920s and early 1930s.

The Original Anna I

Interview with Lotte Lenya

Early in 1933, when Hitler was coming to power, Lotte Lenya and her husband, the composer Kurt Weill, left Berlin for Paris. There they met Edward James, a British millionaire and patron of the arts, who was married to the celebrated Viennese dancer Tilly Losch. James knew of Weill's successful collaboration with Bertolt Brecht on *The Threepenny Opera* and other works, and suggested to the composer that he get together with his former partner to write something for the two women—Losch and Lenya. James was prepared to finance the production.

Weill got in touch with Brecht, who was then living in Switzerland. The playwright, in financial straits and eager to do some work, started to write at once and in about a month's time completed the libretto for *The Seven Deadly Sins*. Brecht's old friend, Caspar Neher, the costume and scene designer, came on from Berlin and stayed with the Weills, while working in close cooperation with the composer. But Brecht arrived in Paris only in time to attend the last few rehearsals and left the city before the play opened.

To direct and choreograph *The Seven Deadly Sins,* Edward James brought in George Balanchine, who had been a dancer and choreographer

Lotte Lenya created the part of Anna I in the original production (1933) and performed it again at the New York City Center in 1958. Here she is shown with Allegra Kent, who danced Anna II in the later production. Miss Lenya's costume was influenced by the German style of the twenties. Photograph: Fred Fehl.

with Diaghilev's company. With Boris Kochno, a former Diaghilev aide, Balanchine had just founded "Les Ballets 1933," and planned to put on at the Théâtre des Champs-Elysées a dance program in which he agreed to include the Brecht-Weill work.

"The rehearsals were a very funny experience," said Miss Lenya. "Balanchine then spoke only Russian. Kochno could handle Russian and French. But the play had been written, and was to be performed, in German. So it was necessary to get an interpreter to translate the lines from German into French for Kochno, who would then translate them from French into Russian for Balanchine; and the tide of translations would run the opposite way when Balanchine wanted to communicate with the performers. A lot of it went on in pantomime." The play is difficult, Miss Lenya feels, because it is full of Brechtian paradoxes; it is not very clear in any language. Balanchine said he didn't understand it then and still doesn't. The music, on the other hand, is crystal clear; it has no embroidery; it is like modern Mozart. Balanchine relied heavily upon it and worked closely with Weill. Balanchine in his youth had intended to become a concert pianist, which is probably why he has always been more interested in wedding music and movement than in story-ballets.

After the company had worked for four or five weeks, Brecht came to Paris to see the final rehearsals. He had never liked ballet as an art form and had written *The Seven Deadly Sins* merely as a potboiler. He hated the production; from his ideological point of view, nothing was right. It was too soft; it was like Hollywood; it had no punch or bite. He screamed and yelled, insulted everyone, and left before the opening, which took place early in June. The reaction of the French critics was mixed.

Later that month "Les Ballets 1933" went to London, and the Brecht-Weill work was done at the Savoy Theatre, under the title of *Anna-Anna*, in an English translation provided by Mr. James. The critical reaction was no better in London than it had been in Paris. But there was one important outcome for Balanchine and for America. Lincoln Kirstein, a wealthy American and an authority on ballet, attended the performances at the Savoy, where six ballets were performed. Kirstein was deeply impressed by what he saw. His interest led to an invitation, which Balanchine accepted, to go to the United States and found the school, which later developed into the New York City Ballet Company, one of the greatest dance organizations in the world.

"It's strange how 'American' *The Seven Deadly Sins* is," said Miss Lenya, recalling the original production, "because in 1933 none of us had been there, Weill, Brecht, Balanchine, or myself. But we had a fantastic curiosity about this country. We read all the literature. We saw every American movie. We heard every American record that came out. We soaked it up."

Concerning the role of Anna I, Miss Lenya remarked: "She is a sort of Greek chorus—she only advises and supervises. As a character she is completely sexless and almost isolated. The actress who plays the part doesn't need much direction, except when she is involved with other characters. She is merely told where to stand and where to move to, but the most important thing for her to remember is that the lyrics and music must be carefully studied, and delivered clearly and sharply without any embroidery. A direct presentation is best because the character's cynicism has a cumulative effect that in itself gives the end of the play a striking and emotional impact."

Balanchine, whose mind is quick to catch visual metaphors, said, "Lenya plays Anna I as if she has her little sister on a golden chain around her neck." It was Balanchine who invented the cloak under which the two sisters made their initial entrance. This was one of the few ideas used in both the 1933 and 1958 versions of the play. Of the six ballets done on the program in 1933, only *The Seven Deadly Sins* may still be seen in anything vaguely approaching its original form. Balanchine could not revive the other ballets, even if he wanted to, because almost as soon as he invents anything, he forgets how it goes; it is only in recent years that he has had written notations and films made of his choreography. He has said, "Ballets are like butterflies, and who wants to see last season's butterfly?" So, although it was called a revival, the 1958 version was actually a new production, freshly conceived. "I've never known anyone to whom ideas come in such profusion," said Miss Lenya. "He's like a race horse, the way he takes off—you almost feel you have to hold him back. With other artists you eventually reach a point where you know, 'Well, that's it, there'll be no more surprises,' but you never see the end of Balanchine's powers."

After singing the role of Anna I, in the English version by Auden and Kallman, at the New York City Center during the 1958–1959 season, Miss Lenya repeated the part in German, the following year, in Frankfurt-am-Main, Germany. She has also recorded the work in German for Columbia Records (KL 5175).[1] In the production at the Frankfurt Opera House, Anna II was danced by Karin von Aroldingen, with direction and choreography by Tatjana Gsovsky. "Miss Gsovsky was well acquainted with the work of Brecht," said Miss Lenya. "She had an excellent understanding of, and feeling for, the play. She turned it into a sort of *Lehrstück* (lesson play), which would have delighted Bert Brecht." Carefully observing Brecht's stage directions, which most choreographers tend to ignore, Miss Gsovsky had a large blackboard set up on one side of the stage, and on it, with a piece of chalk, Anna I wrote, as in a schoolroom, the name of the sin that was to be demonstrated (Sloth, Greed, and so on). At the end of each scene, she would angrily erase the word on the board and write the next one.

Commenting on the dancers—Tilly Losch, Allegra Kent, and Karin von Aroldingen—with whom she has appeared, Miss Lenya said, "Each one was quite different from the others. After all, styles do change in the dance as well as in the expression of emotions, and that changed the entire production. Tilly was lovely, delicate, and romantic; Allegra, a beautiful girl and an excellent technician, had a sharper and more modern style; Karin, a large and healthy girl, was extremely powerful and dramatic in her emotional expression." Miss Lenya was invited to attend one of the final rehearsals of Glen Tetley's balletic production of the play in 1967, and had great praise for Bettina Jonic and Mary Hinkson, both of whom she found to be beautifully expressive and moving.

Concerning the history of the play, Miss Lenya said, "It's fascinating and unbelievable! The original creation came about as the result of sex and money. Edward James and Tilly Losch were having marital difficulties, and he thought he could please her by giving her the 'gift' of a production in which she would shine. Brecht took the job mainly for the money involved. After 'the gift was presented,' Brecht hated it, and James and Losch split up anyway. There's Brechtian irony for you! And to make it even more paradoxical, *The Seven Deadly Sins* has kept on proving itself as a work of art, and has been receiving more and more the kind of attention it deserves."

---

[1] Vocal and orchestral scores of *The Seven Deadly Sins* are published by Schott's Söhne, Mainz, Germany; negotiations are under way for their distribution in the United States by Belwin-Mills, Inc.

During a rehearsal of the final scene of the play, Balanchine stops to explain a dance step to Allegra Kent (Anna II) and marks the beat for her as she rests on his shoulder. The dancers in the background wear masks and wigs. Photograph: Gordon Parks Life Magazine © Time Inc.

Anna II

Interview with Allegra Kent

Allegra Kent joined the New York City Ballet Company at the age of fifteen, having had several years of training before beginning her studies with Balanchine. At nineteen she became a ballerina; the following year she was selected for the role of Anna II in *The Seven Deadly Sins*. The production had a double significance for Balanchine, marking the twenty-fifth year since he had first mounted this work, as well as his anniversary as a choreographer in America.

Balanchine approached the 1958 version of this ballet as if it were a new work, changing almost everything but the lines and the music. Before he works with the dancers, he never knows exactly what he is going to do, but for *The Seven Deadly Sins* he proceeded like a jazz musician improvising on an old tune, making up most of the movements as he went along. He would sit by himself, in the big practice room at the School of American Ballet, where rehearsals were held, and listen intently to Weill's music. Then he would get up, look at the waiting dancers, and say, "Ready." He showed them what he wanted them to do. The dancers tried it, often amazed at the unexpected new steps. Balanchine would clap his hands twice, his signal to stop. He demonstrated again the exact expression of the face, the precise angle of the fingers, and the position of arms and legs. The dancers repeated until he was satisfied and rewarded them with the terse comment "Excellent."

As the leading dancer in the play, Miss Kent received the choreographer's closest attention. In the opening scene, for instance, in order to better observe her movements and comment on them, Balanchine stood in for the man Anna II was attempting to seduce. In another scene he supported her until she achieved the proper stance on the backs of two male dancers; and, later, he beat out with his finger the precise timing she was to observe in relation to the music. Balanchine customarily allows the dancers a certain amount of freedom. In the Gluttony scene, in which Anna II is under contract to keep her weight down, Balanchine asked Miss Kent to improvise some exercises. She went through what she called "some peculiar-looking" calisthenics, which the choreographer liked and kept in.

One of the very few dance effects repeated by Balanchine from his earlier production was backbends; Tilly Losch had been famous for them. This requires the dancer to throw arms and head back and to arch the spine so that the body assumes the shape of a crescent. Balanchine gave Miss Kent several backbends to perform because they suggested abandon, surrender, resignation, and sensuality, all appropriate for Anna II.

After she had mastered the technical details of the part, Miss Kent varied the performance frequently, doing it as she felt it each time. Her authorization for such procedure was Balanchine's directive "Rely on your instincts, and if your instincts are right, the thing will be right." It was only after Miss Kent had reached this level of performance that she began to think of Anna II as a person, and specifically as a pretty "cool" character. In the Avarice scene, for instance, there are several "suicides," but they are more symbolic than literal and are played for comedy or satire, with no sadness or deep feeling involved.

"During rehearsals," Miss Kent remarked, "very little was said about characterization. The story was told as straightforwardly as possible, but in dance terms. It was treated as a ballet, not as a drama. And yet there was much more miming than actual dancing in it; only in the last scene did it begin to resemble a ballet." In this final scene, Anna II, vainly trying to flee the sinner's life, catapulted herself blindly through a doorway covered completely with aluminum foil. The jump was intended to suggest suicide. Miss Kent was caught offstage by a male dancer with unerring skill, but the leap raised qualms in her at every performance.

Miss Kent has appeared in several roles that require acting skill, but always in the context of the dance; among other dramatic works, she mentioned particularly Francisco Moncion's *Pastorale* and Jerome Robbins' version of *Afternoon of a Faun.* She liked doing *The Seven Deadly Sins* as a change from the regular repertoire and particularly enjoyed having to get in and out of a whole wardrobe full of costumes with lightning speed. "It was fun," she said. But one little skirt gave trouble; she suggested that they remake it in black stretch elastic so that it could simply be pulled on and off—the idea worked.

Miss Kent indicated that her approach to *The Seven Deadly Sins* was almost completely instinctual, as is her approach to her art generally. She summed it up by saying, "I feel what I dance, and I dance what I feel."

Designing for Balanchine

Interview with Rouben Ter-Arutunian

Rouben Ter-Arutunian first worked as a designer with George Balanchine when they created *The Magic Flute* for presentation on the NBC television network in 1956. Two years later Balanchine asked Ter-Arutunian to design the production of *The Seven Deadly Sins* he was planning to mount at the New York City Center Theater for the 1958–1959 season. Ter-Arutunian was responsible for creating the scenery, costumes, and lighting.

One glance at the script told the designer that its series of short scenes would necessitate rapid shifts and changes; that the contents required a mood of ironic social criticism; and that the appropriate period would be the 1920s or 1930s. All these elements strongly suggested an expressionistic style. Having lived and studied in Germany and Austria, Ter-Arutunian had gained a deep understanding of expressionism, which looks within to a world of emotional and psychological states and expresses them in distorted outlines, strong colors, and exaggerated forms, as exemplified in the work of such painters as Kirschner, Grosz, Pechstein, Kokoschka, and Feininger. From these painters Ter-Arutunian took hints for the abstract and geometric forms he employed in several scenes, notably Envy, and for the acid colors—grays, browns, and purples—which formed the basis of the visual concept and served as a unifying factor in the production.

Selected line cuts from Ter-Arutunian's sketches. New York City Center production, 1958. Courtesy Rouben Ter-Arutunian.

The Family was seated on a platform, downstage left, and faced front stiffly as if posing for a tintype. They appeared to be in a furnished apartment suggestive of Berlin in the 1930s, the outstanding feature of which was a huge, fringed lampshade of multicolored mosaic glass, that was suspended above them. They were dressed in middle-class, nondescript clothing of the period; the Mother—a basso, with a moustache and a red wig—wore a purple dress with a large floral print. The "house" was erected around them, piece by piece after each scene, as called for by Brecht.

Anna I and Anna II made their first entrance in clothes that could only have emanated from such a home. At the outset the girls were dressed alike (Anna I wore this costume throughout the play): black berets; sleazy, electric-blue, slightly bell-shaped satin skirts; blouses with orange-and-white checks; black woolen stockings; and white "Minnie Mouse" shoes. "The contrast between the shoes and the stockings," said Ter-Arutunian, "built the entire character. They are poor, shabby, tasteless, and pathetic." Anna I, in addition, wore a sweater; the designer felt that this was another "inspired" item of apparel. The sweater was rusty brown with olive-colored triangles and resembled expressionistic wallpaper. Balanchine wanted the two Annas to come forward out of the blackness upstage with their bodies covered by a single cape, so that only their faces would be visible. Ter-Arutunian set up a street lamp that glowed wanly in the early dawn, cast a faint light on the girls' pale faces, and evoked a feeling of pathos.

The opening scene (Sloth) takes place in a public park, suggested by a statue, a fountain, and a bench. The action was played against black curtains; and black drops were used for the changes of scene. Three couples cross during the park scene; Anna II accosts the man each time, while Anna I snaps her camera—her "blackmail weapon." On one occasion a man in a top hat and coat with a fur collar lifts Anna II in his arms as Anna I takes the picture. Other passers-by are two effeminate pimps in tight-fitting, sexually provocative clothing.

The second scene (Pride) takes place in a cabaret, which has the crass and shiny atmosphere of a speakeasy of the 1920s. Four Bankers, who give the impression that they are the Lords of Gangsterdom, are the customers. They sit at a little table and drink champagne; larger-than-life-size champagne bottles are part of the décor. There is also a doorway, elaborately decorated with stars, circles, and arabesques and hung with a beaded curtain. Anna II is brought in on a silver platter, under a cellophane covering, and is served up to the Bankers as the most delectable dish in the night club.

In the scene called Wrath, Anna II makes her appearance in a circus setting as a fetchingly outfitted bareback rider in a ruffled tutu, a little pea jacket, and a cone-shaped hat topped with a pompon. She is mounted on a prop pony, which seems to have originated in a child's fantasy: it is lacy, plumed, and curlicued, and set against an eye-filling sugar-cane background. Here the cruel ringmaster—in high hat, tails, and boots—uses his whip on the pony and arouses the girl's anger.

The central prop for the fourth scene (Gluttony) was a huge scale, on which Anna II could be weighed regularly. This scene consisted mainly of a series of limbering exercises; bending, twisting, and stretching; Anna II curved her body and performed exquisite acrobatics on a mat. Meanwhile Anna I kept watch over her sister with a gun and allowed her an occasional quick lick on a coveted ice-cream cone.

Anger in Los Angeles. Anna II (Allegra Kent) arrives at the movie studio on a "horse" done up in lace against scenery in candy-cane colors. See Ter-Arutunian's sketch. Photograph: Gordon Parks Life Magazine © Time Inc.

In the scene depicting Lust, the most prominent object was a huge brass bed with an ornate, tasseled bedspread. This bedroom in Boston was decadently bawdy but beautiful in design; its strong period flavor also contained an underlying social comment.

In the sixth scene (Avarice), in which Anna II drives men to their ruin and suicide, she is the cool sophisticate of the 1920s. She wears the typical abbreviated sheath; this one is in yellow, the upper part heavily sequined, the lower part in three tiers of fringes; and her sequined hat has a little plume. Her accessories are gloves that reach above her elbows; many long and heavy strings of pearls; and a thick feather boa. She gestures with a cigarette in a very long holder.

For the final scene (Envy) Balanchine wanted great height and cold glitter, and Ter-Arutunian supplied it in superlative degree. He provided a full-stage picture with a chrome and tinsel atmosphere—a sort of "Coney Island of the mind"—with abstract patterns and geometric shapes, and backed with great sheets of aluminum foil. Through a long line of narrow doorways, doll-like men and women emerged—the men in black felt hats, black ties, and dinner jackets; the women in glittering bras and G-strings, pink fringes, and black boots. These figures wore masks; in fact, all the performers in the ballet, except the two Annas and the members of the Family, wore masks.

"The play is intimate enough to be done in a real cabaret," said Ter-Arutunian, "but one gains more than one loses if it is presented on a large stage. The final scene builds to a crescendo of tragic grandeur, with crowded, vibrant movement at its climax. Then comes a tremendous contrast at the last moment of the play. The girls move slowly and silently across a dimly lit stage; chastened and subdued, they are on their way home."

Ter-Arutunian was very happy with the production and went back to see it as often as he could. Of the many operas, plays, and ballets he has designed, *The Seven Deadly Sins* is one of his favorites, but if the Brecht-Weill work is to be done again by the New York City Ballet Company it will have to be entirely reconstructed because, although a ballet company usually stores its scenery and costumes for later use, Balanchine gave Ter-Arutunian's sets and costumes to the San Francisco Ballet Company.

The Norwegian Television Production

Interviews with Ivo Cramér, Guy Krohg, Mona Hofland, and Anne Borg

Ivo Cramér, Choreographer-Director

In 1964 Arild Brinchmann, then in charge of the Norwegian Broadcasting Television Theatre, initiated a production of *The Seven Deadly Sins* and asked Ivo Cramér to direct and choreograph it. Cramér's work was well known in Norway, Sweden, and in many countries on the continent of Europe. He had been Artistic Director of the Musical Section of the Royal Dramatic Theatre in Stockholm, in charge of operas, operettas, musicals, and ballets, not only for the capital but for touring companies that were sent to all parts of Sweden. Of the ballets he himself created, the most celebrated were *The Message* and *The Prodigal Son,* both based on material from the Bible. Cramér thus appeared to be the logical person to direct *The Seven Deadly Sins.*

Shortly after he was asked to do the play for television, Cramér was invited to present it on the stage at the Bergen (Norway) Festival. In preparing it for broadcast and then reworking it for the stage, Cramér became acutely aware of the limitations and advantages of each medium as it related to this work. The handling of the "growing house" is a case in point; the device works more effectively on stage than on television. In the theatre the audience can see at a glance what is going on at home in Louisiana and what the girls are up to in their travels; this provides contrast and conflict. In television it would not do to keep the camera trained throughout on the full stage picture; the result would be too static; but cutting from group to group and to long, medium, and close shots—which is necessary in films and television—weakens the ironic effect of the play's premise.

Cramér also realized, after analyzing Brecht's script, that he could not follow the author's stage directions precisely. Some of the action called for was too complex for ballet and pantomime and would require dialogue to make it clear. Cramér decided to substitute simpler situations, while preserving Brecht's basic statement. The choreographer wished to produce the play as simply as possible, counting on help from the audience's imagination; to stimulate it, he worked closely with his designer, Guy Krohg, to create locale and mood by the use of evocative costumes and a few symbolic props.

For Brecht's complicated "blackmail trick" in the first scene (Sloth), Cramér substituted what he called "seduction by lollipops." The childishness of Anna II at the beginning of the play was emphasized by the clothes she wore and by her delight at receiving gifts of lollipops from older men, who promptly paid up when Anna I threatened to report their advances to the cop who stood under a lamp-post.

The second scene (Pride) posed a problem of another sort for Cramér. The music composed by Weill for this scene is not long enough to cover all the action called for by Brecht; Cramér trimmed the scene to fit the music and built it to the moment when the cabaret dancer ("the old pro") tears the dress off Anna II.

In the third scene (Anger) Brecht calls for a performing horse, but Cramér felt that using a prop horse or two actors in disguise would give the effect of vaudeville. He eliminated the horse and on *The Thief of Bagdad* set introduced a clumsy tailor, who, while repairing the star's pantaloons, pricked him with his needle and was rewarded with a beating. It was this that aroused Anna's anger; she seized the whip and struck the star. Cramér recalled that the Swedish choreographer Birgit Cullberg, in her production of *The Seven Deadly Sins,* handled this scene in quite a different way. Anna's anger was aroused not in a movie studio but in an American restaurant, when a Negro customer is refused service. Cramér objected to the introduction of this note of social protest as being unfaithful to the text.

In the fourth scene (Gluttony) Anna II does not steal a bite from an apple but snatches some cake from the tray of a waitress who is passing by. Following this scene, the Family writes to Anna and tells her she will be able to eat as much as she wants when she gets back to Louisiana. Since Cramér was not able to show the Family and the girls in the same frame, he presented a montage of blown-up letters from the Family and the front page of a newspaper, with headlines about the girls; the character of Anna II was slowly shifting from innocence to sophistication and disillusionment.

Cramér felt that the fifth scene (Lust), as described by Brecht, was too complicated to be retained intact. From the words "the endless nights I heard my sister sobbing bitterly," Cramér got the idea of using a bed as a prop and several other sexual elements for the scene. In her farewell dance with Fernando, Anna II swings her leg between his legs and produces the impression of an Aristophanic phallus, an indication of her complete loss of innocence. But Anna I proves to be just as lecherous as her sister, for at the end of the scene, both girls climb into bed with Edward. The last thing we see is the leg of Anna II hanging over the side of the bed and swinging like a pendulum, a period detail that Cramér had recalled from the German films of the 1920s.

As Brecht described the Avarice scene, the men ruined by Anna II destroyed themselves in various ways and various places. Cramér simplified the action and gave it a farcical twist: Anna herself provided the guns with which her former suitors shot themselves in her presence, and before her very eyes the third victim hanged himself with her feather boa.

Anna's counterparts—the girls called for by Brecht for the final scene— were omitted by Cramér. He limited the people in his cast partly for reasons of economy, partly because of his concept for the conclusion. Male dancers, each representing one of the seven sins, entered and performed with Anna a review of her experiences since leaving home. Although she was exhausted, she seemed ready to go on with the life she had been leading, and the men formed a semicircle around her, a sort of barrier, hemming her in; but Anna I drew her sister out of the circle, and the girls returned to Louisiana.

In the Epilogue, Brecht leaves the girls as they are making their way back home. In both the television and stage versions Cramér showed the girls reaching home, reunited with the Family. The Cullberg version ended with Anna II curling up—like a foetus returning to the womb—under the porch of the house, which her efforts have brought into being, as if she were part of its structural foundation.

Cramér worked on *The Seven Deadly Sins* for three weeks in a rehearsal hall in Oslo and then for four days in a Norwegian Broadcasting studio. He ran through the play over and over again without breaks as if it were being done on the stage. Costume changes and the handling of props had all been worked out in advance, so that the show could be taped in one day in May 1964; the taping was actually completed two hours ahead of schedule. The play was not put on the air, however, until September 1964.

The television taping was done on a Thursday; on Friday Cramér re-staged the play completely for presentation at the Bergen Festival a few weeks later—on the last Sunday in May—where it was performed on the stage. The entrances and exits of the performers, as well as their positions and movements in the various scenes, were altered, according to Cramér, because the orientations of actor to actor and actor to audience differ completely on stage and screen. "For the actor in the theatre," said the choreographer, "the real world is all around the stage but mainly off to the right and left; for the actor on the screen (television or film), the real world is behind the camera. That is why screen entrances and exits from right or left in front of the camera seem flat and two-dimensional, while oblique movement away from, toward, or even past the camera are more dynamic." Cramér admits to having learned a great deal about camera technique, especially about filming dances, from Ingmar Bergman, with whom he has worked.

Ivo Cramér has very strong feelings about *The Seven Deadly Sins:* "I love the idea of satirizing the *petit bourgeois,* but I don't think Brecht has presented his point of view very clearly. Men offer lip service to religion and morality, but are willing to commit sins for gain—he's certainly saying that. But his ethical position is particularly confusing in the last scene; it is almost impossible to extract Brecht's meaning from it. The two Annas seem to be saying about those girls who wish to imitate them, 'They don't know where they're going—but we know where we're going! Don't waste your youth!'

"Kurt Weill's music is better than the libretto. The music has a unified style and build. The story was apparently contrived because Lotte Lenya does not dance and a dancer is needed. The explanation offered in the Prologue of two girls representing one character would be unnecessary if the play had been written for a single actress who could sing as well as dance. As it is, Anna I merely serves as a narrator and remains static throughout, while Anna II is a real and moving character who develops as the play progresses. I don't like the split. I think it's a weakness in the play that keeps it from being done more often. But I'd like to do it again because I'm fascinated by its cynicism and by the amazing number of human details it contains. I'd do it entirely differently, of course, because a new production would mean a new cast with new qualities; old mistakes could be eliminated; and new insights would suggest new approaches to the material. That's the great advantage of ballet and of repertory theatre—an artistic creation can be reworked and improved on."

Guy Krohg, Costume and Scene Designer

Guy Krohg and Ivo Cramér had worked together on several ballets and musicals, and they understood each other's tastes and methods. In planning the Brecht-Weill production, their collaboration was particularly close. They worked in Cramér's hotel room in Oslo (Cramér's home is in Sweden) going through the script and score and listening to the recording innumerable times, while planning the details of design and movement. Since basically the same scenery and costumes were to serve for both the television and stage productions, the greatest simplicity and flexibility were required; the quick changes of scene necessitated an almost bare stage and very selective décor. Many of the effects were achieved by projections on a cyclorama. All hand and set properties were extremely light and mobile and were brought in and removed by the dancers themselves.

Four cameras recorded the action in the television studio: one was directly in front of the main dancing area; the second was mounted on a platform for overhead shots; the third was trained on the Family and the house; the fourth picked up the changing posters on the fence.

In the Prologue only hand props were used; as the girls, leaving home, went along the road, they passed country people who carried various objects —a shovel, a scythe, milk pails. A cloud machine and a wind machine provided visual and sound effects.

For the opening scene in the park, there was a lamp-post, a bench, a skipping rope, and lollipops.

The décor of the cabaret scene was meant to suggest New Orleans in the 1920s. There was a bar, a table, four chairs, and a doorway with a beaded curtain. Dark, dancing shadows on the cyclorama added to the atmosphere. On one side of the set, posters on a fence indicated the place of the action; the fence was a backing for the bed used in the Edward-Fernando scene (it merely had to be swung around). On the other side of the set was the house that grew up around the Family as the play progressed.

For the scene in the movie studio, with its *Thief of Bagdad* set, there was a fake motion picture camera and a large window frame containing a stylized, arabesque design.

The scene depicting Gluttony was set in a gymnasium, where there were enormous parallel bars, fake scales for weighing in, and the big cream cake which the waitress carried by. Before and after this scene the letters exchanged between the girls and the Family were flashed (enlarged) on the screen.

The Edward-Fernando scene created some problems for the designer when he attempted to follow Brecht's directions. Krohg began by showing the façade of some shops and a sidewalk café, but this piece of scenery was too difficult to set up and shift for the television production and had to be eliminated. The scene was played on a bare stage as if on the sidewalk. At one side of the set, however, was a king-sized bed at the foot of which was a U.S. mailbox. At the appropriate moment the action moved into the bedroom: Anna II climbed into the bed on the side closest to the camera; Edward gave Anna I some money, then got into bed upstage of Anna II; Anna I dropped the money into the mailbox, then crawled into the bed on the side farthest from the camera and pulled the cover over her; Anna II dangled her leg from the bed as the scene ended. When the play was done on the stage in Bergen, the façade of shops and café was used and also a "Brechtian curtain." The fence no longer served as a backing to the bed, but, made of very thin and flexible wood, it was attached to the curtain itself and traveled with it. Letters and posters were affixed to the fence between scenes, and the curtain was drawn after each scene.

As depicted on television, Avarice opened with a still photograph on the front page of the *Baltimore Post*; it showed Anna II on a chaise longue, with guns, and a folding screen behind her. As the camera moved in for a close-up, the picture came to life.

The final scene presented a résumé of the entire play in dance form and was performed on a bare stage.

The four singers who comprised the Family were on a two-step platform from the opening of the play; beside the platform was a U.S. mailbox. The little house that went up during the play was constructed of seven pieces of compo-board. After each scene the singers added a piece to the house, so that it was completed for the Epilogue, when the girls returned home. On the stage at Bergen, the little house stood in front of the curtain, and the Family remained there throughout in a dim blue light; behind the curtain was a revolving stage, which made possible the addition of a little more scenery than had been used on television.

Although *The Seven Deadly Sins* was written in 1933, Guy Krohg decided to dress the dancers in the clothes of the 1920s because the play has the flavor of that period.

In the Prologue Anna I wore a traveling cape ample enough to enfold Anna II. Both girls wore straw sailor hats, white sailor blouses, and short navy-blue skirts to suggest youth and innocence. The passers-by wore coarse work clothes: a farmhand in overalls and a straw hat that was raveling, a farm woman in cotton dress and bonnet. All the clothing was symbolic and so constructed as to allow for quick changes; under their costumes the dancers wore leotards.

The girls wore their sailor suits for the scene in the park; the men who made advances to Anna II wore various kinds of coats and hats, and their spats, and celluloid collars and cuffs were easily detachable. The policeman at the lamp-post was in a uniform of American style.

In the cabaret Anna I wore a cloche hat, a short, tight-fitting beaded dress and a feather boa. The colors were dark—black and brown. Anna II was in the classical dance costume for ballet. The "old pro" wore something that looked like a bikini, tricked out with sequins and feathers; she also sported a top hat. In the Prologue this dancer had worn a peasant's dress and had carried a bundle that actually contained the accessories for the "old pro's" costume, into which she had to change as soon as she got out of range of the camera. The bartender was in shirt-sleeves and a colorful vest; he had a high, stiff collar and sleeve garters. The customers, who were seen in silhouette, wore hats of various shapes—Homburg, peaked cap, and so on. After the "old pro" tore away the classical costume, Anna II put on the top hat and danced in her leotards.

The costumes for the movie studio were a sort of "Arabian fantasy"— the men were naked to the waist, and wore huge turbans, wide pantaloons secured at the ankles, and slippers with turned-up toes. The "star" was in bright colors, the tailor in dark colors. The girls wore costumes similar to the men's, but in addition they had ribbons across their brows and wore bras covered with seed pearls. The "cameramen" had peaked caps and on the backs of their shirts the identification "Studio 6." Anna II, as a star, was in classical dance dress. The guards, who were to keep her from eating, wore executioners' outfits and leather skullcaps. The woman who walked through carrying the cake was in a waitress' uniform. The "producer" wore a white shirt and riding breeches and carried a riding crop.

In the scene depicting Lechery, Edward wore a white linen suit and a straw hat; Fernando was in sleek, dark trousers and a silk shirt. Anna I was richly dressed; Anna II was in a simple frock with a low neckline, which showed off her many strands of pearls.

For the Avarice scene, Anna II was on a chaise longue, wearing a dressing gown with ruching at the neck and wrists and a long red feather boa. The three men—her lovers—were variously dressed in the style of the 1920s. A guard stood by; he wore a fantasy costume consisting of a metal breastplate and the plumed helmet of the dragoons, and held a very long lance, with which he disposed of the bodies of the suicides and also helped the last man to hang himself with the feather boa as a noose.

Scene from Ivo Cramér's production. The Family receives remittances from the girls and builds a little house in Louisiana, but the costumes suggest the American west. Courtesy Norwegian Broadcasting.

In the final scene each of the male dancers returned, wearing the costume in which he had appeared earlier, thus creating the visual impression of a summation. Anna I wore an elaborate gown of cloth-of-silver; Anna II, her classical dance costume.

The members of the Family were dressed as countryfolk, with a Western flavor, and wore the same clothes throughout. The mother was in an old-fashioned gingham dress with a large flower pattern, an ample apron, a sunbonnet, and little metal-rimmed spectacles; the father and two sons, who all had heavy moustaches, wore plaid shirts, dark trousers, suspenders, wide belts, low boots, and big hats with wide brims turned up. The two Annas, though dispirited, return home wearing clothes of more sophisticated style than those in which they left.

Mona Hofland, Actress-Singer

Mona Hofland, Norway's most versatile actress, who played Anna I in Ivo Cramér's television and stage productions of *The Seven Deadly Sins*, had also starred as Eliza Doolittle in *My Fair Lady* and in the title role of a highly successful production of *Hedda Gabler*.

Miss Hofland studied ballet as a child and began her career as an actress in 1950 in a theatre in Oslo devoted to the production of modern plays. She made her début as Räina in Shaw's *Arms and the Man* and traveled with the play throughout Norway. The theatre then launched a series of new plays of poor quality and had to close its doors. The house was taken over by the Oslo New Theatre, and Miss Hofland continued with this company until 1963, when she started freelancing. In 1967 she was invited to become a member of the company at the Norwegian National Theatre.

While still connected with the New Theatre, Miss Hofland made her first appearance in musical comedies. She was able to sing but felt she needed coaching. Learning that the American singer, Anne Brown, who had been the original Bess in *Porgy and Bess* was living in Oslo, Miss Hofland phoned her and asked her if she took pupils. Miss Brown said that she did not, but after a short conversation agreed to work with her. "She is not only a great teacher," said Miss Hofland, "but a very wise woman and a warm and charming person. She has since become one of the busiest voice teachers in Oslo." Miss Hofland studied with her for six months and goes to her for coaching whenever she is cast in a musical. Miss Brown helped her with the role of Eliza in *My Fair Lady*. That play was produced in Norway by Lars Schmidt, under the supervision of Axel Otto Normann, who brought in Alfred Solaas as director and Ivo Cramér as choreographer. No basic changes were made, but Solaas and Cramér added many creative touches, so that theirs was not a rubber-stamp version of the American production. The play was presented at the Norwegian Opera House and ran for six months; then, after a summer layoff, it resumed its run at the New Theatre. It was considered a great hit, having chalked up one of the longest runs of any play in Oslo in recent years.

Earlier, at the New Theatre, Miss Hofland had played Hedda Gabler under the direction of Claes Gill, a very sensitive and imaginative producer. When the cast met for the first time, Gill announced that he planned to do a very contemporary production: the décor would be modern, the women would wear short skirts, and so on. At this point, Espen Skjonberg, Miss Hofland's

Scene V (Lust) in the Ivo Cramér production. Anna I (Mona Hofland) and
Anna II (Anne Borg) receive gifts of pearls from their lovers. At the right is
the American dancer, Ronald Frazier. Courtesy Norwegian Broadcasting.

husband, who was to play Judge Brack, suggested to the director that the way
to achieve a contemporary feeling was to use modern psychology, not modern
costumes—the one was internal, the other merely external. Gill agreed and
during rehearsals talked to the actors quietly and at length "about everything
under the sun" in order to stir their imaginations and deepen their under-
standings of their roles; he never gave them specific movements or line-
readings, but worked for spontaneous reactions. About Hedda, Gill said, "She
did not want to be a member of society; she preferred to withdraw and to
exercise remote control over other people." Miss Hofland had many talks
with Gill about what a modern woman might do in the various situations in
which Hedda found herself. The lines of the play were spoken simply and
seriously, but the scenes between Hedda and Brack had an undercurrent of
bantering humor, an ironic bite that brought them close to comedy. "I tried
to make Hedda a well-rounded character, not sentimental but realistic," said
Miss Hofland, "and people told me that for the first time they felt some pity
for her."

In 1964 Mona Hofland was invited by Arild Brinchmann to take part in
the television production of *The Seven Deadly Sins*. She had worked in
television for about a year and had not been too happy with it; nevertheless,
she agreed and got hold of the script, the score of the play, the Lenya recording, and began to study the part of Anna I by herself. After she had
learned the lines and the songs, she had two sessions with Anne Brown, who

helped her to develop the nuances of the character. When she acted the part in the television studio, Miss Hofland, who is accustomed to performing in the theatre, was disconcerted by the absence of audience reaction, but when the part was repeated on the stage at the Bergen Festival there was enormous response. She recalled: "For the first time I began to realize the emotional power in the play. There were moments when the audience sat there tense and spellbound, then suddenly there would be great bursts of laughter and applause. Reactions of the audience are important to the actor; they help him to adjust his performance as he goes on. That's what I missed in the television studio. Acting in front of a camera is like acting in your own room; there's no communication, no response."

Discussing her role in the Brecht-Weill play, Miss Hofland said she thought Anna I felt a struggle going on in her conscience about what she was doing, and forcing her sister to do, for money. But Brecht was not presenting a sociological treatise nor even showing the psychological development of his characters; he was simply drawing a picture of the world as he saw it and of the way people behave in it. Miss Hofland not only liked the play but felt an intense excitement while doing it; she particularly enjoyed working in an ensemble production, with its intermixture of ballet, music, song, and dialogue. She would now like to appear on the stage in other plays by Brecht: "One critic complained, after seeing *The Seven Deadly Sins,* that I hadn't sung my songs in a 'pretty' way. He probably preferred the performance I gave in *My Fair Lady.*"

Anne Borg, Dancer

Anne Borg, leading dancer with the Norwegian Opera Ballet Company, had worked with Ivo Cramér many times before he selected her for the role of Anna II in his productions of *The Seven Deadly Sins.* She had appeared in numerous ballets and operettas choreographed by Cramér and had had a leading part in *The Message,* Cramér's own ballet, with which she went to London for its presentation on BBC-TV.

Although Anna II has only one or two lines and her character is created entirely by gesture and movement, Miss Borg began to study the part by reading the Brecht script and listening to the phonograph recording. From the speeches of Anna I and from the mood and tempo of the music, she was able by indirection to work out a character line for herself. Cramér said very little to her about the characterization of Anna II, but he did want her to alienate herself from the role and suggested that she dye her hair red (she is a natural blonde) as this would distance the character from her ordinary self.

After the play went into rehearsal, Cramér concentrated on the choreography and set the scenes one by one, but not in the order in which they appear in the script; the scene in the park, for instance, was done before the Prologue. All the movement was made to correspond not only to Weill's music but to Brecht's words, and as Anna II and the other dancers sang along throughout, they became aware of what they were supposed to be expressing. As soon as several scenes were set, Cramér arranged them in sequence so that the timing and movement would be exact for the taping. Miss Borg, who had not done much television work before this, found it difficult to judge distances from the camera while concentrating on the music, the movement, and the meaning.

Mona Hofland as Anna I faces the camera; Anne Borg as Anna II tries to entertain the customers with a classical dance; in semidarkness, right, the bored customers; leaning against the bar, left, The Old Pro, who will show Anna II what the customers really want. Ivo Cramér's production for Norwegian television, 1964. Courtesy Norwegian Broadcasting.

Anne Borg and Mona Hofland, as the two Annas, worked closely together during the production, discussing at length their relationship as sisters as well as their split personality. While performing, they never looked directly at each other; Anna I faced the camera when she sang and avoided giving the impression that she was addressing her sister. This device reinforced the idea that Anna I was soliloquizing and that Anna II was an *alter ego*—that the two girls comprised one person, as stated in the script.

Miss Borg found several scenes especially troublesome. Although Cramér had simplified the action in the Edward-Fernando scene, the movement was still extremely complicated and the emotions complex, requiring the utmost concentration. Another scene that caused the dancer some concern was the one in which Anna II drove her lovers to suicide; Miss Borg was not accustomed to playing farce or broad satire and was afraid that the rapid tempo of the action would make what she was doing look silly or, even worse, would not be clear to the audience. Her fears, it turned out, were unfounded.

According to Miss Borg, it is difficult for a dancer to be explicit about the interpretation of a part, because she has been trained to express her role physically and not verbally. Unlike the actor the dancer is not primarily concerned with an analysis of the part, but must learn the steps, the gestures, and the movements while concentrating on and interpreting the music; an *image* of the role is always there, but not in an intellectually detailed or conceptualized way. After the technical work has been mastered, a profounder characterization may be developed.

Miss Borg approached the role of Anna II timorously, first, because she stood in awe of the work of Bertolt Brecht, but even more because she had never worked with anything like it before. She felt that if she failed she would fail badly. But as she progressed in the part her enthusiasm grew and the experience became very exciting. She actually found it more stimulating than doing a classical ballet—*Swan Lake,* for instance—because Brecht's work is composed of flesh-and-blood people and is related to life, while the classical ballet is a highly developed form of art and belongs entirely to the world of make-believe.

Although Brecht states that Anna II ends in triumph, Miss Borg does not quite agree. Anna II set out to assault the world and found it profitable but debasing; the innocent child went through a series of harrowing and maturing experiences in her search for security, to emerge rich and hardened, but probably less secure than when she started out. Though Anna II has achieved a triumph, perhaps, in the eyes of her parents and of the other girls, in her own eyes she has failed. She has been emotionally drained; she is empty. And emptiness was what showed clearly in Miss Borg's face in the last close-up of her. The audience, in fact, was reduced to tears—a reaction that would have been anathema to Brecht, who wished to appeal to the intellect not to the emotions.

Choreography

Interview with Glen Tetley

Using his own dance company, three guest stars, and a vocal quartet, Glen Tetley, dancer and choreographer, presented his own version of *The Seven Deadly Sins* in British Columbia at the Vancouver Festival in July 1967. The Festival Committee commissioned the Brecht-Weill piece after Meredith Davies, conductor of the Vancouver Symphony Orchestra, had seen and been impressed with Tetley's earlier ballet *Pierrot Lunaire,* an abstract work set to Arnold Schoenberg's music. Mr. Davies conducted the orchestra for the performances of *The Seven Deadly Sins* in Vancouver.

After reading the Brecht script, Tetley decided that he would retain the lyrics but would depart from the action as described by Brecht. He wished to reduce the element of mime and to elaborate the dance so that the entire work would be articulated not in representational but in abstract terms. To achieve that end he originally thought of having the lyrics sung in German, but then decided to use the Auden-Kallman translation. From this translation he extracted the character called Adam, who is mentioned in the Lust scene, and developed it into a full-fledged role for a male dancer. Adam would serve as foil and partner for Anna II and, with Anna I and Anna II more highly integrated than in other productions, Tetley could take the play still further along balletic lines.

Tetley spent about a month in the preparation of the ballet and a month in rehearsal. At the very start he was confronted by a difficult

Glen Tetley, choreographer (in shirtsleeves) at a rehearsal. He is describing action and movement to Scott Douglas as Adam left and to Bettina Jonic as Anna I.

problem: scenery, costumes, and company would have to be transported by air from New York to Vancouver on a very limited budget. He approached Rouben Ter-Arutunian, who had designed earlier Tetley ballets, but Ter-Arutunian's estimate exceeded the budgetary allowance. Tetley's problem was solved by Jackie Cassen and Rudi Stern, who could design the décor with kinetic lights; this solution, in turn, altered Tetley's concept of the production. "I was delighted that circumstance brought me to Cassen and Stern," Tetley said, "because the stimulus of seeing their work for other productions and further discussions with them about *The Seven Deadly Sins* projected my thoughts into an entirely different direction—with scenery created entirely by light, the action of the play could be as fluid as a ballet."

The play was to be presented in Vancouver's Queen Elizabeth Theatre, a very large house with excellent lighting equipment. The design worked out by Cassen and Stern, in consultation with Tetley, was as follows: Ten large translucent Fiberglas panels suspended from a pipe in the flies divided the stage roughly in half—front to back—from another pipe, several feet behind the first, were hung ten opaque Cellutone panels, which served as backing for the Fiberglas and acted as screens to conceal the projectors at the rear of the stage. Twelve projectors had been brought in to augment the regular illumination and were set up in specified positions: eight on stage—two at either side and four at the rear—and four out in the house. The projectors were masked and were operated by about ten dance and design students from Vancouver. The students, who were specially trained and supervised during the performance by Cassen and Stern, had to handle about fifteen hundred slides. The hand-painted slides were not static but cast abstract images, which shifted and changed during each scene. The images were actually choreographed; it was for that reason that dance students were employed, their musical knowledge and their sense of rhythm and timing being a great asset. The lights, both standard and projected, were in all the colors of the spectrum and ran from brilliant and hot to dim and cool, according to the sin depicted. In addition to the panels, there were four Plexiglass platforms on stage, which could be used separately or joined together to create all sorts of abstract forms and structures. There were very few realistic props, and no furniture or set pieces, as Tetley wanted to clear the entire space, so that it might work as an environment for fantasy.

Although Tetley considers *The Seven Deadly Sins* a masterpiece, he looks upon it as having a strange, hybrid form for the theatre. Kurt Weill orchestrated it for a full symphony orchestra and included a solo singer and a quartet, so that it does not fit conveniently into either an opera or a ballet repertoire. For the opera it is too short and contains too large an element of dancing, while for the ballet it is too long and makes too many musical and vocal demands. It is a remarkable but unwieldy work.

For the role of Anna I, Tetley chose Bettina Jonic, who had been acclaimed for her singing of Brecht-Weill works at the Edinburgh Festival and in London. The part of Anna II was danced by Mary Hinkson, a member of Martha Graham's company. Adam the Guide, the character created by Tetley, was danced by Scott Douglas, a leading performer with the American Ballet Theater; and the Family (male quartet) was sung by Terence Wolfe, Robert Jeffrey, David Kendall, and Thomas Wright.

Willa Kim, who designed the costumes, had a total concept of black, white, and Mylar[1] that produced a very Brechtian yet very modern impression. The dancers wore white body-tights and stylized white face make-up. Worn over the tights, in the various scenes, were symbolic pieces of costume in Mylar and clear plastic, designed in such a way as to allow the dancers to make rapid changes without interrupting the flow of the action.

Anna I was the only character who wore the same costume throughout the play. Tetley saw her as an evangelist for sin—the reverse of Billy Graham—as a person sensibly and severely garbed. So Bettina Jonic's beautiful head, with its delicate features, was set off by a dress of shiny black material with a small white clerical collar. Adam—the mental counterpart of Anna I and the physical counterpart of Anna II—was a ghostly white figure in snowy tights, gleaming Mylar vest, silver face make-up, and hair covered with glittering dust; he led the other dancers in, encouraged Anna II in the various sins, and rewarded her with a shower of gold at the end of each scene.

Tetley's conception of "the folks back home" also differed from Brecht's. The choreographer saw them as a rapacious family of crows, huddling in a sort of contemporary birds' nest. Their "house" was not built piecemeal

---

[1] A very thin but strong plastic.

during the play, but was a Buckminster Fuller geodesic dome in plastic situated on the right forestage of the theatre. This dome, which resembled an Eskimo's igloo, was about eight feet in diameter and five feet in height, and was sold as a "climbing toy" at F. A. O. Schwarz, Fifth Avenue, New York. Cassen and Stern covered it with silver Mylar, so that it gleamed like chrome, and lit it in such a way as to make it part of the total stage picture. The Family, dressed in fantasy variations of Southern rural clothing made of shiny straw, live inside the dome. As they grow more affluent, they emerge from the dome—the Mother enormously fat, the men awkward —a hypocritical chorus commenting on the action, moving like birds of prey or scavengers, sitting on top of the house or lifting it up and circling about as if they are on a carousel. When, at the end of each scene, Anna II is paid with a shower of glittering, silvery gold plastic "dust," which she tosses at the Family, they reach out for it with grasping claws.

The lighting of the Prologue produced a severe impression; no projections were used, but down-focused spots fell in separate pools, leaving many dark areas on stage. The two Annas make their first entrance advancing out of the darkness upstage. Only their heads are visible, as their bodies are completely covered by an ample black cloth, which unrolls behind them and forms a serpentine pattern as they move. They appear to be two people enclosed in one skin and, as the cloth is stretchable jersey, they move slightly apart from one another without breaking the image. At mention in the lyrics of the home in Louisiana, the dome and Family are "discovered" on the forestage. Anna I (the intellect) stands motionless in reverie, but Anna II (the instincts), remembering the Family, breaks out of the "skin" and rushes about like an animal released from its cage. Anna I tries to enfold her in the cloak, but Anna II slips away and falls onto the Plexiglass platform as if in a trance, and seeming—since the Plexiglass is transparent—to be suspended in air. As Anna I exits, Adam enters in silence, sees Anna II and begins to prod her with his finger; she writhes but does not awaken.

Sloth. The stage suddenly bursts into full light, predominantly pale greens and yellows, choreographed to suggest a breathing, undulating forest. Through the openings between the panels, a chorus of Furies suddenly surges downstage; they wear Medusa wigs (made of tangled shoelaces) and are lighted to cast towering, frightening shadows on the Plexiglass panels behind them. Nightmarish figures—male dancers made up as caricatures of the members of the Family—try to waken Anna II, but it is Adam, continuing to prod her maliciously, who finally stirs her out of her sloth. She dances with the Furies, then performs a slow and seductive *pas de deux* with Adam; at its conclusion he drops a shower of gold dust into her hand. She flings it in the direction of the avaricious Family; and Anna I, having returned, encloses Anna II in her arms.

Pride. The male dancers, wearing plastic shirts with garish designs and ties with brilliant figures painted on them, build a tower of the Plexiglass platforms; the lights playing on the tower from behind turn it into a flashy marquee for a cheap night club. The predominant colors for the scene are hot mauves and pinks. In the club Adam is the master of ceremonies. Anna II wears a dress concocted of bits of lace curtains and muslin, which Anna I strips away, revealing beneath it a dance costume of the 1920s. When two large fans of ostrich plumes are thrown to Anna II from the

Scene from the Tetley production. The Mother (a male dancer in fantasy costume) hovers over Anna II (Mary Hinkson) who has collapsed on the plexiglass platforms. Courtesy Glen Tetley.

Mary Hinkson as Anna II performing her fan dance a la stripteaser Sally Rand against scenery of kinetic light projected on plastic panels. Photograph: Barry Glass.

wings, she goes into an elegant, acrobatic fan dance à la Sally Rand. (The girls in the line wore costumes designed to be amusingly obscene; they wore wild red wigs, big rubber bosoms with black bras that exposed the nipples from which dangled black tassles, and exposed behinds. They danced in silver theoties—typical chorus girls' shoes of the 1930s.) Suddenly the entire company turns into fantasy furniture: the men become a bed for Anna II; the girls, a swaying couch for Adam. Then Anna's costume and fans disappear; there is a reprise of the chorale sung by the Family, while Anna writhes in anguish as if attempting to wipe the slime from her body; then she exits.

Anger. Strong, bright lights are thrown onto the panels in "op-kinetic" patterns, as of circles and dots rushing by. The boys come on in black vinyl motorcycle jackets and helmets, and perform a wild, running dance; flashlights, strapped to their wrists, give the impression of fast-moving night traffic. The girls enter, wearing white vinyl raincoats and hats and carrying placards with no messages on them; they picket. The boys fall into a sort of Parade of the Wooden Soldiers, like a toy Gestapo. And the scene builds into a big Busby Berkeley production number from a Warner Brothers musical. Anna II, in transparent silver, does a tap dance à la Ruby Keeler; the Family picks up the "house" and does a merry-go-round dance. Adam enters and reminds the Annas that they should be working and earning money. The boys and girls fall to the floor and lie on their backs like broken dolls. In a *pas de deux*, Adam subdues Anna II, who strips off her coat and tosses it to Anna I. As Adam pours gold dust over her, Anna II spirals down and sinks to the floor. Like fat birds the members of the Family sit on top of their cage and sing their chorale.

Gluttony. The male dancers appear, looking like overstuffed penguins, or heavy old men in dress suits; they wear plastic age-masks and big vinyl bellies. They carry the Plexiglass platforms as though they were coffins, and then arrange them to form a banquet table. Adam enters with a champagne bottle and glasses, and the old men proceed to get tipsy and do a drunken dance. They suggest Silenus, leader of the satyrs. At first Tetley thought of providing them with phalluses, but that would have symbolized lechery; to emphasize gluttony, they have dinner napkins tied round their necks. Grotesque props are brought on—huge rubber sausages, chickens, and a cake. Anna II, seeming to pop out of the cake, wears a bunny costume and a little apron with maribou trim. The men gorge themselves and attempt to devour her. On their hands and knees, they suggest pigs, and Anna II throws slops to them; then she lies on their backs and they crawl off with her.

Lust. Anna II returns sensuously dressed and bedecked with Van Cleef and Arpels jewelry at her throat, wrists, and fingers. Tetley considered this the central scene of the play, in which Anna II may work out the conflict between love and lust; she will either break the web of the life she has been caught up in or weave it more tightly about herself. Weill's music at this point is strong and percussive. Anna I, an onlooker, leans against the proscenium at one side of the stage; on the same side, but upstage of her, in a warm pool of light, stands a young man, Alessandro (Fernando, in the script). On the other side of the stage, in a pool of cold light, stands Adam (Edward). Anna II, in a dance of desperation, runs backward across the entire length of the stage and is caught in the arms of Adam. She breaks away from him and crosses the dark area in the

Scene IV (Gluttony) in the Tetley production. Mary Hinkson (Anna II) dressed in a scanty costume trimmed with maribou, pops out of a cake, and entertains some drunken old men. The plexiglass platforms here serve as a banquet table. Courtesy Glen Tetley.

center of the stage, joining Alessandro in the warm light. A beautiful section of the music follows; it is tender and nostalgic. Anna puts Alessandro's arms around her, and they dance. At the pure and emotional climax of this *pas de deux*, Anna I reminds her sister that her love belongs to the man who pays. Anna II leaves Alessandro and goes back to Adam, then turns and sees Anna I touching Alessandro. She flies at them, first attacking Alessandro, then seizing her sister and engaging her in a wild fight; they struggle like two animals. Defeated, Anna II returns to Adam and gives herself to him in a violent sexual way, shoving his head into her stomach. Dejected, she returns to her sister—Alessandro has faded away—then drags back to Adam. He covers her with gold dust, lifts her, and carries her out. Anna I exits, too.

Avarice. For this scene Tetley departed completely from the libretto. Neither Anna II nor Adam appear in it. It is as if Anna II, having given herself up to lust, is not only drained but vanquished, and Anna I is the victor. The choreography is abstract; the projections on the panels are "op-kinetic" patterns in black-and-white geometric figures. The music has a recurrent, pulsing measure, as if expressing the body's insistent wanting and greed. Three couples appear (Alessandro is with another girl); all the dancers, in white body-tights, dance in unison. Lighted from one side in ruby (blood color) and from the other in gold, their tall, slender figures look like neon tubes warming up. The dance expresses conflict and violence, building to a wild crescendo as the bodies seem to get hotter and to glow more brilliantly. At the frenetic climax the boys and girls are widely separated; then the girls hurl themselves into the boys' arms like rockets, and the impact takes the dancers offstage.

Envy. At the beginning of the scene, the stage is in total darkness. Then down-focused spots make two paths of light, which are separated from, but parallel to, each other, running from upstage down. Anna I appears at the top of one path; Anna II, at the top of the other. Anna II wears a glittering evening gown, in the style of Paco Rabanne—a heavy, sleeveless dress with a neckline that encircles the throat, and hung all over with silver Mylar discs, as if weighted with a shower of money. The music from the orchestra explodes and the two Annas stalk each other, walking down their respective paths and then up. The Plexiglass platforms have been piled in the center of the stage to represent a low mountain, or pulpit. Anna I ascends to the highest level and begins to sing, as at a revival meeting. As she delivers her "Sermon of Evil on the Mount," Anna II sinks to the floor. The projections flow all over the stage like fire and water. The dancers enter, dressed entirely in white and locked together in a tight group, like ghosts or lost souls in purgatory—a scene by Doré out of Dante. Anna II watches them with envy, but her movements run counter to those of Anna I and the dancers. As the scene draws to a close, the top of the panels begin to glow with a pure, white, heavenly light, while the bottom of the panels are reddened as if by hell-fire; it is an ambivalent image. The boys lift the girls on their shoulders and carry them back through the openings between the panels. With their arms raised toward the sky, the girls' sleeves cast enormous shadows as of angels' wings. In the center of the stage, there is a cluster of lights, which looks like a great jewel; the lights mix, merge, and fade as the scene ends.

One of the final moments of the play in Glen Tetley's production, Vancouver, Canada, 1967. Mary Hinkson as Anna II in a gown hung with glittering mylar discs to suggest wealth; Scott Douglas as Adam, the tempter; and Bettina Jonic as Anna I in a severe black dress with white, clerical collar. Photograph: Barry Glass.

Epilogue. The lighting resembles that of the Prologue—there are pools of light but no projections. Anna I returns to her song about their home in Louisiana. Adam enters very slowly with the long black cloth used at the opening of the play; when he wraps it around Anna II, she crumples. He lifts her in his arms. Anna I covers her sister completely with the cloak and throws an ample fold around her own shoulders. Only her head is visible as she walks toward the "house." She has triumphed! The members of the Family slowly raise their arms to welcome her home. The lights fade out.

Just before the company left for Vancouver, Tetley invited Lotte Lenya to see a final rehearsal of the work and noted, at its conclusion, that she was visibly moved.

Designing with Light

Interview with Jackie Cassen and Rudi Stern

Jackie Cassen and Rudi Stern, who are artists by training, create stage designs primarily with light. Working in the tradition of Thomas Wilfred, the creator of Lumia and a pioneer in the technique of light projection as an art form, Cassen and Stern have been carrying forward his experiments with the aid of advancing technology in materials and equipment. Miss Cassen was acquainted with the late Mr. Wilfred, paid visits to his studio-school in Nyack, New York, and benefited from his discussions and advice.

Interviewed in their studio-loft in lower Manhattan, where they were surrounded by electrical instruments, lamps, bulbs, tubes, screens, plastic and glass, Cassen and Stern appeared to be practicing physicists rather than stage designers. Miss Cassen explained that modern stage décor may be produced entirely by a process called *kinetic light,* which she defined as follows: "Specially designed and painted slides, when projected, are made to cast constantly moving and changing images onto the stage; these images are integrated with, and express the emotions involved in, the dramatic material or music they accompany. It was kinetic light—abstract, fluid, and colorful—that provided the stage settings for Glen Tetley's production of *The Seven Deadly Sins.*"

After consultation with Tetley, Cassen and Stern built a model stage, on which they experimented with the effect of light on the various kinds of plastic materials that were to be used during the performance. They used paper and cardboard figures to represent the actors, singers, and dancers. Without being aware of it, Cassen and Stern were carrying out almost identical experiments with light—even down to the use of a model stage and cut-out figures—to those Gordon Craig had performed early in this century. Concerning his experiments, Craig said that he wanted to study "the lighting of static objects with moving light such as reflections from moving waters, projected colours, and so on; then the effect of light on moving objects, as when figures emerge from shadows, exist briefly in the light, and disappear again into the darkness."

Screens were hung on the model stage (another Craig idea), but Cassen and Stern used plastic materials and miniature front and rear projectors to play upon them. To co-ordinate their work with the text, music, and movement of the Brecht-Weill play, Cassen and Stern read the script with the most careful attention, listened closely again and again to the Lotte Lenya recording, and made frequent visits to the studio where Tetley was working with the members of the cast. Then, for each sin and for the city in which it occurred, the designers decided on the emotional tones they desired and created the colors and movement patterns that would best express them. They were aiming not only for an appropriate evocation of each scene but for a contrast between scenes, so that each would have its own individuality and emotional tone. These preliminary ideas and sketches were discussed with, and approved by, Tetley.

When Cassen and Stern were satisfied with the results they achieved in the model, they set up a section of the stage, life size, in the studio, and dancers were introduced for further experimentation, in an effort to explore all the possibilities of movement and light.

Cassen and Stern started to work on *The Seven Deadly Sins* at the beginning of April 1967, and from then until they left for Vancouver in July, they were occupied with the preparation of slides; about three thousand of these were painted by hand with special care and precision. Then the slides, projectors, Mylar, and other materials were transported to Vancouver by air. The Plexiglass went in sheets and was made up into platforms in the theatre, where the geodesic dome—the "house" in which the Family lived—was trimmed and processed.

Arriving at the Queen Elizabeth Theatre about a week before Tetley and the company, Cassen and Stern supervised the hanging of the screens, the placing of the instruments, and the training of the students who were to handle them. Before the play opened, a classroom was set up in the basement of the theatre where the students were taught not only how to work the projectors and slides but how to use their hands sensitively to produce the fluid movement of light. Miss Cassen conducted these classes, and during the performances she worked with some of the students back-stage while Mr. Stern worked with others in the house. A very elaborate intercom system was set up between them, run by Tetley's stage manager, Maxine Glorsky. Gilbert Hemsley, Jr., designed the setup of the normal stage lighting and supervised the installation of that equipment.

Of all the productions Cassen and Stern have done, they named *The Seven Deadly Sins* as one of their favorites and expressed the wish that New Yorkers might have an opportunity to see it. Meanwhile they continue to work and experiment in the field of designing with kinetic light.

Scene from the elaborate production presented by the State Opera House in East Berlin, February 1968, to commemorate Brecht's birthday. Anna II (Ilse Hurtig) soars while the stock market falls. Photograph: Marion Schöne. Courtesy Deutsche Staatsoper Berlin.

THE SEVEN DEADLY SINS OF THE LOWER MIDDLE CLASS *Ballet Cantata*

BERTOLT BRECHT
English version by W. H. Auden and Chester Kallman

Characters

Anna I
Anna II
The Family
Nightclub Owner, Old Dancer, Star, Director, Ring-Master, Edward, Fernando, Suitors, Passersby, Guests, Dancers, etc.

There are seven scenes, each takes place in a different city in the United States.

Prologue

This ballet cantata is the representation of a journey to be made by two sisters from the southern states who wish to earn enough money to build a little house for themselves and their family. Both girls are called **Anna.** *One of the* **Annas** *is the manager, the other is the artist;* **Anna I** *is the saleswoman,* **Anna II,** *the merchandise.*
On the stage there is a small blackboard on which is shown the route to be taken by the sisters in their tour through seven states; **Anna I** *stands in front of the blackboard with a small pointer in her hand. The stage also represents the ever-changing market-place to which* **Anna II** *is sent by her sister. At the end of each scene, which demonstrates how the seven deadly sins may be avoided,* **Anna II** *returns to the side of* **Anna I.** *Also present on the stage throughout the play is the* **Family** *of the two sisters—father, mother, and two brothers—in Louisiana; the little house, built with the earnings*
that come from the shunning of sins, is erected section by section after each scene, until at the end of the play the **Family** *is completely sheltered.*[1]

Anna I: So my sister and I left Louisiana
Where the moon on the Mississippi
    is a-shining ever
Like you always hear in the songs of
    Dixie.
We look forward to our homecom-
    ing—
And the sooner the better.
Anna II: And the sooner the better.
Anna I: It's a month already since we
    started
For the great big cities where you
    go to make money.
In seven years our fortune should be
    made
And then we can go back.
Anna II: In six years would be so much
    nicer.
Anna I: Our mom and dad and both our
    brothers
Wait in old Louisiana
And we'll send them all the money
    as we make it
For all the money's got to go
To build a little home
Down by the Mississippi in Louisi-
    ana.
Right, Annie?

[1] The stage directions preceding each scene are part of Brecht's original script but were omitted by Auden and Kallman. They are here restored and translated by the editor.—R. G.

531

Anna II: Right, Annie.

I. Sloth
(in committing injustice)

This is the first city on their tour, and in order to get their hands on some money, the sisters work a little racket. Strolling through the local park, they seek out married couples. **Anna II** *rushes up to the* **Man** *as if she knows him, throws her arms around him, reproaches him, and so on, in short, embarrasses him, while* **Anna I** *pretends to restrain her.*

> *[Suddenly* **Anna II** *throws herself upon the* **Woman** *and threatens her with her parasol, which gives* **Anna I** *a chance to extort some money from the* **Man** *on a promise of hauling her sister off. The girls carry out this trick several times in quick succession. Then it happens that* **Anna I,** *while trying to wheedle some money from a* **Man** *she has managed to coax away from his* **Wife,** *and confident that her sister meanwhile is molesting the* **Woman,** *sees to her horror that instead of "working"* **Anna II** *is sitting on a bench and sleeping.* **Anna I** *has to wake her and keep her on the job.]*
>
> *[This scene is mimed and danced while the* **Family** *sings:]*

Family: Will she now? . . . Will our Annie pull herself together?
Lazy Bones are for the Devil's stock-pot—
For she was always quite a one for that armchair;
Unless you came and hauled her off the mattress
The lazy slut would lie abed all morning.
Otherwise, Annie was, we must admit, a most respectful child,
Did what she was told and showed affection for her parents.
This is what we told her when she left home:
"Think of us, and mind you keep your nose down to the grindstone—
Lazy Bones are for the Devil's stock-pot."
O Lord, look down upon our daughter,
Show her the way that leads the Good to Thy reward,
In all her doings prevent her and comfort her,
Incline her heart to observe all Thy commandments,
That her works on earth may prosper.

II. Pride
(in the best of the ego;)
(incorruptibility)

A dirty little nightclub.

> *[***Anna II*** *appears on the stage to the applause of four or five* **Patrons** *who look so dreadful that she is terrified. She is poorly dressed and performs a rather unusual dance; she does her best but gets no response. The* **Patrons** *are immensely bored, they yawn like sharks (their masks show enormous mouths full of frightening teeth); they throw things at the stage and manage to knock out the only light.* **Anna II** *goes on dancing, devoted to her art, until she is dragged off the stage by the* **Owner** *of the place. He sends* **Another Dancer**—*a flabby old slut—onto the stage to show* **Anna** *what she must do to get applause in this place. The old hag dances in a vulgar and sexual way and gets an enormous response.* **Anna** *refuses to dance that way. But* **Anna I,** *who is standing near the stage and was at first the only one to applaud her sister, now weeps over her failure and urges her to dance the way they want her to. She rips off the rather long dress* **Anna II** *is wearing and sends her back to the stage, where the old "pro" teaches her a dance in which she raises her underskirts higher as the au-*

*dience eggs her on with applause.
And then* **Anna I** *leads the shattered girl back to the little blackboard and comforts her.]*

Anna I: So we
Saved up,
Bought ourselves an outfit:
Nighties,
Panties,
Beautiful dresses.
Soon we
Found a
Job that was going,
A job as dancer in a cabaret,
A job in Memphis, the second big
town we came to.
Oh how hard it was for Annie! Beau-
tiful clothes
Can make a good girl particular—
When the drinking tigress meets
Herself in the pool
She's apt to become a menace.
She began talking about Art, of all
things,
About the Art, if you please! of Cab-
aret,
In Memphis, the second big town we
came to.
It wasn't Art that sort of people
came for,
That sort of people came for some-
thing else;
And when a man has paid for his
evening
He expects a good show in return.
Then if you cover up your bosom and
thighs
Like you had a rash,
Don't be surprised to see them yawn-
ing.
So I told my Art-loving sister Annie:
"Leave your pride to those who can
well afford it.
Do what you are asked to do and not
what you want,
For that isn't what is wanted."
Oh but
I had
Trouble, I can tell you,
With her
Fancy

Pig-headed notions.
Many
Nights I
Sat by her bedside
Holding her hand and saying this:
"Think of our home in Louisiana."

Family: O Lord, look down upon our
daughter,
Show her the way that leads the Good
to Thy reward.
Who fights the Good Fight and all
Self subdues,
Wins the Palm, gains the Crown.

III. Wrath
(against meanness)

Anna *gets a job as an extra in a movie.*

[The **Star,** *an actor of the Douglas
Fairbanks type, is jumping a horse
over a flower-box. The animal is
awkward and the* **Star** *whips him
viciously. The horse falls to the
ground and in spite of the blanket
which is placed under him, he
cannot get up. The* **Star** *begins
to whip the beast again and at
that moment the little extra comes
forward and, gripped by wrath,
snatches the whip from the actor's
hand and strikes him with it. She
is immediately dismissed. But*
Anna I *rushes after her and convinces her to turn back, to throw
herself on her knees before the*
Star, *and to kiss his hand, so that
he may put in a good word for
her again with the producer.]*

Family: We're at a standstill! What she's
been sending,
It's not any money a man can build
a home with.
She's as giddy as a cyclone!
All the money goes for her pleasure!
And we're at a standstill, for what
she's been sending
Isn't any money a man can build a
home with.

Won't she settle down to business?
Won't she ever learn to save something?
For what the featherbrain is sending
Isn't any kind of money
A man can build a little home with.

Anna I: We're making progress! We have come to Los Angeles,
And every door is open here to welcome extras.
We only need a bit of practice
Avoiding possible faux-pas
And what can stop us
Going straight to the top then!

Family: O Lord, look down upon our daughter.
Show her the way that leads the Good to Thy reward.

Anna I: If you take offense at Injustice,
Mister Big will show he's offended;
If a curse or a blow can enrage you so,
Your usefulness here is ended.
Then mind what the Good Book tells us
When it says: *Resist not Evil.*
Unforgiving Anger
Is from the Devil.
It took time to teach my sister wrath wouldn't do
In Los Angeles, the third big town we came to
Where her open disapproval of injustice
Was so widely disapproved.
I forever told her: "Practice self-control, Annie,
For you know how much it costs you if you don't."
And she understood and answered:

Anna II: You're so right, Annie.

IV. Gluttony
(satiety, eating for oneself)

Anna *is now a star herself. She has signed a contract which states that she must maintain her present weight, and therefore is not permitted to eat.*

[One day she steals an apple and devours it in secret, but when she is weighed she shows a gain of half an ounce and the **Producer** *tears his hair. From now on her meals are supervised by her sister.* **Two Waiters** *armed with revolvers serve her, and from the general platter she is allowed to take only a little sniff.]*

[This scene is mimed and danced while the **Family** *sings:]*

Family: We've gotten word from Philadelphia:
Annie's doing well, making lots of money.
Her contract has been signed to do a solo turn,
It forbids her ever eating
When or what she likes to eat.
Those are hard terms for little Annie
Who has always been very greedy.
Oh if only she doesn't break her contract—
There's no market for hippos in Philadelphia.
Every single day they weigh her;
Gaining half an ounce means trouble.
They have principles to stand by—
"It's a hundred-and-eighteen that you were signed for;
Only for the weight agreed we pay!"
Gaining half an ounce means trouble,
More than that would mean disaster!
But our Annie isn't all that stupid
And she knows a contract is a contract,
So she'll reason: After all
You still can eat like little Annie
In Louisiana—
Crabmeat! Porkchops! Sweet Corn! Chicken!
And those golden biscuits spread with honey!
Spare your home in old Louisiana!
Think! It's growing! More and more it needs you!
Therefore curb your craving! Gluttons will be punished.
Stop it! Stop it at once! You won't go to heaven.

V. *Lust*
(unselfish love)

Anna *now has a friend [called* **Edward** *in the original,* **Adam** *in the translation] who loves her; he is very rich and gives her gifts of clothes and jewels. But there is another man she adores who takes the jewels from her. Her sister reproaches her and succeeds in getting her to remain true to* **Edward** *and to break with* **Fernando.**

[But one day **Anna II** *passes a café and sees her sister sitting at a sidewalk table with* **Fernando** *who is attempting, unsuccessfully, to make love to her.* **Anna II** *rushes up to them and, before the eyes of* **Edward** *and his* **Friends,** *as well as the gathering* **Onlookers** *and the* **Urchins** *playing in the street, she throws herself upon her sister and wrestles violently with her. The ragamuffins show each other their precious behinds;* **Edward** *runs off in horror. Then* **Anna I** *severely rebukes her sister and sends her back to* **Edward** *after a touching farewell from* **Fernando.]**

Anna I: Then we met a wealthy man in Boston
And he paid her a lot because he loved her;
While I had to keep a watch on Annie
Who was *too* loving, but she loved another:
And *she* paid *him* a lot
Because she loved him.
So I said: "Cheat the man who protects you
And you've lost half your value then:
He may pay once although he suspects you,
But he won't pay time and time again.
"You can have your fun with money
When you've no provider you must face,
But for girls like us it's not funny
If we ever even once forget our place.
"Don't try to sit between two stools,"
I told her;

Then I went to see her young friend
And said: "If you're kind, you won't hold her,
For this love will be your sweetheart's bitter end.
"Girls can have their fun with money
When the money is their own to give,
But for girls like us it's not funny
If we even once forget the way we live."
So I bought him a long one-way ticket
Which it broke his heart to use. (Naturally!)
But when Annie found out my trick, it
Looked like broken bones for me!

Family: O Lord, look down upon our daughter,
Show her the way that leads the Good to Thy reward,
Incline her heart to observe all Thy commandments
That her works on earth may prosper.

Anna I: Now she shows off her white little fanny
Worth twice a little Texas motel,
And for nothing the poolroom can stare at Annie
As though she had nothing to sell.
That's why most girls don't get rich, for
They go bad when they forget their place:
You're not free to buy what you itch for
When you've got a good provider you must face.

Family: Who fights the Good Fight and all Self subdues
Will gain her renown.

Anna I: It wasn't easy putting that in order:
Saying good-bye to young Fernando,
Then back to Adam to apologize,
Then the endless nights I heard my sister
Sobbing bitterly and repeating:

Anna II: It's right like this, Annie, but so hard!

VI. *Avarice*
(by robbery and fraud)

Not long afterwards **Edward** *is ruined by* **Anna** *and shoots himself, but the newspapers give her a lot of flattering publicity.*

[The **Readers** *raise their hats respectfully to her and, newspapers in hand, immediately pursue her in order to ruin themselves. A short time later, a* **Second Young Man,** *cleaned out by* **Anna,** *throws himself out of a window. When a* **Third Young Man** *threatens to hang himself,* **Anna I** *takes matters in hand and rescues the fellow by getting his money back from her sister and returning it to him. She intervenes because people are already beginning to go out of their way to avoid her sister, whose avarice has earned her a bad reputation.*]

[*This scene is mimed and danced while the* **Family** *sings:*]
Family: Annie, so the paper says,
　　Is now set up in Baltimore:
　　Lots of folk seem to be
　　Shooting themselves for her.
　　She must be doing all right
　　And raking it in
　　To get in the news like that!
　　Well, so far, so good:
　　To be talked about helps
　　A young girl up the ladder.
　　Isn't she, though, overdoing it?
　　Some people might think she was
　　　　mean:
　　Folk shy away from a girl
　　Who's said to be mean.
　　Folk give a wide wide berth
　　To those who grab all they can get,
　　Point unfriendly fingers at
　　One whose greed goes beyond all
　　　　bounds.
　　In the measure you give
　　You will surely be given,
　　And as you do, so

Will you be done by:
　　Fair is fair.
　　All must keep this law.
　　We sincerely hope our smart litle
　　　　Annie
　　Also has common sense
　　And will let them keep a shirt or two
　　When she lets them go for good.
　　Shameless hoarders earn themselves
　　　　a bad name.

VII. *Envy*
(of happy people)

Once again we see **Anna** *going through a big city.*

[On her way she catches sight of other **Annas** (all the dancers wear Anna-masks) giving themselves up to slothfulness and so on, for they indulge without regret in all the deadly sins which are denied to **Anna.** "The last shall be first" is the theme of the ballet they now perform: While the other **Annas** move haughtily in the light, **Anna II,** weary and bent, drags herself about with difficulty; but then her rise begins, she dances more and more proudly and, finally, triumphantly, while the other **Annas** fall back and humbly open a pathway for her.]

Anna I: And the last big town we came
　　to was San Francisco.
　　Life there was fine, only Annie felt
　　　　so tired
　　And grew envious of others:
　　Of those who pass the time at their
　　　　ease and in comfort,
　　Those too proud to be bought,
　　Of those whose wrath is kindled by
　　　　injustice,
　　Those who act upon their impulses
　　　　happily,
　　Lovers true to their loved ones,
　　And those who take what they need
　　　　without shame.
　　Whereupon I told my poor tired
　　　　sister

When I saw how much she envied
    them:
"Sister, from birth we may write our
    own story,
And anything we choose we are
    permitted to do,
But the proud and insolent who
    strut in their glory—
Little they guess,
Little they guess,
Little they guess the fate they're
    swaggering to.
"Sister, be strong! You must learn to
    say No to
The joys of this world, for this world
    is a snare;
Only the fools of this world will let
    go, who
Don't care a damn,
Don't care a damn—
Don't-care-a-damn will be made to
    care.
"Don't let the flesh and its longings
    get you,
Remember the price that a lover
    must pay,
And say to yourself when
    temptations beset you:—
What is the use?
What is the use?
Beauty will perish and youth pass
    away.
"Sister, you know, when our life

here is over,
Those who were good go to bliss
    unalloyed,
Those who were bad are rejected
    forever,
Gnashing their teeth,
Gnashing their teeth,
Gnashing their teeth in a gibbering
    void."
Family: Who fights the Good Fight and
    all Self subdues,
Wins the Palm, gains the Crown.

Epilogue

Anna I: Now we're coming back to you,
    Louisiana,
Where the moon on the Mississippi
    is a-shining ever.
Seven years we've been away in the
    big towns
Where you go to make money;
And now our fortune's made
And now you're there,
Little home in old Louisiana.
We're coming back to you,
Our little home down by
The Mississippi in
Louisiana. . . .
Right, Annie?
Anna II: Right, Annie.

CURTAIN

THE
OLD
TUNE

Robert Pinget

Georges Adet as Toupin-Gorman in beret, and Henry de Livry as Pommard-Cream in the French production, of *The Old Tune* (*La Manivelle*) at the Théâtre de la Comédie de Paris, September 1962. Scenery and props are makeshift and backed by draperies, but under stage lighting appear abstract and impressionistic. Photograph: Bernand. Courtesy Georges Adet.

Robert Pinget

Robert Pinget, Swiss novelist and playwright, was born in Geneva of French parents on July 19, 1919. He had two sisters and a brother; his father was a businessman. Though none of his forebears had been involved in literary or artistic pursuits, Robert as a child and young man, wrote innumerable poems. At school he was interested in the classics. Later he took a law degree and obtained a license to practice, then he developed a sudden and deep interest in painting, left Geneva while still in his early twenties, and went to Paris to study at the Ecole des Beaux Arts. As an art student, he adhered to the traditional principles taught at the school, but later developed his own nonrepresentational style. In 1946 he took up permanent residence in Paris where, four years later, an exhibition of his paintings was held at La Galerie du Siècle. He supported himself by working as a journalist. For a short time he lived in London, where he taught French and art.

On his return to Paris, Pinget gave up painting for writing and began to pour out stories, novels, and plays. In 1951 his first book, *Entre Fantoine et Agapa,* was published by Laffont. It was a collection of unusual and far-fetched tales reminiscent of Henri Michaux. The stories were full of comic invention, false reasoning, and a sense of the supernatural, which contained strong elements of realism. In one of the tales, God is called The Supreme Neutron.

In 1952 Gallimard published Pinget's second book, a novel called *Mahu or the Material,* which like his earlier work was compounded of caricature, humor, and fantasy, but completely departed from verisimilitude and coherent narrative. Alain Robbe-Grillet, the avant-garde novelist, who was not personally acquainted with Pinget at the time, wrote a perceptive and complimentary article about *Mahu* and later introduced its author to his own publisher, Jérôme Lindon. Lindon, head of *Editions de Minuit,* has brought out almost all of Pinget's work up to the present time; he is also the publisher of Samuel Beckett, Michel Butor, Nathalie Sarraute, and Claude Simon, the so-called New Wave novelists. Before writing *Mahu,* Pinget had never read the work of any of these authors. Subsequently Pinget and Beckett became close friends and collaborators. When asked to define the New Wave novel, Pinget said it was "a reaction against the traditional novel, which no longer corresponds to the modern writer's way of looking at life or of expressing himself. It is a desire to record the unverifiable, which was born forty years ago with surrealism and the phenomenon of automatic writing." Pinget credited Lindon with bringing this new style of writing to the attention of the public.

In the books that followed *Mahu,* Pinget continued to experiment with and to employ more subjective and unconventional techniques of expression. *Le Renard et la Boussole,* published by Gallimard in 1953, takes place in Israel and contains, in beautiful and flowing prose, a series of meditations on the condition of the Jews, thoughts about human relations, and reflections on the destiny and the ambiguous situation of the writer and artist in general.

There followed in quick succession three important novels, which clearly showed the direction Pinget's thought and technique were taking. *Graal Flibuste* (1957) is an excursion into caricature and mockery, an experiment with the interior voice and with the disarrangement of language. *Baga* (1958) expresses man's disenchantment and disintegration, continues with stylistic exploration, and appears at its conclusion to be overcome itself by a state of inertia. *Le Fiston* (1959)—told in the manner of the "spoken language," with a strange juxtaposition of words, a scrambling of syntax, peculiar punctuation, and unnumbered pages—deals with man's loneliness, with his self-torture, his inability to communicate, his anguished memories, and with the terrifying repetitiveness of experience. For *Le Fiston* Pinget was awarded the Prix Rambert.

Along with several other writers, Pinget was invited by the Ford Foundation to spend six months in the United States in 1959 as a cultural representative of France. He was very much taken with the country and was particularly grateful that the travel grant did not require him to lecture or teach. An inveterate traveler, Pinget has visited Mexico and North Africa, in addition to many European countries.

Pinget's short novel *Clope au dossier* appeared in 1961. It consists of vignettes of provincial life, a series of little autonomous worlds that are tangent to one another, the points of contact being either a place (the bench on which Toupin is installed with his barrel organ, for example) or a given moment. Here the author deals with old age and infirmity, with empty and loveless lives. Commenting on this work, one critic has said, "Pinget is past-master of the art of pushing to the limits of the tolerable a grating form of humor that is born of mental activity, seized, as it were, at the level of the lips, in what ordinary thought and language have often rendered spineless."

L'Inquisitoire (1962), a longer and more comprehensive work, unites the characters and themes of some of the earlier books, and gives the impression of total realism. As Pinget has said, "The real is inexhaustible." On the other hand, the style of the book, which is fugal in musical terms and kaleidoscopic in its visual aspects, actually creates an unreal and dreamlike quality. Nominated for the important Prix Goncourt and awarded the Prix des Critiques, *L'Inquisitoire* became a best seller in France.

Quelqu'un (1965), Pinget's most recent novel, takes place in a squalid boardinghouse and deals with a writer who has misplaced a scrap of paper on which he has made a notation. The search for the piece of paper gives needed unity to the book, in which there is a constant recalling of past time, with the addition of new details interwoven with glimpses into the lives of the various boarders. It is what the author calls an "exposition," or a series of hypotheses, a form of expression he has refined to a remarkable degree. This novel won the Prix Femina.

Pinget's plays have been drawn largely from his novels. From *Le Fiston* came *The Dead Letter* (1959), which was produced at the Thèâtre Récamier in Paris with great success. The play is a variation of the Prodigal Son story, but places its emphasis on man's loneliness and despair, the cruel and senseless aspects of human life, and the ability of the memory both to soothe and to torment.

From his novel *Clope au dossier,* Pinget drew two plays: the one-act *La Manivelle* (1960), which has been performed on stage and radio in many countries; and *Clope* (1961), a full-length play, which has had few productions. Both plays deal with alienation and physical disintegration: Clope, a friendless skeleton of a man, with a hacking cough, lives in a shack in a railway station, and seeks vainly for companionship; Toupin and Pommard, in *La Manivelle,* are worn out with old age but find consolation in their inaccurate memories of the past.

Pinget's other one-act and radio plays include *Architruc* (1961, from his novel *Baga*), *The Hypothesis* (1961), and *About Mortin* (1965). The last-named is a series of eight extended "interviews," with the names of the speakers omitted. These short plays have been presented on stage or radio in Paris, Stuttgart (Germany), and London.

Pinget's work has often been likened to Samuel Beckett's; but Barbara Bray, who is acquainted with both men and who has translated most of Pinget's plays, has said that although there are "important affinities . . . these have been exaggerated and oversimplified."

In an interview with Peter Lennon, which appeared in *The Guardian* (London, November 30, 1965), Pinget contested the idea that the label "dramatist of the absurd" could be usefully applied to either his or Beckett's work. "Don't believe that the world is in any sense absurd," he said. "It is horribly difficult, but not absurd. In fact, over the past few years events have been repeating themselves with terrible logic." When the interviewer asked Pinget why he wrote his novels in either dialogue or monologue form, he replied, "Because it is a simple and practical method of systematically exposing all aspects of a problem."

When he is not traveling, Pinget divides his time between his apartment in Paris and his country home in Touraine, and continues to write novels and plays in his highly personal style.

The Old Tune

An analysis of Pinget's play *The Old Tune* sheds a great deal of light on the trend the drama has taken in recent times. Pinget's complete abandonment of Aristotelian principles, his intermixture of realism with various other theatrical styles, his humorous treatment of serious subjects, and the skeletal brevity of his play are characteristic of the work of almost all avant-garde dramatists.

Pinget, who is a leading exponent of the New-Wave French novel, which presents concrete facts without comment or explanation and without formal structure, has made use of his prose technique in writing his play.

Though his "range of nuance . . . ," as one critic has said, "permits the inclusion of widely disparate fragments of experience in a harmonious whole," one of the salient features of *The Old Tune* is its plotlessness. In order to present what he considers a more authentic picture of real life than is found in conventional drama, Pinget consciously avoids the use of intrigue and suspense. The action in which Gorman and Cream are involved contains no conflict, no crises or climaxes, no resolution, and no dénouement. The situation he offers us is a tenuous confrontation, reflecting a condition of stasis, a waiting, a passing of time, at most, a circular action. Since the play suggests that the future will be nothing but a repetition of the past, a heavy emphasis is placed upon memory. In *Clope au dossier,* the novel from which this play was drawn, Pinget explains what the "heroes" of all his works are trying to do: "For fear of perishing they accumulate between themselves and imminent death as one would [pile up] furniture in front of a door about to be battered down a large number of memories, their defense against the intruder." Yet in *The Old Tune* memory is shown to be nothing more than a gallery of distorting mirrors receding endlessly into the past with the irrationality and inconsistency of a dream. The elusive material of memory never quite comes into focus, and what has been in focus is blurred by subsequent additions. The tiny fragments do not add up to an over-all plot. Life is a series of moments that pass in continuous insignificance; it is lived in a kind of limbo, dim and mysterious. In *The Old Tune* there are striking juxtapositions, held together by associative themes; the discovery and description of old objects, acquaintances, and places gives coherence to the play. Pinget's method lays him open to boring the audience, and so he must find patterns of metamorphosis and progressive discovery or other ways of maintaining the tension. The method is best suited, of course, to a short work.

Gorman and Cream have very little in common with dramatic characters of either the classical or conventional type; they do not exhibit "tragic flaws" or "comic humours," nor do they struggle to attain particular goals or to avoid impending catastrophes. We are not asked to view them as psychological specimens or as case histories; we are not concerned with their personal habits or predilections or even with their ordinary motivations. They are immobile, withdrawn, and flat; their ability to communicate or to progress is impeded by physical handicaps and faulty memories. They are presented primarily in a theatrical and symbolic way, to depict the human condition as the playwright conceives it: each human being is alone, shut within his own incompatible memories, inhabiting in old age the dream world that precedes the dreamless sleep.

The play's dialogue is a more or less feverish argumentation, which gives dynamic quality to the stasis, or near stasis, of the characters. There is no oratory, no declamation; the lines uttered by the old men are staccato, repetitious, circular, and filled with neologisms, spoonerisms, *non sequiturs,* and puns, which shed significant light on the situation and arouse strong feelings of anguish, pathos, and bitter humor. The bareness of plot action and language suggests approaching nothingness, which is emphasized by the use of frequent and extended pauses. The total effect is of a lyrical rendition of actual speech. The extreme economy of the dialogue, as well as its vivid imagery, rhythmical refrains, and measured tempo (mainly *lento*), provide a further link with traditional verse. Its movement in the direction of poetry is one of the most interesting aspects of modern drama, though language and words are becoming increasingly suspect. In Pinget's play *Clope,* the leading character remarks: "Do you know . . . French will soon be a dead language. Too rational. The trend's all toward sensation, instinct, the agglutinisation of language." Thus modern plays often pass beyond poetry and move toward silence and toward mime. The avant-garde dramatist appears to be saying that words do not help men either to communicate with or to understand each other.

The Old Tune, like other very modern plays, does not have a clear-cut theme but is full of implications and ambiguities that enable it to be understood on various levels. Though each playgoer may feel that a particular level is dominant, that does not mean that the other levels do not exist. The modern playwright consciously employs ambiguity to suggest the mystery of life, the inability to understand oneself and others. Audiences brought up on conventional dramatic fare expect the playwright to make a clear statement about life that will enlighten or soothe; they expect him to bring order out of chaos. Confusion ensues when critics and audiences search for hidden meanings in plays whose very purpose is to mirror the chaos of life and its meaninglessness. The task of the playwright today, according to Samuel Beckett, is not to write chaotically, without form, but to find the form that will accommodate the chaos. In Pinget's play *Dead Letter,* there is a pertinent colloquy between a Post Office Clerk and an Old Man:

Clerk: . . . I haven't got a life story.
Old Man: You have to look for the inner meaning.
Clerk: All there is is on the surface. Inner meanings are for people like you. People who've got nothing better to do than keep thinking about the same thing.

If there is no clear theme in *The Old Tune,* there are quite obvious satirical social comments. The characters complain that great sums of money are being poured into atomic research, though no cure for rheumatism has as yet been found; that it is "lunacy" to explore the moon and to go on killing men in the Far East; and that, on a lighter note, it is useless to provide "cultural" advantages, such as lessons in French, for pampered young ladies. There is also a pointed thrust at the two moralities—public and private— of the civil servant in the judge who freely grants divorces while his heart bleeds for the children of broken homes. In short, Pinget does not deal with complex psychological or philosophical issues in a logical, structured way, but presents such concepts in fragmented form and in such a manner as to make them dramatically effective.

What we find to a remarkable degree in *The Old Tune* is the evocation of mood. The atmosphere is heavy with irony, wry humor, and pity. There is deep compassion for man in the human predicament, nostalgia for the past and dreams for the future, dignity in the face of death and a reaching out for communion with the living. Pinget's play exemplifies perfectly, both in form and content, Beckett's remark that "The artistic tendency is not expansive, but contractive. And art is the apotheosis of solitude."

The Production Record

Robert Pinget's play *La Manivelle* (called *The Old Tune* in Samuel Beckett's translation) had its première performance on the Third Programme of the BBC in London on Tuesday, August 23, 1960, at 9:55 P.M., and was rebroadcast on Sunday evening, September 11, at 6:50 P.M. Critical reaction to this radio play was mixed; the acting and direction were praised, but the script was called everything from "a conversation piece" to "a bore." Paul Ferris, writing in *The Observer* (London, August 28, 1960), said:

> Sooner or later any discussion of Third Programme drama productions comes round to saying "beautifully done." Their sound effects are brought in straight from the street, their silences are perfectly timed, their casts are well disciplined. Take that little piece by Robert Pinget, The Old Tune. . . . Wasn't it a little gem? Well, yes, it was: a *very* little gem.

The Old Tune had its American première on March 23, 1961, on the stage of the Royal Playhouse, an off-Broadway theatre in New York. It was done on a double bill with *The Square*, by Marguerite Duras, and had incidental music by Deems Taylor. The play was presented by Rose Lynch, directed by Steve Chernak, and performed by Sy Travers and Jack Delmonte. All the notices were bad except Jerry Tallmer's, which appeared in *The Village Voice* for March 30, 1961. Tallmer wrote:

> The daily critics have put it down and so I suppose it shall die, but "The Old Tune," by Robert Pinget in a translation-adaptation by Samuel Beckett—more Beckett than Pinget, I hazard—is a telling if slender piece of work. Death becomes it well: its subject matter is aging and death, desuetude and deliquesence. But also memory and fondness, loving and nostalgia—and the foolish-fondness of old men straining with weak memories, full of error, for the pictures and pleasures of the past.
> The Royal Playhouse, where at least as of last Saturday night it was receiving its American premiere . . . , cannot be improved upon as a catacomb for its entombment. Once apparently a Lower East Side ballroom, the Royal in 1961 is still festooned with priceless crystal chandeliers, ageless green rep curtains, and down each of its walls there marches a row of something vaguely like cathedral windows; the chairs are provisional and ancient; there's a mysterious area in the back featuring Pepsi-Cola bottles, dust, and the yellowing tatters of publicity puffs for long dead off-off-off-Off Broadway productions. Presiding over this grotto (and the ticket counter) is Rose Lynch, the red-headed proprietress of the theatre and producer of the present effort: a tart and garrulous *concierge* out of 3000 movies we all have seen from France— just as her little auditorium is itself a recreation of the mis-remembered ballroom in "Carnet de Bal," and with the same powerful qualities of evocation. There were eight of us in the audience for the late show Saturday night; eight of us out front, and Rose, and the four actors in the two plays on stage. . . .

In the Beckett-Pinget piece there are two old men, Mr. Gorman and Mr. Cream, mis-remembering the Dublin of their youth. They look out at the chandeliers and at the eight of us and muse, between complaints about the motor cars roaring past. . . . There is loss, there is imagery, there is gain. From the fleeting and transient, something remains. Life. From death, life.

The actors are Sy Travers as Mr. Gorman, Jack Delmonte ("has spent some 40 years in show business, moving with equal facility from the stage to the movies to television and to radio") as Mr. Cream. The director was Steve Chernak. I thought the performance a bit forced, a bit overloud, and essentially excellent. In short, the piece, the play-house, the evening, and the entire gestalt could not have been more down my alley. Or down Beckett's. I think he would have loved it—the whole thing. And I think it was, and is, good theatre.[1]

On September 3, 1962, *La Manivelle* was performed on the stage of the Théâtre de la Comédie de Paris by Georges Adet and Henry de Livry, under the direction of Georges Peyrou. The scenery was created by Fandos, and the costumes were by France Daubrey. The play was well received, the director winning particular praise for his inventiveness.

During January 1964, *The Old Tune* was presented for three week ends (Friday through Monday) at the Judson Poets' Theater in New York; sharing the bill was an abbreviated version of *Pantagleize* by Michel de Ghelderode. The Pinget play was directed by Peter Feldman, with music by Al Carmines, set by Doug Sheer, lighting by Steve Eckers, sound tape by Lee Haring, and sound effects by Marge Saunders; it was performed by Jerry Trichter and Sean O'Ceallaigh.

The Old Tune was presented as the main event of a Sunday evening drama workshop at the Mercury Theatre, Notting Hill Gate, London, on November 22, 1964, under the direction of Alan Simpson. An anonymous newspaper critic wrote:

. . . It was enjoyable *drame vérité*—the kind of thing that Mr. Harold Pinter has attempted in certain revue sketches. . . .

Gorman and Cream meet, as it might be on St. Stephen's Green, exchange cigarettes and memories to the sporadic music of the hurdy-gurdy, and swap news of their children. There is a precise Dublin rhythm to their lament (Mr. Simpson believes that Beckett remains Irish even in his most extra-national work) and a mild gallows humour. Nothing more. Mr. Godfrey Quigley and Mr. Gerry Duggan [the per-formers] both illuminated the metropolitan Celtic twilight.

Students in various countries have found *The Old Tune* to be an imaginative and provocative play and have performed it in both English and French with good results.

---

[1] Reprinted by permission of *The Village Voice,* copyright 1961, The Village Voice, Inc.

Two Interviews with Robert Pinget

By Denise Bourdet

[After the appearance of Pinget's novel *L'Inquisitoire* (1962), Mme. Denise Bourdet interviewed Pinget for the French periodical *La Revue de Paris* (January 1963). The interview was later published in Mme. Bourdet's book *Brèves Rencontres*.][1]

After a few introductory remarks, Pinget began to speak of his work:

Pinget: I have been writing for ten years. I did exercises in style, studies of language. I was seeking to translate into writing the tone and the quality of language as much by constructing a sentence inside out as by removing commas. I even wanted to suppress punctuation, since feeling has none . . .

Bourdet: Nor does private thought.

Pinget: But I had to put in some periods and commas because without them the reader would have been lost. People don't know how to read any more; they read too fast. I read slowly, carefully, always sitting down, comfortably installed, my book placed before me on a table.

Bourdet: I read stretched out, but attentive when I like the book. I have just read the five novels you wrote before *L'Inquisitoire,* which seemed to me to be a summation of the others.

Pinget: I felt obliged, after writing several short books, to turn out a big one. I did not have to torment myself with the usual researches into tone and language, or trouble myself with form, I had the material. . . . I wrote entirely by hand before tapping it out myself twice on the machine. I worked regularly every day, doing nothing but that. I get up rather late but I insist on working for at least an hour before I have my breakfast. I begin again in the afternoon, but after lunch there is a moment that is difficult to get through. I'm sleepy. It's not that I eat too much, but I'm lazy. And, of course, writing is horrible. You see, that's all I do, that's all I want to do, but it's frightful. I ask myself the threatening little question, "Yes or no?" in order to force myself to work, and drive myself by continuing this system of questioning. The Socratic method, in short! . . . I forbid myself, on principle, to work before going to bed, but when I wrote *L'Inquisitoire* it became an obsession and I could not sleep. I turned on my lamp continually and finished by not turning it out at all; the loud voices [of my characters] were everywhere in my room. It was exhausting. It took me a long time to recover from it. . . . As a child and young man I wrote tons of poems. Germaine Taillefer set some of them to music and they were sung with success, it seems, at Carnegie Hall, but I have given up poetry.

Bourdet: At least it has found a place in your books. . . . And you are a great humorist, people laugh a lot when they read your books. They are crammed with words you coin yourself, clichés, ironic remarks, red lights that stop the hurried reader and force him to consider for a moment the situation and the characters.

[1] (Copyright 1963 by Editions Bernard Grasset; the following excerpts are reprinted by permission of Editions Bernard Grasset).

Pinget: I like people to laugh when they read me. I often laugh while I write.

Bourdet: Is irony a mask behind which you conceal your sensitivity?

Pinget: No, it's beyond my control. It wells up from deep inside me. I only notice it after it has appeared. I'm always searching for the truth about people and things, but there are two sides to every truth, and it is the humorous and bizarre side that appears to me first. I like people, but when I want to describe someone I really respect or admire, I am always being taken to task for the barb I put into it. What I am doing, I think, is preventing myself, to as great an extent as possible, from making a value judgment. I prefer sharpness of observation.

Bourdet: Do you see a connection between irony and the art of caricature in drawing or painting?

Pinget: I believe that what gives a portrait its real resemblance to its subject is the element of caricature. Irony does not kill tenderness.

Bourdet: . . . But we don't feel like laughing at many of your comic, burlesque incidents because you have made them pitiful without actually saying so. . . . There are hardly any happy people in [your] work . . . One encounters the physical or moral solitude of the characters on every page. . . . As for yourself, do you seek out solitude, do you like it?

Pinget: I don't like it, but I must adjust myself to it. These days I am becoming a little more sociable. The prizes I most missed getting have drawn me into giving interviews but I have difficulty in communicating with others, and discussion doesn't excite me. I seldom go out though I have a few friends, but I wait until they telephone me before I see them.

Bourdet: If you were afraid of solitude, you would be telephoning them.

Pinget: But I'm lazy, I've already told you that. In the same way, I love music, I even play the cello, but I don't go to concerts. I listen to records at home. Same thing with the theatre, I go very little, although I am interested in it because I've written some plays.

Bourdet: Were you satisfied with the interpretation of the play you adapted from your book Le Fiston, The Dead Letter at the Théâtre Récamier?

Pinget: Yes, though I attended only a few rehearsals. I left before the play opened in order to spend six months in the United States. I was invited by the Ford Foundation to go there with a group of writers.

Bourdet: Did you give some lectures?

Pinget: No, thank God, they were very nice and I wasn't required to. I shall never give any lectures, but the trip was interesting, and I love to travel. Apart from the visits I make to my family in Savoie and the Midi, I often go to England, Spain, and Italy.

Bourdet: Do you think that you are better known abroad than you are in France?

Pinget: I think so, because I've been translated in Italy, the United States, Germany, Sweden, Yugoslavia, Great Britain, and I have been asked to write radio plays for Stuttgart and for the B.B.C. . . . but it's a delusion because, elsewhere as here, I have only a small public. It is true that here [in France] I have never been asked to write anything for the radio or television. . . .

[Concerning his literary tastes and influences, Pinget said:]

Forty years ago . . . I was reading The Pink Library [children's books]; later on, Balzac, whom I prefer to Stendhal; then, like everyone else, Claudel, Giraudoux, Proust, Valéry. Like many others of my generation,

I felt the immense influence of Joyce. Max Jacob and Henri Michaux also impressed me greatly. But what has had the greatest influence upon me is *Don Quixote,* which I re-read often. At the moment I am in the midst of reading Chateaubriand, *Memoirs from Beyond the Grave,* it's beautiful. . . .

By Randolph Goodman, August 1967

Pinget said, "I had just completed my novel *Clope au dossier* when the British Broadcasting Company asked me to write a short radio play for them. I was so deeply involved with the characters and situations in the book that I decided to extract a sequence from it and convert it into a play 'for the ear.' The action and characterization presented no problems, but I had to heighten the dramatic quality of the dialogue. And since the play was to be done in London it would have to be translated into English. I had helped Samuel Beckett with the French versions of his radio plays *All That Fall* and *Embers*—I did the first drafts, then he reworked them, and they were published as a collaboration—and he offered to put my play into English. As he only translates his own material, I considered his offer a great kindness. Beckett wanted to set the scene of the play in Dublin and turn my Parisians into Irishmen; I gave him permission to do so. It is a model translation. It catches perfectly the meaning, mood, and feeling of my play, and even the words are very close to those in French. I called the play *La Manivelle,* which means the crank of a hand-organ, but Beckett renamed it *The Old Tune.*"

After its presentation by the B.B.C. in August 1960, the play was published in a bilingual edition by Editions de Minuit, Paris. Pinget feels that it would be helpful to students if the play could always be published in both languages side by side. Shortly after it appeared in print, it was performed on the radio and stage in several countries in Europe. Because it is inexpensive to mount and because so much of its effect depends upon the skill of the actors and director, it has most often been performed in avant-garde and experimental theatres. It has even proved successful, according to Pinget, when young people play the parts of the old men. Though Pinget had actually discussed with Georges Peyrou, who directed the French stage version of the play, the possibility of casting young actors in the roles of Toupin and Pommard in order to introduce an element of dream or fantasy, they finally decided to use older performers and work for a realistic effect.

Pinget is motivated to write by the sound of language; he notices a sharp difference in the speech of old people, the middle-aged, and the young. Unlike most writers Pinget begins with sounds, which he translates into words, out of which grow characters and situations. The entire process begins with a certain quality of the voice, a particular tone; by listening attentively to it, Pinget is able to create a person, a scene, a full action. This explains his remark to Mme. Bourdet that while writing *L'Inquisitoire* "loud voices were everywhere" in his room. That is how Pinget develops his novels and radio plays, for he feels that the novel is more closely related to radio than to the stage. When he writes directly for the theatre, on the other hand, his background as a painter and his pictorial imagination come into play. Then he frequently starts with a situation, which appears very clearly in his mind; he visualizes every corner of the stage. When the scene is correctly imagined, the characters start to speak of their own volition and Pinget records their speech. Thus it may be said that Pinget never starts from reality but always from the imagination, which is a mutation of reality; yet a sense of the real is always present in his work, because language is his medium and words are inherently descriptive and representational. In paying such close attention to his "voices," Pinget realizes that his approach to writing is more or less mystical. And feeling, as he does, that there is a great difference between writing for the ear and writing for the eye, and that the two forms should be kept separate and distinct, Pinget was genuinely surprised when *La Manivelle,* a play written for radio, managed to succeed on the stage.

Asked whether Samuel Beckett had had any influence upon him as a writer, Pinget replied, "I was writing long before I had read or met Beckett, and it is difficult to assess influences. Beckett is a very scrupulous worker with a genuine theatre-sense (*intelligence du théâtre*); he writes with great precision and a professional conscience. By observing Beckett one can gain more confidence in one's own talent because Beckett provides a model of sensibility as well as of technical skill. He is very inspiring to know and to talk to. Beckett has taught me a great deal about myself and my work; in giving me advice he never stressed his own aims and goals but rather those that were pertinent to me and my ideas. When I write I feel completely independent of Beckett, though there is no denying that we have a more or less similar view of life and deal with many of the same subjects— the passage of time, loneliness, old age, memory—each of us, of course, in his own way."

Pinget views memory, for example, as being almost as important to man as the moments of his life as he actually lives them. Thus the "old tune," the song that recurs intermittently during Pinget's play, suggests that the past lives of the old men were as fragmented and faulty as their memories. The crank of the hand-organ, as the controlling symbol, goes round and round like the ideas and speech of the characters, halting, breaking down, then going forward with its sad, human music.

Directing *The Old Tune* on BBC-Radio

Interview with Barbara Bray

In 1960 the British Broadcasting Company, pioneering a new drama series, which would make available to its radio listeners the latest work of foreign authors, commissioned Robert Pinget to write a short play for presentation on the air. Pinget responded by extracting a section from *Clope au dossier,* the novel he was then working on, and arranging it as a radio script. He had previously written a play called *Clope,* but it did not contain this scene.

The new work, *La Manivelle,* was translated into English by Samuel Beckett and presented under the title of *The Old Tune.*

Barbara Bray, who was then BBC Script Editor for the Drama, was chosen to direct the Pinget play. Mrs. Bray, herself a translator from the French, was excited by Beckett's transference of the action to an Irish setting; she agreed with the critic who said that the play reminded him of "a Justice Shallow scene." Mrs. Bray wished to come as close as possible in her production to what the translator had in mind—the creation of a genuinely Irish atmosphere. Her first problem arose in casting the play; it would not be difficult to find actors with authentic brogues, but both characters—Gorman and Cream—are described as having the cracked voices of old men. It was necessary, therefore, for radio, to find players who not only had Irish accents but whose voices presented clear contrasts in tone and timbre, so that listening audiences could distinguish easily between them.

For the role of Mr. Cream, Mrs. Bray selected Jack MacGowran, who had won distinction in Irish parts on the stage, screen, and television, and whose voice was light, smooth, and lyrical. For the part of Mr. Gorman, Mrs. Bray chose Patrick Magee, an actor who was identified with the plays of Samuel Beckett, as he had taken part in broadcasts of *Endgame* and *All That Fall* and had appeared on the stage in *Krapp's Last Tape;* Magee's voice was deeper, more guttural, and more explosive. Not only were the actors' voices clearly differentiated, but they delineated the characters well.

The two old men are cranky and burdened down by age but Gorman, the organ-grinder and the poorer of the two, comes out as stronger and more aggressive; the voice of Cream, who is the father of a judge and financially better off than Gorman, is fainter and more tenuous. "The characters are beautifully observed," said Mrs. Bray, "and for all their seriousness are extremely funny. They are a good example of Pinget's special kind of comedy. Another such character appears in *Clope*—a young man is in the kitchen peeling potatoes and crying over the death of a young girl." Gorman and Cream express resentment over the loss of their liberty and are attempting to preserve the little left to them; they object to the way people either ignore them or push them around, but their complaints are not expressed in a sentimental way or as unrelieved pathos.

Mrs. Bray found that the play presented some difficulty in production because the thought patterns and transitions are often submerged. The intention of the playwright was not to make the characters sharply distinguishable as black-and-white aspects of old age, but to merge them subtly one with the other. At first each man talks about his own concerns, but as the play progresses each character seems to take over from the other. Their speeches coalesce and give the impression of being one divided monologue; both are singing the same old tune. Mrs. Bray feels that the play would not have worked without the complete collaboration of the actors, not only with each other but with her. They made excellent, imaginative suggestions for the development of the characterizations and for the handling of the dreamlike dialogue.

It is Mrs. Bray's opinion that radio drama can be both more complex and more precise than drama on stage or screen. The visual elements of the production—the physique of the actor, the costumes, scenery, lights, and props—immediately limit the imagination and relegate voices, music, and sound to subordinate positions. The effect of sound is, as it were, diffused by the eye. When the appeal is to the ear alone, even when only two voices are blended with sounds and music, it is possible to create an unlimited number of moods, emotions, and ideas and to achieve more varied and more controlled effects. In radio drama there need be few crude and constricting images, and the listener's imagination may be given absolute and unlimited freedom; he is also more inclined to give the play his undivided attention. In a theatre attention is more or less dissipated by the greater number of distractions. Although phonograph recordings of stage plays resemble radio dramas to some extent, they do not have the same impact as plays specially written to appeal to the ear.

Since a work of art cannot be adapted from one medium to another without undergoing some alteration, Pinget's radio plays, which are poetic in form, emerge on the air as a kind of music, and the key to their production is timing. "The director interpreting a radio script," said Mrs. Bray, "is like a conductor following a composer's score; the means at his disposal are tempo, rhythm, and volume, and a sensitive use of the pause for the dramatic handling of silence as well as of sound. The radio director must create aural patterns that are exactly right; a "beat" too long can be as disconcerting as a wrong note in a musical performance. One great difference between the musical conductor and the radio director is the amount of technical knowledge and equipment that the director must work with. There are complicated light and hand signals which the director must use to cue in voices, music, and sound effects, and to indicate pauses. And the sound effects as well as the music must be chosen and timed."

Pinget's play called for a hand-organ and a tune played haltingly on it; there were also intermittent traffic noises. Mrs. Bray rented an old barrel organ for the production and had it fitted out with "The Bluebells of Scotland," the tune chosen by Beckett. The program opened with traffic noises to set the scene, and these gave way to the music of the organ. The lines were spoken slowly, dreamily, and were occasionally interrupted by the sound of the traffic. Early in the play Gorman mentions bluebells, which recalls the past; then he utters the phrase "When you think . . ." This is followed by a ten-second pause; the silence is broken by the tune from the barrel organ, but it falters, and the traffic noises come up. Two or three times more the words "When you think . . ." return as a refrain and act as a cue for the music and the traffic noises. At the end of the play the music rises with a note of defiance and triumph. The running time of the play as performed was 32 minutes, 40 seconds; it took more than two full days of rehearsal in the studio, though the actors were highly expert and though scripts, in radio, are not memorized but read.

According to Mrs. Bray, the drama directors at the BBC, have complete freedom in producing their plays, thus, she was able to take a thoroughly experimental approach to the Pinget script. She had in her head what she called "a primitive justification of the drama," what she considered the "perfect form"; however, she kept the conception fluid and her ideas changed as the rehearsals progressed, particularly since the program was done collaboratively. The patterns in measured sound were not timed mechanically but were felt, and grew out of the emotions and tensions of each moment of the play.

Although radio drama as an art form has, unfortunately, been neglected in the United States, there are still large listening audiences in Britain. There the radio directors feel a special responsibility to young writers and actors, to help the beginning professional not only to earn a living but to learn the techniques of his craft. Many writers, actors, and directors have moved on from radio to television, films, and theatre. Mrs. Bray believes that no medium is better suited than radio to the presentation of poetic-musical drama, in which the imagination is given free play.

Mr. Gorman on the Radio

Interview with Jack MacGowran

Jack MacGowran, Dublin-born actor and star of British stage, screen, and television, was trained at the Abbey and Gate Theatres in his native city and studied mime in Paris, before making his first appearance in London. MacGowran has played leading roles in virtually all of Samuel Beckett's plays and in many of Sean O'Casey's and has given numerous readings from, and lectures on, the works of both playwrights. Consequently, the actor was offered one of the two leading roles, that of Mr. Cream, in *The Old Tune,* which Barbara Bray was producing for the British Broadcasting Corporation.

MacGowran liked the play very much and was particularly impressed that Beckett had been able to transform Pinget's French characters into true Dubliners, and to fill their speech with pure Celtic rhythms, without doing injury to the play's meaning. This suggested that the little work had universal qualities. The actor also found the play's situation extremely appealing: here were two old men, widely separated by class, meeting on common though shaky ground. They had had similar interests in the past but little concern with the world then going on about them; now they are equally oblivious to the present, but try to recreate the past that has disappeared. Their attempt to do the impossible is paradoxical, pathetic, and absurd.

The music which Gorman extracts with such difficulty from his hand organ has more significance for him than does the world, with all its traffic noises. Grinding away at the hurdy-gurdy is a routine that Gorman must go through compulsively because the tune, in becoming audible, signifies survival. It is his link with the past; that is why the play is called *The Old Tune.* The last sentence in Beckett's novel *The Unnameable,* according to MacGowran, seems relevant to both the organ and the organ-grinder: "I must go on . . . I can't go on . . . I'll go on . . . ." To some extent this is Pinget's comment on the human condition: it is not progressive, it merely persists. Early in their lives there was an affinity between Gorman and Cream; in middle age they drifted apart; finally they meet in the equality of old age—and the circle closes; they have merged in the human situation. Yet a contradiction remains: the old men live on memories that are no longer sure, for they are made up in large part of fantasy.

Although MacGowran was a vigorous man in his early forties when he played Mr. Cream, he was well qualified by experience and technique to portray a decrepit old fellow of seventy-six. He had begun his career on the stage at the Abbey Theatre in Dublin, where it was customary, MacGowran explained, to start young people off playing character roles. The fame of the Abbey was based on the work of its character actors, such as Maire O'Neill and Barry Fitzgerald, and the theatre wished to maintain that tradition. The directors of the Abbey Theatre also felt that the actor who began by playing character parts would be better equipped later on to play straight roles. A "character" takes a young actor away from his own personality, stretches his imagination, and allows him to experiment with various techniques while creating the part. The young actor at the Abbey was also asked to observe the older and more experienced players with particular attention in order to become involved in the portrayal of feeling, especially as it affected the use of the voice. To increase the range and flexibility of his voice, in preparation for playing character parts, the beginner was subjected to intensive vocal training.

"But in addition to being properly trained," said MacGowran, "an actor must be observant. When I go to the park, I often watch old people, and I've heard many conversations exactly like those in Pinget's play. I was friendly with Jack B. Yeats, the poet's brother, a man of eighty, and I used to study him carefully. Sean O'Casey and my father also contributed something to Mr. Cream. In fact, the character as I played him was a composite recollection of many old men I'd met and listened to."

MacGowran had noticed that when an old person's memory fails, his eyes seem to glaze. Such an effect might be achieved by mimicry alone, but to make it meaningful and convincing the actor must call into play not only a visual image but all the emotions related to the situation. The actor "sees and hears" the character he is portraying and must identify with him. As an example of what he meant, MacGowran said that his father had been ill for seven years before he died and that he, the son, had tended him. While in a semicomatose state, his father had often spoken of the past in a weak and quavering voice. When, as Mr. Cream, MacGowran was called upon to talk of bygone days, he used the hesitant and quavering voice he knew so well. His emotional involvement with the dying man, a blood relative, had deepened his feeling for, and identification with, the fictional character, and it strongly influenced his performance.

MacGowran had noticed, too, that pace and rhythm differ greatly in the old and the young. As age advances, the mind and tongue slow down; there is a loss of vitality; and consequently it takes longer for messages to travel from the brain to the voice of an older person. Interrupting the slow pace, however, there may be little bursts of speed, when the recollection becomes clearer for a moment or when emotions, such as anger or self-disgust, are aroused. Old people find it difficult to accept and adjust to new forms; they prefer to retain the familiar ones, which are preserved in their memories of the past. All of these factors—internal and external—are fused in the creation of a role and help to make it three-dimensional and believable.

The *Old Tune* in Paris

Interview with Georges Peyrou and Georges Adet

La Manivelle (The Old Tune) had its stage première in Paris on September 3, 1962, at the Théâtre de la Comédie de Paris. Two seasoned actors, Georges Adet and Henry de Livry, played Toupin and Pommard, respectively, under the direction of Georges Peyrou.

"The problem I faced in directing the play," said Peyrou, "was to achieve a contrapuntal effect between the realistic moments of the present and the poetic moments of the past, and, on occasion, the conscious mixture of the two. To get the results I wanted, I had to make maximum use of music, lights, and sound effects."

As the play opened, Old Toupin was seated on a park bench, on an otherwise bare stage, cranking a nostalgic French tune out of his hand organ. The play of lights from the passing traffic crisscrossed the stage in such a way as to give the impression not only of active life in the present but of the strange illumination of a dream; it was an effort to create the illusion simultaneously of reality and unreality for the actors and for the audience. Generally, the stage lighting for the present was harsh; for the past, subdued. The critic for *Avant-Scène*, a French theatre magazine, commented, "Peyrou has had the idea for a very ingenious play of lights." More often, however, the traffic lights, as well as traffic noises, were used during the play as a leitmotif for the present, while music served to evoke the past. The music of the barrel organ, it should be noted, was heard extensively at the beginning and end of the play; at other times only a few faltering notes were ground out.

The music, according to Peyrou, is related to the words "When you think . . ." and represents the past of each individual, his experiences and emotions; it symbolizes the spiritual quality of man and, briefly but comprehensively, signifies Life. By the sudden interjection of the sharp roar of traffic, Peyrou attempted to suggest the impingement of the modern mechanical world upon the human being—the attack of reality on the dream. To Peyrou, however, the play seems to indicate that the interior life triumphs over the exterior. "Not only do the characters account their memories and fantasies as more important than their day-to-day existence," said the director, "but at the play's end an optimistic note is sounded. I don't know if this is the point Pinget intended to make, or whether he would agree with me, but here is my view: The individual lives of men mean nothing. It is the music and poetry they create that is important. Human beings die out, but art remains; in other words, the music rises above the traffic noises."

Before *La Manivelle* went into rehearsal, Peyrou and Pinget discussed the production in detail. Pinget was then toying with the idea of having two young actors play the parts of Toupin and Pommard and of having them recount their memories as if in a dream of old age. The director agreed that such an approach would add several levels of meaning to the play but might prove to be too complex and confusing for the audience. They decided that it would be more direct and effective to have older men playing the parts.

Peyrou considers Robert Pinget a significant writer and *La Manivelle* an important play, if viewed as a work belonging to a special genre; it is not a conventional drama, but "a poem for the theatre," comparable to those created by Maeterlinck and Beckett. "But in their points of view and attack," said the director, "Beckett and Pinget are quite unlike each other. Beckett is metaphysical and complex; Pinget, more ingenuous and direct. While I was directing *Architruc,* a short play by Pinget that was done on the double bill with *La Manivelle,* I had an opportunity to observe the thinking of the two men. At the very end of *Architruc,* the figure of Death appears. Pinget called for 'a skeleton wrapped in a shroud, carrying a scythe.' When this apparition appeared on stage, Beckett, who happened to be attending the rehearsal, objected to it as being too obvious; he thought that Death should be represented, perhaps, as a concierge or a postman, but Pinget did not agree. To me, this seemed to sum up the difference in the approach of the two playwrights."

As *La Manivelle* was produced on a very limited budget, the scenery and costumes had, of necessity, to be of the utmost simplictiy. "Fortunately," said Peyrou, "the play could be done very well on a practically bare stage, and yet it proved to be more successful than many I have done at much greater expense. Although I had directed about thirty plays before mounting *La Manivelle,* I think there is a clear indication of the merit of this little play in the fact that it has drawn the greatest attention to my work. Given the beauty and originality of Pinget's script, much of the credit for our success must go to the actors who turned in remarkably sensitive performances."

Georges Adet, who appeared in the part of Toupin in Pinget's play, had been a member of the Comédie Française just before World War II, when the organization was under the direction of Edouard Bourdet. After Bourdet's retirement, Jacques Copeau took over. When Paris was occupied by the Germans, Adet left the company, feeling that the administration was licking the boots of the Nazis. "The Comédie Française is a beautiful place in which to play," said Adet, "but like all state institutions it is full of intrigues." The actor formed his own troupe, took pupils, and played for the Red Cross. After the liberation of Paris, he joined a touring company, *La Tournée Baret,* and appeared in Jules Romains' play *Dr. Knock.* Adet's most famous role, however, was Harpagon in Moliere's *L'Avare,* which he acted not only at the Comédie Française but in many other theatres in France, England, Switzerland, Belgium, and other foreign countries for a total of fifteen hundred performances. And in 1968 he played it again.

Although Adet is a man in his late seventies, he displays great vitality and youthful spirit on stage, and plays men of fifty to ninety with verve and pleasure. An extremely meticulous technician, he will rehearse day and night until he feels he has control of his part, but is never really satisfied. There is a strong strain of irony in his acting, and he is known for the vivid and incisive manner in which he delivers his lines. Adet willingly agreed to take part in Pinget's one-act play, which is a measure of this actor's dedication to his art, since he does not hesitate to accept roles that are small and do not pay very well if he considers them interesting or challenging.

In 1957 Adet created the role of Nagg in Samuel Beckett's play *Fin de Partie (Endgame)* in its world première at the Royal Court Theatre, London. The actor performed the part in French to great applause.

"As characters, Toupin and Nagg bear a great resemblance to each other," said Adet, "and I acted them in much the same way, that is, naturalistically with strong personal identification and the use of 'interior images.' But their creators have presented the two men in very different ways: Pinget's ancient organ-grinder, who has wound up, figuratively speaking, on society's dust-heap, is depicted in a realistic setting; Beckett's decrepit old man is shown literally living and dying in an ashcan and thus becomes part of a visual metaphor. The characters' names also point up the difference in the way these playwrights think: Toupin and Pommard, in Pinget, are conventional, old French names of no special significance; but Nagg and Nell, in Beckett, seem to contain extensional meanings, if not actual puns (Nagg, a grumbler, or a worn-out old horse; Nell—knell—a mournful sound, a funeral bell)."

In the presentation of Pinget's play, no sharp distinction was drawn between the rich man and the "beggar" (Adet's word); on the contrary, what was stressed was the strong similarity of the two men as hapless human beings. Their characters and their lines seemed to merge, the intention being to create the illusion of identity and universality.

"Although the director has the basic concept for the production," said Adet, "he chooses the actors he thinks will best be able to carry out his ideas, so the actor becomes an important collaborator. Together the actor and director analyze the character and work out the interpretation of the role—that was the way Peyrou and I worked in *La Manivelle*. Of course, the more experienced and creative the actor, the more he can contribute to the characterization."

Directing at the Judson

Interview with Al Carmines

Al Carmines, associate minister and director of the arts program at the Judson Memorial Church in New York, composed and performed the music for the production of *The Old Tune* presented in the church's choir loft in 1964. Carmines feels that religion and drama should be as closely associated in the modern world as they were in ancient Greece and in the Middle Ages and that the theatre today can have a revitalizing effect upon the church.

Carmines' musical education began with piano lessons; he studied from the age of eight to eighteen, and along the way learned to play the accordion, saxophone, and pipe organ. He has never had any formal training in harmony, counterpoint, or composition. While a student at Swarthmore College, he entertained at parties and later performed nonprofessionally for various groups and organizations. In his senior year at college, Carmines met Paul Tillich, the theologian, who had come to the campus to lecture. They talked, and Tillich told the young man, "You are incurably religious whether you are a believer or not." Carmines thought about the conversation,

Al Carmines at the piano. Photograph: Peter Moore.

enrolled at the Union Theological Seminary, and became an ordained minister in 1961. That year he was hired as assistant to the Reverend Howard Moody at Judson and was put in charge of the church's arts program. The connection between theatre and religion was not a new idea at this church; in 1958 Carmines had seen there what he thinks was New York's first Happening, put on by Allan Kaprow.

Almost immediately upon assuming his duties, Carmines, with the help of poet-playwright Robert Nichols, inaugurated the Judson Poets' Theater, with the express purpose of introducing new talents in writing, directing, acting, and dance. The offerings were to be of a poetic and experimental nature, with the stipulation that they should be able to be produced on a limited budget. Carmines has said, "The church gives us $200 a year. Nobody working with the theatre gets paid. Admission is free, but the audience makes contributions. We figured out that it averages 35¢ a head."

As he was starting his theatre program, Carmines happened to see an off-Broadway production of *Waiting for Godot;* he considered it one of the most important experiences of his life. "Seeing Beckett's play for the first time," he said, "vistas opened." He began to read the Irish playwright in depth, but did not wish to produce his plays, as Beckett was an established writer and Carmines preferred to provide opportunities for new dramatists, some of whom were writing in Beckett's vein. One such Beckett-like play soon came to his attention. It was George Dennison's *Vaudeville Skit,* which dealt, in pathos and humor, with three hoboes.

"In the summer of '62," Carmines recalled, "Lawrence Kornfeld, who became our resident director, was rehearsing Dennison's play. I dropped in one day to see how things were going and found the actors 'cutting up.' Larry had not been able to get them into the proper frame of mind. He asked me to improvise some vaudeville music to set the mood. I began to imagine a hobo act and that reminded me of Beckett, and when I think of Beckett I think of funny-sad music. I began to play, making it up then and there. Larry and the actors liked it and said, 'Keep it in.' So all at once, Dennison's play became a musical and, at the age of twenty-four, I became a composer."

Carmines began to work at the piano "like mad" and has turned out the music for five or six plays a year, each year, since then. With a rich gift for melody he has written in a variety of styles ranging from Gregorian chant to honky-tonk piano.

Carmines is attracted to plays that deal with people's problems, but not to conventional problem plays. The play must be exciting, funny, alive, and the music, like the music of Kurt Weill, one of his favorite composers, should have a sharp edge.

Carmines came upon *The Old Tune* when it was published in the *Evergreen Review* in 1961. Though he had never heard of Robert Pinget, Beckett's translation caught his eye, and he liked the play itself. He found it both amusing and touching in the best "Beckett manner." He kept the play in mind for production at the Judson and in 1963 turned it over to director Peter Feldman.

It was decided that it would be too expensive, if not impossible, to acquire a real barrel organ equipped with appropriate music for Gorman to play, and that it would be more practical for the actor to use a prop, while the music was played offstage. Before composing a melody, Carmines had to work out the sound of a hand organ. After some experimentation, he was able, by manipulating the stops, to produce on the pipe organ the exact tone of a barrel organ. He then began to write the song; he wanted something sad yet light, the usual "happy-sad" music associated with Beckett. Recalling the music he had composed for *Vaudeville Skit,* he again wrote in a minor key. Carmines has said, "Some of my happiest music is in a minor key."

The Old Tune actually gave the composer what he called an "Edith Piaf feeling"—warm, earthy, and full of pain. Beckett has so long been associated with France that Carmines thinks of him as a Continental writer, not as an Irishman, and as more moderate, temperate, subdued—less "exuberant"—than such writers as Yeats and Joyce. Carmines was pleased with the music he composed for the play; with its French feeling and hurdy-gurdy sound, it summed up his feelings about Beckett. Pinget, the original author of the play, is still an unknown quantity to the composer.

As audiences entered the theatre for performances of *The Old Tune,* Carmines was at the organ playing music of his own composition as well as traditional songs. At one performance, when he started to play "East Side, West Side," Feldman rushed up and said that the audience would think that the play was set in New York, and he had been trying to suggest a generalized locale. Carmines segued immediately into another tune.

As a composer Carmines works in an unconventional way. In his apartment in Greenwich Village, not far from Judson, he is at the piano from one to four in the morning. He is back at the church office at ten and puts in a full day attending to his pastoral duties, leading study groups, visiting the sick, and so on. Only about ten percent of his music is on paper; the rest is taped, so that he won't forget it. Although he pleads pressure of work, as well as a personal disinclination to writing his music down, he goes through the time-consuming processes of teaching his music by rote to the singers, dancers, and actors and of playing it himself at performances. "There is another reason why I like to keep it fluid," said Carmines. "During the show I can introduce variations and modulations in tempo, volume, and length, and fit the music precisely to the action on stage." It is only when someone else plays his music that he has to "go to the trouble" of writing it down. When asked what the melody he had written for *The Old Tune* was like, he had to work it out at the keyboard from memory. To paraphrase Chekhov, "Carmines composes as a bird sings."

In his review of *The Old Tune,* which appeared in the *New York Post* (January 14, 1964), Jerry Tallmer said, "The real magic in the production is the music provided by Al Carmines, a far-away blend of barrel organ and carousel."

"An Old Tune," original music composed by Al Carmines for the production presented by the Judson Poets' Theatre at the Judson Memorial Church, New York, January 1964. Courtesy of Al Carmines.

The Old Tune at the Judson

Interview with Peter Feldman

Peter Feldman, who directed The Old Tune at the Judson Poets' Theater in New York in January 1964, had served for two years as assistant director to Julian Beck and Judith Malina at the avant-garde Living Theatre, and had then become cofounder and codirector, with Joseph Chaikin, of the highly experimental Open Theatre. Feldman had directed his first play at the Judson in 1963; when he was invited back the following year, Al Carmines, who runs the theatre program there, brought the Pinget play to his attention.

"I liked The Old Tune very much," said Feldman. "I found it harrowing, deeply moving, and yet funny. It seemed to me to embody several important aspects of absurdist thinking: the inevitability of mortality, the lack of discernible purpose in life, and the futility of trying to hang on to anything, including a memory, all this in the context of a very funny series of exchanges between two odd old ducks. The treatment of futility in a comic manner keeps the play from being 'nihilistic,' since comedy is the celebration of vitality itself.

"I read the play carefully several times and began to set down my ideas about it. I keep a notebook in which I record all the thoughts that occur to me concerning the play I am working on. The Old Tune posed a special problem as it had originally been written for radio and my main concern was to make it come alive for a theatre audience. I was afraid the play would seem "talky" and static unless I could find ways to get the men off the park bench and work out some interesting movement. I am visually oriented as a director, probably because of my work with the Living and Open Theatres, where a heavy emphasis is placed on movement and gesture. The physical life on stage would, of course, have to grow out of the core of the play and not look as if it had been 'pasted' on to it. I never make final decisions in advance of production but try to develop appropriate physical and visual images during rehearsals with the aid of my actors.

"The casting problem of the play was to find the kind of actors most rare in the off-off-Broadway movement: good character actors who will work for nothing. We are often heard to say that we don't have to worry about money, since we never have any. That gives us the freedom to experiment without endangering someone's investment, but it also sets up a serious limitation which is most noticeable in the quality of the acting. Young people—even highly talented ones—will act for the experience; but competent older players cannot be attracted on the same basis. If the mature actor has been successful, he is 'untouchable'; if unsuccessful, he is usually out of circulation. I have never been happy working with amateurs or 'non-actors,' the kind most frequently seen off-off-Broadway. I believe absolutely in craft and technique. So it was just a stroke of good luck that enabled me to cast The Old Tune with two excellent performers."

There came to Feldman's mind one day an actor by the name of Jerry Trichter, who had done fine work in many off-Broadway productions. Trichter was an elderly man, tall and gaunt, with a rich flexible voice; he could perform with authority in a wide emotional range and was sure to evoke sympathy in the role of Gorman. For the part of Cream, there were no candidates. Feldman does not like auditions or readings, as they are ordinarily held, because of their strained and unnatural atmosphere; he prefers to cast actors whose work he already knows or can judge from something in which they are presently appearing. But one day Feldman decided to sit in on the readings that Larry Loonin was holding at the Judson for his production of *Pantagleize,* which was to be presented on the same bill as *The Old Tune.* One of the actors who turned up for the audition was Sean O'Ceallaigh, a man of about thirty who gave a convincing demonstration of advanced age; he had acted professionally in Ireland and had done some amateur work in Canada. He was a lively, talkative person, whose speech patterns were sharper and more rapid than Trichter's and whose physical and emotional characteristics presented other contrasts. Feldman offered O'Ceallaigh the part of Cream.

"Sean had a natural, though faint, Irish accent." Feldman said, "Jerry's diction had no local coloration but I didn't ask him to assume a brogue. I was more interested in the cadences of their speech than in their accents. The men talk to each other in a telegraphic way, obliquely, and with constant interruptions. It is a speech pattern that actually demonstrates the uselessness of speech as a means of communication; their talk only divides the men. But, waiting at the edge of death, huddled together over the hand organ as Gorman plays it, they achieve a rapport without words. This, incidentally, is a visual point that a radio play cannot make.

"Pinget/Beckett write dialogue in the European tradition of naturalism, using everyday speech, not as American naturalists do to emphasize its banality, but in the manner of Synge and O'Casey, to celebrate its inherent poetry. The actors had a tendency to 'smooth out' the dialogue by inserting connectives (*and, but, because, so*), which I was careful to remove in order to preserve the staccato rhythm of the playwright's lines."

In pointing up the contrasts between the two men, the director took his cues from the script, then put his imagination to work. Gorman, the organ-grinder, is the poorer of the two. Feldman assumed that the old man was a pensioner who had to supplement his income by being a street musician; he also decided to make Gorman blind, for visual interest (sighted people are fascinated by the movements of the blind), for sympathy, and for contrast. With a wistful air Gorman sits on the public bench in his shabby old clothes. Cream, the father of a judge, looks well fed, wears a coat with a fur collar, and yet shows concern about money. When Cream drops a cigarette, Gorman feels about for it with his hand and finds it—but they cannot smoke, for neither of them has a match. For all their differences these men are actually in the same boat—lonely, neglected, and drifting toward death. To make this point, Pinget differentiated the men only as much as was absolutely necessary; the actors, thinking to heighten the conflict, tended to exaggerate the differences, which the director, aware of the fragility of the play, had to tone down.

Feldman frequently puts his actors through a series of improvisations, but he did not resort to them for this play. He worked directly from the dialogue and the business called for in the script. As the rehearsals proceeded, he found the characters becoming more complex and more interesting. The two old men, meeting after many years and trying to recreate the past, retreat into a common memory, with which their individual memories do not coincide; this calls into question the value of memory itself. Yet it is through their memories, faulty as they are, that they establish their identities and certify their very existence. Of the two, Cream seems to have the poorer memory; Gorman, though more alert, is less articulate. When he finds it difficult to express himself in words, he turns the crank of the hand organ, and the music becomes an extension of what is going on in his mind.

Pinget does not call for a specific song. For this production, Al Carmines composed an original melody in the tempo of a slow waltz, reminiscent of songs heard in French cafés. "What I liked about the tune," said Feldman, "was its Truffaut-like quality, a peculiar nostalgic sentimentality, here placed at the service of a vision which is essentially not sentimental. The play deals compassionately with nostalgia, but is not in itself nostalgic. If it were, it would be merely bathetic." In addition to introducing the music at the points called for in the script, the director found other moments at which to start up the song. As the Passersby went out, Gorman remembered that he should have been playing and suddenly turned the crank; he played, too, as he spoke of his wife, until Cream interrupted him, at which point Gorman's speech and music would stop simultaneously. That the music was not identifiably Irish, as it might have been—played on a barrel organ in Dublin as it was—did not disturb the director, who preferred to evoke a generalized locale and mood.

The creation of mood was one of Feldman's greatest concerns. In order to achieve the dream quality he wanted, he relied not only on the music of the barrel organ but on the tempo of the speeches. As in the plays of Maeterlinck and Chekhov, special attention had to be paid to the introduction and handling of pauses. The director filled some of them with significant bits of business, others with sounds, and still others with a pregnant silence during which the old men were lost in thought. The mood was further heightened by the modulation of lights. To indicate, for instance, that Gorman was retreating into the memory world of the past when he ground out the music, the director introduced at those moments a special lighting effect: the regular lights dimmed, and dappled half-shadows, half-patterns, were projected onto the stage. This change of lighting was the first visual effect to grow out of the business of the play; a similar effect was the use of double beams of light, which swept across the stage at intervals to represent the headlights of automobiles and were accompanied by the roaring sound of motors, as they raced past. The old men reacted angrily, with raised fists, to these intrusive lights and sounds, as though they were an imminent threat to life; they also seemed to suggest that other people were going somewhere and leaving them behind. Sitting in the cold, bleak light of a street lamp, the old men were unaware of the traffic light at the other side of the stage, which blinked occasionally from red to yellow to green. "Although it is not called for in the script," said the director, "I introduced the traffic light as a kind of visual metaphor. It was meant to remind the viewer that the old men were not alone in the world, that a complicated life was going on around them, a life increasingly regulated by mechanisms like traffic lights. No wonder the old men felt alienated."

The one element of the production with which the director was unhappy was the scenery. He had envisioned something impressionistic, feeling that the set should be as fragmentary as the language, the relationships, and the memories. "I wanted anything but absolute naturalism," Feldman said.

"What I got was a complete city street lined with buildings and an archway leading to an alley! Otherwise the production seemed to make good sense. The play is actually a hybrid: naturalist-impressionist-absurdist; and since I am interested in 'total' theatre, I can see myself doing it again but entirely differently. It would be a highly eclectic, dramatic collage, with the dialogue interrupted by scenes of street life, visions out of the past, and film and slide projections of those aspects of the world which disturb or threaten the old men. It would not be a faithful rendition of the text, but in its own way might prove as interesting and as valid in the theatre."

In Feldman's estimation, *The Old Tune*, despite its extreme brevity, merits attention because of the evocative quality of its language, the universality of its characters, and the seriousness of its theme. Like so many other modern plays, Pinget's work offers a dark and disturbing view of man's existence, but it achieves artistic distinction because of its author's poetic conception, humor, and fine sensibility.

THE OLD TUNE *A Radio Play*[1]

ROBERT PINGET
English Text by Samuel Beckett

(Cast
Mr. Gorman, 73 years old
Mr. Cream, 76 years old
First Passerby, a young man [mute]
Second Passerby, another young man [mute]

Scene: A bench in a public place within earshot of heavy traffic. A morning in spring.)

(**Gorman,** *seated on the park bench, plays the barrel-organ and strikes it with his hand when it jams.)*
[Background of street noises. In the foreground a barrel-organ playing an old tune. 20 seconds. The mechanism jams. Thumps on the box to set it off again. No result.]

Gorman: *[Old man's cracked voice, frequent pauses for breath even in the middle of a word, speech indistinct for want of front teeth, whistling sibilants.]* There we go, bust again.
[Sound of lid raised. Scraping inside box.] Cursed bloody music! *[Scraping. Creaking of handle. Thumps on box. The mechanism starts off again.]* Ah about time!
(**Gorman** *cranks the barrel-organ.)*
[Tune resumes. 10 seconds. Sound of faltering steps approaching.]
(**Mr. Cream** *enters.)*

Cream: *[Old man's cracked voice, stumbling speech, pauses in the middle of sentences, whistling sibilants due to ill-fitting denture.]* Well if it isn't—
[The tune stops.]
—Gorman my old friend Gorman, do you recognize me Cream father of the judge, Cream you remember Cream.

Gorman: Mr. Cream! Well I'll be! Mr. Cream!
[Pause.]
Sit you down, sit you down, here, there.
[Pause.]
Great weather for the time of day Mr. Cream, eh.

Cream: My old friend Gorman, it's a sight to see you again after all these years, all these years.

Gorman: Yes indeed, Mr. Cream, yes indeed, that's the way it is.
[Pause.]
And you, tell me.

Cream: I was living with my daughter and she died, then I came here to live with the other.

Gorman: Miss Miss what?

Cream: Bertha. You know she got married, yes, Moody the nursery-man, two children.

Gorman: Grand match, Mr. Cream, grand match, more power to you. But tell me then the poor soul she was taken then was she.

Cream: Malignant, tried everything, lingered three years, that's how it goes, the young pop off and the old hang on.

[1] Parentheses enclose stage directions added by the editor.—R.G.

Gorman: Ah dear oh dear, Mr. Cream, dear oh dear.

  [Pause.]

Cream: And you your wife.

Gorman: Still in it, still in it, but for how long.

Cream: Poor Daisy yes.

Gorman: Had she children?

Cream: Three, three children, Johnny the eldest, then Ronnie, then a baby girl, Queenie, my favourite, Queenie, a baby girl.

Gorman: Darling name.

Cream: She's so quick for her years you wouldn't believe it, do you know what she came out with to me the other day ah only the other day poor Daisy.

Gorman: And your son-in-law?

Cream: Eh?

Gorman: Ah dear oh dear, Mr. Cream, dear oh dear.

  [Pause.]

Ah yes children that's the way it is.

  [Roar of motor engine.]

They'd tear you to flitters with their flaming machines.

Cream: Shocking crossing, sudden death.

Gorman: As soon as look at you, tear you to flitters.

Cream: Ah in our time Gorman this was the outskirts you remember, peace and quiet.

Gorman: Do I remember, fields it was, fields, bluebells, over there, on the bank, bluebells. When you think . . .

  *[Suddenly complete silence. 10 seconds. (**Gorman** cranks the barrel-organ.) The tune resumes, falters, stops. Silence. The street noises resume.]*

Ah the horses, the carriages, and the barouches, ah the barouches, all that's the dim distant past Mr. Cream.

Cream: And the broughams, remember the broughams, there was style for you the broughams.

  [Pause.]

Gorman: The first car I remember well I saw it here, here, on the corner, a Pic-Pic she was.

Cream: Not a Pic-Pic, Gorman, not a Pic-Pic, a Dee Dyan Button.

Gorman: A Pic-Pic, a Pic-Pic, don't I remember well, just as I was coming out of Swan's the bookseller's beyond there on the corner, Swan's the bookseller's that was, just as I was coming out with a rise of fourpence ah there wasn't much money in it in those days.

Cream: A Dee Dyan, a Dee Dyan.

Gorman: You had to work for your living in those days, it wasn't at six you knocked off, nor at seven neither, eight it was, eight o'clock, yes by God.

  [Pause.]

Where was I?

  [Pause.]

Ah yes eight o'clock as I was coming out of Swan's there was the crowd gathered and the car wheeling round the bend.

Cream: A Dee Dyan Gorman, a Dee Dyan, I can remember the man himself from Wougham he was the vintner what's this his name was.

Gorman: Bush, Seymour Bush.

Cream: Bush, that's the man.

Gorman: One way or t'other, Mr. Cream, one way or t'other no matter it wasn't the likes of nowadays, their flaming machines they'd tear you to shreds.

Cream: My dear Gorman do you know what it is I'm going to tell you, all this speed do you know what it is it has the whole place ruinated, no living with it any more, the whole place ruinated, even the weather.

  [Roar of engine.]

Ah when you think of the springs in our time remember the springs we had, the heat there was in them, and the summers remember the summers would destroy you with the heat.

Gorman: Do I remember, there was one year back there seems like yesterday must have been round 95 when we were still at Cruddy, didn't we water the roof of the house every evening with the rubber jet to have a bit of cool in the night, yes summer 95.

Cream: That would surprise me Gorman, remember in those days the rubber hose was a great luxury a great luxury, wasn't till after the war the rubber hose.

Gorman: You may be right.

Cream: No may be about it, I tell you the first we ever had round here was in Drummond's place, old Da Drummond, that was after the war 1920 maybe, still very exorbitant it was at the time, don't you remember watering out of the can you must with that bit of a garden you had didn't you, wasn't it your father owned that patch out on the Marston Road.

Gorman: The Sheen Road Mr. Cream but true for you the watering you're right there, me and me hose how are you when we had no running water at the time or had we.

Cream: The Sheen Road, that's the one, out beyond Shackleton's sawpit.

Gorman: We didn't get it in till 1925 now it comes back to me the wash-hand basin and jug.

[Roar of engine.]

Cream: The Sheen Road you saw what they've done to that I was out on it yesterday with the son-in-law, you saw what they've done our little gardens and the grand sloe hedges.

Gorman: Yes all those gazebos springing up like thistles there's trash for you if you like, collapse if you look at them am I right.

Cream: Collapse is the word, when you think of the good stone made the cathedrals nothing to come up to it.

Gorman: And on top of all no foundations, no cellars, no nothing, how are you going to live without cellars I ask you, on piles if you don't mind, piles, like in the lake age, there's progress for you.

Cream: Ah Gorman you haven't changed a hair, just the same old wag he always was. Getting on for seventy-five is it?

Gorman: Seventy-three, seventy-three, soon due for the knock.

Cream: Now Gorman none of that, none of that, and me turning seventy-six, you're a young man Gorman.

Gorman: Ah Mr. Cream, always the great one for a crack.

Cream: Here Gorman while we're at it have a fag, here.

[Pause.]

The daughter must have whipped them again, doesn't want me to be smoking, mind her own damn business.

[Pause.]

Ah I have them, here, have one.

Gorman: I wouldn't leave you short.

Cream: Short for God's sake, here, have one.

[Pause.]

Gorman: They're packed so tight they won't come out.

Cream: Take hold of the packet.

[Pause.]

Ah what ails me all bloody thumbs. Can you pick it up.

[Pause.]

Gorman: Here we are.

[Pause.]

Ah yes a nice puff now and again but it's not what it was their gaspers now not worth a fiddler's, remember in the forces the shag remember the black shag that was tobacco for you.

Cream: Ah the black shag my dear Gorman the black shag, fit for royalty the black shag fit for royalty.

[Pause.]

Have you a light on you.

Gorman: Well then I haven't, the wife doesn't like me to be smoking.

Cream: Must have whipped my lighter too the bitch, my old tinder jizzer.

Gorman: Well no matter I'll keep it and have a draw later on.

Cream: The bitch sure as a gun she must have whipped it too that's going beyond the beyonds, beyond the beyonds, nothing you can call your own.

[Pause.]

(**First Passerby** enters and crosses.)

Perhaps we might ask this gentleman.

[Footsteps approach.]

Beg your pardon Sir trouble you for a light.

[Footsteps recede.]

(First Passerby *exits.)*

Gorman: Ah the young nowadays Mr. Cream very wrapped up they are the young nowadays, no thought for the old. When you think . . .

[Suddenly complete silence. 10 seconds. (Then **Gorman** *cranks the barrel-organ.) The tune resumes, falters, stops. Silence. The street noises resume.]*

Where were we?

[Pause.]

Ah yes the forces, you went in in 1900, 1900, 1902, am I right?

Cream: 1903, 1903, and you 1906 was it?

Gorman: 1906 yes at Chatham.

Cream: The Gunners?

Gorman: The Foot, the Foot.

Cream: But the Foot wasn't Chatham don't you remember, there it was the Gunners, you must have been at Caterham, Caterham the Foot.

Gorman: Chatham I tell you, isn't it like yesterday, Morrison's pub on the corner.

Cream: Harrison's, Harrison's Oak Lounge, do you think I don't know Chatham, I used to go there on holiday with Mrs. Cream, I know Chatham backwards Gorman, inside and out, Harrison's Oak Lounge on the corner of what was the name of the street, on a rise it was, it'll come back to me, do you think I don't know Harrison's Oak Lounge there on the corner of dammit I'll forget my own name next and the square it'll come back to me.

Gorman: Morrison or Harrison we were at Chatham.

Cream: That would surprise me greatly, the Gunners were Chatham do you not remember that?

Gorman: I was in the Foot, at Chatham, in the Foot.

Cream: The Foot, that's right, the Foot at Chatham.

Gorman: That's what I'm telling you, Chatham the Foot.

Cream: That would surprise me greatly, you must have it mucked up with the war, the mobilisation.

Gorman: The mobilisation have a heart it's as clear in my mind as yesterday the mobilisation, we were shifted straight away to Chesham was it, no Chester, that's the place, Chester, there was Morrison's pub on the corner and a chamber-maid, Mr. Cream, a chamber-maid what was her name, Joan, Jean, Jane, the very start up of the war when we still didn't believe it, Chester, ah those are happy memories.

Cream: Happy memories, happy memories, I wouldn't go so far as that.

Gorman: I mean the start up, the start up at Chatham, we still didn't believe it, and that chamber-maid what was her name it'll come back to me.

[Pause.]

And your son by the same token.

[Roar of engine.]

Cream: Eh?

Gorman: Your son the judge.

Cream: He has rheumatism.

Gorman: Ah rheumatism, rheumatism runs in the blood Mr. Cream.

Cream: What are you talking about, I never had rheumatism.

Gorman: When I think of my poor old mother only sixty and couldn't move a muscle.

[Roar of engine.]

Rheumatism they never found the remedy for it yet, atom rockets is all they care about, I can thank my lucky stars touch wood.

[Pause.]

Your son yes he's in the papers the Carton affair, the way he managed that case he can be a proud man, the wife read it again in this morning's *Lark.*

Cream: What do you mean the Barton affair?

Gorman: The Carton affair Mr. Cream, the sex fiend, on the Assizes.

Cream: That's not him, he's not the Assizes my boy isn't, he's the County Courts, you mean Judge . . . Judge . . . what's this his name was in the Barton affair?

Gorman: Ah I thought it was him.

Cream: Certainly not I tell you, the County Courts my boy, not the Assizes, the County Courts.

Gorman: Oh you know the Courts and the Assizes it was always all Six of one to me.

Cream: Ah but there's a big difference, Mr. Gorman, a power of difference, a civil case and a criminal one, quite another how d'you do, what would a civil case be doing in the *Lark* now I ask you.

Gorman: All that machinery you know I never got the swing of it and now it's all Six of one to me.

Cream: Were you never in the Courts?

Gorman: I was once all right when my niece got her divorce that was when was it now thirty years ago yes thirty years, I was greatly put about I can tell you the poor little thing divorced after two years of married life, my sister was never the same after it.

Cream: Divorce is the curse of society you can take it from me, the curse of society, ask my boy if you don't believe me.

Gorman: Ah there I'm with you the curse of society look at what it leads up to, when you think my niece had a little girl as good as never knew her father.

Cream: Did she get alimony?

Gorman: She was put out to board and wasted away to a shadow, that's a nice thing for you.

Cream: Did the mother get alimony?

Gorman: Divil the money.

[*Pause.*]

So that's your son ladling out the divorces.

Cream: As a judge he must, as a father it goes to his heart.

Gorman: Has he children?

Cream: Well in a way he had one, little Herbert, lived to be four months then passed away, how long is it now, how long is it now.

Gorman: Ah dear oh dear, Mr. Cream, dear oh dear, and did they never have another?

[*Roar of engine.*]

Cream: Eh?

Gorman: Other children.

Cream: Didn't I tell you, I have my daughters' children, my two daughters.

[*Pause.*]

Talking of that your man there Barton the sex boyo isn't that nice carryings on for you showing himself off like that without a stitch on him to little children might just as well have been ours Gorman, our own little grandchildren.

[*Roar of engine.*]

Gorman: Mrs. Cream must be a proud woman too to be a grandmother.

Cream: Mrs. Cream is in her coffin these twenty years Mr. Gorman.

Gorman: Oh God forgive me what am I talking about, I'm getting you wouldn't know what I'd be talking about, that's right you were saying you were with Miss Daisy.

Cream: With my daughter, Bertha, Mr. Gorman, my daughter Bertha, Mrs. Rupert Moody.

Gorman: Your daughter Bertha that's right so she married Moody, gallous garage they have there near the slaughter-house.

Cream: Not him, his brother the nurseryman.

Gorman: Grand match, more power to you, have they children?

[*Roar of engine.*]

Cream: Eh?

Gorman: Children.

Cream: Two dotey little boys, little Johnny I mean Hubert and the other, the other.

Gorman: But tell me your daughter poor soul she was taken then was she.

[*Pause.*]

(**Second Passerby** *enters and crosses.*)

That cigarette while we're at it might try this gentleman.

[Footsteps approach.]

Beg your pardon Sir trouble you for a light.

[Footsteps recede.]

(**Second Passerby** *exits.*)

Ah the young are very wrapped up Mr. Cream.

Cream: Little Hubert and the other, the other, what's this his name is.

[Pause.]

And Mrs. Gorman?

Gorman: Still in it.

Cream: Ah you're the lucky jim Gorman, you're the lucky jim, Mrs. Gorman by gad, fine figure of a woman Mrs. Gorman, fine handsome woman.

Gorman: Handsome, all right, but you know, age. We have our health thanks be to God touch wood.

[Pause.]

You know what it is Mr. Cream, that'd be the way to pop off chatting away like this of a sunny morning.

Cream: None of that now Gorman, who's talking of popping off with the health you have as strong as an ox and a comfortable wife, ah I'd give ten years of mine to have her back do you hear me, living with strangers isn't the same.

Gorman: Miss Bertha so sweet and good you're on the pig's back for God's sake, on the pig's back.

Cream: It's not the same you can take it from me, can't call your soul your own, look at the cigarettes, the lighter.

Gorman: Miss Bertha so sweet and good.

Cream: Sweet and good, all right, but dammit if she doesn't take me for a doddering old drivelling dotard.

[Pause.]

What did I do with those cigarettes?

Gorman: And tell me your poor dear daughter-in-law what am I saying your daughter-in-law.

Cream: My daughter-in-law, my daugh-ter-in-law, what about my daughter-in-law?

Gorman: She had private means, it was said she had private means.

Cream: Private means ah they were the queer private means, all swallied up in the war every ha'penny do you hear me, all in the bank the private means not as much land as you'd tether a goat.

[Pause.]

Land Gorman there's no security like land but that woman you might as well have been talking to the bedpost, a mule she was that woman was.

Gorman: Ah well it's only human nature, you can't always pierce into the future.

Cream: Now now Gorman don't be telling me, land wouldn't you live all your life off a bit of land damn it now wouldn't you any fool knows that unless they take the fantasy to go and build on the moon the way they say, ah that's all fantasy Gorman you can take it from me all fantasy and delusion, they'll smart for it one of these days by God they will.

Gorman: You don't believe in the moon what they're experimenting at?

Cream: My dear Gorman the moon is the moon and cheese is cheese what do they take us for, didn't it always exist the moon wasn't it always there as large as life and what did it ever mean only fantasy and delusion Gorman, fastasy and delusion.

[Pause.]

Or is it our forefathers were a lot of old bags maybe now is that on the cards I ask you, Bacon, Wellington, Washington, for them the moon was always in their opinion damn it I ask you you'd think to hear them talk no one ever bothered his arse with the moon before, make a cat swallow his whiskers they think they've discovered the moon as if as if.

[Pause.]

What was I driving at?

[Roar of engine.]

Gorman: So you're against progress are you?

Cream: Progress, progress, progress is all very fine and grand, there's such a thing I grant you, but it's scientific, progress, scientific, the moon's not progress, lunacy, lunacy.

Gorman: Ah there I'm with you progress is scientific and the moon, the moon, that's the way it is.

Cream: The wisdom of the ancients that's the trouble they don't give a rap or a snap for it any more and the world going to rack and ruin, wouldn't it be better now to go back to the old maxims and not be gallivanting off killing one another in China over the moon, ah when I think of my poor father.

Gorman: Your father that reminds me I knew your father well.

[Roar of engine.]

There was a man for you old Mr. Cream, what he had to say he lashed out with it straight from the shoulder and no humming and hawing, now it comes back to me one one year there on the town council my father told me must have been wait now till I see 95, 95 or 6, a short while before he resigned, 95 that's it the year of the great frost.

Cream: Ah I beg your pardon, the great frost was 93 I'd just turned ten, 93 Gorman the great frost.

[Roar of engine.]

Gorman: My father used to tell the story how Mr. Cream went hell for leather for the mayor who was he in those days, must have been Overend yes Overend.

Cream: Ah there you're mistaken my dear Gorman, my father went on the council with Overend in 97, January 97.

Gorman: That may be, that may be, but it must have been 95 or 6 just the same seeing as how my father went off in 96, April 96, there was a set against him and he had to give in his resignation.

Cream: Well then your father was off when it happened, all I know is mine went on with Overend in 97 the year Marrable was burnt out.

Gorman: Ah Marrable it wasn't five hundred yards from the door five hundred yards Mr. Cream. I can still hear my poor mother saying to us ah poor dear Maria she was saying to me again only last night, January 96 that's right.

Cream: 97 I tell you, 97, the year my father was voted on.

Gorman: That may be but just the same the clout he gave Overend that's right now I have it.

Cream: The clout was Oscar Bliss the butcher in Pollox Street.

Gorman: The butcher in Pollox Street, there's a memory from the dim distant past for you, didn't he have a daughter do you remember.

Cream: Helen, Helen Bliss, pretty girl, she'd be my age, 83 saw the light of day.

Gorman: And Rosie Plumpton bonny Rosie staring up at the lid these thirty years she must be now and Molly Berry and Eva what was her name Eva Hart that's right Eva Hart didn't she marry a Crumplin.

Cream: Her brother, her brother Alfred married Gertie Crumplin great one for the lads she was you remember, Gertie great one for the lads.

Gorman: Do I remember, Gertie Crumplin great bit of skirt by God, hee hee hee great bit of skirt.

Cream: You old dog you!

[Roar of engine.]

Gorman: And Nelly Crowther there's one came to a nasty end.

Cream: Simon's daughter that's right, the parents were greatly to blame you can take it from me.

Gorman: They reared her well then just the same bled themselves white for her so they did, poor Mary used to tell us all we were very close in those days lived on the same landing you know, poor Mary yes she used to say what a drain it was having the child boarding out at Saint Theresa's can you imagine, very classy, daughters of the gentry Mr. Cream, even taught French they were the young ladies.

Cream: Isn't that what I'm telling you, reared her like a princess of the blood they did, French now I ask you, French.

Gorman: Would you blame them Mr. Cream, the best of parents, you can't deny it, education.

Cream: French, French, isn't that what I'm saying.

[Roar of engine.]

Gorman: They denied themselves everything, take the bits out of their mouths they would for their Nelly.

Cream: Don't be telling me they had her on a string all the same the said young lady, remember that Holy Week 1912 was it or 13.

[Roar of engine.]

Gorman: Eh?

Cream: When you think of Simon the man he was don't be telling me that.

[Pause.]

Holy Week 1913 now it all comes back to me is that like as if they had her on a string what she did then.

Gorman: Peace to her ashes Mr. Cream.

Cream: Principles, Gorman, principles without principles I ask you.

[Roar of engine.]

Wasn't there an army man in it?

Gorman: Eh?

Cream: Wasn't there an army man in it?

Gorman: In the car?

Cream: Eh?

Gorman: An army man in the car?

Cream: In the Crowther blow-up.

[Roar of engine.]

Gorman: You mean the Lootnant St. John Fitzball.

Cream: St. John Fitzball that's the man, wasn't he mixed up in it?

Gorman: They were keeping company all right.

[Pause.]

He died in 14. Wounds.

Cream: And his aunt Miss Hester.

Gorman: Dead then these how many years is it now how many.

Cream: She was a great old one, a little on the high and mighty side perhaps you might say.

Gorman: Take fire like gunpowder but a heart of gold if you only knew.

[Roar of engine.]

Her niece has a chip of the old block wouldn't you say?

Cream: Her niece? No recollection.

Gorman: No recollection, Miss Victoria, come on now, she was to have married an American and she's in the Turrets yet.

Cream: I thought they'd sold.

Gorman: Sell the Turrets is it they'll never sell, the family seat three centuries and maybe more, three centuries Mr. Cream.

Cream: You might be their historiographer Gorman to hear you talk, what you don't know about those people.

Gorman: Histryographer no Mr. Cream I wouldn't go so far as that but Miss Victoria right enough I know her through and through we stop and have a gas like when her aunt was still in it, ah yes nothing hoity-toity about Miss Victoria you can take my word she has a great chip of the old block.

Cream: Hadn't she a brother?

Gorman: The Lootnant yes, died in 14. Wounds.

[Deafening roar of engine.]

Cream: The bloody cars such a thing as a quiet chat I ask you.

[Pause.]

Well I'll be slipping along I'm holding you back from your work.

Gorman: Slipping along what would you want slipping along and we only after meeting for once in a blue moon.

Cream: Well then just a minute and smoke a quick one.

[Pause.]

What did I do with those cigarettes?

[Pause.]

You fire ahead don't mind me.

Gorman: When you think, when you think . . .

> [Suddenly complete silence. 10 seconds. (**Gorman** cranks the barrel-organ.) Resume and submerge tune a moment. Street noises and tune together crescendo. Tune finally rises above them triumphant.]

(CURTAIN)

THE
APES
SHALL
INHERIT
THE
EARTH

Werner Aspenström

Scene from *The Apes* as presented at the Colorado State University Theatre, Fort Collins, December 1965. Various images were projected on the panel at the rear. Courtesy Charles D. Haller, Colorado State University.

Werner Aspenström

Karl Werner Aspenström, prize-winning poet, playwright, and author, was born on November 13, 1918, in Norrbärke, in the province of Dalecarlia, Sweden. His parents were Anna Eriksson and Karl Aspenström; the father, a farm worker, died at an early age and left his family in straitened circumstances. As a small child growing up in a rural community, Karl Werner developed an almost mystical attachment to nature. As a student in the local elementary school, he took special interest in reading and writing, despite the scarcity of books.

In 1936, at the age of eighteen, the boy entered the Folk High School in Sigtuna (a city located southeast of Norrbärke, between Uppsala and Stockholm); there he read voraciously, and there he discovered poetry. He rebelled, however, against the intense idealism, nationalism, and conservatism that prevailed at the school; he had a pronounced tendency toward pessimism, which found an outlet in social criticism. Ideas of social reform dominated his thoughts. For a time he joined a number of other students who considered themselves syndicalists (militant socialists). Completing his studies in Sigtuna in 1938, he entered Stockholm University, which granted him a bachelor's degree in 1941 and the degree of Master of Arts in 1945. The following year he married Signe Lund, who is a painter, and a daughter and son—Anna and Pontus—were born of the marriage. Aspenström and his family spend their summers on the island of Kymmendö, where Strindberg lived for a time.

While still a student at the university, Aspenström began his professional career as a critic and reporter. He wrote numerous articles for newspapers and magazines on such subjects as religion, morals, politics, and poetry. He has always had a deep interest in the theatre and a strong dramatic talent. At one time he considered becoming an actor, but he has devoted his life to writing and has demonstrated that he is primarily a poet; not only is he the author of at least six volumes of verse, but all his prose works and plays are strongly imbued with his poetic vision.

In 1964 Aspenström's little collection called *Sixty-Six Poems* appeared. In a preface to the volume, the poet made the following remarks about his life and work:

> Why do you write poetry? That's a question which is sometimes asked and which invites another in response: Why don't you write poetry? Why do you suppress the poetic impulse that was active in you

at least twice in your early life, even if it didn't manifest itself in writing? The first time was in childhood, those happy days before grammar existed, when you began to give things names, to play with words and expressions—distorting old ones and discovering new ones. The second time was during the teen-years, when your heart was full of undefined but explosive feelings which sought release. In 999 cases out of 1000, people let these gifts slip away; they choose another sort of language, other means of expression. Why is it considered more natural for a twenty-year-old to be able to drive a car than to write a sonnet?

I don't know when it became customary to ask writers why they write. It is certain that in this time of Freud and Adler, the question has taken on an insinuating undertone. People think they already know the right answer: The poem is an act of compensation, the imagination supplies what life denies us. There is something to that idea; the point of departure for an artistic creation is often an experience of need, alienation, restraint, but such feelings do not determine its direction or aim. The roots of the tree don't explain its leaves. One might just as correctly claim that art is a sign of an over-abundant energy of life, an excess which we can find even in animals: the turkey-cock could probably manage without the red ruffle on his throat.

What is decisive, however, is that no matter what the original reason for the poem, it is linked with other life processes, other expressions of will: one wants to disturb and reform the world in one way or another; one wants to make gray things glisten; one wants to explore and investigate, perhaps claiming "to write in order to find out why I write." Mayakovsky believed that poetry begins where there's a purpose. (As far as I'm concerned, the line "I walk alone down the road" has a purpose; it says, "Girls ought to take walks with poets." It's no fun for a man alone, you see!) Oh, let us give verse such power that it will move people to band together in cooperatives! Yesenin's opinion, expressed in a polemic against Mayakovsky, is one that many might well agree with: "His poetry has a purpose, mine has a reason. I don't know what reason."

The pair of opposites, Life-Art, which has bothered so many of us for so many generations, seems in the sixties to be on the way to dissolution. In today's paper, I read an interview with a composer, through whose window wafted voices from a school-yard not far off: "[John] Cage listens and says that it's beautiful. He remembers having heard a similar composition by Lutoslawski. And he's absolutely serious; he says it with obvious sincerity. This is *his* music. Cage is the first man in the history of music who has seriously claimed that one can listen in this way: there is no boundary between art and life."

My first attempts at poetry came at the usual age—the early teen-years. My environment was not literary, which is another way of saying that there weren't many books around. In a cupboard, there were about ten adventure stories and a thick book dealing with the [First World] war, with pictures in it. The temperance society in the neighboring village had a library of sixty or seventy novels. We were kids who read anything and everything we could get our hands on. My sister, who was a few years older than I, wrote poems about moose and woodland lakes, in the manner of Dan Andersson. My own first poems were unrhymed and mostly about catastrophes, evil forebodings and omens. Without doubt, they were very clumsy attempts and yet they stand out in my memory as being more "genuine" than the idealistic, juvenile, and generally miserable imitative verse that for the most part filled my first book [*The Preparation* (1943), which the poet has excluded from his bibliography—R.G.]. On the other hand, you can't always trust your memory.

It wasn't until I was eighteen years old that I first set foot in a larger library, which was at the folk high school. Theoretically, I knew that millions of books had been written, but to see with my own eyes a part of this multitude was something else again and sort of a shock. I realized immediately that you had to limit yourself and stake out a mining concession in one area, any area,. in order to get a foothold. I started to read everything available about Babylonian-Assyrian culture, and soon discovered that a great deal of prior knowledge, which I lacked, was necessary.

I came in contact with modern and avant-garde poetry comparatively late. I can't say that I was saved, but I was set free. Over the years, as a member of the editorial staff of the magazine *The Forties* and as a writer for the daily press, I engaged to a certain extent in the defense of literary movements. I lived in an attic wallpapered with poems from all centuries and decades, not predominantly brand new ones. One of the household gods should be named, though: Bertil Malmberg. To create a style is always praiseworthy; to break with your style, as Malmberg did at the end of his long literary career, is, I believe, even more awe-inspiring. Among the works by contemporaries which especially fascinated me was Ragnar Thoursie's *The Enamel Eye*. But the overshadowing literary experience for me was encountering primitive poetry, the most significant at that time being Christer Lind's interpretations in *The Path and the Rainbow* (1943).

The supernatural plays an important part in primitive poetry. In some cases it's simply a question of art serving a useful purpose: an aid in driving away sickness, bringing rain, checking the flow of blood, winning victories in war, snaring game for hunters. No western man dares any longer to attribute such magic power to poetry, but that doesn't mean that poetry hasn't retained much of its magic character for us. The difference is that whereas people in the past turned sorcery outward, we turn it inward; we try by the enchantment of the fable and the persuasiveness of the rhythm to hold fast to a reality which is constantly slipping away. That's about the way I felt it, for example, in the introductory poem in *Snow Legend,* and that was my line of reasoning afterwards. But that way of thinking no longer convinces me. It goes without saying that poetry sometimes has a restraining effect, and just as often obscures rather than clarifies, undermines rather than fortifies. Everyone who has lived for any length of time in complete seclusion, relating only to words and to mental images, knows that poetry has a capacity for attracting ghosts instead of driving them away.

The authors of the forties got a reputation for being pessimists, in my case not unearned. To explain this, people have invoked "the condition of the times"; the war and the destructive powers of human nature it revealed—revealed once again, that is; the isolation and passivity in which neutral Sweden lived; the influence of writers like Kafka, and so on. This "time-factor," which is dearly loved by historians, reminds one quite a bit of "ether," the hypothetical substance, capable of explaining everything, to which the scientists of ancient times constantly referred. Now we are rid of ether. I don't believe that my poems would have been much different, insofar as their content is concerned, if they had been written during another period. I was already grappling with the Deluge Motif, for example, when I was fifteen or sixteen, before I knew much about the world situation and when I knew still less about how poetry should be written. "The times" can block or stimulate certain individual predispositions, but they can't change a person's turn of mind, or determine his basic emotions.

I'd like most of all to write only bright poems, if not white, then verdant, utopian, ascending poems. But death wins in all divisions, we know that; it's a commonplace fact. What's remarkable is that life, in spite of it, advances all the time. That's what one ought to write about. I reproach myself for not having held my ground better against my own melancholy. But writing poetry is not primarily an act of the will: you have to be true to your emotion. The problem of sincerity is basically a problem of "inner acoustics." It would be much easier if poetry were only a matter of craftsmanship, a customer service, if it only involved constructing a useable word-apparatus for the customer-reader, or a mirror device in which the present could view nothing but the present.

The selection [in *Sixty-Six Poems*] covers poems from 1945 to 1960. The premise underlying their choice was that they must fill a volume whose size required extensive exclusion. One difficulty is what to do with poems which have died for the author but not for the reader—in case one knows anything about him. The death of a poem can depend on other, later poems and later experiences which extinguish it, or simply on the fact that the earth has spun around the sun so many more times. According to the opinion currently in favor, the reader accounts for half the poem. If a poem opens itself up and has meaning for a reader, it would be arrogant of the author to exclude it; it would amount to canceling the reader's share, his experience, his response. A complete balance is restored by those other poems which seem to have meaning for the author but which no critic and perhaps no other reader has ever noticed.

—Translated by Cameron Brown

Aspenström's first book was a collection of short stories entitled *Boundless Is Our Adventure* (1945); this was followed by a collection of essays and journalistic pieces, *The Cry and the Silence* (1946). Other prose works are *Foreboding*, a novel (1953), *The Brook*, memories of childhood (1958), *Contradictions*, essays (1961), *The Yellow Paw*, a children's book illustrated by his wife (1965), and *Summer*, essays dealing with nature and the island of Kymmendö (1968).

His volumes of poetry include: *Snow Legend* (1949), *Litany* (1952), *The Dogs* (1954), *Poems under the Trees* (1956), *The Day and the Night* (1961), and *The Stairs* (1964).

Among his works for the stage, which have been published, are *Four*

Plays in One Act (1955); *Theater I*, seven one-act plays (1959); *Theater II*, seven one-act plays (1963); *Theater III*, which includes *The Night of the Fools, The House*, and *The Spiders* (1966), *Isadora, or The Voyage to Berlin* (1966), and *Job* (1968). The dramatic works have been performed on stage, radio, and television in Sweden and in various foreign countries. Aspenström's books are published by Albert Bonniers Förlag, Stockholm.

One of the first prizes Aspenström was to win was awarded him by Bonniers in 1946, and in the same year his script *The Fire* won a prize in a contest for radio plays. In addition to many minor prizes and scholarships, Aspenström has won the following major awards: The Ovralid prize for Literature (1958); the Carl Michael Bellman prize, offered by the Swedish Academy for excellence in poetry (1959); recognition by the Society of the Nine, a signal honor (1967); and the important Signe Edblad-Eldsh Award, made by the Swedish Academy and presented by the King of Sweden (1968).

Aspenström's ideas are profound, subtle, beautifully expressed, and pertinent to contemporary life; they should, therefore, have universal appeal, but actually are little known outside of Sweden. A volume of poems in French and one in German, three or four plays translated into various languages, including English—this represents the sum total of his rather large output available to foreign readers. The problem lies in the difficulty of precise rendition. Poetry and humor have always resisted effective translation, and Aspenström's highly individualistic style is compounded of lyricism, symbolism, fantasy, irony, and satire. In many respects his plays resemble those of the absurdist and avant-garde writers: they are short, they do not have conventional plots or characterization, and the dialogue is not logically structured; their strong appeal lies in their ability to evoke mood and feeling, to communicate ideas by means of image and suggestion, movement and rhythm. *The Apes Shall Inherit the Earth*, for example, stands at the very frontier of nonverbal drama. To achieve the reputation he deserves, Aspenström must await the arrival of a gifted poet-translator.

The Apes Shall Inherit the Earth

After *The Apes* was published—in *Theater I* (1959) in Swedish and in *The Tulane Drama Review* (1961) in English—Aspenström was asked when he had written the play. The questioner was obviously seeking sources and "influences," as he pointed out that Samuel Beckett had made use of a tape recorder in *Krapp's Last Tape* (1959), and that the Russian space-dog Laika (mentioned in the original Swedish but not in the English translation) was sent into orbit in 1959. Aspenström replied:

"To give an exact answer as to when the play came into being is not easy. I often have many projects in work at the same time. I make a draft, put it aside, catch sight of it again after a shorter or longer period, develop it, but perhaps only partially, because I get another idea. There are certain things, of course, that I write at one go. Regarding *Det eviga* [The Eternal, the play's title in Swedish], the idea itself must have been in my mind for a couple of years, but I believe the play was written, in all essentials, some time during the spring or summer of 1958. When plans materialized to publish a collection of my plays, I obviously changed certain details, cut out some things and added others. I suppose it was while I was preparing the script for the printer that 'Laika' entered the play. I remember that when I first read about Beckett's tape-recorder—it was a small item on the cultural page of the newspaper *Dagens Nyheter*—my play had already been finished for quite a while. I recall this particularly because I knew then precisely what would happen: If some day, contrary to all expectations, *Det eviga* should be produced, they would look up the records and talk about influences. That's happened to me before. There is nothing so very remarkable about employing a tape-recorder; I imagine that tape-recorders have served some theatrical function in perhaps hundreds of plays all over the world. It's a new device that has proved to be useful, and everyone can discover that for himself."

A closer look at *The Apes* discloses that there were deeper "influences" at work upon Aspenström than tape recorders and space-dogs. All his life, apparently, the playwright has reacted with horror to the brutality and wastefulness of war. As a sensitive and imaginative child living in a community where a book was a rare commodity, there was nevertheless in his home a thick and fully illustrated volume dealing with World War I. And while he was a student at Sigtuna High School, during the Nazi build-up to World War II, he was further confused and tormented by the conflict between what was being taught at the school and what was going on in the real world.

The principal of the high school, Dr. Manfred Björkqvist, later to become Bishop for the See of Stockholm, was a theologian-philosopher who wrote books on Christian humanism and took a highly idealistic stand on world affairs. But in the school he was a severe disciplinarian and crushed the radical group to which Aspenström belonged for a time. This aroused deep resentment in the students involved. The works of such writers as Rydberg (who wrote legends about the apostles) and Tegnér (who was celebrated for his Christian-Platonic verse) were emphasized in the curriculum. One poem by Tegnér, *Det eviga*, which preached that the Good, the True, and the Beautiful are eternal, apparently made a deep impression on the underprivileged, nineteen-year-old boy. Recalling this period of his life, Aspenström has said:

"We sat there in the evenings in our unheated classrooms, or in the men-servants' quarters, cramming Esperanto [an artificial international language, whose use, its inventor *hoped,* would promote world peace]! The more daring among us sent letters by means of it to various parts of the world; I myself corresponded with people in South America and Japan. We also went to the Mission House to look at slides of invalids from World War I and began to hate the international munitions makers, who were responsible, it seemed to us, for almost all the evil on earth. I know that for many this education in idealism was consoling and stimulating, and something might be said for it, but some were trapped by its rhetoric and sentimentality. . . . Naturally, I have since re-read Rydberg and Tegnér and many others on the Eternal Verities, and as a matter of fact I'm actually not a very reliable anti-idealist; I suppose my views are pretty ambivalent."

Aspenström's rebellion against idealism extended to organized religion; he saw in it one of the most frequent causes of war in recorded history. He attacked "religious manipulators who traded on people's fears in war-time and who even claimed that a religious renaissance was in the offing." He ridiculed the notion that only Christians lead moral lives and, curiously enough, quoted Tegnér to make his point: "Don't forget that high on the list of history's noble men stand many heathen names." In an article he wrote in 1942, Aspenström said that "modern man has more and more begun to find valid life-values outside of religion. . . ." His prediction that "secularization will not result in either nihilism or spiritual homelessness" is open to question, but few would quarrel with his observation that "there are innumerable and precious values in the universe which man must fight for and preserve." Social institutions may go under, but there is still the individual and his duty! This is idealism of an existential variety.

The original title of Aspenström's play was *The Three Apes.* (The title for the version in this volume was adopted by the translators from a remark made by Tennessee Williams who, when asked to explain the meaning of his play *A Streetcar Named Desire,* is said to have replied: "The apes shall inherit the earth.") That Aspenström decided to change the name of his play to *The Eternal*—which was the title of Tegnér's poem—suggests an ironic intention. If the Good, the True, and the Beautiful are eternal, why does man persist in attempting to destroy himself? And if only apes remain after man disappears from earth, what significance will the eternal verities have for them? Is that the survival of the fittest? Darwin, we note, appears upside down!

Obviously, it is not an accident that the play takes place in what was once a schoolroom: that is where man should have received the fruits of his cultural heritage and his ethical concepts. From the slides and sounds we learn that some effort was made to inculcate them, but the overwhelming pollution of the modern world—also presented visually and aurally—defeated the educational process. Eventually, all the objects in the schoolroom were reduced to a meaningless pile of junk. In the quick juxtaposition of the ideal and the real—the Apollo Belvedere shown side by side with the mutilated war veteran—we have Aspenström's concise but penetrating comment on his experience at Sigtuna.

The Apes has no plot in a traditional sense—no exposition, development, climax, or conclusion; it is not even episodic. In many respects it resembles a Happening: the action is disjointed, even lacking a pattern. Yet the play is not improvised; it is prepared and rehearsed. Aspenström approves of directors altering this play in any way that will heighten its impact, whether it means introducing slides and lines relating to current events in the news or staging the play in a manner different from that described in the text. Though written for presentation on a proscenium stage, there is no reason why it could not be done in arena style, or even in an actual (or simulated) classroom, with the audience occupying the schoolroom chairs and the apes acting around them, thus creating Environmental Theatre. In her production of the play in Sweden, Ellen Bergman achieved a dynamic response by having the apes circulate among the audience.

The apes are in no sense conventional characters. The playwright suggests that the First Ape is a bully, the Second a glutton, and the Third an "artist"; but these are merely hints, far from traditional characterization, which involve motivation, development, and so on. The apes more properly belong in the realm of parody or symbol. As long ago as 1836, Georg Büchner, in his seminaturalistic play *Woyzeck,* shows his protagonist at the fairgrounds where he sees an ape dressed as a man and recognizes him as a brother. O'Neill's Yank, in *The Hairy Ape* (1922), feeling a similar kinship, embraces a gorilla in the zoo. Brecht's *In the Jungle of Cities* (1923), depicts no actual beast, only men acting bestially, but the metaphoric title draws a parallel between urban areas and the habitat of apes. The deterioration of ideals, morals, and institutions, in so-called civilized society, brings the image of the ape almost spontaneously to the playwright's mind.

Although lines are spoken in the play, there is no dialogue, no communication, merely disembodied voices electronically produced. In a nonverbal play such as this, the emphasis is shifted to gesture, movement, and other visual elements, which relate the work to mime and dance, action painting and sculpture. With "apes" as performers, the movement and dance are necessarily only quasi-human, and a clearly irrational element enters the picture.

It is interesting to note that *The Apes* is based on the deluge motif—"the horror that may befall all of us unless we take heed in time"—which has haunted Aspenström since his fifteenth or sixteenth year and which served as the basis for his very first play, *The Place is Wrapped in Smoke,* and for such later plays as *The Ark, The Unfinished Flyswatter,* and *The Spiders.* But it is almost pointless to discuss this writer's work on a thematic or didactic level, since his plays so closely resemble fantasy, dream, and poem. Actually, included in *The Apes* is a poem, beginning with the line "Perhaps it is true that God is dead," which was written earlier than the play and which is said to have motivated the writing of the play. Aspenström thought it would provide an exciting climax for a dramatic work, and expressed a wish to be allowed to speak the lines himself. Perhaps he thought that the allusions and implications in his play, if uttered in his own voice and in poetic form, would have a more direct effect on the mind and emotions of the spectator.

The Production Record

In 1959, the year of its publication in Stockholm, *Det eviga* was produced on television by the Swedish Broadcasting Corporation. The performance took place on November 23, with three live monkeys in the roles of the apes. The play was done in a highly abbreviated form and attracted more attention as a novelty than as a serious artistic effort.

In December 1965, on a bill of three one-act plays (the other two were by Brecht and Ionesco), *The Apes Shall Inherit the Earth* was presented in the United States at the Colorado State University Theater, at Fort Collins, under the direction of C. David Haller. The production was mounted in Johnson Hall, which is used for lectures as well as for plays, thus preserving the locale called for in the script. The stage was cleared of scenery, except for several ladders and trunks, a tape recorder, and a slide projector. Unable to secure some of the slides suggested by the playwright, Professor Haller substituted others (a practice of which Aspenström approves), among them the picture of a Bunny from *Playboy Magazine*. At the conclusion of the play, the face of Darwin, rather than that of the Mona Lisa, remained on the screen upside down and, superimposed upon it, a detail from Michelangelo's painting on the ceiling of the Sistine Chapel—the fingers of Adam and God reaching out toward each other—also upside down, suggesting that all creation was topsy-turvy. After the voice on the tape said for the last time, "Love you so–o–o . . . ," the Beatles were heard singing at a deafening pitch, "I Want to Hold Your Hand"—then, suddenly, silence fell. The production was well received, though some members of the audience were confused by the unconventionality of the play. Robert J. Rubel, drama critic for the *Colorado State University Collegian* (December 3, 1965), remarked in his review: "The fear that the 'virtual' world that was presented would perhaps some day become the real world was indeed a thought that must have run through every mind in the audience. So realistic was the portrayal of the eerie scene when the apes start to play with the tape-recorder and the slide projector, that I, at least, was stunned into thought. And then the picture of a hydrogen bomb explosion flashed on the screen."

During February and March 1966, *Det eviga* was given for several matinee and evening performances at the Atelier Theatre in Göteborg, Sweden, under the direction of Ellen Bergman; three young performers—one male and two female—played the apes.

In an article in the Swedish theatrical publication *Teaterronden* (November 7, 1966), Claes Hoogland compared Ellen Bergman's version of *The Apes* with the earlier television production:

> When the play was done on TV in 1959 with real apes, people said, "This is precisely how human beings behave." At the Atelier Theatre, the ballet-pantomime . . . was created by realistically masked young actors, and then people said, "This is precisely the way apes behave!" Was that the playwright's intention? In his script no clear and specific relationship is shown between the pictures and sounds produced and the apes' reactions. Perhaps he is merely pointing out the futility of the cultural expressions which we usually call eternal. Leonardo [da Vinci] and Amadeus [Mozart] don't mean a thing to baboons! Perhaps Aspenström goes a step further and wishes to imply that our relationship to our cultural traditions is like that of these gay apes; we rummage among the unsorted pictures and archives, nod with recognition at the Mona Lisa or the atom-mushroom, and then go on with the futilities near at hand.

On the evening of March 26, 1969, *The Apes* was given an elaborate and dynamic production by five students at the School of Theatre Arts, Columbia University, in New York. The play was presented in the Nave Theatre (Myles Cooper), with Robert Keesler, David Krohn, and Rebecca Nahas playing the apes; scenery and lighting were by Bil Mikulewicz; and direction was by Michael Hassett.

A Short Discourse on Short Plays

Article by Werner Aspenström

The dramatist who chooses to write brief plays should not count on receiving letters of invitation from the managers of big theaters which are reserved for the works of important playwrights; instead he should pray fervently that in Hades there will be a little chamber theater which will eagerly accept his output.

What our theatre managers want—which, it must in justice be said, they consider their audiences prefer—is a long or short *novel* stalking about on the stage decked out in dialogue. Actors, too, prefer to appear as full-length figures, characters conceived on a grand scale; they wish, in short, to portray "living people."

It is maintained, furthermore, that there should be a basic minimum length for plays, that just as in a sexual encounter the onlooker is entitled to a preparation, a climax and a relaxation, so all plays must take enough time to arouse the spectator to the proper pitch, at which point the candy wrappers will stop crackling in the theatre. But is this absolutely necessary? Should the theater audience be so different from concert audiences, who by no means demand symphonies and oratorios seven days a week but at times may be offered a full evening program of sonatas, études, impromptus, and other abbreviated musical forms? Should it be less disciplined than the sports public which can find satisfaction in both the chronicle history of the cross-country run and in the concentrated vignette of the one-hundred-yard dash?

The intensity of the dramatic experience has nothing to do with its length or duration; if it had, no one would be afraid of a flash of lightning. Imagine that you are lying in the grass behind your house, watching the clouds advance across the sky slowly like a procession of camels. All around you there is a restful Sunday quiet, as if the days of high drama were no more. Suddenly you hear two little girls start a strange game on the other side of the fence. One of them is your own daughter. They pretend that their parents have dressed up as wild animals and are on their way to a masquerade party when they are shot and killed. The children are now orphans and act out the harrowing scene of their loneliness and fear. The time it takes to perform this improvised, miniature play is roughly ten minutes and yet it may be that it has provided a theatrical experience more memorable than O'Neill's four-hour peeling of an Ibsen onion. No criticism is intended of the latter method, but it is obvious that onions can be handled in different ways and no constitutional law exists decreeing a correlation between dramatic effectiveness and length of script. To peel an onion slowly to the accompaniment of interminable dialogue is theatre; to cut it quickly with a knife and to show up the halves without dialogue is theatre; to be silent about human fate and the human soul and to speak only of an all-pervasive emotional atmosphere is theatre; to show duels and battles and female choruses lamenting over dead warriors is theatre; even a bird's lonely cry over the silent sea or a dog baying at the silent moon may be theatre, if silence and cry are attuned to each other—but it is not advisable to write a five-act play on that subject.

—Translated by Leif Sjöberg and Randolph Goodman

Live Apes on Swedish Television

Interview with Thorbjörn Axelman

During 1959 the Swedish Broadcasting Corporation presented as one of its regular features a television program called *Prisma,* which consisted of short subjects both documentary and dramatic. Thorild Anderberg was the producer of the program and Thorbjörn Axelman compiled and edited the material used on the show.

Mr. Axelman had read Werner Aspenström's play *Det eviga* and saw its possibilities for presentation on the air. "Werner Aspenström's play attracted my attention," said Mr. Axelman, "because I have always been interested in the dramatic treatment of contemporary problems. With the world situation what it is, I, like most other people, have wondered about man's fate. *Det eviga* supplies one answer, in fantasy form and in a rather melancholy mood."

Live ape fingering the violin in the Swedish television production, Stockholm 1959. Courtesy Swedish Broadcasting.

Mr. Axelman broached the subject of a television presentation to the playwright, who agreed to allow the play to be done, with the suggestion that live apes be used as performers. The idea seemed at first to impose insuperable problems; after some thought and discussion it was decided that it would be necessary to film the play and, by careful editing, to fit the action of the animals, as much as possible, to the requirements of the script. Mr. Axelman explained that Aspenström's wish to use live apes stemmed from the playwright's interest in experimenting with dramatic form. "He is trying to move drama into the realm of abstract art," said Mr. Axelman. "By piling junk on the stage and placing real animals in an imaginary situation, he produces the effect of a theatrical collage." The live animals blurred the line of demarcation between life and art and transformed the play, in a sense, into a Happening. In addition to being grotesque in themselves, live apes would point up in burlesque fashion the resemblance between animals and men.

Mr. Axelman was excited by Aspenström's idea and took it to the show's producer, who went along with it. Ilgars Linde was chosen to direct the film. Mrs. Linde, the director's wife, was a schoolteacher, who was able to get permission for her classroom to be used, when school was not in session, for the shooting of the picture; there the cameramen—Bengt Nordwall and Jan Hugo Norman—and the technical crew set up their lights and equipment.

Three small female apes were borrowed from the Skansen Zoo for five hours; they were let loose in the schoolroom, which was stocked with slide projector, tape recorder, a violin, and the other props called for in the play. With the cameras trained on them, the animals were allowed to roam about at will for some time, and were then individually set to tinkering with specific props; one ape managed to get the violin under his chin in the proper position and to draw the bow across the strings. Clever editing produced a very convincing impression that the apes really were manipulating the tape recorder and the slide projector, watching the pictures and listening to the music, and drawing specific sounds out of the violin. Mr. Axelman complied as exactly as possible with Aspenström's wishes in choosing the slides and the music and in using the author's own voice reading the poem, "Perhaps it is true that God is dead," at the end of the play. One feature of the production was the introduction of clips from various news broadcasts in the recognizable voices of well-known Swedish radio announcers.

While the play was being filmed and edited, Mr. Axelman realized that the use of live apes had turned Aspenström's unconventional script into a more extreme dramatic genre. The dramatist was shown a rough cut of the film and was pleased with what he saw, but he, too, realized that the use of live animals had altered his original conception and had resulted in what appeared to be merely excerpts, or shorthand flashes, from the text. Aspenström gave his approval, however, and the film was then edited into its final form. Its playing time on the air was only eight minutes and forty-eight seconds.

Broadcast under the title of "Experimental Theatre by Werner Aspenström," the television version of *Det eviga* resembled nothing so much as the Theatre of Chance. According to the Chance theory of art—which began with such futurists and dadaists as Marinetti, Jean Arp, and Marcel Duchamp, and whose spokesman in our time is John Cage—there should be a "simultaneous presentation of unrelated events." Much of the beauty and surprise in drama of this sort arises out of accidental gestures, movements, and relationships. It is the equivalent of Jackson Pollack's action painting and Alexander Calder's mobile sculpture and fulfills the requirements set down in *The Theatre and Its Double* by the theatrical visionary Antonin Artaud, who wrote:

> . . . Instead of continuing to rely upon texts considered definitive and sacred, it is essential to put an end to the subjugation of the theatre to the text, and to recover the notion of a kind of unique language half-way between gesture and thought. . . . Once aware of this language in space, language of sounds, cries, lights, onomatopoeia, the theatre must organize it into veritable hieroglyphs, with the help of characters and objects, and make use of their symbolism and interconnection in relation to all organs and on all levels.

Many viewers felt, Mr. Axelman said, that the television version of *Det eviga* was unusual and amusing, but very few saw it as an example of serious drama.

The Apes in Göteborg

Interview with Ellen Bergman

Ellen Bergman, an imaginative director, teacher, and coach, runs the Atelier Theatre in Göteborg, Sweden. There she mounted a production of *Det eviga*, which she presented in a series of special performances during February and March 1966. Unlike the television version of the play, which took only eight minutes and forty-eight seconds, Mrs. Bergman's production ran for a little over a half-hour. This director's training as dancer and mime enabled her to introduce a great deal of inventive business and movement— as well as exciting images and sounds—which added to the humor and significance of the play.

While preparing her production, Mrs. Bergman decided that it would be helpful for everyone involved if the behavior of real apes could be studied at close range; so, she and the three members of her cast went to the zoo. They were amused and astonished to note how closely the gestures, movements, facial expressions, and even the emotional reactions of the animals, resemble those of human beings. One ape became impatient and jealous, for example, when a human visitor talked too long to the keeper who fed the animals; another ape displayed anger when someone touched the keeper, the animal clearly indicating that she considered the keeper her personal property! What they observed at the zoo, the director and actors made use of in their production.

Mrs. Bergman's actors—a young man and two young women—were specially chosen for their agility and their skill at miming, since they were

Scene from *The Apes* (*Det eviga*) in the Ellen Bergman production at the Atelier Theatre, Göteborg 1966. The apes were played by three young performers: Gelly Hovedskou, on the ground eating lice; Peder Kinberg, giving a Hitlerian salute; and Barbro Skantz, with violin. Courtesy Ellen Bergman.

not required to speak any lines. The actors wore furry ape costumes in various shades of brown, with heavy, dark facial make-up; they had bare hands and feet. There were no "characterizations" beyond the traits suggested by Aspenström. The First Ape (Peter Kindberg) was large and aggressive, occasionally fell into a Hitlerian salute and strut, and had a tendency to push the others around. The Second Ape (Gelly Hovedskou) had a heavy body and an insatiable appetite; she munched continually and tested every-thing for its edibility. The Third Ape (Barbro Skantz) was of slighter build; sensitive and artistic, she persisted in trying to get a tune out of a violin and scraped away over and over at the same notes. This last, "romantic," ape suggested man's cultural beginnings and also, perhaps, his indestructible aesthetic yearnings. Superimposed on these human traits was the simian behavior studied at the zoo, the tumbling, leaping, grabbing, and shoving, which did not fail to elicit comments from all the critics. Tord Bäckström, for one, noted, ". . . The apes continue to follow their impulses . . . fight, copulate, or pick fleas from each other. . . . The sudden changes in their varying moods, the shifts from brooding passivity to outbursts of unexpected vitality, the swaying and arm-swinging plasticity—all of it gives the required measure of illusion."

For the slide projector sequence, Mrs. Bergman arranged a brief chrono-logical pictorial history of the world from the Stone Age to the present, which would have been appropriate for a classroom; to this she added actual news photos, such as the atom bomb cloud shown in contrast to a real mushroom growing out of the ground. The apes reacted variously as each slide appeared, but their response was almost unanimous and most intense when the images were of a violent or phallic nature.

For the tape-recorder sequence, the director used the most topical items available. "Each morning," said Mrs. Bergman, "the latest news was taped from reports that came over the radio, and selected items were played on the tape recorder during that day's performance. These current events kept the audience's interest and excitement high." As a change from the usual bulletins about Vietnam and other trouble spots in the world, an especially exciting item turned up during the run of the play. In January 1966, about a month before The Apes opened, an American airplane crashed in mid-air, and the hydrogen bomb it was carrying fell into the sea off the southeast coast of Spain. All during February and March (when the play was being presented), United States warships searched in vain for the missing bomb; on March 8, the American ambassador to Spain held a highly publicized "swim-in" off the coast of Palomares to prove to the world that the Mediterranean had not been contaminated by radioactivity. Some sailors refused to go into the water to swim, however, although their officers boasted that they were not afraid and that no harm would come to them. "This news had been reported on the radio in the morning," said Mrs. Bergman, "and when it turned up during the performance later in the day, the reaction in the theatre was enormous, particularly since there were many Americans in the audience."

The recorded music used in the production was specially selected to show the apes' contrasting reactions to it. When a section of Mozart's Rondo in D Major was heard, the Third Ape responded by performing some dance steps that resembled a minuet, then attempted to teach them to the other apes, who couldn't quite manage to follow. But when the rock-and-roll music came on (an excerpt from "Mess Around," performed by a jazz group called The Animals), all three apes immediately picked up the beat and fell almost instinctively into a popular dance called The Monkey, which seemed as natural to them as their own movement.

In Mrs. Bergman's production the apes recognized no separation between the stage and the auditorium but moved at will up and down the aisles through the audience. They sat in empty seats beside the paying customers, turned their glances toward the stage, applauded in an exaggerated manner, and looked the persons next to them square in the eye while they scratched themselves, searched for lice, and ate the lice. Some of the playgoers were frightened or disgusted and hated the play; others laughed uproariously and loved it. A number of people walked out. Critic Bernt Eklundh said, "One felt slightly embarrassed by the wild mating cries of the apes, and their fondling, and staring at the audience. . . . When they dropped their masks and acknowledged the applause of the public, one felt relieved that they were human beings with attractive faces." The critic Lena Boberg, who had a similar reaction, observed that the feelings of embarrassment and uneasiness that were aroused while she watched the apes were "an interesting phenomenon," but she preferred not to investigate the fact further, because of her uncertainty and fear as to what she might discover.

When asked what she thought of the television version of *Det eviga*, which had used live apes, Mrs. Bergman said that it was an interesting experiment that in no way did justice to the play. The viewer unfamiliar with Aspenström's script would never have got the point of it from what he saw on the screen. To begin with, the classroom showed no signs of destruction or decay; the bright and shiny room in the local schoolhouse gave the impression that the action was taking place in the present. And the action itself depended almost entirely on the whims and limited abilities of the animals. The brevity of the television version—it ran under nine minutes—made the play seem insignificant, and its importance was further reduced by its being merely one item sandwiched between several others on the program. Finally, the live apes seemed more of a distraction than an aid, since the viewer could not help focusing his attention on the clever antics of the animals rather than on the central meaning of the play.

Mrs. Bergman tried to avoid all these errors when she staged her own production. She had been attracted to the play in the first place because it depicted so clearly man's overwhelming and persistent dedication to acquisitiveness and aggression and his total disregard for moral considerations and human life. As a director Mrs. Bergman felt that the play's unusual theme and technique required unusual treatment, and so, despite its brevity—though it ran slightly over a half-hour in her version—she decided not to include it in a bill of one-acters or to offer it as a curtain-raiser, but to present it by itself on certain evenings during the week at either 6 or 8 P.M., and at Saturday and Sunday matinees at 3. Certainly no attempt was made to appeal to the average taste of television audiences, as the critic Ake Perlström recognized when, in his review of Mrs. Bergman's production, he said that it was "charged with melancholy on account of our predicament, and bitterness toward those who deal so carelessly with the fate of the world and the love of life, which, at least for the moment, we feel. . . . *Det eviga* depicts mankind as a lost and forgotten race that once, in its pride, called itself *homo sapiens*. It is an extremely excruciating situation that Werner Aspenström has here given dramatic expression."

The Apes at Columbia University

Interview with Michael Hassett and Bil Mikulewicz

On Wednesday evening, March 26, 1969, *The Apes Shall Inherit the Earth* was presented for a single performance in the Nave Theatre, at the School of Theatre Arts, Columbia University, New York.

The production was a director's project, for which Michael Hassett was responsible; Mr. Hassett worked in close co-operation with Bil Mikulewicz, who designed the scenery and lighting. In order to arrive at a production concept, Hassett read through the play carefully several times and took note of the images that formed in his mind during the reading process. The idea that struck him most forcefully was that the play dealt with a dead civilization, which had been a meaningless one and, to judge from the pictures to be shown on the slide projector, had been bent on its own destruction, for the images depicted mounting violence, leading directly to the mushroom cloud.

"At this early stage in my planning," Hassett said, "I was confronted by a puzzling problem: whether to follow the playwright's specific directions in the script and have the apes react as if with understanding to the images on the screen and to the sounds from the tape recorder; or to allow them to behave in more 'apelike' fashion, responding to lights and sounds, but not to the meanings involved."

Hassett decided to pursue the latter course and to work for the complete alienation and self-centeredness of the animals. He wanted their activity to be unrelated not only to what they saw and heard but also very largely to each other. They would attend to their own basic needs, the needs of primitive creatures, and behave like infants in a nursery. "I felt that the pictures and sounds should present no observable continuity or pattern, but should merely create the impression of a confused culture," said Hassett, "while the behavior of the apes might very well have a tenuous line of action: first a search for food, then sex, then free play, and finally boredom and departure."

Hassett cast the play from among the acting students in the school; the First Ape was played by Robert Keesler, the Second Ape by David Krohn, and the Third Ape by Rebecca Nahas. Since the script is nonverbal, the director did not have to trouble himself with his actors' speech, nor were there any problems concerning their physical appearance as their bodies and faces were completely covered by the ape costumes borrowed for the occasion from the New York Shakespeare Festival. The actors looked like the legitimate offspring of King Kong. Hassett was very careful, however, to choose actors with vitality, agility, strong imaginations, and a gift for mime. David Krohn, the ape who climbed the walls, had actually been trained as dancer and acrobat. Rehearsals were conducted along improvisational lines; the director suggested images and emotions, and the actors interpreted them. Then, taking their cues from the pictures and sounds, as well as from each other, the actors continued to work improvisationally during the actual performance and achieved some very unusual and striking effects.

The play was presented on a thrust stage, which was piled high with an incredible jumble of objects; and the floor was strewn with autumn leaves, which reached the feet of the spectators in the first row of the theatre.

Bil Mikulewicz, the designer, said "I wanted to create the effect of complete clutter, disaster, and unreality. There were very few places in the play where we needed specific props or aids. Of course, we made use of the light booms, the vertical pipes for mounting spotlights, but not for their intended purpose; the booms are fixed to the walls on the stage and in the house, and the Second Ape climbed them and swung from them. The other essentials were a slide projector, a cheap tape recorder, a bag of sandwiches, and a garbage can; beyond that we threw in anything we could lay hands on to suggest chaos. Strindberg's play *The Stronger* was put on just before *The Apes,* on the same bill; the set for that play consisted of French doors, and four iron tables and six chairs of the kind seen in old-fashioned ice-cream parlors. We kept that set, and into it threw a large desk, an old refrigerator,

Robert Keesler as the First Ape, holding a garbage pail, climbing the walls, and howling in the exciting production mounted in the Nave Theatre, Columbia University, March 1969. The play was directed by Michael Hassett, The scenery and lighting were designed by Bil Mikulewicz.

piles of flats, and lots of other incongruous objects, including a piano. During the violent action of our play, one of the iron tables was knocked over and the top came off with a thud; our slide projector was also thrown off center by a falling flat, and there were other moments in the play when total destruction seemed imminent. The autumn leaves with which we covered the floor were collected in four shopping-bags from the grounds at Fort Tryon Park; when we picked them up, they were damp, and crawling with insects. We had to clean them up and dry them out on the radiators at the school before strewing them around.

"As far as the lighting was concerned," Mikulewicz continued, "I wanted it to be as unreal as the scenery, so I set my lights in an arbitrary fashion and allowed the rays to shoot off in random directions. This produced a number of dark areas, some dim ones, and some very bright ones; the apes, who were constantly on the move, went in and out of these areas and were seen in various intensities of light. This produced a weird and sometimes frightening effect. With Michael [the director], I selected the pictures for the slide projector from a number of newspapers and magazines; we had shots of Malcolm X, Charles de Gaulle, the Mona Lisa, four different views of Christ, lots of undraped female flesh, the American flag, many handshakers and smilers, and public monuments, such as the Statue of Liberty, defiled with graffiti. We even had a picture of the professor in charge of directing at the school, which we "borrowed" from his office without his knowledge. The slides were projected continuously at eight-second intervals.

"I thoroughly enjoyed working on this production," Mikulewicz concluded, "because it cleared naturalism out of my system—naturalism has a cramping effect on me."

The music and speech on the tape was a pastiche made up of bits of Mozart, of grand opera, of rock-and-roll, and of an André Kostelanetz rendition of "Love Is a Many-Splendored Thing;" the interspersed talk included snippets from a pretentious discussion on theories of art, a lecture on Vietnam, Gielgud reciting from Shakespeare, Eisenhower speaking, and someone shouting, "Kill, kill, kill!" The tape was prepared by the director, with the assistance of Dale Swanson.

The Apes, as produced by Hassett, did not allow the audience to sit back complacently and relax; at every moment the spectators were jolted, frightened, or amused. To begin with, the entrance of each ape provided a shock. Shortly after the lights came up on stage, the heavy draperies that covered the back wall began to billow; suddenly they were pulled aside, and a huge black ape (the Second Ape) was seen swinging from a pipe near the ceiling. He dropped to the floor and came hurtling downstage, kicking and overturning the objects in his path with a furious din. This was the cue for the entrance of the First Ape, who came crashing through a window high up on the wall, toward the rear of the theatre, on the left side. The windowpane had been removed, and black matte board inserted in its place; the ape smashed through this with such force that several members of the audience sprang out of their seats and withdrew to another part of the house. The audience was electrified when, to a man, they turned around and saw the enormous ape looming in the window; they could feel the cold gusts of air that came in behind him. After the initial shock the people in that part of the house put on their coats and kept them on during the rest of the performance. Those who had left their seats did not return to them—they actually seemed afraid to. The Third Ape entered from the right side of the stage and knocked over a pile of chairs that had been stacked up just inside the door.

The apes now roamed around in search of food, looking under objects, overturning and breaking them; picking up morsels and tasting them. Then the Second Ape came upon a bag of stale sandwiches; the other apes chased him, but he went up the wall, dropping the sandwiches as he climbed; those below immediately seized the food, tussled for it, and ate it.

In their progress around the room, the apes accidentally set off the slide projector and the tape recorder, which continued to work simultaneously until the end of the play. When, at various times, the lights or the sounds became particularly intense in brightness or volume, the apes felt threatened and took fright. Then they scampered for safety—one hid under a bench, another climbed up the wall, the third retreated into a corner; occasionally, they reached for objects that would serve as weapons. When the threat had passed, they relaxed, roamed some more, and munched on what they found. At one moment, when a delicate Mozart melody issued from the tape recorder, the First Ape lay down as if to take a nap, and the audience roared with laughter.

Then a "sexual" sequence followed; this consisted of the courtship practice of grooming and delousing. The director had come upon a description of this procedure in a book dealing with the sexual behavior of primates. The First Ape picked lice from the Third Ape and stroked her until she tired of the courtship, ran off, and perched on top of a piano, which stood against the right wall. The First Ape followed her, but she stamped her feet on the keyboard and produced loud, discordant sounds, which frightened the other two apes, who attempted to attack her as if she were an enemy.

Suddenly, one of the apes came upon a garbage can with a lift-lid worked by a foot-pedal; he began to play with it, and the other apes got into the game. Each tried to take possession of it, the larger ape kicking off the smaller one, until the First Ape decided that the can belonged to him and made off with it. He pounded on it as if it were a drum and paraded upstage to the back wall, where he climbed the pipe to get out of reach of the Third Ape, who had followed him. Meanwhile, the Second Ape, in frustration, started to smash everything in sight; he finally picked up the tape recorder and marched around with it while it continued to play; the light on the instrument made it clear to the audience that the machine was real and not a prop. Then the Second Ape raised the tape recorder above his head and flung it to the ground with all his might, so that it smashed completely. This sent a gasp through the house. It was the director's comment on mechanical culture and aroused the looked-for reaction in the audience.

For their exit the apes used a door on the left side of the theatre, which opened on a courtyard. Finding nothing more of interest to keep him there, the First Ape pulled open the door and went out; then the other two apes scampered after him. The door was left open, and a sharp wind came in, stirring the draperies and sweeping the dry leaves around with a rasping sound; a cold, empty feeling, one of utter desolation, was created as the play came to an end. The entire production took a little over twenty minutes.

"The reactions to the production and some of the interpretations placed on it by members of the audience were very interesting," Michael Hassett said. "The professor in charge of directing asked me whether I had intended to suggest (1) that the apes were a revitalizing force, with pagan vitality, who would make a fresh start after the destruction of our corrupt and exhausted civilization; or (2) that the seeds of our destruction were there in the apes who preceded us, that we have inherited their violence and irrationality, and that they are the primal cause of our depravity and destructiveness? I couldn't give a definitive answer to this question.

"Loud and intemperate laughter was one of the sounds on our tape, and it happened to be ringing out at the moment the machine was smashed. One member of the audience, who spoke to me after the performance, saw the sudden cutting off of the laughter as the basic theme of the play: it was the final dehumanization of man!

"Just after the sound went dead, the American flag blowing in the breeze flashed onto the screen; the flag like the laughter had come up entirely by chance. But later another member of the audience congratulated me for having timed my ironic visual statement so beautifully!" At which point Bil Mikulewicz added his own ironic comment: "Can't you understand why we have God?"

Scene from the Michael Hassett production at Columbia University. The apes root among the dried leaves, knock over furniture, and play with the objects they find.

THE APES SHALL INHERIT THE EARTH

WERNER ASPENSTROM
English version by Leif Sjöberg and Randolph Goodman

Characters

First Ape
Second Ape
Third Ape

A lecture hall with benches and a speaker's platform.

Apparently the room has been deserted for a long time. The windows gape emptily; faded autumn leaves have accumulated in piles on the floor; the walls are discolored and stained as though by chemicals and fire; and huge spider webs cover the pendant lamps. On the platform, which is one step above floor level, there is a lectern and a table on which stands a slide projector; on the wall above the platform, hangs a film screen askew. At the other side of the room there is a small table with a tape-recording machine on it.

[Outside the windows there is hazy, late afternoon sunlight, and a dead quiet and calm. Then indistinguishable figures move back and forth past the windows. Suddenly the shrill chirping and chattering of birds is heard. Then one of the figures puts its head through a window and we see that it is a huge ape. He looks curiously about, retreats, then appears again accompanied by the **Second Ape.** *They climb into the room. The* **First Ape** *is taller, heavier, and more aggressive than the* **Second Ape,** *who chews on his fist as if he were hungry. They move aimlessly about the room, one pulls at the rotting curtains, the other tries sitting on a bench; they test and taste whatever piques their curiosity. The* **First Ape** *leaps onto the speaker's platform and leans on the lectern; the* **Second Ape** *begins to root among the leaves as if seeking for food and occasionally nibbles on a morsel of some sort.*

Then a **Third Ape** *approaches the window; he is small and shy, peers in hesitantly for a long time, finally takes courage and climbs in. Having entered, he rambles about like the others, sits on the benches, crawls under them, and scratches among the leaves on the floor. Suddenly the* **Third Ape** *discovers a strange object; brushing the leaves aside, he raises it up. It is a violin. He turns it from side to side. What can it be? He shakes it and bangs it, puts his eye to the opening and tries to see inside. Inadvertently drawing his fingers across the strings, there is a loud pizzacato. Hearing the sound, he gets so frightened that he drops the instrument, but his curiosity getting the better of him, he picks it up again and draws his fingers across the strings over and over. As the twanging and screeching sounds emerge, he becomes more and more charmed and shuffles his feet in what appear to be clumsy dance steps. The other two rush* up to the **Third Ape** and try to snatch his plaything from him, while he resists. But his attempts to defend himself are of no avail, and while they wrestle for the object the strings snap one after the other until only one is left.

The sun disappears as if behind a cloud and the wind rises, stirring the leaves on the floor. The wind moans and the apes are frightened; they drop the violin and hide themselves under the benches. When the wind begins to die down, they crawl out of their hiding places and continue their rambles, each going off in a different direction. The **Third Ape** stumbles upon the violin, picks it up, and drags it about with him.

The **First Ape** mounts the platform and begins to tinker with the slide projector. All at once a light goes on and a picture of the Mona Lisa appears on the screen. The apes do not know how to react. The **Third Ape** seems frightened and cautiously retires toward the window. The other two apes move closer to the screen in order better to acquaint themselves with the creature there. When the **First Ape** tries to touch the picture, he stands in the beam of light and his shadow falls on the screen. There appears to be a fourth ape in the room! The **First** and **Second Apes** bare their teeth and growl menacingly. The **Second Ape,** wanting to ingratiate himself with the **First Ape** who is apparently the leader, rushes forward and strikes the image on the screen. What business do you have here? Get out!

The **First Ape** moves aside and the Mona Lisa is again visible. Where did the intruder go? Behind the screen, perhaps! No, he is not there. They get tired of searching. The **First Ape** returns to the slide projector and again tampers with it; as he strikes a button, the Mona

Lisa begins to vanish and the screen is shared by the image of Hitler in Nazi uniform, his arm raised in an angry gesture, his mouth roaring imprecations. The **Second** and **Third Apes** take seats in the first row of benches and look on as the pictures change. The **First Ape** bangs his paw up and down mechanically on the releasing button. At first the change of pictures is slow and fumbling. The slides are helter-skelter, sometimes upside down, askew, or cracked. One or two fall to the floor and smash. As the show progresses, the **First Ape** gets nimbler and nimbler until the pictures pass with such speed that we can hardly make out what they represent.[1]]

The picture of Hitler is followed by one of rooftops with a maze of television aerials.

Then the Leaning Tower of Pisa.

An Eskimo in front of an igloo.

The Taj Mahal.

The face of a baby, smiling.

An atomic mushroom of smoke.

Manhattan with the skyscrapers upside down.

A boxing match at the moment when one fighter has struck his opponent a smashing blow to the jaw.

[The apes applaud this enthusiastically.]

A long, sleek Cadillac.

Demonstrators with protest signs.

A closeup of a soldier with half his face shot off.

[Suddenly outside the window a bird begins to sing.]

Enlarged picture of an ant dragging the body of a dead ant.

A tropical forest with a tiger leaping in midair.

[The apes growl at this.]

A sailing vessel on a quiet, moonlit sea.

A jet bomber in the sky.

The Apollo Belvedere.

[1] The director may, if he wishes, select other pictures and arrange them differently in order to achieve the desired effect.—W.A.

A war veteran sitting on a street corner, all his limbs missing but the stump of one arm which he stretches out with its beggar's bowl.

[How boring! The apes yawn loudly; they had certainly expected something more interesting! The **Second Ape** *begins to delouse himself. Finding what he was looking for, he puts it in his mouth and munches contentedly. Meanwhile, more pictures go by.]*

The Pope on a golden throne.
Darwin upside down.

[The apes lose interest until the images begin to fly by with maddening speed—]

landscapes, human faces, machines, churches, bacteria, folk dancers, butterflies, nebulae—

[Then they chatter and squeak with delight.

The **Second Ape** *catches sight something edible on the floor, darts after it, and retires into a corner with his find. The other two apes immediately cast themselves upon him, but they are a moment too late. He has already put the morsel into his mouth and smacks his lips with pleasure. The slide projector is a forgotten toy; on the screen the Mona Lisa again languishes upside down.*

The **First Ape** *finds a round piece of wood resembling a toilet seat into which he sinks his teeth, then makes a wry face and casts it away. The* **Third Ape** *retrieves it, tastes it, and also throws it away. When the* **Second Ape** *has finished his little tidbit, he starts looking around for more, gives up the search, and catches sight of a table in a corner. He tries to break the wheels off the machine that stands on the table. They ought to be edible! It turns out to be a tape recorder. The* **First Ape,** *who considers that he has proprietary rights to everything, immediately pushes the* **Second Ape** *aside and scrutinizes the strange object with*

a technical and expert eye. Didn't he make that other gadget work just a moment ago? After he has fiddled with the new machine for a while, the wheels begin to turn. First we hear a grinding and crackling sound from the loudspeaker; gradually we make out a few bars of a sacred aria by Mozart.[2] The tape runs faster and faster until the music becomes a continuous humming sound.

The **First Ape** *triumphantly handles the machine so that sometimes the tape runs at lightning speed and sometimes at a snail's pace; in between, we are able to make out disjointed phrases and melodic fragments. We hear:]*

A bit of a stirring march.

Announcer's Voice: . . . free parking, free alterations, free refreshments, free . . .

Newscaster: . . . the retiring president spoke warmly and charmingly. He said the greatest achievement of his term of office was the preservation of peace . . .

A few bars of rock-and-roll.

Sportscaster: *[Shouting, with cheering crowds in background.]* . . . in the home stretch . . . neck and neck . . . Last Supper is coming up . . .

A Spanish tango.

Salesman: . . . enjoy our cut-rate excursion to the Moon . . . rockets leave every . . .

Medical Lecturer: . . . there are three common uses for LSD . . .

Announcer: . . . pause for station identification . . .

Female Voice: . . . feel deserted? Our six-volume set called *Loneliness* will . . .

Scientific Lecturer: . . . as the paleontol-*feet in what appear to be clumsy dance steps. The other two rush* ogists say, "If the remains stink, give them to the zoologists; if not, they belong to us." . . .

Prolonged laughter.

[2] Preferably the "Laudate Dominum" from the *Vesperae solennes de confessore.*—W.A.

Exciting jazz music with jungle drums.[3]

[The **Third Ape,** *who is obviously musically gifted, gets up and starts to jog about on the floor.]*

Female Voice: *[Sticky-sweet.]* . . . and ate him *all* up. Now, children . . .

Sportscaster: . . . the muddy track . . .

Soft strains of a cello.

Psychologist: . . . to Worried Mother: Homosexuality is only . . .

Western Jamboree singers.

Preacher: . . . a prayer for our men who gave their lives to preserve democracy on Mars . . .

Announcer: . . . We pause for station identification . . .

[There is a long silence during which the **First Ape** *deserts the tape recorder and sits down beside the other two. The monologue that now follows should be read without a break.][4]:*

Male Voice: Perhaps it is true that God is dead, that man is merely the ugly picture of a mocking beast scrawled on a blackboard, that a giant sponge will arise from the earth, and man will be erased in a cloud of dust . . . Fire and ice, then the world will begin anew . . .

[The three apes are not especially interested. There are, after all, more important things than poetry, aren't there? The **First Ape** *scratches his back; the* **Third Ape** *lends a hand. One must stand in well with the authorities! The* **Second Ape** *has become aware of the pendant lamp and cannot tear his eyes from it. What sort of fruit can that be? Edible, I wonder? He stands up on the bench then makes a terrific leap. He fails to reach the lamp and tumbles to the floor. He returns to the bench, puzzled, and sits down back to front.]*

[3] The drum solo, for example, from Benny Goodman's "Sing, Sing, Sing."—W.A.

[4] I should like to recite this poem myself for use in performance.—W.A.

Male Voice: *[Continues.]* . . . Yet I love this very Jerusalem with its crumbled walls. I love the starry skies as one loves a comfortable old hat, and the meadows of the earth as one loves a pair of worn-out slippers. The sun, the moon, and the lakes in which sun and moon shrink miraculously so that I can fondle them and turn them in my hand like the gold and silver coins which the old king gave us pensioners . . . Unknown listener, you who believe yourself to be the child of a time of incomparable triumphs and incomparable catastrophes—you are only a child! Passionately you clasp your rag doll to your breast and beg her for something she cannot grant you:

"Oh, stay with me!
Never, never go—
I love you so-o-o!
I love you so-o-o!
I love you so-o-o . . ."

The machine is stuck; then the sound suddenly dies.

[The three apes make a final aimless tour through the room, rooting about among the leaves. No, there is nothing more to be eaten here, nothing more to be learned. The **First Ape** *and the* **Second Ape** *depart. The* **Third Ape** *starts to follow, then just as he is perched on the window sill he recalls something, jumps down, picks up the violin, plucks at the single remaining string, smiling idiotically as he does so. Then he puts the instrument down tenderly on a pile of leaves as if it were an object of great value. The tape recorder rotates with a quiet hum;* Mona Lisa *still hangs upside down on the film screen. A bird begins to sing outside the window. The* **Third Ape** *drops out of sight. The room is once more deserted.]*

CURTAIN

FOR FURTHER STUDY

General Works on Theatre and Drama

Bentley, Eric (ed.). *The Theory of the Stage: An Introduction to Modern Theatre and Drama*. Baltimore: Penguin Books, 1968.

Clark, Barrett H. (ed.). Rev. by Henry Popkin (ed.). *European Theories of the Drama*. New York: Crown Publishers, Inc., 1965.

Cole, Toby (ed.). *Playwrights on Playwriting*. New York: Hill and Wang, Inc., 1961.

—, in collaboration with Helen Krich Chinoy. *Actors on Acting*, rev. ed., New York: Crown Publishers, Inc., 1969 and *Directors on Directing*, rev. ed., Indianapolis: Bobbs-Merrill, Co., Inc., 1963.

Gassner, John. *Directions in Modern Theatre and Drama*. New York: Holt, Rinehart and Winston, Inc., 1965.

Gorelik, Mordecai. *New Theatres for Old*. New York: E. P. Dutton & Co., Inc., 1962.

Henrik Ibsen

Fjelde, Rolf (ed.). *Henrik Ibsen*. Englewood Cliffs, N.J.: Prentice-Hall, Inc., 1965.

Shaw, George Bernard. *The Quintessence of Ibsenism*. New York: Hill and Wang, Inc., 1957.

Valency, Maurice. *The Flower and the Castle*. New York: Crowell-Collier and Macmillan, Inc., 1963. This deals with Strindberg as well as Ibsen.

August Strindberg

Dahlström, Carl E. W. L. *Strindberg's Dramatic Expressionism*. New York: Benjamin Blom, 1965.

Lamm, Martin (ed.). *August Strindberg*. Tr. by Harry G. Carlson. New York: Benjamin Blom, 1970.

Mortensen, Brita M. E., and Brian W. Downs. *Strindberg: An Introduction to His Life and Works*. London: Cambridge University Press, 1965.

Anton Chekhov

Magarshack, David. *Chekhov the Dramatist*. New York: Hill and Wang, Inc., 1960.

Simmons, Ernest J. *Chekhov, a Biography*. Boston: Atlantic-Little Brown, 1962.

Valency, Maurice. *The Breaking String*. New York: Oxford University Press, 1966.

George Bernard Shaw

Bentley, Eric. *Bernard Shaw*. New York: New Directions, 1957.
Shaw, G. B. *Shaw's Dramatic Criticism, 1895–1898*. A selection by John F. Matthews. New York: Hill and Wang, Inc., 1959.
Shaw, G. B. Dan H. Laurence (ed.). *Letters*, Vol. I, New York: Dodd, Mead & Company, Inc., 1965. Volume II is in preparation.

Eugene O'Neill

Cargill, Oscar, N. Bryllion Fagin, and William J. Fisher (eds.). *O'Neill and His Plays: Four Decades of Criticism*. New York: New York University Press, 1961.
Gelb, Arthur, and Barbara Gelb. *O'Neill*. New York: Harper & Row, Publishers, 1962.
Leech, Clifford. *Eugene O'Neill*. New York: Grove Press, Inc., 1963.

Bertolt Brecht

Brecht, Bertolt. *Brecht on Theater*. Ed. and Tr. by John Willett. New York: Hill and Wang, Inc., 1964.
Esslin, Martin. *Brecht: The Man and His Work*. New York: Doubleday & Company, Inc., 1961.
Willett, John. *The Theatre of Bertolt Brecht*. New York: New Directions, 1959.

Robert Pinget

Bann, Stephen. "Robert Pinget." *London Magazine*, Vol. IV, No. 7, October, 1964, pp. 22–35.
Esslin, Martin. *The Theatre of the Absurd*. New York: Doubleday & Company, Inc., 1961.
Guicharnaud, Jacques, and June Guicharnaud. *Modern French Theatre (from Giraudoux to Genet)*. New Haven: Yale University Press, 1967.

Werner Aspenström

Kirby, Michael. *Happenings*. New York: E. P. Dutton & Co., Inc., 1966.
Törnqvist, Egil. "Poet in the Space Age: A Theme in Aspenström's Plays." *Scandinavian Studies*, Vol. 39, No. 1, February, 1967, pp. 1–15.
Tulane Drama Review, Vol. 6, No. 2 (The Modern Drama in Sweden), Winter, 1961.

Index

Italic numbers denote pages on which illustrations appear.